STUDY GUIDE

to accompany

Economics

4th EDITION

Paul Wonnacott
University of Maryland

Ronald Wonnacott
The University of Western Ontario

JOHN WILEY & SONS
New York   Chichester   Brisbane   Toronto   Singapore

Preface

This *Study Guide* is designed to be used with the introductory economic textbook, *Economics*, by Paul Wonnacott and Ronald Wonnacott. This *Study Guide* makes no attempt to be self-contained; it is a supplement to, not a substitute for, the textbook.

Each chapter is designed for you to read and work through after reading the corresponding chapter in the text. Each chapter of this *Study Guide* contains seven sections:

- **Learning Objectives.** This section lists the things that you should know after you have studied the chapter in the text and in the study guide. The purpose of this section is twofold. First, it provides a direction and focus as you study the chapter. Second, it provides a checklist to test your understanding after you have completed the chapter.

- **Major Purpose.** This section sets out the basic ideas that will be developed in the chapter.

- **Highlights of Chapter.** This section contains a summary of the important points in the chapter. Its main purpose is to reinforce the textbook by adding illustrative examples and going over the main points from a somewhat different perspective. To a student learning a subject for the first time, everything may seem equally important. This section helps identify the most important ideas in the chapter.

- **Important Terms: Match the columns.** This section lists the important concepts in the chapter, along with a definition or explanation of each. Your task is to match each term with its definition or explanation. Before

looking in the right-hand column, you should try to remember the definition first.

- **True-false questions.**

- **Multiple choice questions.**

- **Exercises.**

The last three sections are designed to help you learn by doing, and to provide a check on your understanding of the chapter. (They may also help you with your exams directly. The questions in the study guide are included in the computerized testbank available to teachers who are making up exams. If teachers wish, they can use questions taken directly from the study guide.)

After going over these three sections, you should check the answers at the end of the chapter in the study guide. Note that each answer refers you to the page in the textbook which covers the point addressed in the question. If you get the wrong answer, you should reread the relevant page in the text. (Note: we have tried to exercise great care in checking the answers, but cannot absolutely guarantee that every answer is correct. We have found and corrected two wrong answers in the proofs; it is conceivable that we have missed a few.)

About half the chapters include a *crossword puzzle* that includes some of the key terms in the text. We hope that you will find them entertaining, and that they will act as a final check on your understanding of the concepts in the chapter. The completed crossword puzzles are reproduced at the end of this study guide.

We would like to thank Ron Blue for the care and imagination with which he has designed and produced this *Study Guide*.

Paul Wonnacott
Ronald Wonnacott

Contents

Preface

STUDY GUIDE

to accompany

Economics

4th EDITION

PART 1

BASIC ECONOMIC CONCEPTS

ECONOMIC PROBLEMS AND ECONOMIC GOALS

LEARNING OBJECTIVES

After you have studied this chapter in the textbook and study guide, you should be able to

✔ List five major economic goals

✔ Describe, in broad terms, what has happened to U.S. unemployment, inflation, growth, and the distribution of income in recent decades

✔ Distinguish the views of Adam Smith and J. M. Keynes with respect to the proper role of the government

✔ Define terms such as inflation, deflation, recession, and efficiency

✔ Distinguish between *allocative efficiency* and *technological efficiency*

✔ Describe briefly how changes in relative prices may contribute to allocative efficiency

✔ Explain why it is harder to identify the problems created by inflation than those created by unemployment

✔ Explain the distinction between equity and equality

✔ Explain how some goals may be *complementary*, while others are in *conflict*

If you have studied the appendix to Chapter 1 in the textbook, you should also be able to

✔ Describe some of the ways in which people may be misled by graphs

✔ Explain the advantage of using a ratio (or logarithmic) scale

✔ Explain the difference between a nominal and a real measure

MAJOR PURPOSE

The major purpose of this chapter is to provide a broad overview of *economic developments* and *economic objectives*, as a background for the more detailed topics of the following chapters. Five major economic objectives are discussed:

- high employment,

- a stable average level of prices,

- efficiency,

- equity, and

- growth.

You should gain some understanding of the problems which have arisen in the U.S. economy, and why it is not always easy to solve these problems. In particular, it may be difficult to deal with problems when the government has a number of goals, some of which are *in conflict*. That is, solving one problem may make others more difficult to solve. For example, inflation generally gets worse as the unemployment rate falls.

HIGHLIGHTS OF CHAPTER

Economics is one of the social sciences—it involves the systematic study of human behavior. The aspect of behavior which interests economists is how people earn a living, and the problems which may make it difficult for them to do so. In the words of Alfred Marshall, economics is the study of people "in the ordinary business of life."

The objective of *economic theory* is to discover and explain the basic principles and laws that govern economic life. Economic theory helps us to understand questions such as: Why are some prices higher than others? Why does the average level of prices rise? Why are some people richer than others? What causes large-scale unemployment?

Economic policy addresses such questions as: How can the government reduce inflation? How can it reduce the unemployment rate? What steps can individuals take to increase their incomes, or reduce the risks of unemployment? How does a business increase its profits?

Economic theory and economic policy go hand-in-hand. Just as a physician needs to know how the human body works in order to heal patients, so the economic policymaker needs to understand economic theory in order to prescribe economic policies that will be successful. Scientific studies of how things work are often inspired by a policy motive—to do something about problems. Thus, scientists strive to unlock the mysteries of the human cell in order to find out why cancer occurs, and ultimately to be able to cure cancer. Similarly, studies of how the economy works are often motivated by the desire to solve economic problems, such as recession and large-scale unemployment.

ECONOMIC POLICY

Perhaps the most hotly contested issue in all of economics is the question of how much the government should intervene in the economy. Many of those in government are motivated by the desire to promote the public welfare. After all, the policies that they promote will be their monument in history. But well-meaning policymakers do not always adopt policies that work in practice. Furthermore, the government may be used to benefit individuals or groups at the expense of the public as a whole.

Adam Smith attacked many governmental interventions in the economy as being contrary to the public interest. Even though tariffs benefited the protected sectors of the economy, they inflicted higher costs on consumers, and acted as a drag on efficiency. Smith conceived of the private economy as a self-regulating mechanism. By pursuing their own interests, individuals would regularly contribute to the common good. There was no need for extensive government interference to ensure that things would come out all right.

A century and a half later, J. M. Keynes was skeptical of Smith's message of laissez faire. Things were not coming out all right. The economy was in a deep depression, with many people out of work. It was the responsibility of the government, said Keynes, to do something about this tragic situation. He recommended government spending on roads and other public works as a way to provide jobs.

ECONOMIC GOALS

Full employment is one of the major economic objectives. Four others are also described in this chapter:

- a stable average level of prices,
- efficiency,
- an equitable distribution of income, and
- economic growth.

Other goals might be added to this list, for example, economic freedom, economic security, and the control of pollution.

The first two goals—full employment and stable prices—come under the heading of maintaining a stable *equilibrium* in the economy. There has in fact been considerable instability in the U.S. economy. The most notable disturbance occurred during the Great Depression of the 1930s, when output and employment dropped sharply, and remained at very low levels for a full decade. During World War II, there was an effort to produced as many munitions as possible. Unemployment ceased to be a significant problem, but prices began to rise substantially. Since the end of World War II in 1945, we have avoided severe disturbances comparable to those from 1929 to 1945. However, there have been periodic recessions, with rising unemployment. Inflation was severe during the late 1940s and the 1970s. During the decade of the 1970s, the average level of prices doubled.

Of the major economic problems, unemployment is perhaps the most obvious. When employment declines, we have less output to enjoy. We not only forego the output which might have been produced, but we also must face the demoralization that comes with unemployment.

The problems with inflation are less obvious. When people buy goods, they obviously dislike higher and higher prices. But there are two sides to every transaction—the buyer's side, and the seller's. With widespread inflation, not only do the prices of what we buy increase. Wage rates also go up, as well as the prices of what we sell. It is not so clear whether individuals are net gainers or net losers.

However, there are certain segments of the population who do lose. Those who have pensions set in money terms lose: As prices rise, their pensions buy less. (However, some pensions, including the Social Security pensions paid by the government, are increased to compensate for inflation.) Those who own government bonds or other interest-bearing securities lose. Through the years, they receive payments whose value becomes smaller and smaller as prices rise. On the other hand, people who have borrowed can benefit: They repay their loans in money whose value has declined.

Inflation generates a feeling that the economic system is unfair. There are arbitrary redistributions of income and wealth, such as the gains to debtors and losses to bond owners. Inflation can also make it more difficult to make wise and well-informed decisions. *Prices* provide an important source of information to the business executive and consumer. During periods of rapid inflation, when all prices are rising at a brisk pace, the message carried by prices may be obscured. It becomes more difficult to make good decisions.

If inflation accelerates to very high rates—such as 1,000% per year—it becomes known as *hyperinflation*. Money is losing its value so rapidly that people may refuse to accept it. Because money is practically useless, sellers may feel compelled to barter their products for other goods. Such barter transactions are very cumbersome and time-consuming.

Most inflations do not accelerate into hyperinflation. Hyperinflation is relatively rare, except for losers during wartime or early postwar periods. There are, however, a few cases where countries have very rapid rates of inflation even though they have not been defeated in a war—for example, present-day Brazil.

There are two important types of efficiency. *Technological efficiency* means getting the most output from a given set of inputs (labor, machinery, raw materials). *Allocative efficiency* occurs when the economy is producing the best combination of outputs, using the lowest-cost combination of inputs. Allocative efficiency means producing the goods and services which the consuming public wants most. It is possible for an economic system to produce "white elephants" in a technologically efficient manner. But this system would not be producing what people want; it would not be allocatively efficient. Similarly, if everyone were a lawyer, and nobody a doctor, there would be allocative inefficiency—even if everyone were a superb lawyer.

Equity means *fairness*, and that raises the question of what fairness means. There can be obvious disagreements. Those with low incomes are likely to argue that a more equal distribution of income would be fairer. Those with higher incomes often argue that their high incomes are the result of hard work; it is fair for them to be paid more because they have worked harder.

Many people would, however, agree that the government should take some steps to help those who are poverty-stricken, for example, by taxing the rich to provide services for the needy. The question arises, however, as to how far this process should be taken. Clearly, if the government confiscated all incomes above the average, and gave the revenues to low income people, then it would severely interfere with the incentive to work hard. (This would also greatly increase the incentive to cheat on taxes!) Even less drastic steps to redistribute income can decrease incentives, and thus decrease the size of the national "pie." The size of the pie depends in part on how it is cut up.

Economic growth is often advocated for its own sake. In a growing economy, we enjoy more goods and services. Furthermore, growth may make it easier to meet other goals, such as reducing poverty. However, we should not simply assume that the more growth, the better. Growth comes at a cost. Most obviously, if we produce more machinery and equipment to help us grow, then we will give up the current consumer goods that might have been produced instead of the machinery and equipment.

COMPLEMENTARY AND CONFLICTING GOALS

Some goals—such as a high level of employment and an elimination of poverty—are *complementary*. Progress on the one contributes to progress on the other. If jobs are provided for people, they are less likely to be poor.

Other goals are *in conflict*. If people buy more goods and services, they will help to increase the number of jobs. But they will also make it easier for sellers to raise their prices. Thus, if the government takes steps to encourage spending, it may help ease one problem (unemployment) while making another worse (inflation). In such circumstances, good policies may be particularly difficult to develop.

IMPORTANT TERMS: MATCH THE COLUMNS

Match the term in the first column with the corresponding explanation in the second column.

_____ 1. Laissez faire
_____ 2. Great Depression
_____ 3. Labor force
_____ 4. Population
_____ 5. Recession
_____ 6. Duty
_____ 7. J. M. Keynes
_____ 8. Adam Smith
_____ 9. Inflation
_____10. Deflation
_____11. Allocative efficiency
_____12. Technical efficiency
_____13. Complementary goals
_____14. Conflicting goals
_____15. This can help promote allocative efficiency

a. Put forward the idea of the "hidden hand."
b. Pursuing one helps in attainment of other
c. When large-scale unemployment existed
d. A change in relative prices
e. A tax on an import
f. Pursuing one makes other more difficult to attain
g. A decrease in the average level of prices
h. A broad decline in production, involving many sectors of the economy
i. Avoiding sloppy management and wasted motion
j. Total number of people in a country
k. Put forward the idea that government should spend for public works when necessary to get economy out of depression, and restore full employment
l. Sum of those employed and those unemployed
m. An increase in the average level of prices
n. Leave the economy alone
o. Producing the best combination of outputs, using the lowest-cost combination of inputs

TRUE-FALSE

T   F   1.   Adam Smith argued that the government should build public works whenever needed to reduce the rate of inflation.

T   F   2.   By definition, a depression occurs whenever the output of the nation falls.

T   F   3.   During the great depression of the 1930s, the unemployment rate rose above 15% of the labor force.

T   F   4.   The Employment Act of 1946 required the government to provide a job for anyone who wanted one but could not find employment from a corporation.

T   F   5.   Since 1970, recessions have been much less severe than those of the 1950s and 1960s.

T   F   6.   A recession is a decline in total output, employment, and income, and is marked by a widespread contraction in *many* industries.

T   F   7.   Changes in the average level of inflation make an important contribution, since they are the key to improvements in allocative efficiency.

T   F   8.   The percentage of the population living in poverty has declined slowly but consistently since 1960.

T   F   9.   Over the past three decades, there has been a consistent trend in the United States: the rich have gotten richer, and the poor have gotten poorer.

T   F   10.   Inflation is caused by a decline in purchases by consumers.

MULTIPLE CHOICE

1.   Since 1900, output per capita in the United States:

a. has approximately doubled, while the length of the work week has declined
b. has grown approximately sixfold, while the length of the work week has declined
c. has approximately doubled, while the length of the work week has remained stable
d. has grown approximately sixfold, while the length of the work week has remained stable
e. has remained stable, while the length of the work week has declined sharply; all the gains have come in the form of more leisure

2.   Between 1960 and 1987, which country grew most rapidly:

a. France
b. Italy
c. Japan
d. United States
e. West Germany

3.   By the phrase, "invisible hand," Adam Smith was expressing the idea that

a. there are no economic conflicts among nations
b. there would be no economic conflicts among nations, if countries would eliminate tariffs
c. there are no conflicts between what is good for an individual, and what is good for society as a whole
d. by pursuing their own individual interests, people frequently promote the interests of society
e. business executives have a natural interest in keeping prices down, and preventing inflation

4.   Suppose that the U.S. government is considering increasing the tariffs on imported steel. Which organizations in the United States are **most likely** to **oppose** such an increase?

a. steelworkers union and autoworkers union
b. General Motors and Caterpillar
c. steelworkers union and the U.S. Treasury
d. U.S. Steel and the U.S. Treasury
e. U.S. Steel and General Motors

5. In his *General Theory*, Keynes' principal concern was with the goal of:

   a. stable prices
   b. low unemployment
   c. allocative efficiency
   d. technological efficiency
   e. an equitable distribution of income

6. Unemployment is likely to be highest during

   a. war
   b. peacetime prosperity
   c. rapid growth
   d. recession
   e. depression

7. Between 1929 and 1933, during the early part of the Great Depression, total output in the United States:

   a. declined about 30%
   b. declined about 20%
   c. declined about 10%
   d. declined about 5%
   e. remained approximately stable; the Depression represented an interruption of growth, not an actual decline in output

8. Which of the following is counted as being un-employed:

   a. someone who has just retired at age 65
   b. a full-time student not looking for a job
   c. someone who has recently graduated from college, and is looking for his or her first full-time job
   d. convicts in prisons
   e. all of the above

9. A moderate rate of inflation (of, say, 4% per annum)

   a. creates no problems in the economy
   b. hurts people living on fixed money incomes
   c. hurts people who have borrowed money
   d. occurs whenever money wages rise more rapidly than prices
   e. is likely to be caused by war

10. The key role in promoting allocative efficiency is played by changes in

    a. the average level of prices
    b. the rate of inflation
    c. the rate of growth
    d. relative prices
    e. the distribution of income

11. Economists distinguish changes in the **average** level of prices and changes in **relative** prices. Changes in the average level of prices are generally considered

    a. undesirable, while changes in relative prices can perform a useful function in promoting efficiency
    b. undesirable, but changes in relative prices are even more undesirable, since they hurt some people while helping others
    c. undesirable, but changes in relative prices are neither good nor bad; they just happen
    d. desirable, but the government should attempt to prevent changes in relative prices
    e. desirable, but changes in relative prices are even more desirable, and the government should take steps to increase changes in relative prices

12. Suppose that every factory worker were in the job best suited for him or her, and they were working as productively as possible, but were producing cars that nobody wanted to buy. This would be an example of

    a. Technical inefficiency and allocative inefficiency
    b. Technical efficiency and allocative inefficiency
    c. Technical inefficiency and allocative efficiency
    d. Technical efficiency and allocative efficiency
    e. Technical efficiency and allocative efficiency, but slow growth

13. During the past two decades, the prices of computers have fallen, while the price of oil has risen. As a result, manufacturers and other businesses have used more computers, and have conserved on energy. This switch toward more computers and less energy is an illustration of:

    a. allocative efficiency
    b. technological efficiency
    c. the effects of inflation
    d. a less equal distribution of income
    e. a more equal distribution of income

14. Which is the best example of **technological** inefficiency

    a. producing too many cars, and not enough housing
    b. slow growth
    c. inflation
    d. inequality of incomes
    e. sloppy management

Chapter 1 Economic Problems and Economic Goals

15. **Equity** in the distribution of income means:

    a. equality
    b. fairness
    c. more for everyone, as a result of growth
    d. more for those who can't work
    e. more for those who work hard

16. Suppose that the incomes of all families are perfectly equal. Then the poorest 10% of the families will get what share of total income

    a. 5%
    b. 10%
    c. approximately 15%
    d. 20%
    e. 25%

17. Which of the following pairs is the clearest example of conflicting goals:

    a. less unemployment and less inflation
    b. less unemployment and less poverty
    c. less unemployment and more growth
    d. less unemployment and more efficiency
    e. more efficiency and less poverty

18. If, during the coming six months, there is a boom in the purchases of machinery by businesses, then we would be most likely to observe

    a. an increase in the rate of inflation, and a decline in the rate of unemployment
    b. a decrease in the rate of inflation, and a decline in the rate of unemployment
    c. an increase in the rate of inflation, and an increase in the rate of unemployment
    d. a decrease in the rate of inflation, and an increase in the rate of unemployment
    e. a decrease in inflation, growth, and unemployment

19. Economists study

    a. inflation
    b. unemployment
    c. efficiency
    d. poverty
    e. all of the above

(Appendix)

20. A reason for using a logarithmic or ratio scale on the vertical axis of a chart is that this

    a. makes it easier to start measuring from zero
    b. allows readers to quickly see when the rate of increase was most rapid
    c. avoids the necessity of choosing an arbitrary beginning year
    d. shows when profits were at a maximum
    e. shows when profits were at a minimum

EXERCISES

1. In the following passage, choose the correct word or phrase in the brackets.

   Economic history is a story of both progress and problems. Some evidence of progress shows up in Figure 1-1 in the textbook. Here we see that output per person has increased by approximately (100%, 200%, 500%) since 1900, and about (25%, 75%, 150%) since 1960. If we were to look at total output of the economy—rather than at output **per person**— we would find that total output has increased by (an even greater percentage than output per person, a somewhat smaller percentage).

   The right-hand panel of Figure 1-1 shows another source of gain. Not only have we produced more, but we have done so with a shorter workweek. The decline in the workweek occurred mainly in the period from (1900 to 1950, 1950 to 1989). Notice also the very sharp drop between 1925 and 1935.

   This decrease was the result of (a much more rapidly improving economy which allowed more leisure, the depression which reduced the demand for output, a loss of the work ethic).

   Successes and problems also show up in Figure 1-3 in the textbook. The (upward trend in output, downward trend in unemployment, both) since 1950 show(s) how things have improved. One of the problems is shown by the vertical shaded bars, which mark periods of (recession, depression, inflation, poverty). During such periods, (the unemployment rate increases, output declines, both).

   Figure 1-4 shows the average level of prices. A rise in this curve is an indication of inflation. The more rapid is inflation, the steeper is the curve. We see that inflation was very rapid between (1950 and 1960, 1960 and 1970, 1970 and 1980).

Finally, Figure 1-5 shows the percentage of the population living in poverty; a decline in the percentage is a sign of success. Observe that, at the beginning of the period shown, the incidence of poverty declined, from about (15%, 22%, 30%) in 1960 to about (5%, 8%, 11%) when it reached its low point in the 1970s. Largely as a result of the deep recession of the early 1980s, the percentage living in poverty increased to about (15%, 22%, 30%) by 1983.

2. In Figure 1-3 in the textbook, how many recessions have there been since 1946? This is an average of one every _____ years.

How long was the longest period between recessions? The shortest? Does this suggest that expansions die more or less regularly, as a result of old age?

The length of each recession is shown by the width of the colored vertical bars. Which two recessions were longest?

Did these two long recessions come after relatively long expansions, or relatively short ones? Does this suggest that a long expansion is most likely to end in a long recession?

ANSWERS

(Note: page numbers after answers to Multiple Choice and True-False questions provide references to passage on which the question is based.)

Important Terms:	1 n, 2 c, 3 l, 4 j, 5 h, 6 e, 7 k, 8 a, 9 m, 10 g, 11 o, 12 i, 13 b, 14 f, 15 d

True-False:
1 F (p. 5)
2 F (p. 7)
3 T (p. 8)
4 F (p. 8)
5 F (p. 8)
6 T (p. 9)
7 F (p. 11)
8 F (p. 12)
9 F (p. 12)
10 F (p. 13)

Multiple Choice:
1 b (p. 3)
2 c (p. 3)
3 d (p. 5)
4 b (p. 5)
5 b (p. 6)
6 e (p. 7)
7 a (p. 7)
8 c (p. 7)
9 b (p. 10)
10 d (p. 10)
11 a (p. 10)
12 b (pp. 10-11)
13 a (p. 11)
14 e (p. 11)

15 b (p. 11)
16 b
17 a (p. 13)
18 a (p. 13)
19 e (p. 14)
20 b (p. 20)

Exercises:

1. 500%, 75%, an even greater percentage than output per person, 1900 to 1950, the depression which reduced the demand for output, upward trend in output, recession, both, 1970 and 1980, 22%, 11%, 15%.

2. 8, 5.5, approximately 8 years (1961-69) although the expansion late 1982 may eventually prove to be longer, about one year (1981-1982), they do not seem to die of old age (there is no apparent tendency for a recession to come regularly after an expansion of four or five years), 1973-75 and 1981-1982, the first came after three years of expansion (1970-1973) while the second came after one year (1980-1981), no — severe recessions seem as likely after sort expansions as after long ones (again suggesting that recessionary forces do not build up in a steady or consistent way).

Across

1. college degree
4. his *Wealth of Nations* was an early classic (2 words)
9. getting the most from efforts
11. shedder of light
12. preposition
16, 18. keeping government to a minimum
19. assist
20. the _____ countries, also known as the third world
24. this company helps you to talk to your friends at home
25. above
26. fairness
27. charged particle
29. during hyperinflation, this becomes practically worthless
31. advocated government spending to restore full employment
33. represents workers
34. losers in war often suffer this

Note to students: answers to crossword puzzles are at
the end of the Study Guide.

Down

1. exist
2. labor organization
3. be ill
4. objective
5. the economic disease of the 1930s
6. indef. article
7. provider of long-distance telephone services
8. artificial (abbrev.)
10. a business degree
13. important source of information
14. an economic problem
15. international institution lending to developing nations
17. rise in average level of prices
21. needed when looking for a job
22. large, powerful
23. early economist (see inside cover of text)
25. individuals
28. number
29. 1st person, possessive
30. holds corn or missiles
31. he wrote the words to "The Star-spangled Banner"
32. its price skyrocketed in 1970s

Chapter 1 Economic Problems and Economic Goals

APPENDIX

This appendix provides additional information and practice for those who have already studied the appendix to Chapter 1 in the textbook.

Graphs

During rainy spells, sales of lawn furniture decline. A simple version of the relationship between weather and the sales of lawn furniture is illustrated in Figure 1.1 below.

The two measures used in this graph—sales of furniture and rainfall—are examples of **variables**. A variable is something that can change, or vary, from time to time or from place to place. For example, the amount of rain in April is generally different from the amount in July.

The statement that the sales of lawn furniture decline during rainy weather means that there is a relationship between the two variables in Figure 1.1. In particular, it means that when rainfall increases, sales decline. This idea can be illustrated in the figure.

The two *axes*, marked with numbers, meet at the origin 0. The *vertical axis* shows the quantity of lawn furniture sold. The *horizontal axis* shows the amount of rainfall. The relationship between the two variables is

Figure 1.1

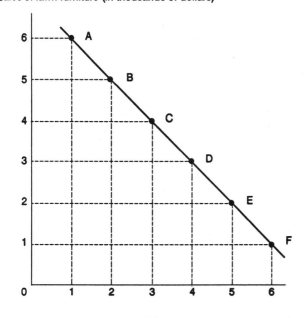

Sales of lawn furniture (in thousands of dollars)

Amount of rainfall (inches per month)

depicted by the line marked with the letters *A* through *F*. For example, point *A* shows that when the rainfall is one inch per month (measured along the horizontal axis), there are $6,000 worth of sales of lawn furniture (measured up the vertical axis). Likewise, at point *B*, 2 inches of rainfall result in sales of $5,000. In this way, each time you read a point on the line you get one bit of information. These "bits" are shown in Table 1.1.

Table 1.1

Point	A	B	C	D	E	F
Rainfall	1	2	3	4	5	6
Sales	6	5	4	3	2	1

Thus, the rule for reading the graph is as follows. If you want to find out how much furniture will be sold when there is some particular amount of rain (say, 3 inches), go along the horizontal axis to 3 units. Then go directly up to the line. This shows sales of $4,000 worth of furniture when the rainfall is 3 inches. Question 1 at the end of this appendix provides an exercise in reading graphs.

Slope

Figure 1.1 shows not only that rainfall and sales are related. It shows the direction of that relationship. Specifically, when rainfall increases, sales decrease. In other words, sales are **negatively** or **inversely** related to rainfall. This negative relationship means that the line in Figure 1.1 slopes downward to the right. As you move to the right (as rainfall increases), the height of the line decreases (sales decrease). For example, by comparing points *A* and *B*, we see that when rainfall increases from 1 to 2 inches, sales decrease from $6,000 to $5,000.

A **positive** or **direct** relationship is illustrated in Figure 1.2; both variables change in the same direction. When snowfall increases, sales of skis increase, too. This means that as we move to the right (more snow), the line slopes upward (more sales of skis).

A graph such as Figure 1.2 shows not only the *direction* of the relationship between the two variables; it also shows the *strength*. For example, it shows that when snow increases by 1 inch (from 2 to 3 inches), 2,000 more skis are sold. The *strength* of the relationship is shown by **the slope** of the line. The slope of the line is defined as the

Chapter 1   Economic Problems and Economic Goals

13

Figure 1.2

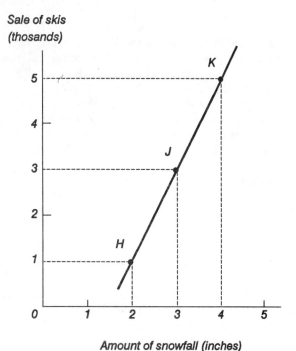

Sale of skis (thosands)

Amount of snowfall (inches)

Figure 1.3

Sales

Snowfall

amount by which the height of the line changes when you go one more unit to the right on the horizontal axis. In Figure 1.2, the slope is 2; a 1 unit increase in snow causes a 2 unit increase in the sales of skis. Alternatively, the slope of a line between two points (such as H and K in Figure 1.2) is defined as the *rise* (that is, the vertical change of 4 units) *divided by the run* (the horizontal change of 2 units). Again, we see that the slope of the line is 2 (that is, 4 divided by 2).

Observe that ski sales respond much more strongly to snow in Figure 1.2 than in Figure 1.3. In Figure 1.3, the much weaker response is illustrated by the relatively flat curve; when snowfall increases by 1 unit, ski sales increase only a half unit; the slope is only 1/2.

Back in Figure 1.1, an increase in one variable (rain) caused a decrease in the other variable (sales of lawn furniture). The line slopes downward; that is, the slope is negative. (For example, between points A and C, the rise is -2 while the run is 2; thus the slope is -1.) A negative slope thus means that the two variables are negatively or inversely related.

In summary, the slope of the line shows two ideas—the direction and strength of the relationship between two variables. The *direction* of the relationship depends on whether the line slopes up or down—that is, whether the slope is positive or negative. The *strength* of

the relationship depends on the steepness of the line. Questions 3 and 4 at the end of this appendix deal with the concept of slope.

Linear Equations

Sometimes the relationship between two variables is shown not by a graph, but by an equation. For example, suppose that you are told that my expenditures on consumer goods (C) each month depends on my income (Y) according to the equation:

$$C = \$400 + 0.50Y$$

(Economists almost always use the letter Y for income. I is used to denote investment.)

In simple English, this equation says that I spend $400 plus half of my income that month. As my income varies from month to month, the equation tells you how my expenditures will vary. Whatever my income (Y) is, you can figure out how much I am likely to spend for consumer goods (C).

For example, choose some convenient value for my income, like Y = 1,000. Then substitute this into the equation to get C = 400 + 0.5 x 1,000 = 400 + 500 = 900. This tells us that when my income (Y) is 1,000, my expenditures on consumer goods (C) is 900. Now choose any other convenient value, like $Y = 1,100$. Substituting this into the equation indicates that when my income is 1,100, my expenditures on consumer goods is $C = 400 + 0.5 \times 1,100 = 950$. Each time you choose a value of Y and make this substitution you thus get one bit of information. These two bits are shown in Table 1.2. As an exercise, fill in the rest of the table.

Figure 1.4 shows this relationship in a graph. The slope of the line is 0.5. This is because every time my income increases by $100 (shown as a move of one unit along the horizontal axis), I spend another $50 (shown as a rise of 0.5 of a unit). In contrast, the equation $C = 400 + 0.75Y$ represents the behavior of individuals who spend $400 plus three quarters of their income. In this case, the slope of the line would be 0.75, because every increase of $100 in income would cause an increase of $75 in consumption.

In general, any equation of the sort $C = a + bY$ represents a line with a slope equal to b. Such an equation is a **linear** equation. For example, the linear equation illustrated in Figure 1.4 has $a = 400$ and $b = 0.5$.

The number b (in this example, 0.5) is known as the **coefficient** of the variable Y. It indicates the slope of the line. The number a (400) shows how high the line is where it meets the vertical axis (point A). Thus, a is often called the **vertical intercept** of this equation. For example, the vertical intercept in Figure 1.4 is 400; this corresponds to the equation where $a = 400$.

At this time, you should do questions 5 and 6, which deal with linear equations.

Curves

So far we have drawn only straight lines. A straight line is easy to use because it has a *constant* slope. For example, in Figure 1.1, the slope of the line is the same between A and B as it is between any other two points on the line.

However, sometimes a relationship is described better by a curve, like the one in Figure 1.5 which illustrates how a student's final grade depends on how many hours he or she spends studying during the average week. A curve does not have a constant slope; as you move to the right on this curve, it gets flatter. For example, the first hour of studying causes an increase in the grade by 30 points—from 20 to 50. However, the second hour makes it rise by only 20 more (to 70), and the third hour causes an increase by only 5 more points. Each move to the right by 1 hour per week causes a smaller increase in the grade. In this example, it would obviously be impossible for the relationship to continue in a straight line in the way it began . The first hour caused an increase of 30 points. Four hours obviously couldn't cause an increase of 120 points, for the simple reason that the exam has a maximum grade of 100 points.

In this curve, as before, the slope is still identified as the amount by which the height of the curve changes as you go one more unit to the right along the horizontal axis. But in this case, the slope changes as you go to the right. For the first hour, it is 30; for the second, 20; then 5, and so on.

Figure 1.4

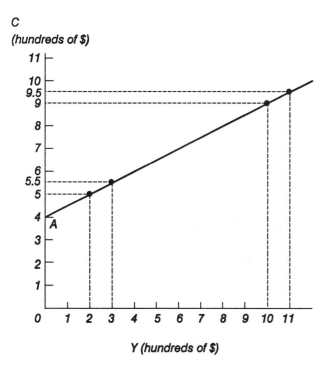

C
(hundreds of $)

Y (hundreds of $)

Table 1.2											
Y	100	200	300	400	500	600	700	800	900	1000	1100
C										900	950

Figure 1.5

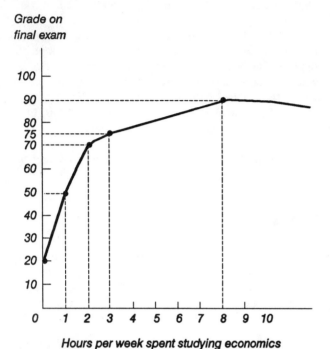

Grade on final exam

Hours per week spent studying economics

Figure 1.6

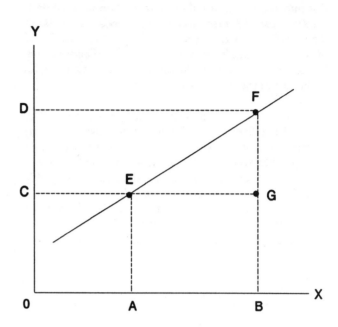

The decreasing slope in Figure 1.5 indicates that as the student spends more and more time studying, each additional hour may raise the grade, *but not by as much as the previous hour*. The first hour raises the grade by 30 points, the next by only 20. This is an example of diminishing returns; the payoff (in terms of a higher grade) diminishes as a person studies more and more.

Notice that, according to Figure 1.5, the curve reaches its maximum. No matter how much time the student spends studying, he or she can't get more than 90. Indeed, after 8 hours, the student gets tired and stale. Any more time with the books will be counterproductive. The slope of the curve becomes negative; each additional hour results in a lower grade.

Other Graphs

Sometimes, in presenting a general argument, we don't bother to put numbers on the axes. For example, the linear relationship in Figure 1.6 shows no numbers (except for the 0 at the origin). Without numbers, we can't tell exactly how strong the relationship is between the variables X and Y. But the graph still provides important information — that the relationship is linear, with a constant direction and slope. In this diagram, we can put in letters as points of reference. Point E represents OA units of X, and its height is measured as OC units of Y.

When describing the movement from E to F along the line, it helps to look at triangle EFG. The change in X is the difference between distance OB and OA; that is, distance AB. Likewise, the change in Y can be read from the vertical axis as CD, or from the triangle as distance GF.

The Ratio Scale

In the standard diagram (such as Figure 1.2) each vertical increase of one notch represents the same increase — in this example, an increase of 1,000 skis. Equal distances along an axis represent equal changes in the variable.

There is, however, an important exception to this rule, illustrated in Figure 1.7. Going the first notch up the vertical axis represents an increase in population from 25 to 50 million, or a change of 25 million. The second notch represents an increase of 50 million — from 50 to 100 people. Here, each notch represents a constant *percentage* change — specifically an increase of 100% in population. Such a diagram, where equal moves along an axis measure equal *percentage* changes, is known as a **ratio scale** or **logarithmic scale**.

In economics, a ratio scale is used most frequently along the vertical axis, with time shown on the horizontal axis (as in Figure 1.7). Such a diagram is used when we're interested in the percentage rate of growth of something—for example, the percentage rate of growth of population or the percentage increase in prices. When such a curve becomes steeper, the percentage rate of increase in population or prices is becoming greater. We can identify the period when the rate of growth was the most rapid. It is the period when the curve is the steepest.

QUESTIONS

1. Point *A* in Figure 1.8 has a height of _____ and lies distance _____ to the right of the origin. Thus, it indicates that when there is a light rainfall of _____ centimeters during rush hour, _____ thousand workers will arrive to work on time. If rain is heavier, at 6 cm., only _____ thousand workers will be on time. With a very heavy rain of 10 cm., _____ thousand workers will be on time.

Figure 1.7

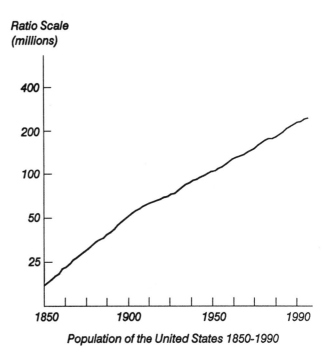

Population of the United States 1850-1990

2. From Figure 1.2 fill in Table 1.3

Table 1.3

Amount of snow	2	3	4
Sales of skis			

3. There are six different lines in Figure 1.9. In Table 1.4, fill in the slope of each line.

Table 1.4

Line	a	b	c	d	e	f
Slope						

Figure 1.8

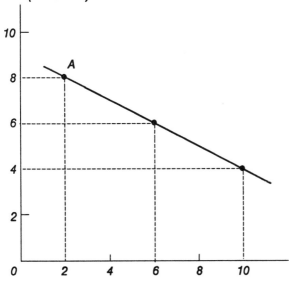

Rainfall during rush hour (centimeters)

Figure 1.9

Figure 1.10

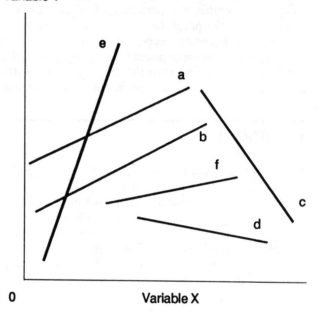

4. Which of the lines in Figure 1.10 show a positive relationship between variables X and Y? _____ .
   When X increases by 1 unit, which of these lines shows the greatest increase in Y? _____ . When X increases by 1 unit, which of these lines shows the greatest decrease in Y? _____ .

5. Consider two variables, X and Y, that are related according to the linear equation $Y = 8 - 2X$. From this equation, fill in Table 1.5.

Table 1.5

X	0	1	2	3	4
Y					

Draw the line representing this equation in Figure 1.11.

The slope of this line is _____ .

The vertical intercept is _____ .

Figure 1.11

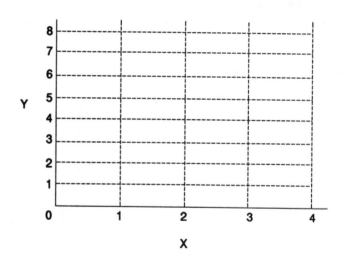

6. The following linear equations show how one variable, Y, depends on another variable, X.

(a) $Y = 90 + 10X$
(b) $Y = 50 + 15X$
(c) $Y = 80 - 5X$
(d) $Y = 3X$
(e) $Y = -10 + 5X$
(f) $Y = 50$

Line _____ has the largest vertical intercept and line _____ has the largest slope.

When X increases by 1 unit, which line shows the largest increase in Y? _____.

When $X = 0$, the highest line is _____.

Which equations show a positive relationship between X and Y? _____.

Which a negative relationship? _____.

What is the slope of (f)? _____.

Which line has a vertical intercept of zero? _____.

Which line passes through the origin? _____.

ANSWERS

Table 1.2, completed:

Y	100	200	300	400	500	600	700	800	900	1000	1100
C	450	500	550	600	650	700	750	800	850	900	950

1.   8, 2, 2, 8, 6, 4

2.   **Table 1.3 completed:**

Amount of snow	2	3	4
Sales of skis	1	3	5

3.   **Table 1.4 completed:**

Line	a	b	c	d	e	f
Slope	1	3	-1	-3	-3	0

4. $(a, b, e, f), e, c$

5.   **Table 1.5, completed:**

X	0	1	2	3	4
Y	8	6	4	2	0

-2, 8

6. $a, b, b, a, (a, b, d, e), c, 0, d, d.$

CHAPTER 2

SCARCITY AND CHOICE
The Economic Problem

LEARNING OBJECTIVES

After you have studied this chapter in the textbook and study guide, you should be able to

✔ Understand why the combination of limited resources and unlimited wants requires us to *make choices*

✔ Define the three major *factors of production*

✔ Explain the *difference* between *real capital* and *financial capital*, and explain why economists focus on real rather than financial capital when studying the productive capacity of the economy

✔ Explain the functions of the *entrepreneur*

✔ Explain the concept of *opportunity cost*, and explain how it is related to the production possibilities curve (PPC)

✔ Explain why the PPC slopes downward to the right

✔ Explain why the PPC usually bows outward from the origin

✔ Explain a circumstance in which the PPC might be a straight line, instead of bowing outward

✔ Explain why production occurs within the PPC if there is large-scale unemployment

✔ Explain the difference between a high-growth and a low-growth policy, using a PPC with capital goods on one axis and consumer goods on the other (Figure 2-5 in the textbook)

✔ Explain why it is impossible to develop a theory without simplifying

MAJOR PURPOSE

The major purpose of this chapter is to introduce the concept of *scarcity*. Because of limited resources, we cannot have all the goods and services that we want. We must therefore *make choices*, picking some items and foregoing others. This idea—that we face scarcity and therefore have to make choices—is at the center of economics. A standard definition of economics is "the study of the allocation of scarce resources to satisfy alternative, competing human wants."

The ideas of scarcity and choice are illustrated by the *production possibilities curve*. This illustrates the idea of scarcity because we are limited to a point on (or within) the curve; we cannot go outside the curve with our present resources and technological capabilities. The curve also illustrates the need to make *choices*. When we pick one point on the production possibilities curve, we pass over all the other points, and forego the goods which we might have had if we had picked some other point.

This chapter applies the production possiblities curve to illustrate the *choice between consumer goods now and consumer goods in the future*. We can forego some consumer goods now and use the resources to produce capital equipment instead. The additional capital will help us to produce even more consumer goods in the future.

Finally, this chapter provides an introduction to *economic theory*. Economic theory *must* be a *simplification* of the real world. If we strove for a complete theory which took into account all the complexities of our world, we would get bogged down in a swamp of detail. When we simplify, we should keep in mind a central question: Does our theory include the most important relationships in the economy, or *have we left out something of critical importance?*

HIGHLIGHTS OF CHAPTER

Scarcity is one of the most important concepts in economics. Scarcity requires us to *make choices*; we cannot have everything we want. Why? The answer is that our resources are limited, while our wants are not.

When we make choices, we pick some goods and services, and forego others. If we pick a college education, for example, we may have to put off buying a car for several years. The *opportunity cost* of our education is the car and other goods and services which we forego to pay tuition, room, and board. Similarly, for the society as a whole, opportunity cost is an important concept. For example, when we decide to produce more weapons, we forego the consumer goods and services we might have produced instead. Individuals, corporations, and governments are continuously making choices among the options open to them.

The ideas of scarcity, the need to make choices, and opportunity cost are summarized by the *production possibilities curve* (PPC). The PPC shows the options from which a *choice* is made. The fact that we are limited by the PPC, and cannot pick a point outside it with our present resources and technology, illustrates the idea of *scarcity*. The *slope* of the PPC shows how much of one good we must forego when we choose more of another. In other words, the slope shows the *opportunity cost* of choosing more of a specific good.

The PPC has two important properties. First, it slopes downward to the right. This means that, if we decide to produce more of one good, we give up some of the other. The idea that there is an opportunity cost when we produce more of one good is illustrated by the downward slope of the PPC curve.

The second feature of the typical PPC curve is that it is *bowed out*—that is, it is *concave* to the origin. This is so because resources are *specialized*. If we decide to produce more and more wheat, we will use land which is less and less suited to the production of wheat, even though it was very good for producing cotton. For each additional unit of wheat, we will have to give up more cotton. Thus, the outward bend in the PPC illustrates the idea of *increasing opportunity cost*.

Under certain circumstances, however, the PPC need not bow outward. It is possible that two goods might require the same set of resources in their production. For example, radios and telephones might take the same combination of resources in their production—the same combination of copper, plastic, silicon, labor, etc.—in which case the PPC would be a *straight line*. In this particular case, the *opportunity cost of radios would be constant* in terms of the telephones foregone. (The opportunity cost of both radios and telephones might nevertheless still increase, in terms of the food or clothing foregone. In other words, the PPC would be a straight line if we put radios and telephones on the two axes, but would bow out if we put radios on one axis and food on the other.)

It is worth emphasizing that a downward slope and an outward bow are two *different* features. A PPC can slope downward without bowing outward—as in the example of radios and telephones. A downward slope means that the opportunity cost is *positive*. An outward bow means that the opportunity cost *increases* as more of a good is produced.

One of the important choices facing the society is the choice between consumer goods and capital goods. If we produce only a little capital, we will be able to enjoy a large quantity of consumer goods now. But, with little investment, we will have slow growth. In other words there is a *tradeoff between a high current level of consumption and high growth*. This tradeoff or choice is illustrated when we draw a PPC curve with consumer goods on one axis and capital goods on the other. For example, Figure 2-5 in the textbook illustrates the difference between a high-growth and a low-growth strategy. A high-growth strategy requires that a sizable fraction of our resources be committed to investment in plant and equipment (capital goods). But this makes possible a rapid growth—that is, a rapid outward movement of the PPC.

This chapter provides a brief introduction to economic theory. When we develop economic theories, we *must* simplify. The world is much too complex to describe in all its detail. The objective of theory is to strip away the nonessential complications in order to see the important relationships within the economy. Theory should not be dismissed because it fails to account for everything, just as a road map should not be discarded as useless just because it doesn't show everything. But, because of simplifications, theory must be used carefully. Just as last week's weather map is useless for planning a trip in a car, so the theory which helps to explain one aspect of the economy may be inappropriate or useless for explaining others.

Finally, this chapter explains the distinction between *positive* and *normative* economics. Positive or descriptive economics is aimed at explaining what has been happening and why. Normative economics deals with policies; it deals with the way things *ought* to be.

IMPORTANT TERMS: MATCH THE COLUMNS

Match the first column with the corresponding phrase in the second column.

_____	1. Economic resources	a. Outward bow of PPC
_____	2. Financial capital	b. Choices open to society
_____	3. Real capital	c. Specialized resources
_____	4. Increase in real capital	d. Stocks and bonds
_____	5. Entrepreneur	e. Straight-line PPC
_____	6. PPC	f. Organizer of production
_____	7. Opportunity cost	g. Basic inputs used in the production of goods and services
_____	8. Increasing opportunity cost	h. Investment
_____	9. Constant opportunity cost	i. Alternative foregone
_____	10. Cause of outward bow of PPC	j. Machinery, equipment, and buildings

TRUE-FALSE

T   F   1.   Resources are said to be scarce because they are incapable of producing all the goods and services that people want; therefore, choices must be made.

T   F   2.   Wants were *unlimited* during the early days of the study of economics in the eighteenth and nineteenth centuries. But they are no longer unlimited in the affluent countries of North America and Western Europe.

T   F   3.   Suppose that a production possibilities curve meets the clothing axis at 5 units of clothing, and at 20 units of food. This illustrates that the society can have a total of 5 units of clothing plus 20 units of food, but no more.

T   F   4.   The production possibilities curve bends outward because resources are not uniform in quality; some are better at producing one good than the other.

T   F   5.   Just as it is possible to select a combination of goods inside the PPC, so it is possible to choose a combination of goods that lies outside the PPC.

T   F   6.   An increase in the quantity of labor causes the production possibilities curve to move outward from the origin.

T   F   7.   Suppose that two countries, A and B, were identical in 1979. Suppose that, between 1979 and 1989, the economy of A grew at 4% per annum, while B grew at 3% per annum. Then, from that fact, we may conclude that economy A was allocatively more efficient than B during the 1979-1989 period.

T   F   8.   *Positive* economics is the study of how policymakers can achieve desirable (that is, *positive*) social goals.

MULTIPLE CHOICE

1. Economists often speak of wants being *unlimited* because:

   a. the cost of living has increased; it costs more to meet our basic needs now than it did twenty years ago
   b. more people live in the cities now than in an earlier age, and it is more expensive to live in cities than on the farm
   c. even though our incomes have risen, we still want *more*; we do not believe all our wants are satisfied
   d. resources such as oil have become scarcer because we have been using them up
   e. as people's incomes have risen, they have decided to take more leisure, and work fewer hours

2. By real capital, economists mean:

   a. real estate, particularly land
   b. plant and equipment
   c. the real value of bonds, adjusted for inflation
   d. the real value of common stock, adjusted for inflation
   e. both (c) and (d)

3. The production possibilities curve has one major purpose: to illustrate the need to:

   a. stop inflation
   b. cut taxes
   c. cut government spending
   d. make choices
   e. stop pollution

4. The textbook has a picture of a production possibilities curve (PPC), joining six points.

   a. All six points are equally desirable, since they all represent full employment
   b. All six points are equally desirable, since they all are consistent with zero inflation
   c. All six points are equally desirable, since they all provide for some growth
   d. All six points are possible, but the PPC curve doesn't give enough information to tell which point is best
   e. Only one of the six points is presently achievable; the others can be achieved only if the economy grows

5. An **outward bow** in the production possibilities curve illustrates what concept:

   a. scarcity
   b. unlimited wants
   c. increasing opportunity cost
   d. unemployment
   e. inflation

6. The opportunity cost of a good is measured by:

   a. the slope of the PPC
   b. how far the PPC is from the origin
   c. the slope of a line from the origin out the the PPC
   d. how far the economy is operating within the PPC
   e. how fast the PPC is shifting outward

7. Suppose the production possibilities curve is a straight line if goods X and Y are put on the axis. Then we know that:

   a. X and Y are really the same good
   b. the problem of scarcity has been solved
   c. we can have all the X and Y we want without incurring an opportunity cost, even though the general problem of scarcity has not been solved
   d. the opportunity cost of X is zero, in terms of Y foregone
   e. the opportunity cost of X is constant, in terms of Y foregone

8. We speak of a production possibilities curve as a *frontier* because:

   a. we can produce within it or on it, but not beyond it with presently available resources and technology
   b. it reflects the concept of scarcity, and goods were particularly scarce for U.S. settlers on the western frontier in the 19th century
   c. it is no longer relevant, now that the U.S. frontier has been tamed and we have an affluent society
   d. unemployment problems provide the frontier for economic research
   e. differences among resources provide the frontier for economic research

9. Suppose that the society has only one objective, to maximize growth. Then, the best choice among the five points shown on Figure 2.1 is:

   a. A
   b. B
   c. C
   d. D
   e. E

Figure 2.1

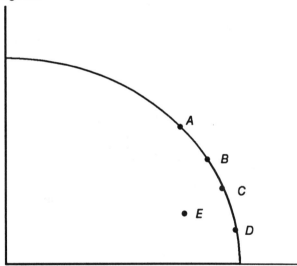

Capital goods

Consumer Goods

10. In Figure 2.1, a growth of the economy can be illustrated by:

   a. a move from point A to B
   b. a move from point B to A
   c. a move from point A to E
   d. a move from point D to E
   e. an outward shift of the production possibilities curve

11. In Figure 2.1, suppose that the economy is originally at point E. Then there will be:

   a. rapid growth
   b. no capital formation
   c. more capital formation than at points A, B, or C
   d. a high rate of unemployment
   e. rapid inflation

12. The production possibilities curve generally bends outward because:

   a. sensible people want to divide their purchases; they want to choose some food and some clothing
   b. there are economies of large-scale production
   c. most people have a comparative advantage in the production of at least one good
   d. there is much less unemployment now than during the Great Depression of the 1930s
   e. resources are not uniform in quality; some are better for producing one good than the other

NOTE: THE NEXT FOUR QUESTIONS ARE BASED ON TABLE 2.1

Table 2.1
Production Possibilities

Products:	Options:					
	A	B	C	D	E	F
Capital goods	0	1	2	3	4	5
Consumer goods	25	24	21	16	9	0

13. In Table 2.1, the opportunity cost of the second unit of capital goods is how many units of consumer goods?

   a. 1
   b. 3
   c. 5
   d. 7
   e. 9

14. Given the options in Table 2.1, a total output of 5 units of capital goods and 25 units of consumer goods:

   a. is unattainable at present
   b. represents a situation of large-scale unemployment
   c. can be achieved only if the economy achieves technological efficiency
   d. can be achieved only if the economy achieves allocative efficiency
   e. can be achieved only if the economy achieves both allocative and technological efficiency

15. Given the options in Table 2.1, a total output of 2 units of capital goods and 10 units of consumer goods:

   a. is unattainable at present
   b. represents a situation of large-scale unemployment
   c. can be achieved only if the economy achieves technological efficiency
   d. can be achieved only if the economy achieves allocative efficiency
   e. can be achieved only if the economy achieves both allocative and technological efficiency

16. The choice of option C rather than B:

   a. represents a mistake, since only 23 total units are produced (that is, 2 + 21) rather than 25 (that is, 1 + 24)
   b. represents a mistake, since consumers have fewer goods
   c. means that there will be more unemployment
   d. represents a choice of more growth
   e. represents a choice of less growth

17. The production possibilities curve shifts outward, away from the origin:

   a. if the number of workers increases
   b. if the skill of workers increase
   c. if there is more capital
   d. if technology improves
   e. if any of the above happens

18. Oil now being pumped in a pipeline is an example of:

   a. the land resource, because oil comes out of the ground
   b. real capital, because it has been produced in the past and will be used in the production of other goods
   c. financial capital, because it is valuable and is worth money
   d. financial capital, because it can be used as collateral for bank loans
   e. financial capital, because it was costly to pump out of the ground

EXERCISES

1. Consider the following production possibilities table:

Table 2.2

	Options:							
	A	B	C	D	E	F	G	H
Consumer goods	0	1	2	3	4	5	6	7
Capital goods	23	22	20	17	13	9	5	0
Opportunity cost of consumer goods		1	2					

a) Complete the third line, showing the opportunity cost of each additional unit of consumer goods.

b) Draw the PPC on Figure 2.2.

Figure 2.2

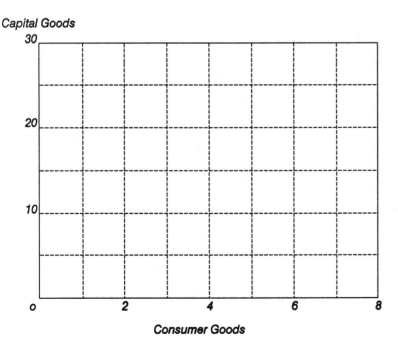

Consumer Goods

c) What is unusual about this curve?

d) In the range between points A and D, the PPC (bows outward, bows inward, is a straight line). This shows that opportunity cost is (increasing, decreasing, constant) in this range. However, between points D and G, the curve (bows outward, bows inward, is a straight line). This shows that opportunity cost is (increasing, decreasing, constant) in this range.

2. Consider a hypothetical economy with a labor force of 10,000 workers, each of whom can be put to work building either houses or roads. Each worker is available for 2,000 hours per year. Thus, there are 20 million labor hours available during the year to produce houses and roads. Table 2.3 shows how many labor hours it takes to build various quantities of houses. For example, in order to build 18,000 houses, 15 million labor hours are needed. Likewise, Table 2.4 indicates how many labor hours are needed to build various amounts of roadway. In Figure 2.3, only one point, A, on the PPC has been plotted. It shows that if no houses are built, the 20 million labor hours can be used to produce 1,000 miles of road. Using the data in Tables 2.3 and 2.4, plot four other points, and draw a PPC to connect them.

Table 2-3

Millions of labor hours	Thousands of houses
20	20
15	18
10	14
5	8
0	0

Table 2-4

Millions of labor hours	Hundreds of miles of road
20	10
15	9
10	7
5	4
0	0

Figure 2.3

ANSWERS

Matching columns:	**1 g, 2 d, 3 j, 4 h, 5 f, 6 b, 7 i, 8 a, 9 e, 10 c**

True-False:	**1 T** (p. 26)
	2 F (p. 26)
	3 F (p. 28)
	4 T (p. 29)
	5 F (p. 29)
	6 T (p. 30)
	7 F (p. 31)
	8 F (p. 33)

Multiple Choice:	**1 c** (p. 26)
	2 b (p. 26)
	3 d (p. 27)
	4 d (p. 28)
	5 c (pp. 28-29)
	6 a (pp. 28-29)
	7 e (p. 29)
	8 a (p. 29)
	9 a (p. 32)
	10 e (p. 32)
	11 d (p. 29)
	12 e (p. 29)
	13 b (p. 29)

Exercises

1. a) 3, 4, 4, 4, 5.

   c) over part of its range, it is a straight line (between D and G).

   d) bows outward, increasing, is a straight line, constant.

2. Four other points are:

	B	C	D	E
Hundreds of miles	9	7	4	0
Thousands of houses	8	14	18	20

SPECIALIZATION, EXCHANGE, AND MONEY

LEARNING OBJECTIVES

After you have studied this chapter in the textbook and study guide, you should be able to

✔ Explain why specialization and exchange go hand in hand

✔ Explain why barter is inferior to exchange with money

✔ Explain why people may nevertheless revert to barter in some circumstances

✔ Give an example of Gresham's law

✔ Explain the two major reasons why there can be gains from specialization and exchange

✔ Explain the difference between absolute advantage and comparative advantage

✔ Explain why a country may have an absolute advantage in a product without having a comparative advantage in that product

MAJOR PURPOSE

In this chapter, we study specialization, exchange, and money. People specialize and engage in exchange because there are gains from doing so. By specializing, people can achieve higher standards of living. There are *two major sources* of gain from specialization:

- *comparative advantage*, and
- *economies of scale*.

These two phenomena are the forces that motivate specialization and exchange; that is, they are the *twin engines that drive commerce.*

Money, on the other hand, *is the oil* which makes the machinery of commerce run smoothly, with a minimum of friction. Without money, people would engage in cumbersome barter. But, if some money helps to make the system work smoothly, we should not conclude that more money would make it work even better. Just as too much oil can gum up an engine, so too much money can

Chapter 3 Specialization, Exchange, and Money

cause difficulty. Specifically, it causes inflation. The Federal Reserve (the central bank of the United States) acts as the chief mechanic. Its task is to create the right amount of "oil" [money]—neither too much, nor too little. The operations of the Federal Reserve will be considered in detail in Chapter 12.

HIGHLIGHTS OF CHAPTER

One reason for economic progress has been an increase in *specialization*. Individuals, cities, and countries are now more specialized than they were a hundred years ago. When production is specialized, people engage in exchange, selling the products they produce to buy the wide variety of goods and services that they want to consume. We live in a highly interdependent economy, in which each of us depends on the specialized production of others.

Specialization and exchange would be very cumbersome without money. It is easy to imagine the difficulties that would arise if we tried to do without money and engaged in barter exchange instead. Barter requires a *coincidence of wants*—people engaging in exchange must each be able to provide a good or service that the other wants. Furthermore, for barter to work, there must be some rough equivalence in the value of the two goods or services to be exchanged. To buy toothpaste, a farmer would scarcely offer a cow in exchange. However, with money, such problems of indivisibility do not arise. The farmer may sell the cow for $1,000 and spend just a bit of the money to buy toothpaste, using the rest for a wide variety of other purchases. Money provides people with *general purchasing power;* money can be used to buy any of the wide variety of goods and services on the market. Those wishing to make exchanges no longer have to search for unlikely coincidences (such as the ill-clad farmer looking for someone who not only has clothes to exchange, but who also wants to get beef in return).

Because it is so useful for those who wish to engage in exchange, money is used even in rudimentary societies with little or no government. The prisoner-of-war camp provides an example of such a simple society. However, governments have gotten deeply involved in the monetary system. Every country uses paper money printed by the central bank or treasury.

One reason for the government to be involved in the monetary system is that the government can provide a *uniform* currency. In the United States, for example, every $1 bill (Federal Reserve Note) is worth the same as every other dollar bill. This uniformity of the money stock is very convenient. When selling something for $1, we only

have to find out if the buyer has a $1 bill. Except for the rare cases where counterfeiting is suspected, we do not need to ask the much more complicated question of whether the dollar bill is inferior to some other dollar bill.

In passing, we might note that the United States has not always had a uniform currency. In the 19th century, privately-owned banks issued currency. The value of this currency depended on the soundness of the bank that issued it. Thus, sellers did have to worry about the value of the dollar bills they accepted. Similar problems have arisen throughout history. For example, when gold coins were in use, their value could depend on the amount of gold they contained. Before the development of modern methods of producing coins with hard edges, such coins were sometimes *clipped*. That is, people chipped off bits before spending them. As a result, not every coin was worth the same as every other coin of the same denomination. People had to examine the physical condition of the coins they were accepting.

In addition to providing a uniform currency, the Federal Reserve has the responsibility of providing an appropriate quantity of money. If too many dollar bills are created, there will be "too much money chasing too few goods." Inflation will result; the dollar will decline in value. On the other hand, if the quantity of money is allowed to decline sharply, spending will decline. Sellers will have a very difficult time finding buyers. Sales will fall, unemployment will rise, and prices will be under downward pressure. The authorities do not always perform their monetary duties well. In some countries—for example, Brazil—prices are galloping ahead by more than 100% per year. This reduces the convenience of money. If prices are rising rapidly, sellers feel under pressure to spend their money as soon as possible, before its value declines significantly.

With the proper quantity of money, the monetary system can work very smoothly, making transactions very convenient. But this is all that money does—it makes exchange convenient. It is not the reason why exchange is desirable in the first place.

There are two reasons why specialization and exchange can yield benefits. The first is *comparative advantage*. The notion of comparative advantage is illustrated in the textbook by the example of the gardener and the lawyer. The lawyer has an absolute advantage in both the law and gardening; she can do both quicker than the gardener. It follows that the gardener has an absolute disadvantage in both the law and gardening—he is slower at both. However, the gardener has a comparative advantage in gardening, while the lawyer has a comparative advantage in the law. Comparative advantage provides the basis for *mutually beneficial* trade. *Both* the gardener and the lawyer can gain from specialization and exchange. (Details are provided in Box 3-3.)

Two points should be emphasized.

- Absolute advantage is not necessary for gain; the gardener can gain by specializing in gardening, even though he is not the best gardener.
- A person (or a nation) cannot have a comparative disadvantage in everything.

In the simple case of two people and two activities (law and gardening), if one person has a comparative advantage in one activity, the other person *must* have the comparative advantage in the other activity.

Economies of scale provide the second major reason why there are gains from specialization and exchange. Economies of scale exist if an increase of $x\%$ in all inputs (labor, machinery, land, steel, etc.) leads to an increase of more than $x\%$ in output. Economies of scale are the major reason why big firms have an advantage in many industries, such as automobiles and main-frame computers. Economies of scale are the major reason why costs per unit of output often decline as more is produced. For example, a car company can produce 100,000 cars at a much lower cost per car than if it produces 1,000 cars. Clearly, if a person tried to put together a car in the back yard or in a small shop, it would be very expensive. There are gains when car production is left to the specialists.

IMPORTANT TERMS

Match the first column with the corresponding phrase in the second column.

_____	1.	Barter	a.	Acting as medium of exchange
_____	2.	Required by barter	b.	Bad money drives out good
_____	3.	General purchasing power	c.	Reason the lawyer gains by practicing law
_____	4.	A function of money	d.	Exchange of one good or service for another
_____	5.	Inflation	e.	Reason costs per unit fall as more is produced
_____	6.	Cause of inflation	f.	Money
_____	7.	Absolute advantage	g.	Adam Smith's pin factory
_____	8.	Comparative advantage	h.	Good can be produced with fewest resources
_____	9.	Economies of scale	i.	Coincidence of wants
_____	10.	Example of economies of scale	j.	Fall in value of money
_____	11.	Gresham's law	k.	Too much money chasing too few goods

TRUE-FALSE

T F 1. One reason that barter is inconvenient is that many commodities cannot easily be divided into smaller parts.

T F 2. Monetary systems develop only when there is a strong national government, since strong national governments are required to provide money with value.

T F 3. Suppose that, in the prisoner-of-war camp with its "cigarette money," the value of cigarettes rises compared to the value of other items (such as beef, etc.). Such an increase is known as inflation.

T F 4. Comparative advantage is the reason why wheat is grown in Nebraska, and not in the city of Chicago.

T F 5. If everyone had the exactly the same talents and training, and exactly the same quantity of capital, then economies of scale would not exist.

T F 6. In the absence of a government, money is valuable only if it is useful. Therefore, cigarette money would be used exclusively in transactions between smokers in the prisoner-of-war camp.

T F 7. Economies of scale are the primary reason why coffee is grown in Brazil rather than New England.

T F 8. Even if everyone has the same abilities, specialization may be beneficial if there are economies of scale.

MULTIPLE CHOICE

1. One of the problems with barter is that it requires a *coincidence of wants*. This means that:

   a. everybody must want money
   b. everybody must want the same good
   c. at least two people must want the same good
   d. everybody must want my good, before I am able to exchange it
   e. for there to be an exchange between individuals A and B, individual A must want what B has, while B must want what A has

2. When a monetary system first replaces barter, it becomes possible for the first time to distinguish between:

   a. a good and a service
   b. the buyer and the seller
   c. private entrepreneurs and the government
   d. owners of capital and workers
   e. all of the above

3. Money is said to represent *general purchasing power* because:

   a. it can be used to buy any of the goods and services offered for sale
   b. the government guarantees its value
   c. the government is committed to accept money in payment of taxes
   d. Gresham's law no longer is valid
   e. Gresham's law applies to other goods, but not money

4. When we draw a diagram showing the circular flow of payments between households and businesses, the two major markets we show are:

   a. goods and services
   b. capital and labor
   c. capital and land
   d. consumer goods and economic resources
   e. products made by private entrepreneurs, and those provided by the government

5. In the present-day United States, what would an economist consider to be the *medium of exchange*?

   a. Supermarkets
   b. Corner drug stores
   c. The Sears, Roebuck catalogue
   d. Real estate brokers
   e. Dollar bills

6. When the best-tasting cigarettes started to disappear from circulation in the prisoner-of-war camp, this was an example of:

    a. economies of scale
    b. absolute advantage
    c. comparative advantage
    d. inflation
    e. Gresham's law

7. In the prisoner-of-war camp, in which cigarettes acted as money, suppose that the quantity of cigarettes coming into the camp remained constant, while the quantity of all other goods decreased. Then the most probable result would be:

    a. a rise in the value of cigarettes, measured in terms of other items
    b. a fall in the prices of other goods, measured in terms of cigarettes
    c. inflation
    d. deflation
    e. bad money driving out good money

8. Suppose that a building supervisor can lay bricks more rapidly and better than a bricklayer. Then, considering only these two individuals, we may conclude that:

    a. the bricklayer has an absolute advantage in bricklaying
    b. the supervisor has an absolute advantage in bricklaying
    c. the bricklayer has a comparative advantage in bricklaying
    d. the supervisor has a comparative advantage in bricklaying
    e. we can't tell which of the above is true without knowing how much brick cost, compared to the wage for bricklayers

9. The theory of comparative advantage was put forward by:

    a. Adam Smith
    b. John Maynard Keynes
    c. David Ricardo
    d. David Hume
    e. Karl Marx

10. Suppose that there are only two countries, A and B, and only two goods, food and clothing. If country A has a comparative advantage in the production of food, B is most likely to have a comparative advantage in:

    a. food also
    b. clothing
    c. both food and clothing
    d. neither food nor clothing
    e. we don't have enough information to decide

11. Suppose 10 workers with 1 machine can produce 100 TV sets in a month, while 20 workers with 2 machines can produce 250 TV sets in a month. This is an example of:

    a. technological efficiency
    b. allocative efficiency
    c. economies of scale
    d. comparative advantage
    e. absolute advantage

12. Suppose that (1) there are economies of scale in the production of each good, and (2) land and labor have specialized capabilities—for example, land and the climate give Brazil a comparative advantage in coffee. Then the gains from specialization will probably be:

    a. larger than if either (1) or (2) had existed alone
    b. small, since (1) and (2) tend to offset each other
    c. negative, since the combination of (1) and (2) create confusion
    d. about the same as with (1) alone, since (2) doesn't make much difference
    e. about the same as with (2) alone, since (1) doesn't make much difference

13. When tariffs among countries are reduced, this generally leads to gains from:

    a. economies of scale
    b. wider use of money rather than barter
    c. comparative advantage
    d. (a) and (b)
    e. (a) and (c)

EXERCISES

1. This exercise illustrates the idea of comparative advantage. Assume the following. A doctor working on home repairs can fix a leaky faucet in 10 minutes. A plumber takes 15 minutes. Then the (doctor, plumber) has an absolute advantage in plumbing. The doctor's time is worth $80 per hour in the practice of medicine. The plumber is paid $20 per hour.

   Suppose the doctor's house has six leaky faucets. If he fixes them himself, it will take _____ minutes. Thus, to fix the faucets, the doctor will use $_____ worth of his time. If the plumber is hired to fix the faucets, he will take _____ minutes, which is (longer, shorter) than the doctor would take.

   The cost in this case is $ _____, which is (more, less) by $_____ than if the doctor fixed the faucets himself. The (doctor, plumber) has a comparative advantage in plumbing.

2. Table 3.1 shows how many cars can be produced in a country with various amounts of inputs. Each unit of input represents a specific quantity of labor and capital. Table 3.2 provides similar information for TV sets. Table 3.1, by itself, illustrates the idea of (comparative advantage, absolute advantage, economies of scale, none of these). Table 3.2, by itself, illustrates the idea of (comparative advantage, absolute advantage, economies of scale, none of these). Suppose that the economy has 5 units of inputs to be devoted to cars and TV sets. Plot the PPC for these 5 units of input in Figure 3.1. How is the shape of the PPC different from the PPCs in Chapter 2? _____

   The opportunity cost of producing cars (increases, decreases, remains constant) as more are produced.

Table 3.1 Production of cars

Number of Cars (millions)	Units of input
1	1
3	2
6	3
12	4
20	5

Table 3.2 Production of TV sets

Number of TV Sets (millions)	Units of input
20	1
40	2
60	3
80	4
100	5

Figure 3.1

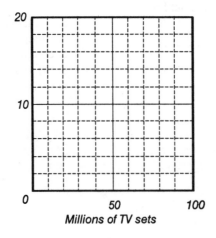

Millions of cars

Millions of TV sets

ESSAY QUESTIONS

1. The textbook explains why comparative advantage can mean that there are benefits from specialization and exchange. But it does not explain why specific people or nations might have a comparative advantage. How would you explain Iowa's comparative advantage over New England in producing corn? Why does Pennsylvania have a comparative advantage over most of the other states in the production of steel? Why does Taiwan have a comparative advantage in the production of transistor radios and TV sets?

2. Why do you think that most economists are usually in favor of reducing tariffs and other barriers to international trade? Why might anyone oppose the reduction of tariffs? The president has generally been more strongly in favor of freer trade than have individual members of the House of Representatives. How might this be explained?

3. There are disadvantages associated with specialization, as well as advantages. What are they?

ANSWERS

Matching columns: 1 d, 2 i, 3 f, 4 a, 5 j, 6 k, 7 h, 8 c, 9 e, 10 g, 11 b

True-False:
1 T (p. 37)
2 F (p. 39)
3 F (p. 40)
4 T (p. 41)
5 F (p. 42)
6 F (p. 40)
7 F (p. 41)
8 T (p. 43)

Multiple Choice:
1 e (p. 37)
2 b (p. 37)
3 a (p. 37)
4 d (p. 39)
5 e (p. 39)
6 e (p. 40)
7 c (p. 40)
8 b (p. 41)
9 c (p. 41)
10 b (p. 41)
11 c (p. 43)
12 a (pp. 41-43)
13 e (p. 43)

Exercises

1.   doctor,
60,
$80,
90,
longer,
$30,
less,

$50,
plumber.

2.   economies of scale,
     none of these,
     it bows inward,
     decreases.

Figure 3.1, completed

Millions of cars

Millions of TV sets

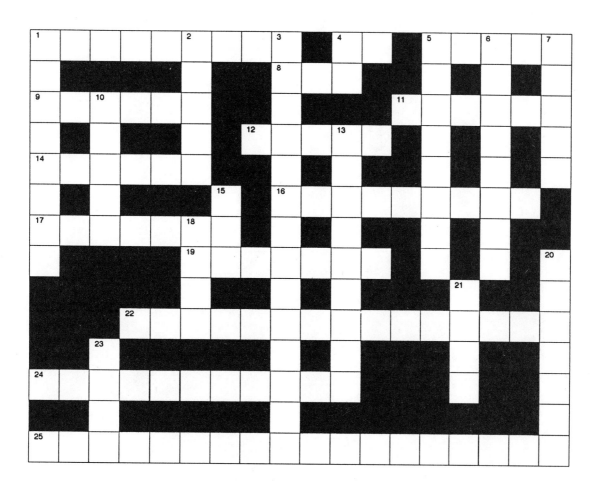

Across

1, 4, 5. reason why there are gains from specialization
8. it's mightier than the sword
9. covering of spun silk
11. Princeton; also, capital of Bahamas
12. top of the cake
14. in a light spirit; jauntily
16. *really* bad
17. his 300-year old law worked in the Prisoner-of-war camp
19. factor of production, which has itself been produced
22. attribute of money (2 words)
24. for beneficial trade, this type of advantage is good enough
25. required for barter (3 words)

Down

1. if people specialize, this becomes necessary
2. oil for the wheels of commerce
3. a way of increasing living standards
4. above
5. because of this, not all our wants can be met
6. this advantage is desirable, but not necessary for specialization
7. if all incomes are _____, top 10% of population get 10% of total income
10. production possibilities _____
13. a type of economics
15. doctors' organization (abbrev.)
18. sharp (Lat.)
20. what someone does in an economy with no money
21. item produced for exchange
23. all

CHAPTER 4

DEMAND AND SUPPLY:
The Market Mechanism

LEARNING OBJECTIVES

After you have studied this chapter in the textbook and study guide, you should be able to

✔ Explain why the demand curve slopes downward to the right

✔ Explain why the supply curve slopes upward to the right

✔ Explain why a price that begins away from equilibrium will move to equilibrium

✔ List and explain three things that can shift the demand curve and four that can shift the supply curve

✔ Give one example each of a pair of goods that are *(1)* substitutes in use *(2)* complements in use *(3)* substitutes in production, and *(4)* complements in production. In each case, you should be able to explain why the pair fits into the category.

✔ Explain the distinction between product markets and markets for factors of production

✔ Explain how the factor markets can help answer the question, *For whom?*

✔ Explain how changes in factor markets can affect what happens in a product market, and vice versa

✔ Explain the main strengths and main shortcomings of the market mechanism as a way of answering the questions, *What? How?* and *For whom?*

MAJOR PURPOSE

This chapter is one of the most important in the book. It introduces the concepts of *demand* and *supply*, which help us to understand what is happening in the market for a specific product. The demand curve illustrates how buyers respond to various possible prices:

At lower prices, they buy more. On the other hand, sellers react negatively to low prices: They offer less for sale. This response of sellers is illustrated by the supply curve.

When drawing a demand or supply curve, we isolate the effect of *price alone* on the behavior of buyers and sellers. Of course, many other things besides price can affect their behavior. When we draw a demand or supply curve and look at the effect of price alone, we make the *ceteris paribus* assumption—that all these other things do not change. In cases where they do in fact change, we are no longer on a single demand or supply curve; the demand or supply curve *shifts*.

Other important concepts introduced in this chapter are:

- the concept of *equilibrium*,
- *surplus* and *shortage*, and
- *substitutes* and *complementary goods*.

HIGHLIGHTS OF CHAPTER

In every economy, some mechanism is needed to decide three major questions: *What* will be produced? *How* will it be produced? And *for whom* will it be produced? There are two major ways of answering these questions:

- through the market—that is, through voluntary exchanges between buyers and sellers, and
- through governmental decision-making.

(Other ways are sometimes used—for example, in a family or in a monastery. But we are not primarily interested in these alternatives.)

All nations have some reliance on markets and some reliance on governmental decision-making. However, there are substantial differences among nations. In the United States, the market is the most important mechanism, although the government does play a significant role in modifying the outcome of the market. In the U.S.S.R., government plays a much more central role, although there is some reliance on markets.

The central feature of a market is *price*. Different prices for different goods provide *incentives* for producers to make some goods rather than others, and incentives for consumers to purchase cheap goods rather than expensive ones. *Prices* also provide *signals* and *information* to buyers and sellers. For example, the willingness of buyers to pay a high price acts as a signal to producers, showing that people are eager to obtain the product.

To study how buyers respond to different prices, we use a *demand curve* or *demand schedule*. This curve or schedule shows the quantity of a specific good that buyers would be willing and able to purchase at various different prices. The demand curve slopes downward to the right, illustrating that people are more eager to buy at lower prices. A major reason is that, at a lower price, people have an incentive to *switch* away from other products and buy the product whose price is lower instead.

On the other side of the market, the supply curve shows how much sellers would be willing to offer at various prices. It slopes upward to the right, because sellers will be increasingly eager to sell as the price rises. Again, the willingness to *switch* is an important reason for the slope. If the price of a good is higher, firms have an incentive to drop other products, and make more of this good instead.

What happens in the market depends on both demand and supply. To find the *equilibrium* price and quantity, we put the demand and supply curves together, to find where they intersect. At this price, the quantity offered by sellers is equal to the quantity which buyers want to purchase. There is no unfulfilled demand to pull prices up, nor any excess offers to pull prices down.

When the price is not at its equilibrium, there are pressures for it to change. If the price is below its equilibrium, for example, there are eager buyers who are unable to find the good for sale. In other words, there is a *shortage*. Producers notice this and conclude that they can sell at a higher price. The price rises to its equilibrium level. On the other and, if the price is initially above its equilibrium, there is a *surplus*. Eager sellers are unable to find buyers. They are willing to sell at a lower price. The price falls to its equilibrium.

When we draw a demand or supply curve, we are looking at the way in which buyers and sellers respond to price, and to price *alone*. In practice, of course, buyers and sellers are influenced by many other things than the price of the good—for example, buyers generally purchase more when their incomes rise, and sellers are less willing to sell when the costs of their inputs rise. But these other things are held constant when a single demand or supply curve is drawn. This is the important assumption of *ceteris paribus*, that other things do not change. If they do change, the demand or supply curve *shifts*. For example, an increase in income generally causes a rightward shift in the whole demand curve. However, in the case of inferior goods, the demand curve shifts left; when people can afford better alternatives, they do so.

If the demand curve shifts to the right while the supply curve remains stable, then both price and quantity will increase. On the other hand, if the supply curve shifts to the right while the demand curve remains stable, then quantity will increase but price will fall. In brief, *a change in demand makes price and quantity change in the same direction, whereas a change in supply markets price and quantity move in opposite directions*. In practice, of course, many things can happen at once; often the demand and supply curves both shift. In this case, it becomes more difficult to predict what will happen.

Supply and demand theory is often used to study the market for a single good. However, there are strong connections among markets. When a price changes in one market, it can change conditions in other markets. For example, an increase in the price of gasoline in the 1970s caused a decline in the demand for large cars. This is an example of *complementary goods*—large cars and gasoline are used *together*. When the price of gasoline increases, the demand for large cars shifts left.

Whereas gasoline and cars are complements, some other products—such as bus tickets and train tickets—are *substitutes*. A person wanting to travel to the next city can go either by train or by bus. The higher is the train fare, the more people will use busses instead. Thus, a higher price of train tickets causes the demand for bus tickets to shift to the right.

Goods may also be substitutes or complements in production. Substitutes in production are goods which use the same inputs; the inputs can be used to produce either the one good or the other. For example, land can be used to produce either wheat or corn. If there is a crop failure abroad and the United States exports much more wheat, the price of wheat will be bid up. Farmers will be encouraged to switch out of the production of corn and produce additional wheat instead. The supply curve for corn will shift to the left.

On the other hand, complements are produced together. For example, wheat and straw are produced together. If the price of wheat is bid up, more wheat will be produced. In the process, more straw will be produced as a by-product. The supply curve of straw will shift to the right.

The question of *what* will be produced is decided primarily in the product market. To throw light on the other two questions—*how?* and *for whom?*—we look first at the markets for inputs. For example, the market for labor helps to answer these two questions. If the demand for labor is high compared to its supply, then wage rates will be high. Thus, wage rates are much higher in the

United States than in India because there are fewer workers for each unit of land and capital in the United States. As a result of the high wage, producers in the United States have an incentive to use only a little labor, and substitute capital instead. In an Indian factory, in contrast, many more things are done by hand because of the low wage rate. The wage rate not only helps to determine how things are produced, but it also helps to determine who gets the product. Because wage rates are high in the United States, the American worker can buy and consume many more products than the Indian worker.

Observe that high wage rates affect what the worker can buy; with high wages, workers are more likely to buy TV sets and homes. This means that wages—determined in the factor markets in the lower box in Figure 4-8 in the textbook—have an impact on the demand for TV sets, homes, and other products in the upper box. Thus, there are important connections among markets.

Finally, this chapter summarizes the strengths and weaknesses of the market as a mechanism for answering the three central questions—What, How, and For Whom? The strong points of the market are that:

- it encourages producers to make what consumers want,

- it provides people with an incentive to acquire useful skills,

- it encourages consumers to conserve scarce goods,

- it encourages producers to conserve scarce resources,

- it provides a high degree of economic freedom, and

- it provides buyers and sellers with information on market conditions, including local conditions.

The market mechanism is also subject to major criticisms:

- some people may be left in desperate poverty,

- markets don't work in the case of public goods such as defense and the police,

- monopolies and oligopolies may have the power to keep production down and keep prices up,

- the market does not provide a strong incentive for producers to limit pollution and other negative side-effects,

- a market economy may be unstable (although government policies will not necessarily increase stability), and

- producers may simply be satisfying a want that they have created in the first place through advertising.

To evaluate the market, it is important to compare it with the alternatives which exist in fact, not with some ideal, unattainable system. The textbook outlines a few of the problems which can arise when the government sets prices—in particular, the problem of black markets and shortages. A number of countries that have interfered very heavily in economic activity—such as the Soviet Union—have run into severe problems, including shortages.

IMPORTANT TERMS

Match the first column with the corresponding phrase in the second column.

_____ 1. Capitalism	a. All the producers of a single good
_____ 2. Monopoly	b. If price of A rises, demand for B increases
_____ 3. Oligopoly	c. Surplus
_____ 4. Perfect competition	d. Free enterprise
_____ 5. Industry	e. Demand for this declines as income rises
_____ 6. Firm	f. Nothing else changes
_____ 7. Excess supply	g. Goods used together
_____ 8. Excess demand	h. Market with only one seller
_____ 9. Inferior good	i. Where every buyer and seller is a price taker
_____10. Complementary goods	j. Shortage
_____11. Substitutes	k. A single business organization, such as General Motors
_____12. *Ceteris paribus*	l. Market dominated by a few sellers

TRUE-FALSE

T F 1. Perfect competition exists only when the government fixes the price, so that no single buyer or seller is able to influence the price of the good.

T F 2. Perfect competition will not exist in a market if there is only one seller, or if there is only one buyer.

T F 3. In a perfectly competitive industry, every buyer and seller takes the quantity as given, and is left with only a pricing decision.

T F 4. Even if there are many buyers, imperfect competition can exist in a market.

T F 5. Even if there are many sellers, imperfect competition can exist in a market.

T F 6. In a capitalist economy, most of the capital equipment is owned by the government.

T F 7. A surplus drives the price down; a shortage drives the price up.

T F 8. If the price of wheat increases, the supply curve of straw will probably shift to the right.

T F 9. The demand curve for Pepsi Cola will probably shift to the right if the price of Coke rises.

T F 10. If the price of paper increases, the supply curve of books will probably shift to the right.

T F 11. If demand increases while supply decreases, the price will increase.

T F 12. If the demand curve shifts to the right, the result will be an increase in the quantity sold and an increase in the market price.

T F 13. If both the demand and supply curves for a product shift to the right, we can expect the quantity sold to increase, but we cannot be sure whether the price will rise or fall.

T F 14. One essential characteristic of a free enterprise economy is that the government make it easier to enter businesses freely by subsidizing new businesses.

T F 15. Factor markets are different from the markets for most goods, in that goods markets are generally perfectly competitive, while the markets for factors are usually monopolized.

MULTIPLE CHOICE

1. Economists sometimes speak of a *free* market. By *free*, they mean:

    a. prices are low
    b. people do not have to pay admission to the marketplace
    c. transactions take place with little or no government interference
    d. the government is not a buyer or seller in the market
    e. there is perfect competition in that market

2. The U.S. government uses four major ways to influence What will be produced, How, and For Whom. It uses every one of the following except one. Which one does not belong on this list?

    a. Spending
    b. Taxes
    c. Regulation
    d. Comprehensive central planning
    e. Public enterprises

3. What is the most important characteristic of perfect competition?

   a. Each seller has at least one powerful competitor to worry about
   b. There is at least one powerful, efficient producer who acts to keep prices down
   c. Every buyer can go to at least three or four sellers to see who has the lowest price
   d. Every buyer and seller is a price taker; none has any power to set price
   e. There must be many buyers, and at least three or four sellers

4. A market with one seller and a few buyers is an example of:

   a. monopoly
   b. oligopoly
   c. perfect competition
   d. technological inefficiency
   e. a black market

5. It is most accurate to speak of General Motors as:

   a. a plant
   b. a firm
   c. an industry
   d. a monopoly
   e. a perfect competitor

6. A surplus of wheat exists when:

   a. wheat production is lower than last year
   b. wheat production is higher than last year
   c. wheat production exceeds the production of all other grains combined
   d. the quantity of wheat demanded exceeds the quantity supplied
   e. the quantity of wheat supplied exceeds the quantity demanded

7. Suppose that a surplus exists in a market. Then we may conclude that:

   a. the price is below the equilibrium
   b. the price is above the equilibrium
   c. the government has imposed a price ceiling
   d. the quantity demanded has decreased
   e. the quantity supplied has increased

8. When we draw the demand curve for a product, we assume that:

   a. there are many sellers
   b. there are only a few sellers
   c. all *supply shifters* are held constant
   d. all *demand shifters* are held constant
   e. both (c) and (d)

9. When incomes increase, the demand curve for an individual good:

   a. usually shifts down
   b. always shifts down
   c. usually shifts to the right
   d. always shifts to the right
   e. doesn't move, since only price affects demand

10. Suppose that we know that an increase in the price of good A will cause a rightward shift in the demand curve for good B. Then we may conclude that:

    a. producers of A and B use the same set of inputs
    b. consumers of A and B have the same levels of income
    c. consumers of A and B have different incomes
    d. A and B are complementary goods
    e. A and B are substitutes

11. Tennis rackets and tennis balls are:

    a. substitutes
    b. complementary goods
    c. inferior goods
    d. independent goods
    e. monopolistic goods

12. Apples and textbooks are:

    a. substitutes
    b. complementary goods
    c. inferior goods
    d. independent goods
    e. monopolistic goods

13. Which illustrate best the idea of substitutes in production?

    a. Copper and aluminum
    b. Wheat and rye
    c. Wheat and bananas
    d. Beef and leather
    e. Cream and sugar

14. Peanuts and tobacco can be grown on similar land. Therefore, they are:

   a. substitutes in production
   b. joint products
   c. inferior goods
   d. normal goods
   e. an oligopoly

15. Suppose that the demand for beef increases. This is most likely to cause:

   a. a rightward shift in the supply curve for beef
   b. a leftward shift in the supply curve for beef
   c. a fall in the price of beef
   d. a fall in the price of leather
   e. an upward shift in the demand for leather

16. In a typical market,

   a. an increase in demand, with no change in supply, will result in a fall in price
   b. an increase in demand, with no change in supply, will result in a decrease in quantity
   c. an increase in demand, with no change in supply, will result in an increase in both price and quantity
   d. an increase in supply, with no change in demand, will result in a decrease in quantity
   e. an increase in supply, with no change in demand, will result in an increase in price

17. Suppose that, between year 1 and year 2, the demand curve and the supply curve for wheat both shift to the right. From this information, we may conclude that, in year 2:

   a. the quantity of wheat sold will be larger, while the price will be higher
   b. the quantity of wheat sold will be larger, while the price will be lower
   c. the quantity of wheat sold will be larger, while we

do not have enough information to tell if the price will be higher or lower
   d. the quantity of wheat sold will be smaller, while we do not have enough information to tell if the price will be higher or lower
   e. we do not have enough information to tell what will happen to either the price or the quantity

18. Incomes are determined primarily in the markets for:

   a. goods
   b. services
   c. factors of production
   d. machinery
   e. parts

19. The advantages of the market mechanism (as contrasted to government controls) as a way of deciding What? How? and For whom?) include:

   a. prices provide incentives for producers to make what the public wants
   b. prices provide incentives for producers to conserve scarce resources
   c. prices provide incentives for consumers to conserve scarce goods
   d. high wages in skilled occupations act as an incentive for workers to undertake training
   e. all of the above

20. A black market is most likely to exist when:

   a. the government controls the price of a good
   b. the supply of a good is controlled by a monopolist
   c. the supply of a good is controlled by two or three producers
   d. the government imposes an excise tax on a good
   e. the government urges producers to produce more to promote the general welfare of the public

EXERCISES

1. Using the demand schedule in the first two columns of the table below, plot the demand and supply curves in Figure 4.1. Label the axes, and mark in appropriate numbers on each axis. Then fill in the last column of the table.

   a. The equilibrium quantity is _____.
   b. The equilibrium price is _____.
   c. At the equilibrium price, what is the surplus or shortage shown in the last column? _____. Does this confirm that this price is an equilibrium?
   d. Now suppose that the government sets a price of 60. At this price, there will be a (surplus, shortage) of _____.

Figure 4.1

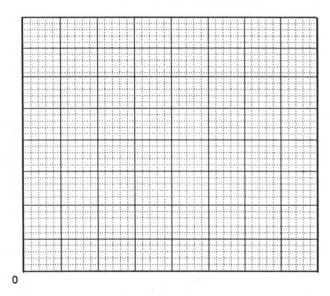

Price of Hamburgers	Quantity Demanded	Quantity Supplied	Surplus (+) or Shortage (−)
	(thousands per week)		
$1.40	200	700	
$1.20	240	600	
$1.00	300	500	
$0.80	400	400	
$0.60	600	300	
$0.50	800	250	

2. Figure 4.2 illustrates some of the issues that arise when the government undertakes price supports (for example, in agriculture). D shows the demand curve, and S_1 the supply curve. Initially, the equilibrium quantity is _____ million bushels, and the price is _____. Now suppose that the government passes a rule that says that wheat cannot be sold at a price less than P_3. The result of this law will be a (surplus, shortage) amounting to _____ million bushels.

If all the government does is set a high price, not all wheat farmers will be better off. Those who are better off will be those who (cut back production, sell their wheat at the high price). On the other hand, some will be worse off, specifically those who (are unable to sell their wheat at the high price, sell their wheat at a low price). To ensure that wheat farmers are better off, the government can (buy the surplus wheat, reduce the price to P_1).

Figure 4-2

Millions of bushels

Now, suppose that the government undertakes irrigation projects to help agriculture in dry areas. This will cause an increase in supply from S_1 to S_2, and the (surplus, shortage) of wheat will (increase, decrease) to million bushels. The government will find the costs of its price support program (increasing, decreasing). If it now eliminates the price support, the free market price will settle at _____.

3. Suppose that supply is given by the equation:

$$Q = -30 + 4P$$

This supply is plotted in Figure 4.3 in the following way. First, choose some convenient value for P, such as 10. Put this value into the equation to get $Q = -30 + 40 = 10$. This means that when $P = 10$, $Q = 10$, so that point A is on the supply curve. Then, choose another value of P, say $P = 15$. Substituting this into the equation, we find that the corresponding $Q = $ _____. This is plotted as point B. The supply relationship is a straight line; there are no squared terms or other reasons for supply to bend. Thus, with the two points A and B, we can draw the straight-line supply S_1.

Figure 4-3

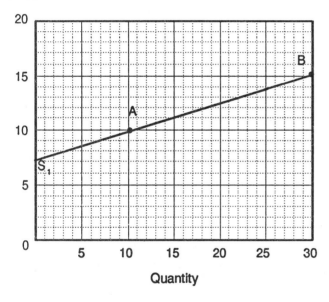

Price

a. Suppose that demand is also a straight line:

$$Q = 20 - P$$

Then, if $P = 15$, $Q = $ _____, and if $P = 5$, $Q = $ _____. Plot demand in Figure 4-3 and label it D_1. On this figure, we see that the equilibrium price is _____ and the equilibrium quantity _____. Confirm these figures by solving the two equations algebraically, to find P and Q.

b. Suppose now that income increases and demand consequently increases, with 15 more units being demanded at each price. Thus, the new demand is

$$Q = 35 - P$$

To plot this new demand, we find two points. For example, if $P = 15$, $Q = $ _____, and if $P = 5$, $Q = $ _____. Plot the new equilibrium demand, labelling it D_2. At the new equilibrium, $P = $ _____ and $Q = $ _____. Again, confirm these numbers by solving the demand and supply equations. The price has (increased, decreased), and the quantity has (increased, decreased) as a result of this increase in demand.

c. Now, suppose we are back with the original demand, D_1, but that supply is now:

$$Q = -10 + 2P$$

If $P = 10$, $Q = $ _____, and if $P = 15$, $Q = $ _____. Plot this new supply and label it S_2. With supply S_2 and demand D_1, the equilibrium price is _____, while quantity is _____. Again, confirm these numbers by solving the demand and supply equations.

d. Finally, suppose that demand shifts from D_1 to D_2, while supply remains at S_2. At the new equilibrium $P = $ _____ and $Q = $ _____. When the demand curve shifted this time, why is it that the price rose more, and the quantity less, than in part (b)?

Answer:_____.

ESSAY QUESTIONS

1. A demand or supply curve applies to a specific time and a specific location. For example, the market for milk in Washington, D.C., is not the same thing as the market for milk in Baltimore. Would you expect the price of milk in these two cities to be similar? Precisely the same? Explain.

2. Suppose that, as a result of an increase in the population of Washington, there were an increase in the demand for milk in that city. If you were an all-powerful social planner, you would probably want to persuade people in Baltimore to give up some of their milk in order to provide for the higher number of people in Washington. What sort of rationing

scheme might you devise to accomplish this goal? How would you know how much to allocate to each family? How large a staff do you think you would need?

Suppose, alternatively, that you allowed market forces to work freely. What would happen to the price of milk in Washington? What would happen to the quantity? How would the changing conditions in Washington affect the supply curve for milk in Baltimore? What would happen to the price of milk in Baltimore? To the quantity? Draw demand and supply curves for Washington and Baltimore to illustrate what is happening. Would your intentions as a social planner be carried out by the market instead? Which policy—rationing or the market—works more efficiently? Are there any disadvantages to the more efficient system?

3. The prices printed on a restaurant menu apply whether the restaurant is crowded or half empty on any particular evening. If you ran a restaurant,

a. would you charge higher prices on Friday and Saturday evenings, when the restaurant is crowded, than on other evenings?

b. would you charge higher prices during the evening than for an identical meal at lunch? Why or why not? (Or, under what circumstances might you?)

c. Does McDonalds behave in the way you have suggested? How do you explain that?

ANSWERS

Matching columns: 1 d, 2 h, 3 l, 4 i, 5 a, 6 k, 7 c, 8 j, 9 e, 10 g, 11 b, 12 f

True-False:
1 F (p. 48)
2 T (p. 48)
3 F (p. 48)
4 T (p. 48)
5 T (p. 48)
6 F (p. 47)
7 T (p. 51)
8 T (p. 55)
9 T (p. 53)
10 F (p. 55)
11 T (p. 54)
12 T (p. 55)
13 T
14 F (p. 47)
15 F

Multiple Choice:
1 c (p. 46)
2 d (p. 47)
3 d (p. 48)
4 a (p. 48)
5 b (p. 49)
6 e (p. 51)
7 b (p. 51)
8 d (p. 52)
9 c (p. 53)
10 e (p. 53)
11 b (p. 53)
12 d (p. 53)
13 b (p. 55)
14 a (p. 55)

15 d (p. 55)
16 c (p. 56)
17 c (pp. 52-56)
18 c (p. 58)
19 e (p. 59)
20 a (pp. 59-60)

Exercises

1   a.   400,
    b. $0.80,
    c.   zero, yes,
    d.   shortage, 300.

2.   120, P_2, surplus, 40, sell their wheat at the high price, are unable to sell their wheat at the high price, buy the surplus wheat, surplus, increase, 80, increasing, P_1.

3.   30,
    a.   5, 15, 10, 10,
    b.   20, 30, 13, 22, increased, increased,
    c.   10, 20, 10, 10,
    d.   15, 20, because S_2 is steeper than S_1.

Figure 4.1 Completed

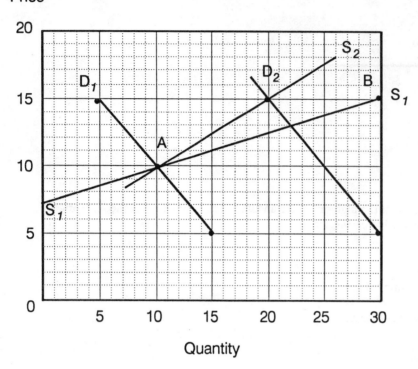

Price

Quantity

CHAPTER 5

THE ECONOMIC ROLE OF THE GOVERNMENT

LEARNING OBJECTIVES

After you have studied this chapter in the textbook and study guide, you should be able to

✔ Describe the four ways in which the government affects the economy

✔ Explain the difference between government spending for goods and services, and transfer payments

✔ Explain the difference between a progressive and a regressive tax, and give an example of each

✔ Describe the five major reasons for government intervention in the economy

✔ Explain the objectives that should be kept in mind when designing a tax system

✔ Explain the difference between the *benefit principle* and the *ability to pay principle*

✔ Explain why the U.S. tax system is less progressive than we might guess by looking at the income tax schedule

MAJOR PURPOSE

The major objective of this chapter is to explain how the government affects the economy. It does so in four ways: spending, taxation, regulation, and the operation of public enterprises. In the United States, public enterprises are much less important than in other countries, and the other three are the principal ways in which the government affects the economy.

There are a number of reasons for government intervention in the economy.

- The government provides *public goods* — that is, goods that cannot be provided by the private sector because everyone can enjoy them, regardless of who pays for them. An example is police protection; we all gain the benefits from an orderly society, whether we pay taxes or not.

- The government can control or discourage externalities, such as pollution. Free markets don't work very well in polluting industries, since they provide no incentive to keep pollution down.

- The government provides merit goods—such as education—that it considers particularly important for the society.

- The government provides programs to help the poor.

- Another important objective of the government is to promote stability.

HIGHLIGHTS OF CHAPTER

The government affects the economy in four major ways:

- spending,

- taxation,

- regulation, and

- public enterprises.

There are some public enterprises in the United States—for example, the Tennessee Valley Authority and the Post Office. However, public enterprise is much less important in the United States than in many other countries, as we saw in Chapter 4. This chapter therefore concentrates on the first three points.

SPENDING

In dollar terms, government spending has risen very rapidly in the United States, from $100 billion per year in 1955 to $1,640 billion by 1988. However, if we look at the size of the government relative to the economy, we get a much less spectacular picture. Indeed, government *purchases of goods and services* have remained approximately stable as a percentage of GNP in the past three decades; increases at the state and local levels have been offset by decreases at the federal level. Nevertheless, if transfer payments are included, government spending has been going up as a percentage of GNP. In other words, the increase in the size of the government reflects mainly the increase in transfer payments, of which social security is the most important program.

TAXES

The primary purpose of taxes is to raise the revenues to finance government spending programs. Per-

sonal income taxes and social security taxes are by far the largest revenue raisers—by a wide margin. Social security tax revenues have grown very rapidly, doubling between 1980 and 1988, and further increases are scheduled for the coming years. These large increases have been necessary to finance the large increases in pensions and other benefits under the social security system.

On most income—up to a maximum of $48,000 in 1989—the social security tax is *proportional*; it is a flat 15¢ on each $1 in income. However, no tax is collected on incomes over the $48,000 maximum, which means that the social security tax is somewhat *regressive*. That is, it is a smaller percentage of an income of $80,000 than of an income of $40,000. Nevertheless, the overall social security system is *progressive*, because the benefits to lower income people are greater, compared to the taxes they have paid, than the benefits of higher income people.

Income tax rates are generally *progressive*—the tax rate on high incomes is generally larger than the tax rate on low incomes. However, the overall tax system is less progressive that the tax rates suggest, both because of the existence of regressive taxes such as social security, and because of "loopholes"—various tax deductions or tax credits. The term "loophole" implies that the deduction or credit is undesirable, and there is considerable debate over what is desirable and what is not. One item sometimes put on the list of loopholes—the provision that homeowners can deduct the interest on their mortgages from their taxable incomes—has such overwhelming political support that it is rarely questioned. (President Carter once hinted that the interest rate deduction might be eliminated, but there was such a storm of protest that he quickly dropped the idea.)

The Tax Reform Act of 1986 closed a number of loopholes, while it also reduced tax rates. The Act was intended to be *revenue neutral*—the increases in tax revenues from the closing of loopholes were designed to compensate for the lower tax rates. By lowering tax rates and plugging loopholes, the government hoped to make the economy more efficient. People now have a greater incentive to engage in productive activities, and less incentive to hunt for loopholes (both because they are harder to find, and because the gains—in terms of taxes saved—are smaller once they are found).

Other than raising revenues, there are a number of other objectives that should be considered in designing a tax code.

- One objective is *equity*, or fairness. As we suggested in Chapter 1, there is some controversy over just what is fair. Nevertheless, discussions of fairness usually begin with one of two approaches to taxation:

° *Ability to pay*. According to this idea, taxes should be imposed according to income or wealth; people with high incomes should pay more because they are better able to do so. The progressive income tax is one application of this principle. (The inheritance tax is another.)

° *Benefit principle*. According to this idea, taxes should depend on who benefits most from government programs. Those who benefit most should pay the most.

- *Simplicity* is an important objective in the tax system. Discussions of tax reform in recent years have often centered around the criticism that the income tax has become hopelessly complicated. Unfortunately, the Tax Reform Act of 1986 made a complex tax system even more complicated. Even some ex-commissioners of the Internal Revenue Service find the income tax too complicated for them to make out their own forms; they get professional help.

- *Neutrality*. As a starting point, most economists believe that the tax system should be designed to disturb market forces as little as possible. It should not capriciously introduce incentives for people to change their behavior in order to avoid taxes.

- *Meeting social objectives*. Nevertheless, in some cases it may be desirable to encourage people to change their behavior. For example, in order to encourage people to give to charities, the government allows people to deduct their contributions to charities from their taxable income. Taxes may also be used to discourage businesses from polluting the air or water.

REGULATION

More direct means are available for encouraging some behavior, and discouraging other activities. For example, there are regulations limiting the amount of pollutants that factories are allowed to discharge into the air and water. In the early days of regulation about a hundred years ago, the government took steps to discourage monopolistic behavior by the so-called "robber barons" of the time. Other regulations are aimed at protecting the safety of workers and discouraging discrimination.

Government regulations are generally aimed at reducing major problems. Nevertheless, regulation has been a source of controversy. There are two major problems with regulation:

- regulatory agencies may require major reporting efforts from business, and sometimes generate expensive red tape of little value; and

- regulatory agencies sometimes come under the control of the industry they are supposedly regulating.

The government may be the means for an industry gaining oligopolistic or monopolistic power.

REASONS FOR GOVERNMENT ACTIVITY

The government becomes involved in the economy for many reasons. Here are the five most important:

- Governments often provide goods and services which the private sector would otherwise fail to provide or would provide only with difficulty and at a high cost. Roads are one example. If the roads within a city were run by private entrepreneurs, motorists would have to stop frequently to pay tolls. National defense is unlikely to be organized and paid for privately. There is a problem of *free riders* — people who let others pay because they will reap the benefits even if they don't contribute. If people benefit whether they pay or not, we have an example of a *public good*.

- The government may intervene when *side effects* prevent people from making socially desirable decisions. For example, vaccinations protect not only the individuals who are vaccinated; they also protect the public from communicable diseases. Smallpox has been eradicated by the combined action of governments and international organizations.

Benefits that go to people other than those who are vaccinated (or their doctors) are known as an *external benefits*. There also can be *external costs*, such as the cost to people downwind from a polluting factory. Just as the government encourages activities with external benefits — such as vaccinations — so it may discourage those with external costs.

- The government may provide *merit* goods or services, such as education, that it considers very desirable from a social viewpoint.

- The government has programs to *help the poor;* for example, food stamps and welfare programs.

- The government may increase or decrease its expenditures in order to *promote economic stability*. For example, during a period of high unemployment, it may undertake public projects in order to provide jobs.

There have been substantial changes in attitudes toward government activity. Between 1930 and 1960, there was a strong upward trend in government activity. One reason was to protect people from the insecurities that were particularly obvious during the depression.

During the 1980s, there has been a movement to reduce the role of government in some countries, such as Britain. The government has sold — or *privatized* — much of the housing and some of the businesses that it owned.

IMPORTANT TERMS

Match the first column with the corresponding phrase in the second column.

_____ 1. Transfer payment
_____ 2. Progressive tax
_____ 3. Proportional tax
_____ 4. Average tax rate
_____ 5. Marginal tax rate
_____ 6. Deficit
_____ 7. Privatization
_____ 8. Externality
_____ 9. Public good
_____ 10. Neutral tax

a. Tax paid divided by income
b. One that takes the same percentage of high and low incomes
c. Sale of government-owned businesses
d. One that takes a higher percentage of high incomes
e. People get the benefit of this, regardless of who pays
f. Expenditure by government, for which government receives no good or service in return
g. Tax which leaves market forces undisturbed
h. Side effect of production or consumption
i. Excess of expenditures over revenues
j. Percentage of additional income paid in tax

TRUE-FALSE

T F 1. Payments to the unemployed are a form of transfer payment.

T F 2. If we include all levels of government (federal, state, and local), then government spending on goods and services is more, as a fraction of national product, than it was even at the height of World War II in 1943-44.

T F 3. Since 1960, transfer expenditures by the federal government have risen, both as a fraction of total federal government expenditures and as a fraction of national product.

T F 4. Defense expenditures have risen consistently as a percentage of national product since the beginning of the conflict in Vietnam.

T F 5. A tax is progressive if high-income people pay a larger percentage of their income than low-income people.

T F 6. Suppose that a state imposes a tax of 5% of all income. Because it "hits the poor as hard as the rich," such a tax is regressive.

T F 7. Suppose that a state imposes a sales tax of 5%. Because high-income people buy more than low-income people, they will pay more sales tax. Therefore, such a tax is progressive.

T F 8. According to the benefit principle of taxation, government expenditures should be undertaken whenever they benefit the public.

T F 9. According to the ability to pay principle of taxation, only those who have enough income that they are able to save should be required to pay taxes.

T F 10. The term "merit good" is used in describing a feature of the British economy. Specifically, a "merit good" is one which the upper class consumes more heavily than the lower classes.

MULTIPLE CHOICE

1. Which of the following is the best example of government expenditure for goods or services

    a. salaries of judges
    b. social security pensions paid to the elderly
    c. welfare payments
    d. unemployment compensation
    e. the progressive income tax

2. The two largest categories of expenditure for the federal government are:

    a. interest and education
    b. education and social security
    c. defense and interest
    d. defense and social security
    e. defense and education

3. Social security plus medicare expenditures together are equal to approximately what percent of GNP?

    a. 1%
    b. 5%
    c. 12%
    d. 18%
    e. 25%

4. As a percentage of GNP, defense expenditures:

    a. have grown rapidly since 1960
    b. have grown slowly and steadily since 1960
    c. have declined slowly and steadily since 1960
    d. decreased between 1960 and 1979, but rose between 1979 and 1983
    e. fell rapidly from 1979 to 1989

5. More than two thirds of federal government expenditures are made up of three large categories. Those three categories are:

    a. defense, education, and social security
    b. defense, education, and agriculture
    c. defense, social security, and agriculture
    d. social security, agriculture, and interest on the national debt
    e. social security, defense, and interest on the national debt

6. Of the following, which provides the largest source of revenue for the federal government?

    a. sales taxes
    b. corporate income taxes
    c. personal income taxes
    d. customs duties
    e. excise taxes on cigarettes and alcohol

THE NEXT TWO QUESTIONS ARE BASED ON TABLE 5.1

**Table 5.1
Income taxes
(hypothetical)**

Income	Tax
$10,000	$1,000
$20,000	$3,000
$30,000	$5,000

7. For a person with an income of $20,000, the **average** tax rate in Table 5.1 is:

   a. 10%
   b. 15%
   c. 20%
   d. 30%
   e. we don't have enough information to tell

8. For a person with an income of $20,000, the **marginal** tax rate in Table 5.1 is:

   a. 10%
   b. 15%
   c. 20%
   d. 30%
   e. 50%

9. If a tax takes $1,000 from someone with an income of $10,000, and $2,000 from someone with an income of $50,000, that tax is:

   a. neutral
   b. progressive
   c. regressive
   d. proportional
   e. marginal

10. The social security tax is:

    a. neutral
    b. marginal
    c. mildly progressive
    d. highly progressive
    e. regressive

11. Last year, the government's debt increased by the amount of last year's

    a. tax revenues - expenditures
    b. interest payments
    c. transfer payments
    d. surplus
    e. deficit

12. During the past decade, the federal government has

    a. run a surplus every year
    b. run a surplus most years, but not every one
    c. had about the same number of surpluses as deficits
    d. run a deficit most years, but not every one
    e. run a deficit every year

13. In his successful campaign for the presidency in 1988, Mr. Bush unequivocally promised:

    a. no new taxes
    b. an increase in defense spending, over that advocated by President Reagan
    c. a comprehensive national health insurance program by 1990
    d. a most favored nation trade treaty with the Soviet Union by 1990
    e. all of the above

14. According to the "neutrality" principle of taxation,

    a. income taxes should be progressive
    b. taxes should be imposed only on goods about which people are neutral (that is, neither very enthusiastic nor very negative)
    c. taxes should be imposed on tobacco and alcoholic beverages
    d. taxes should be designed to disturb market forces as little as possible
    e. the government should rely on the corporate profits tax, not the personal income tax

15. The Tax Reform Act of 1986 was designed to help achieve the objectives of greater:

    a. fairness and simplicity
    b. fairness and neutrality
    c. simplicity and neutrality
    d. simplicity, neutrality, and revenue
    e. fairness, simplicity, neutrality, and revenue

16. The agency of the federal government that requires corporations to disclose information about their financial positions is the:

    a. FTC
    b. EPA
    c. EEOC
    d. FAA
    e. SEC

17. A public good:

    a. creates no positive externalities
    b. creates no negative externalities
    c. cannot be produced by a private corporation
    d. can be enjoyed by all, even those who do not pay for it
    e. must be provided by the federal government if it is to be provided at all

18. Which of the following is the best example of a negative economic externality:

   a. an increase in the international price of oil
   b. an increase in the international price of grain
   c. air pollution created by a steel mill
   d. the rise in the price of steel when the government requires steel mills to reduce pollution
   e. vaccinations

19. Which of the following is designed specifically to be **non-neutral**:

   a. a proportional income tax
   b. a general sales tax of 5%
   c. a tax on polluting activities

   d. all of the above
   e. none of the above

20. The presence of externalities means that

   a. a tax system that seems to be progressive will in fact be regressive
   b. a tax system that seems to be regressive will in fact be progressive
   c. the market system will generally not work as well as it would in the absence of externalities
   d. the rich will generally get richer, and the poor poorer
   e. the federal government will find it much more difficult to balance its budget

EXERCISES

1. The table below shows two different taxes — tax A and tax B. For each of these taxes, fill in the column showing the average tax rate at various incomes, and the marginal tax rate. Also note on the last line whether the tax is proportional, regressive, or progressive.

2. Suppose that a family with an income of $35,000 pays $5,000 in interest on its mortgage, and is allowed to deduct that $5,000 from its taxable income. As a result, taxable income falls from $35,000 to $30,000. This would mean a reduction of $_____ in tax payable under Tax A, and a reduction of $_____ under Tax B. Thus, the higher is the marginal tax rate, the (greater, less) is the tax saving from a deduction.

Income		TAX A		TAX B	
		Average Rate	Marginal Rate	Average Rate	Marginal Rate
$10,000	$1,500	_____%		$1,500 _____%	
			_____%		_____%
$20,000	3,000	_____%		3,500 _____%	
			_____%		_____%
$30,000	4,500	_____%		6,000 _____%	
			_____%		_____%
$40,000	6,000	_____%		9,000 _____%	
Type of tax:		_____		_____	

ESSAY QUESTIONS

1. During the past 15 years, there has been a controversy over the appropriate scope of government regulation. Take the government agencies on pp. 74-75 in the textbook, and divide them into three lists — agencies that you consider clearly desirable, those that are clearly undesirable, and ones you are not sure about. (You are not required to put any particular number on any of the lists. One or two of the lists may be blank if there are no such agencies.) In each case, explain briefly why you put the agency on the list you did.

2. In most communities, the following services are provided by the local government:

   a. Police
   b. Elementary education
   c. Street cleaning
   d. Garbage collection

   Could these be provided by private enterprise? Is there any advantage in having them provided by the government? Would there be any advantage in having them provided by the private sector?

3. What externalities are created by individuals:

   a. driving on a highway
   b. mowing their lawn
   c. smoking in a theater

   In each case, do you think that the government should do anything to encourage or discourage the activity? If so, what, and why? If not, why not?

ANSWERS

Matching columns: 1 f, 2 d, 3 b, 4 a, 5 j, 6 i, 7 c, 8 h, 9 e, 10 g

True-False:
1 T (p. 67)
2 F (p. 67)
3 T (pp. 67-68)
4 F (p. 68)
5 T (p. 69)
6 F (p. 69)
7 F (p. 69)
8 F (p. 72)
9 F (p. 73)
10 F (p. 76)

Multiple Choice:
1 a (p. 67)
2 d (p. 68)
3 b (p. 68)
4 d (p. 68)
5 e (p. 68)
6 c (p. 69)
7 b (p. 69)
8 c (p. 69)
9 c (p. 69)
10 e (p. 70)
11 e (p. 70)
12 e (p. 70)
13 a (p. 71)
14 d (p. 72)
15 b (p. 73)
16 e (p. 74)
17 d (p. 76)
18 c (p. 76)
19 c (p. 76)
20 c (p. 76)

Exercises

1. Tax A.
    Average rates: 15%, 15%, 15%, 15%.
    Marginal rates: 15%, 15%, 15%.
    The tax is proportional.

    Tax B.
    Average rates: 15%, 17.5%, 20%, 22.5%.
    Marginal rates: 20%, 25%, 30%.
    The tax is progressive.

2. $750, $1,500, greater.

PART 2

AN INTRODUCTION TO MACROECONOMICS:
High Employment And A Stable Price Level

CHAPTER 6

MEASURING NATIONAL PRODUCT AND NATIONAL INCOME

LEARNING OBJECTIVES

After you have studied this chapter in the textbook and study guide, you should be able to:

✔ State the relationship between gross investment, net investment, depreciation, and the change in the stock of capital

✔ State the major differences between GNP and NNP, between NNP and National income, between National income and Personal income, and between Personal income and Disposable personal income. (See Fig. 6-3 in the textbook)

✔ State the relationship between nominal GNP, real GNP, and the GNP deflator. That is, you should understand equation 6-6.

✔ Explain why the GNP deflator is not exactly the same as the consumer price index

✔ Explain why real GNP is a better measure of how we are doing than is nominal GNP

✔ Explain why real GNP is nevertheless not a very good way to measure how well we are doing

✔ Explain why it is so hard to calculate a more comprehensive measure of economic welfare

✔ Explain why the *underground economy* exists, why its size may have increased in recent years, and why this is of concern to economists

MAJOR PURPOSE

Macroeconomics is about the *overall magnitudes* in the economy—total output and the average level of prices. The main purpose of this chapter is to provide an introduction to macroeconomics by explaining how total output and the average level of prices are measured. In calculating total output—or GNP—we want to *count everything* that is produced *once, but only once*. This means that there is an important problem to be avoided—the problem of double counting. This problem can be avoided by counting only final products such as TV sets, and excluding intermediate products such as the wire and chips that went into the TV set.

Another important objective of the chapter is to draw a *distinction between nominal* (or current-dollar) *magnitudes and real* (or constant-dollar) *magnitudes*. Through time, GNP measured in dollar terms goes up rapidly. This rapid increase is the combined result of two things:

- there is an increase in the quantity of goods and services that we are producing, and

- the prices at which these goods and services are sold are going up.

The first of these is desirable; the second is not. To see what is happening in real terms, national product accountants eliminate the effects of inflation. They do this by measuring the GNP of each year in the prices of a single base year, 1982.

HIGHLIGHTS OF CHAPTER

This chapter explains how national product is measured, in both *real* and *nominal* terms. It also explains some of the limitations of GNP as a measure of economic welfare.

To calculate the total output of the nation, we must somehow add apples and oranges, steel and airplanes, haircuts and medical services. The only reasonable way to add up different goods and services is to add together the total amount of money spent on each of them. Thus, when we put together a measure of national product, we use *market prices* as a way of judging the comparative importance of each product. A car selling for $10,000 contributes as much to national product as do 20,000 bottles of Coca-Cola selling for $.50 each.

When we measure national product, we want to measure everything produced in the economy (except for illegal products). However, we have to be careful. If we took the value of all the cars produced in the economy, plus all the steel and all the tires, then we would be exaggerating our output. Why is that? The answer is: because much of the steel and many of the tires were used by car manufacturers to produce their cars. We didn't produce a car plus four tires, but the car into which the four tires went.

To *avoid double counting* of tires, steel, and other intermediate products, national product accountants concentrate on *final products*. These are placed in four main categories:

- consumer expenditures for goods and services,

- investment,

- government purchases of goods and services, and

- net exports (that is, exports minus imports).

Investment is perhaps the trickiest of these four to understand precisely. The first important point is that we are dealing with the production of capital goods—buildings, machines, etc.—and not what Wall Streeters mean by investment. That is, we do not include financial investments—such as the purchase of common stock—in the investment category of GNP. The reason is straightforward. When individual A buys 100 shares of common stock from B, there is simply a transfer of ownership, not a direct increase in production. (Of course, the ability of firms to issue stock or bonds may help them to finance new factories, and these new factories are included in GNP.) Recall that this distinction between financial capital (such as stocks and bonds) and capital goods (such as factories) was made back in Chapter 2.

A second complication with investment is that it includes some intermediate products, such as steel, tires, or wheat. Specifically, it includes the increases in our inventories of such products. These inventory increases are something we have produced during the year. They are not included elsewhere—for example, they have not yet been used in the production of consumer goods. They have not yet been included when we count consumer goods. Therefore, they are counted here, in the investment category.

The final complication is that, when we count all the factories and machines produced during the year, we are in an important sense exaggerating what we have produced. The reason is that existing factories and machines have been wearing out and becoming obsolete during the year. What we should be measuring is not the total production of capital goods during the year, but only the increase in our capital stock. In other words, it would make sense to include only the increase in the stock of equipment, plant, and residential buildings, just as we include only the increase in the stocks of inventories.

This leads to the distinction between net investment and gross investment. Gross investment (I_g) is total output of plant, equipment, residential buildings, and increases in inventories. Net investment (I_n) is just the increase in our stock of plant, equipment, residential buildings, and inventories. The difference between the two is depreciation (Figure 6-2). GNP includes gross investment; NNP includes net investment. Accordingly, the difference between GNP and NNP is also depreciation (Figure 6-3).

Other important magnitudes—national income, personal income, and disposable personal income—are also shown in Figure 6-3. While you should not try to memorize the numbers on that figure, you should know the differences between the five major measures. You should also have a general idea of the magnitudes. For example, you should know that personal saving is less than 10% of disposable income; it is not 20% or 30%.

We have seen that market prices provide a feasible way to add various products. But, when we use market prices, a complication arises. Today, a person can use $100 to buy food, or clothing, or other things. The relative prices of food, clothing, or other things represents the relative amounts that people pay for the various goods; it is a way of measuring their relative value. But a person can't shop now out of the Sears catalogue of 1970. A car bought for $10,000 now is not worth four times as much as the car that sold for $2,500 in 1965. Money has lost some of its value as a result of inflation.

This raises an important problem. We want to use GNP figures as one measure of how well the economy is performing, of how large the economy is now as compared to the way it was 5 or 10 years ago. If we simply used GNP measured at current prices, we would not know what to do with the comparison. Does a higher GNP today reflect success; are we producing more? Or does it simply reflect our failure to prevent inflation? In practice, it is likely to reflect both.

In order to separate the undesirable increase in prices from the desirable increase in output, national product accountants calculate constant-dollar GNP. That is, they calculate what GNP would have been if prices had remained what they were in a single base year. Such constant-dollar or real GNP figures represent what has been happening to output over time.

Although real GNP is an important measure of the performance of the economy, it has major defects which mean that we should not concentrate single-mindedly on increasing real GNP. A lot of important things don't appear in GNP—the quality of the physical environment, the stability of the political system, or the degree of social harmony, to name but a few. Because of limits of GNP as a measure of welfare, some economists have considered the possibility of a broader measure, to include important features of our economic performance that are left out of GNP. This attempt has not been very successful. The problems are apparently insoluble. In particular, it is not clear how leisure should be counted. In the period studied by Nordhaus and Tobin per capita real NNP rose 90%, while leisure per capita rose 22%. It is not clear what this means, in terms of an overall measure. Were we more than 90% better off, since we had 90% more goods and more leisure too? Or was the improvement only some average of the 90% and the 22%? The answer is not obvious. The most promising approach is therefore not to search for some comprehensive single measure of welfare, but to look at a number of measures simultaneously—for example, not only real NNP, but also literacy, life expectancy, infant mortality, etc.

IMPORTANT TERMS

Match the first column with the corresponding phrase in the second column.

_____ 1. GNP
_____ 2. NNP
_____ 3. National Income
_____ 4. Disposable income
_____ 5. Depreciation
_____ 6. Real investment
_____ 7. Financial investment
_____ 8. Intermediate product
_____ 9. Value added
_____ 10. Deflate
_____ 11. Underground economy

a. Personal income - [income taxes and other personal taxes]
b. Good intended for resale or further processing
c. Production of plant, equipment, and housing, and changes in inventories
d. NNP + depreciation
e. Remove the effects of inflation from a time series
f. NNP - sales taxes
g. Unreported income
h. GNP - NNP
i. $C + G + I_n + X - M$
j. Acquisition of bonds and corporate stocks
k. Sales minus cost of intermediate products bought from outside suppliers

TRUE-FALSE

T   F   1.   The easiest way to calculate GNP is to add the sales of all corporations.

T   F   2.   Gross private domestic investment includes all the money spent on U.S. stock exchanges during the year, but it excludes money spent by Americans on foreign stock exchanges.

T   F   3.   It is possible for inventory investment to be negative during a year.

T   F   4.   It is possible for gross investment in plant and equipment to be negative during a year.

T   F   5.   GNP can be determined by adding sales taxes to NNP.

T   F   6.   It is possible for net exports to be negative during a year.

T   F   7.   Suppose that there are no sales taxes in an economy. Then personal income will be the same as national income.

T   F   8.   If real GNP has gone up and the price index has gone up, then we can be sure that nominal GNP has gone up.

MULTIPLE CHOICE

1. Which of the following is the best example of an intermediate product?

    a. a road
    b. steel
    c. bread
    d. a TV set
    e. an automobile

2. In the GNP accounts, which of the following is included as a final product

    a. a plane bought by the government
    b. government expenditures to resurface roads
    c. purchases of washing machines by households
    d. purchases of washing machines by laundromats
    e. all of the above

3. Suppose that a firm sells its output for $40,000. It pays $22,000 in wages and salaries, $10,000 for materials bought from other firms, $3,000 for interest on its bonds, and it has profits of $5,000. Then its value added is:

    a. $18,000
    b. $22,000

    c. $30,000
    d. $35,000
    e. $37,000

4. In the GNP accounts, increases in inventories are

    a. excluded, since they are made up mostly of intermediate goods
    b. included as part of the consumption category, since they are made up mostly of consumer goods
    c. included as part of the government category, together with other miscellaneous items
    d. included as part of the investment category
    e. included as an item separate from C, I, and G

5. Suppose we know $C + I_g + G$. Then, to get GNP, we should:

    a. add depreciation
    b. subtract depreciation
    c. add the increase in inventories
    d. add sales taxes
    e. add exports and subtract imports

6. Last year, the XYZ manufacturing corporation issued $10 million in new common stock, and used $8 million of the proceeds to build a new factory. The other $2 billion was used to repay bank loans, and replenish XYZ's deposits at its banks. As a result, GNP went up by:

a. the $8 million spent for the factory
b. the $10 million in new common stock
c. $12 million
d. $18 million
e. $20 million

7. The GNP statistics show that gross investment in 1988 was $766 billion, while depreciation was $506. We may conclude that:

a. net investment was $1,272 billion
b. net investment was $260 billion
c. net investment was -$260 billion
d. net investment was negative, but we don't know how much
e. inventory accumulation was negative

8. Some years ago, the Department of Commerce published a statistical report that, in 1932, gross private domestic investment in the United States was $1.0 billion, while depreciation was $7.6 billion. What conclusion may we come to?

a. net investment was larger than gross investment
b. net investment was negative; the capital stock was smaller at the end of the year than at the beginning
c. most investment was in the form of inventory accumulation
d. imports were larger than exports
e. there is something wrong with the statistics; maybe the Department of Commerce got gross investment and depreciation mixed up

9. Suppose that gross investment has been 10% of GNP, but then it falls to zero during the current year. In the current year:

a. depreciation is the same size as inventory accumulation
b. depreciation is the same size as gross investment
c. depreciation is also zero
d. net investment is also zero
e. net investment is negative

10. Consider the following **incorrect** definition. National Income equals the sum of: wages and salaries,

rent and interest, proprietors' income, net exports, and corporation profits. To make this statement **correct**, one item should be deleted. This item is:

a. wages and salaries
b. rent and interest
c. proprietors' income
d. net exports
e. corporation profits

The next 6 questions are based on the following table, which shows national product in a simple economy with only guns and butter

	Production of guns	Price of guns	Production of consumer goods	Price of consumer goods
1982	200	$1,000	1,000	$500
1990	250	$2,000	2,000	$1,500

11. In this simple economy, current-dollar GNP in 1982 was:

a. $700,000
b. $1,250,000
c. $1,900,000
d. $3,500,000
e. $4,200,000

12. In this simple economy, current-dollar GNP in 1990 is:

a. $700,000
b. $1,250,000
c. $1,900,000
d. $3,500,000
e. $4,200,000

13. Suppose that 1982 is the base year in this simple economy. Real GNP in 1990 is:

a. $700,000
b. $1,250,000
c. $1,900,000
d. $3,500,000
e. $4,200,000

14. Suppose that 1982 is the base year in this simple economy. In this economy, the GNP deflator in 1990 is:

    a. 162.5
    b. 250
    c. 271
    d. 280
    e. 300

15. In this economy, the average level of prices rose how much between 1982 and 1990?

    a. 150%
    b. 171%
    c. 180%
    d. 200%
    e. 280%

16. In this economy, real GNP rose how much between 1982 and 1990?

    a. 52%
    b. 79%
    c. 152%
    d. 179%
    e. 204%

17. This year's nominal GNP measures

    a. this year's output at base-year prices
    b. this year's output at this year's prices
    c. NNP less depreciation
    d. National income less depreciation
    e. NNP less sales taxes

18. Suppose that, since the base year, all prices have risen by 100%. This year's current-dollar GNP is $2,000 billion. Then constant-dollar GNP is

    a. $4,000 billion
    b. $3,000 billion
    c. $2,000 billion
    d. $1,000 billion
    e. $500 billion

19. Suppose we divide current-dollar GNP for 1986 by constant-dollar GNP for 1986. Then the resulting figure is a measure of

    a. inflation during 1986
    b. real output during 1986
    c. nominal output during 1986
    d. the GNP price deflator for 1986
    e. depreciation

20. Last year, Sam Brown spent each Saturday from May to November building a new wing on his family home. In last year's GNP:

    a. the full market value of the wing is included
    b. the lumber, windows, paint, and other materials he bought at the store were included, but the value of his labor was not
    c. the full market value of the wing was included, plus an additional 10% if the Commerce Department's survey found that he actually enjoyed building the wing
    d. the wing was not included at all, since it was not a market transaction
    e. the wing was not included at all, since it probably is not as good as one built by a professional builder

EXERCISES

1. Suppose you have the following incomplete data:

C	$900
I_g	400
Wages and salaries	800
Interest and rent	100
Corporate profits (after taxes)	250
Personal taxes	350
Depreciation	50
G	450
Corporate income taxes	150
Contributions to social security	0
Sales taxes	200
Transfer payments	200
Undistributed corporate profits	150
Proprietors' income	400

Compute the following:

NI	_____
NNP	_____
GNP	_____
X - M	_____
Personal income	_____
Disposable personal income	_____
I_n	_____

2. Suppose a country produces two goods, a consumption good and an investment good. The first two rows of Table 6-1 give the current-dollar value of the total production of the two goods. Fill in the next row indicating nominal GNP each year. The next two rows indicate the market prices of the two goods each year. Fill in the next two rows giving the number of units of each good produced each year. Then fill in the final four rows, using 1982 as the base year.

Table 6-1

	1982	1985	1990
Current-dollar value of C production	200	450	600
Current-dollar value of I production	100	150	200
Nominal GNP			
Price of C	5	9	10
Price of I	20	25	40
Quantity of C production			
Quantity of I production			
Constant-dollar value of C production			
Constant-dollar value of I production			
Real GNP			
GNP deflator			

ESSAY QUESTIONS

1. In what ways does GNP **overstate** economic well-being? In what ways does it **understate** economic well-being?

2. Do the per-capita NNP figures of two countries give a measure of their relative economic welfare? Explain the major deficiencies of NNP as a way of comparing welfare in different countries.

3. "Transfer payments to the poor and the elderly are **not** included in the G segment of national product. But the assistance to the poor and elderly make very important contributions to economic welfare. Therefore, transfer payments should be added, to get a better measure of GNP." Do you agree or not? Explain why.

ANSWERS

Important Terms: 1 d, 2 i, 3 f, 4 a, 5 h, 6 c, 7 j, 8 b, 9 k, 10 e, 11 g

True-False: 1 F (p. 84)
2 F (p. 86)
3 T (p. 86)
4 F (pp. 86-88)
5 F (p. 88)
6 T (p. 88)
7 F (pp. 87, 89)
8 T (p. 92)

Multiple Choice: 1 b (p. 84)
2 e (pp. 84-86)
3 c (p. 84)
4 d (p. 86)
5 e (p. 87)
6 a (p. 86)
7 b (p. 88)
8 b (p. 88)
9 e (p. 88)
10 d (p. 90)
11 a (p. 92)
12 d (p. 92)
13 b (p. 92)
14 d (p. 93)
15 c (p. 93)
16 b (p. 93)
17 b (p. 92)
18 d (p. 93)
19 d (p. 93)
20 b (p. 94)

Exercises

1.

NI	1,700
NNP	1,900
GNP	1,950
$X - M$	200
Personal income	1,600
Disposable personal income	1,250
I_n	350

2.

Table 6-1

	1982	1985	1990
Nominal GNP	300	600	800
Quantity of *C* production	40	50	60
Quantity of *I* production	5	6	5
Constant-dollar value of *C* production	200	250	300
Constant-dollar value of *I* production	100	120	100
Real GNP	300	370	400
GNP deflator	100	162	200

CHAPTER 7

FLUCTUATIONS IN ECONOMIC ACTIVITY

After you have studied this chapter in the textbook and study guide, you should be able to

✔ Describe the four phases of the business cycle

✔ Describe the major features of the Great Depression of the 1930s

✔ Explain the major features of recent business cycles—for example, what happens to profits, investment, and the purchase of consumer durables during recessions?

✔ Explain how the unemployment rate is calculated

✔ Explain why the unemployment rate may understate the problem of unemployment during a recession

✔ Explain why the productivity of labor is adversely affected by recessions

✔ State what Okun's Law is

✔ List the three major types of unemployment, and explain how they are different

✔ Explain potential GNP and the GNP gap

MAJOR PURPOSE

This chapter describes the two major macro-economic problems—**unemployment** and **inflation**. These two problems are closely related to **economic fluctuations**. During recessions, when output is declining, fewer workers are needed by business and the unemployment rate increases. During a rapid expansion, when spending by businesses and consumers is rising rapidly,

inflation generally becomes more severe. Economic conditions were most unstable in the United States during the period between the two world wars. Between 1929 and 1933, output collapsed and the unemployment rate shot upward.

This chapter explains how the business cycle is divided into its four phases:

- **recession,**
- **trough,**
- **expansion, and**
- **peak.**

It also describes how unemployment rises, while output and profits decline during recessions. Inflation generally declines during the later part of recessions and during early recoveries.

This chapter explains how the unemployment rate is calculated, and the various major types of unemployment. **Cyclical** unemployment is the result of fluctuations in overall economic activity. Reducing this type of unemployment is one of the major objectives of economic policy. **Frictional** unemployment results from the normal turnover of the labor force; some amount of frictional unemployment is inevitable. **Structural** unemployment arises when the labor force does not have the type of skills needed for available jobs, or if workers live a long distance from available jobs. This type of unemployment is more severe than frictional unemployment. To escape structural unemployment, people must move or switch to different types of work.

The U.S. economy is quite flexible and changes rapidly. Even in the best of times, the unemployment rate does not get down to zero. It is not possible to identify any specific, unchanging unemployment rate as "full employment." During the 1960s, the government believed that it would be possible to lower the unemployment rate to 4% without generating strong inflationary pressures; 4% was therefore generally taken as the "full-employment target." During the 1970s, 4% seemed unachievable; discussions of full employment focussed on the unemployment range between 5.5% and 6%. During the 1980s, this figure has been revised downward.

The most important characteristics of recessions are higher unemployment and declining output. The shortfall of output below the economy's potential is known as the **GNP gap**; it is a measure of output lost because of slack in the economy.

HIGHLIGHTS OF CHAPTER

The business cycle has four phases. During a **recession**, economic activity declines, and the unemployment rate increases. Economic activity reaches its low point at the **trough**. This is followed by the **expansion** phase, which ends at the upper turning point or **peak**. The key to identifying a business cycle is to tell when a recession has occurred. Not every downward jiggle is called a recession; the downward movement must be significant. The National Bureau of Economic Research decides whether downturns are significant enough to be called recessions. Its starting point is historical: Is the downward slide as severe as the declines of the past which have been called recessions? A simpler rule of thumb has often been used as a quick and ready method of identifying a recession: Has real GNP declined for two or more quarters? While this rule of thumb can be used to identify most recessions, it is not foolproof. Output did not decline for two quarters during the recession of 1980.

The most severe downturn in history occurred between 1929 and 1933 as the economies of the United States and many other countries collapsed into the Great Depression. In this chapter, the main events of the Great Depression are summarized. Although the depression may seem like ancient history, it remains a lesson in how badly things can go wrong. It thus provides a reason for studying macroeconomics. If things can go this badly when macroeconomic policy is mismanaged, it is important to have some idea of what macroeconomic policy is all about.

Between 1929 and 1933, the unemployment rate in the United States rose to almost 25%, real GNP fell 30%, and the average level of prices declined more than 20%. The production of capital equipment, buildings, and consumer durables fell particularly sharply. On the farm, the depression caused a collapse of prices. On international markets, commodity prices also collapsed. International trade fell precipitously, by about two thirds in nominal terms between 1929 and 1933.

Recent recessions have been much *milder* than the downturn of 1929-33. Some have been very short and mild indeed—for example, the recession of early 1980. However, there has been no noticeable tendency for recessions to become progressively more mild over the past four decades. Two recent recessions were severe—those of 1973-75 and 1981-82.

The unemployment rate is calculated by the Bureau of Labor Statistics, as a percentage of the labor force. The unemployed are people who are out of work who

- are temporarily laid off but expect to be recalled,
- are waiting to report to a new job, or

- have been looking for work in the previous four weeks.

If people without jobs do not meet one of these conditions, they are considered to be out of the labor force. The labor force is made up of those with jobs, plus those who are unemployed according to the above criteria.

During recessions, it becomes harder to find a job. As a result, those out of work may become discouraged and stop looking for work. In this case, they drop out of the officially-measured labor force and out of the ranks of those who are counted as unemployed. Consequently, the unemployment rate may understate the unemployment problem during recessions. Nevertheless, the unemployment rate is one important indicator of what is happening during recessions.

During recessions, as sales of products fall, businesses lay off some employees. However, they are often reluctant to lay off highly skilled workers, since these workers may take jobs elsewhere and be unavailable when sales recover. Hence, employment does not fall as much as output. There is a decline in output per worker—that is, in the **productivity of labor**.

As the unemployment rate increases during recessions, so does the number of those who have been unemployed for a long period of time. Not only are more people unemployed, but the hardship faced by the average unemployed person also becomes more severe.

Not all groups are affected equally by unemployment. The unemployment rate for teenagers—particularly minority teenagers—is much higher than for adults.

No matter how prosperous the economy becomes, it is not possible to eliminate unemployment altogether. *Frictional* unemployment represents those who are temporarily unemployed because they are looking for a better job, or because of adjustments associated with a dynamic, changing economy. In a changing economy, there is always some frictional unemployment.

Thus, if full employment is to be a meaningful goal, it cannot be defined as an unemployment rate of zero. There is some debate over the unemployment rate that should be considered full employment. During the 1960s, an unemployment rate of 4% was frequently looked on as representing full employment. Most economists put the figure higher—at 6% or even 7%—during the 1970s. During the 1980s, the figure identified as full employment was reduced to the range between 5% and 5.5%. Chapters 13 and 14 will investigate the idea of full employment in detail.

Potential GNP is estimated as the GNP path along which the economy would move if there were no business cycles and a high level of employment were maintained continuously. The shortfall of actual GNP below the estimated potential is the **GNP gap**. It provides an estimate of the output lost because of recessions.

IMPORTANT TERMS

Match the first column with the corresponding phrase in the second column.

_____ 1. Recession
_____ 2. Trough
_____ 3. Peak
_____ 4. Underemployed
_____ 5. Discouraged workers
_____ 6. Okun's Law
_____ 7. Frictional unemployment
_____ 8. Structural unemployment
_____ 9. Cyclical unemployment
_____ 10. Potential GNP
_____ 11. GNP gap

a. To reduce this unemployment, people must move or acquire new skills
b. Downward movement of the economy, usually lasting two quarters or more
c. Those who have dropped out of the labor force because they were unable to find work
d. Potential output less actual output
e. Observation that unemployment rate moves less strongly than output during the business cycle
f. Turning point at the end of a recession
g. What output would be if the economy were at full employment
h. Unemployment associated with adjustments in a changing, dynamic economy
i. Discouraged workers plus those who are not kept busy because demand is low
j. Turning point as a recession is about to begin
k. Unemployment caused by recessions

TRUE-FALSE

T   F   1.   During the Great Depression, the prices of agricultural products fell much more than the prices of manufactured products.

T   F   2.   Recessions in the U.S. economy have become consistently less and less severe over the past three decades.

T   F   3.   Inflation responds to changes in business conditions. During rapid expansions of real output, the rate of inflation generally increases, and it generally decreased during recessions. However, inflation does not respond immediately; it responds with a lag.

T   F   4.   In percentage terms, investment fluctuates less than consumption, but more than total GNP, during the typical business cycle.

T   F   5.   During the business cycle, consumer spending for durable goods fluctuates more than consumer spending for nondurable goods.

T   F   6.   People temporarily laid off, but waiting to be recalled, are included among the unemployed.

T   F   7.   During a recession, as workers are laid off, the remaining workers can use the best equipment. Therefore, productivity of those remaining at work generally increases rapidly during a recession.

T   F   8.   According to Okun's Law, recessions occur regularly, at intervals of between 5 and 7 years.

MULTIPLE CHOICE

1. Between the peak of 1929 and the trough of the Great Depression in 1933, U.S. real GNP fell by approximately:

    a. 30%
    b. 15%
    c. 10%
    d. 5%
    e. 2%

2. Which of the following is a turning point in the business cycle?

    a. Expansion
    b. Recovery
    c. Peak
    d. Recession
    e. Depression

3. A simple, unofficial definition of recession has often been used by economists and journalists. According to this definition, a recession occurs when seasonally-adjusted real GNP falls for at least:

    a. one month
    b. two months

    c. three months
    d. two quarters
    e. four quarters

4. Between the peak of 1929 and the trough of the Great Depression in 1933, the prices of agricultural commodities:

    a. rose about 15%, in spite of the decline in the prices of most other goods
    b. remained stable, in spite of the decline in the prices of most other goods
    c. remained stable, in spite of the increase in the prices of most other goods
    d. fell about 10%, or slightly less than the average of other prices
    e. fell much more than the average of other prices

5. During the collapse into the Great Depression between 1929 and 1933, the imports of most countries:

    a. declined by a greater percentage than GNP
    b. declined by about the same percentage as GNP
    c. declined by a smaller percentage than GNP
    d. remained approximately constant
    e. increased, in spite of the general decline in GNP

6. During the typical recession,

   a. profits, wages, and prices all fall sharply
      (normally by 10% or more)
   b. profits fall sharply, while wages and prices
      respond only slowly
   c. wages fall sharply, while prices and profits
      respond only slowly
   d. prices fall sharply, while wages and profits
      respond only slowly
   e. profits, wages, and prices all normally rise by
      10% or more

7. During the typical recession,

   a. government spending falls more than
      consumption
   b. government spending falls more than investment
   c. consumption falls more than investment
   d. investment falls more than consumption
   e. consumption and investment generally increase,
      but at a slow rate

8. During recent decades, one sector of GNP has accounted for much of the downward movement
   during recessions. Recent recessions are therefore
   often referred to as:

   a. export recessions
   b. import recessions
   c. inventory recessions
   d. government recessions
   e. consumption recessions

9. The labor force includes:

   a. only those who are employed
   b. those who are employed, plus the unemployed
   c. the total population, less retirees
   d. the total population, less retirees and students
   e. the total population, less retirees, students, and
      government workers

10. Assume that the population is 200 million, the labor
    force is 100 million, and 90 million people are
    employed. Then, the unemployment rate is:

    a. 4.5%
    b. 5%
    c. 9%
    d. 10%
    e. 55%

11. Which of the following groups is **not** counted as
    being unemployed?

    a. People who have left school and are still looking
       for their first job
    b. People who are reentering the labor force, and
       are still looking for jobs
    c. People who are on temporary layoff, but are not
       looking for jobs because they expect to be
       recalled in the near future
    d. People who have been recently fired, and are
       looking for new jobs
    e. Retired people

12. Suppose a person lost a factory job six months ago,
    spent 3 months in a fruitless search for work, and
    then stopped looking. In the collection of official
    statistics, such a person is considered:

    a. still employed in the factory job
    b. structurally unemployed
    c. cyclically unemployed
    d. frictionally unemployed
    e. out of the labor force

13. Who best fits into the category of the
    "underemployed"?

    a. College students
    b. High school students
    c. Government workers
    d. Executives of major corporations
    e. People who can only find part-time work when
       they want full-time work

14. The productivity of labor is:

    a. output divided by the number of hours of labor
       input
    b. the extra amount produced by skilled workers, as
       compared to unskilled workers
    c. the extra amount produced by people with colege
       degrees, as compared to those without degrees
    d. the increase in the amount produced by the
       typical factory worker during the twentieth
       century
    e. the increase in the amount produced by the
       typical farm worker during the twentieth century

15. Okun's Law refers to what phenomenon?

   a. Employment fluctuates by a greater percentage than output during the business cycle
   b. Output fluctuates by a greater percentage than employment during the business cycle
   c. Investment fluctuates by a greater percentage than consumption during the business cycle
   d. Inventories fluctuate by a greater percentage than gross investment during the business cycle
   e. Investment fluctuates by a greater percentage than government spending during the business cycle

16. During a recession, the number of long-term unemployed (more than 15 weeks):

   a. rises, by a greater percent than the overall number of unemployed
   b. rises, but by a smaller percent than the overall number of unemployed
   c. is quite stable, since some of the unemployed get work as the labor force is reshuffled
   d. falls, since some of the unemployed get work as the labor force is reshuffled
   e. falls, since the government is most willing to help the unemployed during recessions

17. According to the official definition of unemployment, which of the following groups has the highest unemployment rate?

   a. Men
   b. Women
   c. Teenagers

   d. College students aged 20 and over
   e. Retirees

18. A major objective of macroeconomic policy is to reduce:

   a. cyclical unemployment
   b. frictional unemployment
   c. labor mobility
   d. product innovations
   e. all of the above

19. During the past three decades, the unemployment rate generally considered to represent "full employment":

   a. has been stable at 0%; at no other rate is there "full employment"
   b. has been stable, at about 4%
   c. has fallen, from about 10% to about 4%, as the economy recovered from the Great Depression
   d. has fallen, from about 8% to about 4%
   e. first rose from about 4% to 6% or 7% during the 1970s, and then fell to about 5.5% during the 1980s

20. Suppose that the unemployment rate this month is 10%. Then we can conclude that:

   a. the economy is still declining into a recession
   b. the economy is at the trough
   c. the economy has passed the trough, and is now in a recovery
   d. actual GNP is less than potential GNP
   e. potential GNP is less than actual GNP

EXERCISES

1. During recessions, output declines. So does employment (by even more than output, but by less than output). The relationship between changes and output and changes in unemployment is known as (Keynes' Law, Okun's Law). This relationship is reflected in a (rapid rise in productivity, fall in productivity) during the typical recession.

When a recession becomes very severe, it is called a (depression, stagnation). This occurred during the 1930s. At that time, prices fell, particularly those of (manufactured goods, agricultural commodities). Output declined very sharply, especially the output of (manufactured goods, agricultural commodities). There was a particularly sharp decline in the output of (consumer goods, capital goods). At that time, (cyclical, frictional, structural) unemployment was very high.

2. Figure 7.1 shows fluctuations in real output. Recessions occurred during the time periods _____ and_____, and expansions during the periods _____ and _____. Peaks occurred at _____ and _____, while troughs occurred at _____ and _____.

Figure 7-1

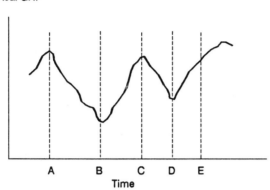

Real GNP

A   B   C   D   E

Time

ESSAY QUESTIONS

1. Explain why, during a recession:

   a. production of consumer durable goods decreases more than production of consumer nondurables
   b. production of capital goods decreases more than production of consumer nondurable goods
   c. output generally declines more than employment
   d. labor productivity generally declines

2. Explain the conceptual difference between structural and frictional unemployment. Explain also why it may be difficult in practice to distinguish whether specific unemployed individuals are part of "structural" or "frictional" unemployment. Might it also be difficult to tell if specific individuals are part of "frictional" or "cyclical" unemployment? Why or why not?

ANSWERS

Important terms: **1** b, **2** f, **3** j, **4** i, **5** c, **6** e, **7** h, **8** a, **9** k, **10** g, **11** d

True-False: **1** T (p. 103)
2 F (p. 103)
3 T (p. 105)
4 F (p. 107)
5 T (p. 107)
6 T (p. 108)
7 F (p. 109)
8 F (p. 110)

Multiple Choice: **1** a (p. 100)
                        2 c (p. 102)
                        3 d (p. 102)
                        4 e (p. 103)
                        5 a (p. 104)
                        6 b (p. 105)
                        7 d (p. 107)
                        8 c (p. 107)
                        9 b (p. 108)
                        10 d (p. 108)
                        11 e (p. 108)
                        12 e (p. 108)
                        13 e (p. 108)
                        14 a (p. 109)
                        15 b (p. 110)
                        16 a (p. 110)
                        17 c (p. 111)
                        18 a (p. 112)
                        19 e (p. 115)
                        20 d (pp. 115-116)

Exercises

1.   but by less than output, Okun's Law, fall in productivity, depression, agricultural commodities, manufactured goods, capital goods, cyclical.

2.   AB, CD, BC, DE, A, C, B, D.

CHAPTER 8

AGGREGATE DEMAND AND AGGREGATE SUPPLY:
Classical and Keynesian Equilibria

LEARNING OBJECTIVES

After you have studied this chapter in the textbook and study guide, you should be able to

✔ Explain why we should not just assume that aggregate demand and supply curves look like demand and supply curves for an individual product

✔ Draw the aggregate demand curve of classical economists, and explain why it slopes downward to the right

✔ Explain why classical economists drew the aggregate supply function as a vertical line

✔ Explain why the simple version of the Keynesian aggregate supply curve is a reversed L, and what the explanation is for the horizontal section

✔ List the four major components of aggregate demand that Keynesians consider in detail to determine what is happening to aggregate demand as a whole

✔ Explain why classical economists believed that equilibrium would occur at full employment, while Keynesian economists believed that equilibrium might occur either at full employment or with large-scale unemployment

✔ Summarize how classical economists explained the Great Depression of the 1930s

✔ Summarize the three major propositions in Keynes' *General Theory*, including his major policy conclusion

✔ Summarize the major points of agreement between Keynesians and those in the classical tradition, and the major points of disagreement

Chapter 7 provided an overview of macroeconomic problems—fluctuations in the overall level of production, periods of high unemployment, and the problem of inflation. The purpose of this chapter is to begin a study of *why* these macroeconomic problems arise. In explaining macroeconomic events, **aggregate supply** and **aggregate demand** are useful tools, just as supply and demand are useful in figuring out what is happening in the market for individual products such as hamburgers, shoes, or wheat.

The Great Depression of the 1930s was caused by a collapse in aggregate demand. The milder business cycles of recent decades have been caused primarily by more moderate fluctuations in aggregate demand. Thus, a more stable aggregate demand is the key to reducing fluctuations in output and employment.

HIGHLIGHTS OF CHAPTER

When studying the market for a specific good (such as apples or hamburgers), we use demand and supply curves. To study the overall behavior of the economy as a whole—changes in total output and the average level of prices—we likewise use **aggregate demand and aggregate supply curves**.

There are major differences between demand and supply in an individual market, and aggregate demand and aggregate supply for the economy as a whole. The major difference is that when drawing a demand or supply curve for, say, hamburgers, we are looking at what happens when *only* the price of this one good changes. (Recall the *ceteris paribus* assumption—that everything else remains unchanged.) Thus, an increase in the price of hamburgers represents a change in *relative* prices; the price of hamburgers rises *relative* to the prices of other goods. Consumers and producers respond to the change in relative prices. Consumers *switch* away from hamburgers and buy hot dogs or other products instead. Such switching is the major reason that the quantity of hamburgers is smaller when the price is higher. Similarly, producers have an incentive to switch. When the price of hamburgers rises, producers have an incentive to make hamburgers instead of other products. Their willingness to switch from other products, and to produce hamburgers instead, is the principal reason why the supply curve slopes upward to the right.

On the other hand, when we look at *aggregate* demand and aggregate supply, we are looking at the responses of buyers and sellers when the *overall* level of prices rises. In simple terms, we are looking at what happens when all prices rise by, say, 10%. Since *all* prices are rising, there is no change in relative prices. Thus, there is no reason for either buyers or sellers to switch as a result. Switching does *not* provide a reason for the slope of the aggregate demand or aggregate supply curve.

Nevertheless, classical economists believed that the aggregate supply curve sloped downward to the right. The reason was that a fall in the average level of prices would increase the purchasing power of money. When prices fell, people would be able to buy more goods and services with the money in their pockets and their bank accounts. Therefore, they would buy more.

However, classical economists did not draw the aggregate supply curve sloping upward to the right. Instead, they believed that it was vertical, at the full-employment or potential quantity of output. If, starting at full employment, all prices—including the price of raw materials and labor—were to increase by, say, 10%, then producers would have no incentive to produce more. They would get 10% more for their products, it is true, but they would have to pay 10% more for their inputs. Because they had the same incentive to produce, the total amount offered for sale would remain constant, regardless of the general level of prices.

Equilibrium occurred at the intersection of aggregate demand and aggregate supply. Because classical economists drew the aggregate supply curve as a vertical line at the full-employment output, they believed that there would be full employment whenever the economy was in equilibrium. This raised a question: How was the depression to be explained? Within the classical framework, large-scale unemployment could be caused by disturbances that resulted in a temporary **disequilibrium**. During the early 1930s, the economy moved away from its full employment equilibrium as a result of the reduction in the money stock and a fall in aggregate demand. Classical economists believed that full employment could be restored by a decrease in wages and prices, which would lead to a new equilibrium at a lower overall price level, or by an increase in the money stock, which would bring aggregate demand back up.

Keynes saw the world differently. He believed that there could be a *long-lasting equilibrium* with high unemployment. The simplest way to illustrate this is with the reversed-L aggregate supply function. In the horizontal range, prices and wages are downwardly rigid. If aggregate demand is so low that it leaves the economy in this horizontal range, then an unemployment equilibrium can persist. The solution to the depression, said Keynes, was to increase aggregate demand. The best way to get an increase would be through direct government action. The government had the responsibility, said Keynes, to increase its spending and thereby increase overall demand, leading the economy back toward full employment. (This major policy conclusion of Keynesian economics will be explained in detail in Chapter 10.)

The theoretical frameworks of both classical and Keynesian economics are still important, since they are both still used—in modified form—by present-day economists. In spite of the different approaches, there is a widespread agreement among economists on a number of central points:

- A sharp decline in aggregate demand can cause large-scale unemployment, as it did during the depression.

- More moderate fluctuations in aggregate demand can cause milder business cycles and temporary periods of high unemployment.

- If aggregate demand can be stabilized, the amplitude of business cycles can be reduced.

- When the economy is already at full employment, any large increase in aggregate demand will cause inflation.

Nevertheless, differences remain both in theoretical approach and in policy conclusions between Keynesian economists and those in the classical tradition. Most important are the following differences:

- Although most economists now believe that both monetary and fiscal policies are important, those in the classical tradition (monetarists) emphasize monetary policy, while those in the Keynesian tradition generally emphasize fiscal policies.

- Keynesians believe that the government has the responsibility to **manage aggregate demand** by changing fiscal and monetary policies from time to time, in order to stabilize demand and minimize business fluctuations. Monetarists believe that active management is more likely to destabilize than to stabilize aggregate demand. They generally advocate a **policy rule**—the authorities should aim for a slow, steady increase in the stock of money. They believe that this will result in a slow, steady increase in aggregate demand and keep the economy at or close to full employment, without causing inflation.

MPORTANT TERMS

Match the first column with the corresponding phrase in the second column.

_____ 1. Purchasing power of money
_____ 2. Downward rigidity of prices
_____ 3. Long run
_____ 4. Classical aggregate supply
_____ 5. Keynesian aggregate supply
_____ 6. The classical equilibrium
_____ 7. Cause of unemployment
_____ 8. Cause of inflation
_____ 9. Monetarist
_____10. Monetarist policy
_____11. Keynesian policy

a. Decline in aggregate demand
b. Money rule
c. Vertical line
d. Active demand management
e. What a dollar will buy
f. Present-day classicist
g. Too much aggregate demand
h. This occurs at full employment
i. This accounts for the horizontal section of Keynesian aggregate supply function
j. Reversed L
k. In classical economics, the period when prices and wages adjust to their equilibrium levels

TRUE-FALSE

T   F   1.   The aggregate demand curve slopes downward to the right because people switch way from services, and buy goods instead, when the average price of goods declines.

T   F   2.   Even if relative prices remain stable, the aggregate demand curve can nevertheless slope downward to the right.

T   F   3.   Classical economists explained the Great Depression as the result of a fall in the money stock, and downward stickiness of wages and prices.

T   F   4.   According to classical economists, brief recessions represented periods of disequilibrium, but the economy could be in an unemployment equilibrium during a major depression.

T   F   5.   According to classical economists, full employment could have been reestablished during the 1930s, but this would have required that both of two conditions be met: (1) a large increase in the money stock, and (2) flexibility of wages and prices.

T   F   6.   The major theoretical innovation in Keynes' *General Theory* was the proposition that the economy could reach an equilibrium with large-scale unemployment.

T   F   7.   Sticky wages and prices are the reason for the horizontal section of the Keynesian aggregate supply curve.

T   F   8.   One major shortcoming of Keynesian economics is that it assumes prices are permanently fixed. Inflation therefore cannot be explained within this theory.

T   F   9.   Those who believe that there should be a policy rule are most likely to advocate a slow, steady increase in the money stock.

T   F   10.   Monetarists advocate a slow, steady increase in the money stock because they believe that the economy will work best with a slow, steady inflation.

MULTIPLE CHOICE

1. When we draw a classical aggregate demand curve, what do we put on the vertical axis?

   a. total quantity of goods demanded
   b. total quantity of goods and services demanded
   c. full-employment output
   d. the quantity of money
   e. the average level of prices

2. There is an important reason why we cannot conclude that the aggregate demand curve must slope downward to the right, just because the demand for an individual product slopes downward to the right. The reason is:

   a. there are no "other goods" for consumers to switch from
   b. relative prices rather than absolute prices are on the axis
   c. inflation-adjusted prices rather than relative prices are on the axis
   d. real prices rather than nominal prices are on the axis
   e. nominal prices rather than real prices are on the axis

3. According to the classical approach, people buy more goods and services when the price level falls (*ceteris paribus*) because:

   a. they switch among products when prices fall
   b. the purchasing power of their money has increased
   c. the purchasing power of their money has decreased
   d. the economy is coming out of a recession
   e. potential GNP has increased because of past investment

4. When the price level doubles, then the purchasing power of the dollar:

   a. also doubles
   b. increases, but only by 50%
   c. doesn't change much
   d. falls 50%
   e. falls 100%

5. Which of the following was put at the center of aggregate demand analysis by classical economists?

   a. money
   b. government spending
   c. the government's tax revenues
   d. tax rates
   e. investment

6. According to classical economists, the aggregate supply curve was:

   a. upward sloping, like the supply curve for wheat
   b. downward sloping, like the supply curve for wheat
   c. vertical, at potential GNP
   d. an L
   e. a reversed L

7. According to classical economists, when the economy was at equilibrium, then real GNP would be:

   a. about 10% above the level in the most recent recession
   b. above potential GNP
   c. at potential GNP
   d. below potential GNP
   e. either (c) or (d), but we can't tell which without information on aggregate demand

8. According to classical economists, the Great Depression represented:

   a. a disequilibrium caused by a fall in the quantity of money
   b. a disequilibrium caused by a fall in exports
   c. a disequilibrium with the twin problems of high inflation and high unemployment
   d. an equilibrium with the twin problems of high inflation and high unemployment
   e. an equilibrium with large-scale unemployment and falling prices

9. According to classical economists, if the economy suffers from a high level of unemployment, full employment can be reestablished by

   a. an increase in the productive capacity of the economy
   b. an increase in the price level
   c. a decrease in the price level
   d. an increase in the money stock
   e. either (c) or (d), or a combination of the two

10. According to classical economists, the best thing the government could do to prevent recessions and depressions would be to:

    a. cut government spending
    b. increase government spending
    c. provide a steady increase in the money stock
    d. promote investment
    e. promote imports

11. According to Keynes, the primary cause of large-scale unemployment is:

    a. high prices
    b. low prices
    c. high exports
    d. low exports
    e. inadequate aggregate demand

12. According to Keynes, when the economy was at equilibrium, then real GNP would be

    a. about 10% above the level in the most recent recession
    b. above potential GNP
    c. at potential GNP
    d. below potential GNP
    e. either (c) or (d), but we can't tell which without information on aggregate demand

13. In its simplest form, the Keynesian aggregate supply function was

    a. upward sloping, like the supply curve for wheat
    b. downward sloping, like the supply curve for wheat
    c. vertical, at potential GNP
    d. an L
    e. a reversed L

14. Consider the reversed L aggregate supply function of Keynesian economics. The effects of an increase in aggregate demand will differ, depending on where the economy begins. Specifically, an increase in aggregate demand will lead to:

    a. an increase in prices if the economy starts in the horizontal section, but an increase in output if it starts in the vertical section
    b. an increase in prices if the economy starts in the vertical section, but an increase in output if it starts in the horizontal section
    c. an increase in prices if the economy starts in the horizontal section, but a decrease in prices if it starts in the vertical section
    d. an increase in prices if the economy starts in the vertical section, but a decrease in prices if it starts in the horizontal section
    e. an increase in prices if the economy starts in the horizontal section, but a decrease in employment if it starts in the vertical section

15. The Keynesian and classical aggregate supply functions are similar in that they both

    a. have a horizontal range
    b. have an intermediate, upward-sloped range
    c. are based on the assumption of downward price rigidity
    d. are based on the assumption of price stickiness
    e. lead to the conclusion that a large increase in aggregate demand will cause inflation if the economy is already at full employment

16. According to Keynes,

    a. a collapse in investment demand was the primary cause of the depression, and an increase in investment demand provided the best hope of recovery
    b. a collapse in government spending was the primary cause of the depression, and an increase in government spending provided the best hope of recovery
    c. a collapse in investment demand was the primary cause of the depression, but an increase in government spending provided the best hope of recovery
    d. a collapse in government spending was the primary cause of the depression, but an increase in investment demand provided the best hope of recovery
    e. a collapse in government spending was the primary cause of the depression, but an increase in saving provided the best hope of recovery

17. The principal cause of the Great Depression of the 1930s was:

    a. a collapse in aggregate demand
    b. a collapse in aggregate supply
    c. a collapse in prices
    d. a collapse in government spending
    e. the outbreak of the Second World War

18. Those in the classical and Keynesian traditions agree that:

    a. a decline in aggregate demand was the principal cause of the Great Depression
    b. a decline in the money stock was the principal cause of the Great Depression
    c. a decline in investment demand was the principal cause of the Great Depression
    d. fluctuations in aggregate supply have been the major cause of fluctuations in output and employment in recent decades
    e. the government has the responsibility to manage aggregate demand actively

19. Shifts in aggregate demand, rather than shifts in aggregate supply, seem to be the primary reason for fluctuations in output. We come to that conclusion because declines in output are usually associated with:

    a. rising inflation
    b. declining inflation
    c. more unemployment
    d. less unemployment
    e. increases in government spending

20. Some macroeconomists propose that the authorities adhere to a *policy rule*. The most common proposal of the proponents of a rule is for a moderate, steady increase in:

a. the quantity of money
b. potential GNP
c. the average level of prices
d. tax rates
e. government tax revenues

EXERCISES

1. In Figure 8.1, AS$_1$ represents the part of the aggregate supply function above point *A*. A classical economist completing this function would draw the dashed section shown as (AS$_a$, AS$_b$). However, a Keynesian economist would be more likely to complete it with (AS$_a$, AS$_b$).

Suppose that AD$_1$ is the initial aggregate demand curve. Then the initial equilibrium will be at point _____, where the equilibrium quantity of output will be OQ__. According to (classical, Keynesian, both) economists, there will be full employment at this initial equilibrium.

Figure 8.1

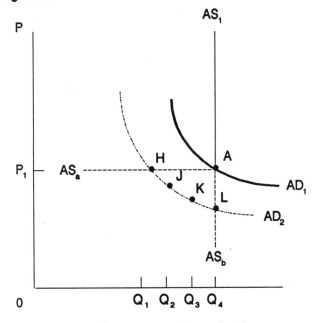

Now suppose that aggregate demand collapses to AD$_2$. According to classical economists, the economy will move in the short run to a point such as _____. However, this point does not repre-

sent a new equilibrium, since (the economy is not at full employment, prices are below P$_1$). If aggregate demand remains at AD$_2$, prices will (rise, fall), and the economy will move a new equilibrium at point _____. At this new equilibrium, there will be (full employment, large-scale unemployment).

In the face of a fall in aggregate demand from its initial AD$_1$ to AD$_2$, Keynesians see a different outcome. In the short run, the economy will move to point _____. If aggregate demand remains stable at AD$_2$, the long-run equilibrium will be at point _____, with output OQ__. With this output, there will be (full employment, large-scale unemployment).

2. On many matters, Keynesian economists and those in the classical tradition agree. However, there are still some disagreements. Mark each of the views below with a **C** if it is more likely to be held with those in the classical tradition, or with **K** if it is more likely to be held by Keynesians:

___ a. Money is by far the most important determinant of aggregate demand
___ b. The government should manage aggregate demand to reduce cyclical swings in the economy
___ c. Even when the unemployment rate is high, wages and prices will move down only slightly, if at all
___ d. Following a rule, rather than periodically adjusting policies, is more likely to lead to a stable economy
___ e. The best policy to follow is to increase the quantity of money at a slow, steady rate
___ f. Large-scale unemployment represents a temporary disequilibrium.

ESSAY QUESTIONS

1. Using diagrams, explain briefly how classical economists drew the aggregate demand and aggregate supply curve. What might cause a depres-

sion? How might the economy move out of a depression and to full employment?

2. Summarize the three main points in Keynes' *General Theory*. Which points, if any, might a classical economist agree with?

ANSWERS

Important terms: **1 e, 2 i, 3 k, 4 c, 5 j, 6 h, 7 a, 8 g, 9 f, 10 b, 11 d**

True-False:
1 F (p. 119)
2 T (p. 120)
3 T (p. 121)
4 F (p. 123)
5 F (p. 123)
6 T (p. 124)
7 T (p. 125)
8 F (p. 125)
9 T (p. 129)
10 F (p. 129)

Multiple Choice:
1 e (p. 119)
2 a (p. 119)
3 b (p. 120)
4 d (p. 120)
5 a (p. 120)
6 c (p. 121)
7 c (p. 121)
8 a (p. 123)
9 e (p. 123)
10 c (p. 124)
11 e (p. 124)
12 e (p. 125)
13 e (p. 125)
14 b (p. 125)
15 e (p. 126)
16 c (p. 127)
17 a (p. 128)
18 a (p. 128)
19 b (p. 128-29)
20 a (p. 129)

Exercises

1. AS_b, AS_a, A, OQ_4, both, J, the economy is not at full employment, fall, L, full employment, H, H, OQ_1, large-scale unemployment.

2.   a. C,   b. K,
     c. K,   d. C,
     e. C,   f. C.

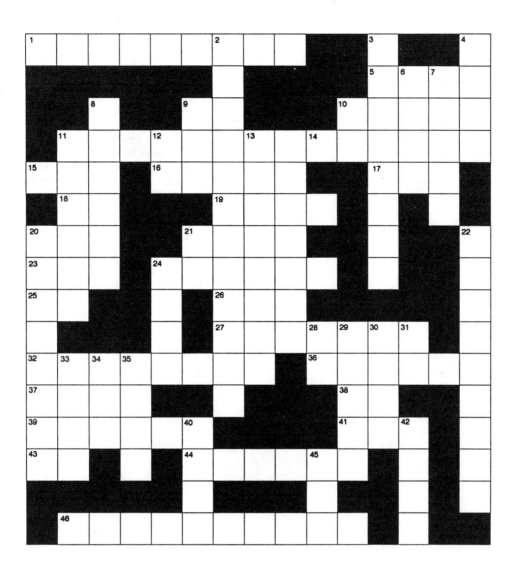

Across

1. to reduce fluctuations, some economists recommend this (2 words)
5. an early economist who was interested in money
9. not (French)
10. builder
11. an important economic objective (2 words)
15. a metal
16. a fruit, or a computer
17. before
18. road (abbrev.)
19. one of the three factors of production
20. in cards, it's either high or low
21. to banks or pension funds, this is important
23. where lawyers sometimes go, either during work or after
24. he revolutionized the study of macroeconomics
25. two directions (abbrev.)
26. peace (Russian)
27. according to Marx, capitalism would do this to workers
32, 36. according to classical economists, these were one reason why the depression lasted so long
37. Greek letter, now means something very small
38. third "person"
39. they decide who will be president
41. unhappy
43. the (Spanish)
44. according to Keynesians, this is the best type of policy
46. money has this type of power

Down

2. a major economic problem
3. this describes the Great Depression
4. type of income
6. someone who gets the good of a product
7. too much of this causes inflation
8. a football player
9. Lenin's economic program (abbrev.)
10. first person, possessive
11. one of the two major policies for managing aggregate demand
12. the (French)
13. some advocate this for managing economy
14. providers of finance
20. rough and hard

21. exist
22. the intellectual ancestors of the monetarists belonged to this school
24. what the guy in 8 down does
28. British political party (abbrev.)
29. _____, ye prisoners of starvation!
30. when you look for a job, you need this
31. major European political and economic organization
33. fiscal policy is a _____ for managing aggregate demand
34. major U.S. corporation (abbrev.)
35. a French city, the scene of a major battle in World War II
40. part of a window
42. Roosevelt's New _____
45. from (German)

CHAPTER 9

EQUILIBRIUM WITH UNEMPLOYMENT: The Keynesian Approach

LEARNING OBJECTIVES

After you have studied this chapter in the textbook and study guide, you should be able to

✔ Explain the relationship between disposable income and consumer expenditures

✔ Explain what the MPC is, and why it is the same as the slope of the consumption function

✔ Explain why, when we put disposable income (or national product) on the horizontal axis, we can also measure disposable income (or national product) as the distance up to the 45° line

✔ Derive the saving function from the consumption function

✔ Explain the relationship between the MPC and the MPS

✔ Explain why equilibrium national product is found where the aggregate expenditures function cuts the 45° line

✔ Explain what will happen if national product is greater or less than this equilibrium quantity

✔ Explain the difference between a leakage and an injection, and give an illustration of each

✔ Express the equilibrium condition for national product in three different ways, and explain why these three different statements amount to the same thing

✔ Explain why there may be large-scale unemployment when the economy is in equilibrium

✔ Explain why an increase in investment has a multiplied effect on aggregate expenditures and national product

✔ Write the two equations for the multiplier in the simple economy with no taxes or international transactions

MAJOR PURPOSE

Chapter 8 presented the main outlines of Keynesian and classical economics. The purpose of this chapter is to explain the central proposition of Keynesian economics — **that the economy may reach an equilibrium with large-scale unemployment.** This happens when aggregate spending is too low to buy all the goods and services that could be produced by the economy at full employment. When aggregate spending is too low, businesses can't sell many of their products. Lacking sales, they cut back on production and lay off workers.

Aggregate demand is made up of four major components: personal consumption expenditures, investment demand, government purchases of goods and services, and net exports. In order to present the simplest explanation, this chapter deals with an economy with only consumption and investment — that is, the government and the foreign sectors are ignored in this chapter. (They are considered in Chapter 10.) Furthermore, investment demand is not explained here; we simply assume that investment demand exists, and see what happens when it changes. (The reasons for a change in investment demand will be studied in Chapter 17 and in the appendix to Chapter 18.)

Thus, consumption is the only type of spending studied in detail in this chapter. The main determinant of consumption is disposable income: When people have more income, they generally spend more. This has important implications for what happens when **investment** demand increases. People are put to work producing factories and machines. Their incomes rise. Therefore they consume more. Therefore, an increase in investment demand causes — or **induces** — an increase in consumption demand, too. As a result, an increase in investment demand has a *multiplier effect* — national product goes up by a multiple of the increase in investment.

HIGHLIGHTS OF CHAPTER

This chapter introduces the basic framework of Keynesian theory. The major innovation of Keynes was the proposition that the economy could reach an equilibrium with large-scale unemployment. National product would not automatically move to the full-employment level; it could stay much below that level if aggregate demand were low. This conclusion provided the reason for his policy conclusion: Since a policy of laissez faire might result in large-scale unemployment, it was up to the government to adopt policies designed to bring aggregate demand up to the full employment level. (This policy conclusion will be studied in Chapter 10.)

As we saw in Chapter 8, there are four components of aggregate demand:

- personal consumption expenditures,
- investment demand,
- government purchases of goods and services,
- and net exports.

However, to make things simple, this chapter deals with an economy with only consumption and investment.

Consumption expeditures (C) depend on disposable income (DI). The relationship between C and DI is known as the **consumption function.** This function has three main characteristics:

- As DI increases, so does consumption. This means that the consumption function *slopes upward.*
- The change in C (ΔC) is less than the change in DI (ΔDI). The change in C, as a *fraction* of the change in DI, is known as the **marginal propensity to consume** (MPC). This fraction, $\Delta C / \Delta$DI, is also the *slope* of the consumption function. Because the MPC is less than one, the slope of the consumption function is likewise less than one.
- At very low levels of DI, C is larger than DI. That is, people spend more than their incomes; they *dissave.* They do this by running down their assets or by borrowing.

These characteristics are illustrated in Figure 9-2 in the textbook.

In order to simplify the discussion, the consumption function is also given a fourth characteristic: It is drawn as a *straight line* in textbooks. This means that the MPC is constant. The evidence on consumer behavior shown in Figure 9-1 suggests that the MPC need not in fact be constant. Thus, we should file away in the back of our minds that we have made a simplifying assumption that is not necessarily correct.

Saving may be identified by drawing a 45° line on the consumption function diagram. The 45° line is equidistant from the two axes; measuring up to the 45° line gives the same number as measuring horizontally to the line. Because we measure disposable income on the horizontal axis, we may also measure disposable income in an upward direction; it is they height of the 45° line. Saving is zero at the point where C = DI—that is, the point where the consumption function and the 45° line intersect.

In simple terms, saving equals DI - C. (It is standard procedure to use this simple relationship, and ignore the interest paid to consumers shown on Figure 6-3 in the textbook.) Thus, a saving function can be derived directly from the consumption function. Specifically, the height of the saving function (Figure 9-3) is the vertical distance between the consumption function and the 45° line (Figure 9-2).

- As DI increases, so does saving. This means that the saving function *slopes upward*.

- The change in S (ΔS) is less than the change in DI (ΔDI). The change in S, as a *fraction* of the change in DI, is the **marginal propensity to save** (MPS). This fraction, $\Delta S/\Delta$DI, is also the *slope* of the saving function. Because the MPS is less than one, the slope of the saving function is likewise less than one.

- When people have very low incomes, S is negative. That is, people *dissave*.

Because each \$1 of additional disposable income is either consumed or saved, MPC + MPS = 1.

To see a simple illustration of equilibrium, we look at a simple economy in which there is no depreciation, no government, and no international transactions. In such an economy GNP = NNP, and we can talk simply of national product, NP. Furthermore, in the absence of taxes and transfers, NP = NI = DI, and we can therefore redraw the consumption function with NP measured along the horizontal axis or up to the 45° line.

When we add investment demand (I^*) vertically to the consumption function, we get the **aggregate expenditures function**, which shows how aggregate spending depends on national product. Equilibrium occurs where AE = NP—that is, where the AE function cuts the 45° line. At this point, producers are able to sell what they produce. If national product were larger—say at L in Figure 9-5 in the textbook, then production would be greater than aggregate expenditures. Unsold goods would pile up in **undesired inventory accumulation**. In order to reduce their undesired inventories, businesses would cut back on orders from suppliers and reduce their production. Output would fall back to its equilibrium at K. At equilibrium, aggregate expenditures may fall below the level needed for full employment. That is, equilibrium national product K may be to the left of full-employment point F, as shown in Figure 9-5. Figure 9-5 is one of the half dozen most important diagrams in the book.

The circumstances under which there is equilibrium may be stated in three different ways, all of which amount to the same thing. Equilibrium occurs when:

- AE = NP, as shown by the intersection of AE and the 45° NP line in Figure 9-5. At this point of intersection, there is a demand for all the goods and services produced. That is:

- Undesired inventory accumulation equals zero, and $I = I^*$.

- $S = I^*$, as shown in Figure 9-6.

If investment demand increases, the additional investment demand is added vertically to the AE function; the AE function shifts upward. As a result, national product increases. As it does so, incomes increase. People spend more. Thus, a \$1 increase in investment demand leads not only to \$1 more in the output of capital goods; it leads to more output of consumer goods and services, too. Overall output increases by a multiple of the \$1 increase in investment. This is the important *multiplier* concept. Specifically, the multiplier is equal to ΔNP/ΔI^*. In the simple economy, this equals 1/MPS. Details on the multiplier are given in Figure 9-11 in the textbook.

IMPORTANT TERMS

Match the first column with the corresponding phrase in the second column.

_____ 1. Marginal Propensity to Consume
_____ 2. Marginal Propensity to Save
_____ 3. Saving
_____ 4. Equilibrium national product
_____ 5. Undesired inventory accumulation
_____ 6. A leakage
_____ 7. An injection
_____ 8. Multiplier

a. Saving
b. NP = AE
c. 1/MPS
d. I minus I^*
e. $\Delta C/\Delta DI$
f. I^*
g. DI - C
h. 1 minus MPC

TRUE-FALSE

T   F   1.   If the MPC is constant, then the MPS is equal to the MPC.

T   F   2.   The slope of the aggregate expenditures function is equal to the MPS.

T   F   3.   The slope of the saving function = 1 - MPC.

T   F   4.   If the consumption function is a straight line, then the MPC is greater than 1.

T   F   5.   Businesses respond to undesired inventory accumulation by increasing their orders for goods.

T   F   6.   If national product is above its equilibrium, then actual investment is greater than desired investment.

T   F   7.   If undesired inventory accumulation is positive, then actual national product exceeds equilibrium national product.

T   F   8.   Because all goods must be demanded if they are to be produced, the slope of the aggregate expenditures schedule equals 45°.

T   F   9.   The higher is the MPC, the larger is the multiplier.

MULTIPLE CHOICE

1.   In Keynesian theory, aggregate demand is studied as the sum of four components, including each of the items below **except one**. Which one?

   a. Personal consumption expenditures
   b. Personal saving
   c. Investment demand
   d. Government purchases of goods and services
   e. Net exports

2.   Saving equals zero when:

a. C + I^* = National Product
b. C + I^* = Aggregate expenditures
c. Personal income = disposable income
d. Consumption = disposable income
e. MPC = 1

3.   The slope of the consumption function is equal to

   a. the MPC
   b. the MPS
   c. the MPS + 1
   d. the multiplier
   e. 1/(the multiplier)

4. If the MPC is three quarters, then an increase in disposable income will cause:

   a. consumption to rise by three times the increase in disposable income
   b. consumption to rise by four times the increase in disposable income
   c. consumption to increase, while saving decreases
   d. consumption to decrease, while saving increases
   e. consumption and saving both to increase, with consumption increasing more than saving

5. Suppose that the consumption function is a straight line. Then:

   a. consumption is a constant fraction of income
   b. saving is a constant fraction of income
   c. the MPC is constant
   d. the MPC becomes smaller as income becomes smaller
   e. the MPS becomes smaller as income becomes smaller

6. If the slope of the consumption function rises, then we may conclude that:

   a. the slope of the saving function has fallen
   b. the marginal propensity to save has risen
   c. the marginal propensity to consume has fallen
   d. the multiplier has become smaller
   e. undesired inventory accumulation has become larger

7. The aggregate expenditure function shows how spending increases in real terms as:

   a. prices fall
   b. prices increase
   c. real national product increases
   d. saving increases
   e. unemployment increases

8. Actual investment minus investment demand equals:

   a. one
   b. zero
   c. inventory investment
   d. undesired inventory investment
   e. desired inventory investment

9. Suppose that, in a simple Keynesian system, national product exceeds its equilibrium quantity. Then:

   a. aggregate expenditures exceed national product
   b. investment demand exceeds saving

   c. actual investment exceeds investment demand
   d. the multiplier equals 1
   e. MPC = MPS - 1

10. National product is at its equilibrium when:

    a. aggregate expenditures = $C + I^* + G$
    b. aggregate expenditures = national product
    c. saving = undesired inventory accumulation
    d. saving = desired inventory accumulation
    e. government spending = tax revenues

11. When undesired inventory accumulation equals zero:

    a. $S = 0$
    b. $I = 0$
    c. $I^* = 0$
    d. government spending = tax revenues
    e. national product is at its equilibrium level

12. In *The General Theory*, Keynes argued that

    a. a market economy might reach equilibrium with large-scale unemployment
    b. large-scale unemployment is caused by inadequate aggregate demand
    c. the best way to cure large-scale unemployment is by increasing government spending
    d. all of the above
    e. none of the above

13. Suppose that saving is greater than investment demand. Then

    a. there must be full employment when the economy is in equilibrium
    b. there must be large-scale unemployment when the economy is in equilibrium
    c. national product is greater than the equilibrium
    d. national product is less than the equilibrium
    e. undesired inventory accumulation is negative

14. In the circular flow of spending:

    a. investment is an injection, and saving a leakage
    b. saving is an injection, and investment a leakage
    c. saving and investment are both leakages, and consumption is an injection
    d. saving and investment are both injections, and consumption is a leakage
    e. consumption and saving are both leakages, and investment is an injection

15. The condition for equilibrium may be stated in three different ways—in each of the following ways except one. Which is the exception?

a. aggregate expenditures = national product
b. $I = I^*$
c. $S = I^*$
d. $S = I$

16. When investment demand increases, which of the following functions shifts upward:

a. aggregate supply
b. aggregate expenditures
c. consumption
d. saving
e. leakages

17. Consider a simple economy, with no government or international trade, and with an MPC of 0.9. According to the multiplier theory, if investment demand increases by $100 billion, equilibrium national product will rise by a multiple of the $100 billion. Specifically, equilibrium national product will rise by

a. $1,000 billion, made up of the original $100 billion in investment plus an additional $900 billion of investment stimulated by the initial investment
b. $1,000 billion, made up of the $100 billion in investment plus $900 billion in consumption as consumers move along the consumption function
c. $500 billion, made up of $100 billion in investment plus $400 billion in consumption
d. $500 billion, made up of the original $100 billion in investment plus an additional $400 billion of investment stimulated by the initial investment
e. $500 billion, made up of $100 billion in investment, $200 billion of consumption, and $200 billion of government spending for goods and services

18. Consider a simple economy, with no government and no international trade. Then if the MPC = 0.9, the multiplier is:

a. also 0.9
b. 1
c. 5
d. 10
e. 100

EXERCISES

1. Figure 9.1 below shows a simple economy with only two types of expenditure—consumption and investment. In this economy, equilibrium occurs at point _____, with national product of _____. At this national product, consumption is distance _____, desired investment is distance _____, actual investment is distance _____, saving is distance _____, and undesired inventory accumulation is _____. Now, suppose that national product is equal to OC. At this national product, consumption is distance _____, desired investment is distance _____, actual investment is distance _____, saving is distance _____, and undesired inventory accumulation is distance

_____.

In this diagram, we can also tell the size of the multiplier. If, from an initial point of equilibrium, investment were to fall to zero, the equilibrium point would move to _____. That is, when investment demand fell by distance _____, national product would fall by distance _____. Thus, the size of the multiplier is distance AB divided by distance

_____.

We can also tell the MPC in this diagram. Specifically, it is distance _____ divided by distance EF.

Figure 9.1

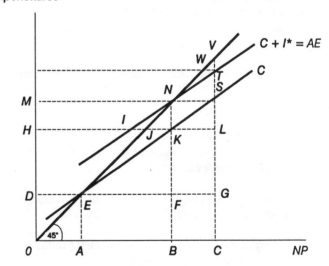

2. Table 9.1 below represents the same type of simple economy studied in this chapter. Suppose that the MPC = 0.8. Fill in the second column, giving the consumption expenditures at each level of disposable income DI. Suppose that desired investment is 40. Now fill in the third column, giving aggregate expenditures at each level of disposable income DI. Now fill in the fourth and fifth columns, giving (respectively) the amount of saving and the amount of undesired inventory accumulation at each quantity of national product. Then fill in the sixth column, giving S minus desired investment. What is the equilibrium national product in this economy?

Table 9.1

(1) DI (= NP)	(2) C	(3) Aggregate expenditures	(4) Saving	(5) Undesired inventory investment	(6) S minus desired investment
0	20	_____	_____	_____	_____
100	_____	_____	_____	_____	_____
200	_____	_____	_____	_____	_____
300	_____	_____	_____	_____	_____
400	_____	_____	_____	_____	_____
500	_____	_____	_____	_____	_____

3. Suppose that the consumption function is C = 25 + 0.75DI. In other words, if DI = 100, then C = 25 + 0.75x100 = 100. Plot the consumption function in Figure 9.2. Plot the corresponding saving function in Figure 9.3. Now suppose that desired investment is 25. Plot this investment in Figure 9.3, and plot the aggregate expenditures function and the 45° line in Figure 9.2. The MPC equals _____, the MPS equals _____, the multiplier equals _____, and the equilibrium national product is _____.

Now suppose that desired investment increases by 25; it is now 50. Plot the new aggregate expenditures function in Figure 9.2 and the new desired investment in Figure 9.3. The new equilibrium national product is _____. At the quantity of NP that used to be equilibrium, aggregate expenditures are now [more, less] than NP by quantity _____, saving is now [more, less] than desired investment by quantity _____, and undesired inventory accumulation equals _____.

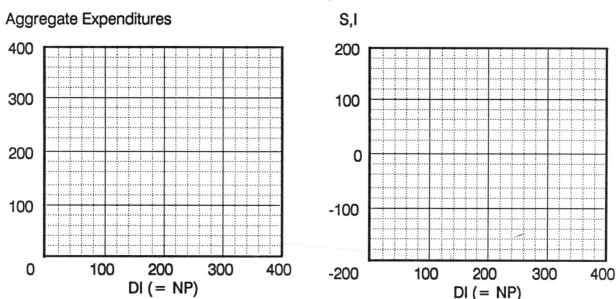

Figure 9.2

Aggregate Expenditures

DI (= NP)

Figure 9.3

S,I

DI (= NP)

4. Suppose that the MPC is 0.5 and that investment expenditures increase by 400 (that is, desired investment increases by 400). In the first column of Table 9.2, fill in the expenditures at each round, as in the table accompanying Figure 9-11 on p. 147 in the text. In the second column, fill in the cumulative total of expenditures (investment plus consumption) up to and including that round. The total expenditures in *all* the rounds, if the series is continued indefinitely, will be _____.

Table 9.2

		(1) Change in aggregate expenditures	(2) Cumulative total
Fiirst round	Investment of		
Second round	Consumption of		
Third round	Consumption of		
Fourth round	Consumption of		
Fifth round	Consumption of		
Sixth round	Consumption of		
Seventh round	Consumption of		

ESSAY QUESTIONS

1. In the textbook, disposable income is the main determinant of consumption expenditures. But consumption can depend on other things, too. What other variables do you think are important, and why? (Hints: What beside disposable income determines the expenditures of a retiree in Florida? Does it make sense for a student to consume more than his or her disposable income? Why?)

2. In the textbook, the level of investment is initially assumed to be constant, and then it is assumed to change without explanation. What do you think would be the important determinants of investment? Would investment demand depend on national product? *If so*, how would this change the way in which Figures 9-5 and 9-6 were drawn in the textbook? Would it make the economy more or less stable through time? *If not*, why do you think other determinants are more important than national product?

ANSWERS

Matching columns: **1 e, 2 h, 3 g, 4 b, 5 d, 6 a, 7 f, 8 c**

True-False: **1 F** (p. 137)
2 F (pp. 138, 141)
3 T (p. 139)
4 F (p. 139)
5 F (p. 140)
6 T (p. 141)
7 T (p. 141)
8 F (p. 141)
9 T (p. 148)

Exercises

1.   N, OB, BK, KN, KN, KN, zero. CS, ST, SV, SV, TV. E, KN, AB, KN. FK.

2.

Table 9.1 Completed:

(1) DI(=NP)	(2) C	(3) Aggregate expenditures	(4) Saving	(5) Undesired inventory investment	(6) S minus desired investment
0	20	60	−20	−60	−60
100	100	140	0	−40	−40
200	180	220	20	−20	−20
300	260	300	40	0	0
400	340	380	60	20	20
500	420	460	80	40	40

Equilibrium national product is 300.

3.   0.75, 0.25, 4, 200, 300, more, 25, less, 25, -25

4.

Table 9.2 Completed:

	(1)	(2)
First round Investment of	400	400
Second round Consumption of	200	600
Third round Consumption of	100	700
Fourth round Consumption of	50	750
Fifth round Consumption of	25	775
Sixth round Consumption of	12½	787½
Seventh round Consumption of	6¼	793¾

The total expenditures in all rounds will be 800.

Part 3

AGGREGATE DEMAND POLICIES

CHAPTER 10

FISCAL POLICY

LEARNING OBJECTIVES

After you have studied this chapter in the textbook and study guide, you should be able to

✔ Explain why an increase in government spending causes an increase in aggregate expenditures

✔ Explain why a cut in tax rates causes an increase in aggregate expenditures

✔ Explain why a $100 change in government spending can have a more powerful effect on equilibrium national product than a $100 change in taxes

✔ Explain why taxes have nevertheless become the primary tool of fiscal policy

✔ Explain why an increase in tax rates causes the aggregate expenditures function to become flatter, thereby decreasing the size of the multiplier

✔ Give an illustration of an automatic stabilizer, and explain how it acts to stabilize the economy

✔ Describe how the full-employment budget is measured

✔ Explain what the full-employment budget is used for

✔ Explain why the government may destabilize the economy if it attempts to balance the budget every year

✔ Explain why a large and growing national debt can be a problem

MAJOR PURPOSE

The principal cause of recessions and depressions is the instability of aggregate expenditures. The authorities have two tools with which to stabilize aggregate expenditures — fiscal policy and monetary policy. Fiscal policy, in turn, can be subdivided under two headings — changes in government spending and changes in tax rates. The major purpose of this chapter is to explain how these two fiscal policy tools can be used to influence aggregate expenditures.

Government spending for goods and services constitutes one of the components of aggregate expenditures, and an increase in such spending therefore increases aggregate expenditures directly. If, during a depression, the government builds new roads, people will be put to work building the roads and providing materials to construction companies. The initial increase in output and employment will be followed by a multiplier effect, as those engaged in roadbuilding activities find that their incomes are higher and therefore buy more consumer goods.

A change in tax rates does not affect aggregate spending in the same way; taxes are not a component of aggregate expenditures. However, a cut in tax rates leaves the public with more disposable income, and therefore encourages consumption spending.

Ideally, the government should cut taxes to fight recessions and raise taxes to fight inflation, thereby stabilizing the path of demand. In practice, however, the U.S. government has had only partial success in using its fiscal policy tools.

HIGHLIGHTS OF CHAPTER

This chapter explains how the government can change its expenditures or tax policies in order to influence aggregate spending and equilibrium national product.

During a depression or severe recession, aggregate expenditures arc below the full-employment output. If we look at the height of the aggregate expenditures function at the full-employment national product, we will find that it lies below the 45° line. The vertical distance between the two lines, measured at the full-employment NP, is the **recessionary gap**. This is the amount by which the aggregate expenditures curve should be shifted upward to get the economy to full employment. The government can eliminate a recessionary gap of, say, $10 billion by increasing its spending by that amount.

Government spending, like investment spending, contributes directly to aggregate expenditures. Furthermore, a change in government spending has the same multiplied effect on equilibrium national product as do changes in investment. Once government is included in the economy, the aggregate expenditures function represents the vertical addition of $C + I^* + G$.

Changes in tax rates also affect national product, but not in the same direct way, because taxes are not a component of aggregate expenditures. However, changes in taxes affect disposable income and therefore affect consumption. For example, an increase in tax rates reduces the disposable income of the public, thereby discouraging consumption. As a result, the consumption function is lowered, and the aggregate expenditures function is likewise lowered.

An increase in tax rates also has a second important effect on the consumption function and aggregate expenditures. Not only do these functions become *lower;* they also become *flatter*. The reason is that an increase of, say, 10% in taxes will take more income from the public if national product is large than if it is small. Therefore, the larger is national product—that is, the further we go to the right in the 45° diagram—the greater will be depressing effect of taxes on consumption.

In an economy with a high tax rate, the consumption function is quite flat, and this means that consumers respond weakly to a change in national product. A relatively small amount of consumption is induced by a change in investment or government spending. The multiplier is small. Fluctuations in investment have only a weak effect on aggregate expenditures. Because the existence of taxes means that the multiplier is smaller, the economy is **stabilized automatically**. Tax rates do not have to be adjusted for taxes to have a stabilizing effect. Automatic stabilizers mean that the government deficit *automatically* tends to increase during recessions.

While these automatic deficits help to stabilize the economy, they introduce two important complications into fiscal policy. First, they present a **trap** for the policy maker. If the government follows a superficially-plausible strategy of trying to balance the budget every year, it will end up destabilizing the economy. As the economy swings into recession, deficits will automatically appear. If the authorities raise taxes or cut spending in an attempt to balance the budget, they will be following precisely the wrong fiscal policy; they will be depressing aggregate expenditures further, and adding to the depth of the recession. President Hoover and the Congress fell into this trap in 1932 when they imposed a substantial tax increase. This added to the downward momentum of the economy. One of Keynes' major objectives was to warn against such blunders. He argued that it is important for fiscal policy to be **aimed at balancing the economy, not the budget**.

The second complication is the problem of **measuring** fiscal policy. Deficits automatically increase during a recession. Just because deficits rise during recessions, we should not conclude that the authorities are following counter-cyclical fiscal policies; they may be doing nothing. In order to determine what is happening to fiscal *policy*, some measure other than the actual budgetary surplus or deficit is needed. The **full-employment budget** provides such a measure. This budget gives a measure of the deficit or surplus that would occur with current tax rates and spending programs **if** the economy were at full employment. Because the full-employment budget is always measured at full employment (regardless of where actual output is), it does not automatically swing into deficit when the economy moves into a recession. However, the size of the deficit or surplus does change when tax rates or spending programs are changed. In brief, the full-employment budget changes when policies change; it does not change when the economy falls into recession. It therefore may be taken as a **measure of fiscal policy**.

Keynesian economists showed how the old objective of balancing the actual budget could lead to the wrong policies. But if the President and Congress are not held responsible for balancing the budget, what will restrain their spending? One possibility would be to have a guideline that would require restraint, while avoiding the trap of balancing the budget every year. Suggested guidelines include:

- balancing the full-employment budget every year,

- balancing the actual budget over the business cycle, with surpluses during prosperity to offset the deficits during recessions, or

- limiting federal government spending to, say, 21% of GNP.

While all of these options have been discussed, none has become a firm basis for policy. The question of restraint has become increasingly important in recent years. Government deficits grew rapidly during the 1980s, and are now running more than $100 billion per year.

When the government runs deficits, it borrows the difference between its expenditures and receipts. That is, it issues bonds or shorter-term securities. A $150 billion deficit therefore leads to a $150 billion increase in the national debt. The high deficits of recent years have made the national debt soar. A national debt is different from a personal or corporate debt, because we "owe most of it to ourselves." That is, even though we as taxpayers have to pay interest on the debt, we also receive most of the interest payments. We may not always be aware of this, because some of the interest payments are not obvious to us. For example, government bonds may be held by our pension funds, and the interest is paid into our pension funds without our necessarily being aware of the fact.

However, the national debt does raise a number of problems, particularly if it is increasing rapidly:

- Some of the debt may *not* represent what we owe to ourselves; some government bonds may be held by foreigners. In this case, the nation is less well off. In the future, we will be taxed to make interest payments to foreign countries. This aspect of the national debt has attracted much attention in recent years. Much of the increase in U.S. government debt has been purchased by foreigners. Only a few years ago, we were major international creditors. That is, U.S. assets abroad were much larger than foreign claims on the United States. However, by 1985, we had dissipated our creditor position; according to official statistics, we became net international debtors for the first time since 1914.

- Even when we own our government's bonds, and pay interest to ourselves, the debt is not problem-free. To pay the interest, the government levies taxes. The public has an incentive to alter its behavior to avoid the taxes. When this happens, the economy generally becomes less efficient. This decrease in efficiency is known as the *excess burden* of taxes.

- If the national debt rises high enough, the government may find it very difficult to collect enough taxes to pay the interest. It may simply borrow more and more, to service the ever-growing debt. In other words, the debt may *grow on itself*. Again, this is an issue which has attracted much greater attention during the 1980s because of the combination of rising debt and high interest rates. Interest on the national debt rose from 1.4% of GNP in 1975 to an estimated 3.3% by 1985. (See Table 10-1 in the textbook.) Although this figure has leveled out, it remains much higher than it was at any time prior to 1980.

- Finally, as interest payments balloon, the government may be tempted to print money to meet these payments. If it does so to any great extent, this will add to inflationary pressures in the economy. (The government prints money via a complicated procedure. The U.S. Treasury issues bonds, and the Federal Reserve prints money to buy these bonds. This is a subject that will be studied in the next few chapters.)

IMPORTANT TERMS

Match the first column with the corresponding phrase in the second column.

_____ 1. Ressionary gap
_____ 2. Output gap
_____ 3. Excess burden of tax
_____ 4. An injection
_____ 5. A leakage
_____ 6. Deficit
_____ 7. Full-employment surplus
_____ 8. Automatic stabilizer
_____ 9. Policy trap

a. Negative surplus
b. The decrease in economic efficiency when people change their behavior to reduce their taxes
c. Any tax or spending program that makes the budgetary deficit rise during recession, even if no policy change is made
d. Vertical distance from the aggregate expenditures function up to the 45° line, measured at full-employment NP
e. $R_{FE} - G_{FE}$
f. The annually-balanced budget
g. Government purchases of goods and services
h. Full-employment NP - actual NP
i. Taxes

TRUE-FALSE

T   F   1.   An increase in government spending of $100 million will increase equilibrium national product by more than $100 million.

T   F   2.   An increase in tax rates reduces equilibrium national product.

T   F   3.   An across-the-board increase in income taxes by, say, 5% has an effect similar to an increase in a lump-sum tax: It causes the consumption function to move down, but it does not change its slope.

T   F   4.   An automatic stabilizer acts to stabilize the size of the government's surplus or deficit.

T   F   5.   A decline into recession causes an increase in the deficit in the actual budget.

T   F   6.   If the government tries to balance the full-employment budget every year, it will fall into a policy trap; it will increase the severity of recessions by raising tax rates or cutting spending during recessions.

T   F   7.   When the economy moves into a recession, the actual budget automatically moves toward deficit, but the full employment budget does not.

T   F   8.   An increase in government spending to build roads will move both the actual budget and the full-employment budget toward deficit.

T   F   9.   A cyclically balanced budget requires the full-employment budget to be balanced every year.

T   F   10.   Foreign held debt imposes no burden, because we pay foreigners with exports of goods and services, and exports make the economy stronger.

MULTIPLE CHOICE

1. The recessionary gap is:

   a. the amount by which actual GNP falls short of equilibrium GNP
   b. the amount by which actual GNP falls short of full-employment GNP
   c. the vertical distance from the aggregate expenditures line to the 45° line, measured at equilibrium national product
   d. the vertical distance from the aggregate expenditures line to the 45° line, measured at the full-employment national product
   e. the vertical distance from equilibrium national product to the aggregate expenditures function

2. When the economy is in equilibrium, the vertical distance between the aggregate expenditures function and the 45° line is equal to:

   a. the output gap
   b. the recessionary gap
   c. investment demand
   d. saving
   e. zero

3. Suppose that the recessionary gap is $10 billion, and it is expected to remain at that amount into the future if no action is taken. The appropriate policy to eliminate this $10 billion gap is:

   a. a cut in taxes of $10 billion
   b. a cut in government spending of $10 billion
   c. an increase in taxes of $10 billion
   d. an increase in government spending of $10 billion
   e. an increase in government spending of $10 billion x the multiplier

4. There is a relationship between the recessionary gap and the output gap. Specifically, the output gap is the recessionary gap:

   a. times the multiplier
   b. divided by the multiplier
   c. times the average tax rate
   d. divided by the average tax rate
   e. minus the average tax rate

5. Suppose that MPC equals 0.75 and that all taxes are lump-sum taxes. If national product is $3,000 billion and full-employment national product is $3,400 billion, then the output gap is:

   a. $100 billion
   b. $400 billion
   c. $600 billion
   d. $700 billion
   e. $1,600 billion

6. To stimulate aggregate expenditures during a severe recession, the appropriate fiscal policy is:

   a. an increase in taxes and/or an increase in government spending
   b. an increase in taxes and/or a decrease in government spending
   c. a decrease in taxes and/or an increase in government spending
   d. a decrease in taxes and/or a decrease in government spending
   e. a decrease in government purchases and/or a decrease in transfer payments

7. A $100 billion increase in government spending for goods and services has:

   a. the same effect on aggregate expenditures as a $100 billion increase in taxes
   b. the same effect on aggregate expenditures as a $100 billion cut in taxes
   c. a weaker effect on aggregate expenditures than a $100 billion cut in taxes
   d. a stronger effect on aggregate expenditures than a $100 billion cut in taxes
   e. no affect on aggregate expenditures; it effects only the "supply side" of the economy

8. In a diagram with aggregate expenditures on the vertical axis and national product on the horizontal axis, an across-the-board cut of one half in all income tax rates will cause the consumption function to become:

   a. lower, with no change in slope
   b. lower and flatter
   c. lower and steeper
   d. higher and flatter
   e. higher and steeper

9. An increase in income tax rates:

   a. makes the aggregate expenditures function steeper, and therefore lowers the size of the multiplier
   b. makes the aggregate expenditures function steeper, and therefore raises the size of the multiplier
   c. makes the aggregate expenditures function flatter, and therefore lowers the size of the multiplier
   d. makes the aggregate expenditures function flatter, and therefore raises the size of the multiplier
   e. lowers aggregate expenditures, but has no effect on the size of the multiplier

10. When we include international transactions in our model of the economy, the multiplier becomes:

   a. larger, because exports are an injection
   b. larger, because imports are an injection
   c. larger, because of the interaction between taxes and imports
   d. smaller, because the aggregate expenditures function now slopes downward
   e. smaller, because the leakage into imports increases as national product increases

11. When we include the government and international transactions in our model of the economy, equilibrium occurs when:

   a. $S + T + M = I^* + G + X$
   b. $S + T + X = I^* + G + M$
   c. $S + T + X + M = I^* + G$
   d. $S + G + M = I^* + T + X$
   e. $S + G + X = I^* + T + M$

12. An illustration of the term "automatic stabilizer" is provided by:

   a. the tendency of tax collections to rise as the economy moves into a recession
   b. the tendency of tax collections to fall as the economy moves into a recession
   c. increases in tax rates as the economy moves into a recession
   d. decreases in tax rates as the economy moves into a recession
   e. public works designed to get the economy out of a depression

13. In which of the following cases does the government fall into a "policy trap" and make the economy more unstable?

   a. it cuts taxes as the economy falls into a recession, since its deficits will increase as a result
   b. it increases tax rates as the economy falls into a recession, since it will depress aggregate expenditures
   c. it increases spending as the economy falls into a recession, since its deficits will increase as a result
   d. it attempts to balance the full-employment budget every year, since this will strongly destabilize aggregate expenditures
   e. it moves toward a full-employment deficit during recessions, since this will strongly destabilize aggregate expenditures

14. The principal purpose of the full-employment budget is to measure:

   a. changes in fiscal policy
   b. the size of the recessionary gap
   c. the size of the output gap
   d. the cut in taxes needed to get the economy to full employment
   e. the increase in taxes needed to get the economy to full employment

15. The full-employment budget:

   a. differs from the actual budget because it does not include transfer payments
   b. differs from the actual budget because it includes transfer payments, whereas the actual budget does not
   c. is in surplus whenever the economy falls short of full employment
   d. is more likely to show a surplus than is the actual budget
   e. is less likely to show a surplus than is the actual budget

16. Since 1960, fiscal policy has:

   a. been strongly stabilizing, particularly in 1964-69, when increases in spending promoted a strong, non-inflationary recovery
   b. been strongly stabilizing, particularly in the early 1980s, when large tax increases were the reason for lower inflation
   c. been strongly destablizing, particularly in the early 1980s, when large tax increases caused surpluses and made the recessions worse
   d. been strongly destabilizing, particularly in 1975, when large tax cuts made the deficits bigger and made the recession worse
   e. had a mediocre record, sometimes stabilizing, and sometimes destabilizing the economy

17. Suppose that a tax cut improves the efficiency of the economy and shifts the aggregate supply curve to the right. The most likely results are:

   a. an increase in both output and inflation
   b. an increase in output, but lower inflation
   c. a decrease in output, but higher inflation
   d. a decrease in both output and inflation
   e. there is no basis for a conclusion; each of the above is equally likely

18. The term, "excess burden of taxes," refers to what?

   a. taxes become burdensome whenever they exceed 10% of GNP
   b. personal income taxes are more obvious, and therefore more burdensome, than taxes on corporate profits
   c. personal income taxes are more obvious, and therefore more burdensome, than sales taxes
   d. people may alter their behavior to avoid paying taxes, thereby reducing the efficiency of the economy
   e. taxes must be raised, not only to repay the principal on the government debt, but also to pay interest

19. The U.S. government cannot "go broke" because:

   a. it has the power to tax
   b. it has the power to issue bonds whenever needed to repay its debt
   c. it has the power to print money, and bonds are repayable in money
   d. it has gold stocks equivalent to its long-term debt outstanding
   e. the constitution limits the size of the debt

20. A number of guidelines have been proposed as a way of exerting restraint on the government. Which of the following possible guidelines provides the greatest opportunity for an active fiscal policy aimed at reducing the amplitude of business fluctuations?

   a. balance the actual budget every year
   b. balance the full-employment budget every year
   c. balance the actual budget over the business cycle
   d. allow the government to increase spending whenever an increase in tax receipts pushes the budget into surplus
   e. none of the above allow any active countercyclical fiscal policy

EXERCISES

1. Figure 10.1 below shows a consumption function in an economy with no taxes. Its equation is $C = 200 + 0.5DI$, where units are billions of dollars and DI stands for disposable income. In the no-tax economy, DI = NP. The MPC equals _____. Now suppose that the government imposes a *lump sum* tax of $200 billion is collected. When NP = $400 billion, DI = $_____ billion, and C = $_____ billion. When NP = $600 billion, DI = $_____ billion, and C = $_____ billion. Plot this consumption function in the same diagram. The new consumption function is (flatter than, steeper than, has the same slope as) the initial consumption function.

Figure 10.1

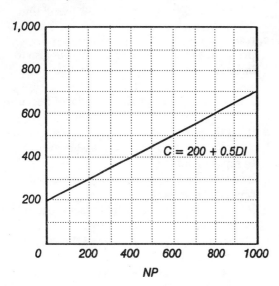

Consumption

$C = 200 + 0.5DI$

NP

Figure 10.2

C, I*, G

National Product

Now suppose that the lump-sum tax is eliminated, and replaced with a proportional tax: T = (1/3)DI. The marginal tax rate is _____. When NP = $300 billion, T = $_____ billion, DI = $_____ billion, and C = $_____ billion. When NP = $600 billion, T = $_____ billion, DI = $_____ billion, and C = $_____ billion. Plot this new consumption function on the same diagram. This new consumption function is (flatter than, steeper than, has the same slope as) the initial consumption function. How do you account for the different behavior of the slope here, compared to what happened when a tax was imposed in the previous paragraph?

2. Figure 10.2 shows aggregate expenditures and its components. In this economy, equilibrium is at point _____, with national product = _____. At this equilibrium, government purchases of goods and services (G) amounts to distance _____, I* = _____, and I = _____. Personal saving (S) equals (DE, DF, we don't have enough information to say).

Now, suppose that national product is at the disequilibrium amount NP4. I* = _____, while I = _____, and undesired inventory (accumulation, decumulation) = _____.

Now, suppose that this disequilibrium quantity NP4 represents the full employment output. There is a recessionary gap equal to distance _____. The appropriate fiscal policy is an (increase, decrease) in government purchases of goods and services amounting to distance _____.

3. The government's tax revenues increase as national product increases, and fall during recessions. This means that the budget automatically tends to move into (surplus, deficit) during recession.

The automatic (surpluses, deficits) during recessions introduce two major complications into fiscal policy. First, they present a (opportunity, trap) for the policy maker. If the government follows a superficially-plausible strategy of trying to balance the budget (every year, over the business cycle), it will end up (stabilizing, destabilizing) the economy. As the economy swings into recession, (surpluses, deficits) will automatically appear. If the authorities (raise, lower) taxes or (raise, lower) spending in an attempt to balance the budget, they will be following the (correct, wrong) fiscal policy; they will be (slowing the decline of expenditures, depressing aggregate expenditures further), and (adding to, reducing) the depth of the recession.

This was illustrated most clearly in (1932, 1942, 1961, 1981) when tax rates were (increased, cut) substantially. This (reduced, added to) the downward momentum of the economy. One of Keynes' major objectives was to (show how fiscal policy could be used in this manner to restore full employment, warn against such blunders). He argued that it was important for fiscal policy to be aimed at balancing the (budget, economy, both, neither).

The second complication is the problem of measuring fiscal policy. (Surpluses, Deficits) *automatically* increase during a recession. Just because (surpluses, deficits) rise during recessions, we should not conclude that the authorities are following counter-cyclical fiscal policies; they may be doing nothing. In order to determine what is happening to fiscal *policy*, some measure other than the actual budgetary surplus or deficit is needed. The (actual, full-employment, long-term) budget provides such a measure. This budget gives a measure of the deficit or surplus that would occur with current tax rates and spending programs *if* the economy were at (equilibrium, full employment). Because it is always measured at (equilibrium, full

employment), this budget does not automatically swing into (surplus, deficit) when the economy moves into a recession. However, the size of the deficit or surplus does change when tax rates or spending programs are changed. In brief, this budget changes when policies change; it does not change when the economy falls into recession. It therefore may be taken as a measure of fiscal policy.

Keynesian economists showed how the old objective of balancing the (actual, full-employment) budget could lead to the wrong policies. But if the President and Congress are not held responsible for balancing this budget, what will restrain their spending? One possibility would be to have a guideline which would require restraint, while avoiding the trap of balancing the (actual, full-employment) budget every year. Suggested guidelines include

(1)_____

(2)_____
or
(3)_____

ESSAY QUESTIONS

1. For each of the following, state whether you agree or disagree, and explain why:

   a. A tax acts as an automatic stabilizer only if it makes the aggregate expenditures function flatter.
   b. Whenever the aggregate expenditures function becomes flatter, the multiplier is lower.
   c. Automatic stabilizers reduce the size of the multiplier.

2. Critically evaluate the following statement: "Any system of unemployment insurance will be completely useless as a way of reducing business cycles. Even though the payment of benefits to the unemployed will help to raise aggregate expenditures during recessions, the contributions (taxes) to support the system will lower aggregate expenditures."

ANSWERS

True-False:

1 T (p. 164)
2 T (p. 166)
3 F (p. 168)
4 F (p. 171)
5 T (p. 171)
6 F (pp. 172-173)
7 T (p. 173)
8 T (p. 173)
9 F (pp. 173, 179)
10 F (p. 178)

Multiple Choice:

1 d (p. 165)
2 e (p. 165)
3 d (p. 165)
4 a (p. 165)
5 b (p. 165)
6 c (p. 167)
7 d (p. 167)
8 e (p. 168)
9 c (p. 168)
10 e (p. 170)
11 a (p. 170)
12 b (p. 170)
13 b (p. 171)
14 a (p. 172)
15 d (p. 173)
16 e (p. 173)
17 b (p. 175)
18 d (p. 177)
19 c (p. 178)
20 c (p. 179)

Exercises

1. 0.5, $200, $300, $400, $400, has the same slope as. 1/3, $100, $200, $300, $200, $400, $400, flatter than, here the tax increases with NP while it did not do so with the lump-sum tax in the previous paragraph.

2. F, NP$_3$, EF, DE, DE, we don't have enough information to say [Note: the reason is that, in equilibrium, $I^* + G = S + T$. The diagram tells us what G and I^* are. But we can't tell what S is unless we also know T.] GH, GH + JK, accumulation, JK, JK, increase, JK.

3. [Note: this exercise is based partly on the chapter highlights section.] deficit. deficits, trap, every year, destabilizing, deficits, raise, lower, wrong, depressing aggregate expenditures further, adding to, 1932, increased, added to, warn against such blunders, economy. Deficits, deficits, full-employment, full employment, full employment, deficit. actual, actual, (1) balancing the full-employment budget every year, (2) balancing the actual budget over the business cycle, with surpluses during prosperity to offset the deficits during recessions, or (3) limiting government spending to a fixed percentage of GNP.

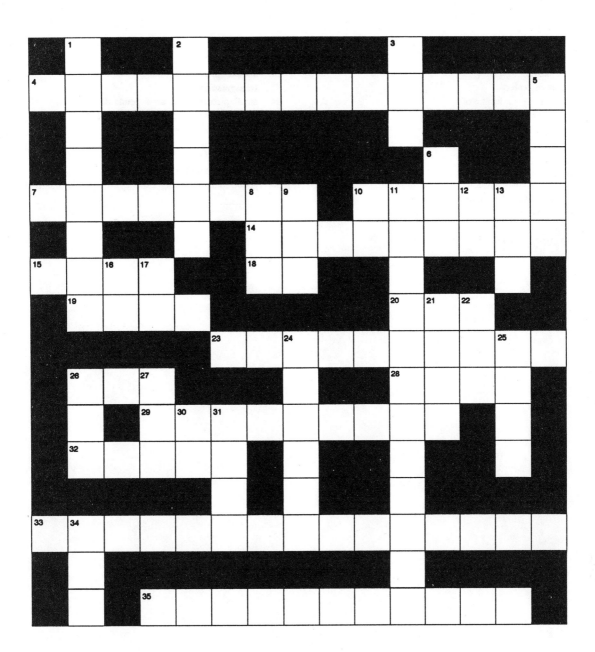

Across

4. a way to combat a depression (2 words)
7, 10. if the government aims for this every year, it may destabilize the economy
14. when NP exceeds its equilibrium, there is undesired _____ accumulation
15. when the government runs a deficit, the national _____ rises
18. a continent (abbrev.)
19. what you do with disposable income that you do not spend on consumption
20. change in saving, divided by change in disposable income
23. change in equlibrium national product, divided by change

in government spending for goods and services
26. the party of George Bush
28. one of the factors of production
29. investment or government spending
32. a quantity theorist of the early 20th century (see inside cover of text)
33. fiscal and monetary policies can be used to manage this (2 words)
35. largest component of national product

Down

1. saving and taxes
2. huge bodies of water
3. national income + sales taxes
5. he was a billionaire
6. an insecticide
8. one (German)
9. this carries the code of life (abbrev.)
10. to _____, or not to _____
11. to reduce this, deficit spending may be desirable
12. between Boardwalk and Baltic Avenue
13. make a mistake
16. college degree
17. a popular type of entertainment (abbrev.)

21. should precede action
22. transgression
24. small picture worn as a pendant
25. remove errors from a manuscript
26. NNP + depreciation
27. a medium-sized mammal
30. not so
31. famous student of psychology
34. government spending can be used to fill the recessionary _____

CHAPTER 11

MONEY AND THE BANKING SYSTEM

LEARNING OBJECTIVES

After you have studied this chapter in the textbook and study guide, you should be able to

✔ Describe the three basic functions of money

✔ Explain the differences between M1 and M2

✔ Explain why a bank might want to hold only fractional reserves, rather than reserves equal to 100% of its deposit liabilities

✔ Explain why fractional-reserve banking leads to the risk of a bank run, and why no bank can withstand a severe run without outside help

✔ Explain in detail how an individual bank responds to an increase in its reserves, and how the overall banking system can increase money by a multiple of the increase in reserves. (The explanation requires use of balance sheets.)

✔ State the formula for the deposit multiplier

✔ Give two reasons why the actual expansion of deposits is likely to be less than indicated by this formula

MAJOR PURPOSE

The major purpose of this chapter is to explain how the banking system creates money. The details of money creation, as set out in the various tables in this chapter, are important. A number of specific conclusions are also important:

- Even though the banking system can create money equal to a multiple of its reserves, an individual bank cannot do so.

- Instead, an individual bank receiving a deposit of $100 can create money by lending only a fraction of this $100 (specifically, $100 x 0.8, if the required reserve ratio is 0.2).

- The bank sees nothing particularly magical or peculiar about such loans, even though they result in an increase in the money stock.

- Fractional-reserve banking developed as a natural result of the desire to make profits.

- Fractional-reserve banks can be subject to runs. Because each bank holds reserves equal to only a fraction of its deposit liabilities, no bank can withstand an all-out run without outside help, no matter how sound the bank was originally.

- Bank runs are not only unfortunate for the banks and individual depositors who are too late to get their funds; they also can have strong adverse effects on the economy. Because reserves are being withdrawn from the base of the monetary pyramid, bank runs cause strong downward pressures on the money stock. One of the major tasks of the monetary authorities is to prevent bank runs and instability of the monetary supply, as we shall see in the next chapter.

HIGHLIGHTS OF CHAPTER

This chapter introduces the basic concepts of money and banking, as a background for studying monetary policy in the next chapter.

Money performs three interrelated functions:

- It is a **medium of exchange**; that is, it is used to buy goods and services.

- It is a **standard of value**; that is, we keep accounts, quote prices, and sign contracts in dollar terms.

- It is a **store of value**; that is, you can hold money for future purchases rather than spending it right away.

The basic definition of the money stock, M1, includes items which are used as money in everyday transactions—coins, paper currency, checking accounts in banks and similar financial institutions, and travelers' checks. Each of these items represents wealth to the holder; if you have $100 in your pocket, you are better off than you would be without it. In this way, money is different from a credit card, which represents a convenient way to run up debt, rather than an asset. Thus, even though credit cards (and the corresponding lines of credit) are often used to make purchases, lines of credit are not included in the money stock.

M2 includes M1 plus noncheckable savings deposits, small time deposits, money market deposits, and money market mutual funds. Although such assets are not used in an unrestricted way to make purchases,

they can be quickly switched into M1. Thus, they can have a powerful effect on people's spending behavior. When we are concerned about the relationship between "money" and aggregate demand, we often use the broader definition of money, M2.

Commercial banks and similar financial institutions—such as savings and loan associations—accept deposits, using most of the proceeds to make loans. They hold reserves equal to only a fraction of their deposit liabilities. **Fractional-reserve banking** developed centuries ago, when financial institutions realized that they could cover their costs and make profits from the interest on loans. Through history, fractional-reserve banks have been plagued by the problem of runs, which have not only been dangerous for them, but have also disrupted the economy. One conspicuous example occurred in 1932-33, when the U.S. banking system collapsed, adding to the downslide into the depression.

Even in olden times, when there were no required reserve ratios, banks kept reserves to use as working balances and to meet unexpected withdrawals; such reserves provided some protection against a run. Now, the function of reserves is not to provide protection against a run. Rather, it is to give the authorities control over the money stock. The Federal Reserve, which is the central bank of the United States, is empowered to set reserve requirements within limits specified by Congress. If the required reserve ratio is, say, 0.10, then a $100 withdrawal from a bank deposit will reduce the required reserves by only $10. The other $90 will have to be obtained elsewhere by the bank, most likely by reducing its portfolio of loans or bonds. In other words, reserves in this case would only provide one tenth of the funds needed to meet the withdrawal.

If there is a required reserve ratio specified by law, then the banking system as a whole can increase its deposit liabilities by as much as 1/R times any increase in its reserves. Tables 11-4 to 11-9 in the text explain in detail how banks do this. These tables are not repeated here, but they are of central importance in any study of the monetary system. They often appear on examinations. Students should go over them particularly carefully, together with the balance sheets in the exercises below. Warning: **The the multiple expansion of bank deposits is one of the most important and difficult concepts in introductory economics.**

The deposit multiplier, D = 1/R, shows the *maximum* increase in deposits that can occur when the banking system acquires additional reserves. In practice, the actual increase is likely to be much less, for two reasons. Most important is that, as people acquire more checking deposit money, they are likely to want to hold some of the additional money in the form of currency. When they make withdrawals from their banks, the reserves of banks are reduced. The second reason is that banks may hold excess reserves rather than lending all they are permitted. In recent years, excess reserves have been very small, and this second point represents only a minor complication. However, it was quite important back in the 1930s, when excess reserves at times amounted to almost half of total reserves. There were two reasons for the very large holdings of excess reserves. Interest rates were very low, which meant that bankers didn't forego much interest when they kept excess reserves. Second, bankers were frightened to lend to businesses, since so many businesses were going bankrupt. The failure of banks to lend more of their excess reserves was unfortunate, since more lending and more money would have promoted economic recovery.

We here have one illustration of the difference between what is good for an individual or an institution and what is good for the economy as a whole. Risky bank lending would have increased the money stock and contributed to economic recovery. But it could have meant financial suicide for any bank making risky loans. Bankers cannot be expected to commit suicide for the public good. It is up to the Federal Reserve, not up to individual banks, to see that the money stock is at the right level to keep aggregate demand close to its desired path. How the Fed does this will be studied in the next chapter.

(A second example of the conflict between what is good for the individual and what is good for the overall economy occurs during a bank run. Each individual has an incentive to be first in line. But severe bank runs can disrupt the economy.)

IMPORTANT TERMS

Match the first column with the corresponding phrase in the second column.

_____ 1. Currency	a. Assets - net worth
_____ 2. M1	b. Deposit liabilities x R
_____ 3. Liquid assets	c. Major reason for risk of runs
_____ 4. Liabilities	d. Actual reserves - required reserves
_____ 5. What a single bank can prudently lend	e. Coins, paper currency, and checking deposits
_____ 6. Required reserves	f. Increase in reserves x $1/R$
_____ 7. Maximum increase in deposits	g. Short-term government securities
_____ 8. Fractional-reserve banking	h. Coins and paper currency

---

TRUE-FALSE

T   F   1.   Checking deposits held by manufacturing corporations — such as General Motors — are included in the money stock (M1).

T   F   2.   Reserve deposits held by the Chase Manhattan bank are included in the money stock (M1).

T   F   3.   Fractional reserve banking was invented by the Federal Reserve.

T   F   4.   In the modern U.S. banking system, most commercial banks reserves are held in the form of gold.

T   F   5.   When General Motors deposits $100,000 in the Chase Manhattan bank, the resulting deposit appears as an asset on the G.M. balance sheet, and the same deposit appears as a liability on the Chase Manhattan balance sheet.

T   F   6.   If a commercial bank receives a deposit of currency, then its actual reserves and excess reserves both increase by the same amount (specifically, by the amount of the deposit).

T   F   7.   If a commercial bank receives the deposit of a check drawn against an account in another bank, then its actual reserves and its excess reserves both increase as a consequence.

T   F   8.   A bank may prudently lend the amount of its excess reserves x 1/R.

T   F   9.   Banks are more likely to hold excess reserves during a depression than during prosperity.

T   F   10. Bank deposits are normally equal to reserves x 1/R. However, they can be larger than that during depressions, when more money is needed to stimulate recovery.

MULTIPLE CHOICE

1. Between 1929 and 1933, during the early part of the Great Depression:

   a. the quantity of money rose, but aggregate demand nonetheless collapsed
   b. the quantity of money fell, but prices nevertheless rose moderately
   c. there was hyperinflation, even though the money stock fell
   d. the quantity of money fell, and this contributed to the downturn
   e. the quantity of money increased at a slow, steady rate, as advocated by monetarists, but the depression nevertheless occurred

2. Even though credit cards are used by many people in making purchases, they are not included in M1. A major reason is that:

   a. credit cards are a way of going into debt, whereas the components of M1 represent assets
   b. credit cards had not yet been invented when money was defined
   c. some credit cards are issued by stores (such as Sears), whereas all money is issued by banks
   d. credit cards are much less liquid than M1
   e. credit cards don't affect consumer expenditures, whereas M1 does

3. Checking deposits make up approximately what fraction of the money stock (M1) in the United States:

   a. 1%
   b. 10%
   c. 25%
   d. 50%
   e. 70%

4. Checking deposits are included in the money stock M1:

   a. only if they are owned by individuals
   b. if they are owned by individuals or non-bank corporations (such as IBM or a local car dealer)
   c. if they are owned by individuals, other banks, or the Federal Reserve

   d. if they are owned by individuals, other banks, or the U.S. Treasury
   e. if they are owned by individuals, the Federal Reserve, or the U.S. Treasury

5. Suppose we know M1, and want to calculate M2. To do so, which of the following do we add to M1?

   a. coins
   b. paper currency
   c. checking deposits
   d. noncheckable savings deposits
   e. Treasury bills

6. In the balance sheet of a business:

   a. Assets = Liabilities
   b. Assets = Liabilities + Net Worth
   c. Assets = Liabilities - Net Worth
   d. Liabilities = Assets + Net Worth
   e. Any of the above may be correct; it depends on the health of the business

7. The primary reason why the activities of early goldsmiths developed into "fractional reserve banking" was the desire to:

   a. keep the money stock down to a fraction of its earlier level, in order to restrain inflation
   b. increase the quantity of money, in order to finance the growth of trade
   c. provide a more stable money system, in order to reduce the size of business fluctuations
   d. provide a broader range of financial services to their customers
   e. increase profits, by lending out some of the gold deposited with them

8. A bank run is most likely to occur at a time when:

   a. government surpluses are high
   b. tax rates are high
   c. many non-bank businesses are going bankrupt
   d. investment by non-bank businesses is large
   e. banks have reserves equal to 100% of their deposit liabilities

9. During a bank run, there can be a conflict between the interests of the individual and the interests of the society as a whole. Specifically:

   a. each depositor has an incentive to get in line, even though bank runs can weaken the economy
   b. each depositor has an incentive to make additional deposits because of the high interest rates, but high interest rates are undesirable for the society as a whole
   c. it is even more important for society than for the individual depositor that unsound banks be closed down
   d. even though a run at a specific bank causes a contraction at that bank, the overall economy nevertheless expands because of the improved competitive position of other banks
   e. all of the above

10. The Federal Reserve performs all the following functions *except one*. Which is the exception? The Fed:

    a. issues paper currency
    b. conducts fiscal policy
    c. controls the quantity of money in the United States
    d. acts as the federal governmment's bank
    e. acts as a bankers' bank

11. In the balance sheet of the typical commercial bank, the largest asset is:

    a. reserve deposits
    b. loans
    c. checking deposits
    d. time deposits
    e. net worth

12. Commercial banks are required by law to hold reserves. These reserves are specified as percentages of a bank's:

    a. total assets
    b. total liabilities
    c. deposit liabilities
    d. holdings of government securities
    e. net worth

13. Suppose that the required reserve ratio is 10% and that a person deposits $100 of currency in his or her bank. Then that single bank can create

    a. $80 in additional money by lending $80
    b. $90 in additional money by lending $90
    c. $100 in additional money by lending $100
    d. $1,000 in additional money by lending $1,000
    e. no additional money; it takes the actions of the whole banking system to create more money, not just one bank

14. Suppose that the required reserve ratio of a commercial bank is represented by the fraction R. Suppose that this commercial bank receives a deposit of currency of $100. Then, as a result, *this single commercial bank* can make a loan of as much as:

    a. $100 / R
    b. $100 x R
    c. $100 / (1-R)
    d. $100 x (1-R)

15. When a commercial bank makes a loan to the local drug store

    a. the bank's assets increase
    b. the bank's liabilities increase
    c. the money stock increases
    d. the amount of checking deposits increases
    e. all of the above

16. Suppose that someone in New York, who banks at the Citibank, sends a check for $1,000 to someone in California, who deposits it in the Bank of America. The required reserve ratio is R. In the process of check clearing, the reserves of Citibank will:

    a. increase by $1,000, while those of the Bank of America will decrease by $1,000
    b. decrease by $1,000, while those of the Bank of America will increase by $1,000
    c. increase by $1,000 x R, while those of the Bank of America will decrease by $1,000 x R
    d. decrease by $1,000 x R, while those of the Bank of America will increase by $1,000 x R
    e. increase by $1,000 divided by R, while those of the Bank of America will decrease by $1,000 divided by R

17. An increase in the required reserve ratio on checking deposits would most likely cause:

    a. an increase in M1
    b. a decrease in M1
    c. an increase in checking deposits
    d. an increase in bank profits
    e. an increase in the checking deposit multiplier

18. The monetary system is sometimes said to form an inverted pyramid. By this, we mean that:

a. a large quantity of checking deposit money can be built on a small quantity of reserves
b. a large quantity of reserves can be built on a small quantity of checking deposit money
c. a large quantity of currency can be built on a small quantity of checking deposit money
d. checking deposits are the largest component of M1
e. currency is the largest component of M1

19. The deposit multiplier, 1/R, represents the *maximum* amount by which the banking system may increase deposits as a result of an initial increase in bank reserves. (R is the required reserve ratio.) In practice, the actual increase is likely to be less than shown by this multiplier, since:

a. a single bank can increase deposits by less than can the banking system as a whole
b. a single bank can increase deposits by more than can the banking system as a whole
c. as the banks expand their loans, the public will decide to deposit more currency in their bank accounts
d. banks may hold less than the required reserve ratio; with a smaller actual reserve ratio, the expansion of deposits is likewise smaller
e. banks may hold excess reserves, and the public may decide to hold more currency as the quantity of money increases

20. Banks are most likely to hold significant quantities of excess reserves when:

a. their profits are high
b. the economy is in a boom
c. the economy is growing slowly and steadily
d. the economy is in a mild recession
e. the economy is in a depression

EXERCISES

1. a. If I deposit $100,000 in currency into a checking deposit in bank A and the required reserve ratio is 20%, then the immediate increase in bank A's total reserves is $ _____ and the immediate increase in bank A's required reserves is $ _____ . Thus, the immediate increase in bank A's excess reserves is $ _____ . As a result of this transaction, the total amount of currency in the hands of the public has [increased by $ _____ , decreased by $ _____ , not changed], the total amount of checking deposits held by the public has [increased by $ _____ , decreased by $ _____ , not changed], and the total amount of M1 has [increased by $ _____ , decreased by $ _____ , not changed].

    b. Suppose bank A now lends all its new excess reserves. The borrower writes a check against the proceeds of the loan, and this check is deposited in a checking deposit in bank B. When this loan is made and this check is deposited and cleared, the effect is to make bank A's total reserves [increase by $ _____ , decrease by $ _____ , remain unchanged], to make bank A's required reserves [increase by $ _____ , decrease by $ _____ , remain unchanged], to make bank A's excess reserves [increase by $ _____ , decrease by $ _____ , remain unchanged], to make bank B's total reserves [increase by $ _____ , decrease

by $ _____ , remain unchanged], to make bank B's required reserves [increase by $ _____ , decrease by $ _____ , remain unchanged], and to make bank B's excess reserves [increase by $ _____ , decrease by $ _____ , remain unchanged]. As a result of this loan, the total amount of checking deposits has [increased by $ _____ , decreased by $ _____ , not changed].

    c. If the process of lending continues until all excess reserves have been eliminated throughout the banking system, then as a result of the whole process, starting with my initial deposit, the total quantity of currency in the hands of the public will have [increased by $ _____ , decreased by $ _____ , not changed], the total quantity of checking deposits in the hands of the public will have [increased by $ _____ , decreased by $ _____ , not changed], the total quantity of M1 in the hands of the public will have [increased by $ _____ , decreased by $ _____ , not changed], and the total quantity of M2 in the hands of the public will have [increased by $ _____ , decreased by $ _____ , not changed].

2. Show what happens as a direct result of each of the following transactions by filling in the appropriate numbers for that transaction in the balance sheet. Each balance sheet should represent the **change** in assets and liabilities of *all* banks as a group. In each case, suppose that the required reserve ratio on checking deposits is 20% and on all other deposits is 10%. Each transaction should be considered separately from all the others.

a. Someone deposits $25,000 in currency into a checking deposit.

b. Someone withdraws $100,000 in currency from a noncheckable savings account.

c. Someone switches $200,000 from a checking deposit to a noncheckable savings deposit.

d. A bank lends $40,000 to someone who immediately takes the proceeds of the loan in the form of currency.

e. A bank lends $100,000 to someone who uses that $100,000 to pay off a loan to someone who puts the $100,000 into a noncheckable savings deposit.

Balance Sheet a

Change in assets		Change in liabilities	
Loans	_____		
Total reserves	_____		
Required reserves	_____	Checking deposits	_____
Excess reserves	_____	Other deposits	_____

Balance Sheet b

Change in assets		Change in liabilities	
Loans	_____		
Total reserves	_____		
Required reserves	_____	Checking deposits	_____
Excess reserves	_____	Other deposits	_____

Balance Sheet c

Change in assets		Change in liabilities	
Loans	_____		
Total reserves	_____		
Required reserves	_____	Checking deposits	_____
Excess reserves	_____	Other deposits	_____

Balance Sheet d

Change in assets		Change in liabilities	
Loans	_____		
Total reserves	_____		
Required reserves	_____	Checking deposits	_____
		Other deposits	_____
Excess reserves	_____		

Balance Sheet e

Change in assets		Change in liabilities	
Loans	_____		
Total reserves	_____		
Required reserves	_____	Checking deposits	_____
		Other deposits	_____
Excess reserves	_____		

ESSAY QUESTIONS

1. Why are bank runs most likely to occur during a depression or severe recession? Are bank runs most damaging to the economy at such times, or would they be more damaging during a period of prosperity? Why?

2. Deposits in most banks and S&Ls are now covered by federal insurance. If your bank doesn't have the money, the federal government will make good, up to a maximum of $100,000 per deposit. As a result, runs on banks and other financial institutions have been *much* less common than they were during the 1930s, prior to federal deposit insurance. Nevertheless, runs still occasionally occur. Why do you suppose they still do?

3. By his term "invisible hand," Adam Smith suggested that self-interested actions tend to benefit society. This chapter has explained two cases where pursuit of self-interest lead to undesirable results for the society as a whole. What are these two cases, and why does self-interest lead to socially undesirable outcomes? Can you think of any way to deal with these problems?

4. Individual bankers often argue, "We don't create money; we just lend money that has already been deposited with us." Is this correct? If so, explain why. If not, explain why not.

ANSWERS

Matching columns: **1 h, 2 e, 3 g, 4 a, 5 d, 6 b, 7 f, 8 c**

True-False: **1 T** (p. 189)
                          2 F (p. 189)
                          3 F (p. 191)
                          4 F (p. 194)
                          5 T (p. 196)
                          6 F (p. 196)
                          7 T (p. 197)
                          8 F (p. 198)
                          9 T (p. 202)
                          10 F (p. 201-202)

Multiple Choice: **1 d** (p. 187)
                          2 a (p. 188)
                          3 e (p. 189)
                          4 b (p. 189)
                          5 d (p. 190)
                          6 b (p. 191)
                          7 e (p. 192)
                          8 c (p. 193)
                          9 a (p. 193)
                          10 b (p. 193)
                          11 b (p. 194)
                          12 c (p. 194)
                          13 b (pp. 195-198)
                          14 d (pp. 195-198)
                          15 e (p. 196)
                          16 b (p. 197)
                          17 b (p. 201)
                          18 a (p. 202)
                          19 e (p. 202)
                          20 e (p. 202)

Exercises

1   a. $100,000, $20,000, $80,000, decreased by $100,000, increased by $100,000, not changed.
    b.   decrease by $80,000, remain unchanged, decrease by $80,000, increase by $80,000, increase by $16,000, increase by $64,000, increased by $80,000.
    c.   decreased by $100,000, increased by $500,000, increased by $400,000, increased by $400,000 (note: M1 is included in M2).

Balance Sheet a

Change in assets			Change in liabilities	
Loans		0		
Total reserves		25,000		
			Checking deposits	25,000
Required reserves	5,000		Other deposits	0
Excess reserves	20,000			

Balance Sheet b

Change in assets			Change in liabilities	
Loans		0		
Total reserves		−100,000		
			Checking deposits	0
Required reserves	−10,000		Other deposits	−100,000
Excess reserves	−90,000			

Balance Sheet c

Change in assets			Change in liabilities	
Loans		0		
Total reserves		0		
			Checking deposits	−200,000
Required reserves	−20,000		Other deposits	+200,000
Excess reserves	+20,000			

Balance Sheet d

Change in assets			Change in liabilities	
Loans		+40,000		
Total reserves		−40,000		
			Checking deposits	0
Required reserves	0		Other deposits	0
Excess reserves	−40,000			

Balance Sheet e

Change in assets			Change in liabilities	
Loans		100,000		
Total reserves		0		
Required reserves	+10,000		Checking deposits	0
Excess reserves	−10,000		Other deposits	100,000

CHAPTER 12

THE FEDERAL RESERVE AND THE TOOLS OF MONETARY POLICY

LEARNING OBJECTIVES

After you have studied this chapter in the textbook and study guide, you should be able to

✔ Describe the organization of the Federal Reserve

✔ Describe how the Fed can use each of its three major tools to affect the size of the money stock

✔ Explain how open market operations change the balance sheets of the commercial banks and the Federal Reserve

✔ Explain how open market operations affect not only the size of the money stock, but also interest rates

✔ Give an example which shows why the yield (interest rate) on a treasury bill falls when its price rises

✔ Explain why a restrictive monetary policy usually does not involve an open market sale, but rather just a reduction in the rate of purchases on the open market

✔ Explain why large changes in the required reserve ratio would be very disruptive, and give an historical example

✔ Explain why a margin requirement may add to the stability of the stock market, even if the margin requirement is never changed

✔ Explain why federal deposit insurance reduces the risk of a run on banks

✔ Explain why stabilization of the interest rate may be a "trap" for the Federal Reserve, just as aiming for an annually balanced budget may be a trap for fiscal policymakers

MAJOR PURPOSE

There are two major tools for controlling aggregate demand—fiscal policy and monetary policy. Fiscal policy, which involves changes in tax rates and in government spending, is in the hands of the Congress and the President. Monetary policy, which involves changes in the rate of growth of the money stock, is in the hands of the Federal Reserve. The major purpose of this chapter is to explain how the Federal Reserve (the "Fed") can influence the money stock.

As we saw in Chapter 11, most of the money stock consists of checking deposits in banks and other similar institutions. The amount of money that banks can create depends on the quantity of reserves that they own and on the required reserve ratio. The Federal Reserve has three principal tools with which it can influence the quantity of money:

- It can **purchase securities on the open market**. When it does so, it increases the reserves of the banks.

- It can **change the discount rate**, changing the banks' desire to borrow from the Fed. Since the reserves of banks increase when they borrow from the Fed, changes in the discount rate influence the total quantity of reserves that the banks hold.

- It can **change the required reserve ratio**, thereby changing the quantity of deposits that can be created on any given reserve base.

HIGHLIGHTS OF CHAPTER

The Federal Reserve is the central bank of the United States. It is the "bankers' bank," and it is responsible for controlling the quantity of money. When the Federal Reserve was established, there were deep concerns over the power of centralized financial institutions, and therefore the Fed is decentralized. There are twelve Federal Reserve districts, with a Federal Reserve Bank in each district. In Washington, there is a Board of Governors with seven members. The most important policy body of the Fed—the Federal Open Market Committee (FOMC)—is made up of seven members of the Board, plus five of the presidents of the regional Federal Reserve Banks. At meetings of the FOMC, these five presidents explain to the other members of the FOMC the economic and financial conditions in their districts. (So do the other regional bank presidents, who are non-voting members of the FOMC.) Thus, conditions in the various regions are considered as the FOMC develops monetary policy.

The Fed has three major tools with which it can affect the quantity of money:

- **open market operations**

- **changes in the discount rate**, and

- **changes in the required reserve ratios**.

Open market operations are the most important tool; they are used for the every-day, "bread and butter" activities of the Fed.

When the Fed buys securities worth, say, $10 million on the open market, bank reserves increase by the same $10 million. Because the banks have additional excess reserves, they are able to make loans; the money stock can increase by a multiple of the $10 million. As we saw in Chapter 11, the *maximum* increase in the money stock is the $10 million times $1/R$, where R is the required reserve ratio. However, in practice, the actual increase is not likely to be this great. As banks make loans and the quantity of money increases, the public is likely to want not only more checking deposits, but more currency too. People therefore withdraw some currency from their bank accounts. When they do so, the reserves of banks decline and the amount of money they can create likewise declines.

The maximum increase in the money stock depends on the size of the open market operation ($10 million in the above example) and on the required reserve ratio. It does not depend on whether a commercial bank, a non-bank corporation, or an individual sells the securities to the Fed. However, the details of the way in which the money supply increases will vary, depending on who the seller is. If a non-bank corporation—such as IBM—or an individual is the seller, then the money stock will go up immediately as a result of the open market purchase. For example, if IBM sells the $10 million in securities which the Fed buys, IBM will deposit the proceeds from the sale in its checking deposit, and its holdings of money will therefore increase by $10 million. IBM's bank will now have larger deposit liabilities, and its required reserves will rise—by $10 million times the required reserve ratio. If this ratio is, say, 15%, the bank will have $8.5 million of excess reserves (the $10 addition to reserves less the increase of $1.5 million in required reserves). It will safely be able to lend the $8.5 million. There will be a series of expansions: $10 million + ($10 x 0.85) million + ($10 x 0.85^2) million, and so on.

On the other hand, if a commercial bank sells the $10 million in securities, there is no initial increase in the quantity of money, since the checking deposits held by the public have not been affected. Required reserves likewise remain unchanged, but the banks have $10 million in excess reserves. They can therefore lend the full $10 million, again initiating an expansion of $10 million + ($10 x 0.85) million + ($10 x 0.85^2) million, and so on. Although the initial, first round effects of the two types of transaction are different, their ultimate effects on the money stock will be the same.

Thus, when the Fed buys securities on the open market, the money stock increases. If the Fed sold securities on the open market, it would likewise cause a multiple decrease in the money stock. However, this would cause *very* tight monetary conditions. In our growing economy, the money stock can grow at a moderate rate without causing inflation. Therefore, when the Fed wants to tighten monetary conditions, it normally does not sell securities. Instead, it simply *reduces the rate of purchases* on the open market.

When it buys securities on the open market, the Fed bids their prices *up*. But this is just another way of saying that it bids interest rates *down*. As a result of the Fed's purchase, the banks have excess reserves. As they make loans or buy bonds with these reserves, the banks bid interest rates down even further.

Changes in the discount rate are the second major tool of the Fed. By cutting the discount rate, the Fed encourages banks to borrow more. When they borrow more, their reserves increase. Thus, a cut in the discount rate is an expansionary policy; increases in the rate are a restrictive policy. The Fed is sometimes spoken of as the **lender of last resort**; the banks can go to the Fed to borrow reserves if they are temporarily short and cannot get funds elsewhere.

The third major tool of the Fed is a change in the required reserve ratio. As we have seen in Chapter 11, checking deposits can be as much as $1/R$ times reserves, where R is the required reserve ratio. By changing R, the Fed can thus change the size of the deposit multiplier. Relatively small changes in R can have a powerful effect on the size of the money stock. In order to avoid disruption of monetary conditions, the Fed is now careful to make only small changes when it does adjust R.

The Fed also has a number of other ways of influencing monetary and financial conditions. It imposes **margin requirements**, limiting the amount that can be borrowed by those who are buying stocks or bonds. The Fed has the power to adjust these requirements, but it has in fact kept the rate on stocks stable at 50% in recent years. For requirements to have a stabilizing effect, it is not necessary that they be adjusted. A steady 50% rate means that stockholders will not be wiped out by moderate reverses in the stock market, and will not be forced to dump their stocks. If they had been able to borrow, say, 90% of the value of the stock, their rush to get out of the stock market could change a small retreat into a stock market collapse.

Finally, the Fed can influence bank behavior by **moral suasion**—suggestions to bankers regarding appropriate policy.

When the Fed purchases securities on the open market, it creates money "out of thin air." Our money is not backed by gold. Money retains its value because the Fed limits its supply; money is scarce. Checking deposits are backed not only by the assets of the banks, but also by the Federal Deposit Insurance Corporation. Insurance is important for individual depositors; it offers them protection. It is also important for the stability of the system as a whole: Federal insurance greatly reduces the risk of a run on banks.

At times in our history, money has also been backed by **gold** (and silver). This system had one great advantage, in that it limited the amount of money that could be created, and thus acted as a restraint on reckless, inflationary expansions in the money stock. However, it had two great defects.

- Increases in the quantity of gold played a function similar to open market purchases in the present system; they increased bank reserves, and permitted a multiple increase in the money stock. However, there was no assurance that the amount of gold mined or imported from abroad would provide the amount of money needed for a full-employment, non-inflationary economy.

- The banking system was vulnerable to runs. Whenever gold reserves were withdrawn from the base of the monetary pyramid, there was a powerful contractionary effect on the quantity of money. In other words, the gold standard could make financial crises and recessions worse—as it did in the early 1930s. This was the major reason for the abandonment of the gold standard.

Finally, this chapter explains how the Fed faces a **policy trap**, somewhat similar to the fiscal trap of attempting to balance the budget every year. If the Fed follows a policy of stabilizing interest rates, its policy is **passive**. It increases the money stock in response to rising demands from the public for funds. Responding in such a passive way can be a great mistake. The money supply may go up particularly rapidly during prosperity, when people are clamoring for loans. This can make the prosperity turn into an inflationary boom. A passive response can also add to a downturn.

IMPORTANT TERMS

Match the first column with the corresponding phrase in the second column.

_____ 1. The Federal Reserve
_____ 2. Open market operation
_____ 3. Example of restrictive policy
_____ 4. Example of the expansive policy
_____ 5. U.S. Treasury
_____ 6. Discount rate
_____ 7. Prime rate
_____ 8. Price of a treasury bill
_____ 9. Margin requirement
_____ 10. Legal tender
_____ 11. Fiat money
_____ 12. Attempt to stabilize interest rates

a. Money unbacked by gold or silver; it is money because the government says so
b. Helps to stabilize stock market
c. Interest rate on Fed's loans to commercial banks
d. Creditors must accept this money in repayment of debts
e. This rises when interest rate falls
f. Central bank of the United States
g. Possibly, a monetary policy trap
h. Reduction of discount rate
i. Purchase or sale of government securities by the Fed
j. A bank's publicly-announced interest rate for short-term loans
k. This institution initially issued securities bought or sold in open market operations
l. Increase in the required reserve ratio

TRUE-FALSE

T   F   1.   Although the Federal Reserve is technically independent of the President, in fact the Fed is closely influenced by the President because the members of the board are appointed by the President for four-year terms which coincide with the presidential term.

T   F   2.   Open market policy is determined by the Federal Open Market Committee, which meets in Washington However, actual open market operations are carried out by the New York Federal Reserve Bank.

T   F   3.   If the required reserve ratio of the commercial banks is 10%, then an open market purchase of $1 million by the Federal Reserve permits the banks to increase their checking deposits by a maximum of $10 million.

T   F   4.   The appropriate strategy for the Federal Reserve during a depression is to sell government bonds, to make low-risk, sound assets available for the commercial banks to buy.

T   F   5.   When commercial banks repay their discounts (borrowings from the Fed), the result is an increase in their excess reserves.

T   F   6.   When the Fed sells securities to the commercial banks, it increases their earning assets, and thus makes possible an increase in the money stock.

T   F   7.   When the Fed increases its purchases of government securities, it is engaging in an expansionary act; when it sells government securities, it is engaging in a restrictive act.

T   F   8.   If the interest rate doubles, then the price of a treasury bill falls by 50%.

T   F   9.   Federal Reserve notes (the paper currency of the United States) are backed dollar for dollar with gold held by the Fed.

T   F   10.   The existence of federal insurance for bank depositors reduces the danger of bank runs. Indeed, one of the major purposes of such insurance is to reduce this danger.

MULTIPLE CHOICE

1. The Federal Reserve *cannot* do one of the following. Which one?

   a. change the tax rate on profits
   b. change the discount rate
   c. change the required reserve ratio
   d. change margin requirements
   e. buy securities on the open market

2. When the Fed purchases securities on the open market, the securities it buys are:

   a. common stock of the U.S. corporations whose stocks are included in the Dow-Jones industrial average
   b. corporate bonds
   c. securities issued by state governments
   d. securities issued by the federal government
   e. any of the above; since it is a transaction on "the open market," the Fed buys whatever is offered for sale at the best price

3. As a result of an open market operation by the Fed, the amount of checking-deposit creation will be larger, the higher is the:

   a. required reserve ratio
   b. discount rate
   c. fraction of securities purchased from commercial banks, rather than the general public
   d. fraction of securities purchased from the general public, rather than from commercial banks
   e. volume of securities purchased by the Fed

4. If the Fed purchases $100,000 of government securities on the open market and the required reserve ratio is 20%, then the maximum increase in commercial bank reserves is:

   a. $20,000
   b. $100,000
   c. $200,000
   d. $400,000
   e. $500,000

5. When the Fed purchases a $100,000 Treasury bill from a manufacturing corporation, and that cor-poration deposits the proceeds in a checking deposit in its bank (Bank A), then:

   a. Bank A's total reserves rise by $100,000
   b. Bank A's excess reserves rise by $100,000
   c. Bank A can safely lend $100,000
   d. the liabilities of the Fed increase by $500,000
   e. all of the above

6. Suppose that (a) the Fed purchases a $100,000 government security on the open market, (b) the required reserve ratio is 20%, (c) IBM sells the security, and (d) IBM deposits the proceeds from the sale in its commercial bank. The effect of this single transaction will be to increase the *excess* reserves of the commercial banking system banks by:

   a. $20,000
   b. $80,000
   c. $100,000
   d. $200,000
   e. $500,000

7. Suppose that *(a)* the Fed purchases a $100,000 government security on the open market, *(b)* the required reserve ratio is 20%, *(c)* IBM sells the security, and *(d)* IBM deposits the proceeds from the sale in its commercial bank. The effect of this single transaction will be to increase the money stock by:

   a. zero
   b. $20,000
   c. $100,000
   d. $200,000
   e. $500,000

8. When the Fed purchases a $100,000 Treasury bill from a commercial bank, as a result:

   a. the bank's total reserves rise by $100,000
   b. the bank's excess reserves rise by $100,000
   c. the bank can safely lend $100,000
   d. the Fed's assets increase by $100,000
   e. all of the above

9. During a depression, the best strategy of the Federal Reserve is to:

   a. sell government bonds, to make low-risk, sound assets available for commercial banks to buy
   b. sell government bonds, in order to reduce the size of the government's deficits
   c. sell government bonds, in order to increase aggregate demand
   d. buy government securities
   e. exhort banks not to lend to businesses, in order to reduce their risks of loss

10. The Fed *tightens* monetary conditions by *lowering*:

    a. required reserve ratios
    b. the margin requirements on stocks
    c. the discount rate
    d. the interest rate on Treasury bills
    e. the rate at which it is buying securities on the open market

11. The discount rate refers to:

    a. the penalty paid by risky bank borrowers; that is, the amount of interest they pay in excess of the prime rate
    b. the rate at which banks write off bad loans
    c. the rate at which assets lose their real value as a result of inflation
    d. the rate at which money loses its value as a result of inflation
    e. the rate of interest that the Fed charges on loans to commercial banks

12. If the required reserve ratio is 20%, and if commercial banks borrow $100 million from the Federal Reserve, then the effect on commercial bank reserves is:

    a. an increase of $100 million
    b. an increase of $500 million
    c. a decrease of $100 million
    d. a decrease of $500 million
    e. no change

13. If the price of a Treasury bill falls, then

    a. all interest rates certainly fall
    b. all interest rates probably fall

    c. the interest rate on this bill certainly falls
    d. the interest rate on this bill probably rises
    e. the interest rate on this bill certainly rises

14. If the price of a $100,000 Treasury bill with 1 month to maturity is $99,000, then the annual yield on that bill is approximately:

    a 1%
    b. 3%
    c. 4%
    d. 6%
    e. 12%

15. When the Fed purchases Treasury bills on the open market:

    a. the quantity of bank reserves falls ·
    b. the interest rate on Treasury bills rises
    c. the price of Treasury bills rises
    d. the risk premium on business loans usually rises
    e. required reserves of banks fall ·

16. In 1936 and 1937, the Fed doubled required reserve ratios. This action:

    a. helped speed up the recovery then under way
    b. was the single most important reason for the recovery from the Great Depression
    c. would have promoted recovery, if it had been backed up with open market sales
    d. was a cause of a recession within the Great Depression
    e. had no effect because banks held excess reserves

17. A margin requirement tends to make the stock market less unstable:

    a. only if it is backed up by open market operations
    b. only if the margin requirement is increased during an upswing in stock prices, and decreased during a downswing in stock prices
    c. only if the margin requirement is decreased during an upswing in stock prices, and increased during a downswing in stock prices
    d. only if the margin requirement is decreased whenever the rate of business bankruptcy increases
    e. even if it is kept perfectly stable, at (say) 50%

18. The Federal Reserve issues paper currency which acts as money in the United States. It is most accurate to say that this money is "backed" by Federal Reserve assets in the form of:

a. loans to member banks
b. U.S. government securities
c. gold
d. required reserves of the commercial banks
e. the value of Federal Reserve buildings

19. Under the old gold standard system (such as that in the United States in the 1920s):

a. the need for gold reserves limited the creation of money
b. the knowledge that money was backed 100% by gold created confidence
c. the knowledge that money was backed partly by gold created confidence and prevented runs on banks

d. the government was forbidden to issue bonds unless it held 100% backing for those bonds in the form of gold
e. the money stock was just a small fraction of the quantity of gold

20. There are two traps facing macroeconomic policy makers. Specifically, they are quite likely to destabilize aggregate demand if they attempt to:

a. balance the full employment budget every year, and stabilize interest rates
b. balance the actual budget every year, and stabilize interest rates
c. balance the full employment budget every year, and stabilize the money stock
d. balance the actual budget every year, and stabilize the money stock
e. stabilize the growth in reserves and in the money stock

EXERCISES

1. Suppose that the required reserve ratio on all deposits is 20 percent.

   a. In balance sheets A, show the initial effects of an open market purchase of $10 million in government securities by the Fed. The seller is a manufacturing corporation that deposits the proceeds immediately in its bank.

   b. In balance sheets B, show the ultimate effects of the above transaction after the maximum expansion of loans and deposits. Assume that banks keep all increases in reserves in the form of deposits in the Fed.

   c. In balance sheets C, show the initial effects of an open market purchase of $10 million in government securities by the Fed. The seller is a commercial bank. (Is the initial change in the money stock the same as in part a? Why or why not?)

   d. In balance sheets B, show the ultimate effects of the transaction in part c, after the maximum expansion of loans and deposits. Assume that banks keep all increases in reserves in the form of deposits in the Fed. (Compare the results with the results in b.)

Balance Sheets A

Federal Reserve System		All commercial banks	
Federal government securities _____	Federal Reserve notes _____ Deposits of banks _____ Net worth _____	Loans _____ Total reserves _____ Required reserves _____ Excess reserves _____	Deposits _____

Balance Sheets B

Federal Reserve System		All commercial banks	
Federal government securities _____	Federal Reserve notes _____ Deposits of banks _____ Net worth _____	Loans _____ Total reserves _____ Required reserves _____ Excess reserves _____	Deposits _____

Balance Sheets C

Federal Reserve System		All commercial banks	
Federal government securities _____	Federal Reserve notes _____ Deposits of banks _____ Net worth _____	Loans _____ Gov. securities _____ Total reserves _____ Required reserves _____ Excess reserves _____	Deposits _____

Balance Sheets D

Federal Reserve System		All commercial banks	
Federal government securities _____	Federal Reserve notes _____ Deposits of banks _____ Net worth _____	Loans _____ Gov. securities _____ Total reserves _____ Required reserves _____ Excess reserves _____	Deposits _____

2. (This exercise is only for those who have studied Box 12-1 in the textbook.) Consider a bond with a face value of $100 and with an annual coupon of $10. In the table below, fill in the approximate price of the bond under different assumptions regarding its term to maturity and current market rates of interest. What does this example suggest regarding the relationship between (a) the term to maturity and (b) the size of price changes in response to a change in interest rates?

Term to maturity

Rate of interest	1 year	2 years	Perpetuity
8%	_____	_____	_____
10%	_____	_____	_____
12%	_____	_____	_____

ESSAY QUESTIONS

1. With an example, show how, if you buy shares on 50% margin, your gains would be higher if the price doubles than if you bought for cash. (Ignore brokerage fees, interest on the loan, and dividends on the stock). What would happen if the price fell by 50%?

2. (This question is especially for those who have studied Box 12-2 in the text and also exercise 2 in this Study Guide). Savings and loan associations (S&Ls) have traditionally held most of their assets in the form of mortgages on homes, with initial terms of 25 or 30 years. Suppose that many mortgages are made when interest rates are 8%. Then suppose that interest rates in the financial markets rise to 12%. What happens to the value of the mortgages held by an S&L? Suppose the S&L continues to offer low interest rates to depositors, because that is all it can afford to pay since it is receiving low interest on mortgages made in previous years. Will any difficulties arise for such an S&L?

ANSWERS

Matching columns: **1 f, 2 i, 3 l, 4 h, 5 k, 6 c, 7 j, 8 e, 9 b, 10 d, 11 a, 12 g**

True-False:
1 F (p. 207)
2 T (p. 208)
3 T (p. 209)
4 F (pp. 210-211)
5 F (p. 211)
6 F (p. 211)
7 T (p. 211)
8 F (p. 212)
9 F (p. 215)
10 T (p. 217)

Multiple Choice:
1 a (p. 206)
2 d (p. 206)
3 e (pp. 206-207)
4 b (pp. 208-209)
5 a (p. 209)
6 b (p. 209)
7 c (p. 209)
8 e (p. 210)
9 d
10 e (p. 211)
11 e (p. 211)
12 a (p. 211)
13 e (p. 212)
14 e (p. 212)
15 c (p. 212)
16 d (p. 212)
17 e (p. 214)
18 b (p. 215)
19 a (p. 217)
20 b (p. 220)

Exercises:

1. Balance Sheets A

Federal Reserve System		All commercial banks	
Federal government securities $10 million	Federal Reserve notes 0 Deposits of banks $10 million Net worth 0	Loans 0 Total reserves $10 million Required reserves $2 million Excess reserves $8 million	Deposits $10 million

Balance Sheets B

Federal Reserve System		All commercial banks	
Federal government securities $10 million	Federal Reserve notes 0 Deposits of banks $10 million Net worth 0	Loans $40 million Total reserves $10 million Required reserves $10 million Excess reserves 0	Deposits $50 million

Balance Sheets C

Federal Reserve System		All commercial banks	
Federal government securities $10 million	Federal Reserve notes 0 Deposits of banks $10 million Net worth 0	Loans 0 Government securities −$10 million Total reserves $10 million Required reserves 0 Excess reserves $10 million	Deposits 0

Balance Sheets D

Federal Reserve System		All commercial banks	
Federal government securities $10 million	Federal Reserve notes 0 Deposits of banks $10 million Net worth 0	Loans $50 million Government securities −$10 million Total reserves $10 million Required reserves $10 million Excess reserves 0	Deposits $50 million

2. The exact answers are:

Term to maturity			
Rate of interest	1 year	2 years	Perpetuity
8%	$101.85	$103.57	$125.00
10%	$100.00	$100.00	$100.00
12%	$ 98.21	$ 96.62	$ 83.33

The longer the term to maturity, the greater is the change in price of the bond for any given change in market interest rates. (Note: market interest rates on long-term bonds generally fluctuate much less than market rates on shorter term securities. This dampens the fluctuations in long-term bond prices somewhat. Nevertheless, long-term bond prices still fluctuate much more than the prices of shorter-term securities.)

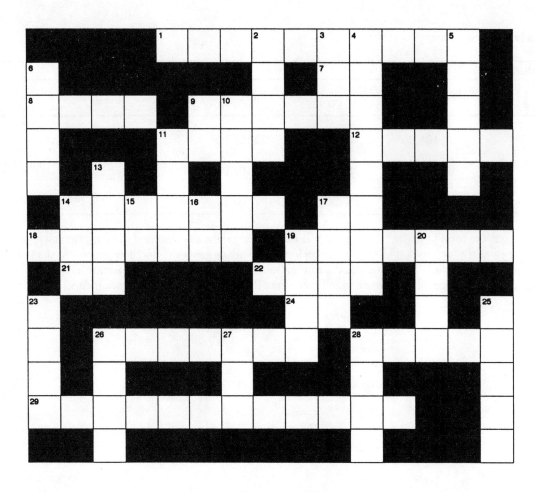

Across

1, 7, 8, 9. the principal tool for controlling the quantity of money
11. what we do with income we don't spend
12. each
14. checking deposits form an inverted _____ on a base of bank reserves
17. third person
18, 19. central bank of the United States
21. not (French)
22. unbacked paper currency is _____ money
24. a university degree
26, 28. by changing this, the Federal Reserve can have a powerful effect on the quantity of money
29. by raising this, the Federal Reserve can discourage banks from borrowing (2 words)

Down

2. by keeping money _____, the Federal Reserve can protect its value
3. part of the foot
4, 28. if the Fed tries to stabilize this, it may destabilize the economy
5. one of the functions of money is to act as a _____ of value
6. in the early days of the Federal Reserve, this was at the base of the inverted monetary pyramid
9. mother
10. useless; of no _____
11. if the Fed lets the quantity of money _____, the result is rapid inflation
13. Dr. Jekyll's alter ego
14. it's mightier than the sword
15. regarding
16. a university degree
17. Alan Greenspan is the _____ of the Federal Reserve
19. be carried or transported by
20. a type of income
23. fearless and daring
25. the Fed sometimes engages in jawboning, or _____ suasion
26. interest rates generally are high on bonds with a high

_____
27. bankers fear this

Part 4

GREAT MACROECONOMIC ISSUES:
Aggregate Supply

CHAPTER 13

HOW CAN INFLATION AND UNEMPLOYMENT COEXIST?

LEARNING OBJECTIVES

After you have studied this chapter in the textbook and study guide, you should be able to

✔ Summarize the experience of the United States with inflation and unemployment since 1960

✔ Explain why demand-management authorities sometimes feel that they face a policy dilemma

✔ Explain the two major reasons why the (short-run) Phillips curve can shift upward

✔ Explain the difference between cost-push inflation and demand-pull inflation, and explain why cost-push inflation can lead to higher prices and higher unemployment

✔ Explain why demand-management authorities face a very difficult problem when there is a large upward shift in the Phillips curve (such as in 1973-1974 and 1979-1980)

✔ Explain why inflation can accelerate to higher and higher rates if the authorities try to keep unemployment below the natural rate

✔ Explain why many economists believe that the long-run Phillips curve is vertical

✔ Explain why Milton Friedman argues that, "There is *always* a *temporary tradeoff* between inflation and unemployment; there is *no permanent tradeoff.*"

✔ Explain why the process of reducing inflation can be painful

MAJOR PURPOSE

For several decades following the Great Depression, macroeconomists concentrated on the management of aggregate demand. When the economy was declining into a recession, they advocated expansive demand policies to keep output and employment at high levels. When inflationary pressures were strong, they advocated tighter policies to restrain demand and keep inflation down.

However, during the past two decades, the economy has from time to time given conflicting signals. There have been bouts of **stagflation**—that is, periods when high unemployment was combined with rapid inflation. The high unemployment suggested that demand should be expanded; the rapid inflation indicated the opposite. To understand this complex economy, we must look not only at aggregate demand, but also at aggregate supply. Our purpose in Chapter 13 is to study aggregate supply and, in doing so, to explore stagflation.

The simplest way to approach aggregate supply is the one presented earlier, in a diagram with real national product on the horizontal axis and the average level of prices on the vertical axis. However, this is not the approach most commonly used. Instead, economists generally begin with a diagram with the two macroeconomic problems—unemployment and inflation—on the axes. The smooth curve traced out by historical data during some periods, such as the 1960s, is known as a **Phillips curve**. However, the Phillips curve has not been stable in recent decades. One of the major purposes of this chapter is to try to explain why the Phillips curve shifts.

HIGHLIGHTS OF CHAPTER

When the demand for a specific commodity—such as wheat—changes, there is a movement *along* the supply curve (as illustrated in Figure 4-7 on p. 56 of the textbook). Similarly, when *aggregate* demand changes, the economy moves along the *aggregate* supply curve. Thus, when we study aggregate supply in this chapter, we are studying how the economy responds to a change in aggregate demand. This is an important and puzzling topic. From time to time, the economy has suffered from **stagflation**—a combination of high unemployment and high inflation. In such circumstances, it is not clear what the authorities should do. If they take steps to increase aggregate demand in an attempt to increase output and employment, they may get more inflation instead. If they restrain demand in an attempt to reduce inflation, they may get more unemployment. Making sense of the aggregate supply puzzle is an important topic; it is the main purpose of this chapter.

To study aggregate supply, it is possible to use the aggregate supply curve introduced in Chapter 8, with real national product (Q) on the horizontal axis and the average level of prices (P) on the horizontal axis. However, this is not the approach most commonly used. Instead, economists generally begin with a diagram with the two macroeconomic problems—unemployment and inflation—on the axes.

When historical data are plotted on such a diagram in Figure 13-3, two main conclusions stand out:

- Between 1961 and 1969, the points trace out a smooth curve, sloping upward to the left. This is known as a **Phillips curve**.

- Since 1970, the observations have been above and to the right of that Phillips curve. We have gotten more unemployment *and* more inflation. Strong movements in a "northeast" direction (upward and to the right) occurred between 1969 and 1970, between 1973 and 1975, and between 1978 and 1980.

During the 1960s, when most economists believed that the Phillips curve being traced out by the data represented a stable relationship, authorities felt trapped on the horns of a **dilemma**. If they expanded aggregate demand briskly, they would get more output and employment. But inflation would rise. On the other hand, if they restrained demand in order to keep inflation down, the unemployment rate would remain at high. They hoped to escape from this dilemma by using expansive aggregate demand policies to reduce unemployment, and incomes policies to directly restrain inflation. (Incomes policies will be studied in Chapter 14.) They were not entirely successful. Inflation in fact did increase as output expanded and unemployment declined. The economy in fact did move upward as it moved to the left in Figure 13-3 in the text.

Shifts in the Phillips Curve

Even worse problems were to come in the 1970s, as both inflation and unemployment increased. Two of the three strong movements to the "northeast" in Figure 13-3 coincided with the spiralling price of oil on the international markets. This suggests one explanation for the stagflation since 1970: Rising oil prices shifted the Phillips curve upward, and meant more inflation combined with more unemployment. Inflation was caused by the *upward push of costs*.

Oil prices certainly do not provide the whole explanation, however. The first major movement to the northeast, between 1969 and 1970, occurred while international oil prices were stable at a very low level. In fact, there was something of a glut on the international oil market.

To explain this early episode of stagflation, we must look elsewhere. The **accelerationist theory** provides the most generally accepted explanation.

The Accelerationist Theory

The accelerationist theory, put forward in the late 1960s by Ned Phelps and Milton Friedman, has one core idea. The Phillips curve—such as that observed in the 1960s—is fundamentally unstable. If the authorities attempt to reduce the unemployment rate to a very low level, they will succeed, but *only temporarily*. In particular, they will succeed only during the interval between the time when demand is expanded and the time when contracts are renegotiated to take the resulting inflation into account. When people renegotiate contracts, they will demand compensation for inflation; wages and other contractual prices will be adjusted upward. Inflation will accelerate; a **wage-price spiral** will gain momentum. This is illustrated by points H, J, and K in Figure 13-7 of the text. At each of these points, actual inflation is higher than people expected when they negotiated contracts. For example, at H, people expected zero inflation (as illustrated by the Phillips curve), but get 2% instead. They then renegotiate contracts on the expectation of 2% inflation. But, with higher costs, businesses raise prices; the economy moves to J. People expect 2% inflation; they get 4% instead.

How, then, can we return to macroeconomic equilibrium, once the wage-price spiral has begun? **Equilibrium occurs only when people get the amount of inflation they expected.** This happens if the rate of inflation stabilizes. For inflation to stabilize, the authorities must depart from their single-minded attempt to keep unemployment low; they must introduce a degree of restraint in aggregate demand policies. As restraint occurs, businesses will find it hard to raise prices more and more rapidly; inflation will indeed level off. However, as it becomes harder to sell goods, output will increase more slowly and the unemployment rate will rise.

Once people get the amount of inflation they expect, the unemployment rate will move back to its **natural** or **equilibrium** rate, illustrated by point N in Figure 13-8 of the text. A central proposition of the accelerationist theory is that this equilibrium rate of unemployment doesn't depend on the rate of inflation; once people adjust completely to inflation, the inflation rate doesn't affect their behavior. They are neither more nor less willing to work, and businesses are neither more nor less willing to hire them. Because the equilibrium rate of unemployment isn't affected by inflation—once people have gotten used to it—the *long run Phillips curve is vertical* (Figure 13-9, p. 236). In the short run, the central bank can lower the rate of unemployment by an inflationary policy. But in the long run, their willingness to accept an inflation rate of, say, 6% will not result in any gain in output and employment. There is a **short-run tradeoff** between the goals of low inflation and low unemployment, but there is **no long-run tradeoff**.

Just as low unemployment is associated with an acceleration of inflaton, so high unemployment is associated with a deceleration of inflation. If aggregate demand is too low to buy the goods and services being offered at the current rate of inflation, output will fall and businesses will settle for smaller increases in price. This is illustrated by point V in Figure 13-10 of the text (p. 238). V is not a good place to be; the unemployed are being used as cannon fodder in the war against inflation. In order to avoid painful periods at points like V, it is important to stop the inflationary spiral from gathering momentum in the first place. To those who asked in the 1970s how we might get out of stagflation, there was only one easy—although unsatisfactory—answer: Go back to 1965 and do it right this time. Stop inflation from accelerating in the first place. But, of course, we could not go back to 1965 again. The economy was in fact dragged through the severe recession of 1982 before the inflation rate was brought down to 4%—a rate that was still much higher than that of the period from 1955 to 1965.

IMPORTANT TERMS

*Match the first column with the corresponding phrase in the
second column.*

_____ 1. Phillips curve
_____ 2. Tradeoff
_____ 3. Stagflation
_____ 4. Cost-push inflation
_____ 5. Natural rate of unemployment
_____ 6. Accelerationist theory
_____ 7. Market power inflation
_____ 8. A likely cost of reducing inflation
_____ 9. Wage-price guideposts
_____10. Gradualism

a. A policy of the President Nixon
b. View that there is tradeoff in the short run, but not in the long run
c. Unemployment greater than the natural rate
d. Choice between conflicting goals
e. A policy of Presidents Kennedy and Johnson
f. High unemployment combined with high inflation
g. Equilibrium rate of unemployment
h. Relationship between inflation and unemployment
i. Another term for cost-push inflation
j. The rise in the international price of oil is an example

TRUE-FALSE

T   F   1.   According to the aggregate supply function of simple Keynesian theory, large-scale unemployment *or* rapid inflation can exist, but not both simultaneously.

T   F   2.   U.S. data for the 1960s trace out a reasonably smooth Phillips curve, but the data for the 1970s do not.

T   F   3.   The Kennedy administration imposed wage-price guideposts in an attempt to shift the Phillips curve to the right.

T   F   4.   Those who emphasize cost-push inflation are more likely to believe that market power is important than are advocates of the accelerationist theory.

T   F   5.   Even when the unemployment rate is at its natural level, there is still frictional unemployment.

T   F   6.   A high point on the long-run Phillips curve represents a higher rate of inflation than does a low point.

T   F   7.   A high point on the long-run Phillips curve represents a higher rate of unemployment than does a low point.

T   F   8.   According to the accelerationist theory, the economy can be in equilibrium only when the inflation rate is zero; any positive rate of inflation will tend to accelerate.

T   F   9.   If the long-run Phillips curve is vertical, then there is no long-run tradeoff between the objectives of price stability and high employment. A low unemployment rate cannot be "bought" over the long run by a willingness to accept inflation.

MULTIPLE CHOICE

1. In the horizontal range of the Keynesian aggregate supply function, the rate of inflation is:

   a. zero
   b. rising
   c. high and constant
   d. equal to the natural rate
   e. less than the natural rate

2. If we compare the U.S. experience since 1970s with that of the 1960s, we find that, on average:

   a. the rate of unemployment and the rate of inflation have both been lower since 1970 than during the 1960s
   b. the rate of unemployment has been lower since 1970 than during the 1960s, but the rate of inflation has been higher
   c. the rate of inflation has been lower since 1970 than during the 1960s, but the rate of unemployment has been higher
   d. the rate of unemployment and the rate of inflation have both been higher since 1970 than during the 1960s

3. In the United States, "double digit" inflation (that is, inflation of 10% or more) occurred in:

   a. every year from 1966 to 1975
   b. every year from 1973 to 1981
   c. 1971, 1972, and 1973
   d. 1971, 1972, and 1982
   e. 1974, 1979, and 1980

4. The Phillips curve traced out by the U.S. data of the 1960s suggested that there was a policy "tradeoff." Specifically, there seemed to be a conflict between achieving the goal of high employment and the goal of:

   a. an equitable distribution of income
   b. allocative efficiency
   c. technological efficiency
   d. high growth
   e. low inflation

5. Cost-push inflation is different from demand-pull inflation because:

   a. demand-pull inflation involves a rise in every price, whereas cost-push inflation involves a rise in prices only in industries with monopoly power
   b. demand-pull inflation involves a rise in every price, whereas cost-push inflation involves only a rise in the prices of goods, not services
   c. when demand-pull inflation begins, it represents a movement along a short-run Phillips curve, but cost-push inflation is an upward shift of the short-run Phillips curve
   d. demand-pull inflation is accompanied by a rise in unemployment rate, but cost-push inflation by a fall in unemployment
   e. demand-pull inflation is accompanied by a fall in output, but cost-push inflation by an increase in output

6. Economists are most likely to conclude that "cost push" inflation is occurring when a rise in the rate of inflation is accompanied by an increase in:

   a. output
   b. the rate of growth of output
   c. the unemployment rate
   d. an increase in government deficits
   e. an increase in the money stock

7. Which of the following is an important assumption of cost-push theories of inflation?

   a. there is perfect competition
   b. market power is an important feature of the economy
   c. unemployment is below the natural rate
   d. an increase in the money stock is the most important cause of inflation
   e. government deficits are the most important cause of inflation

8. A point to the left of the long-run Phillips curve is unstable because:

   a. workers and others have underestimated inflation; they will demand higher wages and prices when new contracts are written
   b. workers and others have overestimated inflation; they will be willing to settle for lower wages and prices when new contracts are written
   c. monetary policy is unsustainably tight
   d. fiscal policy is unsustainably tight
   e. the unemployment rate is above its natural rate

9. Suppose two points, A and B, are on the long-run Phillips curve. B is higher than A. Then the *real* wage at B is:

a. higher than at A
b. the same as at A
c. lower than at A
c. falling, and so is the real wage at A and every other point on the long-run Phillips curve
e. rising, even though the real wage is falling at A

10. According to the accelerationist theory (that is, the natural rate hypotheses), the short-run Phillips curve shifts whenever there is a change in:

a. the natural rate of inflation
b. the natural rate of acceleration of inflation
c. expectations of inflation
d. the degree of unionization of the labor force
e. the rate at which innovations are being used by businesses

11. According to the accelerationist theory, equilibrium can exist only when:

a. the unemployment rate is at its natural rate
b. the inflation rate is zero, since any non-zero rate of inflation will tend to accelerate
c. the expected inflation rate is zero, since inflation will accelerate otherwise
d. the growth of the money stock is zero, since inflation will accelerate otherwise
e. all of the above conditions are met

12. Which of the following is an assumption of the accelationist theory of inflation?

a. there is downward rigidity in nominal wages
b. inflation is caused mainly by unions
c. inflation is caused mainly by OPEC
d. inflation is caused mainly by an acceleration in investment
e. people's expectations of inflation have an important effect on the contracts they negotiate

13. Suppose we draw a diagram with both a short-run Phillips curve and a long-run Phillips curve. At the point where they intersect:

a. the inflation rate is zero
b. the unemployment rate is zero

c. actual inflation is the same as expected inflation
d. inflation is accelerating
e. the rate of unemployment is rising

THE NEXT THREE QUESTIONS ARE BASED ON FIGURE 13.1

Figure 13.1

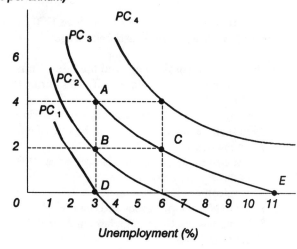

14. In Figure 13.1, the natural rate of unemployment is 6%. Which of the points represents an equilibrium?

a. A
b. B
c. C
d. D
e. E

15. In Figure 13.1, the natural rate of unemployment is 6%. Suppose that the economy is at point A on Phillips curve PC$_3$. To get to that point, contracts have been based on an expected rate of inflation of:

a. zero
b. 2%
c. 3%
d. 4%
e. 6%

16. In Figure 13.1, the natural rate of unemployment is 6%. Last year, the economy was at point A on short run Phillips curve PC3. If contracts are now renegotiated, which of the short-run Phillips curves is most likely to result?

  a. PC_1
  b. PC_2
  c. PC_3
  d. PC_4
  e. either PC_1 or PC_2, but we can't be sure which

17. According to the accelerationist theory, the unemployment rate will be greater than the natural rate when inflation is:

  a. greater than people expected
  b. less than people expected
  c. low and steady
  d. high and steady
  e. zero

18. According to the accelerationist theory (that is, the natural rate hypotheses),

  a. inflation will accelerate whenever the unemployment rate deviates from the natural rate
  b. the short-run and long-run Phillips curves are both vertical
  c. there is a trade-off between inflation and unemployment in the long run, but not the short
  d. aggregate demand policies should be fine tuned in order to prevent inflation from accelerating
  e. an attempt to reduce inflation with more restrictive monetary policies will result in above-normal unemployment during a transition period

EXERCISES

1. Figure 13.2, shown here, represents the Phillips curve for year 1, when the expected rate of inflation is zero. The natural rate of unemployment is _____%. If unemployment is at the natural rate, the rate of inflation will be _____ in year 1. If, alternatively, the unemployment rate is 3%, the actual rate of inflation will be (more, less) than the expected rate by _____%.

Figure 13.2

Inflation (%) vs Unemployment (%)

Suppose now that the expected rate of inflation is 2% in year 2. Draw the Phillips curve for year 2 in Figure 13.2. If the rate of unemployment is still 3% in year 2, the rate of inflation will be _____%.

If, on the other hand, inflation is 3% in year 2, the rate of unemployment will be about _____%. Now suppose that the rate of inflation is kept at 3% indefinitely, into years 3, 4, 5. . . . The expected rate of inflation will eventually become _____%, and the rate of unemployment will move to _____%. Alternatively, if aggregate demand policies are aimed at keeping the unemployment rate at 3%, the rate of inflation will _____.

2 a. Suppose that the economy is initially at point A on Phillips curve 1 in Figure 13.3. Then the curve shifts to Phillips curve 2. If policymakers pursue restrictive monetary and fiscal policies that keep the rate of inflation from increasing, then unemployment will (increase, decrease) by amount _____. If, on the other hand, they keep the rate of unemployment stable by following more expansive policies, then inflation will (increase, decrease), by amount _____.

Figure 13.3

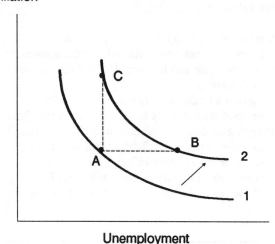

b. Suppose this shift in the Phillips curve is caused by workers observing a rate of inflation higher than they expected. Then, according to the natural rate theory, the rate of unemployment at *A* was (more than, less than, the same as) the natural rate. The attempt by the policymakers to go to point *C* will cause the Phillips curve to _____ when contracts are renegotiated.

ESSAY QUESTIONS

1. According to the accelerationist theory, the rate of unemployment cannot be kept permanently below the natural rate by an expansive aggregate demand policy. Explain why. Can the rate be kept permanently above the natural rate by a restrictive aggregate demand policy? Explain why or why not.

2. The short-run Phillips curve indicates that when unemployment rises, inflation should fall. But in some years, both inflation *and* unemployment rise. How would an accelerationist explain this? Is there any other explanation?

ANSWERS

Important terms: **1 h, 2 d, 3 f, 4 j, 5 g, 6 b, 7 i, 8 c, 9 e, 10 a**

True-False: **1 T** (p. 226)
2 T (p. 229)
3 F (p. 230)
4 T (pp. 232, 234)
5 T (pp. 233-236)
6 T (p. 236)
7 F (p. 236)
8 F (p. 236)
9 T (p. 237)

Multiple Choice: **1 a** (p. 226)
2 d (p. 229)
3 e (p. 229)
4 e (p. 230)
5 c (p. 231)
6 c (p. 231)
7 b (p. 232)
8 a (pp. 234-236)
9 b (pp. 235-236)
10 c (p. 236)
11 a (p. 236)
12 e (p. 236)
13 c (p. 236)

Exercises

1.   5, 0, more, 3, 5, 4, 3, 5, become more and more rapid.

Figure 13.2 Completed:

2   a. increase, *AB*, increase, *AC*

b. less than, shift further up

CHAPTER 14

HOW DO WE DEAL WITH THE INFLATION-UNEMPLOYMENT DILEMMA?

LEARNING OBJECTIVES

After you have studied this chapter in the textbook and study guide, you should be able to

✔ Explain why the natural rate of unemployment can change

✔ List the policies that have been suggested to reduce the natural rate of unemployment

✔ Explain the major purposes of incomes policies

✔ Describe briefly the incomes policies of the past 30 years

✔ Explain the pros and cons of an incomes policy

✔ Explain why the indexation of wages may permit the authorities to reduce the rate of inflation without causing a long period of high unemployment

✔ Explain why the indexation of wages may nevertheless make the inflation problem worse

✔ Explain how profit sharing might make the economy more flexible, and reduce the severity of unemployment during recessions

✔ Explain what can happen if people anticipate the effects of policies, specifically why (1) the wage-price spiral might be speeded up, and (2) why the adjustment to a lower rate of inflation might be speeded up and made less painful

✔ Explain why it is important for the Federal Reserve to maintain credibility

✔ Explain the difference between adaptive expectations and rational expectations

✔ Explain why aggregate demand policies might become ineffective if people's expecations are rational

✔ Criticize the conclusions of rational expectations theorists

✔ Describe briefly how European experience with unemployment has differed from U.S. experience over the past three decades

MAJOR PURPOSE

The previous chapter explained how unemployment and inflation could coexist. Chapter 14 explains the policy issues raised by the desired to achieve low unemployment and low inflation simultaneously. One approach is to try to reduce the equilibrium or natural rate of unemployment by steps aimed at improving the flexibility and efficiency of the labor market. (Even though the long-run Phillips curve is vertical, it is not set in concrete. The equilibrium rate of unemployment can change if labor market institutions change.) The chapter reviews efforts to keep the inflation rate down by **incomes policies** — that is, by direct restraints on wages and prices.

This chapter also elaborates one of the conclusions of the previous chapter — that the short-run Phillips curve can shift when people's expectations change. If people try to anticipate the effects of policies, the wage-price spiral may be greatly speeded up, thus weakening the power of aggregate demand policies to bring down the unemployment rate, even in the short run.

HIGHLIGHTS OF CHAPTER

This chapter explains some of the policy issues raised by the short-run and long-run Phillips curves. The chapter covers four main topics:

- Policies to **reduce the natural rate** of unemployment

- Incomes policies to **control inflation** without creating high unemployment

- Other policies to **ease the transition** to lower inflation

- The ways in which **expectations** may be formed, and how the inflation-unemployment tradeoff depends on expectations.

Policies to Reduce the Natural Rate of Unemployment

The natural rate of unemployment need not be constant; it rose between the 1960s and 1970s and has fallen over the past decade. A number of proposals have been made to reduce the natural rate.

- **Abolish the minimum wage?** Critics of the minimum wage point out that it raises the cost of hiring unskilled teenagers and therefore reduces the number of jobs offered to them. Proponents of the minimum wage argue that it is only fair to pay a reasonable wage to workers. It is unlikely that congress would take the strong symbolic step of abolishing the minimum wage. However, as the wage is set in dollars ($3.35 per hour), it is eroded by inflation. The real minimum wage declined during the 1980s, and this worked to reduce the natural rate of unemployment.

- **A two-tiered minimum wage?** A two tiered minimum wage is sometimes suggested as a way to reduce the negative effect on employment: Employers could pay less while workers are learning their jobs. This proposal was endorsed by President Bush and was included in 1989 legislation to raise the minimum wage. However, the president vetoed the legislation on the ground that the increase in the minimum wage would create unemployment.

- **Less discrimination.** This would reduce the unemployment rate, as well as making the economy more fair. (Note that the objectives of fairness and low unemployment may be in conflict when a higher minimum wage is being considered. However, a reduction in discrimination raises no such conflict — steps toward fairness also reduce the unemployment rate.)

- **Training programs** that help the unskilled prepare for jobs.

- The government as the **employer of last resort?** This proposal would mean a major change in the way the labor market works: The government would offer a job to anyone who could not get one in the private sector of the economy. This proposal is very controversial; it could be quite expensive and could cause a less efficient economy. There is much less support for this proposal now than there was during the 1970s.

Incomes Policies

Incomes policies are sometimes used in an effort to ease the transition to a lower rate of inflation. For example, the wage-price freeze of the Nixon administration was intended to break inflationary expectations without an extended period of high unemployment. At other times, incomes policies are used to stop inflation from gathering momentum in the first place—for example, the wage-price guideposts of the Kennedy and Johnson administrations.

Incomes policies are controversial. Proponents say that they are the only compassionate way to deal with the inflationary problem—the only alternative is to use the unemployed as draftees in the war against inflation. Opponents say that incomes policies may do more harm than good. For example, by suppressing inflationary pressures temporarily, they may provide the illusion of success, with the authorities unwittingly continuing expansive policies as underlying inflationary pressures build up. The result can be an explosion of inflation. Critics also point out that, by interfering with the price system, incomes policies can reduce the efficiency of the economy. Proponents agree that incomes policies may create some problems, but these problems are minor compared to the unemployment caused if inflation is fought solely by restraints on aggregate demand.

Other Policies to Ease the Transition to Lower Inflation

During the 1970s, some economists suggested that the economy could move to a lower rate of inflation without high and persistent unemployment if wages were indexed. If wages are indexed, they are adjusted for changes in the cost of living. Wage indexation became much more common during the 1970s, when inflation was becoming both higher and more erratic.

Indexation may make it easier to unwind inflation without long periods of unemployment; money wages are more flexible, and respond more quickly to restrictive aggregate demand policies. But they are a two-edged sword. They can speed up a wage-price spiral. Indexation—which represents a way in which labor tries to protect itself from erratic inflation—tends to make inflation even more erratic.

Indexation is aimed at adjusting nominal wages in order to stabilize real wages. In contrast, **profit sharing** introduces flexibility into real wages. If workers receive a signficant share of their income in the form of bonuses tied to profits, labor costs move with the business cycle. During recessions, profits and bonuses—and therefore labor costs—fall, encouraging businesses to cut prices in order to maintain sales and output.

Expectations

To explain the basics of the acceleration theory, the last chapter used a very simple assumption—people expect the inflation of today to continue into the future. But expectations can be more complicated. If people not only respond to current inflation, but also **anticipate** the effects of policies, a wage-price spiral can be greatly speeded up. In negotiating their contracts, people do not simply compensate for past inflation; they compensate for expected future inflation, which can exceed the present rate. The result can be a very rapid upward shift in the short-run Phillips curve (Figure 14-1 in the text).

During a period of restraint, the short-run Phillips curve can also shift very rapidly, but now in a downward direction. People take into account not only the reduction in inflation that has already occurred, but the reduction expected for the future. The rapid downward shift of the short-run Phillips curve can cause a much quicker transition to low inflation, thus reducing the overall cost in terms of unemployment.

Therefore, **credibility** is important in macroeconomic policy. When tight policies are being followed, people will adjust relatively quickly if they believe that the policies will be firmly pursued. Paradoxically, the way to stop inflation *without* long periods of high unemployment is to convince the public that the Federal Reserve will firmly pursue a policy of restraint, even if it does cause unemployment.

If expectations are **rational**, people make the best forecasts possible with available information on what the authorities are doing and how the economy works. Available information is, however, *not* perfect; people still make mistakes. But they do not keep making the same mistake. Their mistakes are random numbers. (In contrast, people did keep making the same mistake in the simple acceleration theory presented back in Figure 13-7 on p. 234 of the text.)

Some rational expectations theorists argue that demand management policies are useless as a way of reducing cyclical unemployment because, if followed consistently, they will be anticipated by the public. The only way the Fed can affect real output is by creating a surprise—that is, by trickery. But surprises mean that the Fed is behaving in an unpredictable (erratic?) way. As a result, the public is less able to figure out what is going on, and fluctuations in unemployment become larger. It is important for the Fed to *minimize* uncertainty. This, say many rational expectations theorists, can be done if the Fed follows a monetary rule, with a steady, moderate growth in the money stock.

The theory of rational expectations has provided important perceptions regarding some of the limits of policy. However, the conclusions of the rational expectations theorists are subject to two major criticisms (others are given on p. 255 of the text):

- The facts don't fit the theory. According to the main body of rational expectations theory, deviations from the natural rate of unemployment should be random, relatively brief occurances. But this was not true during the deep recession of 1981-1982. And it most decidedly was not the case during the Great Depression of the 1930s.

- A monetary rule does not necessarily lead to the most predictable outcome. If the Fed can identify and offset fluctuations in the economy, it can make the economy more predictable. Therefore, rational expectations theory has left the old question, to be considered in detail in chapter 18: *Can* the Fed best stabilize the economy by a rule, or by active management?

IMPORTANT TERMS

Match the first column with the corresponding phrase in the second column.

_____ 1. Wage-price guideposts
_____ 2. Wage-price freeze
_____ 3. TIP
_____ 4. Escalator clause
_____ 5. Supply shock
_____ 6. Profit sharing
_____ 7. Adaptive expectations
_____ 8. Rational expectations
_____ 9. Ineffective policies
_____ 10. Credibility
_____ 11. Hysteresis

a. Way to provide flexibility in real wages
b. Incomes policy of President Kennedy
c. These mean that people do not make systematic mistakes
d. Failure to go back to the original condition
e. The Federal Reserve should guard this
f. Incomes policy backed with tax incentives
g. These are based on the inflation actually observed
h. Incomes policy of President Nixon
i. Way to stabilize real wages in the face of inflation
j. With indexed wages, this can be a big problem
k. Possible result of rational expectations

TRUE-FALSE

T   F   1. Between the 1970s and the late 1980s, the natural rate of unemployment rose substantially.

T   F   2. Suppose that money wages were constant through time. Then it would be possible to have a continuous downward trend in prices, if productivity rises.

T   F   3. Under the wage-price guideposts of the Kennedy-Johnson years, wage increases were to be kept to 3.2% per year. The 3.2% was the estimated amount needed to compensate labor for the inflation of the previous decade.

T   F   4. The TIP proposal was supposed to work by stimulating aggregate demand.

T   F   5. Wage indexation reduces uncertainty about real wage rates, but increases uncertainty about nominal wage rates.

T   F   6.   A COLA clause in an indexed wage contract provides a fixed amount to cover an increase in the cost-of-living, no matter what the rate of inflation.

T   F   7.   Wage indexation speeds up the response of inflation to an increase in aggregate demand.

T   F   8.   Profit sharing has been adopted in some segments of U.S. business, including parts of the automobile and steel industries.

T   F   9.   If expectations of inflation are *adaptive*, they are correct.

T   F   10. According to the theory of rational expectations, people can make mistakes, but their mistakes are random.

MULTIPLE CHOICE

1. Which of the following is likely to reduce the natural rate of unemployment?

    a. a fall in the proportion of teenagers in the labor force
    b. more emphasis on fiscal policy, and less on monetary policy
    c. more generous unemployment insurance benefits
    d. a rise in the minimum wage
    e. all of the above

2. Some people have proposed introducing two "tiers" into the minimum wage, with a lower wage for those who are newly hired. Proponents argue that, if their proposal were adopted, the result would be:

    a. less teenage unemployment
    b. less unemployment by older workers who might be replaced by teenagers
    c. a rightward shift of the long-run Phillips curve
    d. higher profits
    e. lower profits

3. If the government acted as the *employer of last resort*, it would:

    a. hire people when they completed college
    b. hire people in over 60 years of age who were unable to find jobs
    c. offer a job to anyone who could not find a job elsewhere
    d. require businesses to hire at least 10% more workers whenever the economy was in a recession
    e. all of the above

4. President Carter proposed "real wage insurance." Taxes of workers would be cut if prices increased by more than 7%, provided the workers had agreed to limit their wage increases to 7%. One criticism of this proposal is that it would tend to:

    a. make the income tax sytem less progressive
    b. cause a recession by introducing unexpected changes in fiscal policy
    c. cancel or offset the automatic stabilizing function of taxes by cutting taxes when inflation became more severe
    d. cause undue reliance on fiscal policy, rather than a reasonable combination of fiscal and monetary policies
    e. cause undue reliance on monetary policy, rather than a reasonable combination of fiscal and monetary policies

5. Which of the following policies is most likely to cause black markets?

    a. a tax-based incomes policies
    b. real wage insurance
    c. wage-price guideposts
    d. a price freeze accompanied by restrictive monetary policies
    e. a price freeze accompanied by expansive monetary policies

6. Price controls sometimes create shortages. Shortages are most likely in the markets for:

    a. luxuries, since their prices are likely to be controlled most tightly
    b. necessities, since their prices are likely to be controlled most tightly
    c. luxuries, since producers will realize that they're not very important socially, and cut back on their production
    d. necessities, since there is a tendency for the demand for necessities to increase at the most rapid rate
    e. services, since their prices are harder to control than goods

7. The major case for wage-price guideposts or controls is that:

   a. they are the only way to stop inflation
   b. they are the only way to keep profits from falling when labor unions bargain aggressively for higher wages
   c. they are essential if income is to be distributed in a more equitable way
   d. they help to shift the long-run Phillips curve to the right
   e. if we avoid guideposts or controls and rely solely on tight aggregate demand policies to restrain inflation, there will be a high cost in terms of unemployment

8. Wage indexation *reduces*

   a. the variability of inflation
   b. the response of inflation to a change in aggregate demand
   c. uncertainty about nominal wage rates
   d. uncertainty about real wage rates
   e. both (c) and (d)

9. One argument in favor of the indexation of wages is that it:

   a. means that foreign producers of oil can't make Americans bear the costs of a higher oil price
   b. generally leads to a more stable, predictable rate of inflation
   c. keeps the unemployment rate below the natural rate
   d. keeps the inflation rate below the natural rate
   e. makes possible a quicker, less painful reduction in the rate of inflation

10. Which of the following is the strongest argument against the indexation of wages? Wage indexation:

   a. makes the real wage rate more volatile
   b. makes the rate of inflation more volatile
   c. causes the rich to become richer and the poor poorer
   d. increases the costs, in terms of unemployment, of an anti-inflationary policy
   e. keeps the unemployment rate permanently above the natural rate

11. The term "profit sharing" usually applies to which of the following ideas

   a. the granting of bonuses to workers when profits are high or rising
   b. charitable giving by corporations
   c. the taxation of profits of rich corporations, combined with grants to corporations suffering losses
   d. a proportional profits tax, which takes twice as much from corporations when their profits are twice as high
   e. a progressive income tax, which redistributes profits across the economy

12. Proponents of profit sharing support it on the ground that it would

   a. make the real incomes of labor more flexible, and thus reduce the rate of unemployment during recessions
   b. make the real incomes of labor more flexible, and thus reduce the average rate of unemployment over long periods of time
   c. increase incentives to be more efficient, and thus reduce the rate of inflation during periods of prosperity
   d. increase incentives to be more efficient, and thus reduce the average rate of inflation over long periods of time
   e. all of the above

13. If people anticipate the inflationary or anti-inflationary effects of changes in aggregate demand policies (rather than simply responding to past inflation), the likely result will be

   a. a more unstable inflation rate
   b. a more rapid acceleration of inflation when expansive policies are followed
   c. a more rapid deceleration of inflation when restrictive policies are followed
   d. all of the above
   e. none of the above; anticipations will change the natural rate of unemployment, not the inflation rate

14. If people anticipate the inflationary or anti-inflationary effects of changes in aggregate demand policies (rather than simply responding to past inflation), then

   a. a policy aimed at keeping the unemployment rate above the natural rate will quickly lead to an explosive wage-price spiral
   b. a policy aimed at keeping the unemployment rate below the natural rate will quickly lead to an explosive wage-price spiral
   c. an expansive aggregate demand policy will lead to a permanent reduction in the natural rate of unemployment
   d. an expansive aggregate demand policy will lead to a permanent increase in the natural rate of unemployment
   e. the economy will have a natural rate of inflation, as well as a natural rate of unemployment, because people will have a better idea of what is going on

15. Some economists argue that *credibility* of a restrictive monetary policy is the key to a quick unwinding of inflation. This conclusion is based on the idea that credibility will cause:

   a. the long-run Phillips curve to shift leftward
   b. the long-run Phillips curve to slope upward to the right
   c. the long-run Phillips curve to slope downward to the right, like a short-run Phillips curve
   d. the short-run Phillips curve to shift downward more quickly when restrictive policies are followed
   e. the short-run Phillips curve to become flatter

16. If expectations of inflation are *rational*, people may make mistakes, but

   a. they make mistakes only about the rate of inflation, not about the unemployment rate
   b. they make mistakes only about the actual rate of unemployment, not about the inflation rate
   c. they make mistakes only about the natural rate of unemployment
   d. their mistakes are solely the result of uncertainty about how the economy works, not the result of uncertainty about what the Federal Reserve will do
   e. their mistakes are random

17. According to the theory of rational expectations, if a policy of expanding aggregate demand is foreseen and understood by the public, it will affect:

   a. real GNP extremely strongly, since businesses will have time to prepare new investment projects
   b. prices, but not real GNP
   c. real GNP, but not prices
   d. both prices and real GNP
   e. neither prices nor real GNP, since the Fed can affect output and prices only by trickery

18. According to some proponents of the theory of rational expectations, aggregate demand policies are *worthless* as a way of

   a. lowering the unemployment rate
   b. lowering the rate of inflation
   c. changing people's expectations of inflation
   d. all of the above

19. According to rational expectations theorists, periods when the unemployment rate exceeds the natural rate

   a. cannot exist, because the economy is always on the long-run Phillips curve
   b. cannot exist, because the economy is always a short-run Phillips curve
   c. will be brief
   d. will be very long, if the Fed follows a restrictive policy that the public understands
   e. will be associated with an inflation rate that is higher than expected

20. According to some rational expectations theorists, the Federal Reserve can temporarily reduce unemployment below the natural rate by trickery. However, the Federal Reserve should not do so. The main reason is that a policy of trickery

   a. is dishonest
   b. will increase uncertainty over future policies, and therefore increase future fluctuations in unemployment
   c. will paradoxically decrease uncertainty over future policies, and therefore increase future fluctuations in unemployment
   d. will cause the long-run Phillips curve to shift sharply to the right
   e. will cause the long-run Phillips curve to shift sharply to the left

EXERCISES

1. Suppose labor productivity in an economy increases by 3% per year; the average worker produces 3% more than in the previous year. Assume also that the labor force and population both grow by 1% per year. The nominal wage [can rise by 3% per year without causing inflation, can rise by 4% per year without causing inflation, cannot rise without causing inflation]. If the inflation rate is zero, nominal GNP will rise by an average of _____% per year over the long run, and real GNP will rise by an average of _____% per year.

2. a. In Figure 14.1, an economy in equilibrium with zero inflation is at point _____. After some time at this point, suppose that aggregate demand unexpectedly increases. In the short run, the economy will move to point _____. This is on short run Phillips curve _____, which reflects expectations of inflation of _____ per year.

Figure 14.1

Inflation (percent per annum)

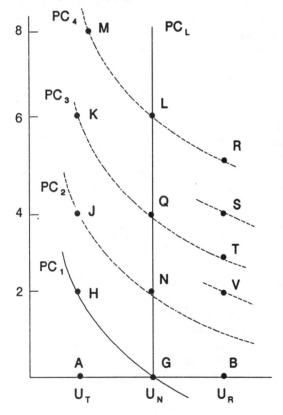

Unemployment rate (percent)

Now suppose that people expect the current rate of inflation of _____ per year to continue. Contracts will be renegotiated, causing the short-run Phillips curve to shift (upward, downward) to _____. If the authorities now expand demand in an effort to keep the unemployment rate at U_T, the economy will move in the short run to point _____. If people continue to expect the current rate of inflation—whatever it might be—to continue, then a demand management policy aimed at keeping the unemployment rate at U_T, will cause the economy to move to point _____ and then to point _____.

b. Suppose that, once the economy has gotten to point J by the process described in part (a), people no longer expect the current rate of inflation to continue, but rather anticipate an acceleration of inflation to 6%. When new contracts are negotiated, the short-run Phillips curve will shift upward from its present position at _____ to _____. Now, policy makers will be able to choose among points _____, _____, and _____, depending on the aggregate demand policies they pursue.

c. Finally, let us go back to starting point G. Suppose now that people have rational expectations. After an extended policy debate, the Federal Reserve decides that it would like to move the economy to point H by and expansive policy. As it pursues an expansive policy aimed at point H, the economy does not move there. Instead, it moves in the short run to point _____—provided that people's expectations are not only rational but correct. If, however, people make errors in forecasting the effects of the Fed's policy, they will move to point _____ or point _____.

ESSAY QUESTIONS

1. Critics argue that the use of wage-price controls is like trying to cure a sick person by using a thermometer that won't register higher than 98.6°. Why? How can wage-price controls lead to a "sicker" economic patient? How would the defenders of wage-price controls respond?

2. List the major criticisms of incomes policies. Now explain whether these criticisms apply more strongly to wage-price guideposts or to a wage-price freeze.

3. Do you believe that profit sharing is desirable? Explain why or why not.

ANSWERS

Important terms: 1 b, 2 h, 3 f, 4 i, 5 j, 6 a, 7 g, 8 c, 9 k, 10 e, 11 d

True-False:
1 F (p. 243)
2 T (p. 246)
3 F (p. 246)
4 F (p. 247)
5 T (pp. 248-249)
6 F (p. 249)
7 T (p. 249)
8 T (p. 250)
9 F (p. 251)
10 T (p. 253)

Multiple Choice:
1 a (p. 244)
2 a (p. 244)
3 c (p. 245)
4 c (p. 246)
5 e (p. 248)
6 b (p. 248)
7 e (p. 248)
8 d (p. 249)
9 e (p. 249)
10 b (p. 249)
11 a (p. 250)
12 e (p. 250)
13 d (p. 251)
14 b (p. 252)
15 d (pp. 252-253)
16 e (p. 253)
17 b (p. 254)
18 a (pp. 253-254)
19 c (pp. 253-255)
20 b (pp. 255)

Exercises

1. can rise by 3% per year without causing inflation, 4%, 4%

2. a. $G, H, PC_1, 0\%, 2\%$, upward, PC_2, J, K, M.

    b. PC_2, PC_4, M, L, R.

    c. Q (note: Q, not N because the aggregate demand which is sufficient to move to H is more than sufficient for point N; the high demand causes a move to Q rather than N), K, T.

CHAPTER 15

HOW DOES INFLATION AFFECT THE ECONOMY?

LEARNING OBJECTIVES

After you have studied this chapter in the textbook and study guide, you should be able to

✔ Explain why unanticipated inflation has much stronger effects on the economy than anticipated inflation

✔ Give examples of those who lose from unanticipated inflation, and those who gain

✔ Explain how the real rate of interest is related to the nominal rate of interest and the expected rate of inflation (equation 15-1)

✔ Explain how the behavior of borrowers and lenders tends to stabilize real interest rates

✔ Give an example of how the after-tax real rate of interest may be negative, even though the pre-tax real rate has remained constant in the face of higher inflation

✔ Explain how borrowers—and particularly purchasers of first homes—can be adversely affected by inflation, even if the real rate of interest remains constant

✔ Explain the difference between a variable rate mortgage and a graduated payment mortgage, and explain how they are designed to deal with different problems

✔ Explain why a high, uncertain rate of inflation can cause problems in the bond market

✔ Explain the problems that can arise if the government uses the real government deficit as a measure of fiscal policy, or if the Fed uses the real quantity of money as a measure of monetary policy

MAJOR PURPOSE

In Chapter 13, we have seen how wage contracts can be adjusted to take account of inflation. The theory of the vertical Phillips curve is based on the view that inflation won't have any affect on the unemployment rate, once people get used to the inflation and adjust to it. This chapter deals with the way in which individuals, businesses, and the government adjust to an inflationary environment. By adjusting, they reduce the effects of inflation on real magnitudes, such as real output and real wages. However, even after two and a half decades of rather rapid inflation, the economy has not adjusted fully to inflation; inflation has significant real consequences. The purpose of this chapter is to study the ways in which the economy does and does not adjust to inflation.

One important set of adjustments is in the market for bonds and other debt instruments. Unanticipated inflation hurts bondholders; they are repaid in less valuable dollars. If they anticipate inflation, however, they can adjust for it. They can withdraw from the bond market until interest rates rise to compensate for inflation. However, even if this happens, with real interest rates remaining constant, inflation can still have important consequences for borrowers and lenders. In particular, the combination of high inflation and high nominal rates of interest means that debt is front-loaded—payments in the early years are high, in real terms. As a result, young people have difficulty buying their first homes.

HIGHLIGHTS OF CHAPTER

In Chapter 13, we began to see how the economy can adjust to inflation. As inflation continues, people come to expect it and change their behavior accordingly. For example, labor unions bargain for a higher nominal wages to compensate for the increase they have come to expect in the cost of living. If people's expectations are accurate, then the inflation need not affect real wages; it will be taken into account by both workers (who will demand higher money wages) and employers (who will be willing to pay higher money wages). In addition, the rate of unemployment may be unaffected; this was the idea behind the vertical long-run Phillips curve of Chapter 13.

The Real Rate of Interest

Adjustments like this may occur not only in the labor market, but also in other markets. Among the most important markets affected by inflation are the markets for corporate bonds, government bonds, mortgages, and other debt instruments. Owners of bonds can be severely hurt by inflation; they are repaid in dollars with smaller value. If they anticipate inflation, they can take steps to protect themselves. They can switch out of bonds and into other assets, such as common stock or real estate. When they do so, bond prices fall; that is, interest rates rise. The rise in interest rates is reinforced by the eagerness of borrowers. Because they will be able to repay in less valuable dollars, they have an incentive to borrow more as inflation increases.

The **real rate of interest** is the rate of interest after account is taken of inflation. It is (approximately) the nominal rate of interest less the expected rate of inflation. For example, if the nominal interest rate is 10%, someone lending $100 today will be repaid $110 in one year's time. If the rate of inflation is 10% during that year, the $110 will buy no more than the $100 would have bought originally. In real terms, the lender has no gain. The nominal interest rate of 10% is no more than enough to compensate for the 10% inflation; the real interest rate is zero (10%-10%). This is not very good from the lender's viewpoint. Lenders are therefore reluctant to make loans, causing a further rise in interest rate. When this happens, the real interest rate becomes positive. Many observers of financial markets believe that the behavior of lenders and borrowers will act to stabilize the real interest rate. Until the early 1970s, evidence suggested that the real interest rate was in fact quite stable. In the early 1980s, however, the real interest rate was high by historical standards.

Even if the real interest rates is constant and inflation is perfectly anticipated, a combination of high inflation and a high nominal interest rate can have an important effect on borrowers and lenders. There are two main reasons for this. One has to do with front loading; the other has to do with the tax system.

The Duration of Debt: Front Loading

Bonds, mortgages, and other types of debt usually specify a constant nominal rate of interest. In a world of zero inflation, a nominal interest rate of 3% represents a real rate of 3%. Someone who has issued a bond with a face value of $100,000 will pay $3,000 in interest each year.

Suppose now that inflation accelerates to 10%, with the *nominal* rate of interest keeping step at 13%. Someone issuing a $100,000 bond now has to pay $13,000 in interest per year. This $13,000 includes $10,000 to compensate for the loss of value by the $100,000 principal over the year. The remaining $3,000 represents a real interest payment. In a sense, $10,000 of the $13,000 may be looked on as a partial repayment of principal. In real terms, the borrower is not only paying interest, but is also repaying part of the principal each year. Payments in early years are very high—the $13,000 represents a lot in the first year, since prices have not yet risen much. The debt is **front loaded.**

During periods of rapid inflation and high nominal interest rates, mortgages are similarly front loaded. As a result, it is very difficult for first-time buyers to afford homes. If they take out a mortgage now, they may face a crushing burden in the early years. This problem would be solved if mortgage payments were graduated—that is, if nominal payments rose through the years to keep real payments stable. Such graduated mortgages are not generally available, nor are they likely to become available. One reason is that they would lead to a rise in the burden of mortgage payments through time if inflation unexpectedly slowed down.

Taxation and Inflation

Taxation is another reason that inflation can have lasting real consequences, even if it is perfectly anticipated. People pay taxes on their *nominal* interest, and can generally deduct their nominal interest payments from their taxable income. In the earlier example, with $13,000 interest on a $100,000 bond, the taxpayer in the 25% bracket would pay a quarter of the $13,000 in taxes, leaving only $9,750, or 9.75% after taxes. This is not enough to compensate for the 10% inflation. The **after-tax real rate of interest** is negative.

Inflation and Uncertainty

Uncertainty is another complication that prevents perfect adjustment to inflation. Periods of *rapid* inflation also tend to be periods of *erratic* inflation. Thus, bond buyers are taking a risk. High nominal interest rates may compensate for the inflation they expected when they bought the bond. But suppose that inflation speeds up unexpectedly. The bondholder will lose. Similarly, there are risks for the borrower: If inflation unexpectedly slows down, the real burden of interest payments increases. Because erratic inflation poses risks for both borrowers

and lenders, a high, erratic inflation may cause the long-term bond market to dry up.

One way to deal with the problem of uncertainty is to have periodic adjustments in interest during the period of the loan. For example, most new mortgages in the United States now have adjustable rates. With the introduction of adjustable rate mortgages, the mortgage market has dealt quite effectively with the problem of *erratic* inflation. But it has not been able to deal with the front-loading problem associated with *high* rates of inflation and interest. Graduated mortgages are unavailable.

Real Magnitudes and Fiscal and Monetary Policies

Finally, this chapter considers how the government itself might respond to an inflationary situation. One question is how we should measure fiscal policy. Some argue that we should look at the changes in the real deficit of the government. When inflation is rapid—say, at 10%—then the first 10% in interest doesn't really represent interest; it represents a partial repayment of the real value of the debt. Thus, a government with a $1 trillion debt and a $100 billion deficit is not running a deficit at all. In real terms, its budget is balanced; the real value of its debt is constant.

This is a rather interesting idea, but it presents a problem. Indeed, it represents a trap that can be added to the earlier list of traps (that is, an annually balanced budget or a monetary policy aimed at a stable nominal rate of interest). Specifically, if inflation increases, the real value of the debt declines. This causes a swing toward surplus in the real budget. If we take the real budget as our guide, we may respond by increasing government spending or cutting taxes. But these steps will increase aggregate demand and make inflation worse.

Similarly, it would be a trap for the Fed to focus on the real quantity of money. During periods of inflation, the real value of the outstanding money stock declines. If the Fed responds by increasing the amount of money in order to restore the real quantity, it will make inflation worse.

Nevertheless, the real debt and the real quantity of money are important. For example, the real quantity of money is an important determinant of how much people will buy. The problem is that real measures must be used *very* cautiously by policymakers. One of the problems with inflation is that it introduces an element of confusion and chaos into the debate over aggregate demand policies.

IMPORTANT TERMS

Match the first column with the corresponding phrase in the second column.

_____ 1. Anticipated inflation
_____ 2. Unanticipated inflation
_____ 3. The real rate of interest
_____ 4. Front loading
_____ 5. Graduated-payment mortgage
_____ 6. Adjustable-rate mortgage
_____ 7. Indexation
_____ 8. Cap

a. A way of dealing with the problem of front loading
b. A limit on indexation
c. This type of inflation has relatively small real effects
d. Automatic adjustment for inflation, as in wages
e. The nominal rate less the expected rate of inflation
f. A way of dealing with the problem of erratic inflation
g. An effect of inflation, even if real interest rates are constant
h. This type of inflation has large real effects

TRUE-FALSE

T F 1. People who have borrowed large sums gain from inflation, particularly when it is unanticipated.

T F 2. People who hold government bonds usually lose from inflation, particularly when it is accurately anticipated.

T F 3. Inflation makes lenders more eager to lend, and borrowers less eager to borrow.

T F 4. It is possible for the real rate of interest on a short-term government bill to be negative, but not the nominal rate of interest.

T F 5. Inflation provides one incentive for borrowers to borrow. The tax system provides another.

T F 6. When nominal interest rates rise, a new mortgage is "front loaded" as a result, if monthly payments on that mortgage are constant in dollar terms throughout the life of the mortgage.

T F 7. A variable-rate mortgage eliminates the "front loading" of mortgages.

MULTIPLE CHOICE

1. Someone who has taken out a mortgage to buy a house will probably

   a. lose from inflation, especially if it was unexpected when the house was bought
   b. lose from inflation, especially if it was expected when the house was bought
   c. gain from inflation, especially if it was unexpected when the house was bought
   d. gain from inflation, especially if it was expected when the house was bought
   e. lose from inflation, but only if there is no mortgage on the house

2. If the nominal rate of interest is 12% and the real rate of interest is 3%, then the expected rate of inflation is:

   a. 18%
   b. 15%
   c. 12%
   d. 9%
   e. 3%

3. Which of the following can be negative?

   a. the nominal rate of interest on short-term securities
   b. the nominal rate of interest on long-term securities
   c. the before-tax real rate of interest on short-term securities
   d. the after-tax real rate of interest on short-term securities
   e. (c) and (d), but not (a) or (b)

4. Between 1981 and 1985, real interest rates were high. The most plausible explanation for the high real rates has been:

   a. the acceleration of inflation between 1981 and 1985
   b. high unemployment
   c. a collapsing stock market
   d. rising tax rates
   e. large government deficits

5. Consider someone in the 25% tax bracket, holding a bank account paying 8% interest. The rate of inflation is 6%. Then the after-tax real return to that individual is:

   a. -2%
   b. 0
   c. 2%
   d. 4%
   e. 6%

6. During periods of rapid inflation, the real value of trading on the long-term bond market generally:

   a. is high, because after-tax real interest rates are high
   b. is high, because nominal interest rates are high
   c. is low, because the real return on bonds is unpredictable
   d. is low, because the real return on bonds is low relative to the real return on short-term securities
   e. increases while inflation is accelerating, but then decreases when inflation levels out

7. Adjustable-rate mortgages are aimed primarily at dealing with the problem created by:

   a. the tendency of homes to depreciate
   b. high inflation
   c. erratic inflation
   d. the combined effects of inflation and taxation

   e. the tendency for real rates of interest to vary with the business cycle

8. A mortgage is most likely to be front loaded if:

   a. nominal interest rates are high, reflecting a high rate of inflation
   b. real interest rates are high
   c. real interest rates are low
   d. inflation decelerates after the house is bought
   e. taxes rise after the house is bought

9. If you had a "graduated-payment" mortgage:

   a. real payments would rise when prices rose
   b. real payments would rise when your real income rose
   c. real payments would rise when the value of the home rose
   d. nominal payments would rise during periods of inflation, keeping real payments stable
   e. nominal payments would rise when your nominal income rose, keeping payments at a constant fraction of your income

10. Suppose that the rate of inflation is steady at 7% per annum. Then over a period of 20 years, the average price level will:

    a. double
    b. treble
    c. quadruple
    d. increase by 500%
    e. increase by 700%

11. "Graduated payment" mortgages (GPM) and "adjustable rate" mortgages (ARM) are aimed at easing two different problems. Specifically, a:

    a. GPM is aimed at reducing the problem of front loading caused by *high* inflation, while an ARM is aimed at the problems created by *erratic* inflation
    b. GPM is aimed at reducing the problems caused by *erratic* inflation, while an ARM is aimed at the problems created by *high* inflation
    c. GPM is aimed at keeping *after-tax* interest rates stable, while an ARM is aimed at keeping *before-tax* interest rates stable
    d. GPM is aimed at keeping *before-tax* interest rates stable, while an ARM is aimed at keeping *after-tax* interest rates stable
    e. GPM is aimed at keeping *nominal* interest rates stable, while an ARM is aimed at keeping *real* interest rates stable

12. The rule of thumb most likely to stabilize real economic activity and prices is:

    a. a slow, steady increase in the real quantity of money
    b. a slow, steady increase in the nominal quantity of money
    c. a slow, steady increase in the real value of the government's debt
    d. a balanced budget every year
    e. a stable nominal rate of interest

EXERCISES

1. a. Suppose that you put $200 into a savings account and keep it there for 1 year, at which time it has grown to $220. Then the nominal rate of interest is _____%. If you expected inflation to be 4% during the year, you anticipated a real rate of interest of _____%. Suppose that inflation turned out to be 6% instead. Then, after the year, you would find that your real return was only _____%.

   b. If you are in a 40% tax bracket, you will pay $ _____ in taxes. Your after-tax nominal rate of interest will be _____%, and your after-tax real return will be _____%

2. Figure 15.1 shows the demand and supply for loanable funds in a non-inflationary situation. The equilibrium rate of interest is _____%. In the same diagram, draw the supply and demand curves that would exist if everyone expected 2% inflation and the economy had adjusted completely to this rate of inflation. The equilibrium nominal rate of interest is now _____%, and the equilibrium real rate _____%. The equilibrium quantity of funds, in real terms, is now (more than, less than, the same as) in the initial situation.

Figure 15.1

Nominal rate of interest (%)

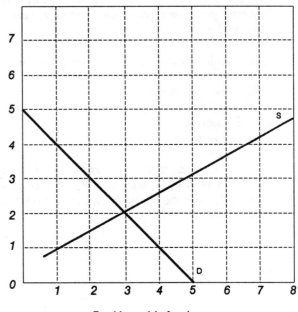

Real loanable funds

ANSWERS

Exercises

1   a.   10, 6, 4
     b.   8, 6, 0

2.   2, 4, 2, the same as

Figure 15.1 completed:

Nominal rate of interest (%)

Real loanable funds

Across

1, 5. unions may use this as a protection against unexpected inflation
7. common preposition
8. the Federal Reserve influences this (2 words)
11, 12. a characteristic of mortgages when inflation and nominal interest rates are high
13. wage-price guideposts may require this
19, 20. a type of inflation
21, 22. policymakers often face this
23. on the interior of
24. used by Presidents Kennedy and Johnson to restrain inflation
27. title given to senior government leaders (abbrev.)
28. during inflation, workers want this done to their wages
30. a source of minerals
31, 32. a way the bond market may respond to erratic inflation

Down

2. combination of inflation and high unemployment
3. small but important part of a machine
4. person who acts on behalf of someone else
5. in a form that is unreadable by unauthorized persons
6. someone in the final year of college
9. an investigative office established by Congress
10. a la _____
12. punctured
14. not very exciting
15. ____ West, young man!
16. a common problem at exam time
17. wall painting
18. this type of bank account is included in money supply, M1
21. what Adam Smith's factory made
25. what people do with goods
26. this is very important in a market economy
27. early monetary theorist (see inside cover of text)
28. man's name (abbrev.)
29. a teachers' organization (abbrev.)

CHAPTER 16

GROWTH AND PRODUCTIVITY:
Why Have They Varied So?

LEARNING OBJECTIVES

After you have studied this chapter in the textbook and study guide, you should be able to

✔ Explain the relationship between total output, total number of hours worked, and productivity

✔ Identify the period in the twentieth century when productivity rose most rapidly, and when it rose most slowly

✔ Summarize Denison's main conclusions regarding:

   1. The reasons for increases in output per person, 1948-73
   2. The reasons for the slowdown of the 1973-81 period

✔ Explain the vicious circle of poverty that can impede the growth of very poor countries

✔ List and explain seven problems that can make it difficult for poorer countries to develop

✔ Explain how ties to the international economy can help countries break out of the vicious circle

✔ Explain some of the secrets of success of the "four tigers" of East Asia

✔ Explain some of the ways in which those four economies are similar, and the ways in which they differ

✔ Explain how foreign borrowing can help to promote economic development, but why it can also cause trouble

MAJOR PURPOSE

The major purpose of this chapter is to study economic growth—that is, the increase in the productive potential of the economy. The chapter deals with two major puzzles—why the U.S. economy has grown so much more rapidly at some periods than others, and why some nations grow so much more rapidly than others.

The key to economic growth is an increase in **productivity**, that is, an increase in output per worker. Economists have been able to identify some of the reasons for changes in productivity — most notably, the increase in the *capital stock* and the improved *education* and *training* of the labor force. But economists do not have a good explanation of why productivity increased so much more slowly after 1973 than during the previous decades.

Some of the most rapidly growing nations in the world are in East Asia. These rapidly growing nations have high rates of saving and investment, and they are strongly export oriented.

HIGHLIGHTS OF CHAPTER

The average productivity of labor is equal to total output (Q) divided by the number of labor hours worked (L). To understand the growth of output, we must look at the increases in labor hours and productivity. Figure 16-1 in the textbook shows these changes since 1800. Over the past century, output has grown at an average rate of a little more than 3% per year. Population has grown more than 1% per year, while labor hours have on average increased at a somewhat slower rate. Productivity has increased at an average annual rate of around 2%.

This increase has not, however, been steady. The improvement in labor productivity was particularly rapid in the quarter century after the Second World War. It was very low — only 0.7% per year — between 1973 and 1981. Since 1981, the productivity performance of the U.S. economy has been reviving.

Observe in Figure 16-1 in the text that productivity has generally improved very rapidly when labor hours were growing slowly, and vice versa. With more people on the job, each works with less capital than would be the case with a lower growth in the labor force. As a result, there is a drag in output per labor hour. When the labor force increases, there are two important effects:

- *total* output increases, since there is an increase in the labor input; and

- output *per labor hour* decreases (or increases more slowly than it otherwise would), since the amount of capital per worker is kept down.

Those who have studied productivity and growth in detail include Edward F. Denison. Denison has estimated the reasons for the increase in output per person employed. The first column of Table 16-1 in the text lists his estimates for the period from 1948 to 1973. The most important

conclusion is that *no single item* accounted for most of the increase. There were a number of sources, each contributing small amounts to the overall increase in output per person. Of the sources identified by Denison, the most important were the increased education of the labor force, the increase in physical capital, greater economies of scale, and an improved allocation of resources. (In passing, observe that Denison's measure — output per person employed — does not correspond precisely to the standard definition of productivity, namely, output per labor *hour*. However the two measures are closely related.)

The second column of Table 16-1 shows Denison's attempt to explain why output per person employed remained stagnant in the period from 1973 to 1981. The most important conclusion here is that Denison's explanations don't in fact explain most of the slowdown. In fact, he explains only a third of the deterioration, leaving a large unexplained residual (1.8%, at the bottom of the last column). The reasons for the poor performance during this period remain something of a mystery, although the increase in the price of oil may have been more important than Denison estimated.

Not only has growth varied considerably from decade to decade; it has also varied considerably from country to country. Some countries have grown very rapidly, while others have grown very slowly.

The very poor nations sometimes seem caught in a *vicious circle of poverty*. When incomes are very low, people have a very difficult time saving. Because almost everything that is being produced is being consumed, the nation does not have many resources to devote to investment in real capital, education, and training. With low capital formation, productivity is stagnant. In addition to low saving and investment (shown in the outer loop of Figure 16-3), a number of other problems may act as drag on output per person and living standards:

- slow improvements in technology,

- small, stagnant markets that make it difficult to capture economies of scale,

- rapid population growth that reduces the amount of capital per person,

- social and cultural barriers to growth,

- a lack of social capital, such as good transportation and communications systems, and

- military conflicts.

The international economy can help countries to break out of the vicious circle by providing

- financial capital to finance real investments,
- technology, and
- markets.

Four of the most rapidly growing economies are in East Asia—South Korea, Taiwan, Hong Kong, and Singapore. These nations have all had very high rates of saving and investment. They have all been strongly export oriented; much of their output has been sold abroad. They have all made extensive use of foreign technology and imported capital equipment. However, the economies have differed in some important respects. The government has been much more directly involved in the economy in Korea than in Singapore or Hong Kong. Large conglomerates dominate the Korean economy, while small and medium sized businesses are the core of the Taiwanese economy.

Borrowing from foreign nations can help to provide the financing for investment and growth. However, if foreign borrowing is not put to good use, it can cause major problems. Borrowers may have difficulty servicing their loans (paying interest and repaying the loans).

IMPORTANT TERMS

Match the first column with the corresponding phrase in the second column.

_____ 1. Average productivity of labor	a. The Soviet Union and Bulgaria
_____ 2. Technological improvement	b. A characteristic of the U.S. economy after 1973
_____ 3. Economies of scale	c. Korea, Hong Kong, Taiwan, and Singapore
_____ 4. Slower growth	d. Q/L
_____ 5. Examples of first world countries	e. The price of one currency in terms of another
_____ 6. Examples of second world countries	f. Low income leads to low saving and investment, which in turn keeps income low
_____ 7. Examples of third world countries	g. An example: the electric power system
_____ 8. Vicious circle of poverty	h. An increase of all inputs by 100% leads to an increase of more than 100% in output
_____ 9. Infrastructure	i. India, Nigeria, Peru, and Indonesia
_____10. The "four tigers"	j. Inventions and better methods of production
_____11. Exchange rate	k. France, Germany, Japan, and Canada

TRUE-FALSE

T   F   1.   If the labor force grows at a rapid rate, this will act as a drag on productivity.

T   F   2.   If the labor force grows at a rapid rate, this will act as a drag on the growth of output.

T   F   3.   Denison found that most of the slowdown in the growth of output per person after 1973 was due to a single cause, the increase in the price of oil.

T   F   4.   If an economy grows at 2% each year, it will double in size in 25 years.

T   F   5.   The rapid increase in the international price of oil in 1973-1974 acted as a drag on growth, since it required some industries to retool

T   F   6.   Three major reasons for an increase in output per worker are investment in real capital, investment in education and training, and improvements in technology

T   F   7.   Gross domestic product (GDP) is the same as gross national product (GNP) except that GNP includes government purchases of goods and services, but GDP does not.

MULTIPLE CHOICE

1. Growth of the economy causes

   a. the long-run Phillips curve to shift to the right
   b. the long-run Phillips curve to become flatter
   c. the aggregate supply curve to shift to the right
   d. an increasing gap between actual and potential GNP
   e. all of the above

2. Since 1920, real GNP in the United States has grown at approximately what rate per year?

   a. 0.5%
   b. 1%
   c. 3%
   d. 6%
   e. 9%

3. In the past two decades, total labor hours worked have grown at a more rapid rate than the population. The major reason has been:

   a. an increase in the average length of the work week
   b. an increase in the participation of women in the labor force
   c. an increase in the number of people working for the government
   d. a very rapid increase in population
   e. an unusually slow growth in population

4. When the number of labor hours increases very rapidly, the most likely effect is:

   a. a slow increase in productivity
   b. a very rapid increase in productivity
   c. a very slow increase in total output
   d. no change in output, since workers have less capital
   e. a decline in output, since workers have less capital

5. Consider an economy in which output *per capita* grows at 2% per year, while population grows at 1.5% per year. Then growth in real GNP is approximately what percent per year:

   a. 2/1.5 = 1.33
   b. 1.5
   c. 2

   d. 1.5 x 2 = 3
   e. 1.5 + 2 = 3.5

6. One of the topics studied by Denison was the change in the quality of the labor force, as measured by education. Denison concluded that the education of the U.S. labor force has:

   a. improved, and this improvement contributed as much to productivity as the increase in machinery and other physical capital
   b. improved, although this improvement contributed less to productivity than the increase in machinery and other physical capital
   c. deteriorated, since SAT scores have fallen
   d. deteriorated, since literacy levels have declined
   e. deteriorated, at least during the 1970s, since labor productivity deteriorated during that decade

7. Output per person increased much more slowly between 1973 and 1981 than in the previous quarter century. According to Denison, what accounted for more than half of the slowdown:

   a. a decrease in labor hours worked by the average worker
   b. a decrease in rate of investment in physical capital
   c. a decrease in rate of investment in education
   d. a smaller increase in economies of scale, because of stronger foreign competition
   e. none of the above

8. For a country in the process of development, a high saving rate is generally

   a. helpful, because it makes resources available for investment
   b. helpful, because it causes a rapid growth of aggregate demand and thus makes it easier to capture economies of scale
   c. harmful, because it causes a stagnation of aggregate demand
   d. harmful, because it promotes imports of consumer goods
   e. unimportant; there is no observable relationship (either positive or negative) between saving and growth

9. A country is overpopulated whenever

   a. the rate of population is increasing by more than 1% per year

   b. real per capital GNP is falling

   c. there are an average of more than 100 people per square mile

   d. any of (a), (b), or (c) exists

   e. we can't conclude that any of the above necessarily means a country is overpopulated

10. The four rapidly-growing economies of Asia, known as the "four tigers," have all had

   a. export-oriented policies

   b. laissez-faire economies

   c. very large and rapidly growing government sectors

   d. very large corporations that dominate the economy

   e. all of the above

11. Countries which faced crises in servicing their foreign debts during the 1980s

   a. were only oil importers, who were adversely affected by spiraling oil prices

   b. were only oil exporters, because they looked forward to large future export earnings and therefore mistakenly thought they could afford to borrow

   c. were only exporters of agricultural products, who were hurt by the fall in the prices of their exports

   d. were only emerging exporters of manufactures, who faced extremely tough competition in breaking into world markets

   e. included all four types of countries: oil importers, oil exporters, exporters of agricultural products, and exporters of manufactured goods

12. According to Thomas Malthus, the wage rate would be depressed to the subsistence level because of

   a. the power of monopolies

   b. the desire of capitalists to exploit the working class

   c. the natural tendency of population to grow more rapidly than the production of food

   d. the long-run downward trend in investment

   e. pestilence, war, and famine

EXERCISES

1. Fill in the blanks.

   a. Denison found that, during the period from 1948 to 1973, the increase in output per worker could be attributed to the following four sources (in addition to the unexplained residual, due partly to technological improvement):

     1._____

     2._____

     3._____

     4._____

   b. Over this period, a small drag on the growth of output per worker was attributable to

   _____

   c. Denison found that he could not explain most of the slowdown in the period from 1973 to 1981. He may have underestimated the effects of:

     1._____

2. A more rapid rate of increase in population leads to a (more, less) rapid rate of growth of output. It generally acts as a (stimulus to, drag on) productivity, because the average worker has less _____ to work with. However, this effect may be offset, or more than offset, by _____, which act to (increase, decrease) productivity as the size of the economy grows.

ESSAY QUESTIONS

1. Since 1966, labor hours (L) increased at a much faster rate than between 1919 and 1966 (Figure 16-1 in the textbook). How do you explain this rapid increase? Would you expect a rapid increase in the next decade? What do you think explains the *inverse* relationship between the growth in labor

input and the increase in labor productivity? On the basis of these answers, do you have any predictions about what will happen to labor productivity in the next decade? How about the rate of growth of out put? Are you confident regarding your last two answers? Why or why not?

2. Recall the "measure of economic welfare" (MEW) introduced in Chapter 6. If this, rather than GNP, were used to measure economic growth and productivity, how would the historical record in Figure 16-1 in the textbook be affected? How would the costs of economic growth be affected?

How do your answers depend on how leisure is treated in MEW?

3. Suppose that a new industrial policy agency is set up by the U.S. government, to assist selected industries. Suppose you are chosen to run this agency. Would you favor assisting new, high-tech industries, or declining industries, or both? Or perhaps neither of these, but some other group of industries? (If so, explain how you would choose your favored industries.) Explain what problems you might encounter in picking industries for assistance, and the problems which might result from your policies.

ANSWERS

Important terms:	**1** d, **2** j, **3** h, **4** b, **5** k, **6** a, **7** i, **8** f, **9** g, **10** c, **11** e

True-False:
1 T (p. 278)
2 F (p. 278)
3 F (p. 280)
4 F (Ch. 15, p. 271)
5 T (p. 281)
6 T (p. 281)
7 F (p. 286)

Multiple Choice:
1 c (p. 277)
2 c (p. 278)
3 b (p. 278)
4 a (p. 278)
5 e (p. 278)
6 a (p. 279)
7 e (p. 280)
8 a (pp. 282-283, 286)
9 e (p. 284)
10 a (p. 288)
11 e (p. 289)
12 c (p. 292, Appendix)

Exercises

1   a.   better educated labor force, increase in physical capital, economies of scale, improved allocation of resources.
     b.   shorter work week.
     c.   higher oil prices.

2.   more, drag on, capital, economies of scale, increase.

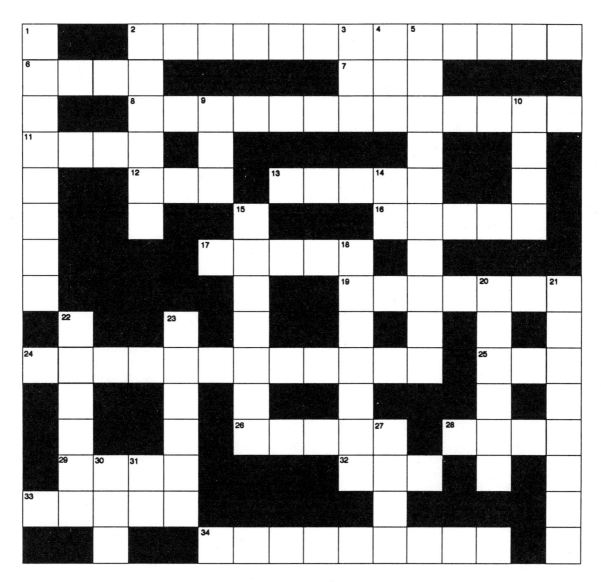

Across

2. what happens when depreciation exceeds gross investment
6. leisure
7. part of the foot
8. has an effect on productivity (2 words)
11. won't he _____ learn?
12. epoch
13. country with rapid economic growth
16. a Nobel prizewinner (see inside cover of text)
17. a major source of innovation (abbrev.)
19. this may suffer, if growth is rapid
24. Q/L
25. pull
26. without this, there would be no production
28. there are many of these in Shakespeare's plays
29. form of capital
32. business organization (abbrev.)
33. bright
34. the most important single contributor to the increase in productivity, according to Denison

Down

1. where bright ideas pay off
2. a Nobel prizewinner (see inside cover of text)
3. they develop the SAT exams (abbrev.)
4. help! (abbrev.)
5. important contributor to growth
9. lots of water
10. important for banks
14. on, in, or near
15. helps workers to produce
18. student of productivity and growth
20. product
21. southern cousin of Russians
22. slowed in 1970s
23. together with demand, this determines price
27. rave
30. a cause of slowdown of 1970s
31. above

GREAT MACROECONOMIC ISSUES:
Aggregate Demand

CHAPTER 17

MONETARY POLICY AND FISCAL POLICY:
Which is the Key to Aggregate Demand?

LEARNING OBJECTIVES

After you have studied this chapter in the textbook and study guide, you should be able to

✔ Explain the three steps in the Keynesian explanation of how a change in the quantity of money can cause a change in aggregate demand

✔ Explain how problems at two of these three steps might mean that aggregate demand will not change much as a result of a change in the quantity of money

✔ Explain how, at the first step, the quantity of money and people's willingness to hold money determine the rate of interest

✔ Explain what the investment demand curve means, and remember what "price" is measured on the vertical axis

✔ Explain the key propositions of monetarists, and the major points of disagreement between monetarists and Keynesians

✔ Explain how deficit spending may lead to a decrease in investment and/or in net exports

✔ Explain why, in spite of strength of the case for using both policies, the United States has nevertheless relied almost exclusively on monetary policy as a demand-management tool in recent years

MAJOR PURPOSE

One of the important controversies of recent decades has been over the relative importance of monetary and fiscal policies. If the economy is heading into an inflationary boom or into a recession, should we turn to fiscal policy to stabilize the economy? Or to monetary policy? Most economists would now say that a *combination* of monetary and fiscal policies is best. However, there has been a sharp debate between Keynesians—who have often emphasized fiscal policy—and monetarists, who have emphasized that money is the key to aggregate demand. The purpose of this chapter is to review the highlights of this debate, and suggest that it is unwise to rely exclusively on either monetary or fiscal policy.

HIGHLIGHTS OF CHAPTER

This chapter deals with the controversy over the relative importance of monetary and fiscal policies. Although most economists take an intermediate position, two extreme views may be identified. One position—the position of strong Keynesians, particularly during the 1950s and 1960s—is that fiscal policy is very important, while monetary policy has little or no effect. The other extreme position—the strong monetarist view—is just the opposite. An earlier chapter explained the Keynesian view of how fiscal policy affects aggregate expenditures. This chapter rounds out the discussion by explaining:

- the reasons why strong Keynesians have dismissed monetary policy,

- the monetarist view as to why monetary policy is important, and

- the monetarist view as to why fiscal policy does not have much effect on aggregate demand.

This chapter also explains why the historical evidence does not give unqualified support to either extreme view; we are left with a case for using both monetary and fiscal policies.

The Keynesian View of Monetary Policy

In the Keynesian view, there are three links in the chain of events whereby an open market purchase can increase aggregate demand. At the *first link*, an open market purchase can cause a *fall in interest rates*. In Chapter 12, we have already seen why. Specifically, the increase in the Fed's demand for bonds will work to bid up the prices of bonds—that is, to bid down interest rates. With excess reserves, commercial banks will be anxious to make loans; this will create additional downward pressure on interest rates. This chapter explains this first link (between an expansive monetary policy and a fall in interest rates) in more detail.

To see how monetary policy affects interest rates, Keynesian economists look at the demand for and supply of money. By the supply of money, they mean the quantity which exists in the economy. By the demand, they mean the *willingness* of people to hold money. This willingness depends in part on interest rates—the lower are interest rates, the more money people are willing to hold. This is

reflected in the downward slope of the demand curve in Figure 17-2 in the text.

Now, suppose that the economy is initially in equilibrium, and that the Fed then increases the quantity of money. At the existing interest rate, people now have more money than they are willing to hold. They try to reduce their money balances. How do they do so? The answer is: by buying bonds. As people buy bonds, bond prices rise. That is, interest rates fall. Once the interest rate has fallen to its equilibrium, people no longer have more money than they are willing to hold; the demand for bonds levels off. (Note that, overall, people don't actually reduce their money balances. Instead, they bid down the interest rate until they are willing to hold the quantity of money in existence.)

The *second link* represents the *effect that a change in the interest rate has on investment*. Interest represents one of the expenses that businesses face in deciding whether to buy machinery or make other investments. If interest rates fall, the costs of investment will accordingly fall, and businesses will be more eager to make investments. The increase in investment as interest rates fall is illustrated by the *investment demand curve*. For example, consider the investment demand curve in Figure 17-3 on p. 299 of the text. If the interest rate is 8%, businesses want to undertake $100 billion in investment. Then, if the interest rate falls to 6% as a result of an expansive monetary policy, businesses will want to increase investment by $25 billion (*ceteris paribus*). In other words, the policy leads to an increase in investment at this second step.

At the *third step*, an increase in investment has a *multiplied effect on aggregate demand*. The theory of the multiplier was explained in detail in Chapter 9.

Keynesian economists foresee two situations in which monetary policy may not have much effect. First, Keynes himself saw a problem at the first step. He was skeptical that monetary policy could be used as a way out of the depression of the 1930s. Interest rates were already very low, and there was not much prospect that they could be lowered significantly with monetary policy. After all, there is a downward limit on interest rates: They cannot be pushed below zero. In other words, in the special case of the depression when interest rates were already low, Keynes believed that the authorities could not rely on monetary policy. They would have to use fiscal policy to get the economy out of the depression.

Some of his followers had a more general skepticism regarding monetary policy; they doubted its effectiveness even during more normal times. Specifically, they foresaw a problem at the second step. They believed that the investment demand curve might be almost vertical. As a result, they were skeptical that changes in interest rates would lead to a significant change in investment. Even if monetary policy did change interest rates at step 1, there might be very little change in investment at step 2.

(The skepticism of some Keynesians over monetary policy lasted through the 1960s. Now, however, almost all Keynesians see an important role for monetary policy. The recent difficulties in actually using fiscal policy—explained toward the end of the chapter—have increased their interest in monetary policy. There has been a move away from polar views and toward more central views.)

The Monetarist View of Monetary Policy

The monetarist view begins with the equation of exchange: $MV = PQ$, where M is the stock of money, V is the velocity of money, P is the average level of prices, and Q is the quantity of output (that is, real national product). This equation is not a "theory," because it is simply true *by definition*. Specifically, V is defined as PQ/M. However, a theory has been built on this equation. This theory—the **quantity theory**—is the proposition that V is stable. If this is so, then a change in the quantity of M will cause an approximately proportional change in PQ, and monetary policy has a strong and predictable effect on nominal GNP.

Monetarism is built on the quantity theory. Five key propositions of monetarism are:

- The money supply M is the most important determinant of aggregate demand and nominal national product PQ.

- In the *long run*, real GNP tends moves to its full-employment level. Consequently, the only long-run effect of M is on P, not on Q.

- However, in the short run, an increase (decrease) in M can cause *both* P and Q to increase (decrease).

- If M is increased at a slow, stable rate, then aggregate demand will also increase at a slow, stable rate.

- Such a slow, stable increase in aggregate demand is the best way to reduce the magnitude of business cycles and keep inflation down. Therefore, the central bank should follow a monetary *rule*, aiming for a slow, steady increase in M.

The Monetarist View of Fiscal Policy

Monetarists doubt that fiscal policy has a strong and predictable effect on aggregate demand. The major reason for this is because of **crowding out**. Suppose that the government spends more, and finances the resulting deficit by borrowing from the public. Interest rates will rise. As a result, businesses will move upward to the left along the investment demand curve; desired investment will decline. Thus, the government spending will crowd out investment; the net effect on aggregate demand will be smaller than foreseen in the simple discussion of Chapter 10. The strength of the crowding out effect will depend on the slope of the investment demand curve. The flatter it is, the more investment will decrease for any increase in the interest rate. Monetarists generally believe that the investment demand curve is quite flat (in contrast to the almost vertical curve of early Keynesians). As a result, they foresee a strong crowding out effect, with little or no net effect of fiscal policy on aggregate demand.

This crowding out argument is based on the assumption that the government sells bonds *to the public*. In this case, there will be no effect on the money stock; this will be an example of **pure fiscal policy**. If, on the other hand, the Fed buys the additional government bonds, interest rates may be kept down and investment and aggregate demand will increase. But the money stock will rise, and a monetarist will consider money, not government spending, to be the cause of the increase in aggregate demand. Thus, if we want to distinguish between the Keynesian and monetarist viewpoints, we should look at a *pure* fiscal policy—a change in G or in tax rates with no change in M—and compare it with what we might call a *pure* monetary policy: an open market operation and a change in M with no change in fiscal policy. If an expansive fiscal policy is accompanied by an increase in M, there is no disagreement: Aggregate demand will increase. Keynesians will generally attribute the increase to fiscal policy, and monetarists to a change in M.

A second reason that deficit spending may have a weak effect on aggregate demand has attracted considerable attention in recent years. An increase in deficit spending by the government can cause an increase in interest rates, encouraging foreigners to buy U.S. bonds and bidding up the price of the U.S. dollar in terms of foreign currencies. U.S. exports are discouraged, and imports stimulated. In other words, a budgetary deficit can cause a deficit in international trade, with the trade deficit offsetting the stimulative effects of the government's deficit spending.

The events of the past quarter century do not give unqualified support to either the strong monetarist nor to the strong Keynesian view. Strong Keynesians were shaken by the events of the late 1960s, when money, not fiscal policy, appeared to be the major engine driving aggregate demand. During the past 15 years, large changes in the velocity of money have shaken the beliefs of strong monetarists.

Now, there is widespread uncertainty over the relative effectiveness of monetary and fiscal policies. Because we do not know exactly how the economy operates, it makes sense to diversify—to use some of each policy, rather than putting all our eggs in one basket. But, while the importance of diversification is widely recognized, we have in fact placed almost exclusive reliance on monetary policy as a demand-management tool in recent years. The reason is that fiscal policy is caught in a political impasse. Many people believe that smaller deficits would be desirable, but there is little agreement on how to achieve that goal.

MATCHING COLUMNS

Match the first column with the corresponding phrase in the second column.

_____	1. Investment demand curve	a.	$MV = PQ$
_____	2. More investment	b.	Possibly, a result of a budget deficit
_____	3. Equation of exchange	c.	Proposition that V is stable
_____	4. Velocity	d.	Relationship between the interest rate and I^*
_____	5. Quantity theory	e.	Change in G with no change in rate of growth of M
_____	6. Crowding out	f.	Caused by a lower rate of interest
_____	7. Pure fiscal policy	g.	More G leads to higher i, which leads to less I^*
_____	8. Trade deficit	h.	PQ / M

TRUE-FALSE

T   F   1. If interest rates fall, people will be willing to hold a larger quantity of money.

T   F   2. According to Keynes, interest rates might be low during a depression. He argued that in this case, expansive monetary policy would not be an effective tool for promoting recovery.

T   F   3. The flatter is the investment demand curve, the more effective is monetary policy as a way of controlling aggregate demand.

T   F   4. Keynesians generally argue that, while the equation of exchange is correct (MV does equal PQ), it is not the best way to analyse changes in demand and output; the equation $Y = C + I^* + G$ is a better place to begin.

T   F   5. According to the quantity theory of money, V is stable through time, and PQ therefore changes by about the same percentage as M.

T   F   6. According to quantity theorists, a change in M will have little or no effect on P in the long run.

T   F   7. According to quantity theorists, a change in M will have a greater effect on P in the long run than in the short run.

T   F   8. The stronger is the crowding out effect, the more powerful will be the effect of fiscal policy on aggregate demand.

T F 9. The flatter is the investment demand curve, the more effective is fiscal policy as a way of controlling aggregate demand.

T F 10. According to monetarists, fiscal policy can have a powerful effect on aggregate demand, provided that changes in government spending are financed by borrowing from the central bank.

MULTIPLE CHOICE

1. According to the Keynesian approach, the effectiveness of monetary policy on aggregate expenditures should be analyzed by looking at three steps. These three steps include each of the following *except* one. That one is:

    a. the effect of monetary policy on the rate of interest
    b. the effect of a change in the interest rate on open market purchases by the Fed
    c. the effect of a change in the interest rate on desired investment
    d. the effect of a change in desired investment on aggregate expenditures

2. Which of the following is most likely to *decrease* when the quantity of money *increases*?

    a. P
    b. Q
    c. $P \times Q$
    d. the interest rate
    e. the quantity of money demanded

3. In the Keynesian approach to monetary policy, if the quantity of money exceeds the quantity demanded, the most likely result is a:

    a. fall in the interest rate
    b. rise in the interest rate
    c. fall in investment
    d. fall in national product
    e. fall in the size of the multiplier

4. Suppose that the amount of money people have exceeds the quantity that they want to hold. Then, according to Keynesian theory, they will try to get rid of excess money balances by:

    a. saving more
    b. buying more goods
    c. buying more services
    d. switching from checking deposits to currency
    e. switching from money into bonds or other financial assets

5. The investment demand curve shows the relationship between:

    a. the rate of interest and the quantity of bonds that people are willing to hold
    b. the rate of interest and the quantity of of money that people want to invest in bonds
    c. the interest rate and desired investment
    d. the interest rate and actual investment
    e. the investment demand curve shows all of the above

6. Keynes believed that an expansive monetary policy might not be very effective as a way to stimulate the economy out of a depression. Monetary policy was most likely to be *ineffective* if:

    a. V were stable
    b. the investment demand curve were flat
    c. the demand curve for money were steep
    d. interest rates were already very high
    e. interest rates were already very low

7. The quantity theory of money is the proposition that:

    a. $MV = PQ$
    b. $MQ = PV$
    c. P is stable
    d. V is stable
    e. according to the quantity theory, all of the above must be true

8. Most Keynesians argue that the equation of exchange, $MV = PQ$

    a. is incorrect, because V does not equal PQ/M
    b. is incorrect, because V is unstable
    c. is incorrect, because M does not equal PQ/V
    d. is incorrect, because M is unstable
    e. is correct, but is not the most enlightening place to begin macroeconomic theory, because V is unstable

9. Keynesians and monetarists are most likely to agree that:

   a. monetary policy is more effective than fiscal policy
   b. fiscal policy is more effective than monetary policy
   c. neither fiscal nor monetary policy can effect Q; the only effect will be on P
   d. the investment demand curve is generally steep
   e. $V = PQ/M$

10. According to the quantity theory of money, a rise in the quantity of money causes an increase in:

    a. the ratio of demand deposits to currency
    b. the ratio of currency to demand deposits
    c. the gold stock
    d. $P \times Q$
    e. Q/P

11. According to the quantity theory of money, a rise in the quantity of money causes:

    a. a rise in P in the long run, and also, possibly, a rise in Q in the short run
    b. a rise in Q in the long run, and also, possibly, a rise in P in the short run
    c. a fall in P in the short run, and a rise in Q in the long run
    d. a rise in both P and Q in both the long run and the short run
    e. a rise in Q in the long run, with no change in P

12. Suppose that the amount of money people have exceeds the quantity that they want to hold. Then, monetarists emphasize that they will try to get rid of excess money balances by:

    a. saving more
    b. buying bonds
    c. buying goods
    d. switching from currency to checking deposits
    e. switching from checking deposits to currency

13. Which of the following views is most likely to be held by a monetarist?

    a. a decrease in the rate of growth of the money stock will cause the level of national product to stay below the full employment level permanently
    b. the money stock should be increased at a steady, constant rate
    c. desired investment is quite unresponsive to changes in the rate of interest
    d. the quantity of money demanded responds strongly to changes in the rate of interest
    e. fiscal policy has a powerful affect on aggregate demand

14. The "crowding out" effect of fiscal policy applies to which of the following ideas?

    a. an increase in G leads to an increase in interest rates, which leads to an increase in I^*
    b. an increase in G leads to a decrease in interest rates, which leads to an increase in I^*
    c. an increase in G leads to an increase in interest rates, which leads to a decline in I^*
    d. an increase in G leads to an increase in I^*, which leads to an increase in interest rates
    e. an increase in G leads to an increase in I^*, which leads to a decrease in interest rates

15. If the investment demand curve is quite flat, then we would expect the effects on aggregate demand of:

    a. monetary policy to be strong while fiscal policy is weak
    b. fiscal policy to be strong while monetary policy is weak
    c. both monetary and fiscal policies to be strong
    d. both monetary and fiscal policies to be weak

16. By "pure" fiscal policies, economists mean:

    a. fiscal policies uninfluenced by special interests
    b. fiscal policies where all changes take place in the non-defense sectors of the government's budget
    c. fiscal policies concentrated in the defense sectors of the government's budget, because these have little effect on the productive capacity of the economy
    d. changes in government spending or tax rates unaccompanied by changes in the rate of growth of the money stock
    e. changes in government spending or tax rates while interest rates are held constant

17. Deficit spending by the U.S. government can lead to U.S. deficits in international trade by the following sequence of events:

   a. budget deficits cause a rise in interest rates, which causes a rise in the price of the dollar in terms of foreign currencies, which causes a rise in imports
   b. budget deficits cause a rise in interest rates, which causes a fall in the price of the dollar in terms of foreign currencies, which causes a rise in imports
   c. budget deficits cause a rise in interest rates, which causes a fall in the price of the dollar in terms of foreign currencies, which causes a fall in imports
   d. budget deficits cause a fall in interest rates, which causes a fall in the price of the dollar in terms of foreign currencies, which causes a rise in imports
   e. budget deficits cause a fall in interest rates, which causes a fall in the price of the dollar in terms of foreign currencies, which causes a fall in imports

18. The recessions of 1980 and 1981-1982 were preceded by

   a. an historically unprecedented decline in the money stock; the Fed was determined to reduce inflation
   b. a slower rate of growth of the money stock; the Fed was determined to reduce inflation
   c. a moderate increase in the rate of growth of the money stock; the Fed was determined to keep the expansion going
   d. a very rapid increase in the rate of growth of the money stock; the Fed was determined to keep the expansion going

   e. a very steady growth in the money stock; the Fed tried to avoid either recession or inflation, but was unsuccessful

19. During the last half of the 1980s

   a. fiscal and monetary policies were both used actively to stabilize the economy
   b. fiscal policy was the primary demand management tool used by the authorities
   c. monetary policy was the primary demand management tool used by the authorities
   d. both fiscal policy and monetary policy were held rigidly constant by political constraints
   e. both fiscal and monetary policies were very restrictive, and the result was a major recession in 1987-1988

20. Fiscal policy was stuck in a "gridlock" in the late 1980s; monetary policy was the only macroeconomic "game in town." The reason was:

   a. the Fed's firm commitment to high interest rates meant that the government could not afford to run deficits
   b. the Fed's firm commitment to low interest rates meant that the fiscal policy could not become expansive without the danger of hyperinflation
   c. there were large surpluses; the president's firm committment to new taxes to "soak the rich" meant that the surpluses would become even larger
   d. there were large deficits, and the president was firmly committed to new taxes to "soak the rich"
   e. there were large deficits, and the president was committed to no new taxes

---

EXERCISES

1. According to the Keynesian approach, money can affect aggregate demand as a result of a three-step process. Specifically, an increase in the quantity of money will lead to:

   a. _____; which in turn will cause

   b. _____; which in turn will lead to

   c. _____.

   Keynesians foresee no problem at the third step. However, problems might occur at each of the first two steps. Specifically, there might be a problem at the first step, particularly if (interest rates were al-

ready very low, interest rates were already high, the rate of inflation were high). There also could be a major problem at the second step, if (the demand for money, the investment demand curve, the consumption function) were steep.

In Keynesian theory, if the amount of money people have exceeds the quantity that they want to hold, they will (buy bonds, buy goods, save more). As a result, (prices will rise, interest rates will fall). Monetarists foresee a different response. If the amount of money people have exceeds the quantity that they want to hold, they will (buy bonds, buy goods, save more). As a result, (aggregate demand will increase, interest rates will fall). In the short run, monetarists believe that this will lead to (higher *P*, higher *Q*, both); in the long run, it will cause (higher *P*, higher *Q*, both). Monetarism is based on the quantity theory of money. That is, it is based on the view that (*M*, *V*, *P*, *Q*, all of them) is/are stable.

2. Suppose that the investment demand curve is very steep. This suggests that monetary policy will be (effective, weak). Specifically, suppose the Federal Reserve engages in a very restrictive policy, selling Treasury bills on the open market. As a result, the prices of bills will (fall, rise), and their interest rates or yields will (fall, rise). This will lead to an (increase, decrease) in *I**, with the size of this effect being very (large, small) because of the steepness of the investment demand curve.

3. In Figure 17.1 below, the curves labelled A and B are two alternative ways the investment demand curve may be drawn. Of the two, curve (A, B) is the one in which *I** is most responsive to changes in the rate of interest. According to curve A, when the rate of interest is 10%, *I** will be _____; when the rate of interest is 5%, *I** will be _____. According to curve B, when the rate of interest is 10%, *I** will be _____; when the rate of interest is 5%, *I** will be _____. If the two economies are identical except for the investment demand, then monetary policy will be more powerful in (A, B), and fiscal policy will be more powerful in (A, B).

Figure 17.1

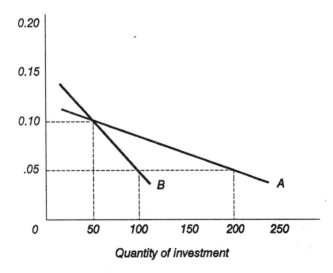

Rate of interest

Quantity of investment

Figure 17.2 shows the 45° line and the line indicating consumption expenditures plus government expenditures for goods and services in either economy A or B. (Assume there are no international transactions.) The slope of this line is equal to _____. This means that the multiplier is equal to _____. [If you have trouble with this point, refer back to Chapter 9.] Suppose that the interest rate in economy A is 10%. Draw the aggregate expenditures line (*C* + *I** + *G*) for economy A. The equilibrium is at a national product of _____. Now suppose that the interest rate decreases to 5%. *I** will (increase, decrease) from _____ to _____ in economy A. Draw in a new aggregate expenditures line. The new equilibrium national product is _____. From your last two answers, confirm the size of the multiplier shown earlier in the paragraph.

Figure 17.2

Aggregate Expenditures

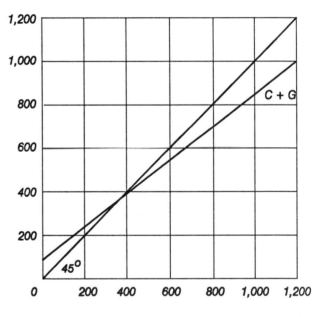

National Product

Now go through the same exercise for economy B. That is, draw in the aggregate expenditures line when the interest rate is equal to 10%, and then when it is equal to 5%. As a result of the fall in the interest rate, investment (increases, decreases) from _____ to _____, and equilbrium national product (increases, decreases) from _____ to _____. By comparing answers, we see that the multiplier is (higher than in A, lower than in A, the same as in A). [Do you see why this is so?] A fall in interest rates from 10% to 5% has (a more powerful, a less powerful, the same) effect on national product in economy B, compared to economy A.

ESSAY QUESTIONS

1. One reason for using both monetary and fiscal policies together is that diversification spreads the benefit or pain. For each of the following policies, explain who the major gainers and losers are, and why.

   a. expansive monetary policy

   b. expansive fiscal policy

   c. restrictive monetary policy

   d. restrictive fiscal policy

2. Suppose one economist told you that the investment demand curve was quite steep, and another told you it was quite flat. Which is more likely to be a monetarist, and which a Keynesian? Explain.

3. "The equation of exchange, $MV = PQ$, is a tautology. Therefore it is useless in helping us understand how the economy works." Evaluate this statement. Also evaluate the following: "The basic Keynesian equation,
Aggregate expenditures $= C + I^* + G + X_n$,
is also a tautology. Therefore it is also useless in helping us understand how the economy works."

ANSWERS

Important terms: 1 d, 2 f, 3 a, 4 h, 5 c, 6 g, 7 e, 8 b

True-False:
1 T (p. 298)
2 T (p. 301)
3 T (p. 301)
4 T (Ch. 9 and p. 302)
5 T (p. 302)
6 F (p. 302)
7 T (p. 302)
8 F (p. 304)
9 F (p. 305)
10 T (p. 305)

Multiple Choice:
1 b (p. 297)
2 d (p. 298)
3 a (p. 298)
4 e (p. 298)
5 c (p. 299)
6 e (p. 301)
7 d (p. 302)
8 e (p. 302)
9 e (p. 302)
10 d (p. 302)
11 a (p. 302)
12 c (p. 303)
13 b (p. 303)
14 c (p. 304)
15 a (p. 305)
16 d (p. 305)

Exercises:

1. a. a fall in the interest rate,
    b. a rise in desired investment,
    c. a multiplied increase in national product,

    interest rates were already very low, the investment demand curve, buy bonds, interest rates will fall, buy goods, aggregate demand will increase, both, higher P, V.

2. weak, fall, rise, decrease, small.

3. A, 50, 200, 50, 100, A, B, 0.75, 4, 600, increase, 50, 200, 1,200, increases, 50, 100, increases, 600, 800, the same as in A (because the multiplier depends on the slope of the aggregate expenditures function, which is the same in the two countries), less powerful.

Figure 17.2 Completed:

Aggregate Expenditures

A: i=5%

B: i=5%

A or B: i=10%

National Product

CHAPTER 18

FINE TUNING OR STABLE POLICY SETTINGS?

LEARNING OBJECTIVES

After you have studied this chapter in the textbook and study guide, you should be able to

✔ Describe the various steps in the active Keynesian approach to aggregate demand management

✔ Explain why lags make it difficult to stabilize aggregate demand through active management

✔ Explain the important role of potential GNP in the active approach

✔ Explain how problems in estimating potential were a major source of difficulty during the 1970s

✔ Explain the case for and the case against a discretionary policy

If your class covers the appendix, you should also be able to

✔ Explain why investment is much more volatile than consumption during the business cycle

✔ Explain why a moderate expansion may be more likely to last than a very rapid expansion

MAJOR PURPOSE

This chapter deals with the one of the major, continuing controversies in macroeconomics: Should aggregate demand policies be adjusted as conditions change, or should the Fed follow a monetary policy rule? On the one side are those in the Keynesian tradition, who argue that aggregate demand should be *actively managed* in pursuit of the goals of high employment and stable prices. On the other side are the monetarists, who generally favor a rule: The Fed should aim for a slow, *steady increase in the money stock*. No matter how well

intentioned the authorities, they do not know enough to stabilize the economy. Discretionary policies do not work in practice. So say the monetarists.

This debate has been dominated by strong advocates of rules on the one hand, and strong opponents on the other. One of the major conclusions of this chapter is that the question before us is not really whether we should chose a rigid, permanent rule that would be followed without regard to "how the chips" fall. There is no way that future policymakers could be bound firmly to such a rule. (Even if it were feasible to enshrine a policy rule in the Constitution, the Constitution could be amended again.) There is, however, a *very* important policy issue which remains—even if rigid, permanent rules are discarded as a logical impossibility. The issue is: Should policies be adjusted frequently in the light of unfolding conditions? Or would we be better off to aim for a stable growth of the money stock and make adjustments only rarely, when very strong evidence for a change accumulates? Unfortunately, the experience of the past quarter century does not provide a clear answer. Sometimes discretionary policies have worked quite well; sometimes they have not. The ambiguous lesson of history is, of course, one of the reasons why the controversy continues.

HIGHLIGHTS OF CHAPTER

Keynes and his followers argued that the government has the responsibility to maintain full employment and reasonably stable prices. Particularly in the early years between 1935 and 1965, Keynesians believed that an untended market economy would suffer from two major problems: Aggregate demand would often be:

- inadequate, and

- unstable.

Authorities should actively intervene to bring **aggregate demand** up to the full employment level, and then manage it on a continuing basis to offset forces of instability.

This idea was particularly influential during the 1960s, a decade that has sometimes been called the "Age of Keynes." Figure 18-1 in the textbook illustrates the general Keynesian demand-management strategy; Figure 18-2 presents the same idea as it was applied in the early 1960s. There were several major steps in bringing aggregate demand up to the full-employment level:

- First, the path of potential GNP was estimated.

- Next, forecasts were made of where actual GNP would go in the absence of policy changes; in other words, the size of the prospective GNP gap was estimated.

- Finally, fiscal and monetary policies were adjusted with the objective of closing the gap in a reasonably brief period.

Until 1965-1966, this strategy was very successful. The estimated GNP gap closed and prices remained reasonably stable. However, by the late 1960s, inflation was accelerating. This was only partly the result of failures in economic analysis. Even more fundamentally, it was a result of political problems that delayed a change in policies. By the mid 1960s, the Council of Economic Advisers was becoming concerned with the growing inflationary pressures. They recommended to President Johnson that taxes be increased in order to restrain aggregate demand and thus reduce inflationary pressures. President Johnson waited several years before actually recommending a tax increase to Congress; he was reluctant to ask the public to pay higher taxes to finance an unpopular war. This was just one extreme example of the problem of lags.

Critics of active management make five major arguments:

- *Lags* in the operation of policies mean that the government, like the panicky helmsman, may overreact to current events.

- Because of lags, policies developed today must be designed to deal with problems several months in the future. But economists are *only moderately successful in their ability to forecast* either the probable course of the economy in the absence of policy changes, or the effects of policy changes themselves.

- *Prices respond even more slowly* than real output when monetary and fiscal policies are changed. As a consequence, there may be an *inflationary bias* to discretionary policies. Decision makers may choose expansionary policies for the short-run benefits of higher output, and worry later about the inflationary consequences.

- Activists may *overestimate potential GNP*. As a result, they may strive to achieve an unattainable goal, creating strong inflationary pressures in the process. Figure 18-4 in the textbook illustrates this argument in general terms; Figure 18-5 applies it to the 1970s.

- The active management of aggregate demand means government meddling in the economy; rules are more consistent with *economic freedom* than are discretionary policies.

Advocates of rules recognize, of course, that it is important to pick the correct rule—one that is consistent with economic stability. It simply won't do to pick any old rule. Some seemingly plausible rules would be a mistake.

For example, the gold standard rule made the banking system vulnerable to runs; it added to the banking chaos of 1931-1933. However, proponents of rules believe that if the money stock were increased at a slow, steady rate, the economy would be more stable than it has been in the past, when proponents of active demand management were in charge. The proposal for a slow, steady increase in the money stock is based directly on the quantity theory of money — that is, on the view that velocity V is stable. If V is in fact stable, then a stable increase in M will mean a stable increase in nominal income PQ.

Opponents of a monetary rule emphasize three points:

- The government would be foolish to adopt rigid rules that may become outdated as circumstances change in unforeseen ways. Indeed, a truly rigid rule is a *logical impossibility*. Future decision makers cannot be bound inflexibly by the present. The *real issue is one of degree:* Will policies be adjusted in the light of a moderate amount of new information, or will policy changes be postponed until the evidence becomes overwhelming? While advocates of policy rules are correct in pointing out that lags create difficulties for discretionary policies, their proposals would increase lags in a major way. The government would be so committed to a course of action that it would not change policy until conditions became very bad indeed.

- There is no guarantee that stable monetary growth will lead to a stable increase in aggregate demand. In the period since 1975, there have been major, unpredictable changes in velocity. For example, there was an abnormal rise in velocity in 1975 a nd 1978 and a sharp decline in 1982. The slowdown in velocity in 1982 made the recession deeper and led the Fed to increase its target for monetary growth. Earlier, in 1979, the Fed had moved toward the monetarist posi-

tion in order to fight inflation more vigorously. In 1982, the Fed backed away from this position in order to combat the recession. It was persuaded to change its monetary target by a moderate amount of evidence — quite rightly so, said the critics of rules.

- The rule advocated by monetarists — a slow, steady growth in the money stock — may lead to aggregate demand that is too low to buy the increasing volume of goods and services that the economy is capable of producing. In other words, the adoption of a rule aimed at slow growth of demand and stable prices may result in high unemployment and slow growth of real output.

Note the contrast between this last point and the fourth point in the earlier list of the criticisms of fine tuning. There is a significant difference in the approach of the two groups to the problems of inflation and unemployment. Advocates of discretionary policies consider monetarists heartless in their willingness to accept unemployment; monetarists consider some Keynesians to be crude inflationists.

As noted earlier, forecasting is required for the implementation of discretionary policies. Some forecasting, either formal or informal, is also needed by businesses that are planning their investment programs. Economic forecasters often use *econometric models*, modified by the results from surveys and the judgment of the forecaster. The record of forecasters is fair. It is much better than would come from a very simple approach, such as projecting the trends of the previous year or so. However, forecasters have not done a very good job in anticipating recessions. In particular, they substantially underestimated the depth of the severe recessions of 1974 and 1982. This is worrisome to the advocates of active demand management. It is particularly important to anticipate recessions, in order to be able to shift to more expansive policies in a timely manner.

IMPORTANT TERMS

Match the first column with the corresponding phrase in the second column.

_____ 1. Potential GNP
_____ 2. GNP gap
_____ 3. V
_____ 4. Policy rule
_____ 5. Recognition lag
_____ 6. Action lag
_____ 7. Impact lag

a. From time weakness begins until time it is recognized
b. If this isn't stable, money rule won't work
c. From time policy is changed until aggregate demand responds
d. Aggregate demand policies are aimed at eliminating this
e. From time weakness is regognized until policies are changed
f. Keep money growth low and stable
g. Target path for those who manage aggregate demand

TRUE-FALSE

T   F   1.   Monetarists advocate that the Federal Reserve aim for a slow, steady increase in the quantity of money.

T   F   2.   Those who advocate activist Keynesian demand-management policies are led by the logic of their position to make an estimate of potential GNP.

T   F   3.   The case for active, discretionary monetary and fiscal policies would be stronger if economists could forecast better.

T   F   4.   The "action lag" is the interval between the time when action is taken, and when the action has its effect on aggregate demand.

T   F   5.   The "recognition lag" is the interval between the time when a problem is recognized and the time when corrective action is taken.

T   F   6.   The inflation rate is a leading indicator.

T   F   7.   If the rate of increase in productivity unexpectedly falls, potential GNP is likely as a result to be overestimated.

T   F   8.   The Council of Economic Advisers overestimated potential GNP by a greater amount in the 1970s than in the 1960s.

T   F   9.   If the potential GNP path is overestimated, active demand managers are likely as a consequence to follow overly stimulative demand management policies.

T   F   10. Because of the errors in estimating potential GNP during the 1970s, almost all economists now believe in a monetary policy rule.

MULTIPLE CHOICE

1. An economist is most likely to favor discretionary aggregate demand policies, rather than a policy rule, if he or she is in which economic tradition?

   a. Keynesian
   b. classical
   c. monetarist
   d. marginalist
   e. libertarian

2. Economists who argue for a policy rule aimed at stabilizing aggregate demand are most likely to favor which rule?

   a. the gold standard
   b. a balanced actual budget
   c. a balanced full-employment budget
   d. a steady growth in the money stock
   e. all the above rules are equally good; the thing that matters is to have *some* rule

3. Milton Friedman is the most famous monetarist. He argues that:

   a. monetary policy should be actively managed to stabilize aggregate demand, but the budget should be kept in balance
   b. the government's budget has no major effect on aggregate demand or on the allocation of resources
   c. both monetary and fiscal policies should be actively managed to stabilize aggregage demand
   d. active monetary and fiscal policies have both been oversold as a way of managing aggregate demand
   e. active monetary policy is the best way to keep full employment without any major risk of inflation

4. Keynes was concerned that:

   a. aggregate demand would be too low, although it would generally be stable
   b. aggregate demand would be unstable, even though it would generally be high enough
   c. aggregate demand was likely to be both too low and unstable
   d. inadequate productive capacity would be the major macroeconomic disease
   e. productive capacity could be kept growing at an adequate rate only if income were redistributed toward those who already had high incomes

5. The discretionary aggregate demand policies followed during the 1960s were aimed primarily at:

   a. increasing the GNP gap
   b. increasing potential GNP
   c. increasing real GNP
   d. increasing prices
   e. reducing prices

6. The discretionary policies of the 1960s involved each of the following steps *except one*. Which is the exception?

   a. estimate potential GNP
   b. forecast the probable course of GNP in the absence of policy changes
   c. forecast the effects of various changes in aggregate demand policies
   d. select the policies aimed at closing the GNP gap in a reasonably brief time
   e. revise the potential GNP path upward, since an even better performance now becomes possible

7. Suppose that the Council of Economic Advisers forecasts a GNP gap of $100 billion for the coming year if no change is made in policies. Then an advocate of:

   a. rules would prescribe a faster growth in the quantity of money
   b. rules would prescribe a faster growth in government spending
   c. active management would prescribe an increase in tax rates, to balance the budget
   d. active management would prescribe an increase in government spending
   e. active management would prescribe an increase in government spending to increase real output, plus a decrease in the money stock to reduce inflation

8. The recognition lag is the lag between the time when

   a. a problem is recognized and the time when corrective action is taken
   b. a problem is recognized and the time when it is corrected
   c. a recession begins and the time when the authorities recognize it has begun
   d. aggregate demand increases and the time when producers recognize that they can raise their prices
   e. aggregate demand increases and producers recognize that they should produce more

9. The time between the beginning of a downturn and the adoption of expansive aggregate demand policies is equal to the:

   a. recognition lag
   b. action lag
   c. recognition lag + the action lag
   d. impact lag
   e. recognition lag + the action lag + the impact lag

10. Monetarists criticize the activist approach to aggregate demand management on the ground that

   a. lags between changes in policy and changes in demand cause policy mistakes
   b. the inflationary effects of an increase in aggregate demand lag after the real output effects; as a result, aggregate demand is stimulated too much and too long in many expansions
   c. aggregate demand managers tend to be too ambitious
   d. all of the above
   e. none of the above

11. The "helmsman's dilemma" illustrates the difficulty of making policy in the presence of:

   a. inflation
   b. deflation
   c. unemployment
   d. low growth
   e. lags

12. Those who advocate policy rules rather than active management argue that active managers tend to:

   a. overestimate potential, and therefore follow inflationary policies
   b. underestimate potential, and therefore follow deflationary policies

   c. underestimate growth, and therefore follow inflationary policies
   d. underestimate the effects of government spending, and therefore rely too much on monetary policy
   e. underestimate the effects of tax changes, and therefore rely too much on monetary policy

13. Sometimes, "everything seems to be going wrong" — that is, output is falling, unemployment rising, and the rate of inflation rising. This is most likely to occur:

   a. early in an expansion
   b. late in an expansion, about 3 or 4 months before the peak
   c. early in a recession
   d. late in a recession, about 3 or 4 months before the trough
   e. at the trough of a recession

14. Potential GNP is most likely to be overestimated when

   a. productivity is improving at an unexpectedly rapid rate
   b. productivity is improving at an unexpectedly slow rate
   c. population is growing
   d. population is stable
   e. population is declining

15. The monetarist case is based on each of the following propositions *except one*. Which is the exception?

   a. the desirable path of aggregate demand is one of steady, moderate growth
   b. the desirable trend of prices is a gradual upward movement, by about 4% per year
   c. the best way to get a steady, moderate increase in aggregate demand is by a steady, moderate increase in the money stock
   d. following a monetary rule increases economic freedom, and probably political freedom, too

16. Opponents of a monetary rule argue that there cannot in fact be a rigid rule because

   a. it would be unconstitutional
   b. the Fed in fact has almost no control over the money stock
   c. money does not affect aggregate demand
   d. money does not affect interest rates
   e. future governments cannot be committed to a rule regardless of the consequences

17. Activists criticize "policy rules" on the ground that

    a. most advocates of policy rules would settle for a rate of growth of aggregate demand that is too low, and a rate of unemployment that is too high

    b. most advocates of policy rules concentrate on fiscal policy, and ignore monetary policy

    c. most advocates of rules concentrate on changes in government spending, and ignore the effects of changes in tax rates

    d. all of the above

    e. none of the above

18. In the face of a large and predictable decrease in V, the best policy for the Federal Reserve is to

    a. increase M

    b. decrease M

    c. increase Q

    d. decrease Q

    e. increase P

19. Suppose that $C = 0.5$ GNP; $I^*_g = 500$; $G = 700$; $X = 300$; and imports are 10% of GNP. Then equilibrium GNP equals

    a. 2,500

    b. 3,000

    c. 3,750

    d. 3,950

    e. 5,200

20. Which of the following is the best leading indicator

    a. increases in the rate of inflation during expansions

    b. decreases in the rate of inflation during recessions

    c. any increases in the rate of inflation during a recession, because this signals a coming expansion

    d. new orders for durable goods

    e. deliveries of durable goods

EXERCISE

1. There are three lags before monetary and fiscal policies affect aggregate demand. First is the _____ lag, next the _____ lag, and then the _____ lag. In addition, there is another lag that occurs after aggregate demand changes. Specifically, the effects of demand on (output, prices) generally lags behind its effect on (output, prices). Critics of active demand management argue that the first set of lags means that policies may destabilize the economy. The second set means that discretionary policies can have an (inflationary, deflationary) bias.

Lags are, however, not the only problem facing the managers of aggregate demand. They also have the difficult task of estimating (the path of potential GNP, the effects of monetary policy on demand, the effects of fiscal policy on demand, all of these). Suppose they overestimate the potential path. This means that, starting from a recession, they are likely to (keep expansive policies too long, abandon expansive policies too soon). The reason is that (the economy will remain below the estimated potential path, they will soon give up trying). As a result, the problem of (inflation, low growth) may become worse.

ESSAY QUESTIONS

1. Suppose that a 4% monetary rule were adopted. Then suppose that the introduction of an electronic transfer system for making payments caused a large increase in the velocity of money. What would happen to the price level? Could this have been avoided if the rule hadn't been adopted? Can you think of a rule that would allow for such contingencies?

2. Presidents have objectives in addition to their economic goals — for example, national defense and getting reelected. How do these other goals strengthen or weaken the case for discretionary policies, rather than a monetary rule?

3. A passage in the chapter highlights section reads as follows: "Advocates of discretionary policies consider monetarists heartless in their willingness to accept unemployment; monetarists consider some Keynesians to be crude inflationists." Explain why these criticisms are made. In the first case, what defense might a monetarist have? (Hint: does it depend on the aggregate supply function?) In the second case, what defense might a Keynesian have? (Hint: does it depend on the relative social costs of unemployment and inflation?)

ANSWERS

Important terms: **1 g, 2 d, 3 b, 4 f, 5 a, 6 e, 7 c**

True-False:
1 T (p. 313)
2 T (p. 314)
3 T (p. 315)
4 F (316)
5 F (p. 316)
6 F (p. 317)
7 T (p. 320)
8 T (p. 320)
9 T (p. 322)
10 F (p. 325)

Multiple Choice:
1 a (p. 313)
2 d (p. 313)
3 d (p. 314)
4 c (p. 314)
5 c (p. 314)
6 e (pp. 314-315)
7 d (Ch. 10 and p. 315)
8 c (p. 316)
9 c (p. 316)
10 d (pp. 315-320)
11 e (p. 317)
12 a (pp. 318-319)
13 c (p. 319)
14 b (p. 320)
15 b (p. 321)
16 e (p. 321)
17 a (p. 322)
18 a (p. 325)
19 a (p. 326)
20 d (p. 328 and throughout chapter)

Exercises

1.   recognition, action, impact, prices, output, inflationary, all of these, keep expansive policies too long, the economy will remain below the estimated potential path, inflation.

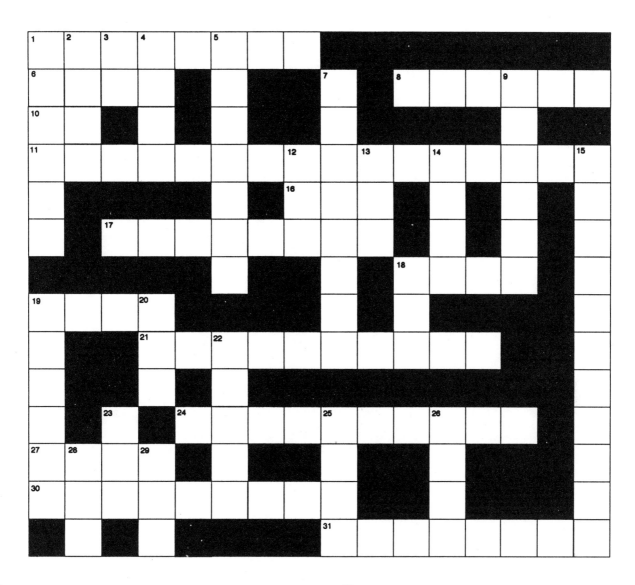

Across

1. someone to whom money is owed
6. holiday season
8. type of lag
10. a chemical element (abbrev.)
11. this is watched by forecasters (2 words)
16. this group has made projections of potential GNP (abbrev.)
17. the _____ of money is the key to aggregate demand, say the proponents of a monetary rule
18. transactions on the _____ market are a key to controlling the quantity of money
19. a healthy economy does this
21. policymakers want to keep this high
24. should we use this, or follow rules?
27. old
30. this level of GNP is sometimes used as a target
31. classical macroeconomics was built on the _____ of exchange

Down

1. demand management policy is aimed at reducing the amplitude of business _____
2. the alternative to active management
3. Keynesian aggregate supply reverses this
4. our condition in the long run, said Keynes
5., 22. peak or trough
7, 25. what monetarists have proposed
9. type of lag
12. here (French)
13. fraction of a week
14. applaud
15. type of lag
18. lengthy lyrical poem
19. eliminating this may be a policy objective (2 "words")
20. spider's home
23. at least six games of tennis
26. researchers should have this
28. U.S. political party (abbrev.)
29. animal's home

CHAPTER 19

FIXED OR FLEXIBLE EXCHANGE RATES?

LEARNING OBJECTIVES

After you have studied this chapter in the textbook and study guide, you should be able to

✔ Identify three sources of demand for a country's currency on the foreign exchange markets, and three sources of supply

✔ Describe four options open to a government when the demand or supply for its currency shifts

✔ Explain why intervention in the exchange market does not provide a permanent solution to disequilibrium in the foreign exchange market

✔ Describe the relationship between the gold stock and the money stock under the gold standard

✔ Describe the mechanism of adjustment under the gold standard, and explain why it is "automatic"

✔ Explain the two major shortcomings of the gold standard

✔ Describe how the "adjustable peg" worked

✔ Explain how problems can arise under the adjustable peg system if people doubt that the present pegged rate will be maintained

✔ Explain the advantages and disadvantages of flexible exchange rates

✔ Explain the ways in which the sharp rise of the dollar between 1981 and 1984 caused problems for the United States

MAJOR PURPOSE

The major purpose of this chapter is to explain the relationship between **international payments** and **macroeconomic policy**. This relationship depends to a considerable extent on the exchange rate system. Under the old **gold standard**, inflows and outflows of gold were a major reason for changes in the money stock, aggregate demand, prices, and unemployment. Changes in aggregate demand which resulted from gold flows were not necessarily best for the domestic economy. A deficit country might go through a painful *deflationary process*, with high unemployment. Under the International Monetary Fund (IMF) system, exchange rates were pegged, but a deficit country could escape the need for a painful deflation by devaluing its currency. The present system of **flexible exchange rates** provides countries with a **greater degree of independence** to follow the aggregate demand policies they think best for their domestic economies. However, problems can still be created by the relationship between domestic policies and international transactions. Large U.S. government deficits, combined with monetary restraint, led to high interest rates in the early 1980s, to a rise in the dollar on the international exchanges, and to severe competititive problems for a number of basic U.S. industries such as autos and steel.

HIGHLIGHTS OF CHAPTER

This chapter deals with the issue of whether a government should regulate the country's exchange rate, and, if so, how. The topic is developed by looking at three historical exchange rate arrangements: the **gold standard** of the 19th and early 20th century; the **pegged-but-adjustable** exchange rate system of 1945-71; and the recent sytem of **flexible** or **floating** exchange rates. As a preliminary topic, the chapter explains the foreign exchange market.

The Foreign Exchange Market

International trade differs from domestic trade for two main reasons:

- International trade must overcome barriers such as tariffs

- International trade involves two or more currencies (national monies).

As a result of the second complication, international trade leads to transactions in the *foreign exchange market*, where one national currency is bought in exchange for another.

Exchange rates are determined in the foreign exchange market. The demand for, say, Canadian dollars, arises when people offer foreign currencies in order to buy Canadian dollars. They want the Canadian dollars in order to buy

- Canada's exports of goods, such as automobiles and newsprint;

- Canadian services, such as hotel accommodations for tourists; and

- Canadian assets, such as Canadian government bonds or shares in Canadian nickel mines.

On the other side of the market, the supply of Canadian dollars arises when people offer Canadian dollars in order to buy foreign currencies. Canadians use foreign currencies to buy

- imports of goods;

- imports of services; and

- foreign assets.

An *exchange rate* is the price of one currency in terms of another. An exchange rate may be quoted either way. For example, $1 U.S. = $1.25 Can. is the same as $1 Can. = $0.80 U.S. To verify this, multiply each side of the first equation by four fifths and switch the two sides.

An equilibrium exchange rate is one at which the quantity of currency supplied is equal to the quantity demanded. When demand for a country's currency decreases (the demand curve shifts to the left), the government has four options:

- Buy the surplus the surplus quantity of the home currency at the existing exchange rate, in order to prevent the exchange rate from changing.

- Decrease the supply by direct actions, such as increasing tariffs or limiting the amount of foreign assets that citizens are permitted to acquire.

- Decrease the supply and increase the demand for the country's currency by more restrictive monetary and fiscal policies. By restraining aggregate demand, such policies will keep prices and incomes down, thereby reducing imports and stimulating exports.

- Let the price of the currency fall to its new equilibrium.

The first option is only a temporary expedient. If the shift in demand is permanent, a country will run out of foreign exchange reserves if it relies solely on this option.

The Gold Standard

The gold standard is an example of a fixed exchange rate system—that is, a system which fixes the exchange rates within narrow limits. If, for example, the pound is worth 4.86 times as much as the U.S. dollar, then nobody will pay much more than $4.86 for a pound, or sell it for much less.

Under the gold standard, there was an **automatic adjustment mechanism** ensuring that there would not be large, persistent internatonal imbalances, with one country ending up with all the gold and the others having none. Specifically, a country losing gold had an *automatic* decrease in its money stock for two reasons:

- Gold itself was one form of money; when gold coins left the country, the money was directly reduced.

- Gold was also a bank reserve.

When banks had smaller gold reserves, their ability to make loans was restricted. As we saw in Chapter 11, the ability of banks to make loans helps to determine the money stock.

The decline in the money stock was the first step in the adjustment process. The remaining steps were as follows: As the money supply fell, aggregate demand, incomes, and prices fell in the deficit countries. This made the country's goods more competitive on world markets, and its trade balance therefore improved. This process was aided by an automatic increase in money and inflation in the surplus countries. With prices rising in the surplus countries, it was even easier for the deficit countries to compete. This process—involving changes in the *relative prices* of the goods of the deficit and surplus countries—tended to continue until balance of payments deficits and surpluses were eliminated and gold flows stopped.

Observe that the gold system worked through changes in domestic demand—that is, the third option in the previous section (although the monetary policy worked automatically in the case of the gold standard). However, even though the gold standard worked to eliminate surpluses and deficits, it had two *major* defects:

- The automatic mechanism could be very costly for a country with a payments deficit because the monetary contraction could cause large-scale unemployment. On the other side, inflationary pressures could be generated in the surplus countries. That is, there could be a **conflict** between the policies needed for a stable domestic prosperity and the monetary changes needed to bring about balance-of-payments adjustment.

- The gold standard could lead to **very unstable** conditions, particularly if there was a run on the gold reserves of banks. This point was explained in detail in Chapter 12.

The Adjustable Peg, 1945-1971

Under the adjustable peg system:

- Countries intervened in their foreign exchange markets as necessary, to keep the exchange rate within 1% of an official "par value."

- Countries with temporary balance-of-payments deficits kept their exchange rates stable by selling reserves on the foreign exchange markets. Countries with temporary balance-of-payments surpluses kept their exchange rates stable by buying foreign currencies, thus increasing their foreign exchange reserves.

- Countries facing a long-term, *fundamental* disequilibrium were to change their official par values. The change in exchange rates would affect the prices of their goods on international markets, and help to eliminate international deficits or surpluses.

There were three major problems with the adjustable peg system:

- It was not clear how to distinguish between a "fundamental" disequilibrium and a "temporary" disequilibrium.

- If a government tried to hold its exchange rate close to the official par when *speculators* believed that there was a fundamental disequilibrium, speculators often made large profits at the government's expense. For example, when a country had a large balance-of-payments deficit, speculators would sell its currency in large quantities.

- The government would have to use its reserves of foreign exchange to buy up the excess supply of its currency, in order to maintain the peg. As reserves dwindled, this strategy became less and less tenable, and the government was forced to devalue. Speculators were able to benefit by selling high before the devaluation, and buying low after the devaluation. The government, however, lost: It bought high and sold low.

Pressures on the exchange rate system led to its abandonment in the early 1970s; most major countries allowed their currencies to float on the exchange market.

Flexible Exchange Rates

A flexible exchange rate is allowed to change in response to changes in the demand and supply for foreign currencies. Flexible exchange rates have a number of advantages:

- When pegged exchange rates break down, flexible rates may be the only feasible option. The lack of a good alternative may be the strongest argument for flexible exchange rates.

- They permit fiscal and monetary policies to be directed primarily toward the important goal of stabilizing the domestic economy, rather than toward maintaining the exchange rate.

- A country following stable domestic policies is insulated from foreign inflation (the *virtuous circle*).

The major disadvantages are:

- Changes in exchange rates may disrupt international trade and investment.

- Many of the large fluctuations in exchange rates since 1973 appear to have served no useful purpose; they have not been necessary to eliminate fundamental disequilibria. The rise in the dollar in the early 1980s put severe pressures on U.S. manufacturing firms, who were faced with very severe foreign competition.

- Depreciation of the currency adds to domestic inflation. A country can fall into a *vicious circle* of depreciation-inflation-depreciation-inflation.

Because of these disadvantages, some of the Western European nations set up the European Monetary System, which provides for pegged rates among their currencies. However, there is more flexibility in this sytem than in the earlier system of pegged rates. For example, rates do not have to be kept so close to the official value.

Recent Developments

The U.S. dollar has fluctuated widely since 1973. Between 1976 and 1978, as inflation accelerated in the United States, the dollar fell sharply on the exchange markets. Fearing that the country was falling into a vicious circle, the administration moved toward more restrained domestic policies.

Between 1980 and the beginning of 1985, the dollar moved much higher on the exchange markets. Large foreign purchases of U.S. assets were the major reason. The high price of the dollar made U.S. goods more expensive to foreigners, and made foreign goods cheaper to Americans buying with dollars. As a result, U.S. industry had difficulty exporting, and faced severe competition from imports into the domestic market.

One reason for foreign purchase of U.S. assets was the high level of U.S. interest rates, which in turn were partly attributable to large U.S. government deficits. Recall the discussion in Chapter 17 of how the government's deficits caused a rise in the exchange value of the dollar and a trade deficit.

IMPORTANT TERMS

Match the first column with the corresponding phrase in the second column.

_____ 1. Foreign exchange
_____ 2. Exchange rate
_____ 3. Par value
_____ 4. Fundamental disequilibrium
_____ 5. Foreign exchange reserves
_____ 6. Devaluation
_____ 7. Depreciation
_____ 8. Speculate
_____ 9. Dirty float

a. Reduction in the par value of a currency
b. Fall in the market price of a currency
c. Buy something in anticipation of a price rise
d. Occurs when governments intervene to influence price of currency
e. Money of another country
f. Officially-chosen exchange rate
g. Price of one currency in terms of another
h. Government's holdings of foreign currency
i. Reason for devaluation

TRUE-FALSE

T F 1. When the Japanese buy Saudi Arabian oil, this creates a supply of yen

T F 2. If the United States cuts its tariffs, this will lead to an increase in imports and an increase in the supply of dollars on the world market

T F 3. Under the gold standard, the adjustment mechanism worked primarily through changes in aggregate demand, not through changes in exchange rates

T F 4. Under the gold standard, a country was expected to change its par value in the event of a fundamental disequilibrium

T F 5. With a pegged exchange rate, sales of reserves are a good way to deal with international deficits, in both the short run and the long

T F 6. Under the pegged system of the IMF, a country was expected to change its par value in the event of a fundamental disequilibrium

T F 7. The gold standard was *automatic*; it would work without government intervention. This means that it was an example of a clean float.

T F 8. Under a pegged exchange rate system, when foreign exchange speculators make profits, governments generally lose

T F 9. By "self-fulfilling expectations," economists mean any speculation undertaken at the recommendation of government authorities.

T F 10. With a flexible exchange rate, central banks have more freedom to combat recessions than they do under the gold standard

MULTIPLE CHOICE

1. Which of the following is a source of *demand* for the U.S. dollar on the foreign exchange markets?

   a. purchases of foreign currencies by the Federal Reserve
   b. U.S. demand for foreign goods
   c. U.S. demand for foreign services
   d. U.S. investment in foreign countries
   e. foreign demand for U.S. exports

2. Which of the following leads to a decline in the demand for British pounds on the foreign exchange markets?

   a. a decrease in British purchases of German chemicals
   b. an increase in the number of U.S. tourists in Britain
   c. a switch by U.S. consumers from British to Japanese cars
   d. an increase in U.S. purchases of British cars
   e. an increase in British sales of textiles to the United States

3. Under the old gold standard, an inflow of gold into the United States worked to:

   a. automatically increase the U.S. money stock
   b. increase the U.S. money stock, but only if the Fed engaged in open market purchases of government securities
   c. automatically decrease the U.S. money stock
   d. decrease the U.S. money stock, but only if the Fed sold government securities on the open market at the same time
   e. automatically increase the U.S. government's deficit

4. Under the old gold standard system, an inflow of gold into the United States caused what sequence of events?

   a. an increase in the U.S. money stock, an increase in the U.S. price level, and an increase in U.S. exports
   b. an increase in the U.S. money stock, an increase in the U.S. price level, and an increase in U.S. imports
   c. an increase in the U.S. money stock, an increase in the U.S. price level, and an increase in spending by foreign visitors to the United States
   d. an increase in the U.S. money stock, an increase

   in the U.S. price level, and a decrease in spending by U.S. visitors to foreign countries
   e. an increase in the U.S. money stock, an increase in the budget deficits of the U.S. government, and an increase in U.S. exports of goods

5. Under the old gold standard, a country faced a *conflict* between the policies needed for domestic stability and those needed for international adjustment when:

   a. it was losing gold and was in a recession
   b. it was gaining gold and was in a recession
   c. its prices were rising and its tariffs were also rising
   d. its unemployment rate was high
   e. its inflation rate was high

6. Under the original IMF system (prior to 1971), the par value of a currency was:

   a. the value of the currency whenever central banks kept bond prices stable
   b. the value of the currency whenever central banks followed a monetary rule
   c. the official price of the currency, usually specified in terms of the U.S. dollar
   d. the value of the currency when policies were up to par, and inflation was low
   e. the value of the currency when policies were up to par, and both inflation and unemployment were low

7. From time to time, speculation a major problem under the adjustable peg system of the early IMF. The major cause of severe speculation was

   a. the wildly fluctuating price of government securities
   b. the wildly fluctuating price of gold
   c. the wild upward and downward movements in the price of oil
   d. speculators would win if the par value were changed, but would not lose much if the par value were held
   e. speculators would win if the IMF made loans to a country to help it maintain the par value of its currency

8. Suppose that a British machine costs £400,000, while the exchange rate is £1 = $2.00. Then the price of that machine, in dollars, is:

a. $800,000
b. $600,000
c. $400,000
d. $200,000
e. $100,000

9. Under the IMF system of adjustable pegs, one problem was that of "self-fulfilling expectations." This meant that:

a. when countries expected to have surpluses, they in fact had them
b. when countries expected to have deficits, they in fact had them
c. when officials expected to avoid a devaluation, they usually succeeded, because of the power of positive thinking
d. when speculators thought that a currency might be devalued, they sold it, increasing the probability that it would in fact have to be devalued
e. when speculators thought that a currency might be devalued, they bought it, increasing the probability that it would in fact have to be devalued

10. Under the IMF system of adjustable pegs, some countries followed "stop-go" aggregate demand policies. A major reason for this was:

a. the short-run Phillips curve sloped upward to the right with a pegged exchange rate; this meant that authorities had to switch policies often
b. the short-run Phillips curve sloped upward to the right with a pegged exchange rate; this meant that authorities had to follow a monetary rule
c. the short-run Phillips curve sloped upward to the right with a pegged exchange rate; this meant that authorities had to rely on monetary policy rather than fiscal policy
d. the short-run Phillips curve sloped upward to the right with a pegged exchange rate; this meant that authorities had to rely on fiscal policy rather than monetary policy
e. a country might restrict aggregate demand when it was losing foreign exchange reserves, and switch to expansive ("go") policies when the balance of payments improved

11. A "dirty float" is called "dirty" because:

a. it is unfair to foreign countries
b. it is unfair to exporters
c. it is unfair to importers
d. it is not "clean;" that is, the central bank intervenes in exchange markets to influence exchange rates
e. it is not "clean;" that is, the central bank departs from the rule of aiming for a steady growth in the money stock

12. Under a flexible exchange rate system, which of the following would be a "vicious circle" for the United States?

a. U.S. inflation causes an appreciation of the dollar on the exchange markets, which causes higher U.S. inflation, which causes more appreciation of the dollar
b. U.S. inflation causes a depreciation of the dollar on the exchange markets, which causes higher U.S. inflation, which causes more depreciation of the dollar
c. higher U.S. interest rates lead to a depreciation of the dollar, which causes even higher interest rates
d. lower U.S. interest rates lead to an appreciation of the dollar, which causes even lower interest rates
e. lower U.S. interest rates lead to an appreciation of the dollar, which causes U.S. interest rates to rebound sharply

13. Suppose that the price of the U.S. dollar rises on the foreign exchange markets. This will:

a. encourage U.S. exports, and slow down inflation in the United States
b. discourage U.S. exports, and make inflation worse in the United States
c. discourage U.S. exports, and slow down inflation in the United States
d. encourage U.S. exports, and make inflation worse in the United States
e. encourage U.S. exports, and ease the U.S. problem of unemployment

14. Suppose that an exchange rate between the United States and Britain is initially in equilibrium, at £1 = $2.00. Now, suppose that domestic prices in the United States double while domestic prices in Britain remain constant. Then, according to the purchasing-power parity theory, the new equilibrium exchange rate will be:

a. £1 = $1.00
b. between 1 = $1.00 and £1 = $2.00, but we can't say exactly where
c. still at £1 = $2.00
d. between £1 = $2.00 and £1 = $4.00, but we can't say exactly where
e. £1 = $4.00

15. Which of the following discourage exports of U.S. goods, and encourage imports of foreign goods into the United States:

a. U.S. inflation and a depreciation of the dollar
b. foreign inflation and a depreciation of the dollar
c. U.S. inflation and an appreciation of the dollar
d. foreign inflation and an appreciation of the dollar
e. a depreciation of the dollar, and an appreciation of foreign currencies

16. Between 1981 and 1985, when the U.S. dollar was rising strongly on the international exchanges:

a. foreigners were acquiring U.S. assets, and the U.S. was running a trade surplus
b. Americans were acquiring foreign assets, and the U.S. was running a trade surplus
c. foreigners were acquiring U.S. assets, and the U.S. was running a trade deficit
d. Americans were acquiring foreign assets, and the U.S. was running a trade deficit
e. changes in exchange rates encouraged more foreigners to visit the United States

17. U.S. macroeconomic policies contributed to the sharp rise in the exchange value of the U.S. dollar between 1980 and 1984. Specifically:

a. expansive monetary and fiscal policies made U.S. inflation higher, and this strengthened the dollar
b. the combination of government deficits and monetary restraint resulted in high interest rates, which encouraged foreigners to buy U.S. assets
c. the combination of government surpluses and monetary restraint resulted in high interest rates, which encouraged foreigners to buy U.S. assets
d. the combination of government surpluses and monetary restraint resulted in low interest rates, which encouraged investment in the United States
e. the combination of government deficits and monetary restraint resulted in low interest rates, which encouraged investment in the United States

18. In the European Monetary System (EMS), exchange rates among the Western European currencies are:

a. permanently fixed, because the gold standard was restored for transactions within Europe
b. permanently fixed by a new international bank that coordinates monetary policies among the European member nations
c. pegged-but-adjustable, with wider bands than under the old IMF system
d. pegged-but-adjustable, with narrower bands than under the old IMF system
e. freely flexible

Note: the following two questions are based on the appendix

19. In the balance of payments of the United States, exports of U.S. goods to Japan are entered as a:

a. positive item
b. negative item
c. long-term capital account item
d. short-term capital account item
e. change in reserve

20. In the balance of payments accounts of the United States, an increase in U.S. official reserve holdings of German marks is entered as:

a. a positive item
b. a negative item
c. a current account item
d. a statistical discrepancy
e. direct investment

EXERCISES

1. The data in Table 19.1 describe the demand and supply of pounds in the foreign exchange market. Plot the demand and supply curves in Figure 19.1, and label the demand curve D1.

Table 19.1

Exchange rate ($ per £)	Quantity demanded (millions of £)	Quantity supplied (millions of £)
$1.25	100	40
$1.50	90	50
$1.75	80	60
$2.00	70	70
$2.25	60	80
$2.50	50	90
$2.75	40	100
$3.00	30	110
$3.25	20	120

a. The equilibrium exchange rate is $ _____ per pound, or _____ per dollar. The equilibrium quantity of pounds sold is _____ million, in exchange for $ _____ million.

b. Suppose now that the demand for pounds decreases by £20 million at each exchange rate. Plot the new demand curve, and label it D_2. The new equilibrium exchange rate is $ _____ per pound. The equilibrium quantity of pounds sold is now £ _____ million, in exchange for

Figure 19.1

$ per £

$ _____ million. If the British government wanted to hold the exchange rate at its *previous* equilibrium (in part a), it would have to (buy, sell) £ _____ million on the foreign exchange markets; that is, it would have to (buy, sell) $ _____ million.

ESSAY QUESTIONS

1. Suppose that, under the adjustable peg, the British government announced that it was going to devalue the pound by 10% in one week. How would this affect the demand and/or supply of pounds today? What would happen to the British government's holdings of dollar reserves? Would there be much risk in speculating today in the market for pounds? Why or why not? Would the government in fact be able to wait for a week before devaluing? Why or why not?

2. In early 1969, there was a public controversy between the German central bank (which wanted to raise the par value of the DM) and the German government (which didn't). What effect do you think this had on exchange markets? Why do you think the central bank took the position that it did? Why do you think the government took the position that it did?

3. Explain how a country might fall into a "vicious circle." Now suppose that the world has only two countries, and they are approximately the same size. If one country is in a "vicious circle," will the other country also be in a "vicious circle" too, or will it be in a "virtuous circle?" Why?

4. Many people believe that there is a relationship between the two large U.S. deficits of the early 1980s — the U.S. government deficits, and the U.S. deficit in international trade. How might one cause the other?

ANSWERS

Important terms: **1** e, **2** g, **3** f, **4** i, **5** h, **6** a, **7** b, **8** c, **9** d

True-False: **1 T** (p. 341)
2 T (p. 341)
3 T (p. 343)
4 F (p. 343)
5 F (p. 344)
6 T (p. 345)
7 F (p. 346)
8 T (p. 346)
9 F (p. 346)
10 T (p. 347)

Multiple Choice: **1 e** (p. 341)
2 c (pp. 341-342)
3 a (p. 343)
4 b (p. 343)
5 a (p. 343)
6 c (p. 344)
7 d (p. 345)
8 a
9 d (p. 346)
10 e (p. 346)
11 d (p. 346)
12 b (p. 347)
13 c (p. 348)
14 e (p. 348)
15 c (p. 350)
16 c (p. 350)
17 b (p. 350)
18 c (p. 352)
19 a (p. 355, appendix)
20 b (p. 356, appendix)

Exercises

1   a. $2.00, £0.50, £70 m, $140 m.
     b. $1.75, £60 m, $105 m, buy, £20 m., sell, $40 m.

Figure 19.1 completed:

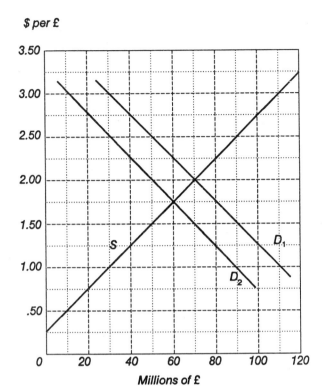

$ per £

Millions of £

Part 6

THE FOUNDATIONS OF MICROECONOMICS:
The Consumer And The Firm

APPLICATIONS OF DEMAND AND SUPPLY: *The Concept Of Elasticity*

LEARNING OBJECTIVES

After you have studied this chapter in the textbook and the study guide, you should be able to

✔ Define and calculate elasticity of demand and elasticity of supply

✔ Describe how a move to a lower point on a demand curve may increase or decrease the total revenue from the sale of a product, depending on the elasticity of demand

✔ Compare the elasticity of two demand curves that pass through the same point, showing why the flatter one is more elastic, and explain why flatness and elasticity are *not* the same when curves *do not* pass through the same point

✔ List four factors that increase the elasticity of demand for a good

✔ List three factors that increase the elasticity of supply for a good

✔ Show how a straight-line supply that is elastic will, when extended, intersect the vertical axis, while a supply that is inelastic will intersect the horizontal axis

✔ Explain how an excise tax will affect buyers and sellers of a good, and why the group that is most sensitive to price (most elastic in its response to a price change) will be able to push the burden of the tax onto the other group

✔ Understand how the government's ability to raise revenue with an excise tax depends on the elasticity of demand and supply for the good being taxed

✔ Show the effects of rent control

✔ Explain why the elasticity of foreign demand for U.S. goods is lower in the short run than in the long run

✔ Define and calculate the income elasticity of demand and the cross elasticity of demand

MAJOR PURPOSE

In this chapter, we begin the detailed study of microeconomics by picking up the supply and demand curves developed in Chapter 4. In that earlier analysis, we saw how a demand curve describes how buyers increase their purchases of a product if its price falls. For some products, this response by buyers will be very strong; for others it may be weak. To illustrate, visualize two demand curves with different slopes that pass through the same point. The flatter one describes buyers who are sensitive to price; they buy much more when price falls. On the other hand, the steeper demand curve describes buyers who are less responsive to price; the amount they buy changes relatively little as price falls. In this chapter we develop a measure—called the *elasticity of demand*—to describe this responsiveness of buyers to price.

A similar concept—*supply elasticity*—is developed to measure the responsiveness of sellers to price. An important question is then addressed: "Why are demand and supply elastic in some cases, but inelastic in others?" Finally, this chapter includes illustrations of how important elasticity may be in answering policy questions such as: Who bears the burden of a sales tax on a product—the buyers or sellers? How much revenue will the treasury raise from this tax? and What are the short-run and long-run effects of rent control?

HIGHLIGHTS OF CHAPTER

In developing demand curves in Chapter 4, it was argued that they slope downward to the right. However, little was said about how steep or flat they may be; or more precisely, about how responsive buyers might be to a change in price. Similarly, in developing supply curves, little was said about how responsive sellers might be. For many problems that can be analyzed with supply and demand curves, it is important to have a simple and handy

description of this sensitivity of buyers or sellers to price. Elasticity is such a measure.

Elasticity of Demand

This is defined as

$$\text{elasticity of demand} = \frac{\%\ \text{change in quantity demanded}}{\%\ \text{change in price}} \qquad (1)$$

To illustrate this formula, suppose that, as a result of a shift in the supply of a good to the right, equilibrium moves downward to the right along the demand curve. With the decrease in the per unit price (the denominator above), there is an increase in the amount demanded (the numerator). If these two are equal—that is, if the price and the quantity demanded change at the same rate, then the elasticity of demand in equation (1) above is equal to 1. Moreover, the *total payment buyers make to sellers does not change*. To see why this is so, suppose that when the price P paid by buyers falls by 20%, the quantity Q that they purchase rises at the same rate. Then the decrease in P is offset by the increase in Q, and there is no change in P times Q, the total payment made by buyers. This is the first conclusion: When the elasticity of demand is 1, there is no change in the total payment by buyers—that is, in the total revenue received by sellers.

Now suppose buyers are *more responsive* to a price change—as in panel *a* of Figure 20.1 below where the quantity they demand increases by 200% (from 400 to 1,200 units) when the price falls by 25% (from $8 to $6). In this case, demand elasticity exceeds 1 in equation (1) above, and there is an *increase* in PQ, the total revenue received by sellers from buyers. In this case, demand is described as "elastic".

Figure 20.1

(a) Elastic demand

(b) Inelastic demand

In panel *b* of Figure 20.1, buyers are *less responsive* to a price change: The quantity demanded increases by only 25% when the price falls by 50%. This is the unresponsive, inelastic case; the elasticity ratio in equation (1) above is less than 1, and there is a *decrease* in the total revenue received by sellers. Before you leave Figure 20.1, it is essential that you are comfortable with the way elasticity and total revenue are related.

In that diagram, slope and elasticity seem to be closely related: The flatter curve in panel *a* is the more elastic. Is this generally true? The answer is yes — but *only if* the two curves being compared pass through the same point. (In Figure 20.1, the common point is A.)

Once you have mastered these simple and essential ideas of elasticity, return to pages 365 and 366 in the text and ensure you understand why, in actual calculations, the midpoint formula should be used.

Elasticity of Supply

This can also be calculated, using a ratio like the one in the equation above. The only difference is the obvious one — quantity demanded is replaced with quantity supplied.

$$\text{Elasticity of supply} = \frac{\text{\% change in quantity supplied}}{\text{\% change in price}} \qquad (2)$$

Whereas elasticity of demand has an important "total revenue" interpretation, elasticity of supply does not. The reason is that a move upward and to the right on *any* supply curve — regardless of its elasticity — will increase total revenue. The one intuitive interpretation of elasticity of supply is this: If a straight-line supply curve passes through the origin, it has an elasticity of supply of 1. If it intersects the vertical axis it is elastic and if it intersects the horizontal axis it is inelastic.

What Determines Demand and Supply Elasticity?

Demand elasticity tends to be greater if

- the product is a luxury rather than a necessity;

- it is a large item in purchasers' budgets rather than a small one;

- it is easy for buyers to replace it with substitutes in consumption;

- we are considering the long-run, rather than the short-run demand.

The elasticity of supply tends to be greater if

- the commodity can be inexpensively stored — that is, if it is not perishable and has low storage costs;
- it is easy for it to be replaced with substitutes in production;
- we are considering the long-run, rather than the short-run supply.

One of the most important of these influences on both supply and demand is time — the short run versus the long run. The reason is simple: If people — whether they are consumers or producers — are given a longer time to adjust to a change in price, they will be able to do more adjusting than if they are only given a short time.

Using Elasticity to Analyze the Burden of a Tax

The first important application of the concept of elasticity is in analyzing whether buyers or sellers bear the burden of a commodity tax. The conclusion from this analysis is important because it applies to any marketplace where two groups face each other, with buyers on the one hand and sellers on the other. The 'inelastic' group that can't back away from the market but must complete the transaction almost without regard to price, will bear more of the burden of a new tax or any other similar disturbance than will the more "elastic group" that is prepared to resist a price change by backing away from the market.

Using Elasticity to Analyze the Amount of Revenue that will be Raised by a Sales Tax

A sales tax will raise the price of the good to buyers, and lower the price received by sellers. Thus typically both are hurt by the price change. If demand and supply are elastic, both buyers and sellers will be sensitive to this price change and will be willing to reduce their purchases and sales. Therefore, the quantity that will be sold will be substantially reduced. The government's revenue (which is this quantity times the tax) will be disappointing.

If demand and supply are inelastic, then buyers and sellers won't substantially cut back their purchases and sales. The quantity sold will not be reduced very much, and government revenues will not be disappointing.

Rent Control

The key issue here is that the supply of apartments is inelastic in the short run, but more elastic in the long run. When the government keeps rents — the price of apartments — below the market equilibrium, the inelastic short run supply means that there will only be a small reduction in the supply of apartments. But in the long run, the more elastic supply means that there will be an even greater reduction in the supply of rental apartments and thus an even more severe shortage. (New apartments won't be built, and some existing ones may be turned into condominiums — that is, sold to new owners who then occupy them and thus take them out of the rental market.)

When rent controls are removed, there is an initial large increase in rents because short run supply is inelastic; there is not yet time for new apartments to be built. Once new apartments are built — that is, once the supply becomes more elastic in the long run — the new units coming into the market will moderate the price increase and eliminate the shortage. Thus tenants benefit in the long run. The problem is: How can a government survive the short run when rents take a big jump? One answer is for the government to gradually phase out controls.

Income Elasticity of Demand and Cross Elasticity of Demand

Just as *price elasticity* of demand measures how much the quantity demanded will respond to *a change in price*, the *income elasticity* of demand measures how much the quantity demanded will respond to a *change in income*, and the *cross elasticity* of demand measures how much the quantity demanded of X will respond to a *change in the price of Y*.

All three of these measures can be described in the following way:

$$\frac{\% \text{ change in quantity demanded of X}}{\% \text{ change in whatever is influencing it}} \quad (3)$$

If the influence on demand in the denominator is the *price* of X, this ratio becomes the *price* elasticity of demand. If the influence in the denominator is *income*, this ratio becomes the *income* elasticity of demand. If the influence in the denominator is the *price of good Y*, this ratio becomes the *cross* elasticity of demand. Note that in each case, the numerator measures how much the demand for X responds to that influence.

IMPORTANT TERMS: MATCH THE COLUMNS

*Match the term in the first column with the corresponding
explanation in the second column.*

_____ 1. Total revenue
_____ 2. Elasticity of demand
_____ 3. Elasticity of supply
_____ 4. Income elasticity of demand
_____ 5. Cross elasticity of demand
_____ 6. Unit elasticity of demand
_____ 7. Joint products
_____ 8. Incidence
_____ 9. Substitutability

a. A measure of how strongly the quantity demanded responds to a change in income. It is defined as the percentage change in quantity demanded divided by the percentage change in income.
b. The percentage change in quantity supplied divided by the percentage change in price, as equilibrium moves from one point to another on a supply curve.
c. The amount of money received by sellers of a product. This also equals the amount of money spent by buyers of the product.
d. A measure of the effect the price of good Y has on the demand for good X. It is defined as the percentage change in the quantity of X divided by the percentage change in the price of Y. This is positive if X and Y are substitutes, and negative if they are complements.
e. The percentage change in quantity demanded divided by the percentage change in price, as equilibrium moves from one point to another on a demand curve.
f. Two products that result from one production process. To illustrate, beef and hides result from the production of beef.
g. When the percentage change in the quantity demanded is exactly equal to the percentage change in price.
h. having other goods that can be used instead
i. burden

TRUE-FALSE

T   F   1.   A move to a new lower price equilibrium on an elastic demand curve means that total revenue falls

T   F   2.   A straight-line demand curve has the same elasticity at each point on the curve.

T   F   3.   If the elasticity of demand is one, then a one percent change in price will lead to a greater than one percent change in the quantity demanded.

T   F   4.   Elasticity of demand is
$$\frac{\% \text{ change in price}}{\% \text{ change in quantity demanded}}$$

T   F   5.   Elasticity of demand describes how responsive buyers are to a change in price, while elasticity of supply describes how responsive sellers are.

T   F   6.   The elasticity of supply is greater in the short run than in the long run.

T   F   7.   The elasticity of demand tends to be higher for luxuries than for necessities.

T   F   8.   The supply of hides tends to be inelastic because hides and beef are joint products.

T   F   9.   The better are the substitutes in production, the more elastic is the supply; and the better are the substitutes in consumption, the more elastic is the demand.

T   F   10.   Over time, demand becomes less elastic, while supply becomes more elastic.

MULTIPLE CHOICE

1. When there is a rightward shift in the supply curve, total revenue:

   a. must rise
   b. must fall
   c. will rise only if the demand curve is elastic
   d. will rise only if the demand curve is inelastic
   e. will rise only if the supply curve is inelastic

2. If people reduce their consumption of coffee by very little, even when its price skyrockets, we can conclude that:

   a. supply is elastic
   b. supply is inelastic
   c. supply has zero elasticity
   d. supply has unit elasticity
   e. demand is inelastic

3. If the elasticity of demand is greater than 1, then a 10% reduction in price will result in:

   a. no change in quantity demanded
   b. an increase of less than 10% in the quantity demanded
   c. a decrease of less than 10% in the quantity demanded
   d. a decrease of 10% in the quantity demanded
   e. an increase of more than 10% in the quantity demanded

4. If the elasticity of supply is 3, then a 1% increase in price will:

   a. reduce the quantity supplied by 3%
   b. increase the quantity supplied by 3%
   c. increase the quantity supplied by 1%
   d. triple the quantity supplied
   e. increase the quantity supplied by one third

5. A move to a new, higher-price equilibrium on a supply curve means that total revenue:

   a. will not change
   b. may rise or remain unchanged
   c. may fall or remain unchanged
   d. must fall
   e. must rise

6. If the price of X goes from $1.50 per dozen to $2.50 per dozen, and suppliers are willing to increase from 9,000 to 11,000 the amount they offer for sale, then the midpoint elasticity of supply is:

   a. .10
   b. .4
   c. .8
   d. 2.5
   e. 4.0

7. If the supply curve for apples shifts to the left:

   a. the rise in price will be greater in the short run than in the long run
   b. the rise in price will be less in the short run than in the long run
   c. the rise in price will be the same in the long and short run
   d. the fall in price will be the same in the long and short run
   e. the price will fall in the short run, and rise in the long run

8. In the long run, the elasticity of demand for foreign travel is high because:

   a. it is a necessity
   b. it is a luxury
   c. airliners can easily switch from transporting goods to transporting people
   d. travel has no substitutes in consumption
   e. travel has no substitutes in production

9. A technological change that shifts the supply curve to the right will cause total revenue to:

    a. rise if demand is elastic
    b. fall if demand is elastic
    c. rise if demand is inelastic
    d. rise if the elasticity of demand is 1
    e. fall if the elasticity of demand is 1

10. If the government places a sales tax on a perfectly competitive good, then the seller will bear the heavier part of the burden, if:

    a. demand is elastic and supply is inelastic
    b. demand is inelastic and supply is elastic
    c. both demand and supply are inelastic
    d. both demand and supply are elastic
    e. the elasticity of supply is infinite

11. The burden of a commodity tax is born entirely by buyers:

    a. in any case
    b. if supply has unit elasticity
    c. if demand has unit elasticity
    d. if demand has infinite elasticity
    e. if demand has zero elasticity

12. A bumper crop will lower farm income:

    a. regardless of demand and supply elasticity
    b. if demand is elastic
    c. if demand is inelastic
    d. if demand and supply have equal elasticity
    e. if demand elasticity is infinite

13. If demand for good X is less elastic than the government estimates, then the revenue it will raise from a sales tax on X will be

    a. impossible to collect
    b. changed, but it is impossible to know in which direction
    c. lower than predicted
    d. higher than predicted
    e. unaffected

14. Annual government revenue from a sales tax will be

    a. higher in the long run than in the short run
    b. lower in the long run than in the short run
    c. higher in states with a small population
    d. higher in states with large cities at the border
    e. none of the above

15. For most renters, government imposition of rent control

    a. provides gains in the short run and the long run
    b. imposes losses in the short run and the long run
    c. provides gains in the short run but losses in the long run
    d. provides losses in the short run but gains in the long run
    e. has no effect

16. Between early 1985 and late 1987, the value of the dollar (relative to the yen)

    a. rose 20%
    b. rose 50%
    c. fell 20%
    d. fell 50%
    e. did not change

17. The income elasticity of demand

    a. is positive for an inferior good
    b. is negative for a normal good
    c. is zero for an inferior good
    d. is negative for an inferior good
    e. a and b

18. If, other things equal, the demand for X falls by 20% while the price of Y increases by 10%, then the cross elasticity of demand, E_{XY}, is

    a. .5
    b. -.5
    c. unknown
    d. 2
    e. -2

19. The income elasticity of demand is the percentage change in:

a. quantity demanded divided by the percentage change in price
b. income divided by the percentage change in quantity demanded
c. price divided by the percentage change in quantity demanded
d. quantity demanded divided by the amount of income

e. quantity demanded divided by the percentage change in income

20. The cross elasticity of demand is the percentage change in the quantity demanded of X divided by the percentage change in:

a. quantity demanded of Y
b. quantity supplied of Y
c. income
d. the price of X
e. the price of Y

EXERCISES

1. a. If equilibrium is at A in Figure 20.2, total revenue is area _____, which is $_____. Total revenue at point B is area _____, that is, $_____. D_1 is (elastic, inelastic, unit elastic) because, as price falls, total revenue (increases, decreases). To be more precise, we can calculate the elasticity of D_1 from the formula:

% change in _____ / % change in _____ =
_____ / _____ = _____

Figure 20.2

b. D_2 is (more, less) elastic than D_1 because the elasticity of D_2 is:

% change in _____ / % change in _____ =
_____ / _____ = _____

2. Draw in a supply curve through point A and mark it S_1. Draw in another supply curve through point B and mark it S_2. Mark the point where S_2 cuts D_2 as F. If supply is initially at S_1, and it shifts to S_2, then the change in price is greater if demand is (D_1, D_2); that is, the change in price resulting from a shift in supply is greater if demand is (more, less) elastic.

3. a. In Figure 20.3, supply curve S_1 is (elastic, inelastic, unit elastic) because it _____. If price rises from P_1 to P_2, then the equilibrium on S_1 moves from point _____ to point _____. On the other hand, for supply curve S_2, this change in price would move equilibrium from point _____ to _____. The quantity response to this change in price is (greater, less) for S_2 than for S_1. S_2 is therefore (more, less) elastic than S_1. It is (true, not true) that if two supply curves pass through the same point—such as A—the flatter one is the more elastic. This conclusion is (the same as, quite different from) the one we arrived at in comparing slopes of demand curves. In general, if any straight line supply curve such as S_2 cuts the quantity axis, it is (elastic, inelastic).

Figure 20.3

Table 20.1

Price per bushel	Millions of bushels demanded	Millions of bushels supplied
$5	25	5
10	20	10
15	15	15
20	10	20
25	5	25

Figure 20.4

Price (dollars per bushel)

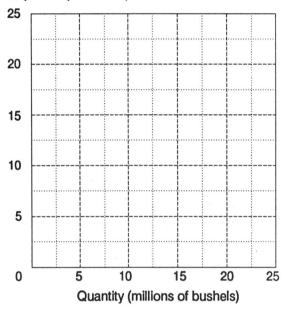

Quantity (millions of bushels)

b. Now consider S_3. As price rises from P_1 to P_2, the quantity response is (greater/less) than for S_1. S_3 is therefore (more, less) elastic than S_1. It is still (true, not true) that if two supply curves pass through the same point — such as A — the flatter one is the more elastic. In general, if any straight line supply curve like S_3 cuts the price axis, it is (elastic, inelastic).

4. Draw in a demand curve through point A and mark it D_1. Draw in another parallel demand curve through point B and mark it D_2. Mark the point where D_2 cuts S_1 as F. If demand is initially at D_1, and it shifts to D_2, then the change in price is greater if supply is (S_1, S_2), that is, the change in price resulting from a shift in demand is greater if supply is (more, less) elastic.

5. a. The data in Table 20.1 describe hypothetical demand and supply curves for apples. Plot these curves in Figure 20.4 and mark them S and D. Mark the equilibrium as point A, where the price of apples is $_____ per bushel, and the equilibrium quantity is _____ million bushels. Suppose the government sets a price floor at $19, making it illegal to sell apples at a price below this. Mark the new equilibrium in Figure 20.4 as B and draw in an arrow showing the excess (demand/supply). Mark this arrow BC.

b. In moving from A to B, the percentage change in price is _____; the percentage change in quantity demanded is _____; and the elasticity of demand is _____. The percentage change in quantity that sellers would like to supply is approximately _____; therefore the elasticity of supply is _____.

6. a. Suppose now that the government cancels its price floor, and instead requires the sellers of apples to pay a sales tax of $10 per bushel. When the buyers now pay $15 per bushel, the sellers get to keep only $_____ per bushel after they pay the $10 per bushel tax. Thus, according to Table 20.1, they will supply _____ million bushels. Fill in the rest of Table 20.2.

Table 20.2

(1) Price per bushel paid by demanders (including tax)	(2) Amount per bushel received by sellers	(3) Millions of bushels supplied
10	$ 0	0
15	_____	_____
20	_____	_____
25	_____	_____

b. Plot the new supply curve in Figure 20.4 and mark it S'. The new equilibrium price (paid by demanders) is $_____, and the new equilibrium quantity is _____. Of the $10 per bushel paid in sales tax, sellers are paying $_____, and buyers are paying $_____.

7. Draw a straight-line demand curve D' passing through point A which is more elastic than D. If this new demand curve were to replace the old demand curve, the equilibrium price *before* the imposition of the tax would be (higher, lower, no different); and the equilibrium quantity before the tax would be (higher, lower, no different). The equilibrium price after the tax would be (higher, lower, no different) than with the old demand curve, and the equilibrium quantity would be (less, more, no different). With the new demand curve, the amount of tax paid by buyers would be (more, less) and the amount paid by suppliers would be (more, less) than with the old demand curve.

ESSAY QUESTIONS

These two questions are a bit more demanding than those in earlier chapters. If you have any trouble with them, come back and answer them after you have read page 479 in the text (question 1) and pages 488 and 489 in the text (question 2).

1. Suppose you are a monopolist (a single seller) and you can set your price. If you discover that the demand for your product is inelastic, would you want to raise your price or lower it? Why? How far would you want to change it?

2. It has been argued that stores issue trading stamps to discriminate against people who cannot be bothered collecting, licking, and redeeming the stamps. These people end up paying a higher price for their purchases than those who use the stamps, because only the users receive a "discount" in the form of the items they get with the stamps. Suppose you were the owner of a large chain of stores and you wanted to engage in this kind of price discrimination. (That is, raise the price to non-users of stamps, and lower it to users.) What would happen to your total revenue if the demand by users of stamps was elastic and the demand by non-users was inelastic? What would happen to your total revenue if the demand by users was inelastic and the demand by nonusers was elastic?

ANSWERS

Important Terms: **1** c, **2** e, **3** b, **4** a, **5** d, **6** g, **7** f, **8** i, **9** h.

True-False:
1 F(p. 368)
2 F(p. 369)
3 F(p. 365)
4 F(p. 366)
5 T(p. 371)
6 F(p. 372)
7 T(p. 370)
8 T(p. 373)
9 T(pp. 370, 373)
10 F(pp. 370, 372).

Multiple-Choice:
1 c(p. 368)
2 e(p. 365)
3 e(p. 365)
4 b(p. 371)
5 e(p. 371)
6 b(p. 371)
7 a(p. 370)
8 b(p. 370)
9 a(p. 368)
10 a(p. 374)
11 e(p. 374)
12 c(p. 374)
13 d(p. 375)
14 b(pp. 370, 375)
15 c(p. 377)
16 d(p. 378)
17 d(p. 379)
18 e(p. 379)
19 e(p. 378)
20 e(p. 379).

Exercises

1   a. P_1AQ_1O, \$20 x 8 = \$160, P_2BQ_2O, \$10 x 10 = \$100, inelastic, decreases, quantity, price, 25, 50, 0.5 (or using the more appropriate midpoint formula, E_d = .333)

      b.   More, quantity, price, 75, 50, 1.5.

2. D_1, less.

3   a.   unit elastic, passes through the origin O, A, C, A, B, less, less, true, the same as, inelastic.

      b.   greater, more, true, elastic.

4. S_2, less.

Chapter 20   Applications of Demand and Supply

223

5   a. $15, 15, supply.

Figure 20.4 Completed

Price (dollars per bushel paid by demanders)

Quantity (millions of bushels)

b.   27%, 27%, 1 (slightly different using the midpoint formula), 27%, 1.

6   a. $5, 5.

Table 20.2 Completed

(1)	(2)	(3)
10	$ 0	0
15	5	5
20	10	10
25	15	15

b. $20, 10, $5, $5.

7.   no different, no different, lower, less, less, more.

CHAPTER 21

DEMAND AND UTILITY

LEARNING OBJECTIVES

After you have studied this chapter in the textbook and the study guide, you should be able to

✔ Show how the market demand curve is constructed by adding up the individual demand curves

✔ Define marginal utility, and show how it is related to total utility

✔ Describe the principle of diminishing marginal utility

✔ Explain consumer equilibrium which occurs when purchases have been made up to the point where marginal benefit has fallen to price

✔ Use the demand curve to illustrate consumer surplus, and to measure how consumers lose when price rises

✔ Use Adam Smith's diamonds/water paradox to explain the importance of total utility as well as marginal utility

✔ Explain how a consumer chooses among goods, showing why the consumer is in equilibrium when the marginal utility of a dollar's worth of any good is equal to the marginal utility of a dollar's worth of any other

✔ Show why purchasers must take into account not only price, but also transactions costs, including search (information) costs

✔ Explain why search costs include not only out-of-pocket costs, but also time costs, and why time costs are also important in using a product

MAJOR PURPOSE

In the last chapter, we measured elasticity of demand and elasticity of supply, and we saw how important they are in analyzing policy problems. In this chapter, we describe the fundamentals of demand; we examine the foundations of the demand curve. (In chapters 23 and 24, the fundamentals of supply will be similarly examined.)

Specifically, the four most important objectives in this chapter are

- to analyze how the consumer facing a given price arrives at equilibrium,

- to examine and measure how much the consumer benefits when the price of a product falls,

- to describe how a consumer makes a choice among several goods, and

- to consider the other costs, in addition to price, that are incurred when someone purchases a good or service.

HIGHLIGHTS OF CHAPTER

The first fundamental characteristic of the demand curve that must be recognized is an obvious one: A market demand curve is simply the sum of all the individual demand curves. This is illustrated in Figure 21-1 in the textbook. In turning to the other characteristics of demand, we begin by examining the demand curve of one individual consumer.

The First View of the Consumer: What does the Demand Curve Tell Us?

Underlying each individual demand curve are the two basic concepts introduced in Chapter 2—scarcity and choice. Thus the consumer can be viewed as choosing between scarce movies and *all* other scarce products— that is, between movies and money, since money is the means of acquiring all other goods. This is the choice that is described by the demand curve for movies, which tells us how much money the consumer is willing to give up to buy one movie, how much more to buy a second, and so on.

Notice that here we are taking a different approach to the demand curve than we did in previous chapters. Earlier we viewed the demand curve as telling us, *at each given price*, how many units (the quantity) that the buyer would purchase. As an example, consider Figure 4-1 on p. 49 of the text. At a given price of $4 we *horizontally* measured the *quantity* (400) that a buyer would purchase. Now, we are viewing the demand curve as telling us, *at each given quantity*, how much money the consumer is willing to pay for another movie—as shown by the set of *vertical* arrows in Figure 21-3a of the text.

Willingness to pay is typically a good indicator of how highly the consumer values each additional movie— that is, willingness to pay measures the *marginal benefit (marginal utility)* of movies. The more a consumer buys, the less marginal utility is derived from another movie. In other words, the further to the right the consumer goes in making more and more purchases in Figure 21-3a, the shorter these vertical arrows of marginal utility (that is, marginal benefit) become. In simplest terms, the more movies you watch, the less interested you become in watching any more. Formally stated, this is the *law of diminishing marginal utility*, which states that as more and more of any product is acquired, *eventually* the utility (or benefit) provided by one more unit must fall.

Consumer Equilibrium

With this background, the equilibrium of the consumer is now easily described. Because the benefit of, say, the third movie—as shown by the left hand arrow in Figure 21-3 of the textbook—is higher than the market price of $4, the consumer buys that movie. For the same reason, the consumer buys a fourth and fifth movie. Purchases cease at six movies because the marginal benefit has fallen to the level of price. (Beyond that, where marginal benefit has fallen below price—that is, below the marginal cost to the buyer—further purchases are obviously not justified.) This then provides an important conclusion: In equilibrium, the consumer purchases up to the point where the marginal benefit of a product equals its price. Thus we can read the quantity a consumer will demand at any price right off the consumer's marginal benefit curve. This confirms our earlier claim that the demand curve is the consumer's marginal benefit curve, that is, marginal utility curve.

Consumer Surplus

Figure 21-3b in the text shows the concept of consumer surplus. In purchasing the third movie, the consumer enjoys a $3 surplus; the individual is willing to pay $7 for that movie, but it only costs $4. Similarly, there is a $2 surplus on the next movie, and so on. The consumer purchasing six movies acquires a surplus equal to all these arrows above the $4 price line, that is, a surplus equal to the area of the shaded triangle. Thus consumer surplus is the area of the triangle to the northwest of the point of equilibrium on the demand curve.

How the Consumer Is Affected by a Change in Price

Figure 21-4 of the text shows how much the consumer benefits from a price reduction. At the original price of $10 and equilibrium at E_1, the consumer surplus is area 1. When the price falls to $6 and equilibrium moves to E_2, the consumer surplus is area $1 + 2 + 3$, for an increase of $2 + 3$—the area enclosed to the left of the demand curve between the old and new price. This is the consumer benefit if the price falls from $10 to $6—or, of course, the consumer loss if the price rises from $6 to $10.

The Second View of the Consumer: The Choice Among Goods

In using the demand curve so far, we have only been studying how a consumer chooses between one product (movies) and money, that is, *all* other products. On page 388 we show how a rational consumer will choose among movies, apples, shoes, and all other items. So we are no longer concentrating on the purchase just of movies; instead we are examining the purchase of each of the available products. Faced with this variety, what does the consumer do? The answer is: Keep purchasing each item until the marginal utility of the last dollar spent on movies is equal to the marginal utility of the last dollar spent on apples, which in turn is equal to the marginal utility of the last dollar spent on shoes, and so on. You can derive this fundamental principle—which appears formally as equation (21-1)—by working your way through the example in Table 21-1. Once you have mastered this, you can then always confirm that the principle in equation (21-1) holds by applying the same sort of reasoning that mathematicians frequently use: Assume that this principle does *not* hold, and then show how the consumer will then change purchases until it *does*. For example, if the consumer is getting more utility from the last dollar spent on movies than on shoes, total utility can be increased by switching purchases from shoes to movies until the utility from the last dollar spent on each *is* equal.

Costs to the Consumer in Addition to Price

The price of a good is not the only cost to a buyer. In addition, the buyer may also face *transaction costs*. These may include dealer or brokerage fees in making the actual purchase, plus any *search costs* (information costs) that must be undertaken. Search costs are the costs incurred in making a purchasing decision. For example, if you are buying a car, search costs will include any out-of-pocket costs of buying magazines that compare cars, plus the "time costs" involved in studying these magazines. There are also time costs in using products once they are purchased. If your new car turns out to be a lemon, you will incur a lot of time costs in taking it back and forth for repair. Thus if your time is worth a great deal, you are more likely to buy a reliable car that minimizes this time cost. In general, it is important in any purchasing decision to consider not only price, but all of these other costs as well.

IMPORTANT TERMS

Match the term in the first column with the corresponding phrase in the second column. But before you do so, write out your own definition of the term in the first column.

_____ 1. Total benefit (total utility)
_____ 2. Marginal benefit (marginal utility)
_____ 3. Indifference curves
_____ 4. Optimal purchase rule
_____ 5. Law of diminishing marginal utility
_____ 6. Consumer equilibrium
_____ 7. Consumer surplus
_____ 8. Search cost (information cost)
_____ 9. Time cost
_____ 10. Transactions cost

a. The additional satisfaction derived from one more unit of a product.
b. Utility is maximized when the utility from the last dollar spent on each good is equal.
c. Another way of explaining how a consumer chooses among many goods.
d. A situation in which the marginal benefit of each good just equals its cost.
e. The difference between the amount that a consumer would be willing to pay for a good and the amount that actually is paid for it.
f. As more and more of a good is consumed, a point is eventually reached where marginal utility begins to decline.
g. The time and money spent in collecting the information necessary to make an informed purchase.
h. The total satisfaction derived from a product.
i. All costs (except price) associated with buying or selling anything, including search costs and other costs such as fees or commissions.
j. The time spent shopping for a good and using it.

TRUE-FALSE

T   F   1.   If marginal benefit has fallen below the price of a good, the consumer has bought too much.

T   F   2.   If a consumer's purchase of a good is less than the equilibrium amount, marginal benefit will still be greater than the price of the good.

T   F   3.   The reason why a demand curve slopes downward to the right is that ultimately each consumer's marginal benefit falls as the individual consumes more.

T   F   4.   Because diamonds sell for a higher price than water, they must provide more total benefit to society.

T   F   5.   When the price of a good falls, the consumer surplus that an individual receives from that good will rise.

T   F   6.   If the price of a good falls, then both marginal and total utility will increase.

T   F   7.   A consumer who gets twice as much marginal utility from a pound of beef as a loaf of bread will be in equilibrium if the price of a loaf of bread is twice as high as the price of a pound of beef.

T   F   8.   Time costs are incurred in using, but not in purchasing, products.

T   F   9.   If a consumer is purchasing only 2 goods, and continues to do so until the ratio of the marginal utilities of these 2 goods is equal to their price ratio, then that consumer is in equilibrium.

T   F   10.   Time-saving devices are more prevalent in low-wage countries than in high-wage countries.

MULTIPLE CHOICE

1. The market demand for a good is the:

   a. vertical sum of the individual demands
   b. average of the individual demands
   c. horizontal sum of the individual demands
   d. vertical product of the individual demands
   e. horizontal product of the individual demands

2. The market demand curve has:

   a. less slope than the individual demand curves
   b. more slope than the individual demand curves
   c. more slope or less; you can't tell in general
   d. the same slope as the individual demand curves
   e. more slope, if the individual demand curves are elastic

3. The height of a demand curve is

   a. the price consumers would be willing to pay plus consumer surplus
   b. the price consumers would be willing to pay minus consumer surplus
   c. the price consumers would be willing to pay minus the price they actually paid
   d. the price consumers would be willing to pay plus the price they actually paid
   e. the price consumers would be willing to pay

4. Marginal utility can be viewed as

   a. the height of the demand curve plus the price consumers actually pay
   b. the height of the demand curve minus the price consumers actually pay
   c. the price consumers would be willing to pay plus the price they actually pay
   d. the price consumers would be willing to pay minus the height of the demand curve
   e. the height of the demand curve

5. A consumer will continue to purchase a good until its:

   a. marginal benefit falls to zero
   b. marginal benefit falls to the level of its price
   c. total benefit falls to the level of its price
   d. total benefit falls to zero
   e. total benefit rises to the level of its price

6. The amount of a good that a consumer purchases should depend on its:

   a. marginal benefit only
   b. search cost only
   c. price only
   d. price and search cost only
   e. marginal benefit, search cost, and price

7. A consumer with diminishing marginal utility for a good will be willing to pay:

   a. more and more for each additional unit
   b. less and less for each additional unit
   c. the same amount for each additional unit
   d. nothing for this good
   e. less than nothing for this good; the individual will have to be subsidized to take it

8. According to the law of diminishing marginal utility:

   a. the utility from another unit can never rise
   b. marginal utility must always be negative
   c. marginal utility must always be positive
   d. marginal utility must rise at first, but eventually it may fall
   e. marginal utility may rise at first, but eventually it must fall

9. If water and diamonds had the same upward-sloping supply curve:

   a. they would certainly sell for the same price
   b. the would be likely to sell for the same price
   c. diamonds would be more expensive
   d. water would be more expensive
   e. no prediction could be made about their prices

10. If we know only the selling price of a perfectly competitive good, then we know:

    a. the total benefit it provides
    b. the total cost of producing it
    c. its total cost and total benefit
    d. the marginal benefit it provides
    e. none of the above

11. If price increases, there is:

    a. a gain to the consumer equal to the area to the left of the demand curve between the old and new price
    b. a loss to the consumer equal to the area to the left of the demand curve between the old and new price
    c. a loss to the consumer equal to the area to the left of the supply curve between the old and new price
    d. a gain to the consumer equal to the area to the left of the supply curve between the old and new price
    e. no effect on the consumer

12. Consumer surplus is a "triangle" with two sides being:

    a. the vertical axis and the horizontal axis
    b. the horizontal axis and the price line
    c. the horizontal axis and the demand curve
    d. the vertical axis and the price line
    e. none of the above

13. In which case do consumers enjoy the least consumer surplus? (Assume in each case that they face the same price and purchase the same quantity.)

    a. demand elasticity is 1
    b. demand is highly inelastic
    c. demand is highly elastic
    d. supply elasticity is 1
    e. supply is highly elastic

14. If the price of good A increases, then:

    a. marginal utility will decrease, and total utility will increase
    b. marginal utility will increase and total utility will decrease
    c. marginal utility will decrease, but by less than total utility decreases
    d. marginal utility will decrease by more than total utility decreases
    e. marginal and total utility will both increase

15. The more willing the public is to bear search costs:

    a. the more variation there will be in price quoted by sellers

    b. the less variation there will be in price quoted by sellers
    c. the higher will be the price quoted by sellers
    d. the greater the overcharging by wholesalers and retailers
    e. the greater the overcharging by retailers, but not wholesalers

16. Time costs are:

    a. greater in a high-income (than a low-income) country, and this is one reason why less reliable cars are purchased there
    b. greater in a high-income country and this is one reason why more expensive and reliable cars are purchased there
    c. less in a high-income country and this is one reason why more expensive and reliable cars are purchased there
    d. less in a high-income country and this is one reason why less expensive and reliable cars are purchased there
    e. less in a high-income country, but this doesn't affect the cars that are purchased there

17. A consumer buying two goods will be in equilibrium if:

    a. the ratio of the marginal utilities of these goods is greater than their price ratio
    b. the ratio of the marginal utilities of these goods is less than their price ratio
    c. the ratio of the marginal utilities of these goods is equal to 1
    d. the ratio of the marginal utilities of these goods is equal to their price ratio
    e. some other condition is met; any condition involving marginal utilities is irrelevant

18. If the price of apples rises, the consumer will buy:

    a. fewer apples, thus increasing his marginal utility from apples
    b. fewer apples, thus reducing this marginal utility from apples
    c. more cherries, thus reducing his marginal utility from cherries
    d. more cherries, thus increasing his marginal utility from cherries
    e. a and c

19. If the marginal utility of a pound of beef is twice as great as the marginal utility of a loaf of bread, then the consumer will be in equilibrium if:

a. the price of a pound of beef is twice the price of a loaf of bread
b. the price of a pound of beef is four times the price of a loaf of bread
c. the price of a pound of beef is half the price of a loaf of bread
d. their prices are the same
e. their prices are related in some other way

20. According to the substitution effect, a fall in the price of apples results in:

a. an increase in the purchases of apples because other goods have become cheap relative to apples
b. an increase in the purchases of apples because apples have become less expensive relative to other goods
c. a decrease in the purchases of apples because apples have become less expensive relative to other goods
d. a decrease in the purchases of apples because the buyer's real income has risen
e. an increase in the purchases of apples because the buyer's real income has risen

EXERCISES

1 a. If the price for the product shown in Figure 21.1 below is $7, then _____ units will be purchased, because this is the quantity where marginal benefit, as given by the height of the _____ curve, is equal to _____. There are two interpretations of any point such as R on an individual's demand curve. The first is that R indicates the *quantity* that will be purchased at a certain price of, say, $7. This interpretation is shown by arrow _____. The second is that R indicates, at a given quantity, the maximum *price* that the buyer is willing to pay for the marginal unit—in this case the 100th unit. This second interpretation is shown by arrow _____. Since this arrow indicates how much the consumer will be willing to pay to acquire that 100th unit, it measures the value the consumer puts on that unit—that is, the (total value of all 100 units, marginal benefit of that 100th unit).

b. The total benefit the consumer gets from all 100 units purchased is area _____, which is the sum of all the (horizontal, vertical) marginal benefit arrows like _____ enclosed beneath the _____ curve throughout the range of quantities between _____ and _____. However, this purchase costs the consumer area _____, which is the quantity of _____ units multiplied by the $_____ price. Therefore, the *net* benefit to the consumer of this purchase is area _____, which is sometimes called _____.

Figure 21.1

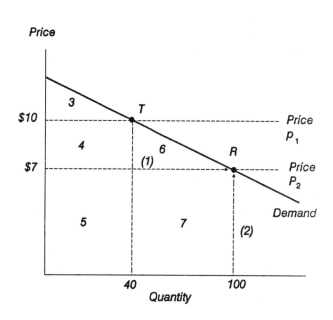

2. If price increases to $10, the new equilibrium is at _____, where the quantity purchased is _____ units. The demand curve between R and T is [elastic, inelastic] because the % change in quantity is (less, more) than the % change in price. The total benefit from this smaller purchase is area _____. However, the cost is area _____, which is the quantity of _____ units times the $_____ price. Therefore, the *net* benefit to the purchaser when price is $10 is area _____.

3   a. Since the net benefit to the purchaser when the price was $7 was area _____, and that benefit was reduced to area _____ when the price rose to $10, the burden of this price increase on the consumer is area _____, which is the area enclosed to the (left, right) of the _____ curve between the old price and the new price.

   b. Let's look at this from another point of view. Because price has risen, the consumer is buying _____ units less. The total benefit the consumer used to get on these units—and has now lost—is area _____. However, the consumer is no longer incurring the cost, shown by area _____, of purchasing these units, since they are no longer being bought. Therefore, the net loss of the consumer on these units that are no longer purchased is area _____. In addition the consumer is hurt because of the greater price that has to be paid on the first 40 units (that *continue* to be purchased). The higher cost to the consumer on these units is area _____, which is the $_____ increase in price times those 40 units.

Thus, in summary, we confirm that the loss to the consumer because of the price increase is area _____. This is made up of a loss of area _____ because purchases are reduced, plus a loss of area _____ because of the higher price that must be paid on purchases that continue to be made.

ESSAY QUESTIONS

1. People derive more benefit from the water they use than they do from all the champagne they drink. Yet champagne costs far more than water. Would champagne be more expensive than water if the two had the same supply curve and were thus equally scarce? Explain your answer.

2. To judge by the amount of time spent, most people seem to derive more utility from watching television than from going to movies. Yet they will pay $4 or $5 to go to a movie, when they could stay home and watch television for nothing. Can you explain this?

3. When Henry Ford invented the mass production of automobiles, what effect do you suppose this had on the typical marginal benefit schedule for horse-drawn carriages? What do you suppose it did to the price and sales of horse-drawn carriages?

4. Heroin addicts find that the more they consume, the more they want. Does this contradict or illustrate diminishing marginal utility? Can you use this heroin example to illustrate the law of diminishing marginal utility?

ANSWERS

Important Terms: 1h, 2a, 3c, 4b, 5f, 6d, 7e, 8g, 9j, 10i.

True-False: 1 T(p. 385)
                      2 T(p. 385)
                      3 T(p. 385)
                      4 F(p. 387)
                      5 T(p. 386)
                      6 F(p. 385)
                      7 F(p. 389)
                      8 F(p. 390)
                      9 T(p. 388)
                      10 F(p. 391)

Multiple Choice: **1** c(p. 383)
                            2 a(p. 383)
                            3 e(p. 385)
                            4 e(p. 385)
                            5 b(p. 385)
                            6 e(p. 390)
                            7 b(p. 385)
                            8 e(p. 384)
                            9 d(p. 387)
                            10 d(p. 385)
                            11 b(p. 386)
                            12 d(p. 386)
                            13 c(p. 386)
                            14 b(pp. 384, 385)
                            15 b(p. 390)
                            16 b(p. 391)
                            17 d(p. 388)
                            18 e(p. 388)
                            19 a(p. 389)
                            20 b(pp. 397, 398, APPENDIX).

Exercises

1   a.   100, demand, price, (1), (2), marginal benefit of that 100th unit.

    b.   3 + 4 + 5 + 6 + 7, vertical, (2), demand, zero, 100, 5 + 7, 100, $7, 3 + 4 + 6, consumer surplus.

2. T, 40, elastic, more, 3 + 4 + 5, 4 + 5, 40, $10, 3.

3   a.   3 + 4 + 6, 3, 4 + 6, left, demand.

    b.   60, 6 + 7, 7, 6, 4, $3, 6 + 4, 6, 4.

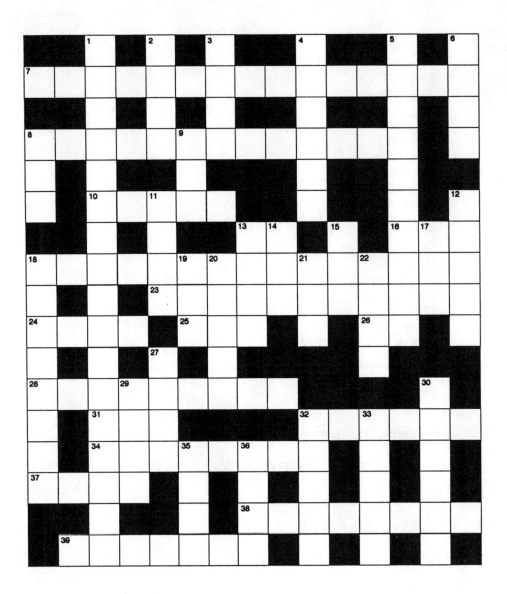

Across

7. benefit of consumers in excess of what they pay
8. beef and leather provide an example of _____ _____ (2 words)
10. laissez _____
13. indefinite article
16. a means of travel
18. benefit from consuming one more unit (2 words)
23. when the price of one increases, the demand for the other increases
24. where people skate
25. sound of disgust
26. 1st person, possessive
28. unresponsive to a change in price
31. bounder
32. an important economic objective is to reduce this
34. price is likely to be _____ when both demand and supply are inelastic
37. member of one of the British Houses of Parliment
38. fundamental reason for study of economics
39. if demand is elastic, total _____ increases when price is reduced

Down

1. this joins all points that provide equal satisfaction (2 words)
2. oxidized iron
3. close
4. area just outside a city
5. measure of how much quantity responds to a change in price
6. a continent
8. what an unemployed person wants
9. official price of a currency under pegged exchange rate system
11. part of the eye
12. an appointment of lovers to meet
13. in addition
14. a fruit covered with a woody shell
15. very successful movie or song

17. devoured
18. the _____ tax rate is the tax rate on additional income
19. central idea
20. all around
21. game without a winner
22. a small piece
27. passing fashions
29. one of the factors of production
30. one of the objectives of economic policy
32. this is used in producing many manufactured goods
33. low business activity
35. ripped
36. the _____ year is the year from which price changes are measured

CHAPTER 22

BUSINESS ORGANIZATIONS:
Proprietorships, Partnerships, and Corporations

LEARNING OBJECTIVES

After you have studied this chapter in the textbook and study guide, you should be able to

✔ Describe the three major types of business organization, and explain the major advantages and disadvantages of each

✔ Describe the ways in which a corporation can raise funds for expansion

✔ Explain the advantages and disadvantages to the corporation of issuing common stock rather than bonds

✔ Explain the advantages and disadvantages of buying common stocks rather than bonds

✔ Explain what the concept of leverage means

✔ Explain how greater leverage can create risks for both corporations and bondholders

✔ Describe the major motives of the people who buy securities, and the major motives of those who issue securities

MAJOR PURPOSES

The major purposes of this chapter are to

- explain the three forms of business organization,

- describe how businesses finance expansion, and

- describe some of the problems that arise in the financial markets.

For big business, the major legal form is the corporation. This provides owners with the protection of **limited liability**. Stockholders are not responsible for the debts of their business, and can lose only the funds they have spent to acquire a share of ownership. Limited liability is one of the reasons why there is such a broad market in common stock, and why it is relatively easy for corporations to raise funds by selling additional stock.

One of the major functions of the markets for financial capital—such as the stock market and the bond market—is to provide funds to new and expanding companies. People have an incentive to buy the securities of rapidly growing, profitable, and financially sound corporations. The capital markets do a fairly good job of providing resources to the most profitable and promising corporations.

The appendix to the chapter explains the two basic types of business accounts—the balance sheet and the income statement.

HIGHLIGHTS OF CHAPTER

There are three major types of business organization:

- The **single proprietorship**, owned and operated by an individual. Many small businesses are single proprietorships.

- The **partnership**, which is quite similar to the single proprietorship, except that there are several owners and operators. With a few exceptions, partnerships are quite small businesses.

- The **corporation**, which is the standard organization for large businesses. The corporation provides **limited liability** to the stockholder-owners. This is a great advantage, because the stockholder-owners don't have to worry about being stuck with the obligations undertaken by the corporation. (In contrast, a partner is liable for the obligations undertaken by the partnership.) Because of limited liability, a large, well-known corporation may be able to sell shares of common stock (that is, shares of ownership) to a wide variety of people. Thus, the corporate form of organization has the advantage of making it *easier to finance growth*. A third advantage of the corporation is that it has *automatic continuity*. When one of the stockholder-owners dies, the stock goes to the heirs. The corporation continues uninterrupted. Because of the protection offered by limited liability,

an heir need not be concerned about accepting the stock.

However, taxes create a disadvantage for the corporate form of business. The corporation pays tax on its profits. Then, when the profits are paid out as dividends to stockholders, the stockholder-owners have to pay taxes on these dividends. Thus, profits distributed to stockholders are taxed twice: once by the corporate income tax, and once by the personal income tax on the stockholders.

Ways in which the corporation can raise funds include

- issuing additional shares of *common stock*, each representing a fraction of the ownership of the corporation;

- *selling bonds*, which is a way of borrowing money for a long period of time from the person who buys the bond;

- issuing shorter-term debt, such as *notes* or *commercial paper*; and

- *borrowing from a bank* or other financial institution.

Each of the first three items can normally be bought and sold in markets. For example, a person who owns stock or bonds of a corporation may sell them to anyone who is willing to buy. Transactions in such securities are usually facilitated by *brokers* or *dealers*. (Brokers bring buyers and sellers together. A bond dealer may be the actual buyer or seller of a bond.) Similarly, government bonds and shorter-term securities may be sold by the present holder to someone else. Thus, if the government or corporation issues long-term bonds, it has a guaranteed use of the funds for a long period of time. But the buyer is not necessarily tying up funds for a similar long period: the bond may be sold at any time. Thus, the financial markets provide **liquidity** to bondholders.

The prices of securities in the financial markets are determined by supply and demand; the prices of common stocks, bonds, and other financial assets can fluctuate as conditions change. The major determinant of the price of common stock is the *expected profitability* of the corporation. The person who buys the share will participate in the good fortune (if any) of the corporation. Even though bonds provide a fixed contract—for, say $12,000 in interest payments each year over 20 years—they may nevertheless fluctuate in value. In the marketplace, people have the choice of buying new bonds or old bonds. If a new bond will pay more interest—say $14,000—then the amount people will be willing to pay for the old bond (with $12,000 interest per year) will go down.

Although interest payments on bonds are set by the bond contract, the payment of interest is not guaranteed. If the issuing corporation runs into trouble, it may not have the funds to pay interest. In this case, the bondholder has the legal right to sue, and may push the corporation into the bankruptcy courts. Even then, there is no assurance that the bondholder will be paid, because the corporation may simply not have enough assets to cover its liabilities. If a corporation is in difficulty, there may be an agreement among bondholders and other creditors to give it more time to pay, and perhaps take smaller interest payments.

Because bondholders are not guaranteed payment, they must be concerned with the prospects that the issuer will in fact be able to make interest payments on schedule, and repay the principal when the bond reaches maturity. If a corporation is shaky, people will avoid its bonds unless they offer an extra amount of interest to compensate for the risk—the so-called **risk premium**. Because of differences in risk, some bonds offer substantially higher interest rates than others. Interest rates can also differ because of the tax law. For example, interest on state and local government bonds is exempt from federal income tax. This makes them attractive, and states and localities can therefore offer lower interest rates on their bonds than do corporations or the federal government.

In deciding which securities to buy, potential bond buyers weigh a number of factors—*risk, return, liquidity, and taxes*. Issuers of securities also have a number of factors to consider. One of their most important decisions is whether they will issue additional common stock or additional bonds. If they issue stock, they will be taking on additional part-owners. Thus, they will have to share their future profits among more people. If they issue additional bonds, they will be increasing the **leverage** of the corporation. If the business does well, the owners will only have to pay the interest; they will not have to share their profits with the bondholders. But they will be legally committed to pay the interest, whether the firm does well or not. Thus, leverage can add to the risks that the company may fail in the future.

The major function of financial markets is to allocate the saving of society to the various investment projects that can be undertaken. On the whole, the financial markets do a fairly good job in allocating funds among various projects. People who buy bonds or stocks have an incentive to put their funds into the corporation with the best prospects. Nevertheless, major mistakes are made. Some mistakes are inevitable in an risky and uncertain world—the best buggy whip manufacturer in American became obsolete with the invention of the motor car. But some mistakes can be avoided if people have more information. This is where the Securities and Exchange Commission plays an important role. It requires corporations to disclose their financial condition. By enforcing a reasonable rule—that information be disclosed—the government can help the private capital markets work better.

IMPORTANT TERMS

Match the first column with the corresponding phrase in the second column.

_____ 1. Proprietorship
_____ 2. Limited liability
_____ 3. Double taxation
_____ 4. Common stock
_____ 5. Bond
_____ 6. Commercial paper
_____ 7. Net worth
_____ 8. Leverage
_____ 9. Book value
_____10. Risk premium
_____11. Broker

a. Chief advantage of forming a corporation
b. A short-term debt
c. Representative of a buyer or seller
d. Net worth divided by number of shares
e. Unincorporated enterprise
f. Debt divided by net worth
g. Yield on Baa bonds minus yield on Aaa bonds
h. Represents ownership in a corporation
i. Assets minus liabilities
j. Long-term debt
k. A disadvantage of forming a corporation

TRUE-FALSE

T   F   1. Partnerships have "unlimited liability." This means that there is no limit to the amount of bonds and other liabilities they can issue.

T   F   2. A partnership with two partners (A and B) has its income taxed twice — once as the income of A, and once as the income of B.

T   F   3. Corporate profits paid out as dividends are taxed twice: once by the corporation income tax, and once by the personal income tax.

T   F   4. A government bond is generally more liquid than a house.

T   F   5. Issuing additional common stock increases the leverage of a corporation.

T   F   6. Issuing more bonds increases the leverage of a corporation.

T   F   7. Businesses that increase their leverage usually do so to reduce the risk of bankruptcy.

T   F   8. The main reason that most state bonds have lower yields than federal government bonds is that their interest payments are not subject to federal income tax.

MULTIPLE CHOICE

1. In a standard partnership, each partner

   a. must pay personal income tax on all the income of the partnership
   b. has unlimited liability, but only for the debts which he or she undertook personally
   c. has unlimited liability, but only for his or her share of the debts of the corporation
   d. has unlimited liability for all the debts of the partnership, including those undertaken by the other partners
   e. can lose the amount of his or her initial investment, but no more

2. The partnership form of business organization:

   a. provides each partner with a liability limited to his or her share of the business
   b. normally issues common stock to raise the funds for expansion
   c. can have a maximum of five partners (since any larger number means that incorporation is required)
   d. does not provide the automatic continuity that a corporation does in the event of the death of one of the owners
   e. is generally used by banks

3. Corporations provide "limited liability." This means that:

   a. the stockholder-owners are not personally liable for debts of the corporation
   b. the corporation is not legally liable for debts of more than one-half its net worth in any one year
   c. officers of the corporation cannot be held legally liable for any fraudulent activities of the corporation
   d. the corporation is legally required to make contributions to the pension fund of its employees only in the years when it is profitable
   e. all of the above

4. The profits earned by a partnership

   a. are taxed twice
   b. are often retained by the firm, in which case they escape taxation
   c. are treated as personal income of the partners, and are therefore subject to personal income tax
   d. are treated as capital gains for tax purposes
   e. are never taxed

5. People sometimes talk of the "double taxation" applying to corporations. Which of the following is subject to double taxation?

   a. interest paid by the corporation
   b. interest received by the corporation
   c. retained profits
   d. dividends paid by the corporation
   e. all of the above

6. One drawback of double taxation of corporate dividends is that such taxation:

   a. is regressive
   b. is progressive
   c. gives a tax preference for corporations to raise funds by borrowing rather than by issuing stock, encouraging corporations to borrow excessively
   d. gives tax preference for corporations to raise funds by issuing stock rather than by borrowing, encouraging corporations to issue excessive amounts of stock
   e. gives a tax preference for corporations to raise funds by borrowing from banks rather than by issuing bonds, and the banking system as a result is destabilized

7. Each share of common stock represents:

   a. a debt of the issuing corporation
   b. an asset of the issuing corporation
   c. a fraction of the ownership of the corporation
   d. a claim on the stocks of inventories held by the corporation
   e. a right to receive dividends, even if interest cannot be paid on bonds

8. Normally, the riskiest type of security to buy is a

   a. federal government bond
   b. short-term debt of the federal government
   c. state government bond
   d. corporate bond
   e. common stock

9. A major purpose of the Securities and Exchange Commission (SEC) is to require corporations to:

   a. issue stock periodically so as to decrease leverage
   b. issue stock periodically so as to increase leverage
   c. issue bonds periodically so as to decrease leverage
   d. issue bonds periodically so as to provide bondholders a stable source of income
   e. make information available to the public

10. Financial leverage is measured by

    a. the trend in net worth, measured in dollars
    b. the trend in debt, measured in dollars
    c. the trend in debt, after adjustment for inflation
    d. the ratio of debt to net worth
    e. the price-earnings ratio

11. Leverage generally adds to the risks faced by:

    a. the stockholders of the leveraged company
    b. the bondholders of the leveraged company
    c. suppliers to whom the leveraged company owes money
    d. the banks which have made loans to the leveraged company
    e. all of the above

12. The net worth of a company is equal to:

    a. assets minus liabilities
    b. liabilities minus assets
    c. profits minus costs
    d. costs minus profits
    e. profits minus taxes

13. A commitment by a bank to lend up to a predetermined limit to a specific customer is known as a

    a. form of leverage over the bank
    b. stock option
    c. commercial paper
    d. line of credit
    e. illegal overdraft

14. Whenever a corporation issues bonds, rather than raising funds by issuing new common stock, it:

    a. increases its leverage
    b. decreases its leverage
    c. decreases the risks faced by stockholders
    d. decreases the risks faced by bondholders
    e. increases the tax it has to pay

15. Yields on U.S. government bonds were:

    a. low in the early 1930s, and high in the early 1940s
    b. low in the early 1930s, and high in the early 1980s
    c. high in the early 1930s, and low in the early 1940s
    d. high in the early 1930s, and low in the early 1980s
    e. very high, by historical standards, in the early 1930s, 1940s, and 1980s

16. In 1932, the yield on high-grade corporate bonds was about 5%, while the yield on lower grade corporate bonds was about 10%. The difference was:

    a. a tax premium
    b. a risk premium
    c. an inflation premium
    d. an incentive for risky businesses to borrow
    e. a sign of the breakdown of capital markets

17. Interest rates on state bonds are generally lower than interest rates on bonds of the federal government. The major reason is that:

    a. the federal government has been running large deficits
    b. the federal government has been running large surpluses
    c. state governments have been running large deficits
    d. Cleveland and New York almost went bankrupt during the 1970s
    e. interest from state bonds is exempt from federal income tax

18. Interest rates on government bonds are most likely to rise during:

    a. recessions
    b. depressions
    c. deflationary periods
    d. periods of rising inflation
    e. the period just prior to income tax time in April of each year

Note: The next two questions are based on the appendix.

19. In the balance sheet of a corporation:

    a. net worth = assets + liabilities
    b. assets = net worth - liabilities
    c. assets = liabilities - net worth
    d. assets = liabilities + net worth
    e. profits = sales - depreciation

20. What appears on the income statement of a corporation?

    a. depreciation
    b. income before taxes
    c. income after taxes
    d. all of the above
    e. none of the above

EXERCISE

1. This exercise is based on the appendix to Chapter 22.

   a. The following numbers apply to the XYZ corporation. Prepare a balance sheet for the XYZ corporation in Table 1. There are no assets and liabilies other than those listed below. However, not all items should be included in the balance sheet. *USE ONLY THE ONES THAT BELONG.*

Accounts payable	$800,000
Sales during year	$1,900,000
Accounts receivable	$900,000
Wages paid during year	$850,000
Long-term bonds of XYZ Corp. outstanding	$1,000,000
Plant and equipment (current value, after depreciation)	$2,000,000
Inventory on hand	$300,000
Revenue from service contracts	$250,000
Bank deposits and other cash items	$200,000
Depreciation during year	$300,000
Net interest paid	$150,000
Other costs	$250,000
Accrued liabilities	$150,000
Number of shares of common stock outstanding	100,000
Holdings of notes issued by ABC corp	$50,000

Table 22.1

Balance Sheet (thousands of dollars)	
Assets	Liabilities
	Net worth
Total Assets =	Total liabilities and Net Worth =

b. Some of the numbers not used in part (a) belong in the income statement. Use them to complete the income statement in Table 2. This corporation pays 30% of its income in taxes.

Table 22.2

Income statement (thousands of dollars)
1. Revenues:
Total:
2. Costs:
Total:
3. Profit before taxes:
4. Tax:
5. Net profit:
6. Addendum: Profit per share:

c. The book value of each share of stock of the XYZ corp. is ($15, $19.50, $20.00, $34.50).

ESSAY QUESTIONS

1. To find net worth, what do we subtract from assets? Is it possible for the net worth of a corporation to be negative? If so, what could we say about the book value of each share of common stock of a corporation with a negative net worth? Would it ever pay to buy shares in a firm with a negative net worth? If it is not possible, explain why not. Specifically, explain what will happen as the net worth of the corporation shrinks toward zero.

2. Suppose that you are in charge of finance for a large corporation. How would you go about raising funds to (a) finance the construction of a large plant, with an expected useful life of 25 years, (b) acquire larger inventories of raw materials, and (c) meet a temporary shortage of cash resulting from a decision by your customers to wait an extra month before paying their bills? Under what circumstances might you issue new common stock rather than borrow? Might it ever be a good idea to cut the dividend by, say, 50% to pay for any of the above? Explain why or why not. Might it ever be a good idea to cut the dividend for other reasons? Explain.

ANSWERS:

Important terms: **1** e, **2** a, **3** k, **4** h, **5** j, **6** b, **7** i, **8** f, **9** d, **10** g, **11** c

True-False:
1 F (p. 400)
2 F (pp. 400-402)
3 T (p. 402)
4 T (pp. 405-406)
5 F (p. 406)
6 T (p. 406)
7 F (p. 406)
8 T (p. 407)

Multiple Choice:
1 d (p. 400)
2 d (pp. 400-401)
3 a (p. 401)
4 c (p. 402)
5 d (p. 402)
6 c (p. 402)
7 c (p. 403)
8 e (p. 405)
9 e (p. 405)
10 d (p. 406)
11 e (p. 406)
12 a (p. 406)
13 d (p. 406)
14 a (p. 406)
15 b (p. 407)
16 b (p. 407)
17 e (p. 407)
18 d (p. 408)
19 d (p. 412, appendix)
20 d (p. 414, appendix)

Exercises:

1.

Table 22.1 Completed

Balance Sheet (thousands of dollars)				
Assets			**Liabilities**	
Cash	200		Accounts payable	800
ABC notes	50		Accrued liabilities	150
Accounts receivable	900		XYZ bonds	1,000
Inventory	300		Total liabilities	1,950
Plant & Equipment	2,000		Net Worth	1,500
			Total Liabilities	
Total Assets =	3,450		and Net Worth =	3,450

Table 22.2

Income statement (thousands of dollars)	
1. Revenues:	
Sales	1,900
Service contracts	250
Total:	2,150
2. Costs:	
Wages	850
Depreciation	300
Net Interest	150
Other	250
Total:	1,550
3. Profit before taxes:	600
4. Tax:	180
5. Net profit:	420
6. Addendum:	
Profit per share:	4.20

1.   c. $15.

CHAPTER 23

THE COSTS OF PRODUCTION

LEARNING OBJECTIVES

After you have studied this chapter in the textbook and the study guide, you should be able to

✔ Explain why, in the short-run, some costs are fixed and some are variable, while in the long run all costs are variable

✔ Define total, variable, fixed, and marginal costs; also average total cost, average variable cost, and average fixed cost

✔ Explain the law of (eventually) diminishing returns, and why this law means that marginal costs must eventually rise

✔ Explain, using a diagram, why a firm's average cost curve is cut at its minimum point, by its marginal cost curve

✔ Show in a diagram how long-run and short-run average costs curves are related to each other by an envelope relationship

✔ Define economies of scale and diminishing returns, clearly distinguishing between the two. You should also be able to explain why a firm may face both

✔ Explain the difference between accounting costs and economic costs, and why opportunity costs must be included in economic costs

✔ Explain why an economist defines costs to include normal profit, but not excess profit

MAJOR PURPOSE

Businesses make profits by selling at a **price that exceeds costs. Price** depends on the type of market in which they sell. (We will consider several types later in chapters 24 through 27.) Now in Chapter 23 we examine

costs with special reference to how they differ in the short run and the long run.

In the short run—the period in which the firm's capital stock is fixed—the key decision is: How much will it cost to increase output when only labor and other variable inputs can be increased, but fixed inputs such as capital cannot? The first half of this chapter is devoted to this question, and we derive a number of measures of cost—such as marginal cost MC and average total cost ATC—that will eventually in later chapters become important tools in examining how firms maximize profits.

Then we turn to costs in the long run when the firm can vary not only its labor input, but also those factors of production such as capital that are fixed in the short run. Thus, in the long run, all costs become variable. Now the picture of how costs vary when the firm changes its output is quite different. In particular, we focus on the quite different way in which its average cost changes. How does its long run average cost compare to its short run average cost?

We also show how the economist's definition of a firm's cost is far broader than an accountant's. For an economist, costs include not only the out-of-pocket costs that accountants take into account, but also implicit costs such as the opportunity costs of the owner's time and capital invested in the firm. Because the opportunity cost of the owner's capital—that is, normal profit—is included by an economist in calculating a firm's costs, any additional (excess or economic) profit is a return that can be earned in this industry above and beyond the return that can be earned elsewhere. Therefore, it is an incentive for more resources to move into the industry.

HIGHLIGHTS OF CHAPTER

In this chapter, we first focus on the short-run—the period in which the firm cannot change the amount of plant and equipment it is using. Then, in a later part of the chapter, we turn to the long run, when the firm is able to vary the amount of capital and equipment it uses.

The Long Run vs the Short Run

In the short run, one or more inputs are fixed. The capital the auto producer has is fixed. The land a farmer has is set. The decision is a narrow one: how much should the firm use of the variable inputs?—in particular labor, the only variable input we consider in detail in this simplified treatment.

In the long run, all inputs are variable. The firm now has to decide not only how much labor it should use, but also how much land and capital it should use. (In this simplified analysis, we assume that there is only one of these inputs—capital.)

The short run when capital is fixed isn't specified in number of years. For a college entrepreneur typing term papers it may take only a matter of days to acquire more capital—that is, a small computer. But for the company generating electrical power the short run may be 10 years or more—the time necessary to build a new power generating plant.

Costs in the Short Run

To understand short-run costs, there is no substitute for working your way across Table 23-1—at least the first three rows for outputs 0, 1 and 2. Thus, in the first row, at an output of zero (in col. 1) there is no variable cost (in col. 3); since the firm is producing nothing, it hires no labor and therefore has no variable costs. But it does have that $35 of fixed cost (in col. 2) that it cannot escape—for example, its capital equipment will depreciate and will have to be insured against fire even if it's producing nothing. Since such charges are incurred regardless of the firm's output, this $35 always remains the same as you go down column 2. However, in column 3, variable costs do rise to $24, then $40, and so on as the firm increases its output and hires more labor.

With this in hand, you can now finish working your way across the first three (or more) rows, showing how each of the figures you calculate appears in Figure 23-1. As you proceed, you cover all the required definitions on page 417 of the text.

The Relationship Between Average and Marginal Costs

MC intersects ATC at the lowest point on ATC. The reason is that initially the marginal value (MC) is below the average value (ATC), so it's dragging the average value down. But when MC rises above ATC (as it does after output 5 in this example) MC begins to pull ATC up. If you follow baseball at all, Box 23-1 will make this idea transparent.

The Short Run Production Function: Marginal Product and Marginal Cost

The law of eventually diminishing returns guarantees that the short-run marginal cost curve MC will ultimately rise (as indeed it does in Figure 23-1b). To understand this law, consider the short-run situation of a firm producing bicycles with a given stock of capital and only one variable factor, labor. As the firm initially hires more labor, each additional worker increases the firm's output by a substantial amount. But ultimately, as its labor force grows and its capital equipment is operated closer and closer to capacity, an additional worker will add only a small amount to the firm's output. All the new employee can do is work on odd jobs or stand around waiting for one of the machines to be free. In other words, the **marginal product of labor** — that is, the number of additional units of output (bicycles) which result from using one more worker — must eventually decrease. This illustrates the **law of (eventually) diminishing returns: If more of one factor (labor) is employed while all other factors (capital, etc.) are held constant, eventually the marginal product of that one factor (labor) must fall.**

In Part 9 of the book, it will become clear that the law of diminishing returns is a key to explaining wages and other income payments. For now, it is important because it explains why marginal costs must ultimately rise. In our example, the law of diminishing returns means that eventually an extra worker in the bicycle factory is able to do only odd jobs and produce very little. Most of his time is wasted. True, the firm can still produce another unit of output; but when it's done by a worker like this who is wasting most of his time, this unit of output comes at a very high marginal cost. Thus the **law of diminishing returns ensures that marginal costs must eventually rise.**

Costs in the Long Run

In the short run, labor is variable but capital is fixed. However, in the long run, both labor and capital are variable. The firm now has to decide how much capital it should install.

Describing this decision by a firm requires knowledge of its cost curves, and Figure 23-4 in the text show how a firm's long-run average cost curve (LAC) can be derived from its short-run average cost curves (SAC). (Each of its SAC curves applies to a specific amount of capital.) Note in that diagram how the firm's LAC curve is the envelope curve enclosing all the SAC curves from below. LAC shows how a firm wishing to produce any specified level of output — say q_4 — can select the appropriate amount of capital. Specifically, the firm minimizes its average cost of producing q_4 at point J by selecting capital stock 4. (SAC_4, of course, is the short run average cost curve that applies if the firm has capital stock 4.) Alternatively, if the firm wished to produce output q_2, it would do so at minimum average cost by producing at G using capital stock 2. Thus the LAC "planning curve" tells the firm what its minimum average cost will be for

each level of output when, in the long run, it is free to select any capital stock.

This then sets the stage for comparing two important economic phenomena.

Economies of Scale and the Law of (eventually) Diminishing Returns

Economies of scale exist when a 10% increase in output requires less than a 10% increase in all inputs — in other words, when input costs increase less rapidly than output. In this situation, the average cost of producing output falls as output increases; LAC slopes downward and to the right. An important conclusion follows: When there are economies of scale, the LAC slopes downward.

Figure 23-6 shows how a firm facing economies of scale — with a downward-sloping LAC shown by arrow e — can also be facing diminishing returns (arrow f). The reason is that diminishing returns occur when the short-run marginal cost curve SMC_1 rises. Although economies of scale refer to falling costs (specifically, a downward sloping LAC) and diminishing returns refer to rising costs (an upward-sloping marginal cost curve) the two are not in contradiction. Diminishing returns apply to the short run, when the firm cannot change its capital stock. On the other hand, economies of scale apply to the long run, when the firm is not constrained in this way and can do better — that is, achieve lower costs — by **changing** its capital stock. To see this in more detail in Figure 23-6, note that in the short run, the firm cannot change its fixed capital stock. Increasing only its labor results in rising marginal cost (SMC_1) — that is, diminishing returns. However, in the long run, when the firm can vary both labor and capital, it can operate on LAC. Because this is falling, the firm enjoys economies of scale.

The Economist's Concept of Cost: Opportunity Cost

The final important topic covered in this chapter is the difference between economic costs and accounting cost. While the accountant looks only at explicit, out-of-pocket costs, the economist also considers implicit costs, such as the opportunity costs of the owner of a firm. One of these opportunity costs is the salary the owner could have earned in another job; another is the interest income or dividends that the owner could have earned by investing her capital elsewhere. This alternative possible income on capital — that is, the opportunity cost of capital — is called the firm's normal profit; it is the amount that is necessary to keep capital in that firm. Because economists thus include normal profit as a cost, when they speak of "profit" they mean excess profit—that is, additional profit above and beyond normal profit. Such above-normal or excess profit is important for the operation of the market system, because whenever it exists, it acts as a signal to attract resources into that industry.

IMPORTANT TERMS

Match the first column with the corresponding phrase in the second column.

_____ 1. Short run
_____ 2. Long run
_____ 3. Short-run production function
_____ 4. Marginal product
_____ 5. Law of (eventually) diminishing returns.
_____ 6. Fixed costs
_____ 7. Variable costs
_____ 8. Total cost
_____ 9. Average total cost
_____ 10. Marginal cost
_____ 11. Opportunity cost
_____ 12. Economic cost
_____ 13. Economic profit
_____ 14. Economies of scale

a. The income an input could earn in its best alternative use.
b. The sum of both fixed and variable costs.
c. Costs that do not vary as output increases in the short run.
d. If more of one factor is employed while all other factors are held constant, the marginal product of that factor must eventually fall.
e. The time period over which the firm's capital stock is variable.
f. The relationship between the amount of variable inputs used and the amount of output that can be produced, when the amount of capital is constant.
g. Explicit accounting costs, plus implicit opportunity costs.
h. Income above normal profits.
i. Doubling all inputs more than doubles output.
j. In the long run, all costs.
k. Cost per unit.
l. The increase in total cost when output is increased by one unit.
m. The time period over which the firm cannot vary its capital stock.
n. The additional output the firm can produce by using one more unit of an input.

TRUE-FALSE

T   F   1.   If output is zero, variable costs must be zero.

T   F   2.   The law of diminishing returns states that the marginal product of any factor must eventually fall if other factors are held constant.

T   F   3.   In a firm's short-run production function, the firm's labor and plant are held constant, while its machinery is allowed to vary.

T   F   4.   The law of diminishing returns is unrealistic because it implies that we could feed the world from our back garden.

T   F   5.   When existing firms earn economic profit, then that industry is attractive for new firms.

T   F   6.   Economic profit is the profit that remains after account is taken of all explicit and implicit costs, including normal profit.

T   F   7.   Diseconomies of scale exist if a 15% increase in output requires a 16% increase in all inputs.

T   F   8.   It is not possible for a firm to be facing diminishing returns if its long-run average cost curve is falling.

T   F   9.   In the long run, there are no variable costs.

T   F   10.   The law of eventually diminishing returns describes a short run situation in which labor varies but fixed factors do not.

T   F   11.   Whereas each indifference curve of a consumer represents a specific number of units of satisfaction, each isoquant in a production function represents only a "higher" or "lower" level of output.

MULTIPLE CHOICE

1. An example of a variable cost is:

   a. wage payments
   b. rental payments on a long-term lease
   c. interest payments on a mortgage
   d. depreciation costs
   e. all of the above

2. As output increases in the short run:

   a. fixed costs increase, but variable costs do not
   b. fixed costs decrease, but variable costs do not
   c. both fixed costs and variable costs change
   d. neither fixed costs nor variable costs change
   e. variable costs increase, but fixed costs do not

3. As output increases in the short run:

   a. fixed cost falls
   b. fixed cost rises
   c. fixed cost has less and less influence on average total cost
   d. fixed costs has more and more influence on average total cost
   e. average fixed cost rises

4. A firm's costs are related in the following way:

   a. average cost ATC cuts marginal cost MC at the minimum point of MC
   b. average cost ATC cuts average variable cost AVC at the minimum point of AVC
   c. MC cuts ATC at the minimum point of ATC
   d. MC cuts total cost at the minimum point of total cost
   e. AVC cuts ATC at the minimum point of ATC

5. If total costs are rising, then marginal cost must be:

   a. rising
   b. falling
   c. positive
   d. negative
   e. zero

6. The law of diminishing returns means that, as output increases in the short run,

   a. fixed cost will eventually fall
   b. fixed cost will eventually rise
   c. marginal costs will eventually rise
   d. marginal costs will eventually fall
   e. marginal costs will eventually become constant

7. In the long-run decisions of a firm:

   a. employment of labor is held constant, while its use of capital is allowed to increase
   b. employment of labor is held constant, while its use of capital is allowed to decrease
   c. use of capital is held constant, while its employment of labor is allowed to vary
   d. both are allowed to vary
   e. neither is allowed to vary

8. To calculate all the short run costs of a firm with two inputs — labor and capital — all we need to know is:

   a. the firm's short run production function
   b. the firm's short run production function and its fixed costs
   c. the firm's short run production function and its wage rate
   d. the firm's short run production function, its wage rate, and its fixed costs
   e. none of the above are enough

9. If a firm's fixed cost is $100, and its total cost is $200 to produce one unit and $310 to produce two, then the marginal cost of the second unit is:

    a. $100
    b. $110
    c. $200
    d. $210
    e. $310

10. If a firm's fixed cost if $100, and its total cost is $200 to produce one unit and $310 to produce two, then its average variable cost for each of the two units is:

    a. $50
    b. $100
    c. $105
    d. $110
    e. $155

11. If a firm's fixed cost is $100, and its total cost is $200 to produce one unit, and $310 to produce two, the firm is:

    a. already facing diminishing returns
    b. not yet facing diminishing returns
    c. not yet facing constant returns
    d. already facing increasing returns
    e. facing constant returns

12. If there are economies of scale:

    a. short run average cost rises
    b. short run average cost is constant
    c. short run average cost falls
    d. long run average cost falls
    e. long run average cost rises

13. If there are diminishing returns:

    a. short run marginal cost falls
    b. short run marginal cost rises
    c. short run marginal cost is constant
    d. long run marginal cost falls
    e. long run marginal cost is constant

14. Fixed costs are:

    a. fixed only in the short run
    b. fixed only in the long run
    c. fixed in both the long and short run

    d. fixed in neither the long nor the short run
    e. variable in the short run

15. In the long run, a firm has to decide on:

    a. how much plant and equipment it uses, but not how much labor
    b. how much plant it uses, but not how much equipment and labor
    c. how much equipment and labor it uses, but not how much plant
    d. how much labor it uses, but not how much plant and equipment
    e. how much of all three it uses

16. A firm's long-run average cost curve is the envelope of its short run:

    a. marginal cost curves
    b. fixed cost curves
    c. average variable cost curves
    d. average cost curves
    e. total cost curves

17. The long run average cost curve is constructed by:

    a. joining the minimum points on all the short run marginal cost curves
    b. joining the minimum points on all the short run average cost curves
    c. joining the minimum points on all the short run average variable cost curves
    d. joining the minimum points on all of the firm's planning curves
    e. none of the above

18. If a firm is simultaneously facing diminishing returns and economies of scale, then:

    a. its long-run average cost curve is falling, while its short-run marginal cost curve is rising
    b. its long-run average cost curve is rising, while its short-run marginal cost curve is rising
    c. its long-run average cost curve is rising, while its short-run marginal cost curve is falling
    d. its long-run average cost curve is falling, while its short-run marginal cost curve is falling
    e. its long-run average cost curve is neither rising nor falling, while its short-run marginal cost curve is rising

19. In reading a long-run production function table, any evidence of:

a. economies of scale would be found along a row, with diminishing returns along a diagonal
b. economies of scale would be found along a diagonal, with diminishing returns along a row
c. both would be found along a row
d. both would be found along a diagonal
e. economies of scale would be found along a column

20. At the long run equilibrium for the firm,

a. an isoquant of the long-run production function is tangent to an equal-cost line
b. an isoquant of the short-run production function is tangent to an equal-cost line
c. an isoquant of the long-run production function intersects an equal-cost line
d. an isoquant of the short-run production function intersects an equal-cost line
e. an indifference curve is tangent to an equal-cost line

21. The opportunity cost of an input is:

a. the most it could earn in its least productive alternative use
b. the least it could earn in its least productive alternative use
c. the most it could earn in its most productive alternative use
d. a or c
e. b or c

EXERCISES

1. Table 23.1 below shows two short run production functions for a firm that uses only 2 factors: labor and capital. Each production function describes the amounts of labor the firm would require to produce various amounts of output. The left panel shows the short run production function if the firm has 20 units of capital; the right panel shows its short run production function if it has 40 units of capital.

Table 23.1

TWO SHORT-RUN PRODUCTION FUNCTIONS

20 units of capital			40 units of capital		
Output	Capital	Labor required	Output	Capital	Labor required
0	20	0	0	40	0
1	20	8	1	40	7
2	20	14	2	40	12
3	20	28	3	40	20
4	20	45	4	40	30
5	20	65	5	40	46
6	20	90	6	40	66

The cost of labor to the firm is $500 per unit and the cost of capital is $250 per unit. Thus, producing say, 3 units of output with 20 units of capital cost and 28 units of labor would cost a total of $19,000; that is, $5,000 in fixed costs (20 units of capital at $250 per unit) plus $14,000 in variable costs (28 units of labor at a $500 per unit wage rate). This $19,000 is entered in Table 23.2 below. Fill in the rest of this table.

Table 23.2

COSTS CALCULATED FROM THE TWO SHORT-RUN PRODUCTION FUNCTIONS IN TABLE 23.1, GIVEN A WAGE OF $500

Output	Total cost	Fixed cost	Var. cost	Avg. cost	Avg. var. cost	Marg. cost	Total cost	Fixed cost	Var. cost	Avg. cost	Avg. var. cost	Marg. cost
0				——	——	0				——	——	0
1												
2												
3	19,000	5,000	14,000	6,333	4,667							
4												
5												
6												

b. If the firm is making a long-run decision and wishes to produce 2 units of output, how much capital should it acquire — 20 units or 40? Why?

c. Answer question (b) if the firm wishes to produce 5 units of output.

2. Table 23.3 below presents average cost figures for 4 of the large number of plant sizes that a firm can select in the long run. (Note that plants B and C have costs similar — but not identical — to those you calculated for the two plants in Table 23.2.) In Figure 23.1, graph the four average cost curves. Label them A, B, C, D and mark the minimum point of each MA, MB, MC and MD. Sketch in a rough long-run average cost curve (LAC) for this firm. Does it pass through all the minimum points? In particular, does it pass through M_A and M_D? Through M_C? Why?

Table 23.3

Out-put	Average cost, if fixed cost is:			
	$2000 Plant A	$5,000 Plant B	$10,000 Plant C	$15,000 Plant D
1	7,100	9,000	13,500	13,900
2	6,700	7,000	8,000	8,500
3	6,800	6,300	6,700	6,900
4	8,000	6,900	6,200	6,600
5	9,600	7,600	6,600	6,500
6	12,000	8,700	7,200	6,600

Figure 23.1

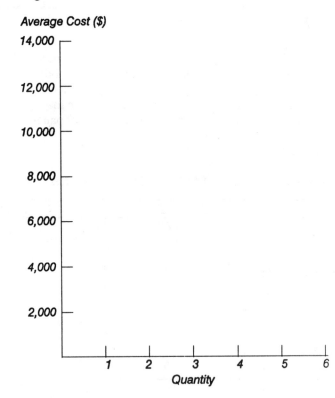

3. Fill in a table similar to Table 23-3 in the textbook, showing how an accountant and an economist would describe the costs and profit of Mark Laporte, who owns and operates a farm. His total revenue in this particular year is $180,000. His expenses include $27,000 he pays to hire farm labor, $12,000 for fertilizer and seed, $10,000 he pays to rent an adjacent farm, and $20,000 for gas and other costs. Although his accountant tells him that, relative to his neighbors, he's extremely successful,

he sometimes considers giving up farming to take a job managing a farm supply business nearby where he has been offered a $65,000 salary. If he did so, he would sell his farm and invest the proceeds in government bonds that would yield a $62,000 per year interest income.

What is his accounting profit and his economic profit? Assuming that he finds farming and managing the farm supply business equally attractive, what would you recommend that he do? Why?

ESSAY QUESTIONS

1. Draw a U-shaped average cost curve. Then draw in the corresponding MC curve and finally the AVC curve. In red show the new curves after a cost-cutting technological innovation. What effect does this have on the firm's supply curve?

2. Would you expect the short run to be longer for a gardening service or a steel company? Explain.

3. In Figure 23-2b in the text, the marginal product curve cuts the average product curve at the highest point on the average product curve. Explain why this must be so, using an argument similar to the one used to establish that the MC curve intersects the ATC at the lowest point on the ATC curve.

4. "The law of diminishing returns ensures a dismal economic future, because it tells us that as the labor force grows, it will eventually produce a lower and lower marginal product." Do you agree? Why or why not?

5. Do you agree with the following statement? Explain why. "If a firm producing 1000 units of output is on its long-run average cost curve then the combination of capital and labor that it is using costs less than any alternative combination which could be used to produce 1000 units of output." Illustrate your answer with a diagram, showing two or three of the other combinations.

6. Are either normal profit or economic profit — or both — included in costs? Explain why.

ANSWERS

Important Terms :   1 m, 2 e, 3 f, 4 n, 5 d, 6 c, 7 j, 8 b, 9 k, 10 l, 11 a, 12 g, 13 h, 14 i.

True-False:
1 T(p. 416)
2 T(p. 421)
3 F(p. 420)
4 F(p. 422)
5 T(p. 429)
6 T(p. 429)
7 T(p. 425)
8 F(p. 427)
9 F(p. 422)
10 T(p. 421)
11 F(p. 433, APPENDIX)

Multiple Choice:
1 a (p. 417)
2 e (p. 416)
3 c (p. 418)
4 c (p. 419)
5 c (p. 418)
6 c (p. 422)
7 d (p. 415)
8 d (p. 422)
9 b (p. 417)

Exercises

1   a.

Table 23.2 Completed

COSTS CALCULATED FROM THE TWO SHORT-RUN PRODUCTION FUNCTIONS IN TABLE 23.1, GIVEN A WAGE OF $500

Output	Total cost	Fixed cost	Var. cost	Avg. cost	Avg. var. cost	Marg. cost	Total cost	Fixed cost	Var. cost	Avg. cost	Avg. var. cost	Marg. cost
0	5,000	5,000	0	____	____	0	10,000	10,000	0	____	____	0
1	9,000	5,000	4,000	9,000	4,000	4,000	13,500	10,000	3,500	13,500	3,500	3,500
2	12,000	5,000	7,000	6,000	3,500	3,000	16,000	10,000	6,000	8,000	3,000	2,500
3	19,000	5,000	14,000	6,333	4,667	7,000	20,000	10,000	10,000	6,667	3,333	4,000
4	27,500	5,000	22,500	6,875	5,625	8,500	25,000	10,000	15,000	6,250	3,750	5,000
5	37,500	5,000	32,500	7,500	6,500	10,000	33,000	10,000	23,000	6,600	4,600	8,000
6	50,000	5,000	45,000	8,333	7,500	12,500	43,000	10,000	33,000	7,167	5,500	10,000

b.   20 units; its average cost will be $6,000, rather than $8,000.
c.   40 units; its average cost will be $6,600, rather than $7,500.

2.   no, no, yes because M_C is the lowest of all the minimum values.

Figure 23.1 Completed

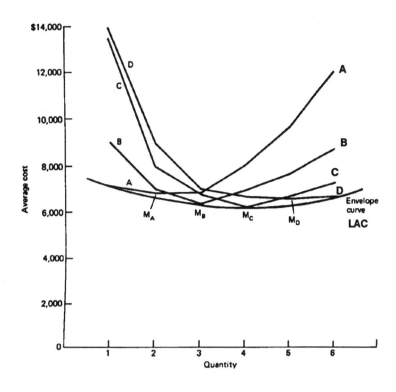

3. The table you derive should look like this:

Table 23.4

Costs and profits, evaluated by:					
1. An accountant			**2. An economist**		
Total revenue		$180,000	Total revenue		$180,000
			Costs:		
Costs:			Explicit:		
Labor	27,000		Labor	27,000	
Fertilizer, seed	12,000		Fertilizer, seed	12,000	
Rent	10,000		Rent	10,000	
Gas, etc	20,000		Gas, etc.	20,000	
Total costs		69,000	Implicit:		
			Owner's salary	65,000	
			Normal profit	62,000	
			Total costs		196,000
Accounting profit		111,000	Economic (above normal) profit		−16,000

His accounting profit is $111,000, but his economic profit is -$16,000.

His best course of action is to sell the farm, buy bonds with the proceeds and take the other job, since he is now earning $16,000 less in farming than he could if he followed this alternative course of action. That is, his economic loss in farming is $16,000; his $111,000 of accounting profit is $16,000 less than his opportunity cost of $65,000 + $62,000 = $127,000.

Part 7

MARKET STRUCTURE AND MARKET ECONOMY

CHAPTER 24

SUPPLY IN A PERFECTLY COMPETITIVE MARKET

LEARNING OBJECTIVES

After you have studied this chapter in the textbook and the study guide, you should be able to

✔ Define perfect competition, explaining each of the five important requirements

✔ Show why the condition for profit maximization by *any firm* is to produce until "marginal cost = marginal revenue"

✔ Show, as one specific case of this general theorem, that the condition for profit-maximization by a *perfectly competitive firm* is to produce until "marginal cost = *price*"

✔ Demonstrate why the short-run supply curve of a perfectly competitive firm is its marginal cost curve (above its average variable cost curve)

✔ Analyze the long run effect of the entry of new firms on an industry's supply

✔ Describe how an industry adjusts to an increase in demand, clearly distinguishing between the short-run increase in price, and the long-term drift of that price back down towards its original level as new firms enter the industry.

✔ Distinguish between case A where, in the long run, price falls all the way back to its original level and case B where it falls back only part way

✔ Explain the underlying conditions that give rise to each of these two cases

✔ Restate this analysis to describe what happens when demand decreases, rather than increases

✔ Show how the gain to producers from a price increase can be read off a supply curve, just as a change in consumer surplus can be read off a demand curve

MAJOR PURPOSES

In Chapter 21 we saw how a demand curve reflects the desire of buyers to acquire a good. In this chapter, our attention turns to *supply*. It will be shown that, in a perfectly competitive market, a supply curve reflects the marginal cost of producing a good. Specifically, just as you can visualize a whole set of marginal benefit arrows rising up to a demand curve, you can also visualize a whole set of marginal cost arrows rising up to a supply curve. To establish this important conclusion, we analyze a profit-maximizing firm's response to various market prices. At each price, the firm will supply a quantity determined by its marginal cost curve (provided its variable costs are covered). Therefore supply reflects marginal cost. We also show the importance in the long run of free entry of new firms into an industry—and free exit by existing firms. Thus, for example, the long term adjustment of a perfectly competitive industry to an increase in demand will involve not only an increase in the output of existing firms but also an increase in the number of firms. This is one of the reasons why the long term supply response by an industry will be more elastic than its short term response.

The final objective in this chapter is to show how the profit position of perfectly competitive producers is affected by a change in market price. We will show that, just as a price increase in Chapter 21 *hurt consumers* by the area to the left of the *demand curve* (between the old and new price) a price increase will *benefit producers* by the area to the left of the *supply* curve (between the old and new price). With this knowledge of how both producers and consumers are affected, we are now in a position to analyze the winners and losers when, say, government intervention affects a market price. The example given is the imposition of a sales tax.

HIGHLIGHTS OF CHAPTER

In our examination in this chapter of what underlies the cost curve—just as in our parallel examination in Chapter 21 of what underlies demand—we assume that rational self-interest is pursued. Specifically, in this chapter, we assume that firms will produce the quantity of a good that will maximize their profit.

First, recall that our description of costs in Chapter 23 equally well describes the costs of a firm producing in perfect competition or in any other form of market. However, the important question "How much will the firm produce?" cannot be answered without specifying the market form. In the text, the market is assumed to be perfectly competitive, and a more complete definition of this market form is now required. So far we have only emphasized that it is a market in which there are so many buyers and sellers that none can influence price. Now we recognize several further conditions—in particular, the requirements that the product is standardized, and that there are no barriers to the entry of new firms or the exit of existing firms.

Supply in the Short Run

The stage is now set for addressing the question: Given the firm's marginal cost (MC) and other cost schedules described in Chapter 23, how much will the firm supply at any given price? The rule for any profit maximizing firm is to produce until its MC equals its marginal revenue MR, where MR is its additional revenue earned from producing one more unit of output.

This general rule—that a firm will produce until MC = MR—can be stated in an alternative way for a perfectly competitive firm: Such a firm will produce until its MC = *price*. (The reason is that such a firm takes the price of its output as given. Therefore, its MR is just the price that it faces. For example, if it sells apples for a price P = \$2 a basket, then each additional basket provides \$2 of extra revenue MR.) This conclusion that a firm continues to produce until MC = P is important. It means that when it is faced with any given market price P, it will supply a quantity of output that can be read off its MC curve; in other words, the firm's supply curve depends on its MC curve. Be sure that you fully understand Figure 24-2 and Table 24-1 in the textbook. These most clearly demonstrate why the firm will produce until MC = P; and why, therefore the firm's supply curve is the same as its marginal cost curve.

In making this statement about the firm's supply, however, we must recognize one important reservation. Price must be above a certain minimum level, or the firm won't supply anything at all. This minimum level is the price that will generate enough revenue to cover the firm's variable costs. More specifically, price must be at least as high as the firm's "shutdown point" on its average variable cost (AVC) curve—that is, at least as high as point K in Figure 24-3 in the textbook. As long as price is at least this high, then in the short run, the firm will supply this product. This is true, even if the price is still below the "breakeven point" (H in the same diagram) where the firm is just barely able to cover its total cost, including both its variable costs and its fixed costs. Even though a firm operating between these two points is incurring a loss, it is still able to cover its variable costs and have at least something left over to cover its fixed costs. Therefore, it is better to continue to operate than to close down altogether. (If it were to close down, it would be worse off because it would be unable to cover *any* of its fixed costs.)

This then leads to the conclusion that, as price falls, the firm's short-run supply curve will follow its MC curve down until it reaches the shutdown point where MC intersects AVC.

The short run *industry* supply curve is the horizontal summation of the short run supply curves of all of the individual firms, as shown in Figure 24-4.

Supply in the Long Run

In the long run (unlike the short run) the firm *can* escape from its fixed costs, because all costs are variable. Therefore it can operate on its flatter long run ATC (envelope) curve. And there is another important difference: In the long run, firms can enter or leave the industry.

In deriving long run supply two cases should be distinguished.

Case A: Long Run Supply is Completely Elastic. (Figures 24-6 and 24-7 in the text.) Suppose new firms can produce at the same cost as old firms. (For this to happen, inputs acquired by new firms would have to be as productive as those used by existing firms; and the industry would have to be small enough so that new firms can purchase inputs without bidding up their price.) In such circumstances, an increase in demand for this industry's output can, in the long run, be met entirely by new firms entering the industry and selling at the same cost and price as old firms. Since supply can increase without any increase in price, the long run supply is completely elastic; an example is S_L in Figure 24-6.

It is true that when demand initially increases, price does rise in the short run, before new firms can enter. It is this increase in price and hence profit to existing firms that becomes the incentive for new firms to enter the industry. As new firms enter, supply shifts to the right. As a result, profit is reduced. This process continues until price falls back all the way to its original level, above-normal profit is eliminated, and there is therefore no incentive left for new firms to enter.

Case B: A rising long-run supply curve. (Figure 24-8 in text.) In this case, price does not fall all the way

back to its original level. The reason is that, as the number of firms in the industry increases, costs rise. This may happen because new firms cannot purchase inputs without bidding up their price, or because these firms cannot acquire inputs of the same quality as those used by existing firms. (For example, new entrants into farming may find that the only available land is less productive.) Because new firms are incurring higher costs, their profits will disappear before price falls all the way back to its original level. At this point, there will be no incentive left for more firms to enter; thus the new equilibrium price will be higher than its original level. In this case, therefore, the long-run supply curve slopes up; an example is S_L in Figure 24-8.

The Benefit to Producers from a Higher Price

When, in response to a higher price, producers move from E_1 to E_2 in Figure 24-9, they acquire two benefits:

- They get a higher price on their original 30 units of sales; thus their profit increases by area 1.

- On the additional 20 units they now sell, their costs are given by the height of the supply curve. But they receive the higher $700 price. Thus profit increases by the difference between the two — area 2. Therefore **when price rises, producers benefit by the area to the left of the supply curve between the old and new price.**

Reprise: The Burden of an Excise Tax

A $1 tax in Figure 24-10 shifts the S curve up from S_1 to S_2, with consumer equilibrium moving from E_1 to E_2.

Consumers lose areas 1 + 2, the area to the left of the **demand** curve between the old and new price.

Producers must take a price reduction (after tax) from $2 to $1.60. Thus they lose areas 3 + 4 to the left of the supply curve.

The treasury gains 1 + 3 of tax revenue — a $1 tax on each of the 3,000 units sold.

Thus there is a transfer of 1 + 3 from consumers and producers to the treasury (i.e., to taxpayers). The rest of the loss (area 3 + 4) is a deadweight loss that goes to no-one. It's the loss because a tax has distorted this market—in particular has reduced the quantity bought and sold from 5,000 to 3,000.

IMPORTANT TERMS

Match the first column with the corresponding phrase in the second column.

1. Perfect competition
2. Short run supply
3. Long run supply
4. Marginal revenue
5. Break-even point
6. Shutdown point
7. Increase in producer surplus
8. Above-normal profit

a. Income in excess of opportunity cost.
b. A market where there are no barriers to entry or exit, and there are so many buyers and sellers of a standardized product that none has any influence over its price.
c. The quantity sold in the time period during which the capital stock is variable.
d. The increase in total revenue from the sale of one more unit. In perfect competition, this is the same as market price.
e. The point at which the marginal cost curve intersects the average variable cost curve. If the price falls below this, the firm will cease operating even in the short run.
f. The point at which the marginal cost curve intersects the average cost curve, and the firm makes a zero profit.
g. The quantity sold in the time period during which the capital stock is fixed.
h. The area to the left of the supply curve between the old and new price

---

TRUE-FALSE

T   F   1.   Marginal revenue is total revenue less the cost that results when one more unit is produced.

T   F   2.   If a competitive firm is producing slightly less than the profit-maximizing amount, then price is greater than marginal cost.

T   F   3.   In the short run, the firm stops producing if price falls below its minimum average total cost.

T   F   4.   As you move up a firm's short-run marginal cost curve to the right, you reach the shutdown point before the break-even point.

T   F   5.   A firm earning a profit maximizes those profits where the vertical distance between its total cost and total revenue curves is minimized.

T   F   6.   If a firm is operating at capacity—that is, with a completely inelastic supply (MC) curve—then an increase in market price will result in no increase in its total revenue or output.

T   F   7.   In the short run, a firm that is operating at its shutdown point is earning no economic profit or loss.

T   F   8.   Unless there are economies of scale, a perfectly competitive firm's short run supply curve cannot slope upward to the right.

T   F   9.   An increase in demand for a perfectly competitive good will result in a short-run increase in the output and profit of existing firms.

T   F   10. If new entrants to an industry can obtain the same quality of inputs as existing firms, and inputs are available at stable prices, then the long-run industry supply will be upward-sloping.

MULTIPLE CHOICE

1. For a perfectly competitive firm, marginal revenue is:

    a. less than the price of its output
    b. equal to the price of its output
    c. greater than the price of its output
    d. greater than the price of its output if the elasticity of demand for its output is greater than 1
    e. not related to the price of its output

2. The short-run supply curve slopes upward because of:

    a. the law of eventually diminishing returns
    b. economies of scale
    c. the upward slope of the marginal cost curve
    d. a and c
    e. b and c

3. In a perfectly competitive industry, there are:

    a. so few buyers and sellers that each one can influence price
    b. so few buyers and sellers that none can influence price
    c. so many buyers and sellers that none can influence price
    d. so many buyers and sellers that each one can influence price
    e. just the right number of buyers and sellers so that each can influence the price

4. In a perfectly competitive market, an individual consumer determines:

    a. price but not the quantity to purchase
    b. quantity to purchase, but not price
    c. neither the quantity to purchase, nor price
    d. both the quantity to purchase, and price
    e. both the quantity to purchase and price, but only if the product is standardized

5. In perfect competition, the demand by individual buyers is

    a. perfectly elastic while the demand facing individual sellers is not
    b. perfectly elastic like the demand facing individual sellers
    c. not perfectly elastic while the demand facing individual sellers is perfectly elastic
    d. not perfectly elastic, nor is the demand facing individual sellers
    e. perfectly elastic while the demand facing individual sellers can be either elastic or inelastic

6. In perfect competition, the per unit profit of an individual firm is:

    a. its total cost minus its total revenue
    b. its total revenue minus its total cost
    c. its average total cost minus the price at which it sells
    d. its average total cost plus the price at which it sells
    e. its selling price minus its average total cost

7. In perfect competition, total profit of an individual firm is its:

    a. marginal revenue minus its average total cost
    b. total revenue minus its average total cost
    c. total revenue minus its total cost
    d. marginal revenue minus its total cost
    e. marginal revenue minus its marginal cost

8. Consider a perfectly competitive industry, where there are many identical firms initially producing with zero (excess) profit. If demand decreases, then in the short run:

    a. each firm will produce more and operate at a loss
    b. each firm will produce more and operate at a profit
    c. each firm will produce more and continue to operate with zero profit
    d. each firm will produce less and operate at a profit
    e. each firm will produce less and operate at a loss

9. The shutdown point is:

   a. the minimum point on the average total cost curve
   b. the minimum point on the average variable cost curve
   c. the minimum point on the marginal cost curve
   d. the minimum point on the average fixed cost curve
   e. the point where marginal cost cuts the average fixed cost curve

10. Beneath a supply curve, you can visualize a set of vertical

    a. marginal revenue arrows
    b. marginal benefit arrows
    c. marginal cost arrows
    d. average cost arrows
    e. average benefit arrows

11. In the short run, the break-even point is:

    a. at the intersection of the marginal cost curve and the average fixed cost curve
    b. below the intersection of the marginal cost curve and the average fixed cost curve
    c. the same as the shutdown point
    d. above the shutdown point
    e. below the shutdown point

12. In the short run, the perfectly competitive firm's break-even point occurs at:

    a. a greater quantity of output than the shutdown point
    b. a smaller quantity than the shutdown point
    c. the same quantity as the shutdown point
    d. a lower price than the shutdown point
    e. the same price as the shutdown point

13. If a firm's total cost and total revenue curves (TC and TR) are plotted, the firm can earn a profit and maximizes it where:

    a. its TC cuts its TR from above
    b. its TC cuts its TR from below
    c. its TC is parallel to, and above its TR
    d. its TC is parallel to, and below its TR
    e. its TC is horizontal

14. Removing restrictions on entry by new firms will:

    a. shift the industry's supply curve to the left
    b. shift the industry's demand curve to the left
    c. shift the industry's supply curve to the right
    d. have no affect on the industry's supply curve
    e. have no affect on the industry's supply and demand curves

15. If demand decreases in a perfectly competitive industry, then price will:

    a. rise in the short run and fall in the long run
    b. rise in the short run and rise further in the long run
    c. fall in the short run and fall further in the long run
    d. fall in the short run and rise back towards the original price in the long run
    e. fall in the short run and thereafter remain constant at that level

16. Suppose demand has increased in a perfectly competitive industry, and each firm has moved to a new short run equilibrium. Then, in the further process of long run adjustment, the individual firm will face:

    a. falling price and decreasing profit
    b. falling price and increasing profit
    c. falling price and constant profit
    d. increasing price and decreasing profit
    e. increasing price and increasing profit

17. For long run industry supply to be completely elastic (horizontal):

    a. the industry must be large enough so that it can influence the price of its inputs
    b. inputs of uniform quality must be available to old and new firms alike
    c. both of the above
    d. neither of the above
    e. it is not possible for an industry supply curve to be completely elastic.

18. The long-run supply curve for an industry will be upward sloping if:

    a. new firms bid up the price of inputs
    b. the quality of inputs deteriorates as new firms purchase more
    c. a or b
    d. neither a nor b
    e. It's impossible for a long-run supply curve to be upward sloping

19. If price rises and output increases, then the gain to the producing firm is:

a. the increase in the firm's revenue, plus the increase in its costs
b. the increase in the firm's revenue, minus the increase in its costs
c. the increase in the firm's revenue
d. the increase in the firm's costs, minus the increase in its revenue
e. the decrease in the firm's costs

20. If price falls, then producers:

a. benefit by the area to the left of the supply curve between the old and new price
b. benefit by the area to the left of the demand curve between the old and new price
c. are worse off by the area to the left of the

demand curve between the old and new price
d. are worse off by the area to the left of the supply curve between the old and new price
e. are not affected

21. When the government imposes an excise tax on a product

a. the consumers' and producers' loss is less than the government's tax collections
b. the consumers' and producers' loss is the same as the government's tax collections
c. the consumers' and producers' gain is the same as the government's loss of tax collections
d. the consumers' and producers' gain is less than the government's loss of tax collections
e. the consumers' and producers' loss is greater than the government's tax collections

---

EXERCISES

1 a. If the price is P_1 in Figure 24.1 below, the quantity supplied will be _____, total revenue will be area _____, average cost will be _____, and multiplying this by the number of units sold yields a total cost of area _____. Thus economic profit will be area _____.

Figure 24.1

b. Alternatively, we can arrive at this same profit by noting that the firm's average revenue is its price P_1, its average cost is _____, and therefore its average profit is _____. Multiplying this by its quantity of output yields its total profit of area _____.

c. If the price is P_2, the firm will supply quantity _____, total revenue will be _____, average cost will be _____, total cost will be _____, and economic profit will be _____. Therefore the (breakeven/shutdown) point is _____.

d. If the price is P_3, the firm will supply _____, total revenue will be _____, average cost will be _____, and total cost will be _____. Therefore total economic (profit/loss) will be _____. If price stays at P_3, then the firm will continue to operate in the _____ run, but not in the _____ run. Despite its loss, it makes this short-run decision because price P_3 is still above the firm's (shutdown/breakeven) point at _____. Another way of viewing this decision is that the firm is operating above its (MC, AC, AVC) curve. Therefore, it can more than cover its _____ costs and thus have some left over partly to cover its _____ costs. Shade in and mark for future reference the firm's profit when its price (in this case P_1) is above the minimum point K on its AC curve; and its loss when its price (in this case P_3) is below K.

2. Table 24.1 describes some of a firm's long-run costs. Fill in the rest of this table. Note in particular that column 3 is to show its envelope curve LAC.

When the price of this firm's output is $70, the firm's long run profit maximizing output is _____, and its economic profit is _____. When the price is $85, the firm's profit maximizing output is _____, and its profit is _____.

TABLE 24.1

A FIRM'S LONG-RUN COSTS

Output	Total cost	Average cost (LAC)	Marginal cost	Total revenue if price equals $70	Economic profit if price equals $70	Total revenue if price equals $85	Economic profit if price equals 85
1	$120		$120				
2							
3							
4							
5							
6							

When price rises from $70 to $85, there is a (gain, loss) to this firm of _____.

3. In Figure 24.2, supply is S₁ in panel b. When D₁ decreases to D₂, price falls from _____ to _____ as the short-run equilibrium of the industry shifts from _____ to _____. Each firm in panel a responds by moving along its supply curve from _____ to _____. Each firm now has a (profit, loss) of _____. As firms therefore

(enter, leave) the industry, the industry supply in panel b shifts from _____ to _____, and industry equilibrium moves from _____ to _____. The initial 30% leftward shift in demand has been offset by a _____% shift in supply, and price (moves to, returns to) _____. Long-run supply is constructed by joining all points such as _____ and _____. It is (completely elastic, unit elastic, inelastic).

Figure 24.2

(a) An individual firm....

(b) ...in a perfectly competitive industry

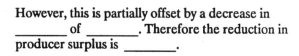

4. If price is P_1, the total revenue of the perfectly competitive industry shown in Figure 24.3 is _____ . If price falls to P_2, its total revenue is _____, for a (decrease, increase) in revenue of _____ .

However, this is partially offset by a decrease in _____ of _____ . Therefore the reduction in producer surplus is _____ .

Figure 24.3

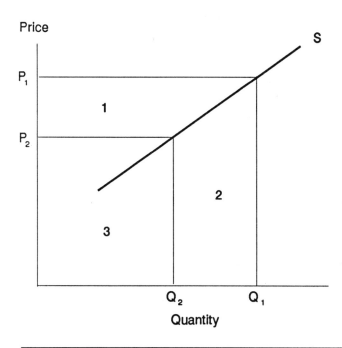

ESSAY QUESTIONS

1. "If a firm's overhead costs increase by, say, 20% because of an increase in its property taxes, its output will not be affected." Evaluate this statement, clearly distinguishing between the short and long run.

2. Draw a U-shaped average cost curve. Then draw in the corresponding MC curve and finally the AVC curve. Show the new curves after a cost-cutting technological innovation. What effect does this have on the firm's supply curve?

3. "In the short run, a perfectly competitive firm will not produce at any point where its average cost is still falling." Do you agree? Why or why not?

4. "If demand for a perfectly competitive product shifts downward, price must fall." Do you agree? Explain, clearly distinguishing between the long and short run.

ANSWERS

Matching Columns: **1** b, **2** g, **3** c, **4** d, **5** f, **6** e, **7** h, **8** a.

True-False: **1** F (p. 440)
2 T (p. 440)
3 F (p. 443)
4 T (p. 443)
5 F (p. 442, BOX)
6 F (p. 440)
7 F (p. 443)
8 F (p. 449)
9 T (p. 447)
10 F (p. 447).

Multiple Choice: **1** b (p. 440)
2 d (p. 442)
3 c (p. 438)
4 b (p. 438)
5 c (p. 439)
6 e (p. 440)
7 c (p. 440)
8 e (p. 448)
9 b (p. 443)
10 c (p. 442)
11 d (p. 443)
12 a (p. 443)
13 d (p. 442, BOX)
14 c (p. 446)
15 d (p. 448)
16 a (p. 447)
17 b (p. 449)
18 c (p. 449)
19 b (p. 451)
20 d (p. 451)
21 e (pp. 451-452).

Exercises

1   a. Q_6, P_1FQ_6O, B, BGQ_6O, P_1FGB.
     b.   B, BP_1, P_1FGB.
     c. Q_5, P_2KQ_5O, P_2, P_2KQ_5O, zero, breakeven, K.
     d. Q_4, P_3SQ_4O, A, AJQ_4O, loss, $AJSP_3$, short, long, shutdown, N, AVC, variable, fixed.

2.

TABLE 24.1 Completed

A FIRM'S LONG-RUN COSTS

Output	Total cost	Average cost (LAC)	Marginal cost	Total revenue if price equals $70	Economic profit if price equals $70	Total revenue if price equals $85	Economic profit if price equals 85
1	$120	120	$120	70	−50	85	−35
2	150	75	30	140	−10	170	20
3	200	66⅔	50	210	10	255	55
4	270	67½	70	280	10	340	70
5	350	70	80	350	0	425	75
6	440	73⅓	90	420	−20	510	70

4, $10, 5, $75, gain, $65.

3. P_1, P_2, G, H, E, T, loss, RSTP$_2$, leave, S_1, S_2, H, J, 30%, returns to, P_1, G, J, completely elastic.

4. 1 + 2 + 3, 3, decrease, 1 + 2, costs, 2, 1.

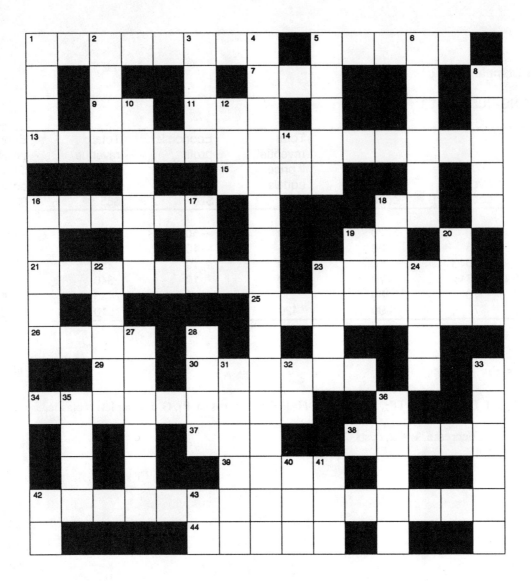

Across

1,5. When you know these, you can calculate marginal costs
7. head of a corporation (abbrev.)
9. be (1st person)
11. in the past
13. the amount an input could earn in its best alternative use (2 words)
15. this grows in a damp, cool place
16. The U.S. government has had a large deficit in its _____
18. first name of President Carter's Secretary of State (abbrev.)
19. a business organization (abbrev.)
21, 23. the relationship of the long-run cost curve to a series of short-run cost curves
25. at this point, losses equal fixed costs

26. sign of affection
29. third "person"
30. overrun and inhabit
34. the sum of fixed and variable costs (2 words)
37. this elasticity is measured between two points on a curve
38. compulsive saver
39. more than a few
42. to maximize profits, a firm equates this with marginal cost (2 words)
44. with this type of floating exchange rate, governments don't accumulate foreign exchange reserves

Down

1. forbid, prohibit
2. get a return or reward
3. what Navy wants to do to the West Point football team
4. a reason why there are gains from specialization (3 words)
5. expenses
6. systematic statement of principles or propositions
8. a barrier to _____ reduces competition
10. things are dead around there
12. please don't chew this in class!
14. be (3rd person)
16. at the _____ even point, profits are zero
17. a number
18. thin rope
19. sever
20. when night falls, so does this
22. go to see

23. hints, signals
24. expression of a choice
27. German concentration camp
28. a size of type
31. economists consider this type of profit to be a cost
32. main character in a 1983 movie
33. elasticity of demand and supply determines who bears the _____ of a sales tax
35. an agency of the U.S. government (abbrev.)
36. this type of cost does not affect marginal cost
40. an important part of President Roosevelt's recovery program (abbrev.)
41. Japanese currency
42. manuscript (abbrev.)
43. a southern state (abbrev.)

CHAPTER 25

PERFECT COMPETITION AND ECONOMIC EFFICIENCY

LEARNING OBJECTIVES

After you have studied this chapter in the textbook and the study guide, you should be able to

✔ Explain why the condition "marginal cost to society = marginal benefit to society" is necessary for allocative efficiency

✔ Explain why perfect competition results in allocative efficiency when there are no externalities

✔ Show how perfect competition tends to promote technical efficiency

✔ Demonstrate, in a diagram similar to Figure 25-3 in the text, that a deadweight loss to society results if either more or less than the efficient quantity of output is produced

✔ Explain why perfect competition tends to promote dynamic efficiency in certain ways; but why, in some other ways, other types of market may provide greater dynamic efficiency

✔ Show not only the great virtues of a perfectly competitive market, but also its limitations; in particular, be able to explain why an efficient outcome is not necessarily best, and why there are many possible efficient outcomes

✔ Explain why speculation sometimes benefits society, and why it sometimes damages society

MAJOR PURPOSE

The primary objective in this chapter is to demonstrate that, under certain conditions, a perfectly competitive market provides an efficient outcome. Thus perfect competition must be studied carefully, even though it doesn't describe a large part of the economy; most products are produced in some other type of market. Specifically, they are produced most frequently in markets between monopoly and perfect competition. Such markets are not efficient, and we will be able to see why in later chapters only if we now develop a full understanding of the conditions under which perfect competition is efficient.

Another important topic of later chapters will be those instances where even perfect competition is not efficient. So efficiency is seldom completely achieved. But it must be understood to ensure that policies to cure inefficiency do indeed move the economy in that direction, rather than making matters worse. Thus understanding what efficiency means and why it is sometimes achieved in perfectly competitive markets is our major task in this chapter.

HIGHLIGHTS OF CHAPTER

You sometimes hear it said that we should learn to cooperate more with each other rather than compete. But the economist will say that, on the contrary, competition is often the best method of ensuring harmony. This is the message of Adam Smith's "invisible hand," as described in Chapter 1. In pursuing our own self- interest, each of us is led by market forces—as if by an invisible hand—to promote the interests of others as well. In this chapter we show how this does indeed often happen in perfectly competitive markets. (In other markets, it often does not.) We also show that, even when they are efficient, perfectly competitive markets do have some shortcomings.

Perfect Competition and Allocative Efficiency

The core idea of this chapter is that, under certain conditions, perfectly competitive markets produce an efficient outcome. Consider first the concept of allocative efficiency, defined in Chapter 1. This requires that the marginal social cost of any activity be equal to its marginal social benefit—otherwise, a net gain can be acquired by changing the level of that activity. For example, if the marginal benefit of producing wheat is less than its marginal cost,—that is, if the benefit of one more bushel of wheat exceeds its cost—then there is a net benefit from producing that additional bushel. The output of wheat should be increased. Moreover, it should continue to be increased until marginal benefit and cost are equal. Only then will the incentive for increasing output disappear; this output is efficient.

Under perfect competition, output is efficient because marginal social benefit (MBs) and marginal social cost (MCs) are equalized. The reason is that under perfect competition, supply equals demand. Supply reflects the marginal cost of producers and demand reflects the marginal benefit to consumers. Therefore the equality of supply and demand means that the marginal cost of producers is equal to the marginal benefit to consumers. Provided these are the only benefits and costs—as care-

fully assumed in equations 25-1 and 25-2 of the text—it follows that the marginal cost to society is equal to the marginal benefit to society, and an efficient outcome results. Thus, in a perfectly competitive market, the pursuit by producers and consumers of their own private interest promotes the interest of society as a whole.

Figure 25-2 is particularly useful in clarifying this. In panel a, consumers pursue their self interest by responding as perfectly competitive price takers to the $10 market price. In panel b, perfectly competitive producers pursue their self interest by also responding as price takers to the same $10 market price. The result in panel c is an efficient outcome for society as a whole. We emphasize that this occurs in perfect competition, because both producers and consumers are price takers, who respond to the same market price.

In succeeding chapters we will examine markets that, for one reason or another, are not efficient. One possible reason is that producers are not perfectly competitive price takers. A second reason is that consumers are not perfectly competitive price takers. In either case, the market is not perfectly competitive, and is therefore inefficient. But there are also two reasons why a market may be inefficient, *even though it is perfectly competitive*. The first is that consumers are not the only ones to benefit from a good; there are benefits that go to others in society as well. (When you buy home improvements, the benefits go not only to you, but also to your neighbors.) The second is that producers are not the only ones who face a cost when a good is produced. (Those living downstream face a cost when a chemical producer dumps waste into a river.) Note that, in each case, inefficiency arises because of the violation of one of the key assumptions made in this chapter.

Perfect Competition and Other Kinds of Efficiency

Perfect competition also tends to promote technical efficiency. Technically inefficient firms that are operating above their AC curves, aren't likely to survive competition with technically efficient firms that are operating on their AC curves.

The situation is different with respect to dynamic efficiency. Discovering innovations that generate economic growth is usually very expensive. The perfectly competitive firm is too small to be able to afford such expenditures. Nor does it have the incentive; a farmer who discovers a new strain of wheat would find that most of the benefit would go to the millions of other farmers.

However, when innovations are discovered, they will be quickly *adopted* by perfectly competitive firms. These firms have no choice: If they don't make these changes, their competitors will drive them out of business.

Other Reservations About Perfect Competition

Efficiency isn't everything. There are problems that the perfectly competitive market doesn't solve. One is how the nation's income should be distributed. Perfect competition provides no answer here. The reason is that for every possible distribution of income there is a different perfectly competitive equilibrium. While each is efficient, the economist has no objective way of deciding which of these efficient outcomes is "best." This is an important point: Make sure you can explain is using Figures 25-1 and 25-6 in the textbook.

Another possible drawback of a perfect competitive market is that it may be subject to severe fluctuations in price and quantity—especially when there is a time lag between the production decision and the delivery of the product to the market. In the case of the hog cycle, the text shows how the expectation that future price will be the same as today's price leads to cyclical fluctuations in price and quantity.

Speculation

The text describes how price fluctuations may be reduced by speculators. For example, if private speculators make accurate forecasts they will tend to iron out fluctuations in the market. They do this by buying when there is an oversupply (and thus keeping price from falling even more) and by selling when there is a scarcity (and thereby keeping the price from rising even higher).

A speculator who succeeds in this strategy will not only make a personal profit, but will also benefit society by helping to iron out the instability in this market. On the other hand, a speculator who gets it wrong—for example, one who buys when the good is cheap and is forced to sell when it is even cheaper—will lose money and will damage society as well. But such individuals typically go out of business.

Another type of speculation that is against the public interest is the attempt to corner a market in order to reduce sales and thus raise price. The resulting contrived scarcity is damaging to society. There may also be costs to society even *if* those who are trying to corner a market don't succeed, if their purchases trigger severe price fluctuations. An example was the apparent attempt by the Hunts to corner the silver market.

IMPORTANT TERMS

Match the term in the first column with the corresponding explanation in the second column.

_____ 1.	Allocative efficiency
_____ 2.	Efficiency loss
_____ 3.	Speculation
_____ 4.	Cornering a market
_____ 5.	*Pareto optimum
_____ 6.	*Pareto improvement
_____ 7.	Technical inefficiency
_____ 8.	Moral hazard
_____ 9.	Dynamic efficiency

*Starred terms are drawn from boxes, appendices, or optional sections of the text.

a. The activity of buying and selling commodities with a view to profiting from future price changes. In perfectly competitive commodity markets, this tends to stabilize prices if forecasts are reasonably good

b. Buying up enough of a commodity to become the single (or at least dominant) holder, and thus acquire the power to resell at a higher price

c. A situation in which it is impossible to make anyone better off without making someone else worse off

d. The loss from producing an amount that is not efficient

e. Any change that benefits someone, without making anyone else worse off

f. Running an activity at a level where marginal social cost equals marginal social benefit

g. Changes taking place at the best rate over time

h. Waste in the production process

i. The problem that arises when people who get insurance take less care in avoiding risk

TRUE-FALSE

T F 1. Perfect competition guarantees an efficient solution.

T F 2. For a good with external benefits, marginal benefit to buyers is less than marginal social benefit.

T F 3. The typical firm in perfect competition must strive to eliminate technical inefficiency because it could be driven out of business otherwise.

T F 4. For each distribution of income, there is a different efficient solution.

T F 5. The best possible distribution of income is the only distribution that can lead to an efficient outcome.

T F 6. The only efficient outcome is the one in which everyone receives the same income.

T F 7. The greater the cost of storing a good, the greater may be the gap in its price between two years.

T F 8. Producers maximize their income by producing at a point of tangency between their production possibilities curve and the highest income line they can reach.

T F 9. A speculator may try to corner a market in order to be able to create a future shortage and thus raise the price.

T F 10. For a good with external costs, marginal cost to producers is greater than marginal cost to society.

MULTIPLE CHOICE

1. In a perfectly competitive market where supply equals demand, the marginal benefit of each consumer will:

   a. be greater than the marginal cost of each producer
   b. be equal to the marginal cost of each producer
   c. be less than the marginal cost of each producer
   d. be less than the average variable cost of each producer
   e. be less than the average fixed cost of each producer

2. A perfectly competitive market generates an efficient outcome if all but one of the following conditions holds. Which of the conditions below does not hold?

   a. social costs are the same as private costs
   b. social benefits are the same as private benefits
   c. consumers equate marginal benefit and price
   d. producers equate marginal cost and price
   e. consumers equate marginal benefit and total cost

3. If more than the efficient output is being produced, then

   a. marginal social benefit MB_S is equal to marginal social cost MC_S
   b. MB_S is less than MC_S
   c. MB_S is more than MC_S
   d. MB_S is zero
   e. MC_S is zero

4. To be efficient, a perfectly competitive market requires that:

   a. benefits from the good are widely dispersed among buyers and non-buyers
   b. all benefits of the good go to its purchasers, with none going to others
   c. costs of the good are borne by all producers and some non-producers
   d. all costs of the good are borne by non-producers
   e. costs of the good are borne by all members of society

5. If a firm is prevented from entering an industry because of failure to obtain a government license, then:

   a. more will be produced at a higher price
   b. more will be produced at a lower price
   c. less will be produced at a lower price
   d. less will be produced at a higher price
   e. less will be produced at the same price

6. In a perfectly competitive market,

   a. price is a rationing device that determines which buyers will acquire a good, and which sellers will produce it
   b. price is a rationing device that determines only which buyers will acquire a good
   c. price determines only which sellers will produce a good
   d. price determines neither the buyers nor the sellers of a good; price determines only how wealthy sellers will be
   e. none of the above

7. Perfect competition is superior to monopoly in terms of:

   a. dynamic efficiency, but not necessarily allocative efficiency
   b. allocative efficiency, but not necessarily dynamic efficiency
   c. allocative efficiency, but not technical efficiency
   d. dynamic and technical efficiency
   e. dynamic and allocative efficiency

8. It is sometimes argued that perfect competition is inferior to other market forms in creating innovation because the typical small firm:

   a. has an incentive, but not the funds to finance large R + D expenditures
   b. has lots of funds, but doesn't have an incentive to spend them on R + D, since it would gain only a small share of the benefits
   c. has neither the funds nor the incentive to spend them on R & D
   d. has both the funds and the incentive to spend them on R & D, but it is just mismanaged
   e. knows that once it has created an innovation, the government will not allow it to be widely applied

9. If we are initially in an efficient, perfectly competitive equilibrium, and we take income from Smith and give it to Jones, then:

   a. the quantities of goods that each will acquire will remain unchanged
   b. there will be a move to a new, efficient equilibrium where Smith acquires fewer goods and Jones more
   c. there will be a move to a new, efficient equilibrium where Jones acquires fewer goods and Smith more
   d. there will be a move to a new, inefficient equilibrium where Smith acquires fewer goods and Jones more
   e. there will be a move to a new, inefficient equilibrium where Jones acquires fewer goods and Smith more

10. If the price in a hog cycle is:

    a. low this year, then there will be decreased production, and price will be even lower next year
    b. low this year, then there will be increased production, and price will be even lower next year
    c. high this year, then there will be reduced production, and price will be even higher next year
    d. high this year, then there will be increased production, and price will be even higher next year
    e. high this year, then there will be increased production, and price will be lower next year

11. In a market with only a few sellers (when some have influence over price) which of the following efficiency conditions for perfect competition is violated?

    a. there are costs of a product to others than producers
    b. there are benefits of a product to others than buyers
    c. sellers equate their marginal cost and price
    d. buyers equate their marginal benefit and price
    e. none of the above

12. Speculation will be most effective in moderating a hog cycle if:

    a. speculators buy pork when it is cheap and sell it when it is dear
    b. speculators sell pork when it is cheap and buy it when it is dear
    c. speculators buy pork when it is cheap and buy it again when it is dear
    d. speculators sell pork when it is cheap and sell it again when it is dear
    e. speculators lose money on the transaction

13. Suppose speculators buy in the first year and sell in the second. Then:

    a. if price is higher in the second year, this speculation results in an efficiency loss for society, but a profit for speculators
    b. if price is higher in the second year, this speculation results in an efficiency gain for society, but a loss for speculators
    c. if price is lower in the second year, this speculation results in an efficiency loss for society, and a loss for speculators
    d. if price is lower in the second year, this speculation results in an efficiency loss for society, but a profit for speculators
    e. if price is lower in the second year, this speculation results in an efficiency gain for society, but a loss for speculators

14. Speculation that stabilizes price and quantity:

    a. is beneficial to society because goods are moved from a year of glut to a year of scarcity when they are valued more highly
    b. is beneficial to society because goods are moved from a year of scarcity to a year of glut when they are valued more highly
    c. is damaging to society because goods are moved from a year of glut to a year of scarcity when they are valued more highly
    d. is damaging to society for other reasons; supplies are not moved from one year to another
    e. has no effect on society

15. A perfectly competitive market is likely to rank:

    a. high in developing new technology but low in adopting it
    b. low in developing new technology but high in adopting it
    c. low in both
    d. high in both
    e. high in neither

16. British deregulation of the London financial markets in 1986:

    a. raised the cost of financial services
    b. left the cost of financial services unchanged
    c. made entry of new firms easier
    d. made entry of new firms more difficult
    e. had no effect on the entry of new firms

17. For a good with an external cost, the

    a. marginal benefit to society is more than the marginal benefit to buyers
    b. marginal benefit to society is less than the marginal benefit to buyers
    c. marginal cost to society is the same as the marginal cost to sellers
    d. marginal cost to society is greater than the marginal cost to sellers
    e. marginal cost to society has an unknown relationship to the marginal cost to sellers

18. At a Pareto optimum,

    a. it is possible to make someone better off without hurting someone else
    b. it is impossible to make someone better off without hurting someone else
    c. many Pareto improvements can still be made
    d. a few Pareto improvements can still be made
    e. none of the above

19. According to economists, moral hazard occurs when:

    a. people stop celebrating religious holidays
    b. those who are insured become more careful in protecting themselves against risk
    c. those who are insured become less careful in protecting themselves against risk
    d. those who are insured don't change their attitude toward risk
    e. a and b

20. Cornering a market is

    a. selling a whole block of city property
    b. selling a large block of the common stock of a company
    c. selling enough of a good to be able to raise its price in the future
    d. none of the above
    e. all of the above

EXERCISES

1. Figure 25.1 shows the supply and demand for wheat. (This question also draws on Chapter 24.)

Figure 25.1

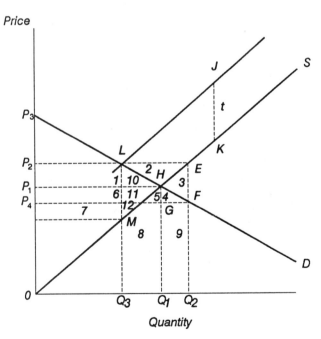

a. The equilibrium price is _____, and the equilibrium quantity is _____. Now suppose that the government imposes a sales tax $t = JK = LM$. The new equilibrium price is _____ and quantity is _____. The efficiency (gain/loss) is $10 +$ _____ because output has been [increased above/reduced below] its efficient level. Consumers [gain, lose] area _____, while producers [gain/lose] area _____. The treasury [gains/loses] area _____. The difference between all the losses and all the gains is a [gain/loss] of area _____, which is recognized to be the _____.

b. Now suppose that, instead of this tax, the government sets a floor price on wheat. It stands ready to buy whatever amount of wheat may be necessary to keep its price from falling below P_2. The new equilibrium price and quantity sold are _____ and _____. The public purchases quantity _____ while the government [buys/sells] quantity _____. The efficiency [gain/loss] is _____ because output has been [increased above/reduced below] its efficient level _____. The cost to the treasury of [increasing/decreasing] its stockpile of wheat is the rectangle with base _____ and height _____.

c. Repeat question b, assuming the government imposes a price floor at P_4.

2. The purpose of this next exercise is to demonstrate the social benefit that can be produced by the existence of markets. Figures 25.2 and 25.3 represent the markets for a manufactured good in Florida and Texas.

Figure 25.2

Figure 25.3

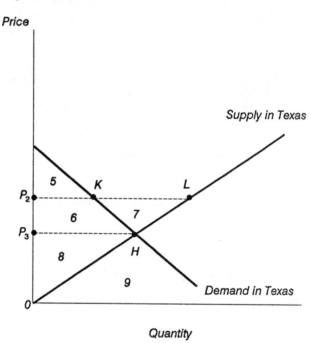

a. Suppose that initially there was no trade between the two states; that is, no market in which people from one state could trade with people from the other. Then the equilibrium price in Florida would be _____ and the equilibrium price in Texas would be _____.

b. Next, suppose that a group of traders organized a market in which Texans could trade with Floridians. Suppose that there were no transportation costs or any other kind of cost to separate the market of the two states. Then there would in fact be only one market that included both states. A single equilibrium price would be established such that the total amount supplied in the two states was just equal to the amount demanded in the two states; (suppose no other states are involved). Therefore, the excess of supply over demand in one state must equal the shortfall in the other. In Figures 25.2 and 25.3 this equilibrium price is _____.

At that price Florida has an excess (demand, supply) of _____. This is an equilibrium price because the excess (supply, demand) of Texas is _____, which is equal to the excess (supply, demand) of Florida.

c. As a result of trade between the two states, consumers in Florida have realized a (gain, loss) of _____, producers in Florida are (worse, better) off by _____; so the net (benefit, loss) to Florida is _____.

d. Consumers in Texas have realized a (gain, loss) of _____, and producers in Texas are (better, worse) off by _____. Therefore, the overall (gain, loss) to Texas is _____.

These two triangles provide estimates of the gains to the two states from creating a market in this good.

ESSAY QUESTIONS

1. In exercise 2 immediately above, who would be the winners and who would be the losers from the opening up of trade between the two states? What sort of arguments do you suppose the losers might propose in favor of a government prohibition of such trade? How could these arguments be countered? Can you imagine any way in which the winners might compensate the losers? Would the total gain in each state be enough so that after such compensation everybody could end up a winner? Would this then be a Pareto improvement?

2. According to the economist's theory of how markets work, butchers provide the public with meat in an economically efficient manner, not because they hate to see people go hungry, but because they are interested in making as large a profit as possible. In this chapter we have seen that this is true in perfect competition where there are so many buyers and sellers that none can affect price. But is it true if there is a monopoly—that is, a single seller with power to raise price? Specifically, suppose there is a monopolist who raises price from P_1 to P_2 in Figure 25.1 above. Is the outcome then an efficient one? Explain your answer.

3. Argue the case that perfect competition tends to promote at least two different kinds of efficiency.

4. Apply the analysis of this chapter to show in a diagram the triangular efficiency loss from a rent control policy.

5. Earlier we stated that the demand and supply of a product are defined in terms of a certain time and certain place. What is the "place," that is, the geographical extent of the market for the firms supplying the following items?

   a. pastries
   b. haircuts
   c. copper

6. The text gave reasons why a perfectly competitive firm would not engage in much R + D expenditure. Is the same true of advertising expenditure? Explain why. Do you think it might make sense for all perfect competitors in an industry to advertise?

ANSWERS

Important Terms: 1 f, 2 d, 3 a, 4 b, 5 c, 6 e, 7 h, 8 i, 9 g

True-False:
1 F (p. 463)
2 T (p. 454)
3 T (p. 460)
4 T (p. 463)
5 F (p. 463)
6 F (p. 463)
7 T (p. 465)
8 T (p. 469, APPENDIX)
9 T (p. 467)
10 F (p. 455)

Multiple Choice:
1 b (p. 456)
2 e (p. 457, Box)
3 b (p. 458)
4 b (p. 457, Box)
5 d (p. 459)
6 a (p. 462)
7 b (p. 460)
8 c (p. 461)

Exercises

1   a. P_1, Q_1, P_2, Q_3, loss, 10 + 11 + 12, reduced below, lose, 1 + 10, lose, 6 + 7 + 11 + 12, gains, 1 + 6 + 7, loss, 10 + 11 + 12, efficiency loss.

       b. P_2, Q_2, Q_3, buys, Q_3Q_2, loss, 3, increased above, Q_1, increasing, Q_3Q_2, Q_3L.

       c.   This floor has no effect because the market price is already above it.

2   a. P_1, P_3.

       b. P_2, demand, BC, supply, KL, demand.

       c.   gain, 2 + 3, worse, 2, benefit, 3.

       d.   loss, 6, better, 6 + 7, gain, 7.

CHAPTER 26

MONOPOLY

LEARNING OBJECTIVES

After you have studied this chapter in the textbook and the study guide, you should be able to

✔ Explain four reasons why monopolies exist

✔ Describe the cost conditions that lead to a natural monopoly, and explain how, in these circumstances, competition will eliminate all firms but one

✔ Show why a monopolist's demand and marginal revenue are quite different from a perfect competitor's

✔ Explain how a monopoly can select its profit-maximizing output by equating its marginal cost and marginal revenue

✔ Demonstrate the alternative method of selecting this output by maximizing the rectangle defined between the firm's average costs and demand curves.

✔ Show why a monopoly produces too low a level of output to achieve allocative efficiency

✔ Explain why the appropriate government policy towards collusive monopoly is to break it up or prevent it from being formed in the first place

✔ Demonstrate why marginal cost pricing is the appropriate government policy towards natural monopoly, provided it is feasible; and why, if it is not feasible, average cost pricing may be used.

✔ Show why, in very special circumstances, price discrimination by a monopolist may benefit all concerned — both the producer and consumers of the product

---

MAJOR PURPOSE

We how now completed our analysis of one extreme of the market spectrum — perfect competition, where there is free entry and so many buyers and sellers that none can influence price. Our focus now turns to the other extreme: monopoly, where a single seller not only can influence price, but can actually *determine* it, subject only to demand conditions. The following questions will be addressed: Under what conditions does monopoly arise? How does the monopolist's price and quantity compare with the perfect competitor's? How efficient is monopoly? What are the government's methods of controlling monopoly? Are there conditions under which a monopoly should be free not just to set its price, but to go beyond this to set several prices that discriminate between buyers?

HIGHLIGHTS OF CHAPTER

Here are the key questions:

Why Does Monopoly Exist?

Monopolies exist for any or all of the following reasons:

- the monopoly may possess something valuable that is not available to a potential competitor (for example, some talent, property, or patent);

- government may have created the monopoly by making competition illegal, as in the case of certain kinds of mail carried by the post office;

- there may be a natural monopoly; or

- the existing sellers may have colluded—that is, agreed to act in cooperation rather than competition.

The case of natural monopoly is perhaps the most important. It exists whenever there are economies of scale through a wide range—that is, whenever a firm has an average cost curve that continues to fall until its output becomes about large enough to satisfy the entire industry demand. (See panel b in Figure 26-1 in the textbook).

How Does a Monopoly Maximize Its Profit, and How Do Its Price and Output Compare with a Perfect Competitor's?

A monopoly, just like a perfectly competitive firm, maximizes profit by choosing the level of output where its marginal revenue (MR) equals its marginal cost (MC). But whereas the perfect competitor's MR equals the market price, the monopoly's MR is less than the market price; that is its MR curve lies below its demand curve. This is because the perfect competitor faces a horizontal demand curve. When the firm sells one more unit the price stays the same; thus the firm's extra revenue MR is just the market price. Compare this to a monopoly, which faces a demand curve that slopes downward to the right.

When this firm sells one more unit, the price *doesn't* stay the same. It falls. Thus the monopoly's extra revenue (MR) is the price that it receives from selling the extra unit, *minus* the loss it incurs because selling this extra unit lowers the price it receives for all the *other* units.

Since the monopoly's MR curve lies below its demand curve, it intersects the MC curve at a smaller output, as you can see in Figure 26-6 in the textbook. Thus, the monopoly exploits its advantage by reducing its output. By making the product scarce, it is able to raise price.

Like the perfectly competitive firm, the monopoly produces where MR = MC only if it is able to cover its costs. This requires that the demand curve overlap the AC curve; that is, the demand curve must not be always below the AC curve.

Is Monopoly Efficient?

The efficient output is the one under perfect competition, where supply (MC) equals demand (the marginal benefit of this good). When competitors collude to form a monopoly, output is reduced because the new monopoly is equating MC, not with demand, but instead with MR which is *below* demand. Because this reduces output below the efficient, perfectly competitive level, monopoly is inefficient. This is the main disadvantage of monopoly. But a complete verdict on any particular monopoly is not possible without also taking into account other factors such as the technical inefficiency that may exist because there is no competition to force the monopoly to fight rising costs. It is also necessary to take into account the transfer of income from consumers to the monopoly that results from the monopoly's higher price. Strictly speaking, we can't be sure whether this transfer is desirable or undesirable, because there is no objective way of comparing one person's gain with another's loss. However, it is often reasonable to assume that these transfer effects cancel; that is, each dollar transferred is valued as highly by the person losing it as the person receiving it. If this assumption is reasonable, then the efficiency loss of monopoly implies a welfare loss.

What Should Government Policy be Towards Monopoly?

To answer this question, it is first necessary to specify what sort of monopoly is being considered. If it is a *collusive monopoly* of firms that would otherwise be highly competitive, then the solution is to break up the monopoly—or better still, prevent it from being formed in the first place. This is a problem of antitrust policy that is discussed in Chapter 28. On the other hand, if it is a natural monopoly because of extended economies of scale, then breaking it up is no longer a simple solution. The reason is that this policy would create smaller-volume firms and thus raise costs of production, and this would impose an unnecessary cost on society. The preferred approach in this case is to leave the firm as a monopoly and continue to benefit from its relatively low costs of production; at the same time, impose a government policy that forces the monopoly to act as though it were a price-taking perfect competitor. That is, take away its market power to raise its price by imposing a ceiling on that price.

The question is, at what level should that price be set? The simple answer is *marginal cost pricing* shown in Figure 26-7 of the text; set the price at the efficient level where the marginal cost of producing this good (MC) equals the marginal benefit it provides—that is, the market demand.

Unfortunately, in many instances this policy is not feasible because forcing the price down this much would turn the monopoly into a money-loser, and drive it out of business in the long run. This is the case examined in Box 26-2, where the government would have to supplement marginal cost pricing with whatever subsidy would be necessary to keep the firm in business; or equivalently, put the firm under government ownership and subsidize its operations in this way. A final alternative which is often used is average cost pricing: Instead of driving the price all the way down to the level required by marginal cost pricing, drive it down only part way—specifically, to the level where demand intersects average cost rather than marginal cost. Because price equals average cost, the firm

breaks even. It is not turned into a money-loser, and the problem of going out of business does not arise.

However, since price is reduced only part way, monopoly inefficiency is only reduced part way; it is not eliminated. There is also a problem which applies not only to average cost pricing, but also to marginal cost pricing—and indeed to any government policy to control natural monopoly. Firms lack adequate incentive to keep costs down: If their costs rise, they know that the government-administered price will rise, because price is tied to costs.

Price Discrimination

So far we have assumed that the monopoly charges a single price to all consumers. But the firm will usually find it more profitable if it can charge different customers different prices—that is, if it can divide its market and charge a higher price to the group of customers with less elastic demand than to those with more elastic demand. Such a pricing policy by a monopoly may be beneficial to all concerned if the firm would not otherwise exist. In that case, allowing the firm to discriminate may not only allow the firm to cover its costs, but also provide a benefit to consumers who would not otherwise be able to buy this product.

On the other hand, if a monopoly quoting a single price *can* exist, then price discrimination can no longer be defended in this way. In this case, it may be justified on other grounds, or it may not. A justified case is charging a higher toll on a highway in rush-hour periods of congestion. An unjustified case arises when a nationwide firm cuts its price in a region to bankrupt a small, emerging competitor in that region.

IMPORTANT TERMS

Match the term in the first column with the corresponding explanation in the second column.

_____ 1. Natural monopoly
_____ 2. Market power
_____ 3. Marginal revenue
_____ 4. Price discrimination
_____ 5. Marginal cost pricing
_____ 6. Theory of the second best
_____ 7. Average cost pricing
_____ 8. Marketing association
_____ 9. Price maker
_____ 10. Economies of scope

a. An agency set up by firms to raise the price of their product
b. The theory of what constitutes an efficient level of output in one industry when, due to monopoly or for other reasons, the level of output in other industries is not efficient
c. The policy of regulating a monopoly's price by setting it at the level where the firm's average cost curve intersects the market demand curve
d. The ability of a seller or buyer to influence price
e. The practice of charging different prices to different customers for the same good; this is one method a monopoly may use to increase its profits or avoid a loss
f. A situation in which there are economies of scale (falling average costs) over such an extended range of output that one firm can produce the total quantity sold at a lower average cost than could two or more firms
g. The policy of regulating a monopoly's price by setting it at the level where the firm's marginal cost curve intersects the market demand curve
h. The additional revenue from selling one more unit of output
i. A monopoly firm that does not have to take price as given, but can instead set it
j. Reduced cost of existing products when new products are added to a firm's line

TRUE-FALSE

T   F   1. An unregulated profit-maximizing monopoly will set a price where marginal cost intersects the demand curve.

T   F   2. Oligopoly—a market dominated by a few sellers—is very rare compared to monopoly.

T   F   3. A profit-maximizing monopolist will set a price above marginal cost.

T   F   4. One cannot be certain that monopoly, with its efficiency loss, is damaging to society without taking into account the monopoly transfer of income.

T   F   5. A likely disadvantage of breaking up a natural monopoly is that it will raise costs of production.

T   F   6. One problem with government ownership or price regulation of a monopoly is this: Once the firm knows that the government will ensure that its costs are covered, the firm will have a reduced incentive to keep its costs down.

T　　F　　7.　If marginal cost pricing is feasible, it will eliminate the efficiency loss from a monopoly.

T　　F　　8.　Government fixing of a free market price may increase efficiency in one set of circumstances, but decrease it in another.

T　　F　　9.　Price discrimination is justified only if the monopolist is already earning at least a normal profit

T　　F　　10.　If a monopoly is formed in a perfectly competitive industry, the resulting monopoly firm will act like a competitive firm.

MULTIPLE CHOICE

1.　An example of a monopoly is

　　a. the auto industry, while an example of an oligopoly is the steel industry
　　b. the auto industry, while an example of an oligopoly is the local natural gas supplier
　　c. the steel industry, while an example of an oligopoly is the local natural gas supplier
　　d. the local natural gas supplier, while an example of an oligopoly is wheat production
　　e. the local natural gas supplier, while an example of an oligopoly is the auto industry

2.　A firm's minimum cost is $30, achievable at 1,000 units of output. This firm will be a natural monopoly if the quantity demanded at a $30 price is about

　　a. 1 million units
　　b. 100,000 units
　　c. 10,000 units
　　d. 2,000 units
　　e. 1,000 units

3.　Economists define market power as

　　a. the ability of a firm to influence federal anti-pollution legislation
　　b. the ability of a firm to influence tax legislation in its home state
　　c. the ability of consumers to purchase imports rather than domestically produced goods
　　d. the ability of a firm to influence Supreme Court decisions
　　e. none of the above

4.　A monopoly's marginal revenue is:

　　a. always positive
　　b. always above average cost
　　c. equal to the height of its demand curve
　　d. less than the height of its demand curve
　　e. greater than the height of its demand curve

5.　Which of the following faces a completely elastic demand?

　　a. IBM
　　b. an individual wheat farmer
　　c. General Motors
　　d. Ford
　　e. an urban transit company that is not subject to government price regulation.

6.　The demand facing a monopoly is

　　a. the same as the total market demand
　　b. to the right of total market demand
　　c. to the left of total market demand
　　d. completely elastic
　　e. more elastic than the total market demand

7.　At the equilibrium output of an unregulated monopoly, marginal revenue is:

　　a. less than marginal cost
　　b. more than marginal cost
　　c. more than market price
　　d. equal to market price
　　e. less than the market price

8.　An unregulated monopoly is inefficient because it equates:

　　a. marginal cost with demand rather than with marginal revenue
　　b. marginal revenue with demand rather than with marginal cost
　　c. marginal revenue with average cost rather than with marginal cost
　　d. average cost with demand rather than with marginal revenue
　　e. marginal cost with marginal revenue rather than with demand

9. If the monopolist is producing more than the profit-maximizing amount, then:

   a. marginal revenue will exceed price
   b. marginal cost will exceed price
   c. marginal cost will exceed marginal revenue
   d. average cost will exceed price
   e. marginal revenue will exceed average cost

10. If a monopoly is maximizing profit, then the marginal cost of producing one more unit is:

    a. equal to its marginal benefit to society
    b. more than its marginal benefit to society
    c. less than its marginal benefit to society
    d. less than its marginal benefit to the monopoly firm
    e. more than its marginal benefit to the monopoly firm

11. If a perfectly competitive industry is monopolized, the result is

    a. higher output and lower price
    b. higher output and the same price
    c. higher output and higher price
    d. lower output and higher price
    e. lower output and lower price

12. The profit rectangle for a monopoly is its quantity of output times

    a. the monopoly's average cost
    b. its price
    c. its price less its average cost
    d. its marginal cost
    e. its price less its marginal cost

13. Monopoly typically results in:

    a. allocative efficiency
    b. technical inefficiency
    c. allocative inefficiency
    d. a and b
    e. b and c

14. When a regulatory agency controls a monopoly by marginal cost pricing, the monopoly's:

    a. price is reduced
    b. output is reduced
    c. profit is eliminated
    d. level of efficiency remains the same
    e. all of the above

15. Which of the following makes zero profit?

    a. an unregulated monopoly charging a single price
    b. an unregulated, price-discriminating monopoly
    c. a monopoly regulated by marginal cost pricing
    d. a monopoly regulated by average cost pricing
    e. a monopoly regulated by variable cost pricing

16. The theory of the second best tells us that monopolizing one industry in an economy where monopoly exists elsewhere will

    a. reduce efficiency
    b. increase efficiency
    c. have no effect on efficiency
    d. have an uncertain effect on efficiency
    e. lower price in that industry

17. Government marginal cost regulation of monopoly is designed to induce the firm to

    a. act like a perfect competitor by reducing output
    b. act like a perfect competitor by taking price as given
    c. produce to the point where above-normal profit finally disappears
    d. produce to the point where normal profit finally disappears
    e. reduce price while holding its output constant

18. A product is not being provided because the potential producer is a monopoly whose demand lies below its average cost curve AC. This problem may be solved by permitting the firm to discriminate and thus:

    a. at least cover its costs
    b. shift its demand above its marginal cost curve
    c. shift its demand above its average variable cost curve
    d. shift its AC curve down so it overlaps demand
    e. shift its demand above its AC curve

19. A government marketing agency that is introduced into a competitive industry will:

    a. typically set quotas to ensure that producers will increase their sales
    b. typically set quotas to ensure that producers will reduce their sales
    c. typically set quotas to ensure that producers will maintain their previous sales levels
    d. not set quotas, but will encourage producers to sell more
    e. encourage the entry of new firms

20. If a discriminating monopolist charges a higher price to the group with the more elastic demand than to the group with the less elastic demand:

a. its profit will increase
b. its profit will decrease
c. its profit will remain unchanged
d. its profit will be zero
e. c and d

21. Average cost price regulation of a public utility by the government:

a. raises problems because the amount of invested capital is difficult to estimate
b. raises problems because a reasonable percentage return on invested capital is difficult to estimate
c. increases efficiency
d. all of the above
e. none of the above

EXERCISES

1 a. If the monopoly shown in Figure 26.1 is unregulated, it will maximize profits by selecting output _____ where _____ equals _____. The price it will quote is _____, the highest price at which this output can be sold. Its profit will be _____ for each of the units it sells, that is, a total profit of area _____. An alternative view of its decision is that it selects the point _____ on the _____ curve that maximizes this profit rectangle. The efficiency (gain, loss) is _____.

Figure 26.1

b. A government regulatory agency that uses marginal cost pricing will set price equal to _____. The firm will respond in the short run by producing _____ output because this is where its _____ curve cuts the price line at P_6. However, in the long run, the firm would produce an output of _____ because at equilibrium T it is operating at a (profit, loss) of _____. To keep it in business the government would have to (provide a subsidy, impose a tax) of _____. This policy would (reduce, increase, eliminate) the previous efficiency loss of _____; that is, it would improve efficiency by _____.

c. If the agency were instead to use average cost pricing, it would set price at _____. The monopolist would produce output _____ and earn a profit of _____. The subsidy now necessary to keep this firm in business would be _____. This policy would reduce the efficiency loss from the original JTN to _____ that is, it would improve efficiency by _____. Compared to marginal cost pricing, this average cost pricing policy improves efficiency (more, less); but it avoids the government problem of having to (subsidize, tax) this firm.

d. With either form of regulation, the monopoly is forced to act like a (perfect competitor, oligopolist, natural monopolist) facing a fixed price.

2. A monopoly has the demand and total cost figures shown in Table 26-1. Fill in this table, ignoring for now the last three columns.

Table 26.1

P	Quantity demanded	Total revenue	Marginal revenue	Total cost	Average cost	Marginal cost	Profit	(1) Net profit with lump-sum tax	(2) Net total revenue with excise tax	(3) Net profit with excise tax
10	0	$0	$0	$2	$___	$0	$	$	$	$
8	1	8		3						
6	2			6						
4	3			11						
2	4			18						

a. The monopoly's fixed cost is _____. It will choose to produce a level of output equal to _____ and charge a price equal to_____. Its maximum attainable profit is _____.

b. Suppose that, in an attempt to capture some of this monopoly's profits for the taxpayer's benefit, the government imposes a lump-sum tax of $5. This tax may be regarded by the monopoly as a fixed cost, because it must be paid no matter how much output is produced. After the imposition of this tax, the monopoly's fixed cost is _____. Fill in the third-last column (1) indicating the monopoly's after-tax profit. After imposition of the tax, the monopoly will choose to produce an output equal to_____ and to charge a price equal to _____. Its maximum attainable after-tax profit will be _____.

c. Suppose that instead of the lump-sum tax, the government decides to impose a 50% excise tax on the monopoly. In other words, the monopoly must now pay the government 50% of its total revenue. In this case, the monopoly's fixed cost is _____. Fill in the second-last column (2), showing the monopoly's after-tax total revenue, and the last column (3), showing its after-tax profit. In this case, the monopoly will choose to produce an amount of output equal to _____, and to charge a price equal to_____. Its maximum attainable after-tax profit will be _____. The amount of excise tax collected from this monopoly will be _____.

d. From the point of view of economic efficiency the (lump-sum, excise) tax is preferable. From the point of view of maximizing the amount of tax revenue collected from the monopoly, the (lump-sum, excise) tax is preferable.

ESSAY QUESTIONS

1. Are economies of scale a barrier to entry? Explain. Is IBM a monopoly? A perfect competitor? Or in a dominant position somewhere in between? Do you think economies of scale give it an advantage over potential competitors?

2. Compare a monopoly and a perfectly competitive firm in terms of their (1) demand and marginal revenue schedules (2) their market power (3) their efficiency, and (4) the appropriate government policy in dealing with each.

3. "Allowing a monopolist to charge some customers more than others is not appropriate because it is unfair to those who have to pay the higher price." Evaluate this statement. Are there any circumstances in which those who pay the higher price could actually benefit?

4. Suppose the only two firms in an industry are considering a merger that would result in a reduction in costs of production through the elimination of wasteful duplication. Is it possible to argue that this government action could increase efficiency? If so, how? Might it decrease efficiency? If so, how?

5. A perfectly competitive firm can sell all it wants at the existing price. Can a monopoly do that? If it tried to, what would happen? Does that mean that a monopoly is more constrained in its decision making than a perfect competitor?

6. Recall our discussion of the elasticity of demand from Chapter 20. If a monopoly's demand function is elastic, then what happens to its total revenue as its output increases? In this case, what can be said about the monopoly's marginal revenue? If the market demand is inelastic what can be said about the monopolist's marginal revenue? In view of this, explain why a monopoly that has discovered that its demand curve is inelastic would want to change its output.

ANSWERS

Important Terms: **1** f, **2** d, **3** h, **4** e, **5** g, **6** b, **7** c, **8** a, **9** i, **10** j

True-False: **1** F (p. 478)
2 F (p. 473)
3 T (p. 478)
4 T (pp. 483-484)
5 T (p. 484)
6 T (p. 486, BOX)
7 T (p. 484)
8 T (p. 488)
9 F (p. 489)
10 F (p. 482)

Multiple Choice: **1** e (p. 473)
2 e (p. 473)
3 e (p. 474)
4 d (p. 476)
5 b (p. 475)
6 a (p. 475)
7 e (p. 478)
8 e (p. 481)
9 c (p. 478)
10 c (p. 481)
11 d (p. 482)
12 c (p. 478)
13 e (pp. 480-481)
14 a (p. 484)
15 d (p. 487, BOX)
16 d (p. 483, BOX)
17 b (p. 484)
18 a (p. 488)
19 b (pp. 481-482)
20 b (p. 489)
21 d (p. 494, APPENDIX)

Exercises

1 a. Q_1, MC, MR, P_2, JK, P_2JKP_3, J, demand, loss, JNT.
   b. P_6, Q_3, MC, zero, loss, P_5VTP_6, provide a subsidy, P_5VTP_6, eliminate, JNT, JNT.
   c. P_4, Q_2, zero, zero, LWT, JLWN, less, subsidize.
   d. perfect competitor.

2.

Table 26.1 Completed

P	Quantity Quantity demanded	Total revenue	Marginal revenue	Total cost	Average cost	Marginal cost	Profit	(1) Net profit with lump-sum tax	(2) Net total revenue with excise tax	(3) Net profit with excise tax
10	0	$0	$0	$2	$____	$0	$-2	$-7	$0	$-2
8	1	8	8	3	3	1	5	0	4	1
6	2	12	4	6	3	3	6	1	6	0
4	3	12	0	11	3⅔	5	1	-4	6	-5
2	4	8	-4	18	4½	7	-10	-15	4	-14

   a. $2, 2, $6, $6.
   b. $7, 2, $6, $1.
   c. $2, 1, $8, $1, $4.
   d. lump-sum, lump-sum.

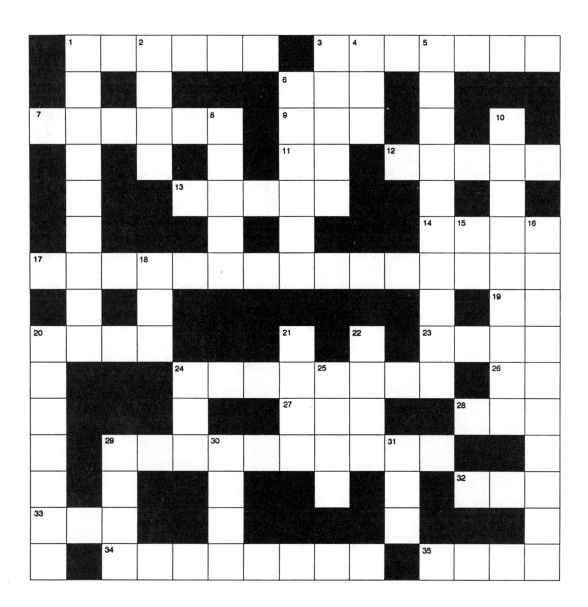

Across

1,3. If perfect competition is to be efficient, this must equal the benefit to consumers
6. a curve frequently used in mathematics (abbrev.)
7. an early marginalist (see inside cover of text)
9. certainly not new
11. an element (abbrev.)
12. a famous quantity theorist (see inside cover of text)
13. a winner of Nobel prize in Economics (see inside cover of text)
14. misfortunes
17. to maximize profits, firm equalizes this and marginal cost (2 words)
19. a state in the Old South (abbrev.)
20. expensive

23. muse of history
24. industry with only one seller
26. above, and touching
27. large body of water
28. final part
29. with perfect competition, this is what every buyer and every seller is (2 words)
32. if the elasticity of demand is _____, total revenue remains constant when the price changes
33. an international organization for labor (abbrev.)
34, 35. the increase in variable costs when one more unit is produced

Down

1. buy or sell in the hope of profiting from a change in price
2. business owned by a group of consumers or producers (abbrev.)
3. Treasury _____ are short-term liabilities of the U.S. government
4. finish
5. this exists when we get the most out of our productive efforts
6, 21. for an efficient solution, this must equal social benefit
8. Chairman of Council of Economic Advisers, 1972-1974
10. an illegal source of market power
15. natural log (abbrev.)

16. the best we can do when there are immutable imperfections in a market (2 words)
18. one of the two Germanies (abbrev.)
20. a type of efficiency
22. this is what a highly progressive income tax would do to the rich
24. "L'etat, c'est _____."
25. one of the four phases of the business cycle
29. the senior dance
30. rock that juts out
31. I (Latin)

CHAPTER 27

MARKETS BETWEEN MONOPOLY AND PERFECT COMPETITION

LEARNING OBJECTIVES

After you have studied this chapter in the textbook and the study guide, you should be able to

- ✔ Clearly distinguish between perfect competition, monopolistic competition, oligopoly, duopoly, and monopoly

- ✔ Explain why the run-of-the-mill firm earns no above-normal profits in the long run in monopolistic competition, and why this market form is not necessarily inefficient, even though fewer firms could produce the same output at lower costs

- ✔ Give two reasons why oligopoly may arise

- ✔ Describe why economies of scale and advertising create barriers to entry

- ✔ Explain why oligopolists have an incentive to collude, and the effect such collusion will have on efficiency

- ✔ Explain why the OPEC countries were able to collude to raise the price of oil during the 1970s without imposing formal production quotas; and why they at least tried to set formal production quotas in the 1980s

- ✔ Describe the kinked demand curve with a diagram

- ✔ Explain why the kinked demand curve would discourage an oligopolist from changing price frequently

- ✔ Explain the concept of price leadership, how it relates to the analysis of kinked demand, and why it is often viewed as "tacit collusion"

- ✔ Give three examples of non-price competition

- ✔ Summarize the arguments for and against advertising

✔ Describe game theory and explain why it may be useful in analyzing duopoly

✔ Explain why the outcome of a game may be influenced by such factors as (i) how easy it is for a player to cheat on a prior understanding and (ii) whether or not the game is repeated

✔ Describe a contestable market, and why this concept is important

MAJOR PURPOSE

The last two chapters have described the two extremes in the spectrum of markets: perfect competition, where there are so many sellers that none has any influence over price; and monopoly, where the single firm is free to set any price it chooses, since it has no competitors to worry about. (A monopoly is restrained only by consumer demand and the possibility of government intervention.) Most American industries do not conform to either of these two extremes, but lie somewhere between, where individual firms have some influence over price. The objective in this chapter is to analyze some of the market forms that lie within this intermediate range. We begin with monopolistic competition, the market closest to perfect competition, and then work our way towards monopoly by considering markets with fewer and fewer firms. Thus we describe oligopoly, a market with several firms, and then duopoly, a market with only two.

In *monopolistic competition* — as in perfect competition — there are a large number of sellers and free entry into the market. However, monopolistic competition differs from perfect competition because each firm produces a differentiated product, and this gives each firm some small degree of influence over price.

Oligopoly is a market dominated by a few sellers, in which (in the absence of government intervention) there is a strong incentive for firms to collude in order to act like a monopolist and raise price. The most prominent example of such collusive behavior is described in this chapter: the Organization of Petroleum Exporting Countries (OPEC) which raised oil price by more than ten times in less than a decade.

In *duopoly*, there are only 2 firms. The importance of how your competitor may react becomes paramount, and game theory will be used to highlight that issue.

HIGHLIGHTS OF CHAPTER

In this chapter we discuss monopolistic competition, oligopoly and duopoly — three of the "imperfectly competitive" market forms that lie between the extremes of monopoly and perfect competition.

Monopolistic Competition

This is closest to perfect competition. In monopolistic competition, as in perfect competition, there is a large number of firms. There is also free entry of firms into the industry, which means that any short-run excess profit for the run-of-the-mill firm will be eliminated in the long run. The important difference between the two market forms is this: Under monopolistic competition, a firm produces a differentiated product and therefore faces a downward-sloping demand curve. Under perfect competition, the firm produces a standardized product and faces a completely horizontal demand curve. Because the sloping demand curve gives a firm in monopolistic competition some influence over price, the firm quotes a higher price, and therefore produces a smaller output than a perfectly competitive firm that cannot raise its price. This restricted output suggests that monopolistic competition is inefficient, but this is not necessarily the case. Lower output by each firm means more firms are satisfying total market demand. Thus the consumer can choose from a wider range of differentiated products. This wider choice may more than make up for the disadvantage of lower output by each firm.

Oligopoly: a Market with a Few Sellers

The smaller the number of sellers, the greater the market power (the influence over price) that can be exercised by each firm. Thus the first task is to define the degree of concentration of the industry. This has traditionally been measured by the proportion of the industry's output produced by the four largest firms. Another measure, called the Herfindahl-Hirschman index, is now often used instead because it takes into account all firms in the industry — not just the four largest.

An oligopoly can arise because an industry is a "natural oligopoly" in which the lowest-cost way of satisfying market demand is with a small number of firms. Alternatively, firms may combine or grow large, not because of cost conditions, but instead because they seek to acquire market power.

Because there are few clear-cut principles governing the behavior of oligopolists, the theoretical analysis is not as straightforward for oligopoly as it is for many other market forms. But the following points are important:

- There is a tendency for oligopolists to collude—that is, to act like a monopolist and raise price so as to maximize the total profits of the industry. To maintain the high price, the product must be made scarce. Therefore each colluding firm is required to restrict its output to a certain quota level. This reduction in output leads to the same sort of efficiency loss as in the case of monopoly. However, it is precisely this reduction in the output of each firm that creates a tendency for collusive arrangements to break down; each firm is asked to reduce its output when it has an incentive to produce more. The reason the individual firm would like to produce more is that, at its restricted level of output, the firm's marginal cost is still below its price. Therefore, it has an incentive to increase its output, if it can get away with such cheating. But if firms do cheat by producing more than their quota of output, the high price cannot be maintained, and the collusive arrangement comes apart.

- When the oligopolistic firm makes a change in, say, its price, it must take into account the possible reaction of its rivals—something that need not even be considered by a monopolist (with no rivals) or a perfectly competitive firm (whose rivals don't even notice what it's doing). This sort of complicated decision-making is what makes the theory of oligopoly so interesting and difficult.

- Oligopolistic firms sometimes face a kinked demand curve. If one firm raises its price, its rivals won't. Instead they'll hope to capture some of its sales. But if the firm lowers its price, its rivals will follow suit to avoid being undersold. In such circumstances, the firm is facing the kinked demand curve shown in Figure 27-6 of the textbook, and it is unlikely to change its price from the kinked level unless underlying cost conditions change a great deal. While the theory of kinked demand is controversial as an explanation of how firms behave, it is very useful in making clear the issues that firms must deal with in making their decisions. For example, the kinked demand analysis in Figure 27-6 can be modified slightly to explain price leadership.

- In an industry with price leadership one firm takes on the role of being the leader in announcing a price change, on the understanding that other firms will follow. This sort of "gentleman's agreement" has often been criticized as a collusive arrangement, with the price leader setting the price at about the level that a monopolist would select. However, it is only "tacit collusion" because there is no communication between the firms, and it is therefore very difficult or impossible to prove that collusion has taken place. (Selling at the same price is not proof of collusion because, after all, that is what perfectly competitive firms do.)

- Oligopolists who wish to avoid potentially destructive price competition have other options, in addition to tacit collusion in the form of price leadership. They can attempt to increase their market share by various forms of non-price competition, such as advertising or R&D expenditure to improve product quality. Advertising in particular is controversial. On the one hand, it may involve wasteful competition, distort people's values, and mislead consumers. On the other hand, it may make consumers better informed and help to promote product quality by making firms fearful of losing the goodwill that they achieve through advertising. Moreover, it provides financial support for the media.

- Oligopolists often succeed in erecting barriers to entry against new competitors. One such barrier is advertising which creates a favorable image of an existing firm that is difficult for new firms to overcome. But the most important barrier to entry may be economies of scale that leave room for only a few low-cost firms in the industry.

OPEC: an example of oligopoly collusion

In many ways, the most interesting and far-reaching example of a collusive oligopoly has been the Organization of Petroleum Exporting Countries, OPEC. This collusive arrangement succeeded in quadrupling oil prices in 1973-1974, and again doubling them in 1979-1980. This was even more remarkable because during the 1970s OPEC did not have to rely on the formal quotas on output that are typically required to keep price up and ensure that the collusive arrangement won't come apart. One of the reasons for this was the dominant role of the Saudi Arabians in producing world-traded oil. For many years they could keep the price up by restricting just their own very large output.

However, by 1985 the Saudis' production had been so far reduced in the attempt to maintain price, that they were unwilling to continue to do this. They turned up their pumps and the price of oil fell sharply, to less than $10 a barrel, compared to the high of $32 a barrel three years earlier. This made other OPEC countries recognize the importance of abiding by quotas. The question is: Will they?

Duopoly: The Insights of Game Theory

In most oligopoly markets, a key issue is "How will competing firms react?" In duopoly, this becomes of paramount importance. Game theory is designed to deal with this issue, and the text provides an example of how it can be applied. In this example, the two firms are both far worse off if they both cut their price than if they both do not. It's in their *collective interest* not to. The problem is that it's in the *individual interest* of each of the firms to cut price and capture market share from the competitor. Game theory describes the possible outcomes, which depend on such questions as:

- *Is the game repeated?* If it is, then the best strategy may be to "stand pat" (p. 514). Avoid price cutting on the first play of the game, in order to increase the chance of avoiding a mutually destructive price war. Stand pat in the hope your competitor will do the same; don't cut your price until your competitor does.

- *How much can each firm trust the other?* The more trust there is (that is, the more each firm can trust the other not to cut price) the more reasonable it is for each to refrain from price cutting.

- *How long does it take for cheating (price cutting) to be detected and for the other firm to retaliate?* The shorter the time period, the less likely it is for either firm to cheat.

Don't Just Count Numbers: The Concept of Contestable Markets

Even if there is only one firm in an industry, it cannot act like a monopolist if the market is contestable, and new firms can freely enter and leave. Then any attempt by the firm to increase price and profit will be met by the free entry of new competitors, and any new excess profit will be competed away.

IMPORTANT TERMS

Match the term in the first column with the corresponding explanation in the second column.

_____ 1. Oligopoly
_____ 2. Concentration ratio
_____ 3. Natural oligopoly
_____ 4. Product differentiation
_____ 5. Cartel
_____ 6. OPEC
_____ 7. Kinked demand curve
_____ 8. Price leadership
_____ 9. Barrier to entry
_____ 10. Monopolistic competition
_____ 11. Contestable market
_____ 12. Payoff matrix

a. The practice in some oligopolistic industries of having one firm announce its price change first, on the unspoken understanding that other firms will follow suit.
b. The ability of each firm to distinguish its product from those of its rivals. Such distinctions may be real or imagined.
c. A market dominated by only a few sellers.
d. A market in which (a) there is a large number of firms, (b) free entry of new ones, and (c) differentiated products. The demand curve facing each seller is quite elastic, but not completely so.
e. The proportion of an industry's output produced by the four largest firms (or, using an alternative measure, by the eight largest firms).
f. Anything that makes it difficult for new firms to enter an industry to compete against existing firms.
g. Any formal agreement among firms to collude in order to set price and/or determine market shares.
h. An industry in which total market demand can be satisfied at lowest cost by a few firms.
i. The demand curve that will face an oligopolist if its rivals will follow it if it cuts its price, but will not follow it if it increases its price.
j. A specific example of a cartel.
k. Table showing the outcomes of a game.
m. A market in which free entry makes even a monopolist act like a perfect competitor.

TRUE-FALSE

T F 1. Monopolistic competition is similar in many respects to perfect competition; but one important difference is that the product is differentiated.

T F 2. Because consumers like variety, we cannot conclude that monopolistic competition is inefficient.

T F 3. The concentration ratio is relatively low in the auto industry.

T F 4. Colluding firms in a cartel typically have an incentive to cheat by producing less than their quotas.

T F 5. All cartels, regardless of where they may exist, are illegal.

T F 6. A large firm acting as a price leader may decide not to retaliate against a small firm that has cut price, for fear that this may initiate a price war with other large firms.

T F 7. Price leadership may be a disguised method of collusion.

T F 8. The kinked demand curve arises mainly in monopolistic competition.

T F 9. The theory of the kinked demand curve doesn't predict the price where the kink will occur.

T F 10. All barriers to entry take the form of economies of scale.

T F 11. Duopoly firms have an individual and collective interest in cutting price if their situation is similar to the prisoners' dilemma.

T F 12. A stand-pat, collusive outcome becomes more likely if a duopoly game is repeated.

MULTIPLE CHOICE

1. Product differentiation by a firm occurs:

   a. only in perfect competition
   b. only in monopoly
   c. in monopoly and perfect competition
   d. in monopolistic competition
   e. in all market structures

2. In the long run a firm in monopolistic competition will:

   a. face a perfectly elastic demand curve
   b. produce more than the amount that minimizes average cost
   c. produce less than the amount that minimizes average costs
   d. produce the amount that minimizes average costs
   e. earn an above-normal profit

3. In monopolistic competition:

   a. there is a standardized product, just like in perfect competition
   b. there is a standardized product, unlike the differentiated product in perfect competition
   c. entry of new firms is restricted, unlike the free entry that exists in perfect competition
   d. entry of new firms is restricted, just as in perfect competition
   e. there is a large number of sellers, just as in perfect competition

4. In monopolistic competition:

   a. there are very few sellers
   b. it is impossible for new firms to enter the market
   c. firms sell differentiated products
   d. all of the above
   e. none of the above

5. The feature of monopolistic competition that drives a firm's profits to zero in the long run is:

   a. production differentiation
   b. price leadership
   c. market power
   d. free entry
   e. collusion by sellers

6. A firm's minimum cost is $10, achievable at 20,000 units of output. The industry will be perfectly competitive if the total quantity demanded of this product at a $10 price is:

   a. 1 million units
   b. 100,000 units
   c. 40,000 units
   d. 20,000 units
   e. 10,000 units

7. If oligopolistic firms collude to raise price:

   a. each benefits, while there is an overall loss to the economy as a whole
   b. the price leader benefits, while the other firms and the economy as a whole lose
   c. each firm and the economy as a whole benefit
   d. each firm benefits, while the economy as a whole is not affected
   e. each firm and the economy as a whole lose

8. General Motors is a:

   a. monopolist
   b. duopolist
   c. oligopolist
   d. monopolistic competitor
   e. perfect competitor

9. A high concentration ratio in an industry typically indicates that:

   a. the dominant firms in the industry have a great deal of market power
   b. no firms in the industry have much market power
   c. no firms in the industry have any market power
   d. the industry is monopolistically competitive
   e. the industry is perfectly competitive

10. Between 1980 and 1985, U.S. industry became

    a. less competitive, because of the decline in international trade
    b. more competitive, because of the decline in international trade
    c. less competitive, because of the growth in international trade
    d. more competitive, because of the growth of international trade
    e. more competitive, despite the decline in international trade

11. The Herfindahl-Hirschman index for an industry where one firm produces 80% of the industry output and the other two produce 10% each is:

    a. .66
    b. 6,600
    c. .88
    d. 8,800
    e. 1.0

12. The biggest surprise about OPEC is that it:

    a. survived for many years without a formal set of production quotas
    b. did not increase the price of oil when it had an opportunity to do so in 1973/1974
    c. has made no further price increases since its spectacular success in 1973/1974
    d. has been able to prevent any price reduction since 1973
    e. includes only countries from the Middle East

13. The success of the OPEC cartel in the 1970s and early 1980s was in substantial part due to:

    a. strong cultural ties among the member countries
    b. the strong sense of political unity among the member countries
    c. close social ties among the member countries
    d. all of the above
    e. the willingness of the Saudis to cut back their production

14. If a firm is at the kink in its demand curve and it raises its price, then:

    a. it will lose market share, but only to those competitors that follow its price increase
    b. it will lose market share to those competitors that don't follow its price increase
    c. its market share will not be affected
    d. its market share will increase
    e. its market share will increase, but only at the expense of those competitors that follow its price increase

15. If all firms sell at the same price:

    a. there must be price leadership
    b. there must be some other form of collusion
    c. the industry must be perfectly competitive
    d. the industry must be an oligopoly
    e. none of the above

16. The growing importance of international trade has:

    a. made U.S. firms more competitive
    b. made U.S. firms less competitive
    c. not affected the competitiveness of U.S. firms
    d. made domestic concentration ratios more meaningful
    e. b and d

17. Price leadership:

    a. only occurs when there is heavy advertising in an industry
    b. is a means of achieving "orderly" price changes in an oligopolistic industry
    c. indicates which senior executive within a firm will make pricing decisions
    d. frequently occurs in perfect competition
    e. frequently occurs in a monopolized industry

18. The kinked demand curve:

    a. helps to explain why oligopoly price has some degree of stability
    b. leaves unanswered the question of how price is established in the first place
    c. is based on the assumption that if a firm lowers its price, its competitors will follow
    d. is based on the assumption that if a firm raises its price, its competitors won't follow
    e. all of the above

19. Which of the following is not true about advertising?

    a. it may involve waste
    b. it may mislead consumers
    c. it provides financial support for the media
    d. it may help to promote product quality by making firms fearful of losing goodwill
    e. it is often undertaken by single firms in a perfectly competitive market

20. In a contestable market:

    a. there is a single firm which can act as a monopolist
    b. there is no free entry
    c. the potential entry of new firms increases the market power of the existing firm
    d. the potential entry of new firms has no effect on the market power of the existing firm
    e. if there is a single firm, it cannot act as though it is a monopolist

21. A payoff matrix shows:

    a. the difference between duopoly and oligopoly
    b. the difference between duopoly and monopolistic competition
    c. the difference between oligopoly and monopolistic competition
    d. the definition of duopoly
    e. how the outcome in duopoly depends on the policy selected by each firm

22. Once firms recognize that a game is to be repeated:

    a. the chance of a collusive, stand-pat outcome decreases
    b. the chance of a collusive, stand-pat outcome increases
    c. the chance of a collusive, stand-pat outcome is left unchanged
    d. both firms will lower their price
    e. both firms will increase their output

EXERCISES

1 a. In Figure 27.1, D represents the total market demand for an industry, with MR_I being the marginal revenue curve that corresponds to D. (For any demand curve, there exists a marginal revenue curve.) MC_A and AC_A are the cost curves for firm A, one of the 5 identical firms in this industry. Draw in the marginal cost curve for the industry, and label it MC_I. Label point R, where MC_I and D intersect, and point S, where MC_I and MR_I intersect. Label as Z the point directly above S on the demand curve.

Figure 27.1

If these firms act like perfect competitors and take price as given, then MC_I becomes the industry (demand, supply) curve, and the industry equilibrium is at point _____. _____ units are sold at price _____, with each firm earning a profit of _____.

b. Now suppose these firms collude to maximize their collective profit, which they will do by equating MC_I and _____, at an output of _____ units. They will sell this output for price _____. That is, the industry will select its profit maximizing point _____ on the demand curve D. Since industry output has been reduced from _____ to _____ units, the output of each individual firm, such as A, must be reduced by the same proportion, from _____ units to _____. Draw in point T, which is the equilibrium for firm A, where this firm is now selling _____ units at price _____. Label as V the point on AC_A directly below T. Shade in the new profit area _____ of firm A.

By colluding, these 5 firms have each (increased, decreased) their profit from _____ to _____. At the same time, the nation as a whole has (lost, gained) because of the efficiency (loss, gain) of area _____ that results because output has been (reduced, increased) to the (efficient, inefficient) level of _____ units from the (efficient, inefficient) level of _____ units where the marginal benefit to society shown by curve_____ equals the marginal cost to society shown by curve _____.

2. Figure 27.2 shows an oligopoly which, along with all its rivals, is currently charging price P and producing quantity Q. This firm faces the kinked demand curve that consists of the segment of D_A above the existing price P and the segment of D_B below the price P. The respective marginal revenue curves are MR_A and MR_B.

a. If the firm increases its output to more than Q, it faces demand curve _____, and its MR curve is therefore (MR_A, MR_B). But if it decreases its output to less than Q, if faces demand curve _____, and its MR curve is therefore (MR_A, MR_B). Therefore its complete MR curve is (MR_A, MR_B, WXYZ).

Figure 27.2

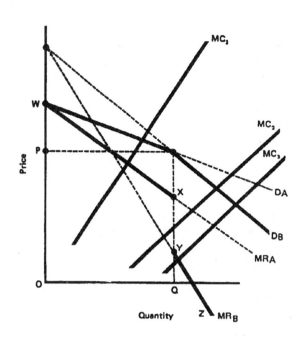

b. If its MC is MC_1, then it will charge a price that is (more than, less than, the same as) P; and it will choose a quantity that is (more than, less than, the same as) Q.

c. If its MC is MC_2, then it will charge a price that is (more than, less than, the same as) P, and choose a quantity that is (more than, less than, the same as) Q.

d. If its MC is MC_3, then it will charge a price that is (more than, less than, the same as) P, and choose a quantity that is (more than, less than, the same as) Q.

e. If its MC is MC_2, we now see why the kinked demand curve results in a stable price. If MC_2 shifts up, but still intersects the vertical segment XY, then the firm will (raise, lower, leave unchanged) the price. Alternatively, if MC_2 shifts down, still intersecting XY, the firm will (raise, lower, leave unchanged) the price. In other words, marginal cost can shift up or down within the range _____ without affecting price at all.

ESSAY QUESTIONS

1. Firms in monopolistic competition have some influence over price. Why don't they use this influence to raise price above average costs and therefore make an above-normal profit in the long run?

2. Will firms in an industry with a high concentration ratio be more or less likely to engage in collusive activity than those in an industry with a low concentration ratio? Why?

3. Oligopoly is a market with a few sellers. But how many is a few? Does it matter if there are 4 or 14? Why? To be specific, compare the situation of an individual U.S. firm if

    a. it has only 3 U.S. competitors, versus

    b. a situation in which it has the same 3 U.S. competitors, plus 2 Japanese competitors, 4 European competitors, and 2 other foreign competitors.

    Would the U.S. firm have the same market power in either case? Would firms be equally able to collude, tacitly or explicitly?

4. Explain why a group of oligopolists might have trouble establishing a collusive price agreement, and then have trouble keeping the agreement from coming apart.

5. It is often argued that advertising increases sales, and this permits lower prices to consumers. Explain the circumstances in which this could occur. Also explain the circumstances in which advertising would increase prices to consumers.

6. What industry characteristics distinguish oligopoly from monopoly? from perfect competition?

7. Explain some of the techniques oligopolists use to avoid price competition.

8. If it is in the collective interests of 2 duopoly firms to avoid price cutting, how can it be in the individual interest of each to engage in price cutting?

ANSWERS

Important Terms: **1 c, 2 e, 3 h, 4 b, 5 g, 6 j, 7 i, 8 a, 9 f, 10 d, 11 m, 12 k**

True-False:
1 T (p. 496)
2 T (p. 497)
3 F (p. 499)
4 F (p. 504)
5 F (p. 507)
6 T (p. 509)
7 T (p. 509)
8 F (p. 507)
9 T (p. 509)
10 F (p. 501)
11 F (p. 513)
12 T (p. 514)

Exercises

1   a.   supply, R, 1,500, P_1, zero.

       b. MR_I, 1,000, P_2, Z, 1,500, 1,000, 300, 200, 200, P_2, P_2TVC, increased, zero, the shaded area, lost, loss, ZSR, reduced, inefficient, 1,000, efficient, 1,500, D, MC_I.

Figure 27.1 Completed

2   a. D_B, MR_B, D_A, MR_A, WXYZ.

       b.   more than, less than.

       c.   the same as, the same as.

       d.   less than, more than.

       e.   leave unchanged, leave unchanged, XY.

Part 8

ECONOMIC EFFICIENCY:
Issues Of Our Time

GOVERNMENT REGULATION OF BUSINESS

LEARNING OBJECTIVES

After you have studied this chapter in the textbook and the study guide, you should be able to

✔ Identify and briefly describe the three legislative acts that form the cornerstone of federal antitrust policy

✔ Explain why it may be advantageous to have large-size firms, and why antitrust action to break them up involves costs as well as benefits

✔ Show how economic efficiency may be promoted if the government on the one hand allows **natural** monopolies to exist (subject to international competition or price regulation), while on the other hand it uses antitrust policies to break up **collusive** monopolies

✔ Describe the three-step process used to determine whether or not a merger should be allowed

✔ Give several reasons why *market-structure* regulation tends to be in the interest of the firms being regulated, rather than in the interest of consumers or the nation as a whole

✔ Explain the two important reasons why it is feasible for a government agency to cartelize an industry, but why it is not possible for a private group of producers to do so

✔ Explain how former Civil Aeronautics Board (CAB) regulations affected the interests of: *(a)* the established airlines, *(b)* the nation as a whole, *(c)* passengers on heavily-travelled trunk routes, and *(d)* passengers on small- city routes. In explaining *(c)* and *(d)*, use the concept of cross-subsidization

MAJOR PURPOSE

This chapter begins Part 8, in which a number of markets are examined to see how well they work. When they don't work well, what sort of government intervention is appropriate? For example, Chapter 28 describes government antitrust intervention when there is a threat by firms to collude in order to restrain trade or monopolize an industry. Chapter 29 describes problems that arise in agricultural markets, and why government intervention in these markets has created a whole new set of complications. Chapter 30 demonstrates how a free market may do

Chapter 28   Government Regulation of Business

an inadequate job of protecting our health, safety and the environment; and how the government is justified in intervening to provide such protection. Government intervention may also be sometimes justified to prevent our resources from too rapid depletion (Chapter 31) and to provide public goods that free markets fail to provide (Chapter 32). Finally, the last two chapters in Part 8 (chapters 33 and 34) deal with the great debate: What are the gains from international trade, and should the government intervene to restrict that trade? Although there are some situations in which such intervention is justified, the broad conclusion is that, with some exceptions, international markets work reasonably well, and there has been too much government intervention in this area in the past.

Chapter 28, to which we now turn, deals with two broad types of government regulation of business:

- **Antitrust laws** that prevent collusion and other restraints to trade. While such laws are necessary, their application is critically evaluated by posing such questions as: Should firms be broken up without regard to the possible effect on costs of production?

- **Regulation of naturally competitive industries**, such as trucking and the airlines, where government regulation in the past has not removed restraints on trade, but instead has created them. Government intervention of this form has often been hard to justify, and is now being phased out with the deregulation of these industries.

HIGHLIGHTS OF CHAPTER

This chapter focuses on several ways in which the government regulates business.

Antitrust

The first category of regulation consists of antitrust laws. The main laws that underlie the government's antitrust policy are:

- The Sherman Antitrust Act (1890), which made collusion illegal;

- The Clayton Act (1914), which banned, for example, interlocking corporate directorates, corporate takeovers that would lessen competition, and tying contracts that force a buyer to purchase a firm's entire product line or nothing at all; and

- The Federal Trade Commission (FTC) Act (1914), which established the FTC to prevent *unfair competition*.

The text also briefly describes the Robinson-Patman Act (1936) and the Miller-Tydings Act (1937), to illustrate how some government laws can have a perverse effect, in the sense that they discourage, rather than encourage competition.

However, for the most part, antitrust legislation does encourage competition—in several ways. For example, it prevents cutthroat pricing below costs designed to drive competitors out of business. The problem with trying to deal with cutthroat competition is that it is never clear whether a firm is setting its price below costs because it is trying to cut the throats of its competitors, or because it is just trying desperately to make sales in a weak market—perhaps in the face of stiff foreign competition. (Moreover, remember that even under perfect competition, a firm might continue to operate with price less than average cost as long as the firm is covering its average variable cost. This is scarcely setting a cutthroat price. Instead the firm is just accepting an unfavorable price that's dictated by the market.)

A second antitrust objective is to prevent firms from colluding to *cartelize* an otherwise competitive industry. But collusion, like cutthroat competition, is difficult to establish in the courts. For example, the fact that all firms in an industry are charging the same price doesn't prove that there has been a conspiracy to fix prices, because uniformity of price occurs in a perfectly competitive market in which there is no collusion whatsoever.

A third objective of antitrust policy is to limit the size of enterprises, by breaking up large firms, and by preventing mergers that create them in the first place. However, it doesn't necessarily follow that the government should automatically block all mergers, because the bigger firms that may be created by mergers may provide **advantages of large size**:

- Because of economies of scale, large firms may enjoy lower costs per unit than smaller firms. Thus, in deciding whether a merger should be allowed, the authorities have to weigh the cost savings against the disadvantage of the increased market power that goes to the new larger firm (Figure 28-1 in the text).

- Large firms can better afford the expenditures on research and development (R + D) which generate growth and technological improvements. Large firms also have more incentive to undertake R and D expenditures, because their large market share allows them to capture a large share of the benefits from any new technique or product they may develop. For example, if GM develops a superior engine, it will acquire millions of dollars of benefits from this in its huge sale of cars; so GM can justify this sort of R + D. However, a Kansas farmer can't justify a similar R + D expenditure to develop a better strain of wheat; the benefits to him would be limited to a few thousand dollars, while the millions of dollars of additional benefit would be spread among thousands of wheat farmers.

Three Steps in Judging a Merger

Figure 28-2 on p. 533 of the text shows that there are three ways that firms can get approval for a merger:

- If the industry is not highly concentrated — that is, if its Herfindahl-Hirschman Index (described on p. 498 of the text) will have a value of less than 1,000. Or

- If there are reasons such as strong foreign competition that prevent the exercise of market power. As another illustration, even a merger leading to a monopoly may be approved if the market is contestable, with free entry of new competitors. Or

- If there are benefits from the merger — such as economies of scale — that are sufficiently strong to offset any disadvantages of the merger.

If none of these justifications can be made, then the merger is not allowed.

Market-Structure Regulation of Price and Entry

One of the most interesting examples of this kind of regulation was the airlines industry, which used to be regulated by the Civil Aeronautics Board (CAB). Now that this industry has been deregulated — and the CAB has disappeared — it is clear that this industry is not a natural monopoly, so that the past regulation of this industry cannot be justified on this ground. Essentially this industry is naturally a fairly competitive one that was made non-competitive when the CAB cartelized it by imposing regulations.

Specifically, the CAB cartelized the airline industry by restricting entry into particular air routes, and by regulating price at a level that was favorable for the airlines. Even though a group of private firms (the airlines) could not have legally cartelized the industry in this way, it was possible for a government agency — the CAB — to do it because:

- any policies of a government agency, such as the CAB, are exempt from antitrust action, and

- when the CAB set prices backed up by the force of law, this eliminated the problem that so often destabilizes other kinds of cartels — namely, the problem of firms cheating by cutting their price. Airlines didn't cut their price because this would have been illegal.

What were the overall effects of CAB regulation? First, it reduced efficiency by raising price and thus reducing the total amount of air travel. Second, its decisions were not taken in the interest of the flying public, but instead were in the interests of the airlines that benefitted from the high price. There was also a *cross-subsidization* transfer from the passengers on the long 'big-city' trunk routes to small-city travellers. That is, the CAB required the airlines to provide small-city service, even in cases where it was not profitable; in compensation, the CAB allowed the airlines to cover their losses by charging a higher price on their profitable trunk routes.

In 1978, Congress empowered the CAB to dismantle its regulations and open the industry up to competition. (Of course, safety regulation remained, administered by the Federal Aviation Administration.) As expected, the immediate effect of deregulation was to reduce price and increase quantity (number of passengers). It had other effects as well.

- Airline efficiency increased, as the companies were able to freely allocate their planes between routes. The large airlines no longer had to fly their big jets half empty into small cities.

- Small cities were served by new companies, flying smaller planes at more frequent intervals. Greater frequency meant that many small-city passengers also benefitted, even though they had lost their *big-airline* service.

- As many new firms entered the industry, some of the less efficient older firms were squeezed out.

- More flying meant increased airport congestion, and increased fears about safety. However, the accident rate actually fell, and travel for Americans became safer for an additional reason. Cheaper air fares due to deregulation induced Americans to switch from dangerous auto travel to safer plane travel.

The problem of how to reduce airport congestion—perhaps by auctioning off landing slots—remained.

IMPORTANT TERMS

Match the term in the first column with the corresponding explanation in the second column.

_____ 1. Cutthroat competition
_____ 2. Price leadership
_____ 3. Interlocking directorate
_____ 4. Tying contract
_____ 5. Fair trade contract
_____ 6. Horizontal merger
_____ 7. Vertical merger
_____ 8. Conglomerate merger
_____ 9. Natural monopoly regulation
_____10. Entry regulation
_____11. Cross subsidization

a. Charging one group of customers more in order to help finance service to another group of customers.
b. The union of firms in the same competing activity.
c. Fixing by a manufacturer of the price that retail stores can charge for its product.
d. The practice in some oligopolistic industries of having one firm announce its price changes first, on the understanding that other firms will follow suit. Such a practice is sometimes suspected of being a form of *tacit* or silent collusion, in which the initial firm sets approximately the same price that a cartel would set.
e. The union of firms in unrelated activities.
f. A contract which requires purchasers to buy other items in a seller's line in order to get the items they really want. (Sometimes called full-line forcing.)
g. This exists when a director sits on a board of two or more competing firms.
h. Regulation of the nation's trucking firms.
i. Pricing below costs in order to drive competitors out of business
j. The union of a firm and its supplier. This happened, for example, when the shoe retailer T.R. Kinney merged with the shoe manufacturer Brown Shoe Co.
k. Setting the price that can be charged by an electric power company or a telephone company.

TRUE-FALSE

T   F   1.   Both criminal and civil antitrust suits can be brought against a firm.

T   F   2.   Predatory or cutthroat pricing is defined as setting price above average cost, but still low enough to put competing firms under pressure.

T   F   3.   Antitrust action that splits up a natural monopoly will lead to lower average costs of production

T   F   4. Full-line forcing is the requirement that purchasers buy a whole line of items in order to get the one they really want. It was prohibited by the Clayton Act in 1914.

T   F   5. So long as the acquiring firm offers to buy the target firm's stock, the management of a target firm will support the merger.

T   F   6. Since AT&T was broken up, there has been an increase in the price of local phone service and a drop in the price of long-distance service.

T   F   7. All takeover bids will be resisted by target companies.

T   F   8. Recently, the Department of Justice has disallowed mergers if the projected Herfindahl-Hirschman index of the industry is more than 1000.

T   F   9. Airline regulation kept airline fares down for the consumer. It was only when regulations were relaxed in the late 1970s that airline fares rose dramatically.

T   F   10. A merger that increases the market power of the new firm will automatically be disallowed by the Department of Justice.

T   F   11. Airline deregulation encouraged people to switch from cars to planes, and this increased accident rates.

MULTIPLE CHOICE

1. In recent years, the market power of large U.S. corporations has

   a. decreased because of the growth of foreign competition
   b. decreased because of the decline of foreign competition
   c. increased because of the growth of foreign competition
   d. increased because of the decline of foreign competition
   e. been unaffected by changes in foreign competition

2. Cutthroat competition is

   a. pricing above cost to drive competitors out of business
   b. pricing at cost to drive competitors out of business
   c. pricing below cost to drive competitors out of business
   d. decreasing advertising in order to put pressure on competitors
   e. restricting sales in order to put pressure on competitors

3. Which of the following increased competition?

   a. the chain store law
   b. establishing the Civil Aeronautics Board
   c. disbanding the CAB
   d. milk marketing orders
   e. none of the above

4. Effective antitrust policy requires that:

   a. Congress pass the necessary laws
   b. government agencies such as the Department of Justice enforce these laws
   c. the courts uphold the laws
   d. all of the above
   e. none of the above

5. An antitrust action that breaks up a natural monopoly may:

   a. restrict benefits from economies of scale
   b. increase benefits from economies of scale
   c. increase benefits from the law of diminishing returns
   d. decrease benefits from the law of diminishing returns
   e. have no economies-of-scale effect

6. In the Alcoa case (1945), Judge Learned Hand stated that industries should be organized into many small firms:

   a. provided this would not raise costs
   b. provided this would not raise costs *by a substantial amount*
   c. regardless of whether or not this would raise costs
   d. provided this would raise costs and therefore product quality
   e. provided this would keep costs constant

7. The increasing strength of foreign competition makes antitrust action against large U.S. firms:

   a. illegal
   b. more necessary
   c. less necessary
   d. neither more nor less necessary
   e. more necessary in some respects, but less in others

8. Interlocking directorates occur:

   a. when directors are forced to sit on the boards of several non-competing companies
   b. when a director is on the board of several competing firms
   c. when directors are forced to hold stock in several non-competing companies
   d. when directors trade inside information
   e. when a director of one company is involved in a takeover bid for another company

9. The Celler-Kefauver Antimerger Act:

   a. prevented a firm from purchasing the physical assets of another firm, if this would *substantially lessen competition*
   b. prevented a firm from taking over another firm by purchasing its common stock
   c. prohibited tying contracts
   d. prohibited full line forcing
   e. legalized interlocking directorates

10. An example of collusion is:

    a. an agreement to fix price
    b. an agreement to restrict sales
    c. an agreement to rig bids
    d. all of the above
    e. none of the above

11. An example of collusion that is beneficial for society as a whole might be

    a. an agreement by producers to reduce sales
    b. an agreement by chemical firms to cooperate in developing pollution-control devices
    c. an agreement by buyers to rig bids
    d. an agreement by producers to fix price
    e. all of the above

12. The practice of price leadership:

    a. makes tacit collusion difficult to detect
    b. is practised by monopolies
    c. is practised only under perfect competition
    d. is used primarily in cutthroat competition
    e. is never practised by oligopolists

13. A merger of a firm and its supplier is called:

    a. a vertical merger
    b. a horizontal merger
    c. a conglomerate merger
    d. a direct merger
    e. an indirect merger

14. In a takeover bid by firm A for firm B:

    a. both the management and stockholders of B are almost certain to welcome the bid
    b. both the management and stockholders of B are almost certain to oppose the bid
    c. the managers may oppose it, even though the stockholders welcome it
    d. the managers of firm A typically employ their golden parachutes
    e. firm A usually regards firm B as a black knight

15. Greenmail is:

    a. the premium paid by a target firm to buy its own stock from a shark
    b. the premium paid by a shark to buy its own stock from a target company
    c. the price reduction a private firm enjoys when it buys its own stock from a shark
    d. the price reduction a shark has to accept when it sells the target firm's stock
    e. none of the above

16. Recently the Department of Justice has allowed a merger if:

    a. entry into the industry is easy
    b. some advantage such as economies of scale more than offsets the disadvantage of increased market power
    c. either a or b
    d. both a and b
    e. neither a nor b

17. Recently the Department of Justice has been prepared to disallow a merger if:

    a. the industry is highly concentrated
    b. entry is not free
    c. the advantages of a merger such as economies of scale do not compensate for the disadvantages such as increased market power
    d. all of the above
    e. none of the above

18. In attempting to organize a cartel:

    a. a government agency is immune from antitrust prosecution, but a private group of producers is not
    b. a private group is immune from antitrust prosecution, but a government agency is not
    c. both groups are subject to antitrust prosecution

    d. neither group is subject to antitrust prosecution, because the antitrust laws don't cover cartels
    e. neither group is subject to antitrust prosecution, because the cartels do not fall under FTC jurisdiction

19. Before deregulation, the CAB conferred a net gain upon:

    a. the established airlines and the nation as a whole
    b. the nation, but not the established airlines
    c. the established airlines, but not the nation
    d. potential new airlines and the economy as a whole
    e. potential new airlines but not the economy as a whole

20. Deregulation of the airlines increased the safety of all U.S. travellers because:

    a. it raised airline fares and thus induced Americans to switch from planes to safer cars
    b. it raised airline fares and thus induced Americans to switch from cars to safer planes
    c. it reduced airline fares and thus induced Americans to switch from cars to safer planes
    d. it reduced airline fares and thus induced Americans to switch from planes to safer cars
    e. it had no effect on airline fares

EXERCISES

This is a review of Chapter 28 and of marginal cost price regulation in Chapter 26.

1   a. Suppose that the total cost for a firm producing widgets equals the fixed cost of $2 million plus a variable cost equal to $4 for every widget produced. Thus the marginal cost of producing widgets is always (constant, increasing, decreasing), and average cost is always (constant, increasing, decreasing.) The widget industry is a _____.

    b. Suppose this firm is being regulated using marginal cost pricing. Then its price would be $_____. Suppose the firm sells 2 million units at this price. Its cost per unit would be $_____, and its loss per unit would be $_____. Therefore the taxpayer would have to pay a total subsidy of $_____ to keep the firm in operation.

    c. If the industry were broken up into two separate firms, each with the same cost structure as before, and each firm were to produce half of this quantity, then the cost per unit would be _____, which is (more than, less than, the same as) before. The loss per unit would be $_____, which is (higher, lower, no different) than before. Therefore the total subsidy required to keep the industry alive would be (higher, lower, no different) than before. Specifically, the total subsidy paid to both firms would be $_____.

    d. After this monopoly is broken up and all necessary subsidies are paid, the firms would (gain, lose, be unaffected), the consumers would (gain, lose, be unaffected), and the taxpayers would (gain, lose, be unaffected). Thus the nation as a whole would (gain, lose, be unaffected). What important principle is illustrated by this hypothetical example?

ESSAY QUESTIONS

1. Discuss the benefits and costs of breaking up a natural monopoly.

2. "Giant companies such as IBM and General Motors still dominate the production of many goods. Thus our antitrust laws cannot have been effective." To what extent do you agree with this statement? Explain your position.

3. "In restricting GM's use of its market power, the competition from Japanese auto companies has been far more effective than our antitrust laws." Do you agree? Explain your position.

4. Evaluate the following FTC ruling on mergers: "...proof of violation [of the antitrust laws] consists of...evidence showing that the acquiring firm's...overall organization gives it a decisive advantage in efficiency over its small rivals": In the matter of Foremost Dairies, Inc., 60 FTC. 944, 1084 (1962).

ANSWERS

Important Terms: 1 i, 2 d, 3 g, 4 f, 5 c, 6 b, 7 j, 8 e, 9 k, 10 h, 11 a

True-False:
1 T (p. 535)
2 F (p. 525)
3 F (p. 528)
4 T (p. 523)
5 F (p. 531, BOX)
6 T (p. 535)
7 F (p. 531, BOX)
8 F (p. 533)
9 F (p. 538)
10 F (p. 533)
11 F (p. 538)

Multiple Choice:
1 a (p. 533),
2 c (p. 525)
3 c (p. 538)
4 d (p. 524)
5 a (p. 528)
6 c (p. 528)
7 c (p. 534)
8 b (p. 523)
9 a (p. 523)
10 d (p. 526)
11 b (p. 525)
12 a (p. 525)
13 a (p. 525)
14 c (p. 531, BOX)
15 a (p. 531, BOX)
16 c (p. 533)
17 d (p. 533)
18 a (p. 536)
19 c (p. 536)
20 c (p. 538)

Exercises

1   a.   constant, decreasing, natural monopoly.

         b. $4, $5, $1, $2 million.

         c. $6, more than, $2, higher, higher, $4 million.

         d.   be unaffected, be unaffected, lose, lose. From the point of view of efficiency, natural monopolies should be regulated rather than broken up.

Across

5, 7, 8. economies of scale and advertising can create these
13. U.S. soldier (Abbrev.)
15. type of competition aimed at eliminating rivals
16. won't he _____ learn?
17. mad, fanatical
18, 21. a major objective of the firm
23. an academic degree
24. on the interior of
25. _____ policies are designed to limit market power
29. at one time, the foundation of the monetary system
30. estimated time of arrival (abbrev.)
31. one
32, 33. when this exists, there are economies of scale
35. goods from foreign countries
36. a source of technological improvement
38, 39. this type of analysis sometimes used to evaluate government regulations
40. an international organization whose purpose is to exercise market power (abbrev.)

Down

1. Lincoln's first name
2. this is greatest in a monopolized industry
3. one reason for the development of monopoly
4. government agency with antitrust responsibilities (abbrev.)
6. income from land or buildings
9. return on an investment
10. the concentration _____ measures the degree to which an industry is dominated by a few sellers
11. one of the major antitrust acts
12. a type of merger
14. citizen of a middle-eastern country
15. what students often do the night before the exam
19. this type of efficiency is generally reduced by monopoly
20. the same (Latin abbrev. used in scholarly reference)
22. correct
25. smallest particle of an element
26. Keynes believed that the objective of balanceng the budget every year represented a policy _____
27. remain
28. light brown
34. this organization became the CIA (abbrev.)
37. Much _____ about Nothing

CHAPTER 29

WHY IS AGRICULTURE A
TROUBLED SECTOR?

LEARNING OBJECTIVES

After you have studied this chapter in the textbook and study guide, you should be able to

✔ Explain why farmers face special problems because agriculture is the one major sector in the economy that is perfectly competitive (or almost so)

✔ List the four major problems facing U.S. farmers

✔ Explain why farm prices are unstable in the short run

✔ Show how the concept of elasticity can throw light on agricultural problems

✔ Demonstrate why farm prices (relative to other prices) have been on a long-run downward trend

✔ Explain how increases in agricultural productivity have affected farm price

✔ Describe the role income elasticity plays in determining the long-run price of agricultural goods

✔ Show how the decline in export markets has affected farmers

✔ Explain why farmers have been facing a heavy debt burden in the 1980s

✔ Describe government price supports for agricultural goods

✔ Explain deficiency payments

✔ Analyze government supply restrictions, and explain why they can be viewed as government cartelization of an agricultural market

✔ Evaluate the effect of each of these programs on efficiency

✔ Explain the effect of each of these programs on equity

✔ Describe the subsidy war in agriculture between the United States and Europe

MAJOR PURPOSE

There are three key questions addressed in this chapter:

- *What are the basic problems of the farming sector?* We will see that some of the problems of farmers can be traced back to the perfectly competitive nature of agricultural markets. Because farmers—unlike oligopolists—have no control over price, their prices fluctuate more in the short run. Moreover, substantial improvements in farm productivity have increased supply, and this has led to a downward long-term trend in agricultural prices.

- *What policies has the government introduced to assist farmers?* There are several, in addition to the one most familiar to the general public—price supports.

- *How efficient and equitable are these policies?* Although the government may have been well-intentioned, it is difficult to give its policies a high score in terms of either their equity or efficiency.

HIGHLIGHTS OF CHAPTER

Why have U.S. farmers, who have been so productive, been in such trouble?

One important key to understanding agriculture is to recognize that its products are sold in perfectly competitive markets. In such markets, increased **productivity** has led to increased supply and lower price. This lower price has made **farmers worse off**, though greatly benefitting consumers. In response to distress on the farm, the government has intervened to keep farm prices up. However, government intervention that works well to keep price **down** in a natural monopoly sometimes doesn't work well in keeping price **up** in a perfectly competitive sector.

Let's now consider in some detail the special problems of farmers that have induced the government to intervene to support agricultural price, even though it generally does not intervene to support prices elsewhere.

The Special Problems of Agriculture

1. *Short-run price instability.* When supply increases from S_1 to S_3 in Figure 29-2 because of a bountiful harvest, farm revenue **decreases** (because of inelastic demand). On the other hand, when supply decreases to S_2 because of a bad crop, farm revenue **increases**. Thus, paradoxically, farmers are often hurt by good crops, and benefit from bad ones.

   The other important message in this diagram is that the inelastic demand for farm products, along with shifting farm supply, leads to serious short-run fluctuations in price—back and forth from P_2 to P_3.

2. *Long-run downward trend in price.* This problem, pointed out in the previous section, is detailed in Figure 29-3a. Over time, large productivity improvements have shifted farm supply to the right from S_1 to S_2, driving down price because the shifts in demand to the right (from D_1 to D_2) have been far less. The reasons for the smaller shifts in demand are (1) U.S. population has not been growing rapidly; and (2) as income has risen, people have tended to spend it on other things than food—that is, the income elasticity of demand for food has been low.

3. *Decline in traditional U.S. export markets.* One of the reasons for this has been the European Common Agricultural Policy (CAP), a program of heavy subsidization and protection of European farmers that has moved Europe beyond the original CAP objective of self sufficiency to a strong net export position. This has meant that traditional U.S. export sales have been damaged, not only in Europe, but also in third markets where U.S. farmers have had to compete with heavily subsidized European exports. (See detail on the "subsidy war in agriculture" at the end of the chapter.)

   Other reasons why U.S. sales in third markets have been disappointing have included population controls and improvements in agricultural productivity in countries like China.

Has this disappointing export performance had an effect on U.S. farm income? Figure 29-4 suggests that the answer is a strong "Yes".

4. *A heavy debt burden*. Farmers who borrowed heavily to purchase land in the booming 1970s at inflated prices found themselves in trouble in the 1980s when (i) farm prices and incomes fell, and (ii) interest rates rose. (See Figure 29-6.) Moreover, farmers couldn't escape from their debt burden by selling some of their land. Its value fell with farm prices, often falling below the value of their mortgages. (See Figure 29-7.)

Government Policies to Assist Farmers

1. *A price support*. When the government raises price from P_1 in Figure 29-8a to a higher price support level P_2, there is excess supply E_3E_2 that the treasury has to buy up, at a cost to taxpayers of the shaded area. Consumers also lose because they are now paying a higher price, while farmers benefit because they are receiving that price increase. Therefore there is a transfer from taxpayers and consumers to farmers.

   There is also an efficiency loss because Q_2 is being produced and this is more than the efficient, perfectly competitive quantity Q_1.

2. *A deficiency payment (panel b of Figure 29-8)*. If the target price under this program is the same P_2, farmers will receive the same increase in income as they again move from E_1 to E_2. The key difference is that instead of buying up the surplus to keep price up, the government now lets the price fall to P_4, and pays farmers a deficiency payment of P_2P_4 per bushel, for a total payment of the shaded area. Once again, taxpayers lose and farmers benefit. However, this time consumers also benefit because the price they face is reduced from P_1 to P_4. Therefore there is a transfer from taxpayers to farmers and consumers.

   There is also the same efficiency loss as under the price support program, since there is the same amount of overproduction (Q_2 rather than the efficient Q_1).

3. *A supply restriction (panel c of Figure 29-8)*. In this case, a restriction on, say, the acreage that can be planted reduces supply from Q_1 to Q_3. This en-forced scarcity raises price from P_1 to P_2. This has exactly the same effect as monopolizing a perfectly competitive industry; in fact, the government has cartelized this industry by enforcing an output restriction on producers. [You may wish to review Figure 27-4, where this story is told in more detail. The one difference is that the collusive oligopoly (cartel) in that earlier diagram maximized industry profit. The government supply restriction here need not necessarily be that severe.]

   Farmers benefit from this supply restriction (for the same reason that firms did in Figure 27-4) — but not as much as with the previous two policies, because they are now selling less (Q_3 rather than Q_2). Consumers lose because price has risen. There is therefore a transfer from consumers to producers. Note that in this case there is *no cost* to the treasury; therefore it will prefer this policy.

   There is an efficiency loss because production has been reduced to Q_3.

4. *Combined programs*. The above 3 programs can be used in combination. For example, in some grains there has been a price support with a deficiency payment added to this, provided farmers restrict their acreage.

Evaluation of These Government Programs

The efficiency losses and transfers from these programs are shown in Figure 29-9. Also consider the following two questions:

- *Do transfers improve equity?* If they went to small, poor farmers they might. However, transfers tend to go to rich farmers. (See Figure 29-10.) The reason is that subsidies are put on bushels of wheat rather than on farmers who need the income. Thus the big, high-income farmers who produce the most wheat get the lions' share of the subsidies.

- *Should poor farmers therefore be directly subsidized instead?* The answer to this is probably yes — although we'll see in Chapter 39 that even this would involve problems.

Now that you have seen how inefficient price supports are, read the counter argument in Box 29-2.

IMPORTANT TERMS

Match the first column with the corresponding phrase in the second column:

_____ 1. CAP
_____ 2. Secular trend
_____ 3. Deficiency payment
_____ 4. Price support
_____ 5. Supply restriction
_____ 6. Buffer stock
_____ 7. Subsidy war
_____ 8. Parity ratio

a. A government policy of keeping the market price from falling below a specified level.
b. The prices farmers receive divided by the prices they pay.
c. Long run tendency.
d. A good that the government accumulates.
e. The agricultural policy of the Europeans that has moved them beyond self sufficiency to become net exporters.
f. Any limitation on a firm's output by the government.
g. Competition between governments in assisting exports.
h. Per bushel subsidy to farmers to raise the price they receive to a certain target level.

TRUE-FALSE

T   F   1.   Government agricultural price supports raise both farm prices and farm incomes.

T   F   2.   U.S. farm price supports provide a subsidy that is larger in dollar terms to the poor farmer than to the rich farmer.

T   F   3.   If more children had stayed on the farm, the problem of depressed farm prices would be less severe.

T   F   4.   Long-run agricultural price can remain unchanged only if both the demand and supply curves stop shifting.

T   F   5.   If birth control methods were more widely accepted in the Far East, the price of rice would be lower.

T   F   6.   The past downward trend in farm prices (relative to other prices) has occurred because improvements in farm technology have shifted the supply curve to the right more rapidly than the demand curve has been shifting.

T   F   7.   When the government increases its stockpile of wheat, its policy is raising the price of wheat.

T   F   8.   If demand for food had been more responsive to rising incomes, there would not have been such a pronounced downward trend in food prices.

T   F   9.   An effective way for the government to reduce its buffer stocks is to introduce a price support.

T   F   10.   Because price supports often subsidize wealthy farmers more than poor farmers, they are not an effective means of increasing equity.

MULTIPLE CHOICE

1. The long-term decline in agricultural prices in the United States might be reversed if:

   a. people began to eat less food
   b. there was a decline in the rate of population growth throughout the world
   c. there was a decline in the price of fertilizers
   d. there were several years of good weather and therefore bountiful crops throughout the world
   e. there was a decline in the rate of technological progress in agriculture

2. Improvements in agricultural productivity tend to:

   a. raise farm prices and income
   b. lower farm prices
   c. raise farm prices, but lower farm income
   d. have no affect on farm prices
   e. have no affect on farm income

3. The base period in farm parity calculations is:

   a. 1900-1904
   b. 1910-1914
   c. 1914-1920
   d. 1920-1924
   e. 1930-1934

4. Some people believe that long-run food prices will rise because:

   a. farmers will stay on the land, rather than taking jobs in the city
   b. the risk of drought in foreign countries will be eliminated
   c. population growth will be reduced in developing countries
   d. the supply curve will shift more rapidly to the right than the demand curve
   e. the supply curve will shift less rapidly to the right than the demand curve

5. Relative to other prices, farm prices have been:

   a. stable in the short run, with a long-term upward trend
   b. stable in the short run, with a long-term downward trend
   c. unstable in the short run, with neither an upward nor a downward long-term trend

   d. unstable in the short run, with a long-term downward trend
   e. unstable in the short run, with a long-term upward trend

6. Increased productivity at IBM has led to:

   a. a cut in its prices and profits
   b. an increase in its prices and profits
   c. an increase in its prices, and a cut in its profits
   d. a cut in its prices, and an increase in its profits
   e. a cut in its prices, and no change in its profits

7. Government price supports have:

   a. raised farm prices and reduced the parity ratio
   b. raised farm prices and kept the parity ratio from falling further
   c. lowered farm prices and kept the parity ratio from rising
   d. left farm prices unchanged, but reduced the parity ratio
   e. left farm prices unchanged, but raised the parity ratio

8. By 1989, the farm parity ratio was:

   a. less than 100, which indicated that the prices farmers pay had fallen relative to the prices farmers receive
   b. more than 100, which indicated that the prices farmers pay had fallen relative to the prices farmers receive
   c. more than 100, which indicated that the prices farmers receive had fallen relative to the prices farmers pay
   d. less than 100, which indicated that the prices farmers receive had fallen relative to the prices farmers pay
   e. about 100, which indicated that the prices farmers receive were about the same as the prices farmers pay

9. Farmers have reason to fear bumper crops worldwide in products in which

   a. demand is inelastic
   b. demand has unit elasticity
   c. demand is elastic
   d. b or c
   e. none of the above, since demand is irrelevant

10. If there is crop failure in a product

    a. with elastic demand, income rises
    b. with elastic demand, income falls
    c. with elastic demand, income remains constant
    d. with inelastic demand, income remains constant
    e. with inelastic demand, income falls

11. If supply

    a. increases more rapidly than demand, price will fall
    b. increases more rapidly than demand, price will rise
    c. increases more rapidly than demand, price will remain constant
    d. decreases more rapidly than demand, price will remain constant
    e. decreases more rapidly than demand, price will fall

12. Interest payments farmers had to pay

    a. rose between 1960 and 1980 and fell in the early 1980s
    b. rose between 1960 and 1980 and rose even faster in the early 1980s
    c. rose between 1960 and 1980 and remained roughly constant in the early 1980s
    d. fell between 1960 and 1980 and remained roughly constant in the early 1980s
    e. fell between 1960 and 1980 and fell even faster between 1980 and 1987

13. In the early 1980s, the interest payments farmers had to pay on their mortgages

    a. fell while the value of their land rose
    b. fell while the value of their land fell
    c. rose while the value of their land fell
    d. rose while the value of their land rose
    e. rose while the value of their land remained roughly constant

14. Recent government programs have

    a. increased the per capita incomes of rich farmers more than poor farmers
    b. increased the per capita incomes of rich farmers less than poor farmers
    c. decreased the per capita incomes of rich farmers less than poor farmers
    d. decreased the per capita incomes of rich farmers more than poor farmers
    e. had no apparent effect on either

15. In the 1980s, carryover stocks of coarse grains and wheat

    a. rose in the United States but fell in the rest of the world
    b. fell in the United States but rose in the rest of the world
    c. rose in the United States but remained constant in the rest of the world
    d. rose in both areas
    e. fell in both areas

16. The recent U.S./Europe subsidy war in agricultural products has been the result of

    a. subsidies by the United States but not by Europe
    b. subsidies by Europe but not by the United States
    c. subsidies by both
    d. subsidies by neither, but taxes by both
    e. other reasons

17. Most of the benefits from government agricultural price support programs go to

    a. farmers renting the land when the programs are announced
    b. those who own farm land when the programs are announced
    c. those who own farm land a decade or so later
    d. farmers renting the farm land a decade or so later
    e. none of the above

18. A world shortage of food due to poor crops would

    a. lower U.S. food prices and reduce U.S. exports
    b. lower U.S. food prices and increase U.S. exports
    c. raise U.S. food prices and reduce U.S. exports
    d. raise U.S. food prices and increase U.S. exports
    e. have little effect on U.S. food prices, but increase U.S. exports

19. Between 1980 and 1985, U.S. agricultural exports

    a. increased while farm income fell further below city income
    b. increased while farm income rose above city income
    c. decreased while farm income rose above city income
    d. decreased while farm income fell even further below city income
    e. decreased while the gap between farm and city income remained roughly constant

20. When the government supports farm price above its free-market level

    a. there is an efficiency gain and a transfer from farmers to taxpayers
    b. there is an efficiency gain and a transfer from taxpayers to farmers
    c. there is an efficiency gain and no transfer
    d. there is an efficiency loss and a transfer from taxpayers to farmers
    e. there is an efficiency loss and a transfer from farmers to taxpayers

21. The one reason for believing that the government might do a better job than private speculators in stabilizing farm price is that

    a. government officials and politicians can use their political experience to make better predictions of future price
    b. politicians become expert at speculating on the future because they have had to speculate with their careers in election campaigns
    c. the government can provide farmers with a future price guarantee, but private speculators cannot
    d. the government does not have to provide the future price guarantee that private speculators do
    e. government officials are speculating with their own money while private speculators are not

---

EXERCISES

1. Figure 29.1 shows the supply and demand for a particular grade of wheat in a particular year in a perfectly competitive market in Chicago.

Figure 29.1

Price

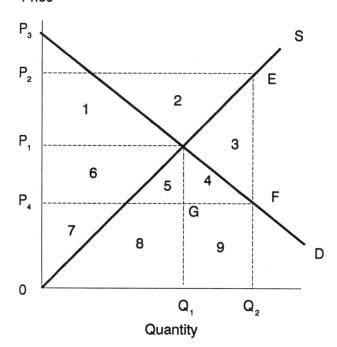

Quantity

    a. The equilibrium price is _____, and the equilibrium quantity is _____. Now suppose that the government, instead of allowing the market to operate freely, buys directly from farmers all the wheat they want to sell at price P₂.

The quantity supplied will be _____. As a result of this government intervention, farmers realize a (gain, loss) of area _____. Shade in this area in the diagram.

    b. Suppose that the government, after buying this wheat, now sells it all on the market for whatever price it will fetch. This price will be _____. This government policy is equivalent to a (price support, deficiency payment, supply restriction).

    c. As a result of this government intervention, consumers realize a (gain, loss) of area _____. Shade in this area in the diagram. If we just consider the effects on consumers and producers (the two shaded areas), we would conclude that there is a net (gain, loss) to the economy as a result of the government's intervention. However, the government has made a (gain, loss) on these wheat dealings. The total amount that the government paid for the wheat is _____ and the total revenue that the government received for selling the wheat is _____. Therefore the (gain, loss) to the government (i.e., the taxpayers) is _____. If this is taken into account along with the effects on producers and consumers, we conclude that the government's action results in a net (gain, loss) to the economy of area _____.

2. Alternatively, we could have even more easily arrived at this conclusion by noting that the government's action (raised, lowered) output from the perfectly competitive amount _____ to the amount _____. According to Figure 25-3a, the result is efficiency (gain, loss) of triangle _____.

ESSAY QUESTIONS

1. The U.S. government will not allow a huge U.S. bank (like the Continental Illinois) or a huge auto company (like Chrysler) to go bankrupt, but it will allow farmers or other small businesses to go bankrupt. Is this government policy fair? Can it be justified on some other grounds?

2. Why might farmers hope that there would be no worldwide bumper crops? Which would result in the highest price of corn in Iowa? a drought (a) everywhere except in that state; (b) everywhere except in the United States; (c) everywhere except in North America; (d) nowhere. Explain.

3. If you are working for the U.S. government, and your only concern is to minimize the money the government has to pay out to farmers, would you prefer a deficiency payment or a price support:

   a if the demand curve is very elastic?

   b if demand is very inelastic?

   Explain your answer.

4. "Food has a higher value than gold because without food we would starve. Yet gold has a far higher price. That doesn't make any economic sense." Critically evaluate.

5. What are some of the pros and cons of government-guaranteed prices for farmers?

ANSWERS

Important Terms :   1 e, 2 c, 3 h, 4 a, 5 f, 6 d, 7 g, 8 b

True-False:
1 T (p. 550)
2 F (p. 552)
3 F (p. 544)
4 F (p. 545)
5 T (p. 546)
6 T (p. 545)
7 T (p. 553)
8 T (p. 544)
9 F (p. 550)
10 T (p. 552)

Multiple Choice:
1 e (p. 545)
2 b (pp. 544-545)
3 b (p. 548, BOX)
4 e (p. 545)
5 d (p. 543)
6 d (p. 548, BOX)
7 b (pp. 548, 550, BOX)
8 d (p. 548)
9 a (p. 544)
10 b (p. 544)
11 a (p. 545)
12 b (p. 549)
13 c (p. 549)
14 a (p. 554)
15 d (p. 555)
16 c (p. 555)

17 b (p. 554)
18 d (p. 554)
19 d (p. 547)
20 d (pp. 550-551)
21 c (p. 553, BOX).

Exercises

1   a. P_1, Q_1, Q_2, gain, $1 + 2$.
      b. P_4, deficiency payment.
      c.   gain, $4 + 5 + 6$, gain, loss, areas 1 through 9 inclusive, $7 + 8 + 9$, loss, 1 through 6, loss, 3.

2.   raised, Q_1, Q_2, loss, 3.

CHAPTER 30

GOVERNMENT REGULATIONS TO PROTECT OUR QUALITY OF LIFE

LEARNING OBJECTIVES

After you have studied this chapter in the textbook and the study guide you should be able to

✔ Identify the agencies that are responsible for protecting our quality of life

✔ Explain why pollution is an externality

✔ Explain why perfect competition does not lead to efficiency when there is pollution or any other kind of external cost

✔ Show the efficiency loss from pollution, in a diagram similar to Figure 30-2 in the textbook

✔ Explain why we cannot and should not attempt to eliminate pollution completely

✔ Demonstrate why the policy of imposing a physical limit on pollution is a far less efficient way of reducing it than imposing a tax on emissions

✔ Show why a third option—imposing physical limits on pollution, but allowing the rights to be bought and sold—is efficient like a tax

✔ Critically evaluate the policy of subsidizing pollution-control equipment

✔ Explain how recycling reduces the pollution problem, and, as a favorable side effect, also reduces the problem of resource depletion that we will be studying in the next chapter

✔ Explain why ensuring that products and jobs are safe requires dealing with a lack of information rather than an externality

✔ Demonstrate why information problems justify government intervention

✔ Show why information problems are more serious for health than for safety

✔ Demonstrate why benefit/cost analysis is important in designing government regulations

✔ Explain why benefit-cost analysis involves many problems; for example this approach often requires us to attach a value to a human life

✔ Demonstrate why government policy becomes inconsistent, with too few lives saved, if no attempt is made to put a rough-and-ready value on a human life

MAJOR PURPOSE

Many people think that environmental pollution is simply a bad thing that should be prevented. They believe that it has nothing to do with economics, and economic considerations such as cost are irrelevant. Pollution, they contend, should be cleaned up, regardless of cost. The objective in this chapter is to show that pollution is, in fact, an economic problem — one that involves many of the principles that have already been developed in this book. Moreover, if economic considerations are ignored, pollution will be much more costly to control. Society will waste valuable resources in the clean-up effort. Or to put the same point another way: Our limited available funds for cleaning up will give us far less improvement in the environment if we ignore costs.

The second objective of this chapter will be to show that creating safe products and safe jobs is also an economic problem. Here again costs cannot be ignored.

HIGHLIGHTS OF CHAPTER

Pollution as an External Cost

Pollution is an external cost, because it is not borne by those responsible for it. For example, when smoke from a factory soils someone's clothes, the factory owner doesn't have to pay the cleaning bill.

Why does a Perfectly Competitive Market Fail to Deal with the Pollution Problem?

When there is an externality like pollution, the "invisible hand" of a perfectly competitive, free market does not provide an efficient outcome. The reason is that there is a violation of one of the conditions in Chapter 25 that allows perfect competition to deliver an economically efficient outcome. The condition that is violated is that the marginal cost to producers (MC) must be the same as the marginal cost to society (MC_S). This condition does not hold when there is an external cost such as pollution, because MC_S is more than MC. The difference between the two is the marginal external cost MC_E, as illustrated in Figure 30-1 in the textbook.

Efficiency requires that the marginal benefit to society (shown by the demand curve) be equal to the marginal cost to society MC_S. In Figure 30-2 of the textbook we see that this efficient outcome is at E_2. However this is not the equilibrium in a perfectly competitive free market. The reason is that, as always in such a market, supply reflects the cost facing producers. But this is only their private cost MC. The external cost of their actions is a cost they don't have to face. Because supply reflects private cost MC only, the perfectly competitive equality of demand and supply is at equilibrium E_1 rather than the efficient E_2. Thus perfect competition is inefficient; too much output of this polluting good is produced (Q_1 rather than the efficient output Q_2). The efficiency loss is measured by the red triangle in this figure. Be sure you can explain this triangle: For each of the units of "excess" output between Q_2 and Q_1, social cost MC_S exceeds benefit D. There is therefore a net cost involved in producing each of these units — with the sum of all these costs being the red triangle.

What Principles Should Guide our Anti-Pollution Policy?

The above analysis suggests a simple way that the government can make a perfectly competitive market efficient. Impose a tax on polluting producers equal to the external cost they are creating; that is, impose tax r in Figure 30-2 of the text. This tax now becomes one of the costs producers have to face. In other words, the "external cost is now internalized," because it has now become a cost that producers have to face. Since producers will have to take this external cost — along with all their other costs — into account in making their supply decisions, the supply curve shifts up from S_1 to S_2. Supply now reflects both internal and external costs, and the perfectly competitive equilibrium of demand and supply is at the efficient point E_2. Thus, with this simple imposition of a tax, the perfectly competitive market does yield an efficient outcome after all. Adam Smith's invisible hand does work, because, with this tax, the government is applying the **appropriate pressure** on the market, and then **letting the market work.**

Figure 30-2 in the text illustrates another important principle: Polluting output can be cut back "too much." Limiting it to Q_3 is even worse than a "hands off" policy that would allow output to continue unrestricted at Q_1. (At Q_3, the efficiency loss FE_2G is even greater than the red efficiency loss at Q_1.)

Antipollution Policies: What has the U.S. Experience Been?

The main policy of the government has not been to tax polluters, but has instead been to impose physical limits on pollution. While this policy has reduced pollution, most economists believe that it has not done so in an efficient, low-cost way for the following reasons:

- The physical limits in some cases have been too restrictive and in other cases too loose, because the Environmental Protection Agency (EPA) has tended to disregard the cost of reducing pollution.

- Even if the total physical limit were to be set correctly (for example, at Q_3 in Figure 30-3 of the text) imposing restrictions on individual polluting firms is a much more costly way of reducing pollution (by, say, a half) than is the imposition of a pollution tax. Under a pollution tax of T, pollution would be cut back by those firms that can do so at least cost—that is, firms to the right of Q_3 that can cut pollution at a cost shown, for example, by the short arrow. Thus the total cost of reducing pollution would be minimized. On the other hand, when a physical limit on pollution is imposed on each firm, some of the reduction in pollution must be undertaken by firms to the *left* of Q_3 at the relatively high cost shown by, for example, the tall arrow. There is the same reduction in pollution, but it is achieved at an unnecessarily high cost.

The EPA has recently begun to introduce a third method which, like a pollution tax, also lets the market work and therefore reduces pollution at minimum cost. This is a policy of imposing a physical limit on pollution but then allowing permits to pollute to be bought and sold at a market price. This "price of polluting" acts as a

deterrent just like the tax T, ensuring that pollution will be cut back at mimimum cost.

A fourth method used by the EPA has been to subsidize pollution-control equipment. However, this has involved problems:

- The government has often failed to ensure that the pollution-control equipment it has subsidized is used effectively.

- Pollution-control equipment provides, at best, an "end-of-pipe" solution that is often more costly than other solutions such as using cleaner inputs. (For example, less polluting Western coal could be used in power plants.) Again, either a pollution tax or a system of tradeable permits would be a lower-cost policy because it would give firms not only the incentive to cure pollution, but also the incentive to find the least expensive cure.

Recycling

This can play an important role in reducing the amount of pollution because it disposes of polluting wastes (such as empty beer cans). Such a policy would also mean that we will need to extract fewer natural resources from our environment. If we produce new beer cans out of old ones, we won't need to mine as much iron ore.

Government Intervention to Ensure Safe Jobs and Safe Products

1. How is this intervention to be justified? If firms under pressure let products or workplaces become dangerous, the health and safety of the firm's customers or labor force may be compromised. This seems like an externality, but it isn't. The damage is not to an innocent bystander (like those living on a polluted river). Instead it is to the firm's customers or labor force who are **parties to the transactions,** and who can consequently take some action to curb the damage the firm is doing to them. For example, airline passengers can avoid an unsafe airline, and workers can insist on a premium wage for dangerous jobs—**provided they know the risks involved.** The evidence is that workers do insist on some premium in risky jobs, but not enough to compensate adequately.

Thus the major problem is the **lack of information** about what risks to health and safety really are. By the time the public finds out an airline is dangerous, lives have been lost. This justifies safety regulations by the FAA. As another example, workers can't know the cancer risks from handling chemicals. This justifies OSHA's intervention to ensure that chemicals are labelled.

2. Risks to health are a greater problem than risks to safety. Workers can see risks to safety such as an unprotected buzz saw, and can insist that it be safely installed. There is much greater information problem with health. A cancer risk from chemicals that may kill people 20 years later cannot be "seen." Therefore government intervention to provide information and to prevent risk is even more strongly justified where there is a health risk than where there is a safety risk; however both are important.

3. The airlines provide two exceptions to these general principles:

   • There is a *huge* information problem with safety in the air. Unlike the case of a buzz-saw, where information about risk becomes available when *one* person is *injured,* information about risk on an airline may become available only after *hundreds* are *killed.* Since the information cost the public faces in this case is so high, the FAA is justified in imposing safety standards

   • The FAA is further justified by externalities. A crash may not only kill the parties to the transaction (the passengers and crew). It may also kill innocent bystanders on the ground who are *not* parties to the transaction. (They have nothing to do with flying.)

Evaluating a Government Regulation with Benefit/Cost Analysis

A regulation cannot be justified just because it has a desirable objective such as improving health and safety.

It must be *effective* in achieving that objective, that is, it must provide substantial *benefits*. And those benefits should exceed its *costs*. The purpose of benefit/cost analysis is to perform just such a test.

One might expect that whenever policy makers are considering a new regulation, they would perform such a benefit/cost analysis. Unfortunately this is not always the case. In some recent legislation, it is expressly stated that regulations must be enforced regardless of their costs.

If we take a benefit/cost approach to analyze a proposed new regulation, it is first necessary to estimate costs, such as the operating costs of the agencies that administer the regulations, and the costs incurred by firms in complying with the regulations.

Even greater problems are encountered in estimating the benefits of a regulation. For example, one of the benefits may be the saving of lives — and no-one wants to put a value on a human life. It is far easier to say that the value of a life is infinite, and leave it at that. But that's not how we value our lives. We all take some small risk with our lives whenever we take a trip in a plane — or, for that matter, an even bigger risk when we travel by car. We don't sit at home and avoid the risk, as we would if we truly believed that our lives had an infinite value. But while it's easy to argue that the value of a life is less than infinite, it's very difficult to be more specific. For attempts to do so, see Box 30-4 in the textbook.

Even if the complete information necessary for a full benefit-cost test is not available, it is still possible to make government policy more effective using fragmentary information. To use an example cited in the text, a regulation imposing an arsenic standard has been saving lives at an estimated cost of $70 million per life. Alternatively, lives could be saved at a cost of only about $100,000 each by building more railroad overpasses. Obviously, we should switch to this policy; if we did, we could save the same number of lives at much lower cost. Or, to put the same point more appropriately, we could use our limited funds to save far more lives.

IMPORTANT TERMS

Match the term in the first column with the corresponding phrase in the second column.

_____ 1. Internal cost
_____ 2. External cost
_____ 3. Social cost
_____ 4. The marginal cost of reducing pollution (MCR)
_____ 5. Marginal cost of having pollution (MCP)
_____ 6. "End-of-pipe" treatment
_____ 7. Recycling
_____ 8. FDA
_____ 9. FAA
_____ 10. EPA
_____ 11. OSHA

a. The cost of reducing pollution by one more unit.
b. The cost that is paid by the producer. Also called private cost.
c. The cost of having one more unit of pollution
d. The cost not paid by the producer (or consumer) of a good, but by someone else.
e. The policy of removing pollutants just before they enter the environment.
f. Agency that deals with pollution
g. Agency that monitors airline safety
h. Agency that monitors conditions in the workplace
i. Agency that banned thalidomide
j. The total cost to society, that is, the sum of internal and external costs.
k. Using materials again rather than throwing them away. This can reduce pollution and preserve natural resources.

TRUE-FALSE

T   F   1.   Restricting industrial growth is one of the best measures for controlling pollution.

T   F   2.   Inefficiency occurs if producers do not take external pollution costs into account.

T   F   3.   Marginal external cost equals marginal social cost minus marginal private cost.

T   F   4.   The main effort of the Environmental Protection Agency has been to collect the taxes that the government has imposed to discourage pollution.

T   F   5.   A pollution tax "internalizes an externality" because the producer is forced to face not only internal costs, but also the external costs imposed on society.

T   F   6.   Without government intervention, the marginal cost of having pollution would be zero.

T   F   7.   Setting an arbitrary physical limit on pollution will always be better than doing nothing at all.

T   F   8.   The problem with pollution is that, in the absence of government intervention, firms view it as an internal cost.

T   F   9.   The Clean Air Act has sometimes been interpreted to mean that the air should not be allowed to deteriorate anywhere — even in states with no air pollution problem.

T   F   10. Benefit/cost analysis is designed to ensure that the total benefits of a policy will equal its total costs.

T   F   11. It makes no sense to impose an arsenic standard that cost $70 million for each life saved, while we are not building the railroad overpasses that could save lives for far less than $1 million each.

MULTIPLE CHOICE

1. An example of an externality being internalized occurs if:

   a. an export firm is required to raise the price of a good it is also selling in the home market
   b. an export firm is required to export less and sell more goods on the home market instead
   c. a producer is forced to face the external cost his product imposes on society
   d. a producer is forced to face the internal cost his product imposes on society
   e. a tax is imposed on the producer equal to the marginal social cost of the good

2. In a perfectly competitive market, the marginal benefit of a polluting good will equal its marginal social costs if:

   a. a tax is imposed on the good equal to its marginal external cost
   b. a tax is imposed on the good equal to its marginal internal cost
   c. a subsidy is provided equal to the marginal internal cost
   d. a subsidy is provided equal to the marginal external cost
   e. the government does not intervene with either a tax or subsidy

3. In a perfectly competitive market for a polluting good where the government is following a "hands-off policy,"

   a. less than the efficient amount will be produced
   b. more than the efficient amount will be produced
   c. the efficient amount will be produced
   d. price will be equal to the efficient level
   e. price will be higher than the efficient level

4. In the face of external costs, efficiency can be achieved in a perfectly competitive market by setting a tax equal to:

   a. the marginal social cost of producing the good
   b. the marginal internal cost of producing the good
   c. the marginal external cost of producing the good
   d. the total social cost of producing the good
   e. the total internal cost of producing the good

5. Airplanes flying low over houses near airports cause "noise pollution." The most efficient policy to deal with this would be to:

   a. rely on the "invisible hand" to take care of the problem
   b. provide a subsidy to each airline depending on the total amount of noise it creates in the affected neighborhoods
   c. impose a tax on each airline depending on the total amount of noise it creates in the affected neighborhoods
   d. impose limits on the number of flights of each airline
   e. subsidize airlines that install noise-abatement devices

6. The marginal external cost of a polluting good is equal to:

   a. its marginal social cost plus its marginal internal cost
   b. its marginal social cost less its marginal internal cost
   c. its marginal internal cost less its marginal social cost
   d. its marginal internal cost or its marginal social cost, whichever is greater
   e. its marginal internal cost or its marginal social cost, whichever is less

7. As time passes, pollution becomes a more difficult problem to deal with because the marginal cost of reducing pollution (MCR):

   a. shifts to the left, while the marginal cost of pollution (MCP) is rising
   b. shifts to the right while MCP is rising
   c. shifts to the right while MCP is falling
   d. shifts to the left while MCP is falling
   e. remains stable while MCP is rising

8. An effluent fee is:

   a. any tax imposed on the wealthy
   b. a special tax on the wealthy who pollute
   c. a tax on each unit of pollution
   d. a subsidy provided to polluters to encourage them to use cleaner fuels
   e. a subsidy provided to polluters who install pollution-abatement equipment

9. Superfund is a multimillion dollar program:

   a. to clean up ground pollution
   b. to clean up industrial air pollution
   c. to clean up air pollution from auto exhausts
   d. to publicize the dangers of pollution to the public
   e. to publicize the environmental benefits of the Environmental Protection Agency

10. If a physical limit is set on the amount of pollutants each firm can emit:

    a. pollution will be cut back at minimum cost — that is, by the firms that can do so least expensively
    b. pollution will cut back at zero cost
    c. the result will surely be an improvement on leaving pollution uncontrolled
    d. the result will surely be inferior to leaving pollution uncontrolled
    e. it is not clear how the result will compare with leaving pollution uncontrolled

11. To determine the appropriate tax on pollution in a lake where there are many polluting industries, the government must have information on:

    a. the marginal cost of reducing pollution (MCR) and the marginal cost of having pollution (MCP)
    b. MCP but not MCR
    c. only the marginal benefit of reducing pollution (MBR)
    d. the marginal cost of pollution control equipment
    e. the marginal benefit of pollution control equipment

12. If one is to argue — along with Ronald Coase — that property rights should be created to deal with water pollution, then the question of who actually owns these rights:

    a. must be resolved by giving them to state governments
    b. must be resolved by giving them to polluting firms
    c. is more important from the point of view of equity, than of efficiency
    d. is more important from the point of view of efficiency, than of equity
    e. is important from neither an equity nor an efficiency point of view

13. If a physical limit is set on the amount of pollutants each firm can emit:

    a. pollution will be cut back, but at a higher cost than necessary

    b. pollution will be cut back, at the minimum possible cost
    c. there will be no change in the amount of pollution
    d. there will be an increase in the amount of pollution
    e. nothing can be said about the pollution that will result

14. The least-cost way of reducing pollution in a lake is to:

    a. encourage all firms to cut back their pollution by the same percentage
    b. force all firms to cut back their pollution by the same percentage
    c. let the firms with the highest profits cut back the most
    d. force the firms with the lowest profits to go out of business
    e. provide an incentive for firms with the lowest cost of reducing pollution to make relatively large cutbacks

15. If permits to pollute in a lake can be bought and sold, and sell for a price T, then pollution will be reduced:

    a. by those firms that can do so at a cost of less than T
    b. by those firms that can do so at a cost of more than T
    c. in equal proportion by all firms
    d. by firms that can externalize this internality
    e. by all firms that are physically able to do so, regardless of the cost

16. Consider the following three policies to reduce pollution:

    1. imposing physical limits on pollution
    2. imposing physical limits on pollution and allowing trade in pollution permits
    3. imposing a pollution tax

    The methods that use the market mechanism are:

    a. 1 and 2
    b. 1 and 3
    c. 2 and 3
    d. 1, 2 and 3
    e. 2 only

17. The government's policy of subsidizing the purchase of pollution control equipment can be criticized because it:

    a. places too great an emphasis on 'end-of-pipe' treatment
    b. places too little emphasis on 'end-of-pipe' treatment
    c. has led to an overemphasis by the government on how efficiently this machinery will subsequently be operated
    d. has been supported by inadequate short-term financing during its construction
    e. none of the above

18. The recycling of wastes:

    a. can reduce the rate of depletion of natural resources
    b. can increase the rate of depletion of natural resources
    c. is economically efficient, no matter how costly it may be
    d. causes pollution
    e. has no effect on pollution

19. Almost all studies estimate the value of a human life in the broad range:

    a. $330,000 to $5 million
    b. $3 million to $6 million
    c. $4.5 million to $15 million
    d. $100 million to $200 million
    e. $1 billion to $3 billion

20. In controlling the release of new drugs

    a. there is a cost of delay for further testing, but no benefit of delay
    b. there is a benefit from delay, but no cost
    c. there is neither a benefit nor a cost from delay, because health is a non-economic issue
    d. there is a cost and benefit of delay; the cost is that lives may be lost because a life-saving drug can't be used yet
    e. there is a cost and benefit of delay, but neither can be specified

21. In their daily decisions, most people implicitly value their own life as worth:

    a. an infinite amount
    b. zero
    c. about half their current year's income
    d. some value between a and c
    e. some value between b and c

22. Workers who take risky jobs:

    a. protect themselves fully by insisting on a higher wage that will completely compensate for the risk
    b. protect themselves partly by insisting on a higher wage that will partly compensate for the risk
    c. don't protect themselves at all
    d. settle for a lower wage
    e. settle for the same wage but lower fringe benefits

EXERCISES

1. Figure 30.1 represents the market for a good that causes pollution

Figure 30.1

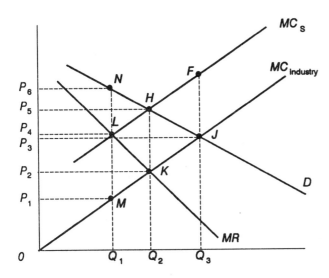

a. If the market is perfectly competitive, output will be _____, market price will be _____, marginal social cost will be _____, and the marginal external cost will be _____.

b. If the commodity produces no external benefits, then the optimal output is _____. This output would be attained under perfect competition if the producers were faced with a tax of _____ per unit. This would result in a market price of _____. Without this tax, the efficiency loss will be area _____.

c. Suppose that these firms were able to collude to form a monopoly. Then the level of output (with no tax) would be _____, the market price would be _____, and the efficiency loss would be _____.

d. Assume that the marginal external cost is constant – i.e., that the lines MC_S and $MC_{industry}$ are parallel, with $LM = HK = FJ$. Now suppose that the government imposes the same tax on the monopolist that it earlier charged to the perfect competitors. In this case, the monopolist will produce an output of _____, it will charge price _____, and the efficiency (gain, loss) will be area _____. Thus a per unit tax on a polluting monopolist (will, will not) necessarily lead to greater efficiency.

2. If pollution is left uncontrolled in Figure 30.2, the amount of pollution will be _____. If the government imposes a tax T to reduce pollution, it will be cut back to _____. Those firms to the (right, left) of Q_1 will stop polluting while those firms to the (right, left) of Q_1 will continue to pollute.

Figure 30.2

MCR = marginal cost of reducing pollution

Quantity of pollution

3. This problem requires Box 30-3 in the textbook.

a. If MCP_1 in Figure 30.3 is the marginal cost of having pollution and MCR is the marginal cost of reducing pollution, then, in the absence of any pollution tax, the quantity of pollution will be _____, MCR will be _____, and MCP will be _____. The economically efficient reduction in pollution is to quantity _____. This will result if firms are charged a tax of _____ per unit of pollution.

Figure 30.3

4. Now suppose that the marginal cost of having pollution is really MCP$_1$ but that the government makes a mistake and estimates it to be MCP$_2$. The government erroneously uses MCP$_2$ and sets the tax on pollution at _____. The resulting quantity of pollution is _____, which is (more, less) than the economically efficient amount. At this level of pollution, MCR is _____ and the true MCP is _____. There will be an efficiency (gain, loss) from the government's estimating error equal to area_____. Thus we (may, may not) conclude that, if the government underestimates the problem it will take inadequate action to counter it; that is, the government will set too low a pollution tax.

b. Now suppose that the marginal cost of having pollution is MCP$_2$ instead of MCP$_1$. Then the economically efficient amount of pollution is _____. This will result if firms are charged a tax of _____ per unit of pollution. The efficient amount of pollution in this case is (more, less) because pollution is (more, less) damaging.

5 a. The two lines in Figure 30.4 below show the marginal cost of reducing pollution MCR for two smoke-polluting firms (which are otherwise identical). Bars are added for detail. Reducing smoke pollution is less costly for firm (A, B). Suppose each firm is presently required by law to limit its output of smoke to 10 units, as shown by the dark vertical line. Both firms together generate 20 units of pollution. Now suppose that a government official decides, after reading this book, to impose a pollution tax instead of limiting each firm's smoke. If he sets the tax at $650 for each unit of smoke emitted, then firm A will (cut back, expand) its emissions to _____ units of smoke, and B will (cut back, expand) its emissions to _____ units. Both firms together generate (more, less, the same) pollution as before. The firm with the higher MCR has (increased, decreased) its pollution and the one with the lower MCR has (increased, decreased) its pollution.

Figure 30.4

Therefore, the tax is (more, less) efficient in keeping down costs than the previous limits on pollution.

6 a. Suppose that a company can produce a car that runs on gasoline, or one that runs on a newly invented fuel that sells for the same price, but that reduces the emission of pollutants by 50 percent. Unfortunately the car using the new gasoline costs $200 more to construct. Suppose that, in all other respects, both cars perform equally well, so that consumers do not care which fuel a car uses; if given the choice, they will buy the car with the lower purchase price. Therefore, with no regulations, the car producer will build the car using (gasoline, new fuel).

Suppose it is also possible to install an "end-of-pipe" pollution control device on all its cars, which also reduces emissions by 50 percent but costs $500. Again, suppose that consumers do not care whether or not a car has this device.

b. Firm A's pollution-reduction costs have (increased, decreased) by _____, while firm B's pollution-reduction costs have (increased, decreased) by _____. Thus the total pollution reduction cost of the two firms has (increased, decreased, stayed the same), while the total amount of pollution by the two firms has (increased, decreased, stayed the same).

Then the auto producer will build the car using (gasoline, new fuel), and (with, without) the device. The cars (will, will not) pollute the atmosphere; but the car companies don't take this into account because this is an (external, internal) cost.

b. Now suppose a government agency wants to cut back auto emissions by 50 percent. So it requires the company to install the pollution-control device. The company will now build cars using (gasoline, new fuel), and with the device. The cost to society of this end-of-pipe reduction in pollution is $_____ per car.

Now suppose instead that the government just requires the auto producer to cut back the emissions from its cars by 50%, leaving it up to the company to decide how to do this. Then the cost to the company of complying with this requirement would be $_____ per car if it installed the device, or $_____ per car if it switched to the new fuel. Therefore, it would choose the (device, new fuel). In this case the cost to society of the reduction in pollution would be $_____ per car.

c. In this example, the policy of telling the company how to reduce pollution is $_____ (more, less) costly per car than the policy of just telling them to do it and leaving all details to them. If instead the agency had told the company to do it by making cars that use the new fuel, the cost to society would have been (more than, less than, the same as) the cost of just telling them to do it. What general rule does this suggest about the relative cost of telling companies to comply compared with telling them exactly how to comply?

7. The Apex Company employs 2000 individuals working on high-steel construction. The firm has to pay its labor force a $1,000 per person wage premium each year in order to attract workers who are willing to risk their lives. The risks on this job raise the mortality rate by 2/1000; that is, the chance a worker will be killed during a year is 2/1000 higher than in other jobs. The question is: Should the government introduce a safety regulation that will reduce the risk by 1/1000, if this regulation costs $1.5 million (including both government administration costs and the compliance cost by the firm)?

To answer this, we need to know the value of a human life. Because each worker is willing to take a 2/1000 chance of losing his life if he is paid $1,000 more, this means that he values his life at ($5 million, $500,000, $1,000, $500) which is his wage premium of $_____ divided by the _____ increase in risk.

Although this can't be predicted precisely in advance, the expectation is that this regulation would be expected to save _____ lives, which is the _____ risk reduction from this regulation times the 2000 workers employed. Since each worker values his life at $_____, the benefit of this regulation is $_____. This is (greater than, less than, the same as) the $1.5 million cost of the regulation. Thus, this regulation (passes, fails) this benefit/costs test, and it would be (introduced, rejected),

If its cost were $500,000 then it would (pass, fail) the benefit/cost test, and it should be (introduced, rejected).

ESSAY QUESTIONS

1. "One advantage of using taxes rather than physical limits to control pollution is that the former policy harnesses the forces of the marketplace to help find an efficient solution, whereas the latter policy does not." Do you agree or disagree? Explain your answer.

2. Explain why, in selecting the specific least-cost method of reducing pollution, private firms will do at least as good a job as government agencies, and often better?

3. Explain how the concept of an external cost (that is, a cost not borne by the decision maker) is illustrated by the following example. When Napoleon, the founder of the conscription system, was told that a planned military operation would cost too many men, he replied: "That is nothing. The women produce more of them than I can use."

4. In recent years a large Canadian distillery has paid for the tickets to enable people to travel free on the Toronto subway system on New Year's Eve. Explain how this self-imposed tax has helped to promote economic efficiency by internalizing an external cost.

5. Show why the value of human life may have to be taken into account in calculating both the benefits *and* costs of regulation by the Federal Drug Administration.

ANSWERS

Important Terms : 1b, 2d, 3j, 4a, 5c, 6e, 7k, 8i, 9g, 10f, 11h

True-False:
1 F (p. 560, BOX)
2 T (p. 561)
3 T (p. 561)
4 F (p. 564)
5 T (p. 561)
6 F (p. 566, BOX)
7 F (p. 561)
8 F (p. 560)
9 T (p. 568)
10 F (p. 572)
11T(p. 573)

Multiple Choice:
1 c (p. 561)
2 a (p. 561)
3 b (p. 561)
4 c (p. 561)
5 c (p. 561)
6 b (p. 560)
7 b (p. 567, BOX)
8 c (p. 564)
9 a (p. 559)
10 e (p. 561)
11 a (p. 566, BOX)
12 c (p. 562, BOX)
13 a (p. 564)
14 e (p. 564)
15 a (p. 564)
16 c (p. 564)
17 a (p. 568)
18 a (p. 569)
19 a (p. 574, BOX)
20 d (p. 571)
21 d (p. 574, BOX)
22 b (p. 570)

Exercises

1. a. Q_3, P_3, Q_3F, JF.
    b. Q_2, HK, P_5, HFJ.
    c. Q_2, P_5, zero.
    d. Q_1, P_6, loss, NLH, will not.

2. Q_2, Q_1, right, left.

3. a. Q_3, essentially zero, Q_3F, Q_1, P_1.
    b. Q_2, P_2, more, less.

4.   P2, Q2, more, Q2E, Q2R, loss, CRE, may.

5   a.   A, cut back, 9, expand, 11, the same, increased, decreased.
        b.   increased, $600, decreased, $700, decreased, stayed the same, more.

6   a.   gasoline, gasoline, without, will, external
        b.   gasoline, $500, $500, $200, new fuel, $200.
        c. $300, more, the same, telling them exactly how to comply will cost more unless the government happens to pick the least-cost method — in which case it doesn't matter.

7. $500,000, $1,000, 2/1000, 2, 1/1000, $500,000, $1 million, less than, fails, rejected, pass, introduced.

CHAPTER 31

NATURAL RESOURCES:
Are We Using Them At The Right Rate?

LEARNING OBJECTIVES

After you have studied this chapter in the textbook and the study guide, you should be able to

✔ Describe the internal and external costs of extracting a common-property resource, and explain why both of these are internal costs if the resource is privately owned.

✔ Explain why a perfectly competitive market in a natural resource may be efficient if the resource is privately owned, but not if it is common-property

✔ Describe the maximum sustainable yield (Box 31-1) and explain why harvests involve no future costs if the population of a species is greater than this; and why problems arise if the population is harvested down to a level below this

✔ Explain why simple projections of the use and availability of resources yield misleading predictions

✔ Give three reasons why population growth continues to be rapid in less developed countries despite the scarcity of resources

✔ Present the case in favor of economic growth, and the case against

✔ Describe how the domestic price of oil was controlled before 1979, and some of the practical problems that were encountered

✔ Explain the efficiency and transfer effects of this policy, and how it affected the amounts of oil produced, consumed, and imported by Americans

✔ Present the arguments for raising the domestic price of oil above the world price

✔ Explain the advantages and disadvantages of each of the three major alternative sources of energy — natural gas, coal and nuclear power

MAJOR PURPOSE

In the last chapter, we saw that there was an external cost—in terms of damage to those living downstream—if chemicals are produced by a factory that dumps wastes into a river. The objective in this chapter is to use much of this same analysis to examine the external cost that is associated with resource extraction—namely, the cost to future generations because less of the resource will be available then. In this analysis, the question of who owns the resource is a critical one. If it is privately owned, then the owner will tend to take this future cost into account (since it's the owner's own resource that is being depleted) and decisions will therefore tend to be efficient. However, if the resource is common-property (publicly owned), then those extracting the resource have no reason to take the future into account. Because they tend to ignore the external cost to future generations, there is an inadequate conservation effort; an inefficiently large quantity of the resource is extracted.

In this chapter, we also return to the case study of oil, one of our most important natural resources. Earlier, in Chapter 27, we examined the attempt by OPEC to keep the world price of oil high; in this chapter, we examine the difficulties and inefficiencies introduced in the 1970s when the U.S. government kept the domestic price of oil low. Why did the government do this, and what was the effect of this policy on oil use? Finally, we examine alternative forms of energy, since these will determine how painful any shortage of oil may be to future generations.

HIGHLIGHTS OF CHAPTER

Since no one owns the fish in the sea, they are a common-property resource, and provide a good illustration of one of the central problems addressed in this chapter: Common-property resources are inadequately conserved in a free, perfectly competitive market. The reason is that fishing involves two costs—(1) the internal costs incurred by those who fish, such as the boats, nets, labor, and so on, and (2) the external cost that falls on future generations because there is less of this resource available to them. If the resource is common-property, fishing firms don't pay any attention to this second cost. Like the polluting firm that ignores its external cost—such as the damage its pollutants do to those living downstream or downwind—the fishing firm that ignores the external costs it is imposing on future generations will produce more than the efficient amount. (Its output decision is influenced by its internal costs, but not by the external costs it creates.)

Policies to Reduce Inefficiency in Resource Extraction

There are three possible ways to reduce inefficiency

- *Set a physical limit on the catch.* The problem with this approach is that it does not use the market mechanism. A government official restricts the catch (perhaps by putting a limit on the size of nets or size of boats); and, as in the case of pollution discussed in the previous chapter, too severe a physical restriction may be worse than no restriction at all. The two alternative ways to increase efficiency do use the market mechanism.

- *Impose a tax or fishing fee* on fishermen according to the number of fish they catch—specifically, impose a tax on them equal to the external costs they generate, just like the tax on polluting firms analyzed in the last chapter.

- *Create property rights;* let the fish be privately owned. While this is not possible in the oceans or Great Lakes, it might be in inland lakes or ponds. (And it certainly is feasible for many other resources—such as timber—that are already privately owned.) Once the schools of fish are privately owned, the owners will take into account both the harvesting costs and the cost of having a reduced catch in the future. (It is *their* future catch that will be reduced.) Thus this future external cost is internalized once the resource is privately owned. Since the private owners will take all costs into account, the result is an efficient one. But it won't be equitable, unless the new owners are charged in some way for the asset (the fish) that they now own.

Special problems of non-renewable resources

Since schools of fish can eventually reproduce themselves, they are a renewable resource. On the other hand, there are other resources, such as coal, oil or base metals that are not renewable. The key questions with such resources are: Will we run out, and if so, when? What can we do to prevent this? Simple projections of present trends point to an eventual doomsday, when rising population overtakes our limited resources. But such projections are oversimplified, because they do not allow for the adjustments that will take place as resources become scarce.

One of the most important kinds of adjustment is this: As a resource becomes more scarce, it becomes more expensive; this, in turn, leads to: (1) a substitution in production for the scarce resource by other factors that are more plentiful; (2) a substitution in consumption by goods that require less of the scarce resource; (3) induced innovation that economizes on these resources; and (4) a reduction in the rate of growth of population because raising children becomes costly as the price of resources rises.

Some have criticized this last point by noting that in the less developed countries, population growth has continued even though most parents can't afford to have children. However, the experience of these countries can be explained by three special factors: (1) poverty is so severe that people have children to provide them with support in their old age; (2) there are religious and social objections in these countries to birth control; and (3) their recent population growth is not just a reflection of birth rates, but also of falling death rates, due to dramatic advances in medical services; however, falling death rates cannot continue to have the impact on population that they have had in the past.

In addition to the question of whether our future growth will be severely restricted by resource scarcity (as the Doomsday models predict) or whether growth can continue because adjustment mechanisms work well, there is another overriding question: Do we really want substantial economic growth? The traditional argument in favor of growth is that it helps to relieve unemployment, reduce poverty, and raise our incomes and those of our children. However, a number of arguments have recently been put forward against continued growth. For example, it has been pointed out that growth contributes to pollution and depletes our natural resources. The main difficulty with such anti-growth arguments is that restricting growth is not the best way to attack these problems. Much more progress is possible if we design policies — such as taxes on polluters or on those firms extracting resources — that deal directly and specifically with each of these problems. In the case of resources, it is important to ensure that they are being priced high enough to provide adequate conservation.

What is the Efficient Pricing of a Nonrenewable Resource?

The answer, illustrated in Figures 31-4 and 31-5, is that its price should keep rising as it becomes scarcer and scarcer; this will generate increasing pressure to conserve, for example, by using substitutes instead. It is important to understand why its price *should not* be the same in each year. This would be inefficient because $100 of a resource this year is worth more than $100 next year; used this year in investment it can grow to more than $100 next year. Therefore it's efficient to use more this year and less next year — and a relatively low price this year and high price next year will generate that pattern.

It is also important to understand why, in a perfectly competitive market, the price of a resource *will not* (as well as *should not*) be the same in each year. If it were, the resource holders would sell it all off this year, and earn interest on the proceeds. (This is better than holding it until next year, selling it then for the same price and earning no interest.) The price difference leaves them indifferent and therefore happy to sell it in either year.

Oil

Recently, this resource has been priced well above the requirements of conservation. Under the influence of OPEC — and in particular, the Saudi Arabians — the world price of oil rose over ten times between 1973 and 1982. To provide some relief to oil users, the U.S. government instituted a policy of holding the domestic U.S. price down below the rapidly-escalating world price. Full detail on the effects of this price ceiling — and the problems it raised — cannot be provided without a diagram, and you should be sure you have mastered Figure 31-6 in the text before proceeding. However, three of the broad effects of this price control policy can be sketched out.

- There were winners and losers. The winners were oil users — from Sunday drivers to the giant power-generating companies and their customers — who benefited because the price of oil was kept down. However, this lower price hurt oil producers in the United States.

- There were two efficiency losses, shown by the two shaded triangles in Figure 31-6. One arose because the low price encouraged oil consumption, while the other arose because the low price discouraged domestic oil production.

- Because the low domestic price of oil encouraged consumption and discouraged production, our requirement for imported oil increased. In turn, this meant heavier demand for OPEC oil and thus allowed OPEC to increase the world price of oil. Paradoxically, the more that the United States tried to keep its domestic price below the world price, the greater was the upward pressure on the world price.

When this policy was phased out by Presidents Carter and Reagan, the U.S. domestic price rose to the world price, and U.S. oil consumption and therefore imports were correspondingly reduced. This falling U.S. purchase of oil was one of the reasons the world price fell. Key questions were:

- to drive the world price even lower, should the United States go one step further and raise the domestic price of oil *above* the world price?

- To what degree would U.S. users turn to other forms of energy such as natural gas and—perhaps most important in the long run—how soon would nuclear fusion be developed to the point where it could, to a substantial degree, replace oil as a source of energy? In early 1989, that date was still a long way off.

IMPORTANT TERMS: MATCHING THE COLUMNS

Match the term in the first column with the corresponding explanation in the second column.

_____ 1. Reservation price
_____ 2. Sustainable yield curve
_____ 3. Maximum sustainable yield
_____ 4. Induced innovation
_____ 5. Dynamic efficiency
_____ 6. Renewable resource
_____ 7. OPEC
_____ 8. Common property resource

a. A resource that is not privately owned.
b. The curve relating the annual increase in a renewable resource (such as fish) to its population size. For any given population, this curve indicates the amount that can be extracted and still leave the population size constant.
c. The international cartel that raised the world price of oil by more than ten times between 1973 and 1982.
d. The largest value on the sustainable yield curve. This is the largest amount of a renewable resource that can be extracted each year without reducing the population size.
e. The height of the supply curve for a privately-owned resource. It includes (1) the cost of harvesting or extraction, and (2) the amount necessary to compensate the owner for the reduction in the resource available in the future.
f. The development of new substitutes for increasingly expensive resources.
g. A resource that reproduces itself naturally (such as fish) or that may reproduce itself with human assistance (such as timber).
h. The result when the price of a perfectly competitive nonrenewable resource rises each year by the amount of the interest rate.

TRUE-FALSE

T F 1. Under perfect competition, the rate of extraction of a privately owned resource is generally greater than the efficient rate.

T F 2. Those harvesting a common-property resource take into account only the harvesting cost — not the cost to society of having less of this resource available in the future.

T F 3. For a common-property resource, supply is determined by the marginal extraction cost only.

T F 4. A competitive equilibrium in the market for a privately-owned natural resource is generally inefficient.

T F 5. If it were possible to tax those who fish for each fish caught, then in theory it would be possible to eliminate the efficiency loss that results because the oceans are not privately owned.

T F 6. An open border to fishermen from foreign countries would make the harvesting of fish more efficient, just as a border open to imports of foreign goods makes production within a country more efficient.

T F 7. When we run out of fresh water, all growth in population must cease.

T F 8. Allowing the domestic price of oil to rise to the world price makes us more dependent on foreign supplies.

T F 9. A case can be made for keeping the U.S. domestic oil price at or below the world price, but no case can be made for keeping it higher.

T F 10. A policy of keeping the domestic price of a resource below the world price results in an inefficiently low level of domestic production.

T F 11. Raising the domestic price of oil above the world price will put upward pressure on the world price.

MULTIPLE CHOICE

1. In a perfectly competitive market, the last unit of a privately-owned resource will be sold for:

   a. more than its reservation price
   b. less than its reservation price
   c. its reservation price
   d. more than its conservation price
   e. less than its conservation price

2. The height of the supply curve for a common-property resource reflects:

   a. the extraction cost
   b. compensation for the reduced amount available in the future
   c. the extraction cost less compensation for the reduced amount available in the future
   d. the extraction cost plus compensation for the reduced amount available in the future
   e. the extraction cost or compensation for the reduced amount available in the future, whichever is larger

3. Which of the following is a common-property resource?

   a. fish
   b. timber on privately-owned land
   c. an oil company's reserves
   d. coal
   e. copper

4. In analyzing resource use, economists use the term 'reservation price' to mean:

   a. the lowest bid a seller will take in an auction
   b. the highest bid a buyer will pay in an auction
   c. the cost of harvesting or extracting a resource today
   d. the amount necessary to compensate for the reduced availability of the resource in the future
   e. c plus d

5. The reservation price of a resource will decrease if:

   a. the expected future cost of extracting the resource rises
   b. the expected future price of the resource rises
   c. the expected future price of the resource remains constant
   d. auction prices have remained constant
   e. auction prices have been rising

6. The problem with Doomsday models (that is, models that predict disaster because a growing population runs out of resources) is that typically:

   a. they are based on the assumption that current trends will continue long into the future
   b. they take inadequate account of the economic adjustments that will occur as resources become scarcer
   c. they take inadequate account of the social adjustments that will occur as resources become scarcer
   d. all of the above
   e. none of the above

7. Which of the following is an argument commonly used in favor of economic growth?

   a. unemployment is likely to be less severe in a rapidly growing economy
   b. faster economic growth helps to economize on scarce natural resources
   c. growth reduces pollution
   d. growth is necessary or our children will run out of natural resources
   e. growth reduces congestion

8. Which of the following is most important in explaining the increase in population in most less developed countries?

   a. the increase in the stock of natural resources relative to the labor force
   b. constant wages

   c. a change in the resource/capital ratio
   d. increasing wealth
   e. advances in medicine that have reduced the death rate

9. Between 1973 and 1982, the world price of oil rose from:

   a. less than $3 a barrel to $13 a barrel
   b. less than $3 to $23
   c. less than $3 to over $30
   d. $13 to $23
   e. $13 to over $30

10. The rapid increase in the price of oil in the 1970s:

    a. could be fully justified as a conservation measure
    b. could be partly justified as a conservation measure, but also reflected the exercise of monopoly power
    c. could not be justified, even in part, as a conservation measure
    d. represented a transfer from OPEC countries to oil importing countries
    e. discouraged U.S. conservation efforts

11. Which of the following is a valid reason for raising the domestic U.S. price of oil above the world price?

    a. it would increase OPEC revenues, and thus allow these countries to strengthen themselves militarily
    b. it would encourage consumers to substitute oil for natural gas
    c. it would put downward pressure on the world price
    d. b and c
    e. none of these reasons is valid

12. Keeping the domestic price of oil below the world price

    a. encouraged production and consumption
    b. discouraged production and consumption
    c. discouraged consumption and encouraged production
    d. encouraged consumption and discouraged production
    e. encouraged consumption, but had no effect on production

13. The fact that a significant reduction of U.S. demand might depress the world price of oil is a point in favor of having a domestic price:

a. below the world price
b. equal to the world price
c. above the world price
d. either above or below, depending upon the elasticity of domestic demand
e. either above or below, depending upon the elasticity of domestic supply

14. Which of the following contributed to the slowdown of the nuclear power industry in the 1970s?

a. concern over how to dispose of radioactive wastes
b. concern over the possible proliferation of nuclear weapons
c. the fear of accidents, such as the one at Three Mile Island
d. higher than expected plant costs
e. all of the above

15. Putting a common-property resource under private ownership may raise which of the following problems:

a. the resource will be harvested too rapidly
b. if the new owners have monopoly power, they may use it to restrict the extraction of the resource more severely than conservation requires
c. if the new owners have monopoly power, they may use it to increase the quantity extracted of the resource
d. unless the new owners are charged adequately for this asset, it is unfair for society to provide them with such a windfall gain
e. b and d

16. The creation of private property rights over what was previously a common-property resource:

a. is not legal for the government to do
b. would raise problems of fairness if the government were to sell these rights to a private owner for a price below their market value
c. would decrease the efficiency of the extraction of the resource
d. would have no effect of the extraction of the resource
e. would freeze in the previous level of inefficiency in the extraction of the resource

17. An efficient pattern of non-renewable resource use requires that:

a. the resource be priced at the same level each year
b. the price falls each year by the amount of the interest rate
c. the price rises each year by the amount of the interest rate
d. the cost of extracting the resource exceeds its price by the amount of the interest rate
e. the cost of extracting the resource is less than its price by the amount of the interest rate

18. If a perfectly competitive nonrenewable resource is being extracted efficiently, and more is extracted next year than this year, then:

a. the demand next year must have unit elasticity
b. the demand this year must have unit elasticity
c. the demand neither year must have unit elasticity
d. the demand must be greater this year than next
e. the demand must be greater next year than this

19. Conservation means:

a. to stop using any of the resource at all
b. to not use any of the resource until it is displaced by a substitute
c. to use it in an efficient pattern over time, starting today
d. to use it in an efficient pattern over time, starting as soon as its price starts to fall
e. to use it in an efficient pattern over time, starting as soon as its price stabilizes

20. Which of the following policies is the least efficient way of responding to a higher world price of oil?

a. limit the growth of GNP
b. conserve more
c. encourage more domestic production
d. intensify the search for alternative sources of energy
e. encourage energy-efficiency technology

21. Allowing the domestic price of oil to increase to the world price results in:

a. increased oil imports
b. efficiency losses
c. no change in efficiency
d. increased domestic consumption of oil
e. reduced domestic consumption of oil

EXERCISES

1 a. Figure 31.1 depicts a perfectly competitive market for a natural resource. The demand curve is D, the marginal cost of extraction is the height of the curve labelled S, and the marginal external (future) cost is the difference between the height of S and S'. The efficient quantity (assuming no external benefits) is _____, and this quantity will be demanded if the price is _____. If the resource is privately owned the price will be _____, the quantity extracted will be _____, and the size of the efficiency loss will be _____.

Figure 31.1

Price

Quantity extracted

b. If the resource is not privately owned the price will be _____, the quantity extracted will be _____, and the size of the efficiency loss will be _____. The efficiency loss could be eliminated by a (tax, subsidy) on extraction equal to _____ per unit.

2 a. In Figure 31.2, a price ceiling of P_1 is imposed on the domestic oil market. Domestic production is _____, consumption is _____, and (exports, imports) are _____. Because importers have to buy oil at the high world price P_2 and sell it domestically for only P_1, the government must compensate them by paying

them a subsidy of _____ per barrel, times the _____ barrels they are importing, for a total government subsidy payment of area _____.

Figure 31.2

Price

Domestic supply = MC

Domestic demand = MB

World price

Controlled domestic price

Quantity

b. When this price control is removed, price becomes _____, domestic production (increases, decreases) to _____ and domestic consumption (increases, decreases) to _____. (Imports, Exports) consequently (increase, decrease) to _____. Consumers (gain, lose) area _____ while producers (gain, lose) area _____ and the government (gains, loses) area _____ of (subsidy, tax) it no longer has to (pay, impose).

c. When all these gains and losses are taken into account, the net (gain, loss) from decontrolling price is _____. This can be broken down into its two components: (1) The efficiency gain of area _____ because consumers are no longer buying oil they value at less than its true cost (the world price); and (2) the efficiency gain of area _____ because domestic firms are now producing oil for less than it previously cost to import. At the same time, there has been a transfer from consumers to _____ and _____.

ESSAY QUESTIONS

1. Explain how the problem of a excessive use of a common property resource is similar to the problem of environmental pollution. To deal with each of these problems, the government sometimes considers quantity restraints. Explain why you think these policies are effective or ineffective in dealing with each of these problems.

2. How does private ownership help to eliminate the inefficiency that exists when a resource is publicly owned (common property)? Would inefficiency be eliminated just as well if ownership were given to a single owner who then had a monopoly? What new problems might be created by allowing the resource to be monopolized?

3. "One of the shortcomings of the market mechanism is that private business interests are concerned, not with the future, but instead with how much profit they can earn right now. We need the government to regulate the rate of extraction of natural resources to protect future generations from being deprived of their rightful share of resources." Do you agree or disagree? Why?

4. (This problem is based on Box 31-1 in the textbook.) "If the population of a species is now greater than the point of maximum sustainable yield, and if firms are now harvesting at a rate just large enough to maintain a constant size of population, then by increasing the rate of extraction they can harvest more now and more in the future." Explain this statement, using a diagram similar to Figure 31-2. If the cost of extraction is zero, what is the opportunity cost of raising the rate of extraction in this situation? Is this a case of being able to get something for nothing?

5. Suppose that scientists working on nuclear fusion make a major breakthrough, which means that fusion is likely to become an economic source of energy by 2010

   a. What would you expect the effects (if any) to be on the world price of oil (1) now, and (2) in 1998?

   b. What would you expect the effect (if any) to be on the U.S. price of natural gas (1) now, and (2) in 1998?

6. "It is not fair for our oil companies to make excess profits on the oil they produce and sell to us within the United States simply because half way around the globe, OPEC has raised the world price. Oil companies in the United States should be forced to sell us the oil we need at a more reasonable price." Which U.S. policy in the 1970s was guided by this sort of philosophy? Does it make sense to you? Did this policy create problems? Explain.

7. The strict auto emission standard imposed by the EPA during the 1970s achieved its primary purpose of reducing pollution. But it had an unfavorable side effect because it increased our consumption of gasoline and thus damaged our attempts to conserve oil. Could the benefits of reduced pollution have been achieved without damaging the conservation effort if a policy of a higher oil price had been implemented instead? Explain.

8. Explain some of the external costs of producing and using oil. In your view, how do these costs compare with those arising from the production and use of natural gas? Coal? Nuclear fission?

ANSWERS

Important Terms :   1 e, 2 b, 3 d, 4 f, 5 h, 6 g, 7 c, 8 a.

True-False:
- 1 F (p. 584)
- 2 T (p. 580)
- 3 T (p. 580)
- 4 F (p. 584)
- 5 T (p. 580)
- 6 F (p. 581)
- 7 F (p. 589)

8 F (p. 590)
9 F (p. 591)
10 T (p. 590)
11 F (p. 591)

Multiple Choice:

1 c (p. 584)
2 a (p. 584)
3 a (p. 580)
4 e (p. 584)
5 a (p. 585, BOX)
6 d (p. 578)
7 a (pp. 588-589)
8 e (p. 588)
9 c (p. 589)
10 b (p. 584)
11 c (p. 591)
12 d (p. 590)
13 c (p. 591)
14 e (p. 593)
15 e (pp. 584-585)
16 b (p. 584)
17 c (p. 586)
18 e (p. 586)
19 c (p. 586)
20 a (pp. 589-592)
21 e (p. 590).

Exercises

1 a. Q_1, P_1, P_1, Q_1, zero.
   b. P_2, Q_2, GLF, tax, P_1P_3.

2 a. Q_1, Q_4, imports, Q_1Q_4, P_1P_2, Q_1Q_4, 5 + 2 + 1 + 3 + 6.
   b. P_2, increases, Q_2, decreases, Q_3, imports, decrease, Q_2Q_3, lose, 4 + 5 + 2 + 1 + 3, gain, 4 + 5, gains, 5 + 2 + 1 + 3 + 6, subsidy, pay.
   c. gain, 5 + 6, 6, 5, producers, the government.

Across

1,4. If a pasture or fishing area is owned in this manner, it may be overused
6. he was a student of Marxism (see inside cover of text)
7. a common type of harmful externality
8. an emission fee is one way to protect our _____
10. the _____ yield is the amount of a renewable resource (for example, fish) that can be harvested while still leaving the population constant
11. one way to reduce the pollution problem is to _____ waste
14. an economist famous for his writings on externalities and on macroeconomics (see inside cover of text)
16. famous hockey player
17. the efficient output occurs where the _____ social cost equals the _____ social benefit
18. what a doctor, lawyer, or teacher provides
19. what people do after studying for a long time
22, 24. one way of dealing with the problem of a scarce natural resource
25. major communications company (abbrev.)
26. in the direction of

Down

1. high prices encourage people to _____ scarce raw materials
2. if people have _____, they may use raw materials too quickly
3. arrest
4, 13. the creation of _____ _____ is one way to discourage the overuse of a natural resource
5. overfishing today creates an _____ cost which will be faced by future fishers
9. this, plus error, is a hard way to learn
10. private cost plus external cost equals _____ _____ (2 words)
12. mistake
14. our _____ is sometimes called "spaceship earth."
15. rock used in the construction of buildings
18. a place to keep money
20. major conglomerate (abbrev.)
21. South American City (abbrev.)
23. yes (Russian)

CHAPTER 32

PUBLIC GOODS

LEARNING OBJECTIVES

After you have studied this chapter in the textbook and the study guide, you should be able to

✔ Demonstrate why a free, perfectly competitive market provides less than the efficient amount of a good with external benefits

✔ Measure, in a diagram like Figure 32-1 in the textbook, the efficiency loss resulting from the private provision of a good with external benefits

✔ Show why efficiency requires a good to be subsidized by an amount equal to the marginal external benefit it provides (assuming that there are not high costs of administering the subsidy)

✔ Define and fully explain the concept of a public good

✔ Construct the marginal social benefit curve (a) for a public good, and (b) for a private good, making clear the difference between the two

✔ Explain why the "free-rider" problem makes it difficult for the government to estimate the benefits of a public good simply by asking people how highly they value it

✔ Give the reasons for believing that when the government provides a good or service—whether or not this is in response to a failure by the free market—major problems remain, such as the problems of bureaucracy; efficiency is still not guaranteed

✔ Show why it may be necessary to view as a public good any wild life species that is becoming extinct

✔ Explain the concept of "option demand" and demonstrate its significance in dealing with such a wildlife species

MAJOR PURPOSE

The last chapter dealt with external costs. In this chapter we use a parallel approach to analyze external benefits—that is, the benefits of a product that are enjoyed by others, above and beyond the internal benefits enjoyed by those who buy it. When external benefits exist, a free perfectly competitive market does not produce an efficient outcome. There is too little free-market production of such a good, just as there was too much production of a good with an external cost in the last chapter. The solution is to subsidize the good with the external benefits, just as the good with the external costs was taxed in the last chapter.

A further objective of this chapter is to extend this analysis of external benefits to describe the concept of a public good. A flood-control dam is an example of a public good, because no-one can be excluded from enjoying its benefits, regardless of who pays for it. Typically, with such a broad distribution of benefits, there are no specific individuals who play a significant enough role as purchasers to be prepared to buy the good. So if it is to be provided at all, the government must purchase it. In this chapter, we describe the difficulties a government faces in trying to decide whether or not such a purchase is justified; and we also describe the more general problems that arise whenever the government provides the public with any good or service. Even when the private market fails, and a good must be provided by the government (if it is to be supplied at all) problems remain.

HIGHLIGHTS OF CHAPTER

Why is there too little production of a good with an external benefit?

The Inefficiency of a Private Market when there are External Benefits

A free, perfectly competitive market delivers less than the efficient output of a product with an external benefit because the marginal cost of the product (supply) is equated to its marginal private benefit (demand), rather than to its marginal social benefit. The reason is that, in deciding on their demand for the product, buyers take account of only the private benefit it will provide them, and ignore the external benefit it will provide to others. With the demand curve therefore reflecting only private benefit, and any external benefit being ignored, it is no surprise that too little is produced, as Figure 32-1 demonstrates. The appropriate government policy is to subsidize this product by the amount of the external benefit it provides (assuming there are not substantial costs in administering the subsidy). Such a subsidy will increase the demand for the product and thus increase its output to the efficient amount.

Public Goods

In the case of products with an external benefit that we have been describing so far — such as gardening — you will receive an external benefit if your neighbor pays $100 for gardening services. But, of course, you will get an even larger benefit if you pay the gardener the $100 yourself in order to have the gardening done on your own lawn rather than on your neighbor's. Thus the benefits you get depend on who buys the service. A public good can be viewed as the extreme case of a good with an external benefit, where the amount of benefit that an individual gets is just as great if someone else buys as it is if he or she were to buy it. In other words, the individual *cannot be excluded* in any way from enjoying it. For example, you get the same benefit from cleaner air, whether or not you help to pay for antipollution measures. That is not true of a private good. You can't enjoy a movie or a restaurant meal unless you pay for it. This is the reason why the benefits of a private good are horizontally summed in Figure 32-2 of the textbook, while the benefits of a public good are vertically summed in Figure 32-3.

The Free Rider Problem

If you will get the same benefit whether or not you help pay for a good, why not be a "free-rider" and not pay at all (or pay as small a share as you can get away with)? The incentive for people to ride free raises problems for an entrepreneur who believes (let's suppose correctly) that the benefits people would get from a public good — such as flood-control dam — exceed its costs and it therefore should be built. How can it be financed, when everyone the entrepreneur asks to contribute to it tries to minimize that contribution by understating the benefits the dam would provide? In short, each individual has an incentive to be a free rider, enjoying the benefits of the dam without contributing to it. Since all individuals have this incentive to understate the benefits of the dam, it appears not to be justified, and does not get built.

Suppose the government, rather than a private entrepreneur, tries to evaluate the dam by asking people how highly they would value it. If they think they will be taxed accordingly to their answer, they will understate. On the other hand, if they think their taxes won't be affected by the project, they will tend to overstate their benefit — as a means of slightly increasing the chance that the project will be undertaken. In this case, they have nothing to lose, since the cost they incur is not affected by their overvaluation.

An Alternative Approach by the Government

In view of the difficulties in trying to get people to answer accurately, the authorities generally reject the approach of asking people for their evaluation of a project. Instead they often use a "benefit-cost" analysis based on a completely different kind of information. To use the example in the text, they may estimate the benefit of a dam by examining how frequently floods have occurred without it, and the average crop loss. This approach may be superior, but it still involves major problems. For example, those who are running this analysis may have a vested interest in having the dam pass the benefit-cost test because they may hope to be employed in its construction. Or they may simply be trying to please their employer—a government that has promised this dam in the last election. They may therefore add benefits—perhaps at an inflated value—until these benefits exceed the costs, and the project is justified. Such an inflation of benefits may be easy, especially if one of the benefits of a flood-control project is to save lives. It is very difficult indeed to attach a dollar value to a human life. (Recall our discussion in Box 30-4 of the textbook.)

Other Problems with Government Expenditure Decisions

More generally, when decision-making shifts from the private marketplace to the government—as indeed it must in the case of a public good which the private market fails to deliver—then a new set of special problems arises:

- Typically, private firms stop producing goods if they are no longer profitable—or if they fail outright from the start—because these firms would lose money otherwise. On the other hand, government projects that are no longer justified are much more difficult to terminate for two reasons: (a) no politician wants to admit that a project may have been a mistake, for fear of losing the next election as a result; and (b) there is no natural check, like the bankruptcy of a private firm, to force termination of a government project.

- Political votes are not as specific and frequent as the economic votes that people cast every day when they are deciding what to buy with their money. Thus private auto

companies get a clear message of the models the public wants and does not want. Not so with public goods. It may be two or four years before the next election when the public can vote on how it likes or dislikes the dam and the other goods and services the government is providing. And even if people do approve of what the government is doing—and vote for it in the next election— it's hard to know whether the election victory is due to the dam the government has built, or its foreign policy or some other completely different issue. (Public opinion polls make this problem less severe, but don't remove it.)

- Special interest groups can exert an inordinate influence on government decision-making. If you have no particular interest in a dam in the Rocky Mountains, it probably doesn't pay you to oppose it, since it may add only a trivial 10 cents to your tax bill. But those directly affected in the area have a strong incentive to support it and lobby for its construction. Thus, a few large benefits concentrated in one area may politically outweigh many small, widely dispersed costs, even if the sum of all these small costs exceeds the benefits economically.

- Politicians are mainly interested in projects with benefits that are obvious to the public and immediate. (If they don't have a payoff before the next election, it may be too late.) Thus politicians often do not take a long-term point of view; there is a tendency for much government effort to be centered on short-term decision-making.

- The job of implementing—and sometimes initiating—government policies is performed by a bureaucracy. There is a constant tendency for bureaus and their budgets to expand, in part because of the incentives for bureau chiefs to expand their personnel. Accordingly, bureaus tend to grow beyond the efficient size. This tendency is not checked by the threat of economic loss or bankruptcy that faces a private firm that overexpands.

IMPORTANT TERMS

Match the term in the first column with the corresponding explanation in the second column.

_____ 1. External (spillover) benefit
_____ 2. Public good
_____ 3. Internal private benefits
_____ 4. Benefit-cost analysis
_____ 5. Option demand
_____ 6. Free riders
_____ 7. Logrolling
_____ 8. Internalizing an externality

a. A product whose benefits are available to everyone, regardless of who pays for it
b. Forcing firms or individuals to face the external costs or benefits they are creating
c. The estimation of the dollar value of the costs and benefits that are likely to result from a particular government policy.
d. Those who cannot be excluded from the benefits of a public good, even though they do not pay their share of its costs
e. The benefit derived from a product by those who do not buy it or produce it
f. The desire to have something available, whether or not we actually use it
g. The benefits from a good derived by the purchaser
h. An agreement by two voters that each will support the other's project

---

TRUE-FALSE

T   F   1.   Internalizing externalities means that producers are forced to face any external costs of their actions; and buyers are allowed to enjoy any external benefits generated by their purchases.

T   F   2.   One benefit of having the government provide public goods such as flood control dams is that these decisions are easily reversible.

T   F   3.   The reason why private firms can't be relied on to produce a public good is that they would externalize the internal benefits.

T   F   4.   The marginal social benefit curve of a public good can be constructed by vertically summing the individual demand curves.

T   F   5.   You cannot be excluded from enjoying the benefits of a public good even if someone else pays for it.

T   F   6.   It is generally more difficult to cut out an expenditure program in the private than in the public sector.

T   F   7.   The public can be more specific in expressing its preferences for goods by voting in elections than by making purchases in the marketplace.

T   F   8.   It may make sense to vote for a party that has promised to make a certain government expenditure, even though you don't want this expenditure at all.

T   F   9.   Politicians prefer policies with costs and benefits that are obscure.

T   F   10.   Government policy should insure than no damage whatsoever occurs to the environment.

MULTIPLE CHOICE

1. In producing two goods (one with an external benefit, the other with an external cost) a free, perfectly competitive market will generate:

   a. too much output of the good with the external benefit, and too little of the good with the external cost
   b. too little output of the good with the external benefit, and too much of the good with the external cost
   c. too little output of the good with the external benefit, and just the right amount of the good with the external cost
   d. too little of both
   e. too much of both

2. Which of the following comes closest to being a private good with no external benefits?

   a. national defense
   b. painting the outside of your house
   c. painting the inside of your house
   d. hiring a gardener
   e. the police force

3. If the government follows a "hands off" policy, then the production of a perfectly competitive good with an external benefit will result in:

   a. marginal external benefit being greater than marginal social benefit
   b. marginal external benefit being equal to marginal social benefit
   c. marginal social cost being equal to marginal social benefit
   d. marginal social cost being greater than marginal social benefit
   e. marginal social cost being less than marginal social benefit

4. If a good has an external benefit, the government can ensure an efficient outcome by introducing a:

   a. tax equal to the external benefit
   b. tax greater then the external benefit
   c. subsidy less than the external benefit
   d. subsidy greater than the external benefit
   e. none of the above

5. If there are substantial administrative costs in subsidizing a good with an external benefit, the government should:

   a. tax it instead, to provide the same result
   b. subsidize the good regardless
   c. cancel the subsidy regardless
   d. cancel the subsidy if the efficiency gain it would produce is less than the administrative costs
   e. cancel the subsidy if the efficiency gain it would produce is greater than the administrative costs

6. The internal benefit of a good is the:

   a. benefit enjoyed by those who haven't purchased it
   b. benefit enjoyed by the individual who has purchased it
   c. benefit enjoyed by free riders
   d. benefit enjoyed by the government, even though the public has purchased it
   e. benefit enjoyed by the public, even though the government has purchased it

7. An example of internalizing an externality occurs when:

   a. a firm building a ski lift buys a restaurant at the bottom of the hill
   b. a firm buys from a domestic supplier a good that it used to buy from abroad
   c. a city government subsidizes exterior home improvements
   d. a and c
   e. b and c

8. In defining the marginal benefit to society of a public good:

   a. the demand curves by individuals are horizontally summed
   b. the demand curves by individuals are vertically summed
   c. the demand curves by individuals are horizontally summed and then vertically summed
   d. we use the same technique that was used to derive the market demand curve for a private good from the individual demand curves
   e. we take the demand curve of the individual who is most eager and able to buy the good

9. With a public good:

   a. anyone can participate in the benefits except the actual purchaser
   b. everyone can participate in the benefits including the actual purchaser
   c. no-one can participate in the benefits except the purchaser
   d. only free riders participate in the benefits
   e. free riders are prevented from participating in the benefits

10. Estimates that the government collects from individuals on how highly they value public projects tend to be unreliable because:

    a. if people feel they will be taxed according to the value they state, they will tend to understate
    b. if people feel they will be taxed according to the value they state, they will tend to overstate
    c. if people feel they will not be taxed according to the value they state, they will tend to overstate
    d. if people feel they will not be taxed according to the value they state, they will tend to understate
    e. a and c

11. A free rider is someone:

    a. who cannot be excluded from enjoying the benefits of a project even though this individual has paid nothing to cover its costs
    b. who can be excluded from enjoying the benefits of a project
    c. who is trying to encourage the government to continue its transportation subsidies
    d. who has paid more than a fair share of the costs
    e. who has paid his or her fair share of the costs

12. Benefit-cost analysis often involves the following problem:

    a. questionable projects that have been promised in an election campaign may be justified by exaggerating benefits
    b. questionable projects that have been promised in an election campaign may be justified by underestimating costs
    c. it is very difficult to place a value on a human life
    d. projects may be evaluated by those with a conflict of interest—for example, engineers who may eventually be employed in building the projects
    e. all of the above

13. Typically, a government bureau that is a monopoly will produce:

    a. too much output, while a private monopoly will produce too little
    b. too little output, just like a private monopoly
    c. too much output, just like a private monopoly
    d. the right amount of output, while a private monopoly will produce too little
    e. too little output, just like a private oligopoly

14. A species of wildlife in the wilderness:

    a. cannot die out unless it is adversely affected by human action
    b. will die out if it is left unprotected
    c. may die out if it is left unprotected
    d. will be prevented from dying out by free market forces
    e. should not be protected by the government because of option demand

15. Suppose you voted for Bush in 1988 because you preferred his foreign policy, even though you thought that the economic policies of Dukakis were superior. Then this illustrates the problem that:

    a. public expenditure decisions are hard to reverse
    b. special interest groups have an inordinate influence on public decisions
    c. bureaucrats are not subject to the normal check of bankruptcy
    d. political votes are difficult to interpret because they are not as specific as marketplace votes
    e. free riders are difficult to deal with

16. Many economists have argued that our farm subsidy programs are inefficient—that what farmers gain from higher food prices is less than what consumers lose. But these programs continue. According to the principles explained in this chapter, which seems the most likely explanation?

    a. food is a public good
    b. the farmers' special interest is politically stronger than the consumers' general interest
    c. the farmers' special interest is politically weaker than the consumers' general interest
    d. consumers do not adequately recognize the benefits of good food and must be forced to pay for them through taxes
    e. farmers have more votes than nonfarmers

17. Reversing a decision is more difficult for a government than a private firm because:

a. this admission of error may damage the government in the next election
b. business executives generally prefer to admit mistakes than to continue to lose money
c. politicians don't directly suffer out of pocket when they continue uneconomic expenditures
d. all of the above
e. b and c

18. Logrolling:

a. never damages the public interest
b. always damages the public interest
c. always promotes the public interest
d. sometimes damages the public interest, and sometimes promotes it
e. has an effect which is impossible to assess, no matter how much information is available on individual preferences

19. If the government asks individuals their valuation of a public good, they will:

a. overstate if the government will tax them according to their stated valuation
b. understate if the government will tax them according to their stated valuation
c. understate if the government will finance the project without taxing them
d. neither understate nor overstate if the government will finance the project without taxing them
e. neither overstate nor understate if the government will tax them according to their stated valuation

20. Option demand is the demand for:

a. a good, not because you want to use it now, but because you may want to use it in the future
b. a good, not because you want to use it now, but because you are certain to want it in the future
c. any public good that provides benefits now and in the future
d. any private good that provides benefits now and in the future
e. a good which is a private good now, but may be a public good in the future

21. In the case of a natural oligopoly, the appropriate role for the government is likely to be to:

a. enforce anti-trust legislation
b. regulate price
c. provide the good itself
d. leave the market alone
e. encourage price discrimination

EXERCISES

1. Figure 32.1 shows the supply curve S and demand curve D for a perfectly competitive good that provides external benefits. Assume for now that there are no external costs of producing this good, and ignore MCs.

a. In an unregulated market, the quantity that is produced is _____ and the market price is _____. If the marginal social benefit curve is MBs, then the economically efficient quantity is _____, and the marginal external benefit is _____.

b. The efficiency loss from relying upon the private market for the provision of this good is _____. The government could eliminate this efficiency loss by offering a per unit (subsidy, tax) of _____ to the producers of this good.

Figure 32.1

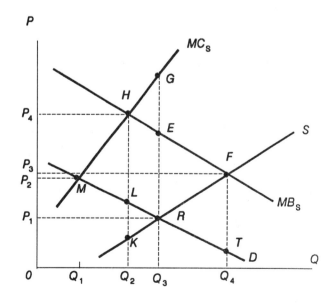

c. Now suppose that the good involves external costs as well as external benefits. (An example would be a dam that provides flood control to farmers downstream but that floods out farmers upstream.) Let the curve labelled MC_S represent the marginal social cost of producing the good. Then the efficient amount of production of the good is _____. At that level of production, the marginal external cost would be _____, and the marginal external benefit would be _____. With no tax or subsidy, the private market would produce (more, less) than the economically efficient amount and the efficiency loss would be _____. This efficiency loss could be eliminated if the government were to (tax, subsidize) the production of the good by _____ per unit.

2. Figure 32.2 shows the marginal private benefit MB_A and MB_B that individuals A and B receive from a public good (a waste-treatment plant). In Figure 32.2c show the marginal social benefit, assuming that A and B are the only members of society affected by the project.

Figure 32.2

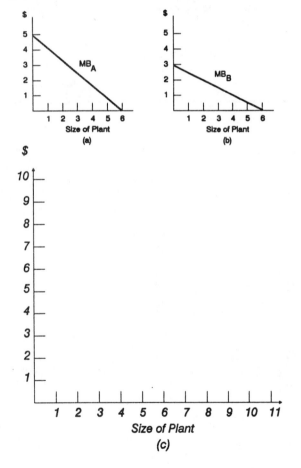

3 a. Suppose that there are 1,000 farmers affected by a proposed dam. Each of them would receive a benefit of $1,000. The social benefit of the dam is $_____. If the dam costs $500,000, it (is, is not) worth building.

b. Suppose you are one of the farmers. The government tells you that it intends to tax farmers according to how much each says the dam will be worth to him or her. If you tell the truth, it will cost you $_____. If you say $2,000 it will cost you $_____. If you say no benefit it will cost you $_____. You will have an incentive to (understate, overstate, reveal accurately) how much it is worth to you. Other farmers (will, will not) have the same incentive to provide this sort of answer, so the chances are that the dam (will, will not) be built — an (efficient, inefficient) outcome.

c. As another example, suppose that the same 1,000 farmers would get the same true benefits from the dam, but now suppose that the cost of building the dam is $1,500,000. In this case the dam (should, should not) be build. But suppose that now the government says that if it goes ahead with the dam it will tax the millions of taxpayers a few cents each to finance it. Your taxes will be scarcely affected. The only question the government has is: Should it go ahead or not? That depends on how highly farmers value it. If the government goes ahead, you will have a net gain (value to you of the dam minus your new taxes) of _____. You will maximize your chances of getting this gain if you (understate, overstate, reveal accurately) your benefit, and thus (increase, decrease) the chance that the dam will be built. Other farmers (will, will not) have the same incentive to give the same sort of answer, so the chances are that the dam (will, will not) be built — an (efficient, inefficient) outcome.

ESSAY QUESTIONS

1. Explain carefully whether or not each of the following might be considered to be a good with an external benefit

   a. The U. S. Olympic Team
   b. Your telephone
   c. Driver safety lessons
   d. Television programs

2. If the government asks people to reveal how much they would benefit from a public good, will they tell the truth? If the government asks them to reveal how much they are being damaged by a good with an external cost, will they tell the truth? Why or why not? How will their answers be affected if the government tells them that it is thinking of providing them with protection from this external cost, with this protection to be financed out of the government's general tax revenues?

3. Many industries pay lobbyists to influence regulatory agencies, congressional committees, and other government agencies and officials in Washington. Sometimes these lobbyists spend a lot of time promoting the idea that their industry is a source of external benefits. Why would the firms in an industry pay lobbyists to do this?

4. Criticize the following statement: "The government should not be providing money for vaccination programs. If people are unwilling to pay the full cost of vaccinations without subsidy, then vaccinations fail the market test and should not be provided at all."

5. Explain why you agree or disagree with the following statement: "You can rely on the government to provide you with the goods you want at a reasonable price just as much as you can rely upon private business firms. The reason is that the party in power wants you to be pleased with what it provides so that you will vote for it in the next election, just as a private business firm wants you to be pleased with what it provides so that you will buy the product again."

6. It has been argued that when the government spends more money, it provides a great deal of benefits to a small number of people and a very small cost to a large number of people (namely, taxpayers). Give an example. Why does a government judge that such a policy is in its interests? Will it necessarily be in the nation's economic interest?

ANSWERS

Important Terms: **1 e, 2 a, 3 g, 4 c, 5 f, 6 d, 7 h, 8 b**

True-False: **1** T (p. 598)
2 F (p. 603)
3 F (p. 603)
4 T (p. 601)
5 T (p. 599)
6 F (p. 603)
7 F (p. 603)
8 T (p. 603)
9 F (p. 603)
10 F (pp. 561, 602).

Multiple Choice: **1** b (pp. 561, 597)
2 c (p. 600)
3 e (p. 597)
4 e (p. 597)
5 d (p. 598)
6 b (p. 597)
7 d (p. 598)
8 b (p. 601)
9 b (p. 599)
10 e (pp. 601-602)
11 a (p. 601)
12 e (p. 602)
13 a (p. 607)
14 c (p. 602)
15 d (p. 603)
16 b (p. 604)

Exercises

1   a. Q_3, P_1, Q_4, ER.

       b.   EFR, subsidy, TF.

       c. Q_2, KH, LH, more, HGE, tax, LK.

2.   a straight line intersecting the vertical axis at $8, and the horizontal axis at 6.

3   a. $1 million, is.

       b. $1,000, $2,000, 0, understate, will, will not, inefficient

       c.   should not, almost $1,000, overstate, increase, will, will, inefficient.

CHAPTER 33

WHAT ARE THE GAINS FROM INTERNATIONAL TRADE?

LEARNING OBJECTIVES

After you have studied this chapter in the textbook and the study guide, you should be able to

✔ Identify the four main sources of gain from international trade

✔ Explain why trade increases competition in the domestic U.S. market and reduces the market power of U.S. producers, thus generating an efficiency gain

✔ Explain why trade makes possible cost reductions because it provides opportunities to exploit economies of scale. Thus income is increased and a wider variety of new products is available

✔ Explain the difference between absolute advantage and comparative advantage

✔ Explain why countries export those commodities in which they have a comparative advantage, and how comparative advantage is determined by opportunity costs

✔ Explain the two respects in which international trade and technological change are similar, and the respects in which they are different.

✔ Measure diagrammatically the gains from international trade using a production possibilities curve as in Figure 33-4 of the textbook, or alternatively, using the supply and demand diagrams shown in Figures 33-6 and 33-7

✔ Show the gains from trade in a supply/demand diagram by comparing the effect of trade on consumers with its effect on producers

✔ Identify the winners and losers from international trade

MAJOR PURPOSE

Americans in Kansas gain from domestic trade with other Americans in Minnesota and New York. Similarly, Americans gain from international trade with the Japanese and French. The reasons are the same in either case. Our purpose in this chapter is to examine the gains from trade from four broad sources:

- increased competition;

- greater availability of products;

- economies of scale; and

- comparative advantage.

This chapter also identifies the *winners* and *losers* from trade. While winners outnumber losers, and the nation as a whole benefits from trade, some Americans are hurt. Their ability to organize themselves and apply political pressure is one of the big reasons why countries maintain restrictions on trade—restrictions that will be examined in the next chapter.

HIGHLIGHTS OF CHAPTER

The two broad questions addressed in this chapter are: Why are there gains from trade? Who are the winners and losers? First, consider why we gain from trade.

The Sources of Gain

- *Increased competition*. There are two important changes that face domestic producers when trade is opened up. First, they face a much larger market; they can now sell to people anywhere in the world. Second, they now face many more competitors. Zenith no longer competes against RCA; instead it now competes with an additional group of producers from Japan, Europe and elsewhere. Because of increased competition, oligopolists such as Zenith and RCA lose much of their market power—their ability to influence price. Thus they move closer to perfect competition, with the increase in efficiency that this implies. Similarly a U.S. monopolist may, as a result of trade, find itself an oligopolist, with several foreign competitors; this industry also moves closer to perfect competition.

- *Greater availability of products*. Trade makes goods available that would otherwise not exist. Boeing might not have been able to develop the jumbo jet if it had been unable to sell it in a world market.

- *Economies of scale*. Without international trade, each country must be self-sufficient; it must therefore produce a wide variety of products in the small quantity necessary just to satisfy its own needs. With international trade, each country can specialize, producing only a few items in large volume and trading to get the rest. Large volume often means reduced cost; that is, there are economies of scale. And reduced cost means that we can produce and therefore consume more. In other words, our real income rises. It also rises because other countries are specializing and reducing their costs. Thus the products we trade for, as well as the goods we produce ourselves, fall in cost.

Not only are costs reduced; in addition, variety may be increased. For example, because of international trade, someone buying a car in the tiny European country of Liechtenstein can choose among Fords, Volkswagens, Datsuns, and many others that are produced elsewhere. Without international trade, consumers wouldn't have this choice. People in Liechtenstein would have to buy cars produced in Liechtenstein. But the market there is so small (the population is less than 30,000), that they would be lucky to have even one auto firm producing one model. There would be little or no variety.

- *Comparative advantage*. To understand comparative advantage, you must first understand absolute advantage. Table 33-3 in the textbook can be used to clarify the difference between the two. In the right-hand column of this table, we see that America has an absolute advantage in food because a worker in America can produce 3 units of food, whereas a worker in Britain can produce only 1. In other words, it only takes a third as many workers to produce food in America as in Britain. The input requirement—that is, the labor requirement—to produce food in America is lower than in Britain. (This is the definition of absolute advantage: a country has an absolute advantage in a good if the input requirement in that country is lower than that in other countries.)

America also has an absolute advantage in clothing. (An American worker out-produces a British worker in clothing by 6 to 4, as shown in the first column of Table 33.3.) Because America has an absolute advantage in producing both goods, absolute advantage cannot be the key to explaining which country will produce what. If it were the key, then America would produce both goods, and Britain neither—and that is inconsistent with the two-way trade we observe.

What then does determine the pattern of production and trade? The answer is: *comparative advantage*. But in which product does America have a comparative advantage? The answer is: food, because this is where American's absolute advantage is greater; a worker in America can out-produce a worker in Britain by 3 to 1 in food, but by only 6 to 4—that is, 3 to 2—in clothing.

Because America has a comparative advantage in food, Britain has a comparative advantage in clothing; that's where Britain's absolute disadvantage is least.

Using a more formal definition, we say that America has a comparative advantage in food if it has a lower opportunity cost of producing food than does Britain. This is indeed the case. In the last row of Table 33.3, we see the high opportunity cost of food in Britain. Since a worker who is now producing 1 unit of food could instead be producing 4 units of clothing, the opportunity cost (the alternative foregone) of producing that 1 unit of food is 4 units of clothing. Compare this to the lower opportunity cost of food in America, derived from the top row in this table: Since an American worker who is now producing 3 units of food could instead be producing 6 units of clothing, the opportunity cost in America of each unit of food is 6/3 = 2 units of clothing. Because America has a lower opportunity cost of

food than does Britain, America has a comparative advantage in food, and will specialize in this. Similar calculations for clothing will show that Britain has a comparative advantage here. With specialization in its products of comparative advantage, both American and Britain benefit, as is demonstrated in the calculations at the bottom of this table.

To sum up: Both absolute and comparative advantage refer to the cost of production. The difference is in how this cost is measured. For absolute advantage, cost is measured in terms of inputs required. For comparative advantage, cost is measured in terms of outputs forgone, that is, opportunity cost.

Here's an intuitive approach that may help you to understand better the gains from trade. Trade is the way a country can inexpensively acquire the goods in which it does not have a comparative advantage. Why produce these goods at home—where their opportunity cost is high—when they can be purchased from another country where their opportunity cost is low?

This gain from trade is further illustrated using the production possibilities curve shown in Figure 33-4 of the textbook. The gain comes when a country uses trade to move from point B to D. But you should be able to break down this move into its two components: (1) the move from B to C, as the country *specializes in food*, and (2) the move from C to D, as the country then *trades food for clothing*.

This production possibilities curve is also useful, as shown in Figure 33-5 in the textbook, when it is used to compare international trade and technological change. Both allow a country to consume a combination of goods lying beyond its current production possibility curve. (Both may also be the source of unemployment that may have to be endured in the short run in order to realize income gains in the long run.)

Finally, the textbook also illustrates the gains from trade using familiar supply and demand diagrams. You should understand clearly why the nation gains from unrestricted exports, as shown in Figure 33-6, and unrestricted imports, as shown in Figure 33-7. We gain on the export side because we sell goods abroad for more than it costs us to produce them (or more than we lose when we switch these goods away from domestic consumption). At the same time, we gain on the import side because we can buy imports for less than it would cost us to produce them inefficiently at home; and imports also allow us to increase our consumption of bargain-priced goods from abroad. For both exports and imports there is a triangular efficiency gain shown in Figures 33-6 and 33-7. You should be able to confirm these gains in a diagram like Figure 33-8 that shows how trade affects consumers and producers. This technique then allows you to fill in the details on the second key question in this chapter:

Who are the winners and losers?

Since opening our borders to an import lowers the domestic price of this good, consumers win and domestic producers lose. On the export side, there is also a conflict between these two groups—although the roles are reversed. Because opening foreign markets raises the price we can charge for our exports, producers win and consumers lose. Whenever trade policy is changed for a specific industry, a conflict between consumers and producers arises. This must be understood before turning to the contentious issues on trade policy discussed in the next chapter.

IMPORTANT TERMS

Match the term in the first column with the corresponding explanation in the second column

_____ 1. Economies of scale
_____ 2. Comparative advantage
_____ 3. Opportunity cost
_____ 4. Absolute advantage
_____ 5. International specialization
_____ 6. Terms of trade
_____ 7. Production gain on an export
_____ 8. Consumption gain on an import

a. country A has this in good X if the opportunity cost of producing X is lower in country A than in any other country.
b. Each country concentrating on one, or a small number of products, and acquiring the others through international trade.
c. Country B has this in good Y if Y can be produced with fewer inputs in country B than in any other country.
d. Falling average cost as output increases. This is one source of gain from international trade.
e. The quantity of good B that must be sacrificed in order to produce another unit of good A.
f. The sale of a product abroad for more than it costs to produce at home.
g. The price a country receives for its exports divided by the price it pays for its imports.
h. The ability to purchase goods abroad more cheaply than they could be produced at home.

TRUE-FALSE

T   F   1.   Comparative advantage ensures that U.S. exports of any good will equal U.S. imports of that same good.

T   F   2.   International trade tends to transform a natural oligopoly into a natural monopoly.

T   F   3.   Although each member country in the European Community imposes tariffs in its trade with other member countries, it may trade freely with the rest of the world.

TABLE 33.1
Output per worker

	clothing	food
in America	10	8
in Europe	2	4

T F 4. In Table 33.1, Europe has a comparative advantage in food.

T F 5. In Table 33.1, Europe has an absolute advantage in both goods.

T F 6. If America has an absolute advantage in a good, then America will necessarily specialize in that good.

T F 7. If America has a lower opportunity cost of producing good X than any other country, then America has a comparative advantage in X.

T F 8. While improved technology allows a country to consume more by moving to a higher production possibility curve, international trade allows a country to consume more without moving its production off its existing production possibilities curve.

T F 9. Large U.S. exports of grains following droughts abroad in the early 1970s benefited U.S. farmers, hurt U.S. consumers, and resulted in an overall efficiency loss.

T F 10. If a country imports oranges, then producers of oranges in that country probably gain from international trade in oranges.

MULTIPLE CHOICE

1. Machinery is:

   a. imported, but not exported by the United States
   b. exported, but not imported by the United States
   c. exported by the United States to Europe only
   d. imported and exported by the United States
   e. neither imported nor exported by the United States

2. Specialization and trade provide gains in

   a. domestic trade only
   b. foreign trade only
   c. domestic and foreign trade
   d. neither domestic nor foreign trade
   e. foreign trade, so long as countries do not have an absolute advantage

3. Which of the following is a possible result of international trade?

   a. a natural monopoly in the domestic market may be transformed into a natural oligopoly in the world market
   b. a perfectly competitive industry may be turned into a natural oligopoly
   c. a natural oligopoly may be turned into a natural monopoly
   d. a perfectly competitive industry may be turned into a natural monopoly
   e. large firms are able to exercise more market power because the size of the market is increased

4. International trade makes domestic firms more competitive in terms of

   a. price
   b. quality
   c. design
   d. the introduction of new products
   e. all of the above

5. International trade will lead a firm to introduce a new product if:

a. trade shifts demand to the right enough so that for the first time demand for the product overlaps its average costs
b. trade shifts demand to the left enough so that for the first time demand for the product overlaps its average costs
c. trade shifts demand to the left enough so that for the first time marginal cost of the product intersects its average cost
d. trade shifts demand to the right enough so that for the first time marginal cost of the product intersects its average cost
e. trade shifts demand to the right enough so that for the first time marginal cost of the product intersects its average variable cost

6. Under international trade we export those goods for which we have a relatively low:

a. materials cost
b. wage cost
c. accounting cost
d. opportunity cost
e. overhead cost

7. The idea of comparative advantage was developed by:

a. Adam Smith
b. Karl Marx
c. David Ricardo
d. Alfred Marshall
e. John Maynard Keynes

8. If America has an absolute advantage in a good, then America:

a. may or may not export that good
b. will necessarily export that good
c. will necessarily avoid exporting that good
d. will necessarily import that good
e. will necessarily avoid importing that good

The next 5 questions are based on the following hypothetical example:

TABLE 33.2
Output per worker:

	clothing	food
in America	6	3
in Europe	4	1

9. In Table 33.2, international trade would induce America to import:

a. food
b. clothing
c. both
d. neither
e. one or the other; we can't say which

10. In Table 33.2, America has an absolute advantage in:

a. both goods, and a comparative advantage in food
b. both goods, and a comparative advantage in clothing
c. both goods, and a comparative advantage in neither
d. neither good, but a comparative advantage in food
e. neither good, but a comparative advantage in clothing

11. In Table 33.2, Europe has an absolute advantage in:

a. both goods, and a comparative advantage in food
b. both goods, and a comparative advantage in clothing
c. both goods, and a comparative advantage in neither
d. neither good, but a comparative advantage in food
e. neither good, but a comparative advantage in clothing

12. In Table 33.2, Europe's opportunity cost of producing food is:

a. 3 units of clothing
b. $6/3 = 2$ units of clothing
c. $6/4 = 1 \, 1/2$ unit of clothing
d. 4 units of clothing
e. 3 units of food

13. If the lower right hand number in Table 33.2 is changed from 1 to 2, then the United States has an absolute advantage in:

    a. both goods, and a comparative advantage in food
    b. both goods, and a comparative advantage in clothing
    c. both goods, and a comparative advantage in neither
    d. neither good, but a comparative advantage in food
    e. neither good, and a comparative advantage in neither

14. A nation's real income can be increased by:

    a. international trade, but not by improved technology
    b. improved technology, but not by international trade
    c. neither technology nor international trade
    d. both technology and international trade
    e. international trade, provided there is protection for competing domestic industries

15. International trade allows a nation to increase its income by:

    a. reaching a point beyond its production possibilities curve (PPC)
    b. reaching a point inside its PPC
    c. reaching along its PPC to a point to the northwest and staying there
    d. reaching along its PPC to a point to the southeast and staying there
    e. staying at the same point on its PPC

16. When the U.S. imports a good:

    a. every American citizen gains
    b. U.S. producers and U.S. consumers of that good benefit
    c. U.S. producers and U.S. consumers of that good lose
    d. U.S. consumers lose, but U.S. producers gain
    e. there is an efficiency gain

17. The efficiency gain from the export of a good reflects a gain to:

    a. consumers, plus a gain to producers
    b. consumers, minus a loss to producers
    c. producers, minus a loss to consumers
    d. consumers only
    e. neither

18. A sudden move to free international trade would be most likely to cause short-term unemployment in which of the following industries?

    a. industries that don't export now, but could in the future
    b. industries that export only
    c. industries that export and sell domestically
    d. import-competing industries
    e. industries in which there are neither exports nor imports

19. Without trade in a world with two countries and two goods, real income will be:

    a. higher in the country that has an absolute advantage in both goods
    b. lower in the country that has an absolute advantage in both goods
    c. higher in the country that has an absolute advantage in neither good
    d. higher in the country that has a comparative advantage in neither good
    e. higher in the country that has a comparative advantage in both goods

20. In a world with two countries and two goods, opening trade will:

    a. benefit neither country
    b. benefit only the country with an absolute advantage in both goods
    c. benefit only the country with a comparative advantage in both goods
    d. be a way for each country to benefit
    e. benefit only the country with a comparative advantage in neither good

EXERCISES

1. Suppose that Figures 33.1 and 33.2 represent the markets for shoes in England and Spain.

   a. Without international trade, the price in England would be _____ and the quantity produced in England would be _____. The price in Spain would be _____ and the quantity produced in Spain would be_____. With trade, price will (rise, fall) in England and (rise, fall) in Spain.

Figure 33.1

Figure 33.2

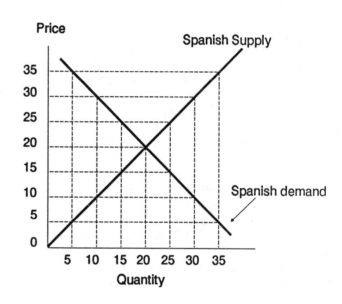

   b. With international trade the single price at which the total demand – that is, the English demand plus Spanish demand – equals the total supply is _____. At that price English demand is _____ and English supply is _____; Spanish demand is _____, and Spanish supply is _____. In this situation, (Spain, England) will export _____ units of shoes. England has a comparative (advantage, disadvantage) in shoes, as reflected by the (lower, higher) price and cost of shoes in England before trade.

2 a. This exercise is designed to help you understand comparative advantage. In Table 33.3, suppose that for country A, each acre of land will produce 100 bushels of wheat or 30 bushels of corn, whereas for country B, each acre of land will produce 40 bushels of wheat of 20 bushels of corn.

   Suppose that each country has 4,000 acres. Fill in Table 33.3, giving the production possibilities for A and B.

TABLE 33.3

A's Production Possibilities		B's Production Possibilities	
Thousands of Bushels of Wheat	Thousands of Bushels of Corn	Thousands of Bushels of Wheat	Thousands of Bushels of Corn
0	_____	0	_____
100	_____	40	_____
200	_____	80	_____
300	_____	20	_____
400	_____	160	_____

b. Plot the PPCs for the two countries in Figure 33.3.

Figure 33.3

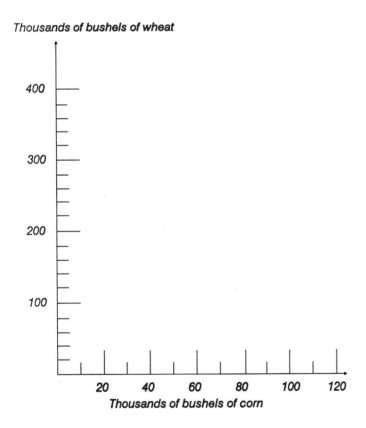

Thousands of bushels of wheat

Thousands of bushels of corn

c. Country _____ has an absolute advantage in producing corn; country _____ has an absolute advantage in producing wheat. Country _____ has a comparative advantage in producing corn; and country _____ has a comparative advantage in producing wheat.
Suppose that, before trade, each country devotes half its land to each product. Then country B will produce and consume _____ thousand bushels of wheat and _____ thousand bushels of corn. Mark this on Figure 33.3. Also mark the production and consumption point for country A.

d. Suppose that A and B were then to trade with each other at the price of 10 bushels of wheat for every 4 bushels of corn. (Note that this ratio of 10:4 is between A's pre-trade domestic exchange ratio of 100:30 = 10:3 cited at the beginning of this question, and B's ratio of 40:20 = 10:5. Therefore, it is a rate of exchange that will make trade beneficial for both countries.) Let's now see precisely why it is in B's interest to specialize in corn and purchase its wheat from A. If it does so, and devotes all its 4,000 acres to corn, B will produce _____ thousand bushels of corn and _____ thousand bushels of wheat. B then keeps the original 40 thousand bushels of corn for its own consumption, and takes the additional 40 thousand it has produced and sells this for _____ thousand bushels of wheat. It is now able to consume the same 40 thousand bushels of corn as before, and 20 thousand (more, less) bushels of wheat. This 20 thousand bushels of wheat represents its (gain, loss) from specialization and trade. Graph B's specialization and trade with arrows in Figure 33.3, clearly indicating B's gains from trade.

Now plot similar arrows for A in Figure 33.3 to show how this exchange also benefits A. (Hint: A moves to the northwest along its PPC in order to produce the 100 thousand more bushels of wheat it needs to exchange with B . When it gives up this wheat to B, it acquires 40 thousand bushels of corn for it; this trade moves it back to the southeast. The question is: Does A go back to its original point or to a point superior to it and thus also acquire a gain from trade?)

Note how the trade arrows for the two countries have the same length and slope. They must; each trade arrow describes the exchange of 100 thousand bushels of wheat for 40 thousand bushels of corn. The only difference in the two arrows is the direction in which they are pointing. (They must point in opposite directions, because an export for one country is an import for the other.) Note also that gains from trade arise because the two PPCs have different slopes, and it's therefore possible to have a mutually-beneficial trade arrow with a slope in between. If the two PPCs had the same slope, then opportunity costs would be the same in both countries. Consequently, neither country would have a _____ advantage, and mutually beneficial trade would (be possible, not be possible). We emphasize that we're concentrating here just on comparative advantage. Economies of scale also provide opportunities for mutually-beneficial trade — but that's another story.

3. In Figure 33.4, D is the U.S. domestic demand curve and MC is the U.S. marginal cost curve for a perfectly competitive good.

Figure 33.4

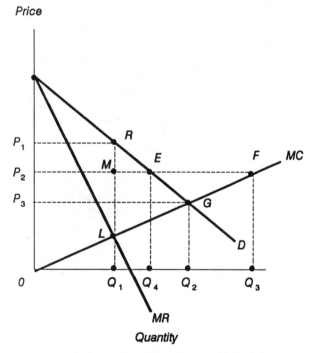

a. Suppose initially that there is no international trade. Then the amount _____ will be produced and the market price will be _____. Suppose now that international trade is introduced, and that it results in a price equal to P2. Then consumption of the good in the United

States will be _____, production of the good in the United States will be _____, and the difference between these amounts will be _____, which will be the amount of the good that the United States (exports, imports).

b. As a result of allowing international trade in this good, producer surplus in the United States has gone (up, down) by the amount _____ and consumer surplus in the United States has gone (up, down) by the amount _____.

Therefore, the net efficiency (gain, loss) to the United States is _____.

c. Suppose next that there is no international trade in the good and that the market in the United States is an unregulated monopoly. Its marginal revenue will be the line _____. The monopolist will produce the amount _____ and will charge price _____. The efficiency (gain, loss) from monopoly will be _____. Suppose now that international trade is introduced and that as a result the firm that used to have a monopoly in the United States is forced to behave as a perfect competitor, taking price as given.

Suppose as before that with international trade the market price is P2. Then consumption of the good in the United States will equal _____, production of the good in the United States will equal _____, and the difference between these two amounts equals _____, which will be the amount of the good that the United States (exports, imports).

d. As a result of allowing international trade in this good, the total revenue received by the producer in the United States has gone from _____ to _____, so the net gain in total revenue equals the rectangle _____, minus the rectangle _____.

e. But the producer's cost has increased by the four-sided figure _____; thus the net gain to the producer equals the triangle _____, minus the rectangle _____. At the same time, consumer surplus (rises, falls) by _____; thus the net gain to the country [that is, the net gain to consumers plus the net gain to the producer] equals area _____. Shade in this area.

f. In this case trade brings two efficiency gains: the standard gain from trade that results even in a world of perfect competition, shown by area

_____ , plus a gain because trade also ends monopoly inefficiency, as shown by area _____ . Both gains make up the area _____ , thus confirming our conclusion in part e.

g. Does this illustrate a special case in which it is possible for international trade in a specific commodity to benefit both the consumers and the producers of that commodity?

ESSAY QUESTIONS

1. Who gains and who loses from a tariff that prohibits the import of a certain good? Do the gains outweigh the losses, or vice versa? Explain.

2. Looking ahead to the next chapter, can you think of any goods that we would not want to export, no matter how great the net economic benefits might be? Hint: Americans now trade military aircraft and equipment with Canada, and this trade provides economic benefits to both countries. Would you recommend that the United States do the same with the Soviet Union?

3. "One of the gains from international trade is that it induces firms to reduce or eliminate technical inefficiency." Is this true? Why? Did we miss this point, or was it covered under one of our four broad sources of gains from trade?

4. Why do the leaders of the United Auto Workers argue that the government should take steps to limit the number of autos imported into the United States? If you were one of these leaders, what would be your attitude towards a similar restriction on U.S. imports of steel? Why?

5. Why might trade between New York and Pennsylvania benefit both states? In your answer, you may want to define the concept of an "export to another state" and an "import from another state."

6. A recent slogan has been "Trade, not aid. If we reduce U.S. restrictions on imports from the less developed countries, they will benefit, and so will we." Do you agree or disagree? Explain why.

7. Can you name any activities in your state that have developed as a result of interstate specialization — that is, specialization between states? Any activities that have developed as a result of international specialization?

8. If the United States and Mexico have an approximate balance in their trade, which country is more dependent on that trade? Why?

9. "There is no trade in cement between Australia and Germany. The reason is that transport costs on so bulky and heavy an item more than cancel out the gains from trade." Explain this statement. Do you agree with it? Does this mean that transport costs influence trade patterns? Explain how high transport costs in a good may explain "cross-hauling" — for example, the export of cement from California to Mexico at the same time as cement is being imported into Texas from Mexico.

ANSWERS

Important Terms: 1 d, 2 a, 3 e, 4 c, 5 b, 6 g, 7 f, 8 h

True-False:
1 F (p. 617)
2 F (p. 614)
3 F (p. 615)
4 T (p. 616)
5 F (p. 616)
6 F (p. 616)
7 T (p. 617)
8 T (p. 620)
9 F (p. 624)
10 F (p. 622)

1 d (p. 613)
2 c (p. 612)
3 a (p. 614)
4 e (p. 614)
5 a (p. 615)
6 d (p. 617)
7 c (p. 615)
8 a (p. 616)
9 b (p. 616)
10 a (p. 616)
11 e (p. 616)
12 d (p. 616)
13 c (p. 616)
14 d (p. 620)
15 a (p. 620)
16 e (p. 622)
17 c (p. 623, FOOTNOTE)
18 d (p. 624)
19 a (p. 618, BOX)
20 d (p. 618, BOX)

Exercises

1   a. $10, 10, $20, 20, rise, fall.
       b. $15, 5, 15, 25, 15, England, 10, advantage, lower.

2   a and b.

Table 33.1 Completed

A's Production Possibilities		B's Production Possibilities	
Thousands of Bushels of Wheat	Thousands of Bushels of Corn	Thousands of Bushels of Wheat	Thousands of Bushels of Corn
0	120	0	80
100	90	40	60
200	60	80	40
300	30	20	20
400	0	160	0

Figure 33.3 Completed

Thousands of bushels of wheat

A's trade

A's specialization

K

A's gain from trade

A's PPC

B's PPC

H

B's gain from trade

B's trade

F

B's specialization

J

L

Thousands of bushels of corn

c.   A, A, B, A, 80, 40.
d.   80, zero, 100, more, gain, comparative, not be possible.

3   a. Q_2, P_3, Q_4, Q_3, $Q_4 Q_3$, exports.
       b.   up, P_2FGP_3, down, P_2EGP_3, gain, EGF.
       c.   MR, Q_1, P_1, loss, RGL, Q_4, Q_3, Q_4Q_3, exports.
       d. P_1RQ_1O, P_2FQ_3O, MFQ_3Q_1, P_1RMP_2.
       e. LQ_1Q_3F, MLF, P_1RMP_2, rises, P_1REP_2, RLFE.
       f.   EGF, RLG, RLFE.
       g.   yes.

Across

1. this type of advantage is sufficient for mutually beneficial trade
5. a government agency that makes recommendations on trade policy (abbrev.)
6, 8. people cannot be prevented from enjoying this, even if they do not help to pay for it
10. thousands of years
12. a barrier to imports
14. total
16, 18. winner of Nobel prize; he studied the problems of majority rule
20. if all barriers to international commerce were removed, this would cease to exist (2 words)
21. symbol for lead
23. he explained theory of comparative advantage
25. this product is both exported and imported by the United States
26. period of time made noteworthy by important events
27. the state of Denmark, according to Hamlet
28. this type of advantage is not necessary for mutually beneficial trade

Down

2, 22. this is measured by slope of production possibilities curve
3. _____ roads are a way of transporting heavy goods
4. major reason for gain from international or domestic trade (3 words)
5. often, these are more powerful than the sword
7. flattery, guff
9. a musical instrument
11, 21. this is reduced by competition from imports
15. because of these people, public goods won't be produced by the free market (2 words)
17. buy the labor of
19. A noted international trade theorist, winner of a Nobel prize
24. according to the _____ law of wages, population pressures would drive wages down to the subsistence level

INTERNATIONAL TRADE: POLICY DEBATES

LEARNING OBJECTIVES

After you have studied this chapter in the textbook and the study guide, you should be able to

✔ Explain the military and political reasons why trade barriers still exist

✔ State three fallacious economic arguments for protection, explaining why they are fallacious

✔ State eight economic arguments for protection that contain some element of truth, and the difficulties with each of these arguments

✔ Describe the multilateral liberalization of our trade over the last 50 years, with special reference to the creation of the GATT and the Kennedy and Tokyo Rounds

✔ Evaluate the European Community (EC) with special reference to the problems it raises for U.S. exporters

✔ Give several examples of non-tariff barriers, explaining why each distorts trade

✔ Describe some of the conflicts that have arisen in U.S.-Japanese trade

✔ Give some of the reasons why companies go multinational

✔ Evaluate multinational corporations (MNCs) in terms of their benefits and costs to host countries

---

MAJOR PURPOSE

Even though the gains from trade have been evident since the days of Adam Smith, and even though tariffs have been on a downward trend over the last 50 years, many trade barriers still remain. We are still a long way from free trade. The primary objective of this chapter is to answer the question "How is it possible for these barriers to still exist? Can they, or can they not, be justified?" We will also address a number of other important, and closely related questions: "What have been the major developments that have moved us towards freer trade? As we have been moving two steps forward, what are the new barriers to trade that have been moving us one step

Chapter 34 International Trade: Policy Debates

back? Why does U.S. trade with Japan remain such a contentious issue? And how do the multinational corporations that span international borders fit into this picture?"

HIGHLIGHTS OF CHAPTER

The trade barriers that remain — and new ones that have been introduced — have been defended by their supporters as "in the national interest." Do the arguments they use make sense?

Arguments for Protection

Two of the arguments for protection — the military and political arguments — have little to do with economics.

The military reason for restricting trade is that weapons and some related goods are vital for our national defense. Under complete free trade, with all countries specializing in their comparative advantage, some military goods might be produced in foreign countries — some of them hostile. Since it would be unacceptable for the nation to find itself dependent on such sources of supply in time of crisis, the production of these goods is protected in the United States as a matter of national security. This military argument does make sense. The major problem it raises is that it is not clear where we should draw the line. Almost any industry can argue that its products are vital for national defense, in one way or another.

The other non-economic reason for protection is political. The loss that results from allowing a good to be freely imported is felt very heavily by the few people who specialize in producing that good; in many cases, their jobs are threatened by the competition of imports. These people will often vote for a politician who promises to restrict such imports. As we saw in the last chapter, the damage to these losers from free trade will be more than offset by the benefits to the winners — all the people who are able to enjoy a wider variety of less expensive goods. But these gains by the winners are widely dispersed over the public as a whole, with the benefit received by each individual being relatively small. Thus winners usually vote for other issues on which they feel more deeply, and the politician who proposes to restrict an import is often elected. Thus trade restrictions that make no economic sense are still introduced for political reasons.

Now let's turn to the economic arguments that have been used to try to justify protection. Some are fallacious, but some contain an element of truth.

1. **"Buy American because it keeps our money at home. When we buy goods from Italy we lose our money to the Italians."** This argument is fallacious. When we buy Italian goods our money eventually comes back when the Italians buy our goods. The Italians want our goods, not our money.

2. **"We can't compete with cheap foreign labor."** This argument is also fallacious. Labor in many foreign countries is less expensive because it is less productive. Our higher productivity means that, on average, we can compete with cheap foreign labor. We do particularly well in goods in which we have a comparative advantage (where our productivity advantage more than offsets our higher wage rate). We can't compete where we don't have a comparative advantage, where our productivity advantage does not offset our higher wage rate.

3. **"Tariffs should be tailored to equalize costs at home and abroad."** This too is a fallacious argument. According to the theory of comparative advantage, we gain from international trade because there are differences in costs between countries. Tailoring tariffs to eliminate these differences would eliminate trade, and all the gains it provides.

4. **"If we buy steel from Pittsburgh rather than Japan, employment will rise in Pittsburgh rather than Japan."** There is a grain of truth in this argument. Restricting imports of steel from Japan may stimulate employment in Pittsburgh, at least in the short run. However, there are two problems. First, Japan may retaliate with her own restrictions against our exports, and this will reduce U.S. employment. Thus we don't get employment gains after all. In short, we are following a "beggar-my-neighbor" policy that doesn't provide employment benefits, but results in shrinking trade and a loss of the gains from trade. Second, blocking out Japanese competition makes it more difficult to control costs and prices in American industries. If American workers don't feel that they have to compete with the Japanese, they will be less restrained in their wage demands. We saw in Chapter 33 that one of the gains from trade is that it makes our economy more competitive. We lose this gain whenever we protect our industries.

5. **"Restricting trade will diversify a nation's economy."** This may be true for some countries.

Trade may lead a country to specialize in producing just a few goods. If world prices drop for these few goods, the country will suffer from having "put all its eggs in one basket." On the other hand, such heavy specialization will put it in a particularly favorable position if those prices rise; a prime example is the group of OPEC countries who produce almost nothing but oil. But these arguments simply don't apply to the United States. A country this large will always produce such a large variety of goods that overspecialization will not be a serious concern.

6. **"We need to protect our infant industries."** This argument is sometimes valid. Without the protection of trade restrictions, some industries may never reach the size where they can realize the economies of scale necessary to compete in world markets. However, there are three difficulties with this argument. (a) Infant industries never seem to grow up. They typically continue to demand protection, and no government wants to lose votes by cutting the apron strings. (b) Even if an industry were to "grow up," it might still not be able to compete effectively. (c) If the infant industry really does have a promising future then why aren't private lenders willing to lend it enough money to survive until maturity?

7. **"Restricting imports may reduce the price we have to pay for them."** This may make sense if the United States buys so much of a good that a cut back in this demand (as a result of a U.S. import restriction) would reduce the world price. While this policy may work if it's applied to an import from a small trading partner, it won't work on a large partner like the European Community. If the EC sees the United States doing this, it can take the same attitude and restrict its purchase of a U.S. good. The price of that U.S. export will then fall. With the price of a U.S. import and a U.S. export both falling, the U.S. may not achieve any price advantage after all. Moreover, for both countries, the gains from trade will shrink.

8. **"Restricting imports may reduce our vulnerability to a cutoff in foreign supplies."** Cutbacks in oil supplies from OPEC countries in the 1970s made clear the force of this argument. But oil is special; for most other commodities, the risk of having our supply cut off is minimal. If one country stops selling to us, we can turn to other sources of supply.

9. **"Use protection to engineer (that is, create) a comparative advantage."** Just as past accumulations of

capital by some nations have given them a comparative advantage in products that require a lot of capital, the accumulation of **human capital** in protected high-tech industries today could give us a comparative advantage in those industries in the future. There is some truth in this, but:

- It is similar to the infant-industry argument, and subject to the same criticisms.

- Like other arguments it assumes that our trading partners won't retaliate.

- Protecting one high-tech industry like computer chips increases the cost of other high-tech industries that use chips. Thus the U.S. computer industry was damaged by U.S. protective measures against Japanese chips.

10. **Protect an industry with positive externalities.** High-tech industries are again a good example. (There were huge external benefits to the broad public when AT&T developed the transistor.) It's true that positive externalities justify a subsidy, but protection may be the worst kind — again since it invites retaliation.

11. **Aggressive reciprocity.** Use the threat of protection to force trading partners to lower their barriers to our exports.

    Super-301 is the U.S. attempt to do this. If it were to succeed, it would be highly beneficial, to us and to other countries that lower their trade barriers. But:

    - If the policy succeeds and the U.S. threat can then be withdrawn, how do you deal with U.S. industries that have developed expectations of protection that must then be disappointed?

    - Every country could feel justified in using this policy, especially since each country views itself as being a "fairer trader" than its partners. In this case, this policy could be a prescription for a trade war.

12. There are only a few strong arguments for free trade. But the many arguments against it are often seriously flawed, and universally assume partners won't retaliate if we protect. So don't just count the number of arguments. The case for free trade is still a strong one.

Nontariff Barriers

There are several kinds:

- **Quotas are quantitative limits on imports.** These include the **voluntary export restraints** that the United States pressured the Japanese into imposing on their exports to the United States. When that pressure was removed and the Japanese were free to drop the VERs, why should they? The United States had shown them how to profitably cartelize their export sales to the United States. Because of this, the Japanese auto companies were making more profit in the United States than in Japan.

  An alternative form of quota is one that a country itself imposes on its imports.

- **Health or quality standards.** An example is the European ban on U.S. hormone-fed beef. How much is this a policy to protect health and how much is it a policy to block out import competition? It is hard to say.

- **Bureaucratic red tape** can be used to discourage imports. An example was the French requirement that all imported VCRs be cleared through the tiny, inland customs house at Poitiers—the same town that Frederic Bastiat used to satirize protection 150 years ago. (See Box 34-1.)

Trade Liberalization

- **Multilateral:** In the Uruguay Round **all countries in the GATT** are now trying to negotiate down trade barriers. This follows the **Kennedy Round** in the 1960s and the **Tokyo Round** in the 1970s which each cut tariffs multilaterally by about one third.

- **Plurilateral:** An example is the European Community (EC) in which **several countries** have gone to free trade. But this raises a problem, because these countries then discriminate against outsiders like the United States. For example, before the EC was formed, U.S. exporters competed on equal terms with the Germans in the French market. (Both faced a French tariff.) With the EC, U.S. exporters still face that tariff while the Germans don't.

- **Bilateral:** Between **two countries only.** Examples include U.S. agreements with Israel and Mexico, and the 1989 agreement to remove all tariffs between the United States and Canada.

The U.S./Japan Trade Problem

The Japanese reduced trade barriers, like other countries, in the Kennedy and Tokyo Rounds, **and have also reduced their barriers on their own** since. Yet informal barriers, such as a Japanese distribution system that absorbs imports very reluctantly, continue to deter Japanese imports. Thus in 1987, U.S. exports to Japan were only 1/3 of the value of Japanese exports to the United States. (True, this is a severe imbalance. However, it is not as bad as it sounds since, in a world of multilateral trade, it is neither likely nor necessarily desirable for bilateral trade flows to balance.) The frustration of Congress led to the Super-301 provision in the 1988 trade bill.

The Multinational Corporation (MNC)

The most important thing to understand about MNCs is why they exist. Why do companies go multinational, by setting up subsidiaries in foreign countries?

- **To acquire resources.** Examples include U.S. oil companies operating in the Middle East.

- **To acquire markets** for products which have been successfully developed and sold in the U.S. market, and which therefore have already had their R&D costs written off.

- **To jump foreign trade barriers.** In selling in a foreign country, it is often less expensive to produce in that country, rather than to produce in the United States and pay that country's tariff, and perhaps high transport costs as well.

- **To get access to lower wages.** This has led to the charge by U.S. labor that MNCs "are exporting U.S. jobs." Or are they creating U.S. jobs? About 1/4 of U.S. exports are components that MNCs export to their subsidiaries abroad.

The world economy has benefited from the development of MNCs in the following ways:

- It is in the interests of any profit-seeking MNC to locate each of its activities in the country that has a comparative advantage. Because MNCs thus help countries to "find their comparative advantage," the MNCs assist in the realization of worldwide real income gains from trade.

- MNCs also assist in the realization of real income gains from economies of scale. In designing another car, a company like Ford finds its costs are lower because it can, say, draw on a design of a Ford car that has already been produced by its German subsidiary.

- MNCs have also helped to raise standards of living by quickly transmitting technological knowledge across borders.

However, many people think that the MNCs now have too much influence over governments. Scandals in which executives of Lockheed paid large bribes to government officials in other countries have illustrated the abuse of economic power by MNCs.

IMPORTANT TERMS

Match the term in the first column with the corresponding explanation in the second column.

_____ 1. Tariff
_____ 2. NTB
_____ 3. Quota
_____ 4. Trade restriction
_____ 5. Protection
_____ 6. "Beggar-my-neighbor" policy
_____ 7. Infant industry
_____ 8. Terms of trade
_____ 9. Aggressive reciprocity
_____ 10. Multilateral
_____ 11. Plurilateral
_____ 12. Bilateral
_____ 13. The General Agreement on Tariffs and Trade (GATT)
_____ 14. EC
_____ 15. Kennedy Round
_____ 16. Tokyo Round
_____ 17. MNC

a. The common market in Europe formed in the late 1950s by Germany, France, Italy, Holland, Belgium, and Luxembourg, and later joined by other countries such as Britain.
b. The policy of imposing barriers to trade in order to shield domestic industries from foreign competition.
c. Between only two countries.
d. A tax imposed on imported goods as they enter a country.
e. The multilateral GATT negotiation in the 1970s that cut tariffs by about a third
f. An industry that has not yet reached the size at which it can capture sufficient expertise and/or economies of scale to compete in world markets
g. A nontariff barrier, that is, any government measure—other than a tariff—that restricts trade.
h. A large corporation with its head office in one country and subsidiaries in other countries.
i. A treaty signed in 1947 that provides for multilateral negotiations to reduce trade restrictions.
j. The use of trade restrictions to reduce imports, increase domestic production, and therefore reduce unemployment.
k. A limit on the number of units of a good that can be imported into a country.
l. Between many countries
m. The multilateral negotiation by GATT countries in the 1960s that reduced tariffs by about a third.
n. The price we receive for our exports, compared to the price we pay for our imports.
o. Any tariff or non-tariff barrier that impedes international trade.
p. Fair trade.
q. Between several countries.

TRUE-FALSE

T   F   1.   Tariffs are often imposed because producers have more political influence than consumers.

T   F   2.   When international trade is opened up in a good, the United States as a whole gains only if we end up exporting that good.

T   F   3.   Diversifying an economy may reduce the gains from trade.

T   F   4.   If the United States were to increase restrictions on imported steel, this would tend to increase employment in Pittsburgh in the short run.

T   F   5.   After an infant industry has been supported by the government for a year or two, political pressure to remove the protection becomes almost irresistible.

T   F   6.   U.S. presidents have been more likely than the Congress to favor a policy of increasing trade barriers.

T   F   7.   Because wages in America are higher, it follows that costs of production are also higher — and this justifies protecting our goods from cheap foreign products.

T   F   8.   One of the strongest arguments for trade restrictions is that they keep us from losing our U.S. dollars to foreigners.

T   F   9.   If the U.S. government were to do nothing about our unemployment problems, this would constitute a "beggar-my-neighbor" policy.

T   F   10.   By restricting its imports, a country may be able to improve its terms of trade. But in practice this may be very difficult to accomplish because other trading countries are often powerful enough to retaliate.

MULTIPLE CHOICE

1. A policy of protecting essential defense industries:

   a. has been opposed by economists since the days of Adam Smith
   b. is sometimes abused by industries that contribute very little to national security but still try to use the defense argument to get protection
   c. is justified as a method of creating employment, but can't be justified in any other way
   d. all of the above
   e. none of the above

2. If we take into account the interests of both producers and consumers, then protection of the auto industry is:

   a. in the interest of the nation as a whole, and in the interest of the state of Michigan
   b. in the interest of the nation as a whole, but not in the interest of the state of Michigan
   c. not in the interest of the nation as a whole, nor in the interest of the state of Michigan
   d. not in the interest of the nation as a whole, but it may well be in the interest of the state of Michigan
   e. not in the interest of Michigan, and has little or no effect on the nation as a whole

3. The strongest political pressure for a change in trade policy usually comes from:

   a. producers lobbying for import restrictions
   b. producers lobbying for export restrictions
   c. consumers lobbying for import restrictions
   d. consumers lobbying for export restrictions
   e. consumers lobbying for a reduction in trade restrictions

4. In dealing with a serious problem of unemployment, a country that trades heavily should normally look first to:

   a. increasing tariffs
   b. increasing quotas
   c. increasing other nontariff barriers
   d. restricting its exports
   e. domestic monetary and fiscal policy

5. With free trade it is likely that the United States would:

   a. give up the production of industrial goods in order to concentrate on agricultural goods
   b. give up the production of agricultural goods in order to concentrate on industrial goods
   c. give up one industry (say electrical machinery) in order to specialize in another, (say, chemicals)
   d. give up the production of some items of electrical machinery in order to specialize in other items of electrical machinery; and do the same in chemicals
   e. in both electrical equipment and chemicals, produce an even wider range of items than at present

6. Which of the following arguments for protection makes economic sense?

   a. we should tailor tariffs so as to equalize costs at home and abroad
   b. when we import, the country loses money that wouldn't be lost if we produced domestically instead
   c. we can't compete with cheap foreign labor
   d. restricting oil imports tends to reduce the world price of oil
   e. all of the above

7. Problems that arise when a country protects an infant industry include:

   a. the industry's cost may never fall below those in foreign countries, because foreigners may enjoy some natural advantage
   b. it may be very difficult to know when infant protection has become an old age pension
   c. the new industry may hire a large number of employees whose voting power may make it difficult to remove protection later — even when it is no longer justified
   d. all of the above
   e. none of the above

8. A beggar-my-neighbor policy involves:

   a. encouraging the purchase of essential materials from abroad
   b. export controls to prevent the sale of our natural resources to foreign countries
   c. import restrictions designed to capture employment from foreign countries
   d. subsidies to encourage imports of foreign natural resources
   e. subsidies to encourage imports of foreign luxury goods

9. Restricting an import to improve our terms of trade is more likely to work if applied to oil imports than if applied to imports from Europe because:

   a. the U.S. is a small buyer of oil
   b. the U.S. is a small buyer of goods from Europe
   c. the Europeans can't effectively retaliate
   d. the Europeans can effectively retaliate
   e. OPEC can effectively retaliate

10. The infant industry argument for protection makes sense if the infant is:

    a. able to compete against foreign firms now, but not in the future
    b. not able to compete against foreign firms now, but will be able to in the future
    c. won't be able to compete now or in the future
    d. will be able to compete now and in the future
    e. won't be able to compete now; the future is irrelevant

11. "If I buy a radio from India, I get the radio and India gets the dollars. But if I buy a U.S.-built radio, I get the radio and the dollars stay here." This argument is:

    a. misleading because the Indians seldom keep the dollars they earn from us in trade; they eventually spend them on our goods
    b. misleading because the dollars I spend buying a U.S.-built radio also leave this country
    c. correct; this is why we should stop trading
    d. correct; we should trade only for political reasons
    e. true for radios, but not for most goods we import

12. In the early 1980s, the U.S. auto industry was having trouble competing with imports, partly because of:

   a. high previous wage settlements, and Japanese voluntary export limits
   b. high previous wage settlements; Japanese voluntary export limits reduced the pressure on the U.S. auto companies
   c. low previous wage settlements; Japanese voluntary export limits reduced the pressure on the U.S. auto companies
   d. high previous wage settlements; Japanese voluntary export limits had essentially no effect on the U.S. auto companies
   e. low previous wage settlements; Japanese voluntary export limits increased the pressure on the U.S. auto companies

13. Trade restrictions on a good will improve our terms of trade if:

   a. U.S. demand for the good is a significant part of world demand
   b. U.S. demand for the good is an insignificant part of world demand
   c. the U.S. industry is a natural monopoly
   d. the lower price that results drives some of our own producers out of business
   e. the U.S. is already self-sufficient in this good

14. U.S. tariffs today are:

   a. higher than in the 1930s
   b. slightly lower
   c. much lower
   d. about the same
   e. higher in most goods, but lower in some

15. The argument that an industry with positive externalities should be protected is most similar to the argument that:

   a. a polluting industry should be taxed
   b. a polluting industry should be subsidized
   c. a polluting industry should be left alone
   d. vaccinations should be subsidized
   e. vaccinations should be taxed

16. The formation of the European Community:

   a. was one of the reasons for the severe scarcity of agricultural goods in the early 1980s
   b. has made it easier for Americans to compete against the French in the German market
   c. has made it more difficult for Americans to compete against the French in the German market
   d. has made it more difficult for Americans to compete against the Japanese in the German market
   e. has had no effect on Americans competing in the German market

17. If an industry has large positive externalities:

   a. it must be protected
   b. it should be protected
   c. it should be subsidized, with protection being the best method
   d. it should be subsidized, but not by protection because this invites retaliation
   e. it should be subsidized, but not by protection because this guarantees against retaliation

18. In the Kennedy Round, participating countries cut their tariffs by about a third. In the Tokyo Round that followed:

   a. almost no further progress was made
   b. no further progress was made
   c. participating countries cut their remaining tariffs by about 10%
   d. participating countries cut their remaining tariffs by roughly another one third
   e. participating countries cut their remaining tariffs by roughly 90%

19. The Tokyo Round resulted in an average tariff reduction of about:

   a. 5%
   b. 15%
   c. 25%
   d. 35%
   e. 45%

20. In 1987, U.S. exports to Japan were:

    a. less than one third U.S. imports from Japan
    b. 33% less than U.S. imports from Japan
    c. about the same as U.S. imports from Japan
    d. 33% more than U.S. imports from Japan
    e. over three times U.S. imports from Japan

21. Nontariff barriers are:

    a. designed solely to restrict trade
    b. designed solely to improve health standards
    c. designed solely for other non-trade reasons
    d. sometimes designed to restrict trade, and sometimes designed to improve health standards; but in either case, they restrict trade
    e. justified so long as they provide a benefit, regardless of their cost

---

EXERCISES

Parts (a) through (e) of this exercise cover the same ground as the appendix to the chapter. You will probably be able to do the exercise and find it helpful, even if you are not being asked to study the appendix. However, if you get stuck, you can refer to the appendix for help. In any case, first try to do the exercise on your own.

1. Figure 34.1 shows the domestic U.S. supply and demand for a good that is traded internationally

Figure 34.1

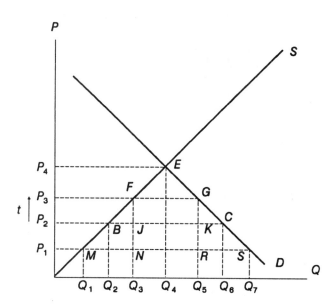

a. Without international trade the price would be _____ and the quantity produced would be _____. If this good is available on the world market at a price P_2, then the price in the United States, under free trade, will be _____. Domestic production will be _____, domestic consumption will be _____, and the country will (import, export) the amount _____. As a result of this international trade, the (gain, loss) to consumers is area _____, while producers are (better, worse) off by area _____. If we consider both producers and consumers, the effect of international trade on the nation, on balance, is an efficiency (gain, loss) of area _____.

b. Suppose that the government imposes a tariff on this good, shown by arrow t. Suppose that this has no effect on the world price of the good. Because of the tariff, the domestic price will (rise, fall) to _____. (Importers who are willing to bring this good in for a price P_2, will need this higher price to compensate them for the tariff t that they now have to pay the government.) The quantity of imports will be _____. As a result of the tariff, consumers (gain, lose) area _____, while producers are (better, worse) off by area _____. Moreover, the government is now collecting a tariff t on imports of _____, for a total revenue of area _____. Therefore, there is a net (gain, loss) to the nation from this tariff of areas _____.

c. Now suppose that, instead of this tariff t, the government imposes an import quota that restricts imports to the quantity FG. With imports of FG, P_2 (is, is not) an equilibrium price, because the demand for this good at price P_2 is (more than, less than) the domestic plus imported supply. Thus price will be (above, below) P_2. P_3 (is, is not) an equilibrium price because, with imports FG, the demand for this good at P_3 is (more than, less than, equal to) the domestic plus imported supply. Thus, this quota of FG is "the quota equivalent of tariff _____, because both raise the domestic U.S. price by _____, and reduce imports to _____.

d. Because of the quota, the price in the domestic market will rise to _____, consumers will (gain, lose) area _____, and producers will (gain, lose) area _____. Suppose that the quota rights are held by foreigners exporting to the U.S. They can then make a profit by acquiring this good outside the United States for _____ per unit and selling it in the United States for _____. The revenue the U.S. government gets from the imposition of this quota is _____. Therefore the net effect on the nation of this quota is its effect on producers and consumers, which is a (gain, loss) of area _____.

e. When the U.S. government imposes an import quota, and gives away these quota rights to foreigners, then a quota will result in a (larger, smaller) amount of (gain, loss) to the U.S. nation than will an equivalent tariff. The additional (gain, loss) from the quota occurs because duty revenue is collected by the U.S. treasury if there is a (tariff, quota), but is not collected if there is this type of (tariff, quota). Instead, this revenue goes as profit to (U.S. producers, foreign holders of quota rights).

ESSAY QUESTIONS

1. When a country is in a severe recession, the demand to reduce imports become stronger. Why? Critically evaluate such a proposal.

2. It is sometimes argued that trade restrictions protect our high standard of living from being eroded by competition from low-income countries. Evaluate this. Do trade restrictions erode our standard of living or increase it, for the nation as a whole? for the industry that's being protected?

3. The watch industry, the chemical industry, the canned crab industry and the lead pencil industry have all, at one time or another, used the national defense argument in seeking protection. Evaluate the claim of each.

4. Explain carefully how a tariff tends to reduce the benefits of international specialization.

5. Consider a tariff high enough, not just to reduce, but to completely prevent imports. How would it affect consumers? producers? the nation as a whole? Would the U.S. treasury collect any duty revenue from such a tariff? from a tariff that only reduces imports?

6. The text argued that a country may improve its terms of trade by restricting imports. In 1973 the oil-producing countries of OPEC managed to improve their terms of trade by restricting their exports. Explain carefully what are the similarities and differences between the "terms of trade" argument for restricting imports and the "terms of trade" argument for restricting exports.

ANSWERS

Match the Columns: 1 d, 2 g, 3 k, 4 o, 5 b, 6 j, 7 f, 8 n, 9 p, 10 l, 11 q, 12 c, 13 i, 14 a, 15 m, 16 e, 17 h.

True-False:
1 T (p. 628)
2 F (p. 624)
3 T (p. 632)
4 T (p. 631)
5 F (p. 633)
6 F (p. 629)
7 F (p. 630)
8 F (p. 630)
9 F (pp. 631-632)
10 T (p. 633)

Exercises

1
a. P_4, Q_4, P_2, Q_2, Q_6, import, BC, gain, P_4ECP_2, worse, P_4EBP_2, gain, EBC.
b. rise, P_3, FG, lose, P_3GCP_2, better, P_3FBP_2, FG, FGKJ, loss, FJB and GKC.
c. is not, more than, above, is, equal to, t, t, FG.
d. P_3, lose, P_3GCP_2, gain, P_3FBP_2, P_2, P_3, zero, loss, FGCB.
e. larger, loss, loss, tariff, quota, foreign holders of quota rights.

Part 9

HOW INCOME IS DISTRIBUTED

CHAPTER 35

WAGES IN A PERFECTLY COMPETITIVE ECONOMY

LEARNING OBJECTIVES

After you have studied this chapter in the textbook and the study guide, you should be able to

✔ Explain why, under perfect competition, the curve showing a firm's demand for labor is the same as the curve showing the marginal revenue product of labor

✔ State two reasons why the labor demand curve might shift to the right

✔ Illustrate how the labor demand curve can be used to show the total income of labor in an industry and the total income of other factors of production

✔ Explain why the height of the labor supply curve for an industry reflects the opportunity cost of labor — that is, labor's wage and productivity in other industries

✔ Explain why, in the absence of externalities, perfect competition in the labor market typically results in an efficient wage and employment level

✔ Measure diagrammatically the efficiency loss that results when a labor market is not perfectly competitive

✔ Explain why one cannot necessarily jump from the conclusion that a perfectly competitive labor market is efficient, to the much stronger conclusion that a free, unregulated labor market is "best"

✔ Explain the effects of a minimum wage in an otherwise perfectly competitive labor market

---

MAJOR PURPOSE

In this chapter, the objective is to use the familiar tools of supply and demand developed in earlier chapters to analyze how wages are determined in perfectly competitive labor markets. The labor market for a specific industry will be perfectly competitive if

(a) there are so many buyers and sellers of labor service that none can affect the wage rate;

(b) labor is standardized, with all workers being equally productive; and

(c) workers are mobile and can move in and out of this industry.

Given these assumptions, the text shows (1) how the labor demand by an industry reflects the productivity of labor in that industry, and (2) how labor supply reflects the wages and productivity of labor in other industries. The conclusion that follows is that perfect competition yields an efficient outcome in a labor market, just as it did in a product market.

A number of real-world complications in labor markets are recognized. For example, in this chapter we study what happens when the government intervenes to set a minimum wage. In the next chapter, assumption (a) above is relaxed in order to show the effects when workers form a union to raise wages — or employers form an association to lower wages. In Chapter 37, assumption (b) is relaxed in order to analyze what happens when workers are not equally productive. Finally, in Chapter 38 we examine what happens when assumption (c) that labor is mobile does not hold — specifically, what happens when discrimination prevents blacks from entering jobs traditionally held by whites?

HIGHLIGHTS OF CHAPTER

As a first approximation, a wage can be viewed just like the price of any other good or service that is traded in the market. In this case, the service is labor, the demanders are employers, and the suppliers are workers.

The Demand for Labor

In defining its demand for labor, a firm begins with its marginal physical product (MPP). This schedule, shown in column 3 of Table 35-1 in the textbook, shows how the firm's output increases — in physical units — as it hires more labor. By multiplying this increase in physical output by the price at which the firm can sell that output, it is possible to calculate the additional revenue the firm receives as it hires more labor. This is called its marginal revenue product (MRP), and is shown in column 5 of Table 35-1. MRP will also be the value of the marginal product (VMP) provided the firm is selling its output in a perfectly competitive market.

The profit-maximizing firm will demand labor up to the point where the MRP is just equal to the wage rate W. The reason is that, if MRP were greater than W, the firm could increase its profits by hiring more workers; and if MRP were less than W, the firm could increase its profits by hiring fewer workers. Thus the MRP curve

shows how much the firm will hire at each possible wage. In other words, the MRP curve is the firm's labor demand curve.

A firm's demand for labor schedule slopes down because of diminishing returns. (Recall this concept from Figure 23-6.) As a firm hires more and more labor (with other factors fixed), it eventually finds that the marginal physical product of labor — and therefore MRP — decreases. In other words, its demand for labor slopes downward.

There are several reasons why a firm's demand curve for labor might shift:

- If the price of the firm's output falls, MRP and therefore the demand for labor will shift down;

- if the marginal physical product of labor shifts up, MRP and the labor demand curve will also shift up. Such an upward shift might occur, for example, if the firm increases the amount of capital it employs; this would make labor physically more productive by providing it with more machinery to work with. Another example might be a technological improvement that allows a firm to get more physical output from its workers. (Often increased capital equipment and technological change go together, but it is possible for one to occur without the other.)

The market demand curve for labor is just the horizontal sum of the demand curves of all the individual hiring firms. This is similar to the summation of the individual demand curves for a good described in Figure 21-1.

Before turning to the supply curve for labor, we pause briefly to consider a further important interpretation of labor demand.

How the Labor Demand Curve Shows the Distribution of Income

The total income of an industry is the sum of the contributions of all workers employed in that industry. That is, in Figure 35-4 in the textbook, it is the sum of all the individual contributions — such as arrows a and b on the left — of all N workers in this industry. In total, this is area 1 and 2 under the labor demand curve. Of this area representing total industry income, rectangular area 2 is labor income, since it is the quantity of employment (the base of this rectangle) times the wage (the height of this rectangle). The rest — that is, area 1 — goes to other factors of production, in the form of rent, interest and profit.

The Supply of Labor

The height of the labor supply curve indicates how much must be paid to attract one more worker into the industry — that is, the worker's transfer price. This is (roughly) the wage and productivity of this worker in another industry. In other words, the height of the labor supply curve is just the opportunity cost of an additional worker.

Is a Perfectly Competitive Labor Market Efficient?

Efficiency requires that labor be hired in an industry up to the point where its marginal benefit is just equal to its marginal costs. (If there are no externalities — as assumed here — then there is no difference between social and private benefits, and no difference between social and private costs.) The marginal benefit of labor is its productivity in this industry, as given by the labor demand curve. The marginal cost of labor is its opportunity cost — that is, its wage and productivity elsewhere; this is given by its supply curve. Since supply and demand for labor are equated in a perfectly competitive labor market, the marginal cost of labor is equal to the marginal benefit of labor, and this market is therefore efficient.

When a labor market has been shifted away from a perfectly competitive equilibrium, there is an efficiency loss that can be measured by the triangle between the demand curve, the supply curve, and the vertical line at the actual quantity of employment. Examples are provided in panels b and c of Figure 35-6 in the textbook. If such triangular efficiency losses are not clear, you may wish to review the similar analysis that was used in Figure 25-3 to show efficiency losses in product markets. It is essential that you understand these fully, because they will be used frequently.

Although a perfectly competitive labor market is efficient, it does not necessarily follow that a free unregulated labor market is "best," for the following four reasons:

- In an unregulated market, employers may discriminate against minorities, and thus violate the mobility assumption of perfect competition; labor is not free to move into any industry.

- In an unregulated market, employers may have market power, thus violating another assumption of perfect competition.

- There may be externalities.

- Even if none of these problems arise — and an unregulated labor market is efficient — it may not be best because of the way it distributes income.

The Effect of A Minimum Wage

There are four effects when a minimum wage (above the existing equilibrium wage) is introduced into a perfectly competitive labor market.

- Employment is reduced.

- Reduced employment leads to an efficiency loss, similar to the red triangle in panel c of Figure 35-6. (The efficiency loss is even more than this if the minimum wage is imposed across all labor markets.)

- Although the wage received by workers who are still employed in this industry rises, the wage of those who no longer have a job here falls (or disappears altogether). Therefore, on balance the overall effect on total labor income is uncertain.

- The amount of income going to other factors of production will definitely decrease, because the higher wage that must be paid to labor will put a squeeze on these other incomes.

While these four effects can be predicted from our theory, there is another effect that experience has taught us: The unemployment created by minimum wage legislation falls most heavily on teenagers — especially those in minority groups.

The important qualifications to this minimum wage analysis include:

- Even if the minimum wage raises total labor income, workers may not feel that they benefit overall from the change. Even though jobs pay better, they are harder to find; and employers paying a higher wage may no longer feel that they can afford the

cost of on-the-job training that is so beneficial to workers.

- The more industries covered by minimum
wage legislation, the greater the unemploy-

ment it will create. The reason is that it
becomes harder for an unemployed person
to find a job elsewhere, because there are
fewer and fewer other jobs available.

IMPORTANT TERMS

*Match the term in the first column with the corresponding
explanation in the second column.*

_____ 1. Marginal physical product (MPP) of labor
_____ 2. Marginal revenue product (MRP) of labor
_____ 3. Opportunity cost of labor
_____ 4. Value of the marginal product (VMP) of
labor
_____ 5. Transfer price of labor

a. The additional revenue that a firm can earn by
hiring one more worker.
b. The wage necessary to induce a worker to change
jobs.
c. The additional number of units of output that a firm
can produce by hiring one more worker.
d. The wage or productivity of labor in another
industry.
e. Marginal physical product of labor times the price
of the employer's product.

TRUE-FALSE

T   F   1.   The marginal revenue product curve shows the cost to the firm of hiring additional workers.

T   F   2.   A profit-maximizing firm that is operating in perfectly competitive labor and product markets will hire
labor to the point where the value of the marginal product equals the wage rate.

T   F   3.   The demand for labor schedule shifts to the right whenever the marginal revenue product of labor
schedule shifts to the right.

T   F   4.   If the marginal revenue product of labor is less than the wage, a perfectly competitive firm can increase
its profits by hiring more labor.

T   F   5.   One effect of an increase in the minimum wage is a decrease in the income going to factors of production
other than labor.

T   F   6.   Even if there is an external cost of employing labor, a perfectly competitive labor market will still be
efficient.

T   F   7.   The marginal revenue product of labor is the amount the firm's revenue increases when it hires one
more worker.

T   F   8.   The value of the marginal product of labor is the same as the marginal revenue product of labor, if the
hiring firm is a monopolist in its product market.

T   F   9.   The demand for labor by an industry is the horizontal sum of the demand by the individual firms in that
industry.

T   F   10.   If the wage rate rises elsewhere in the economy, the wage and employment in a perfectly competitive
industry will tend to rise.

T   F   11.   There is a greater efficiency loss if the minimum wage is applied just to one industry rather than to all industries.

MULTIPLE CHOICE

1. The marginal physical product of labor:

   a. is based on the assumption that the firm uses a given capital stock as the employment of labor increases
   b. is based on the assumption that the use of capital increases by the same proportion as labor employment
   c. shows the additional revenue a firm can earn because it hires one more worker
   d. is set equal to the wage rate by an employer in equilibrium
   e. is the same as the value of the marginal product

2. A firm's demand curve for labor is the curve showing its:

   a. total physical product of labor
   b. average revenue product of labor
   c. marginal physical product of labor
   d. average physical product of labor
   e. marginal revenue product of labor

3. The demand for labor by a firm producing bolts shifts up in response to:

   a. a rise in the price of bolts
   b. a fall in labor productivity in the bolt-making industry
   c. a downward shift in the demand for bolts
   d. a decrease in the stock of machinery in the industry
   e. a decrease in the stock of other investment equipment in the industry

4. A leftward shift in the labor supply schedule may be the result of:

   a. a rightward shift in the marginal revenue product of labor schedule
   b. a leftward shift in the marginal revenue product of labor schedule
   c. higher available wages in other industries
   d. a fall in labor productivity
   e. a falling opportunity cost of labor

5. Perfect competition in a labor market requires the assumption that workers are

   a. so numerous that each individual can affect the wage rate
   b. so numerous that no individual can affect the wage rate
   c. so few that no individual can affect the wage rate
   d. so few that any individual can affect the wage rate
   e. any of the above, since no assumption is required on this

6. If there is a perfectly competitive market for farm labor, and there is a fall in the price of grain and other farm outputs, then there will be:

   a. a shift to the left in the labor supply curve
   b. a shift to the right in the labor supply curve
   c. a shift to the left in the labor demand curve
   d. a shift to the right in the labor demand curve
   e. a and c

7. The value of the marginal product of labor is equal to the marginal revenue product of labor:

   a. always
   b. never
   c. only if the hiring firm is a monopolist in its product market
   d. only if the hiring firm is a perfect competitor in its product market
   e. only if the hiring firm is an oligopolist in its product market

8. The opportunity cost of labor in an industry:

   a. is approximately measured by the height of the labor demand schedule
   b. is approximately measured by the height of the labor supply schedule
   c. decreases as employment in the industry increases
   d. is completely vertical because labor can switch between industries
   e. is the income that capital can earn elsewhere

9. Which of the following will cause a rightward shift in the labor demand by an industry?

   a. an increase in labor productivity in this industry
   b. a decrease in labor productivity in this industry
   c. an increase in the minimum wage
   d. an increase in the transfer price of labor
   e. a decrease in the transfer price of labor

10. Labor demand by a firm will shift to the left if there is:

   a. a decrease in the minimum wage
   b. an increase in the marginal revenue product of labor
   c. a decrease in the marginal revenue product of labor
   d. an increase in wages in other industries
   e. a decrease in wages in other industries

11. The total area under an industry's demand for labor schedule to the left of the existing quantity of employment equals:

   a. the income received by other factors in the industry
   b. the total income of labor in the industry
   c. the total income of labor and all other factors in the industry
   d. total profits in the industry
   e. the marginal revenue received by the industry

12. If the labor supply curve is vertical, then a technological improvement that increases the marginal physical product of labor will cause:

   a. an increase in the wage and no change in employment
   b. an increase in both the wage and employment
   c. an increase in employment and no change in the wage
   d. a decrease in the wage and no change in employment
   e. a decrease in the wage and an increase in employment

13. In a perfectly competitive labor market for an industry, an increase in wages elsewhere in the economy will result in:

   a. a shift to the right in the labor supply curve
   b. an increase in wages and employment in this industry
   c. a decrease in wages and employment in this industry
   d. a decrease in wages, and an increase in employment in this industry
   e. an increase in wages, and a decrease in employment in this industry

14. Which of the following does not affect an individual worker's transfer price?

   a. the wage in the industry from which the worker is moving
   b. the wage in the industry to which the worker is moving
   c. financial moving costs
   d. psychological moving costs
   e. differences in the attractiveness of working conditions in the new and old industries

15. In a perfectly competitive labor market for an industry, there will be an efficiency loss unless labor is hired up to the point where:

   a. the marginal productivity of labor in this industry exceeds its marginal productivity elsewhere
   b. the marginal productivity of labor in this industry is less than its marginal productivity elsewhere
   c. the marginal productivity of labor in this industry is equal to its marginal productivity elsewhere
   d. the marginal opportunity cost of labor exceeds its marginal productivity in this industry
   e. the marginal opportunity cost of labor is less than its marginal productivity in this industry

16. If less than the perfectly competitive number of workers is hired in an industry:

   a. the marginal productivity of labor in this industry will exceed its marginal productivity elsewhere
   b. the marginal productivity of labor in this industry will be less than its marginal productivity elsewhere
   c. the marginal productivity of labor in this industry will be equal to its marginal productivity elsewhere
   d. the marginal opportunity cost of labor will exceed its marginal productivity in this industry
   e. the marginal opportunity cost of labor will be the same as its marginal productivity in this industry

17. In a perfectly competitive labor market:

   a. employers hire labor up to the point where they maximize their profit
   b. employers hire labor up to the point where their marginal benefit is equal to their marginal cost
   c. employees supply labor services up to the point where their marginal benefit is equal to their marginal cost
   d. there is an efficient level of employment
   e. all of the above

18. In perfectly competitive markets with no government regulation, minority groups have tended to be:

    a. first hired, first fired
    b. first hired, last fired
    c. last hired, first fired
    d. last hired, last fired
    e. faced with special problems, unless the individuals concerned were teenagers

19. A minimum wage can increase efficiency if:

    a. there is a major problem with teenage unemployment
    b. all wages in the economy are already above the minimum wage
    c. all wages in the economy are below the minimum wage
    d. all wages in the economy are the same as the minimum wage
    e. the labor market is not perfectly competitive

20. The unemployment created by minimum wage legislation is particularly severe among:

    a. all white workers
    b. teenage whites
    c. white collar workers
    d. minority teenagers
    e. auto workers

21. An economy-wide labor supply curve will "bend backwards" if:

    a. an increase in the wage rate induces labor to work more
    b. workers decide to use their increase in wages to "buy more leisure"
    c. workers decide to use all their increase in wages to buy more goods
    d. the substitution effect of a higher wage dominates the income effect
    e. there is no cost of living allowance in wage contracts

EXERCISES

1   a. Fill in the missing data in Table 35.1 for a hypothetical firm with a given stock of capital, and selling its output in a competitive market at a constant price.

Table 35.1

Number of workers	Total physical output	Marginal physical product of labor	Marginal revenue product (MRP) when price of output is $10 per unit	Marginal revenue product (MRP) when price of output is $15 per unit
0	0			
1	12			
2	19			
3	24			
4	28			
5	30			

If the wage rate is $55 per worker per day, then the firm will want to hire _____ workers if the price of its output is $10, and _____ workers when this price is $15.

b. Fill in the missing data in Table 35.2 for another hypothetical firm, assuming that the wage it faces is $40 per worker per day and the price of its output is $5.

Table 35.2

Number of workers	Total physical output	Marginal physical product	Marginal revenue product
0	0	—	—
1		10	
2		9	
3		8	
4		7	
5		6	

The firm will be willing to hire no more than _____ workers. With this amount of employment, the firm's total revenue will be _____, its total wage payment will be $_____, and the income of other factors will be $_____.

2. Plot the labor demand schedule of this firm in Figure 35.1. Draw a horizontal line at the wage rate of $40 per worker per day. Label as 1 the area representing labor income. Label as 2 the area representing the income going to other factors.

Figure 35.1

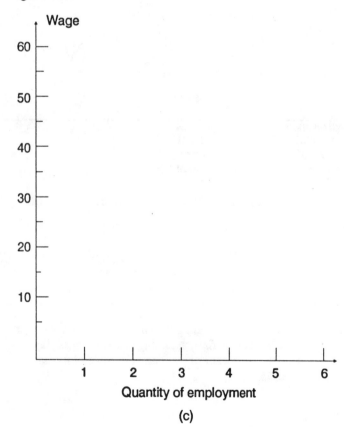

(c)

3. Figure 35.2 depicts a perfectly competitive labor market with no externalities. The equilibrium wage rate is _____, and the equilibrium quantity of employment is _____. Suppose a minimum wage of U is imposed. Then employment will be _____. Next, suppose the minimum wage is H. Then employment will be _____ and the difference between demand and supply will be _____. Fill in Table 35.3.

Figure 35.2

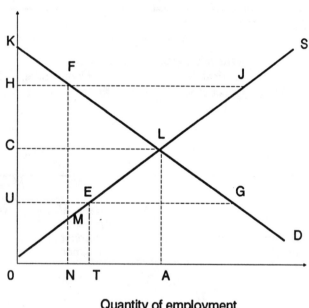

Quantity of employment

Table 35.3

	Efficiency loss is area:	Total labor income is area:	Income of other factors is area:
No minimum wage			
Minimum Wage at U			
Minimum wage at H			

4. (This requires study of the text, especially Box 35-1.) A perfectly competitive labor market is shown in Figure 35.3.

Figure 35.3

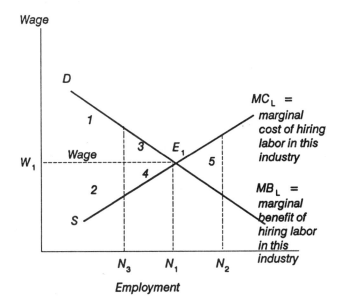

a. The marginal productivity of labor (VMP) in this industry is shown by the _____ curve, while the marginal productivity of labor elsewhere is shown by the _____ curve. The equilibrium is at _____, with wage _____ and employment of _____ workers. At this equilibrium,

employers have (maximized, minimized) their profit by hiring labor up to the point where its marginal benefit – that is, the marginal productivity of labor in this industry as shown by the _____ curve – is equal to the marginal cost the employers face, as shown by _____. At the same time, employees have (minimized, maximized) their own net benefit by offering their labor up to the point where their marginal benefit – as shown by _____ – is equal to their marginal cost, shown by _____. This marginal cost to employees is called a (substitute, opportunity) cost, because it represents their potential earnings in their (least, most) attractive alternative job.

b. If employment is at N_2, there is an efficiency (gain, loss) of area _____ because the N_2N_1 extra workers employed would have (higher, lower) marginal productivity elsewhere – as shown by the _____ curve – than in this industry where their marginal productivity is shown by the _____ curve. On the other hand, if employment in this industry is at N_3, then there is an efficiency (gain, loss) because N_3N_1 workers should be employed in this industry, but are not. These workers would have marginal productivity here shown by the _____ curve compared to their (lower, higher) marginal productivity elsewhere, as shown by the height of the _____ curve. Only at an employment level of _____ can one or the other of these types of efficiency losses be avoided.

ESSAY QUESTIONS

1. "The labor demand schedule slopes down for the same reason that the demand curve for a consumer good slopes down." Explain to what extent this is or is not true.

2. List and explain some influences that could shift the labor supply curve for an industry. In each case, indicate in which direction the shift would occur.

3. Over the past 50 years, the number of domestic servants in the United States has fallen dramatically. Do you think this is because of the price and availability of labor-saving household appliances? Or is it due to rising wages in other occupations? Or do both factors play a role? Explain how each affects the supply and demand for domestic help.

4. Discuss the influences that affect the elasticity of demand for labor, by first reviewing the influences affecting the elasticity of demand for a consumer good discussed in Chapter 20 in the text.

5. How would the supply of labor in a particular market be affected by a decrease in the cost of moving from one city to another?

6. Would you expect labor market discrimination to be more of a problem in a perfectly competitive industry or in a monopolistic industry?

ANSWERS

Match the Columns: 1 c, 2 a, 3 d, 4 e, 5 b

True-False:
1 F (p. 652)
2 T (p. 653)
3 T (p. 653)
4 F (p. 653)
5 T (p. 655)
6 F (p. 660)
7 T (p. 651)
8 F (p. 652)
9 T (p. 654)
10 F (p. 655)
11 F (p. 660)

Multiple Choice:
1 a (p. 652)
2 e (p. 653)
3 a (p. 653)
4 c (pp. 655-656)
5 b (p. 650)
6 c (p. 653)
7 d (p. 652)
8 b (p. 655)
9 a (p. 653)
10 c (p. 653)
11 c (p. 655)
12 a (p. 654)
13 e (pp. 654, 655)
14 b (p. 655, BOX)
15 c (p. 657)
16 a (p. 657)
17 e (pp. 658, 659, BOX)
18 c (p. 661)
19 e (p. 661)
20 d (p. 661)
21 b (p. 664, APPENDIX)

Exercises

1   a.

Table 35.1 Completed

Number of workers	Total physical output	Marginal physical product of labor	Marginal revenue product (MRP) when price of output is $10 per unit	Marginal revenue product (MRP) when price of output is $15 per unit
0	0	—	—	—
1	12	12	120	180
2	19	7	70	105
3	24	5	50	75
4	28	4	40	60
5	30	2	20	30

2, 4.

b.

Table 35.2 Completed

Number of workers	Total physical output	Marginal physical product	Marginal revenue product
0	0	—	—
1	10	10	$50
2	19	9	45
3	27	8	40
4	34	7	35
5	40	6	30

3, $135, $120, $15

2.

Figure 35.1 Completed

3.   C, A, A, N, FJ.

Table 35.3 Completed

	Efficiency loss is area:	Total labor income is area:	Income of other factors is area:
No minimum wage	zero	OCLA	KLC
Minimum Wage at U	zero	OCLA	KLC
Minimum wage at H	FLM	OHFN	KFH

4   a.   D, S, E_1, W_1, N_1, maximized, D, W_1E_1, maximized, W_1E_1, S, opportunity, most.

        b.   loss, 5, higher, S, D, loss, D, lower, S, N_1.

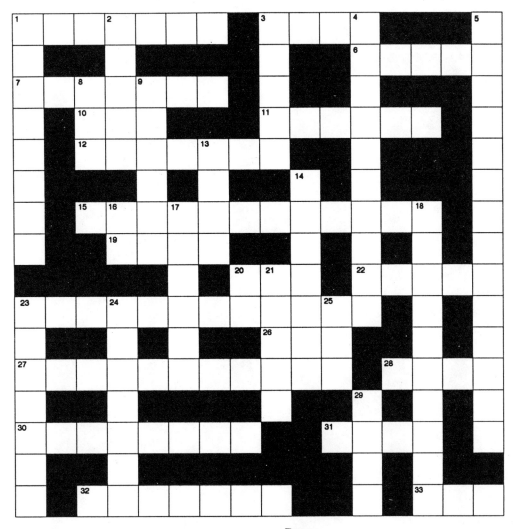

Across

1, 3. proponents say this raises the incomes of the poor; critics say it causes unemployment
6. gas commonly used as a refrigerant
7. he explained the idea of comparative advantage
10. historical period
11. a barrier to international trade
12. one of the arguments for the protection of domestic industry from foreign competition
15. Bastiat suggested that these people might object to the unfair competition from the sun
19. new (German, fem.)
20. a flying mammal
22. "The British are coming," Paul Revere _____
23. the key to rising living standards
26. tool for propelling a boat
27, 28. where this is low, a country has a comparative advantage
30. form an association of workers
31. this type of theory deals with conflicts
32. a third type of efficiency (in addition to allocative and technological efficiency)
33. he is associated with idea that, in aggregate, supply creates its own demand

Down

1, 23. in a perfectly competitive economy, the wage is equal to the value of this
2. picture
3. in an efficient economy, this is avoided
4. the goal of getting the most out of our productive efforts
5. one of the major agruments for tariffs (2 words)
8. ungentlemanly chap
9. do this to oil to produce gasoline
13. African river
14. he suggested that tariffs were equivalent to a "negative railway"
16. one
17. sweet, melodious
18. externalities
20. twice, doubly, involving two (prefix)
21. a good lawyer can often help clients to _____ taxes
24. industry with only two sellers
25. attempt
29. organization for negotiating over tariffs and other trade barriers (abbrev.)

WAGES IN IMPERFECTLY COMPETITIVE LABOR MARKETS

LEARNING OBJECTIVES

After you have studied this chapter in the textbook and the study guide, you should be able to

✔ Describe how and why union membership changed in the various periods of U.S. labor history.

✔ Identify the laws that have been important in encouraging or deterring the U.S. labor movement, and state the major provisions of each

✔ Show in a diagram the inefficiency that results when a union succeeds in raising wages in an otherwise perfectly competitive labor market

✔ Describe, on the other hand, the special ways that a union may improve efficiency

✔ Show, in particular, how efficiency may be increased if a union is formed in a labor market that has previously been monopsonized

✔ Analyze bilateral monopoly, where market power is held by a monopoly (a single seller) on one side of the market, and by a monopsony (a single buyer) on the other

✔ Explain why a strike may occur even though there is a large collective loss from it

✔ Show why there may be large internal and external costs if labor negotiations break down and a strike occurs

✔ Identify three ways of trying to avert an imminent strike

✔ Explain the possible imbalance of bargaining power when a public service union negotiates with a government

✔ State four reasons why workers get different wages.

MAJOR PURPOSE

The key objective in this chapter is to analyze what happens when labor markets are not perfectly competitive. Typically, the result is inefficiency, and this is compared with the efficient outcome when labor markets are perfectly competitive, as described in the last chapter.

Elements of imperfect competition may appear on either side of the labor market. On the one side, workers may form a union which, as a monopoly (a single seller of labor services) is able to raise the wage rate. On the other side, there may be a monopsony firm (a single buyer of labor services) that is able to lower the wage rate. In either case, an inefficiently low amount of labor is hired. The interesting case of bilateral monopoly arises when there is a monopoly (a union) on the workers' side of the market, and a monopsony on the employers side. Illustrations are provided to show how difficult and complicated wage bargaining can be in this case. In particular, special problems arise in any bargaining between a monopoly union of public service workers and their monopsony employer — the government.

HIGHLIGHTS OF CHAPTER

The major topics covered in this chapter include:

- the history of the labor union movement in the United States;

- the effects of introducing a union into an otherwise perfectly competitive labor market;

- the effects of a monopsony (a single buyer) in an otherwise perfectly competitive labor market;

- a description of bilateral monopoly, where a monopoly union bargains with a monopsony employer;

- the reasons why public service employees form a union, but the special problems that then arise; and

- the reasons why wages aren't the same for all workers.

The History of the U.S. Labor Movement

Figure 36-1 in the textbook shows the three distinct periods in U.S. labor history:

1. Prior to 1935, union membership was very low. The key player during this period was the American Federation of Labor (AFL), a collection of craft unions — that is, unions that draw members from any industry, provided they have a common skill. In those early days, strikes were not an effective union tactic because, for example, employers could easily get a court injunction forcing workers back to their jobs. This practice was ended in 1932 by the Norris-LaGuardia Act, which limited injunctions to protecting property and preventing violence.

2. From 1935 to 1945 union membership grew rapidly, aided by two major events:

   - The founding in 1936 of the CIO, a collection of industrial unions. (An industrial union draws its members from a single industry regardless of their skills.)

   - The Wagner Act of 1935 which

     ° made it clear that workers had the right to form a union

     ° prohibited various unfair labor practices of employers

     ° established the National Labor Relations Board (NLRB) to prevent unfair labor practices and to settle disputes between unions.

3. In the period since 1945, union membership has steadily declined as a percentage of the labor force. During the preceding years — that is, the last years of World War II — some people felt that unions had used their newly gained power irresponsibly, in strikes that were damaging to the war effort. As a result, the labor movement entered this post-1945 period facing some public hostility.

   You should be familiar with two major labor laws that were passed during this third period. The first was the Taft-Hartley Act of 1947, which

   - outlawed closed shops in industries engaged in interstate commerce

   - outlawed jurisdictional strikes

   - outlawed the practice of checking off union dues

- imposed restrictions on union leaders that forced them to be financially more responsible

- empowered the President to seek a court injunction forcing strikers to return to work for an 80-day "cooling off" period if there was a strike that endangered national health or safety.

- declared, in its famous section 14(b), that closed ships and union shops are illegal in any state that decides to pass a right-to-work law.

The other major law was the Landrum-Griffin Act of 1959, which imposed even more financial restrictions upon union leaders and strengthened the power of union members to challenge their leaders. This third period of declining union membership extended into the early 80s, when unions came under further pressures. These pressures included stronger—indeed sometimes illegal—management opposition; the severe recession of 1981-2 and the threat by firms to move their plants to the less unionized Southern states or abroad; and the strong action taken by President Reagan in firing air controllers and decertifying their union when they went out on an illegal strike.

The Effects of Unions

A union gives workers a voice in presenting grievances to their employer. It also negotiates with management to establish seniority rules and improve working conditions. These benefit not only the workers but also the employer who is able to offer more attractive jobs and therefore reduce quit rates.

But the main objectives of a union are to protect the jobs and raise the wages of its members. According to recent estimates, unionized workers get 10 - 15% higher wages than comparable nonunionized workers. If a union is established that raises the wage in a previously competitive labor market, there are three main effects:

- there is a reduction in employment and in the income of workers who consequently lose their jobs;

- there is an increase in the wages and incomes of workers who still have jobs, with this increase coming at the expense of other factors of production; and

- there is a triangular efficiency loss that can be measured by the usual geometric technique.

Study Figure 36-2 in the textbook until you can demonstrate these three effects on your own.

Finally, a union tries to protect its members' jobs in several ways. For example,

- It may try to negotiate a shorter work week. If there is unemployment, fewer hours per worker means more workers can get jobs.

- It can press the government to restrict imports. In chapter 34 we saw that this may indeed increase U.S. employment in the short run. However, any employment gains are likely to be wiped out if our trading partners retaliate; and even if they don't, such protection will have damaging effects on the economy.

The analysis in Figure 36-2 of the efficiency loss that results from a union is overly harsh, because in some ways not shown in this diagram, unions improve efficiency. First, by giving workers a voice, unions provide them with an alternative to quitting or being fired when a problem arises. Thus, they save unnecessary costs of labor turnover. Second, by improving working conditions they can reduce the tension between workers and employers, and thus create a more productive atmosphere. Third, a union's bargaining power may simply offset the bargaining power of monopsonist employers; in this case, a union may increase efficiency. (Remember that our earlier discussion of the efficiency losses from a union applies only if the labor market is perfectly competitive otherwise.)

Monopsony

As a single employer of labor, a monopsony tries to exploit its market power by reducing wages. If it succeeds—in an otherwise perfectly competitive labor market—the three main effects will be to

- transfer income from labor to other factors of production;

- reduce employment; and

- create an efficiency loss.

Study Figure 36-3 in the textbook until you can demonstrate these three effects on your own.

Bilateral Monopoly

In this case of "two-sided" monopoly, market power is held both by a union on the one side, and by a monopsonistic employer on the other. This case is the most difficult to analyze.

To illustrate, suppose a union is formed in a labor market where a monopsonist employer has been keeping the wage rate below the perfectly competitive level. In this case, the formation of the union may raise the wage back towards the perfectly competitive level. If this is the outcome, the union will be simply undoing some of the effects of the monopsony. Specifically, the union will

- transfer income back from other factors of production to labor,

- increase employment, and

- reduce the efficiency loss from monopsony. Before reading further make sure you can illustrate these effects with a diagram similar to Figure 36-5 in the textbook.

However, the outcome is not this simple to predict, because there is no guarantee that a newly formed union will only raise wages towards the perfectly competitive level; it may raise wages beyond this. If this happens we can no longer be sure that the union will increase efficiency. This is the basic problem in analyzing bilateral monopoly: We don't know where the wage will be set. All we know for sure is that the wage will be somewhere between the high wage the union seeks, and the lower wage the monopsonistic employer seeks. At what point the wage will be determined within this range depends on the bargaining power of each side. This in turn depends partly on the ability of each to outlast the other in the event of a strike. Thus, the bargaining power of the union depends upon the size of the union's strike fund. The bargaining power of the employer depends upon the size of its inventories of finished goods that it can continue to sell during a strike.

Strikes

In a sense, everyone is damaged by a strike. The employer loses profits, and the labor force loses wages. Nevertheless, strikes do occur, because

- each side may see a strike as a way of getting a more favourable wage rate than the other side's final offer on the eve of the strike;

- each side may want to increase its future credibility and bargaining power by clearly demonstrating that it is prepared to allow a strike to take place; or

- either side may make a bargaining mistake that prevents agreement from being reached before a strike deadline. (Nevertheless, the average U.S. worker spends less than one day a year on strike).

One reason why strikes pose an important issue for public policy is spillovers—that is, costs of strikes to people not involved in the bargaining. For example, a transit strike prevents people from getting to their jobs.

There are several possible ways of averting a strike when the two sides are unable to reach agreement on their own.

- The President may seek a Taft-Hartley injunction that forces workers back to their jobs for an 80-day cooling off period.

- A mediator may be appointed to seek a non-binding compromise solution.

- Both sides may agree to arbitration, in which a third party decides upon a settlement that both sides agree in advance to accept.

Unions of Public Service Employees

Unions in the public sector raise problems because they have such a strong bargaining position, for the following reasons.

- There are large spillover costs to the voting public when public servants such as transit workers or the police go on strike. Thus voters may exert great pressure on the government to settle the dispute.

- Public servants know that, in the last analysis, it is typically easier for a government than for a private company to raise the funds necessary to pay a higher wage. The government can tax or borrow in a way that is not available to private employers.

- A union has much greater bargaining power over a financially weak government than it would have over a financially weak private employer. The reason is that a strike won't force a government out of business, but it might drive a private employer bankrupt, in which case there are no jobs to negotiate about.

- Because public service employees now constitute a large bloc of voters, politicians are reluctant to fight hard against their wage demands.

Because public servants have such a strong bargaining position, it is often suggested that they should not be allowed to strike, or even form a union. But this would raise a problem. If these workers cannot form a union, how can they defend themselves against a monopsonistic employer (the government). If not with a union, what else?

Wage Differences

Wage differences can exist for at least five different reasons: First, there may be dynamic wage differentials. When new job opportunities open up in an industry, wages must rise temporarily to attract workers from other industries. Eventually, the influx of new workers will bring the wages back down. Second, compensating wage differentials give workers more pay for especially hazardous or unpleasant jobs. Third, monopoly or monopsony power may be greater in some labor markets than in others. Fourth, barriers to entry can keep wages artificially high in some jobs. Fifth, those with special talents and skills earn a higher wage because they are more productive, as we shall see in the next chapter.

IMPORTANT TERMS

Match the term in the first column with the corresponding explanation in the second column

_____ 1. Seniority rules
_____ 2. Industrial union
_____ 3. Craft union
_____ 4. Collective bargaining
_____ 5. American Federation of Labor (AFL)
_____ 6. National Labor Relations Act
_____ 7. Congress of Industrial Organizations (CIO)
_____ 8. Closed shop
_____ 9. Union shop
_____10. Open shop
_____11. Right-to-work law
_____12. Jurisdictional dispute
_____13. Checkoff
_____14. National Labor Relations Board
_____15. Monopsony
_____16. Strike fund
_____17. Injunction
_____18. Mediation
_____19. Arbitration
_____20. Dynamic wage differentials
_____21. Compensating wage differentials

a. A collection of industrial unions
b. A union whose members all belong to the same craft or profession, although they may work in different industries. Examples are the plumbers' union and the carpenters' union.
c. The specification of a third party to suggest a compromise settlement in a labor dispute. The third party cannot make binding recommendations.
d. Differences that may arise if labor views some jobs as less attractive than others. (Employers have to pay a higher wage to fill the unattractive jobs.)
e. Preference in hiring and firing to those who have been longest on the job.
f. A union whose members all work in the same industry, or group of industries, although they may belong to different crafts or professions. Examples are the United Auto Workers and the United Mine Workers.
g. An agency that controls unfair labor practices by employers and resolves disputes among unions.
h. A statute making closed ships or union shops illegal.
i. A firm in which anyone hired by an employer must join the union within some specified period.
j. Differences in wages that arise because of changing demand or supply conditions in the labor market. These differences tend to disappear over time as labor moves out of relatively low wage jobs and into those that pay a relatively high wage.
k. A collection of craft unions, formed by Samuel Gompers.
l. Negotiations between a union and an employer over wages, fringe benefits, hiring policies, job security, and working conditions.
m. A court order compelling someone to refrain from a particular act, such as a strike.
n. A firm in which an employer can hire only workers who are already union members.
o. A sum of money owned by a union for the purpose of supporting its members while on strike.
p. A single buyer.
q. The practice of having employers collect union dues by deducting them from workers' paychecks.
r. The Wagner Act of 1935.
s. A conflict between unions over whose members will do specific jobs.
t. A firm in which employees do not have to be in a union.
u. The specification of a third party to suggest a compromise settlement in a labor dispute. The decision of the third party is binding on both labor and management.

TRUE-FALSE

T   F   1.   Bilateral monopoly in the labor market means that employers are exercising monopsony power and labor is exercising monopoly power.

T   F   2.   An industrial union draws its members from any industry, provided they have a common skill (such as plumbing).

T   F   3.   The United Auto Workers is a craft union.

T   F   4.   Samuel Gompers' American Federation of Labor was an attempt to organize labor for a political class struggle, rather than for the pursuit of improved wages and working conditions.

T   F   5.   If wages are reduced below what they would be in perfect competition there will be a loss in efficiency.

T   F   6.   A monopolist in the labor market will seek to raise wages, while a monopsonist will seek to lower them.

T   F   7.   Other things equal, a company producing perishable goods is more vulnerable to strike threats than one producing durable goods.

T   F   8.   The spillover cost of a strike must be less than the internal cost to the industry in which the strike occurs.

T   F   9.   Public service unions have recently been growing less rapidly than other unions.

T   F   10.   Compensating wage differentials would not exist if workers viewed all jobs as equally attractive.

MULTIPLE CHOICE

1. When a union negotiates seniority rules, workers with seniority are typically:

   a. the first to be laid off and the first to be rehired
   b. the first to be laid off and the last to be rehired
   c. the last to be laid off and the last to be rehired
   d. the last to be laid off and the first to be rehired
   e. left unaffected in terms of being laid off or rehired

2. Craft unions draw their membership from:

   a. workers in companies that build pleasure boats
   b. workers in companies that build any boats
   c. all workers in a specific industry regardless of their skills
   d. all workers in a specific industry provided they have the same skill
   e. all workers from any industry provided they have the same skill

3. Unions:

   a. negotiate higher wages
   b. negotiate improved working conditions
   c. have occasionally been getting voting seats on boards of directors
   d. act as a social forum for their members
   e. all of the above

4. Which of the following Acts first made it clear that workers had the legal right to form a union?

   a. Norris-LaGuardia
   b. Taft-Hartley
   c. Landrum-Griffin
   d. Wagner
   e. Sherman

5. Union membership has fallen steadily as a proportion of total employment since 1945, partly because:

   a. employment in heavy industry has decreased as a proportion of total employment
   b. the foundation of the CIO in 1945 reduced workers' incentive to form a union
   c. the foundation of the AFL in 1945 reduced workers' incentive to form a union
   d. the AFL and CIO amalgamated in 1955
   e. much heavy industry had moved to the north

Chapter 36 Wages in Imperfectly Competitive Labor Markets

6. Which of the following acts outlawed closed shops in industries engaged in interstate commerce?

   a. Norris-LaGuardia
   b. Taft-Hartley
   c. Landrum-Griffin
   d. Wagner
   e. Clayton

7. Which of the following provides the greatest barrier to entry into a work force?

   a. open shop
   b. closed shop
   c. union shop
   d. Taft-Hartley Act
   e. right-to-work legislation

8. In a union shop, a firm:

   a. can hire only workers who are already union members
   b. can hire only workers who have already worked in a union shop
   c. can hire only workers who have already worked in an open shop
   d. can hire non-union workers provided they join a union within a brief specified period
   e. can hire any workers, who then have the option of joining or not joining a union

9. Under the two-tiered wage structure that appeared in the 1980s, existing workers receive:

   a. the old wage, while new workers receive a lower wage
   b. the old wage, while new workers receive a higher wage
   c. a new lower wage, while new workers receive the old wage
   d. the same wage as new workers, but greater non-wage benefits
   e. a new lower wage, while new workers receive a higher wage

10. Unions came under pressure in the 1980s because of:

    a. the threat by firms to move their plants abroad
    b. the threat by firms to move their plants to the South
    c. management's stiffer opposition, occasionally in the form of the illegal firing of workers for union activities

d. the deregulation of some industries
e. all the above

11. If a union formed in a perfectly competitive labor market successfully raises wages, then:

    a. income is transferred from other factors of production to all workers
    b. income is transferred from other factors of production to workers who still have a job in this industry
    c. there is an efficiency gain from increased employment
    d. there is an efficiency loss from increased employment
    e. there is an efficiency gain from reduced employment

12. Unions improve efficiency by:

    a. raising wages above what they would be under perfect competition
    b. reducing labor turnover by giving workers the chance to present their grievances rather than quit or be fired
    c. increasing labor turnover by negotiating higher wages
    d. increasing employment above its perfectly competitive level
    e. b and d

13. If a firm can only hire workers who are already union members, it is described as a:

    a. constrained shop
    b. closed shop
    c. union shop
    d. open shop
    e. restricted shop

14. Which of the following is most likely to occur if a union is introduced into a previously competitive labor market with no externalities?

    a. Total income to labor will decrease
    b. The income of some individual workers will increase
    c. Employment in that market will increase
    d. Incomes of non-labor factors of production will increase
    e. An efficiency gain will result

15. The introduction of labor-saving machinery:

   a. may create temporary unemployment, and result in worse jobs for labor in the long run
   b. may create temporary unemployment, but results in higher wages for labor in the long run
   c. may temporarily raise employment, but results in worse jobs for labor in the long run
   d. may create temporary unemployment, and results in lower wages in the long run
   e. has no effect on employment in either the short or the long run

16. Unions may have beneficial effects on efficiency:

   a. by removing labor's collective voice and thus reducing distractions in the workplace
   b. by reducing communication between labor and management, and thus reducing distractions facing managers
   c. by increasing quit-rates
   d. by reducing quit-rates
   e. by increasing management's market power to raise wages

17. Employment will be increased in an otherwise perfectly competitive labor market by

   a. the introduction of a union whose main effect is to raise wages
   b. collusion by employers to act together like a monopsonist
   c. an increase in the minimum wage

   d. the introduction of a closed shop
   e. none of the above

18. A union's negotiating power will be increased most by:

   a. a large union strike fund
   b. a small union strike fund
   c. a right-to-work law
   d. large inventory holdings by the employer
   e. reduced tariff protection on the employer's output

19. In a labor market with a strong union, the creation of a monopsony bargaining association by employers tends to:

   a. raise wages even further
   b. lower wages
   c. transfer income from other factors of production to labor
   d. a and c
   e. none of the above

20. Baseball salaries before-and-after the players' escape from the reserve clause illustrate:

   a. how much unions can raise salaries
   b. how much unions can lower salaries
   c. how much monopsonists can raise salaries
   d. how much monopsonists can lower salaries
   e. the countervailing power of a union

EXERCISES

1 a. In Figure 36-1, MC_L is supply and MB_L is demand in a perfectly competitive labor market with no externalities. The equilibrium wage is _____ and the equilibrium quantity of employment is _____. In perfect competition the income of labor is area _____, and the income of other factors is area _____.

Figure 36.1

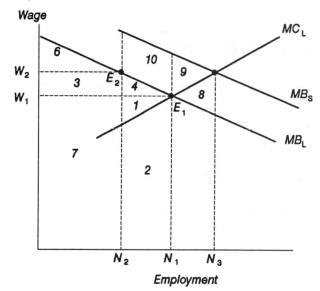

b. Suppose now that a union is formed, which increases the wage to W_2. Then the quantity of employment will be _____, the income going to labor still in this industry will be _____, the income going to other factors will be _____, and the efficiency (gain, loss) will be _____.

c. Now suppose that there is an external benefit from hiring labor in this activity. (To use the example cited in Chapter 35: Suppose the workers being hired are musicians. They provide not only a direct benefit to their employer — the symphony orchestra — whenever they play in a concert, but also an external benefit because of their other contributions to the cultural like of the community.) Because of this external benefit, the marginal social benefit of labor is MB_S rather than just the employers' benefit MB_L. Then the efficient quantity of employment will be _____. In perfect competition the wage will be _____, the quantity of employment will be _____, and the efficiency (gain, loss) will be _____.

d. With this externality, if a union is formed to raise wages to W_2, then the quantity of employment will equal _____ and the efficiency (gain, loss) will equal _____.

2. In Figure 36-2, D represents the demand for labor while area 1 represents the external cost of a strike.

Figure 36.2

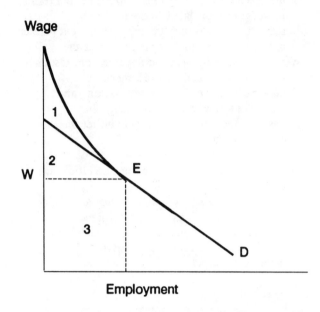

If a strike occurs, the cost to labor — in terms of lost wages — is area _____, while the loss of income by other factors in this industry is area _____. This means that the total internal cost to all factors in this industry is _____. In addition, there is an (external/internal) cost of area _____. Therefore the total cost to society of a strike in this industry is _____. The problem with a strike is that the labor and management participants in the negotiation only take into account (external/internal) costs. No account may be taken of the additional cost to other groups shown as _____. Compulsory arbitration or a Taft-Hartley (closed shop/injunction) may be viewed as a way of injecting the public interest into the negotiations.

ESSAY QUESTIONS

1. "Unions represent just one special form of monopoly, and should not be allowed to exist." What is your position on this? Explain why.

2. Do you think that unions help or hinder the attempt to achieve (a) stable prices (b) an equitable distribution of incomes

3. If there is no union on one side of the market to raise wages, and no collusion or association by employers on the other side of the market to lower wages, compare the bargaining position of the individual worker and the individual employer.

4. Describe the conditions under which an increase in the minimum wage may increase the amount of employment.

5. Describe the spillovers if each of the following went on strike:

   a. Municipal garbage workers
   b. Air traffic controllers
   c. City police
   d. Steel workers

6. In the summer of 1980, the orchestra members of New York's Metropolitan Opera went on strike. Their union leaders thought they had a lot of bargaining power because of the opera's recent financial success. Why might this strengthen the union's bargaining power? Why might that bargaining power also have been strengthened by the knowledge that the opera would be receiving a large income from the nationally televised live performances that were to begin in the fall of 1980? After failing to reach agreement with the union, the management of the opera announced that the whole season would have to be cancelled, and offered to refund the tickets already bought. Eventually, one more round of negotiations was undertaken, agreement was reached, and management announced that the season could proceed after all, but with fewer operas than planned. Do you suppose that the announcement of cancellation of the season helped to speed up a resolution of the strike? Why or why not?

ANSWERS

Important Terms: 1 e, 2 f, 3 b, 4 l, 5 k, 6 r, 7 a, 8 n, 9 i, 10 t, 11 h, 12 s, 13 q, 14 g, 15 p, 16 o, 17 m, 18 c, 19 u, 20 j, 21 d.

True-False:	**1** T (p. 676)
	2 F (p. 668)
	3 F (p. 668)
	4 F (p. 668)
	5 T (p. 674)
	6 T (pp. 672, 674)
	7 T (p. 677)
	8 F (p. 681)
	9 F (p. 683)
	10 T (p. 684)
Multiple Choice:	**1** d (p. 666)
	2 e (p. 668)
	3 e (pp. 665-667)
	4 d (p. 669)
	5 a (p. 669)
	6 b (p. 670)
	7 b (p. 670)
	8 d (p. 670)
	9 a (p. 671)
	10 e (p. 671)
	11 b (p. 672)
	12 b (p. 673)
	13 b (p. 670)
	14 b (p. 672)
	15 b (p. 667, BOX)
	16 d (p. 673)
	17 e (pp. 672, 674)
	18 a (p. 677)
	19 b (p. 676)
	20 d (p. 674)

Exercises

1 a. W_1, N_1, $7 + 1 + 2$, $6 + 3 + 4$.
   b. N_2, $3 + 7$, 6, loss, $1 + 4$.
   c. N_3, W_1, N_1, loss, 9.
   d. N_2, loss, $1 + 4 + 9 + 10$.

2. 3, 2, $2 + 3$, external, 1, $1 + 2 + 3$, internal, 1, injunction.

CHAPTER 37

OTHER INCOMES

LEARNING OBJECTIVES

After you have studied this chapter in the textbook and the study guide, you should be able to

✔ Explain how the public receives an interest income for providing business with debt capital, and how the public receives a profit income for providing business with equity capital

✔ Explain how the demand for loanable funds is related to the marginal efficiency of investment schedule

✔ Show in a diagram how an interest rate ceiling imposed on a perfectly competitive market for loanable funds will affect efficiency and redistribute income

✔ Explain why it is a fallacy to suppose that interest rate ceilings necessarily help poor people

✔ Compare an investment in human capital and an investment in physical capital

✔ Describe the basic roles played by factor prices in a market economy

✔ Explain why it is difficult to measure the rate of return on human capital

✔ Describe estimates of the rate of return on various types of human capital

✔ Define rent and explain why it can be earned not only by land, but by any factor of production

✔ Give three examples of rent, in addition to rent on land

✔ Describe how rent is capitalized in the value of land

✔ Explain why foreign investment in the United States may be beneficial not only to foreign investors, but also to Americans

MAJOR PURPOSE

In the previous two chapters, we analyzed labor income. The objective of this chapter is to analyze other forms of income — specifically, interest, profits, and rent. For example, in discussing interest rates, we see how they are determined by supply and demand in the market for loanable funds. This simple analysis is then extended to show the efficiency and equity effects when the government intervenes to impose a ceiling on interest rates.

While our initial emphasis in this chapter is on the income earned by physical capital, such as buildings and machinery, the focus shifts on page 694 to another important form of capital — human capital in the form of education and training. One form of human capital is a college education, and returns to such an investment are examined. Finally, this chapter analyzes rent — the return to a factor of production above its opportunity cost (that is, above the income it could earn in an alternative activity). Rent is earned not only by land, but also by any other highly productive factor. Examples include the rent earned by highly skilled baseball players or business executives.

HIGHLIGHTS OF CHAPTER

The last chapter was on the income of labor. This chapter is on the *income earned by other factors*, that is, the income earned by capital — physical and human — and the income earned by land.

First, *the income earned by physical capital* such as plant and machinery. This income goes as:

- **interest** to those who have made loans to business to buy plant and equipment — that is, to those who have provided **debt capital** to business;

- **profit** to those who have provided funds to business to buy plant and equipment by buying shares (stock in that business) — that is, to those who have provided **equity capital** to business.

The Rate of Interest

The interest rate may be viewed as a price — the price that equates the demand and supply of loanable funds. The demand for loanable funds reflects the marginal efficiency of investment — that is, the productivity of investment. Whenever you see a demand curve for loanable funds you should visualize it as enclosing the vertical arrows in Figure 37-1 in the textbook, with each of these arrows representing the marginal efficiency of investment.

The supply of loanable funds measures the willingness of savers to part with present income — that is, their willingness to defer present consumption until the future when the loan is repaid. The higher the rate of interest, the greater their reward and the more they are willing to save. Whenever you see a supply curve for loanable funds you should visualize it as enclosing a whole set of vertical arrows (like the one shown in Figure 37-2). Each reflects the value of funds in their alternative use — consumption.

In practice, there is not one rate of interest but many, because of differences in risk. The greater the risk that a borrower will be unable to repay a loan, the higher the rate of interest that this particular borrower will have to pay. Interest rates are also influenced by a number of other factors, such as the expectation of inflation and the length of term of the loan. In addition, the expectation of a change in future interest rates will affect today's interest rates.

An important policy question studied in this section is: What happens if the government imposes an interest-rate ceiling? If the market for loanable funds is perfectly competitive, there are likely to be four main effects of such a policy:

- The public saves less because the interest reward for savings has been reduced. Consequently, fewer loans are made and there is less investment.

- Because investment is reduced, there is an efficiency loss, shown by the familiar triangle in Figure 37-3.

- There is likely to be an additional efficiency loss, because investment funds must be rationed, and the borrowers who do succeed in acquiring the limited funds may not be those with the most profitable investment projects.

- Income is transferred from lenders to those borrowers who are still able to acquire loans. (They now pay a lower interest rate.)

However, it is a fallacy to suppose that interest-rate ceilings necessarily help the poor. The people who benefit are the borrowers who get the limited funds at a bargain price. But these borrowers may be quite rich, while those who don't get funds may be poor.

Normal Profit

Normal profits are earned by owners of equity capital. Normal profit is defined as the return that could be earned in an alternative investment—in this case, the interest the owner could have earned lending these funds out instead.

Factor Prices and the Allocation of Scarce Resources

In a free market, the wage rate screens labor into its most productive use. (Employers with less productive jobs don't hire labor because they can't afford to pay the market wage.) Similarly a free market screens investment funds provided by savers into the most productive investments, i.e., those with the highest MEI. (Businesses that want to invest in less productive projects can't do so, because they can't afford to pay the market interest rate.) In either case, the market price is a rationing device which ensures that the most productive activities will be undertaken.

Human Capital

There are two main forms of investment in human capital:

- formal education, and

- apprenticeship, or on-the-job training.

There are two reasons why investment in human capital may be less than the efficient amount:

- Employers are sometimes reluctant to provide on-the-job training because trainees may quit and take their skills elsewhere.

- There are often external benefits from education. For example, when a highly educated scientist discovers a cure for a disease, it benefits the entire population. Because such external benefits are not taken into account by those making the decision to invest in education, this investment in

human capital may fall short of the efficient level. This underinvestment in human capital provides a justification for government subsidies to education.

In practice, estimating the returns to a college education is very difficult for a number of reasons. For example, people with high incomes tend to have a lot of both education and talent. It's hard to sort out how much of their higher income is due to each.

Further complications arise if we wish to calculate the social return to education. For example, it is difficult to measure the external benefits of education. (How do you measure the benefits to society when a highly educated scientist discovers a new strain of wheat?)

Rent

Perhaps the most important thing to understand about rent is that it can be earned not only by land, but also by other factors of production. It is defined as the earnings of any factor above its opportunity cost. The textbook gives five examples of economic rent:

- The return to agricultural land because of differences in quality.

- The return to urban land because of differences in location.

- The return to mineral deposits because of differences in quality.

- Above-normal profits earned in an industry with barriers to entry.

- The income (above opportunity cost) of an individual with a valuable talent or skill. (See Figures 37-6 and 37-8.)

It is important to understand how rents are capitalized in the value of land. Suppose you own two plots of farm land, and one (A) earns more income—and therefore more rent—than the other (B). A will clearly be worth more; you can sell it for a higher price. But how high will its price go? The answer: it will rise until the rent it earns is about the same percentage return that you can earn elsewhere. For example, if you can rent it out for $200 an acre and the interest rate you can earn by lending out your money instead is 10%, then you will be willing to sell it (and someone else will be willing to buy it) if its price rises to $2,000. Thus rents on land (or on other things such as taxi medallions in the text) determine the values of land, taxi medallions, and so on.

Living in a Global Economy: Foreign Investment in the United States

Just as Americans earn income on their investments in the United States, so too do foreigners who invest here. This is good for them (just as our foreign investments are good for us because we typically earn a good income on them.) But foreign investment also offers benefits to the recipient or host country, that is, foreign investment in the United States also provides *us* with several benefits.

It provides us with funds for investment that cost less than the investments earn. To see why, note that foreign investment in Figure 37-12 shifts the supply of funds in the United States from S to S_T and the amount invested here from Q_1 to Q_2. Those investments provide benefits (returns) of areas 4 + 5, the area of productivity under the D curve. But they cost only 4, the area defined by their interest cost i_2. Thus 5 is a net benefit.

Some of the benefit goes to the U.S. labor force in the form of higher wages. (Our wages are bid up because there is more capital in the United States seeking labor with which to combine.)

The treasury also benefits from the taxes foreign investors pay to the United States.

IMPORTANT TERMS

Match the term in the first column with the corresponding explanation in the second column.

_____ 1. Debt capital
_____ 2. Equity capital
_____ 3. Human capital
_____ 4. Physical capital
_____ 5. Marginal efficiency of investment
_____ 6. Time preference
_____ 7. Roundabout production
_____ 8. Economic rent
_____ 9. Monopoly rent

a. Skills, training, and education of individuals that can be used for producing goods and services.
b. The process of deferring the production of consumer goods, in favor of producing capital goods that can be used in the future to produce even more consumer goods.
c. The above-normal profits accruing to any individual or business because of the possession of monopoly power.
d. Funds that are lent to businesses.
e. The schedule that ranks investments in terms of their percentage return.
f. Funds that go into acquiring a share in the ownership of a business.
g. A desire to consume now rather than in the future. This determines the supply curve for loanable funds.
h. The return to any factor of production in excess of its opportunity cost.
i. The plant, machinery and other forms of equipment that can be used for producing goods and services.

TRUE-FALSE

T   F   1.   Interest income is earned by those who provide equity capital.

T   F   2.   The greater the risk associated with a loan, the lower the interest rate will tend to be.

T   F   3.   An interest rate ceiling benefits all those who wish to borrow.

T   F   4.   A substantial increase in the price of a factor of production will typically induce a firm to change the combination of factors it is using.

T   F   5.   If a ceiling is imposed on the price of any good or service, then any necessary rationing of this good or service is likely to lead to an efficiency loss.

T   F   6.   Factor prices act as a screening device to help allocate factors of production.

T   F   7.   Human capital is like physical capital insofar as it represents an expenditure today that is expected to pay off in the future.

T   F   8.   The costs of a university education include more than living, tuition, and book costs.

T   F   9.   The private rate of return to a university education is not necessarily the same as the social rate of return.

T   F   10.   Very little of the income of basketball star Michael Jordan is rent.

T   F   11.   U.S. treasury tax receipts are higher because of foreign investment here.

MULTIPLE CHOICE

1. What is the annual rate of return on a machine that costs $10,000 and generates enough sales over its 1-year lifetime to cover labor, materials and other costs, plus $12,000?

   a. 120%
   b. 20%
   c. 12%
   d. 10%
   e. 2%

2. The demand curve for loans reflects

   a. the marginal revenue product of labor
   b. the marginal efficiency of investment
   c. either a or b, depending on whether the good being produced is labor or capital intensive
   d. the time preference of savers
   e. none of the above

3. Savers in our society receive an interest return because of their decision to:

   a. buy domestic rather than imported goods
   b. speed up import purchases
   c. delay consumption
   d. speed up consumption
   e. deposit money in a bank savings account rather than to buy government bonds

4. An interest rate ceiling helps all:

   a. the rich who want to lend
   b. the poor who want to lend
   c. the poor who want to borrow
   d. borrowers
   e. those borrowers who can still obtain funds

5. Which of the following is the most likely result of an interest rate ceiling in a perfectly competitive market for loanable funds?

   a. a transfer of income from poor borrowers to some lenders
   b. a transfer of income from all borrowers to some lenders
   c. a transfer of income from rich to poor
   d. a transfer of income from lenders to some borrowers
   e. a reduction in the amount of credit rationing

6. An interest rate ceiling

   a. redistributes income, but has no effect on efficiency
   b. leads to an efficiency gain that is likely to be underestimated by the usual triangular measurement
   c. leads to an efficiency gain that is likely to be overestimated by the usual triangular measurement
   d. leads to an efficiency loss that is likely to be overestimated by the usual triangular measurement
   e. leads to an efficiency loss that is likely to be underestimated by the usual triangular measurement

7. A company in a shaky financial position pays:

   a. a higher interest rate on its borrowing than it would if it were financially sound
   b. a lower interest rate on its borrowing than it would if it were financially sound
   c. the same interest rate on its borrowing as it would if it were financially sound
   d. a higher or lower rate, depending upon the rate of inflation
   e. a lower rate because of the expectation of inflation

8. Because the interest rate is greater than zero, we know that

   a. present goods are worth more than future goods. The reason is that a given amount of present goods can be transformed into more future goods
   b. present goods are worth less than future goods. The reason is that a given amount of present goods can be transformed into more future goods
   c. present goods and future goods have an equal value if interest rates are rising
   d. present goods and future goods always have an equal value
   e. nothing can be said about the relative value of present and future goods

9. A rightward shift in the marginal efficiency of investment is likely to

   a. decrease the rate of interest and decrease the amount of funds loaned
   b. decrease the rate of interest and increase the amount of funds loaned
   c. increase the rate of interest and increase the amount of funds loaned
   d. increase the rate of interest and decrease the amount of funds loaned
   e. increase the rate of interest and leave unchanged the amount of funds loaned

10. An increase by the public in its valuation of current consumption (compared to future consumption) will

   a. decrease the rate of interest and decrease the amount of funds loaned
   b. decrease the rate of interest and increase the amount of funds loaned
   c. increase the rate of interest and increase the amount of funds loaned
   d. increase the rate of interest and decrease the amount of funds loaned
   e. increase the rate of interest and leave unchanged the amount of funds loaned

11. An increase in wages will induce a firm to:

   a. hire more labor
   b. lower its prices
   c. use more labor-saving techniques
   d. use fewer labor-saving techniques
   e. produce more output

12. Minimum wage laws:

   a. discourage on-the-job training of apprentices
   b. encourage on-the-job training of apprentices
   c. increase allocative efficiency
   d. transfer income from workers who still have jobs to other factors of production
   e. transfer income from workers who lose their jobs to other factors of production

13. Recent estimates indicate that the return to a college education has been

   a. below the return to a high school education
   b. the same as the return to a high school education
   c. above the return to a high school education
   d. approximately 15%
   e. c and d

14. A high school education can be viewed as

   a. a bad investment, because it yields a lower return than a college education
   b. a bad investment, even though it yields a higher return than a college education
   c. a bad investment, because it yields a lower return than physical capital
   d. a good investment, even though it yields the same return as a college education
   e. a good investment, because it yields a higher return than physical capital.

15. A college education

    a. must be justified by its consumption benefits, because its investment return is negative
    b. must be justified by its consumption benefits, because its investment return is zero
    c. must be justified by its consumption benefits, because its investment return is positive but near zero
    d. cannot be justified by its investment return alone, because this cannot be estimated
    e. can be justified by its investment return alone, because this is roughly equal to the return on physical capital

16. To estimate the social return to investment in higher education, the private rate of return should be

    a. adjusted downward to take account of government subsidies to higher education
    b. adjusted upward to take account of government subsidies to higher education
    c. adjusted downward to take account of the external benefits of education
    d. a and c
    e. left unadjusted in any of these ways

17. In explaining why the private and social returns to a college education differ, we must take into account

    a. the external benefits of a college education, but not its subsidization by the government
    b. its subsidization, but not its external benefits

    c. both its subsidization and its external benefits
    d. both, but only if they are roughly equal
    e. neither

18. Land may earn rent because it is

    a. productive in growing crops
    b. attractively located for business development
    c. the site of mineral resources
    d. the site of oil deposits
    e. any of the above

19. If the quantity of wheat that can be produced on an acre of land doubles, while the quantity and cost of inputs remain constant, then the rent per acre on this land

    a. increases by 50%
    b. almost doubles
    c. doubles
    d. more than doubles
    e. none of the above

20. The income of the typical physician includes:

    a. rent on innate talents
    b. a return to human capital accumulated in medical school
    c. a return to human capital accumulated as an intern
    d. none of the above
    e. all of the above

EXERCISES

1   a. Figure 37.1 shows a perfectly competitive market for loanable funds. The equilibrium rate of interest in this market is _____ and the equilibrium quantity of loans is _____. In a competitive equilibrium the interest income received by lenders would equal _____.

Figure 37.1

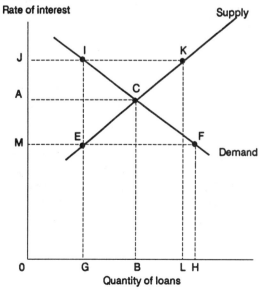

b. If the government imposes an interest rate ceiling at M, then the quantity of loans will be _____, the MEI will be _____, the excess demand for loans will be _____, the interest income received by lenders will be _____, and the size of the efficiency loss will probably be (more, less) than the area _____.

c. If the interest ceiling is set at J, then the size of the efficiency loss will be _____.

2　a. Figure 37.2 shows a perfectly competitive market for a factor of production, where D is the demand curve and S_1 is the supply curve. In a competitive equilibrium, the factor price would be _____, and the quantity of employment of the factor would be _____. The income received by the owners of this factor would equal _____, and the income received by the owners of all other factors would equal _____.

Figure 37.2

Price paid for factor by firms

Quantity of factor

b. Now suppose that a tax is imposed on the owners of this factor, equal in amount to LE per unit of the factor that they are supplying. This would shift the supply curve up vertically by the amount LE, so that the after-tax supply curve is the one labelled S'_1. With the tax, the equilibrium price paid by firms for the factor will equal _____, the equilibrium price received, after tax, by the

owners of the factor will equal _____, the after-tax income accruing to owners of the factor will be _____, the amount of the tax collected will be _____, the income received by other factors will be _____, and the size of the efficiency loss will be _____.

c. Now suppose that there is no tax; instead, suppose that supply shifts from S_1 to S_2. S_2 is (more, less) elastic than S_1. With supply curve S_2 the equilibrium factor price will be (no different, more, less) than with S_1, and the equilibrium quantity of employment of the factor will be (no different, more, less) than with S_1.

d. With S_2 the same tax LE will shift the supply curve up to S'_2. With the tax, the equilibrium price paid by the firms for the factor will be _____, the equilibrium price received, after tax, by owners of the factor will equal _____, the quantity of employment of the factor will equal _____, the after-tax income accruing to owners of the factor will equal _____, the amount of the tax collected will equal _____, the income received by other factors will equal _____, and the size of the efficiency loss will equal _____.

e. To sum up: If we consider the effects of a tax in the face of these two pretax supply curves S_1 and S_2, the one generating the greater tax revenue is (S_1, S_2); the one that produces the smaller efficiency loss from the tax is (S_1, S_2); the one generating the smaller reduction in employment is (S_1, S_2); the one generating the least reduction in the factor's after-tax income is (S_1, S_2), and the one reducing other incomes the least is (S_1, S_2).

ESSAY QUESTIONS

1. The discoverers of insulin, Banting and Best, did not become millionaires as a result of their discovery, despite the fact that it has probably saved millions of human lives. Explain what this means if we wish to compare the private and social rates of return to human capital.

2. Name several influences that affect the position of the MEI schedule, explaining in each case how the schedule is affected, and in what direction, by an increase in that influence.

3. Show how the income of a surgeon can be viewed as partly a wage, partly a return to human capital, and partly a rent. Which of these components would be

increased by the surgeon's success in developing a more advanced surgical technique? By the surgeon's special recognition by the Royal College of Surgeons? How would the rent component be affected if licensing requirements were relaxed to permit more people to practice surgery? Explain.

4. As the interest rate rises, the price of bonds falls. Bearing this in mind, show how an increase in the rate of interest affects potential lenders differently from those who have already lent money by purchasing bonds. Show also how it affects potential borrowers differently from those who have already borrowed money by selling bonds.

5. Suppose that a factor had a totally inelastic supply. What would its opportunity cost be to society? Would it be accurate to classify all its income as rent?

6. Why is it difficult to measure the social rate of return on investment in human capital?

ANSWERS

Matching Columns: 1 d, 2 f, 3 a, 4 i, 5 e, 6 g, 7 b, 8 h, 9 c

True-False:
1 F (p. 688)
2 F (p. 690)
3 F (p. 691)
4 T (p. 693)
5 T (p. 692)
6 T (p. 693)
7 T (p. 694)
8 T (p. 695)
9 T (p. 696)
10 F (p. 697)
11 T (p. 704)

Multiple Choice:
1 b (p. 689)
2 b (p. 689)
3 c (p. 690)
4 e (p. 691)
5 d (p. 691)
6 e (pp. 691-692, BOX)
7 a (p. 690)
8 a (p. 690)
9 c (p. 690)
10 d (p. 690)
11 c (p. 693)
12 a (pp. 661, 694)
13 a (p. 696)
14 e (p. 696)
15 e (p. 696)
16 a (p. 696)
17 c (p. 696)
18 e (pp. 700-701)
19 d (p. 700)
20 e (p. 697).

Exercises

1 a. A, B, OACB.
   b. G, J (or GI), EF (or GH), OMEG, more, ICE.
   c. zero because the ceiling is ineffective.

2 a. A, B, OACB, FAC.
   b. J, G, OGHK, JIHG, FIJ, ICH.
   c. less, no different, no different.
   d. M, N, W, ONTW, NMRT, MFR, RCT.
   e. S_2, S_2, S_2, S_2, S_2.

Across

1. price of land may equal this (2 words)
6. returns in excess of opportunity cost
9. an international organization of the Americas (abbrev.)
11, 12. the desire to have goods now rather than in the future
16. _____ Chi Minh
17. this person is responsible for the production of a newspaper or book
18. one of the factors of production
20. demand payment from
21. one of the authors teaches there (abbrev.)
22. hole in the ground
24. here (Fr.)
25. lyric poem

26. if used carelessly, resources can be _____
28. one
29. a woman's name
31. small piece
32. investment demand (abbrev.)
33. me (Fr.)
34, 36. an economist considers this as part of cost, but an accountant doesn't (2 words)
38. 3.14
39. a key to economic growth

Down

1. this increases as a result of investment
2. a British conservative
3. one cause of inequality
4. poke fun at
5. education is a form of _____ capital
7. out of harm's way
8. industry with only one seller
10. bitter, caustic
12. an advanced academic degree (abbrev.)
13. production with capital is sometimes spoken of as _____ production
14. this is partly consumption, and partly investment

15. a movie character
19. _____ *Kapital* , the chief work of Marx
23. a major reason for an increase in output
26. in a perfectly competitive economy, this equals the value of the marginal product of labor
27. a barrier to international trade
30. a major U.S. corporation (abbrev.)
35. small (prefix)
36. a progressive tax can change the division of the national "_____"
37. A U.S. government agency that regulates the railroads (abbrev.)

CHAPTER 38

INCOME INEQUALITY

LEARNING OBJECTIVES

After you have studied this chapter in the textbook and the study guide, you should be able to

✔ Explain the reasons why some people have more income than others

✔ Explain how the Lorenz curve is constructed and why it provides a good picture of the nation's income distribution

✔ Explain why the Lorenz curve exaggerates the degree of inequality

✔ Identify the government policies that have been designed, at least in part, to make incomes more equal, and specify which of these has been most successful in achieving this objective

✔ Explain why the direct effects of policies designed to increase equality are at least partially offset by their negative indirect effects on incentives

✔ Demonstrate why it cannot be claimed that a free market leads to a fair distribution of income

✔ Demonstrate why complete equality of income is not necessarily fair; that is, show why equality is not the same as equity (fairness)

✔ Explain why it is reasonable to aim for some compromise between the extremes of a free market and complete equality

✔ Show why a conflict often exists between equity and efficiency

✔ Specify at least one policy where these two are not in conflict

✔ Discuss the efficiency and transfer effects of discrimination in a labor market

✔ Describe and evaluate the concept of comparable worth

MAJOR PURPOSES

In the three preceding chapters, we have described how incomes are determined in our society. For example, some people have a higher income because of some innate talent or a large investment in human capital. Others may earn rent from land they own. Our first objective in this chapter is to summarize these economic reasons for differences in incomes, and complete that list with the additional reasons — such as just plain luck — that have not been dealt with in earlier chapters because they don't yield to economic analysis.

Our second objective is to examine the U.S. income distribution that results from all these influences. How much income inequality is there? This question is answered with a Lorenz curve which gives an immediate picture of how much of the nation's income is earned by low-income Americans, and how much by high-income Americans. The conclusion is that a great deal of inequality exists.

The third broad question we then address is: How effective are the government's programs of taxation and expenditure that have, at least in part, been designed to reduce inequality? The answer is that government expenditures have had some effect, but taxes have had very little.

This then provides the background for tackling one of the most difficult issues in economics — the normative question: **"How unequal should incomes be?"** While economists cannot answer that question in a definitive way, they can throw a great deal of light on this issue. Specifically, we show that it is difficult to argue that either (a) income equality or (b) the free-market distribution of income is fair.

Our final objective is to look at one reason for income inequity: discrimination in the labor market. What are its effects on efficiency, and who bears the burden?

HIGHLIGHTS OF CHAPTER

Five broad questions are addressed in this chapter:

- Why is there income inequality?

- How much income inequality exists in the United States?

- How much of this inequality has been eliminated by government expenditures and taxes?

- How much inequality should there be? That is, what is an equitable distribution of income?

- What are the effects of discrimination in the labor market — one of the important reasons why inequity in U.S. incomes persists?

Why is there Inequality?

There are at least eight reasons why some people may have more income than others:

- their greater investment in human capital,

- some innate ability on which they earn rent,

- greater financial wealth, either because they have inherited it or saved it,

- greater market power due to membership in a union or possession of some other form of monopoly power,

- a willingness to work harder or longer hours,

- discrimination in their favor in the labor market,

- good connections and other benefits of family background and

- just plain luck — being at the right place at the right time. To illustrate how costly it can be if you are in the right place at the wrong time, consider the classic complaint of the failing stock-market speculator: "I got all the decisions exactly right; it was just the timing I got wrong."

Which of these influences is most important? Professor Jacob Mincer's surprising reply is that more than half of the differences in income can be attributed to the first factor on this list — differences in human capital.

How Much Inequality is there in the United States?

This question is answered by the Lorenz curve shown in Figure 38-1 of the text. This curve shows the percentage of the nation's income received by the poorest 20% of the population; and by the poorest 40%; and so on. If everyone had exactly the same income each year, then the Lorenz curve would be the 45° "complete-equality" line shown in that diagram. In this case, the poorest 20% would get 20% of the nation's income; the poorest 40% would get 40% of the nation's income; and so on. This is not true for the U.S. Lorenz curve shown in this diagram. Its large bow indicates a substantial degree of inequality.

Actually, this overstates the case. Even if there were perfect equality, with all families receiving exactly the same lifetime pattern of income, there would still be some bow in the Lorenz curve, since it measures income in a single year. The reason is that some families would be at the height of their earning power. They would be observed with far more income in that year than younger families who would be just beginning their careers at a low income.

How Much Do Government Expenditures and Taxes Reduce Inequality?

The difference between the two Lorenz curves in Figure 38-1 in the text shows how much government taxes and expenditures reduce inequality. The surprise is that taxes have had little effect. True, the progressive rates of income tax draw more heavily from the income of the rich. But some other taxes are regressive, and the rich benefit more than the poor from loopholes in the tax system.

Government expenditures are in fact more effective and explain almost all of the reduction in inequality shown in the move from the lower to the upper bow. Why then does so much inequality remain? One reason is that government expenditures like unemployment insurance (UI) first lower the "income earned" distribution giving it a greater bow. (Because of UI, the unemployed are less desperate to get a job and therefore on average take more time before starting to earn an income again; thus the degree of inequality in income earned is **indirectly** increased.) Therefore this brown curve is lower than it would otherwise be. True, programs like UI do then directly raise the income distribution from the brown to the green curve. But it's difficult, on balance, to assess the net effect of these two influences.

Two Other Influences on the U.S. Distribution of Income

1. *Transfers from the young to the old.* These have been increasing because of (a) the expansion of social security which transfers income from young taxpayers to retired beneficiaries and (b) the increase in housing prices. A young couple now has to sacrifice a great deal to make the house purchase that makes the retired sellers rich.

   The net result: It is becoming increasingly difficult for the young to attain the standard of living of their parents.

2. *Is the middle class shrinking?* There have been many anecdotes describing workers who have lost good incomes in heavy industry and now have to take low-income jobs in services such as fast food. Here are the facts:

   - From 1967 to 1987, manufacturing **output** rose as fast as GNP. It was not a shrinking share of GNP.

   - But **employment** in manufacturing fell slightly, which meant it was a shrinking share of total U.S. employment. Thus manufacturing has become like agriculture. Large increases in productivity have meant less employment is required and labor is free to move into services and other sectors.

   - Is this bad? If you're a worker who has lost his manufacturing job, it depends on whether you now have a lower income in fast food or a higher income in finance or computers—and there have been many service jobs created in this latter category

What is a "Fair" or "Equitable" Distribution of Income?

This question cannot be answered with complete certainty, because it is a normative question of "what ought to be," rather than a positive question of "what is." Nevertheless, most people would agree on two points:

- The outcome of the free market has no special claim to being fair. One reason is that there is no way of justifying huge profits to those who can exercise market power and raise price because they operate in markets that are not perfectly competitive. But there are problems that go deeper than this. Even if markets *were* perfectly competitive, it would be difficult to argue that their outcome would necessarily be fair. The example in the text is of the individual who makes no effort or contribution to the nation's output, yet who receives a very high income because he owns inherited agricultural land. The only claim for perfect competition—and it's an important one—is that, in the absence of externalities, it provides an outcome that is efficient. But no claim can be made that this outcome is necessarily fair.

- At the other extreme, complete equality of income would not be fair either, because some people work harder and longer than others, and some people have more dangerous jobs than others. Most would agree that it is fair for such people to have a higher income. After reading this section, it is essential that you be able to explain why equality and equity are not the same. Equality means 'being equal' while equity means 'being fair.'

With these two extremes—the free market's distribution of income and a completely equal distribution of income—being judged unacceptable, what is a reasonable compromise? Here are two of the guidelines suggested in the text:

- Set equality of opportunity as our objective rather than equality of reward. View life as a race that should be fair, with all participants starting out together, although of course, not finishing that way. There should be no handicaps; for example, no one should be denied the opportunity of an education because of discrimination. But this doesn't mean that everyone should be awarded a college degree—that should depend on what people are able to do with their equal opportunity.

- We should modify the rewards of the race. Some must finish last, but they should not be left in an impoverished state.

The Conflict Between Equity and Efficiency

Perhaps the most important concept in this chapter is this: In striving for equity, it must never be forgotten that there is typically (though not always) a conflict between equity and efficiency. To take the extreme case: If everyone were guaranteed an equal income, who would want to fight fires or work the long hours of the computer engineer? Equalizing the nation's income pie would reduce the size of that pie.

The Rawlsian Solution

The ideas of Professor John Rawls discussed in Box 38-1 of the text are of considerable interest because for some time many people thought he had the solution to the problem of what the nation's income distribution should be. Rawls suggests that we imagine everyone to be in an "original position," in which no one knows what his or her particular income will be. Then ask what kind of income distribution reasonable people would choose from behind this "veil of ignorance." They would be choosing a distribution of income—that is, an "income ladder"—without knowing on which of the rungs they themselves would be located.

Rawls argues that in these circumstances, everyone would agree to his "difference principle": There should be complete equality in the distribution of income, unless there is an unequal distribution that leaves everyone better off. But he arrives at this conclusion by supposing that all the people who make this decision would figure that with their luck, no matter what "income ladder" they may choose, they would end up on the lowest rung; so, they would choose an income distribution in which the lowest rung is as high as possible. In other words, they would chose the income distribution with the *largest minimum income*. This is the *maximin* criterion.

In this box, we give examples to show that Rawls' theory only applies to people who won't take a risk under any circumstances. Therefore it just doesn't apply to average Americans—let alone those who visit Los Vegas *in search* of risk. Thus Rawls did not answer the question of what our income distribution should be. To this question, there may never be a clear answer.

Discrimination in the Labor Market: One Important Source Of Inequity

This is of great interest for two reasons:

- discrimination is one of the most distressing sources of income inequity, and

- ending discrimination is one of the few policies where equity and efficiency are not in conflict. Indeed this policy would allow us to improve both.

IMPORTANT TERMS

Match the term in the first column with the corresponding explanation in the second column.

_____ 1. Lorenz curve
_____ 2. Complete equality line
_____ 3. Transfers in kind
_____ 4. Original position
_____ 5. Difference principle
_____ 6. Maximin criterion
_____ 7. Dual labor market
_____ 8. Comparable worth

a. This appears in the Lorenz curve diagram with a 45° slope. The Lorenz curve would coincide with this only if all families received exactly the same income in the year of observation.
b. The theory that income should be equally distributed unless there is some other distribution that makes everyone better off.
c. This exists when there are non-economic barriers such as discrimination that prevent workers in a low-wage secondary market from getting jobs in the higher-wage primary market.
d. This shows the percentage of national income that is received by the lowest-income 20 percent of families, by the lowest-income 40 percent of families, and so on.
e. It is in this location that Rawls would ask everyone to choose the best income distribution, without knowing what his or her position on that income scale will be.
f. Equal pay for jobs that are not necessarily the same, but that have equal value and equally demanding requirements.
g. Payments made by the government, which receives nothing in return. These payments are not in cash, but instead are in the form of goods or services such as food stamps or medical care
h. Making the choice that maximizes the minimum value

TRUE-FALSE

T   F   1.   Transfers-in-kind are those transfers that do not affect the distribution of real income.

T   F   2.   The increasing cost of Social Security is transferring income from the young to the elderly.

T   F   3.   Between 1967 and 1987, U.S. manufacturing output remained roughly constant, while output of the service sector increased.

T   F   4.   Between 1967 and 1987, U.S. manufacturing employment remained roughly constant, while employment in the service sector increased.

T   F   5.   If income is defined broadly to include both money and leisure, then fairness requires that those who take a lot of their income in one form (leisure) should get less in the other form (money).

T   F   6.   The only reason that complete equality is rejected as a target is that this division of the nation's income pie would shrink its overall size.

T   F   7.   Equity is a normative, rather than a positive issue.

T   F   8.   Scientific evidence indicates that complete equality is the only fair way of distributing the nation's income.

T   F   9.   The provable virtues of a free, perfectly competitive market have to do with its equity—not its efficiency.

T   F   10.   Equity requires that everyone be paid the same income.

T   F   11.   It is possible to have an absolutely fair competition, but a bad system of rewards.

MULTIPLE CHOICE

1. How much of the nation's wealth is held by the poorest 25% of the population?

    a. 15%
    b. 12%
    c. 3%
    d. 1%
    e. essentially none at all

2. How much of the nation's wealth is held by the richest 1% of the population?

    a. 2%
    b. 5%
    c. 8%
    d. 13%
    e. 20%

3. Research indicates that, in determining differences in income,

    a. the least important influence is wealth
    b. the least important influence is family background
    c. the most important influence is human capital
    d. the least important influence is luck
    e. the least important influence is human capital

4. The Lorenz curve measures how close the nation's actual income distribution is to

    a. a fair distribution
    b. an equal distribution
    c. the distribution in the previous year
    d. the distribution that would exist if all markets were perfectly competitive
    e. the distribution that would exist if no markets were perfectly competitive

5. The greater the degree of income inequality

    a. the smaller the bow in the Lorenz curve (i.e., the closer the Lorenz curve is to the 45 degree line)
    b. the larger the bow in the Lorenz curve
    c. the steeper the initial slope of the Lorenz curve
    d. the higher the point the Lorenz curve eventually reaches
    e. none of the above

6. What percentage of the total U.S. income (before taxes and transfers) is earned by the lowest-income 50% of U.S. families?

    a. less than 2%
    b. about 5%
    c. about 15%
    d. about 35%
    e. about 45%

7. Because all government taxes taken together are:

    a. highly progressive, they are more effective than government expenditures in making incomes more equal
    b. highly progressive, they are less effective than government expenditures in making incomes more equal
    c. not highly progressive, they are less effective than government expenditures in making incomes more equal
    d. not highly progressive, they are more effective than government expenditures in making incomes more equal
    e. regressive, they are more effective than government expenditures in making incomes more equal

8. Putting an end to racial discrimination is likely to:

   a. increase the bow in the Lorenz curve
   b. decrease the bow in the Lorenz curve
   c. change the Lorenz curve so that its bow is above rather than below the 45° line
   d. make the Lorenz curve start from a different initial point
   e. make the Lorenz curve end at a different point

9. If some individuals acquire more and more human capital, while others do not, then this is likely to:

   a. increase the bow in the Lorenz curve
   b. decrease the bow in the Lorenz curve
   c. change the Lorenz curve so that its bow is above, rather than below, the 45° line
   d. make the Lorenz curve start from a different initial point
   e. make the Lorenz curve end at a different point

10. If we were to pursue only the goal of equity, we would find that our policies would:

    a. always reduce efficiency
    b. often reduce efficiency
    c. always increase efficiency
    d. expand the size of the national income pie
    e. leave the size of the national income pie unchanged

11. It is difficult to argue that the free market would do a completely equitable job of distributing income because:

    a. the free market is often not perfectly competitive; some people raise their income through the exercise of market power
    b. even if the free market were perfectly competitive, it would still often provide luxuries for the wealthy, without providing adequate necessities for the poor
    c. the free market is efficient
    d. a and b
    e. none of the above

12. The most difficult concept for economists to pin down is:

    a. efficiency gain
    b. efficiency loss
    c. equity
    d. equality
    e. inequality

13. A policy of trying to equalize incomes completely has been criticized because it would:

    a. be inefficient
    b. be unfair, because it would give people who work hard the same reward as those who do not
    c. require a change in our present system of inheritance
    d. shrink the national income pie
    e. all of the above

14. The major virtue of a perfectly competitive free market is its:

    a. efficiency when there are no externalities
    b. efficiency when externalities do exist
    c. equity
    d. tendency to ensure equality of income
    e. tendency to ensure equality of wealth

15. A criticism of Rawls' theory is that it:

    a. is based on an unrealistic assumption about how people view risk
    b. concentrates only on the individual (or group) that is lowest on the income scale
    c. doesn't take into account those who are near to, but are not at, the bottom of the income scale
    d. is based on the maximin principle
    e. all of the above

16. John Rawls argues that income should be divided equally:

    a. in all circumstances
    b. in no circumstances
    c. unless an unequal distribution benefits the majority
    d. unless an unequal distribution benefits at least a large minority
    e. unless an unequal distribution benefits everyone

17. According to Rawls' maximin criterion, which of the following income distributions is best?

    a. everyone gets $3,000 per year
    b. everyone gets $5,000 per year except for one person who gets $3,100
    c. half the people get $10,000 per year and the other half get $1,000
    d. everyone gets $20,000 per year except for one person who gets $2,900
    e. everyone gets $40,000 per year except for one person who gets $3,000

18. A labor market is 'color-blind' if:

a. all employers ignore color in making hiring and firing decisions
b. quotas exist which ensure that workers of one color will get a certain percentage of the jobs
c. blacks are last hired, first fired
d. blacks are first hired, last fired
e. blacks are restricted to low-productivity jobs

19. The most likely result of discrimination against men in a perfectly competitive market for nurses' labor is:

a. an increase in the income of male nurses
b. an increase in the income of female nurses
c. a decrease in the wages of female nurses
d. an increase in the income of other factors
e. a reduced supply of female nurses

20. As a result of discrimination against minorities in a perfectly competitive labor market, non-labor factors of production:

a. benefit, because of the transfer they receive from white workers
b. benefit, despite the transfer of their income to white workers
c. gain, because the income they gain from the "minority labor market" exceeds the income they lose in the white labor market
d. lose, because the income they gain from the "minority labor market" is less than the income they lose in the white labor market
e. lose, even though the income they gain from the "minority labor market" exceeds the income they lose in the white labor market

21. The efficiency loss from discrimination in a perfectly competitive labor market:

a. is borne mostly by minorities, whose income is reduced
b. occurs because minorities are employed in more productive activities, while whites are in less
c. occurs because income is transferred from white labor to other factors of production
d. occurs because income is transferred from minority labor to other factors of production
e. occurs because the other factors of production are owned by outsiders

---

EXERCISES

1. Table 38.1 below gives the income distribution of a hypothetical economy, as in panel a of Table 38-1 in the textbook. In Table 38.2 below, fill in the cumulative income distribution in the last row.

Table 38.1

	Lowest 20%	Second 20%	Third 20%	Fourth 20%	Highest 20%
Percent of income	4	6	10	20	60

Table 38.2

	Lowest 20%	Lowest 40%	Lowest 60%	Lowest 80%	Total
Percent of income					

Plot this as a Lorenz curve in Figure 38.1 below, and label it L₁.

Figure 38.1

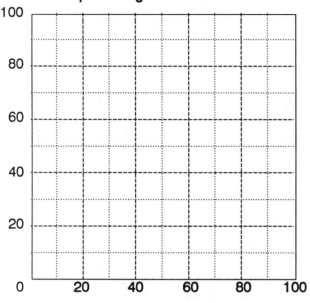

Cumulative percentage of income

Cumulative percentage of families

Suppose that the government then taxes away half the income of every family in the top 20 percent of the income distribution and gives it in equal amounts to every family in the lowest 60 percent of the distribution. Fill in the resulting income distribution in Table 38.3 and the resulting cumulative income distribution in Table 38.4.

Plot the Lorenz curve for income after taxes and transfers in Figure 38.1 and label it L₂. Note how important taxes and expenditures can be in reducing inequality, *at least in theory*.

2. Consider the five following ways of distributing income among five families in an economy:

A. Four families receive $1,000 per year each, and the fifth family receives $600 per year

B. Four families receive $501 per year each, and the fifth receives $3,000 per year

C. Each family receives $500 per year

D. Four families receive $1,100 per year each, and the fifth family receives $5,600

E. Four families receive $5,000 per year each and the fifth receives nothing

Fill in Table 38.5, giving the total national income according to each distribution:

Table 38.5

Distribution	Total national income
A	
B	
C	
D	
E	

Fill in Table 38.6 for each of the distributions, showing the cumulative percentages.

Table 38.3

	Lowest 20%	Second 20%	Third 20%	Fourth 20%	Highest
Percent of income					

Table 38.4

	Lowest 20%	Lowest 40%	Lowest 60%	Lowest 80%	Total
Percent of income					

Table 38.6

	Lowest 20%	Lowest 40%	Lowest 60%	Lowest 80%	Total
Percent of income A					
B					
C					
D					
E					

Draw and label the Lorenz curve for each of these distributions in Figure 38.2.

Figure 38.2

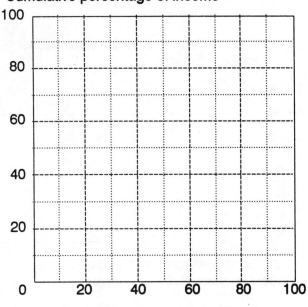

Cumulative percentage of income

Cumulative percentage of families

Indicate in Table 38.7 below the way that these distributions would be ranked according to Rawls' maximin criterion.

Table 38.7

Rank	Distribution
Best	
Second best	
Third best	
Fourth best	
Fifth best	

According to Rawls' ranking, does the best distribution have the largest total income? Does it have the least inequality as measured by the Lorenz curve?

The reason that egalitarians — that is, those who believe in equal incomes — were disillusioned by Rawls is illustrated in Figure 38.2, where we see that Rawls (does, does not) recommend the "complete-equality" distribution _____. Instead he recommends distribution _____, which is one of the (most, least) equal of the distributions.

3 a. Panel *a* in Figure 38.3 shows a perfectly competitive labor market in which there are N_M men and N_F women, and there is no discrimination against women. The equilibrium wage rate is _____, and employment is _____. The income of men is area _____, while women earn _____. The income of other factors of production is _____.

Figure 38.3

(a) Male labor market

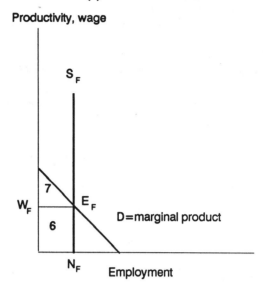

(b) Female labor market

b. Suppose now that there is discrimination against women, and N_F women are forced into the relatively unproductive market in panel *b*. Equilibrium in the main labor market in panel *a* now moves to point _____. In this labor market, men earn an income of _____, while the earnings of other nonlabor factors of production change from original area _____ to _____, for an (increase, decrease) of _____.

c. In the secondary, relatively unproductive labor market in panel *b*, equilibrium is at point _____, with _____ females employed at a wage of _____. Income of females is area

_____, while the income of other factors in this market is _____.

d. When we take *both* markets into account, we conclude that female labor income (increases, decreases) by _____ as a result of discrimination; male labor income (increases, decreases) by _____; and nonlabor income (increases, decreases) by _____. There is a transfer (from, to) male workers (from, to) other factors of area _____. There is a loss overall — that is, an efficiency loss — of _____. Since this efficiency loss is roughly the same as the (loss, gain) to (women, men), we can therefore say that it is borne by (women, men).

ESSAY QUESTIONS

1. "With a problem as perplexing as determining the best income distribution for the nation, the best approach is a simple one that strikes right to the heart of the matter: Make all incomes equal. This is philosophically and morally the fair and just solution." Do you agree? Explain your position.

2. In your view, is it possible for an unequal income distribution to be equitable? Use examples to support your position.

3. Is it fair for Steffi Graf to earn such a high income from doing something — playing tennis — that many others in the world enjoy?

4. In what way do you think the shape of the Lorenz curve would be affected by:

    a an end to racial discrimination
    b some individuals acquiring more and more human capital, while others do not
    c unemployment insurance
    d a highly progressive tax
    e a special new tax on wage income
    f a special new tax on incomes over $100,000

5. Marxists believe in the principle, "to each according to his needs, from each according to his abilities." Do you agree or disagree? Why or why not? Do you think that this principle would lead to a straight-line Lorenz curve? Why or why not? Do you think that a government that tried to put this principle into effect would run into problems?

ANSWERS

Important Terms: 1 d, 2 a, 3 g, 4 e, 5 b, 6 h, 7 c, 8 f.

True-False:
1 F (p. 710)
2 T (p. 711)
3 F (p. 711)
4 T (p. 711)
5 T (p. 713)
6 F (p. 713)
7 T (p. 712)
8 F (p. 715*n.*)
9 F (p. 712)
10 F (p. 712)
11 T (p. 716).

Multiple Choice:
1 e (p. 707)
2 e (p. 707)
3 c (p. 708)
4 b (pp. 709-710)
5 b (p. 710)
6 c (p. 709)
7 c (p. 710)
8 b (p. 720)
9 a (p. 709)
10 b (pp. 712, 720)
11 d (p. 712)
12 c (p. 716)
13 e (pp. 712-716)
14 a (pp. 457, 712)
15 e (pp. 714-715)
16 e (pp. 714-715, BOX)
17 b (pp. 714-715, BOX)
18 a (p. 719)
19 b (p. 718)
20 d (p. 718)
21 a (pp. 719-720).

Exercises

1.   Table 38.2: 4, 10, 20, 40, 100.

Figure 38.1 Completed

Table 38.3: 14, 16, 20, 20, 30.

Table 38.4: 14, 30, 50, 70, 100.

2.

Table 38.5 Completed

Distribution	Total national income
A	$ 4,600
B	5,004
C	2,500
D	10,000
E	20,000

Table 38.6 Completed

		Lowest 20%	Lowest 40%	Lowest 60%	Lowest 80%	Total
Percent of income	A	13	35	57	78	100
	B	10	20	30	40	100
	C	20	40	60	80	100
	D	11	22	33	44	100
	E	0	25	50	75	100

Figure 38.2 Completed

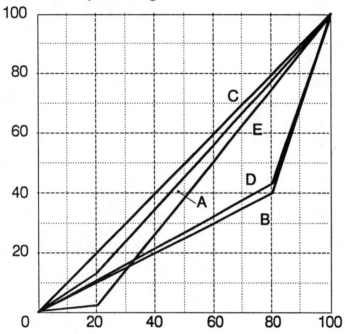

Cumulative percentage of income

Cumulative percentage of families

Table 38.7 Completed

Rank	Distribution
Best	D
Second best	A
Third best	B
Fourth best	C
Fifth best	E

No, no, does not, C, D, least.

3 a. W, N, 3, 5, 1 + 2 + 4.

  b. E_M, 2 + 3, 1 + 2 + 4, 1, decrease, 2 + 4.

  c. E_F, N_F, W_F, 6, 7.

  d. decreases, 5 - 6, increases, 2, decreases, 2 + 4 - 7, to, from, 2, (4 + 5) - (6 + 7), loss, women, women.

GOVERNMENT POLICIES TO REDUCE INEQUALITY:
Can We Solve The Poverty Problem?

LEARNING OBJECTIVES

After you have studied this chapter in the textbook and the study guide, you should be able to

✔ Describe how the poverty line Is defined

✔ Explain why, over long periods of time, our definition of the poverty line tends to drift up to a higher level of real income

✔ State the factors that increase the likelihood of a family being poor

✔ Describe the government policies that attack the causes of poverty, and the policies that reduce its symptoms

✔ Explain the difference between social insurance and welfare programs

✔ Describe the problems with our present welfare system

✔ Explain the concept of the implicit tax in a welfare program and why this is important in evaluating such programs

✔ Critically evaluate the guaranteed minimum income proposal

✔ Argue the case that income maintenance programs are the cure for poverty

✔ Argue the opposite case that such programs are the cause of poverty

✔ Describe how a negative income tax program would work

✔ Explain the theoretical advantages of a negative income tax program

✔ Describe the results of experimental studies on the negative income tax

✔ Explain the objectives of workfare programs such as a wage subsidy

MAJOR PURPOSE

The objective of this chapter is to evaluate what we are now doing—and what we might possibly do in the future—to alleviate the grinding effects of poverty on the poorest individuals in our population. Specifically, we will address three sets of questions:

- How is the poverty line defined, and who are the poor below it?

- What policies does the government now have in place to reduce poverty, and how successful have they been?

- What income maintenance programs have been proposed to replace the present welfare system, and how likely is it that they would be successful?

HIGHLIGHTS OF CHAPTER

Here are the broad questions that are addressed in this chapter.

How is the Poverty Line Defined?

The Department of Agriculture estimates the lowest possible cost of feeding a family with a diet that would be reasonably edible, and that would meet minimal nutrition standards. Since the poor spend about a third of their income on food, the poverty line is defined as three times the cost of this diet. In 1988 the poverty line was $12,075 for a family of four. This poverty line is adjusted every year to take account of inflation. It also drifts higher in real terms over long periods of time because our view of what is barely acceptable tends to expand.

Who are the Poor?

A family is more likely to be poor if it is:

- nonwhite,
- not well educated,
- living in the core of a big city, or
- fatherless.

If a family falls into several of these categories, the chance it will be poor increases.

What are the Government Policies to Reduce Poverty?

Four kinds of government programs attack the causes of poverty, by helping the poor to earn more income:

- policies that subsidize investment in human capital, such as free schooling and subsidies for training workers;

- policies such as the Equal Pay Act of 1963 and the Civil Rights Act of 1964 that are designed to prevent discrimination in the labor market; and

- policies designed to prevent disabling accidents—in particular, policies that increase safety in the workplace.

There are two categories of programs that reduce the symptoms of poverty by providing income assistance:

1. Social insurance programs, such as Social Security, Unemployment Insurance, and Medicare for the elderly. These programs have not been aimed specifically at the poverty problem since they provide benefits to all participants whether or not they are poor. Nevertheless, they still play an important role in reducing poverty.

2. Welfare programs have been designed specifically to alleviate poverty by providing benefits only to the poor. Examples are AFDC (Aid to Families with Dependent Children) and transfers in kind, such as food stamps, housing subsidies, and medical services for the poor (Medicaid).

How Successful have Government Anti-Poverty Policies Been?

Over long periods during this century, poverty has been steadily and substantially reduced. However, in the decade of the 1970s, progress on this front essentially ended, and in the early 1980s the percentage of the nation in poverty increased. This recent experience does not prove that anti-poverty programs have become ineffective. During this period, some of these programs were cut back, so one would expect that poverty would become more severe. The incidence of poverty also increased because of high unemployment.

Nonetheless, these programs have not been as effective as one might have hoped. One reason is that they include an "implicit tax" on any income the poor may earn. When a poor family earns another $1,000 of income, it may consequently have to give up, say, $800 of welfare benefits it receives from the government. (Sometimes it's more than this, sometimes less.) This $800 is called an 80% "implicit tax," because, from the point of view of the poor, it's as though they had $800 of their additional $1,000 of income "taxed away." If they only get $200 net benefit when they go out and earn $1,000, why bother? It is critical that you understand this concept of an implicit tax, and why a high rate of this tax weakens the incentive of the poor to work. For some families in our present welfare system, this implicit tax has been very high indeed—in some instances approaching, or even exceeding, 100%. In such cases, the poor who earn another $1,000 will lose $1,000 of welfare payments from the government. Their income doesn't increase at all; they have no monetary incentive to get a job.

What are the Proposals to Replace the Present Welfare System?

1. *A guaranteed minimum income (GMI).* Under this program, shown in Figure 39-3 of the textbook, the government would guarantee a family a minimum income of, say, $10,000. Any shortfall in the family's earnings would be covered by a payment from the government. The problem with this policy is that it has a built-in 100% implicit tax that leaves no incentive for the poor to go to work. If they do, and earn another $1,000, their welfare payments from the government are reduced by this same amount. It doesn't matter whether they earn $5,000 or $6,000. Their income is fixed by the government at a $10,000 level. So they don't benefit at all when they earn that $1,000 more. Ensure that you fully understand this scheme in Figure 39-3 of the textbook, before you proceed to the more complicated proposal for a negative income tax in Figure 39-5 of the text.

2. *A negative income tax (NIT).* This proposal also provides the poor with a guaranteed minimum income; but in addition it provides them with an incentive to go out and earn income on their own. The implicit tax in this program can be set at, say, 50%, (rather than the 100% implicit tax in the GMI proposal above). Thus a family that earns another $1,000 of income has its payments from the government reduced by only $500. It therefore gets a net benefit of $500, which provides it with an incentive to work. Note that the "income-after-subsidy" line CA that was completely flat in the GMI proposal in Figure 39-3—and therefore provided no incentive to work—has now been replaced by the upward-sloping line CQ in Figure 39-5. Since some of the benefit from increased income can now be kept—it is no longer all lost—there is an incentive to go to work.

If, as its proponents recommend, the negative income tax were to replace the entire inconsistent set of present welfare policies, it would provide another benefit. It would be more equitable because all the poor would be treated alike; all would face the same minimum income, and the same implicit tax. However, this policy would not be problem-free. Like any other anti-poverty program it could not simultaneously achieve the three desirable but conflicting goals of

- providing an acceptable minimum income for everyone,

- preserving the incentive for people to work, and

- keeping costs down.

As an example of how these goals may conflict, suppose the government decides to achieve the first goal by raising the minimum income level from $10,000 to $12,000. This will shift the "income after" line CQH in Figure 39-5 up by $2,000 throughout its whole length, thus increasing the blue "subsidy gap" that the government must fill. Thus this measure may conflict with the objective of keeping costs down.

Unfortunately, the results of experiments suggest that in practice the negative income tax doesn't work as well as many economists had hoped. In fact, compared with even the present welfare system, it has had very disappointing results because it has not been successful in inducing people to work more.

Workfare

Because of the disappointment in the NIT experimental results, attention has turned to workfare policies of paying welfare to the poor only if they are willing to work. One type of workfare policy is a wage subsidy that would help the poor by increasing their wages. Because it would increase the reward for work (the wage rate) it is hoped that this scheme might provide a stronger work incentive. Its main drawback is that it would remove any guaranteed minimum income, and thus would provide no assistance to those individuals who, because of age or disability, cannot work to support themselves. Accordingly, some method would have to be devised to "tag" such people, so that they could qualify for special government support. While such a system would be necessary, it would be far from foolproof. One problem is that some of the able-bodied who do not want to work may try fraudulently to have themselves tagged as disabled.

Concluding Remarks

In the analysis of the GMI and NIT proposals, the focus has been on the cost of a welfare system, in terms of the reduced incentive to work by the *recipients* of welfare. But there is another cost as well — the cost of raising the taxes from the *general public* to finance the welfare expenditure. There is evidence that there is about a 25-35% loss when taxes are raised, because those who are taxed are left with less incentive to work. Make sure — in Figure 39-4 of the text — that you can clearly distinguish between these two costs — that is, the disincentive to work imposed on the public that has to pay for welfare payments, and the disincentive to work of the poor who receive the welfare payments.

IMPORTANT TERMS

Match the term in the first column with the corresponding explanation in the second column.

_____ 1. Poverty
_____ 2. Poverty line
_____ 3. Jobs Training Partnership Act (JTPA)
_____ 4. Equal Pay Act (1963)
_____ 5. Civil Rights Act (1964)
_____ 6. Social Security
_____ 7. Medicare
_____ 8. Medicaid
_____ 9. AFDC
_____10. Food stamps
_____11. Public housing
_____12. Implicit tax
_____13. Guaranteed minimum income
_____14. Negative income tax
_____15. Tagging
_____16. Workfare
_____17. Wage subsidy

a. The identification of those who, because of age or disability, are unable to earn an income, and therefore deserve special support from the government.

b. A program that provides medical services for the poor

c. A proposed government program which would ensure people a minimum income but give them no incentive to work.

d. A program under which the federal government pays local governments to clear slums, build houses, and rent these houses to low-income tenants.

e. The amount of welfare payments lost by a family that earns another dollar of income.

f. A proposal for the government to provide the funds for increasing the wages of low-income earners.

g. An income equal to three times the minimum cost of an adequate diet.

h. Vouchers that provide food for the poor.

i. A program that guarantees everyone a minimum income and provides a work incentive by allowing people to retain part of any income they earn.

j. A program that provides medical services for the elderly.

k. A government program providing welfare to those who work, but not to those who don't.

l. A program to which employers and employees contribute, with benefits paid out to the retired or disabled.

m. A program that provides welfare payments to families with dependent children.

n. A government program providing retraining assistance.

o. The legislation that requires that women be paid the same as men engaged in the same work.

p. The legislation outlawing discrimination in hiring, firing, and other employment practices.

q. Inadequate income to buy the necessities of life.

TRUE-FALSE

T   F   1.   By 1988, only one American family in 20 was below the poverty line.

T   F   2.   There is a larger number of poor blacks in the United States than poor whites.

T   F   3.   The poor are located in the lower left-hand corner of the Lorenz curve.

T   F   4.   Anyone who eats a diet below the requirements of **minimum nutrition** is defined to be below the poverty line.

T   F   5.   The poverty line over time is not adjusted to take **account of inflation**, because inflation is not the problem.

T   F   6.   Medicare provides medical services for the elderly, **and Medicaid** provides medical services for the poor.

T   F   7.   Because the poor can qualify for several government welfare programs, they are sometimes able to raise themselves not only to the poverty line, but above it.

T   F   8.   Transfer programs such as food stamps relieve the symptoms of poverty rather than attacking its causes.

T   F   9.   Under a guaranteed minimum income, all Americans would receive the same income after taxes and subsidies.

T   F   10.   The implicit tax in a welfare system is the sum of the benefits lost divided by the additional earned income.

T   F   11.   By 1980, welfare assistance was greater in kind than in cash.

MULTIPLE CHOICE

1. The people least likely to be suffering from poverty are:

   a. those living in the suburbs who have a high school education
   b. those living in the core area of a big city who have a high school education
   c. those living in the core area of a big city who have a college education
   d. those living in the suburbs who have a college education
   e. those in the core area of a big city who have 6-8 years of education

2. By recent standards, the proportion of the population living in poverty in 1929 was about:

   a. 10%
   b. 20%
   c. 35%
   d. 50%
   e. 65%

3. It becomes impossible to lift all Americans out of poverty, if we define it as:

   a. the bottom half of the U.S. income distribution
   b. any income less than $10,000
   c. the bottom tenth of the U.S. income distribution
   d. a or c
   e. b or c

4. Select the correct word to put in the blank spot: It is _____ better to attack the causes of poverty than its symptoms.

   a. always
   b. usually
   c. seldom
   d. almost never
   e. never

5. The percentage of the U.S. population living in poverty:

   a. decreased until the 1970s, stabilized during the 1970s, and increased in the early 1980s
   b. decreased until the 1970s, stabilized during the 1970s, and has decreased since
   c. has consistently decreased
   d. decreased until 1970, and has increased since
   e. increased until 1970, and has decreased since

6. The program that is most important in maintaining U.S. income is:

   a. Social Security
   b. Aid to Families with Dependent Children
   c. Unemployment Insurance
   d. food stamps
   e. Medicaid

7. Which of the following benefits is in cash?

   a. food stamps
   b. Medicare
   c. Medicaid
   d. Social Security
   e. none of the above

8. Which of the following kinds of government programs relieve only the symptoms of poverty:

   a. those that subsidize investment in human capital
   b. Aid to Families with Dependent Children
   c. antidiscrimination policies
   d. policies to reduce unemployment
   e. safety regulations to prevent disabling injury

9. Allowing Americans a tax deduction for interest payments on mortgages on their homes:

   a. subsidizes those who own homes
   b. subsidizes those who do not own homes
   c. penalizes those who own homes
   d. subsidizes all Americans
   e. penalizes all Americans

10. Which of the following government programs is designed to attack the causes of poverty:

    a. Jobs Training Partnership Act
    b. Social Security
    c. food stamps
    d. public housing
    e. Aid to Families with Dependent Children

11. A guaranteed minimum income:

    a. would increase efficiency by increasing the incentive to work
    b. would be very costly, especially because it would reduce the incentive to work
    c. would cost less than we would expect, because it would increase the incentive to work
    d. would have no effect on the incentive to work
    e. would have no effect on efficiency

12. A guaranteed minimum income has an implicit tax on very low income families of:

    a. 0%
    b. 25%
    c. 50%
    d. 75%
    e. 100%

13. The income-maintenance program that would provide the poor with the largest incentive to work is one in which the 'income-after-subsidy' line:

    a. has zero slope
    b. has a slope close to zero
    c. has a slope of 30°
    d. has a slope of almost 45°
    e. has a slope of 45°

14. The estimated 'leak in the welfare' bucket in the United States is about:

    a. zero when taxes are collected, and 50% when the welfare expenditures are made
    b. 25% when taxes are collected, and 50% when the welfare expenditures are made
    c. 25% when taxes are collected, and 25% when the welfare expenditures are made
    d. 50% when taxes are collected, and 25% when the welfare expenditures are made
    e. 50% when taxes are collected, and zero when the welfare expenditures are made

15. The maximum implicit tax on any family facing the present set of U.S. welfare policies is:

    a. 50%
    b. 80%
    c. just under 100%
    d. 100%
    e. more than 100%

16. A family will have the strongest financial incentive to stop working if the implicit tax it faces is:

    a. zero
    b. so close to zero that the difference is not significant
    c. 50%
    d. almost 100%
    e. more than 100%

17. If a family living in government subsidized housing is required to pay 25% of its income in rent, then for this reason alone it is facing an implicit tax of:

    a. zero
    b. 25%
    c. 75%
    d. 100%
    e. 125%

18. A welfare program that pays you $5,000 if you earn nothing, and $4,500 if you earn $2,000 has an implicit tax of:

    a. zero
    b. 25%
    c. 40%
    d. 50%
    e. 105%

19. Which of the following should offer the greatest work incentive to the very poor?

    a. no taxes or subsidies
    b. the present welfare system
    c. a wage subsidy
    d. a guaranteed minimum income
    e. a and d equally

20. With a negative income tax, an increase in the implicit tax rate will:

    a. increase the slope of the "income-after-tax" line
    b. decrease the slope of that line
    c. leave the slope of that line unchanged
    d. raise the point where the income-after-tax line intersects the vertical axis
    e. lower that point

21. Suppose a negative income tax is set up with the minimum income set at $8,000, and the implicit tax rate set at 50%. In this case, a subsidy would be paid by the government:

    a. to no-one
    b. only to those earning less than $4,000
    c. only to those earning less than $8,000
    d. only to those earning less than $12,000
    e. only to those earning less than $16,000

EXERCISE

Consider the four following tax-subsidy programs:

A. Every family earning less than $5,000 receives enough subsidy to give it an income of $5,000 after taxes and subsidies. On every dollar earned over $5,000, a family must pay a 20% tax.

B. Every family receives a subsidy of $5,000, but then pays a 50% tax on every dollar earned.

C. Every family receives a subsidy of $3,000, but then pays a tax of 30% on every dollar earned.

D. Every family receives a subsidy of $3,000 but then pays a tax of 50% on every dollar earned.

In Figure 39.1 plot the line for each program showing how a family's income after taxes and subsidies is related to its income before taxes and subsidies. For each program, indicate in Table 39.1 the marginal tax rates on income earned above $5,000.

Figure 39.1

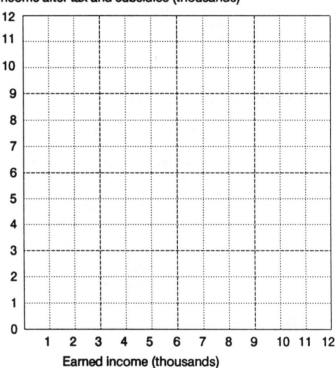

Income after tax and subsidies (thousands)

Earned income (thousands)

Table 39.1

Program	Marginal tax rate on income earned above $5,000
A	
B	
C	
D	

Suppose that the distribution of earned incomes (before taxes and subsidies) in the economy is given by Table 39.2.

Table 39.2

Annual income before taxes and transfers (thousands of dollars)	0	3	5	6	10	15	20	50
Number of families earning this income	1	2	4	4	3	2	1	1

In Table 39.3 fill in the net tax (i.e., tax minus subsidy) paid to each family under each of the programs.

Table 39.3

Income (in thousands)		0	3	5	6	10	15	20	50
Net tax of each	A								
family under	B								
program:	C								
	D								

In Table 39.4 show the total net taxes collected—that is, total taxes collected minus total subsidy paid. Assume that, regardless of the tax-subsidy program that is imposed, there is no change in the incentive of work and therefore the earned income of each family. In other words, the income distribution in Table 39.2 doesn't change, regardless of the tax-subsidy program.

Table 39.4

Programs	Total net taxes
A	
B	
C	
D	

ESSAY QUESTIONS

1. "Social insurance and welfare programs may be desirable, but they are totally unproductive. They don't add anything to the nation's capacity to produce." Do you agree with this statement, or not? Explain your answer. (Use Medicaid as one of your examples.)

2. Use a numerical example to show that if poverty is defined as the income of the bottom 10% of the population, it becomes a meaningless and useless measure of hardship.

3. If you observe that the children of the poor are poor, and that the children of the rich are rich, does this prove the ability of the rich to secure a high income for their children (by providing them, for example, with special educational opportunities)? Or does it reflect different genetic capabilities? Or both? Discuss.

4. If the main ill effect of AFDC is to encourage fathers to leave home so their families can qualify for welfare, what do you think of maintaining the program but disqualifying any family whose father has abandoned them?

5. If the government gave equivalent cash transfers instead of food stamps and other types of assistance in kind, would the recipients be better off? Why? Would their children be better off? Why does the government provide assistance in kind?

ANSWERS

Important Terms: 1 q, 2 g, 3 n, 4 o, 5 p, 6 l, 7 j, 8 b, 9 m, 10 h, 11 d, 12 e, 13 c, 14 i, 15 a, 16 k, 17 f

True-False:
1 F (p. 731)
2 F (p. 726)
3 T (p. 725)
4 F (p. 725)
5 F (p. 726)
6 T (p. 728)
7 T (p. 733)
8 T (pp. 728, 730)
9 F (p. 734)
10 T (p. 733)
11 T (p. 730)

Multiple Choice:
1 d (p. 726)
2 d (p. 731)
3 d (p. 726)
4 b (p. 726)
5 a (p. 731)
6 a (p. 728)
7 d (pp. 728, 730)
8 b (pp. 726, 728)
9 a (p. 730, BOX)
10 a (pp. 726-727)
11 b (p. 734)
12 e (pp. 733-734)
13 e (p. 739)
14 c (p. 737)
15 e (p. 733)
16 e (p. 733)

Exercise

Figure 39.1 COMPLETED

Income after tax and subsidies (thousands)

Earned income (thousands)

Table 39.1 Completed

Program	Marginal tax rate on income earned above $5,000
A	20%
B	50%
C	30%
D	50%

Table 39.3 Completed

Income (in thousands)		0	3	5	6	10	15	20	50
Net tax of each	A	-5,000	-2,000	0	200	1,000	2,000	3,000	9,000
family under	B	-5,000	-3,500	-2,500	-2,000	0	2,500	5,000	20,000
program:	C	-3,000	-2,100	-1,500	-1,200	0	1,500	3,000	12,000
	D	-3,000	-1,500	-500	0	2,000	4,500	7,000	22,000

Table 39.4

Programs	Total net taxes
A	10,800
B	0
C	0
D	36,000

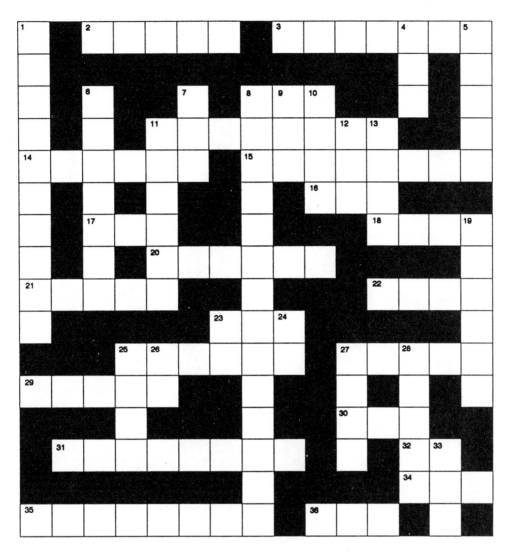

Across

2, 3. education and training are examples of this
8. during a recession, there is a _____ in output
11. program to provide medical services to the elderly
14, 15. this program has been one of the principal reasons for the decline in poverty in the United States
16. an export of Sri Lanka
17. a hard wood
18. strikebreaker
20. fairness
21. assume; take as given
22. an anti-poverty program (abbrev.)
23. a major South American city (abbrev.)
25, 27. a way of illustrating inequality
29. major producer of aluminum
30. tool for cutting wood
31. program to provide medical services to the needy
34. a form of international reserve created by the International Monetary Fund (abbrev.)
35, 36. a way to discourage pollution

Down

1. an anti-poverty program (2 words)
4. a source of revenue for the government
5, 19. this illustrates the idea that something is lost when income is transferred
6. labor, land, and capital are _____ of production
7. snakelike fish
8. one of the causes of poverty
9. frozen water
10. agreement
11. an institution that brings buyers and sellers together
12. regret
13. long periods of time
23. regarding
24. the land of Dorothy's dreams
25. one of the factors of production
26. above, and supported by
27. expense
28. philosopher who suggested that people should disregard their present positions, in order to judge the best distribution of income
33. lyric poem

Chapter 39   Government Programs to Reduce Inequality

CHAPTER 40

MARXISM AND MARXIST ECONOMIES

LEARNING OBJECTIVES

After you have studied this chapter in the textbook and the study guide, you should be able to

✔ Describe the labor theory of value, and the subsistence theory of wages

✔ Explain Marx's concepts of surplus value and the exploitation of the working class

✔ Define and clearly distinguish between socialism and communism

✔ State two predictions of Marx that have not been verified by history

✔ Criticize both the theory and practice of socialism

✔ Explain how capital is raised for investment purposes in a socialist state

✔ Describe the problems associated with central planning

✔ Explain why there is typically less innovation in a socialist state than a free enterprise economy

✔ Explain the problems the Soviets face in setting production targets in their 5-year plans

✔ Describe the "second economy" in the Soviet Union

✔ Describe the problems facing the consumer in an economy that is not closely oriented to the marketplace

✔ Compare the Soviets' disguised unemployment with our overt unemployment

✔ Compare the Soviets' suppressed inflation with our inflation

✔ Explain to what degree the Soviets have succeeded in equalizing incomes, and the problems they have encountered because of the increasing importance of human capital

✔ Explain why growth has been disappointing in the Soviet Union

✔ Describe the ten challenging questions that will have to be faced by the Soviet Union or any other communist country that tries to reform its economic system

MAJOR PURPOSE

Historically, the most influential criticism of the capitalistic, free enterprise system was that set out by Karl Marx. He charged that this system distributes income in an unfair way because it provides income to owners of capital—that is, to "capitalists." In this chapter, we examine Marx's criticism in detail and his proposed alternative: a revolution followed by a socialist state in which capital would be owned by the state on behalf of all the people. We then describe the two most important Marxist experiments—those in the Soviet Union and China. What problems did the Soviets and Chinese encounter? Why is it that the Marxist philosophy that promises so much, delivers so little when put into practice? What will be the major challenges that they—or any other Marxist states—will face in attempting to reform their economies and move towards freer markets?

HIGHLIGHTS OF CHAPTER

This chapter can be broken down into four broad topics:

- Marx's criticism of a free enterprise system;

- the socialist-communist alternative that he proposed;

- the application of Marxism, especially in the Soviet Union; and

- the economic problems the Soviet Union and other Marxist states will face as they attempt to reform their economies by moving toward freer markets.

Marxism

Karl Marx based his philosophy on

- the labor theory of value, and

- the subsistence theory of wages.

He claimed that there is a class struggle in which workers (the "proletariat") are exploited by the capitalists (the "bourgeoisie" who own the capital equipment and other means of production). Instead of enjoying all the fruits of their labor, workers receive just enough to subsist, with the rest going in the form of "surplus value" to the capitalists. According to Marx, the only way of resolving this class struggle is a revolution in which workers forcibly seize the ownership of physical capital from their exploiters. They then set up a socialist state in which there is a dictatorship of the proletariat and capital is owned by the state. In turn this is followed by a communist system in which the state has withered away, and capital and other forms of property are owned by the community as a whole.

One criticism of Marxist theory is that its predictions have not been borne out by history.

- The dictatorship of the proletariat, rather than withering away, has remained powerful in Marxist states.

- Under capitalism workers have enjoyed rising real income rather than the increasing misery predicted by Marx.

Another criticism of Marxist theory is that if capitalists are eliminated, some other way must be found to generate physical capital for investment. The Marxist solution is to generate capital by taxation—in particular, heavy taxes on consumer goods—rather than by personal saving. However, this raises three problems:

- taxes (forced saving) may be more burdensome than voluntary saving;

- when governments invest the funds they have raised, they typically lack the inventiveness of private capitalists; and

- some substitute must be found for the profit motive as a means of allocating capital among different industries.

The concept of profit raises an important issue in the debate between capitalism and Marxism. Supporters of Marxism and capitalism alike generally agree that monopoly profits should not go unchecked. Supporters of capitalism argue that this can be done in a capitalist system by government regulation. Marxists argue that regulation is ineffective because big business interests are so powerful that they end up controlling their own regulators. A capitalist response to this criticism is that big business does indeed have power; and so does the government. But this is better than having all of the power

The Soviet system

Two important features of the Soviet system are:

- most physical capital is owned by the state rather than by private individuals, and

- the decisions on how much of each good to produce and how much to invest in each industry are not made by market forces, but are instead made by a central government planning agency (Gosplan) in its 5-year plans.

These plans set yearly production targets, or quotas, for each industry and—in even more detail—for each plant. There are three major problems with central planning of this sort:

- It is difficult for the government to determine a set of consistent output quotas. For example, the right output for the steel industry depends on the output of those industries that use steel, such as machinery and autos. But at the same time, the right output for the machinery industry depends on the output of those industries that use machinery, such as steel. How do you solve for the output of either steel or machinery when each depends on the other? The answer is that it is not easy. Although there are mathematical techniques for solving such problems, it is seldom possible for a planning agency to get the quotas just right. Consequently bottlenecks—such as a shortage of steel—are common in the Soviet Union.

- Consumers' wants tend to be ignored in the Soviet system. When steel is in short supply, it goes to produce bridges or machinery, not refrigerators for consumers. Thus consumer goods are in chronic short supply, and this leads to the long lineups that are a feature of Soviet life. Another reason the Soviet consumer is short-changed is that each production manager tends to concentrate on satisfying a quota rather than on producing the types of goods that consumers want. (For more on the plight of the Soviet consumer, see Box 40-1 in the textbook).

- It is not clear that the Soviet degree of central planning could be made to work without a repressive Soviet-style political dictatorship. Marxists reply that our freedom is enjoyed only by the rich and powerful. And they point to one apparent advantage of central planning: It produces very little measured unemployment. However, critics point out that if someone is working to produce unwanted goods this really constitutes "disguised" unemployment.

The 5-year plans of the Soviet Union have emphasized rapid growth. For example, between 1950 and 1970, the average rate of growth of Soviet GNP was almost 5%, which far exceeded the 3% growth rate in the United States. However, the reason for this was not that the Soviet Union has a better system for generating growth. Instead it was due to the fact that investment in the Soviet Union has run about 30% of GNP, compared to 15% in the United States. When one compares the Soviet Union with a country like Japan that also invests this high a percentage of its GNP, Soviet growth does not compare favorably. Moreover, despite the heavy diversion of its GNP into investment, Soviet growth has recently become particularly disappointing; it has fallen close to zero.

There have been 4 reasons for this poor performance.

- **Inefficiency** exists because firms aren't under competitive pressure. They are not subject to our **hard budget restraint**—that is, bankruptcy if they continue to lose money. Instead they face a **soft budget restraint**; the government will bail them out.

- **Poor development and adaptation of new technology.** Because their objective is to meet a quota, Soviet managers don't experiment. If you don't experiment in our system, you go out of business.

- **Isolation from the world economy.** Little competition from imports means there is no pressure in the Soviet Union to match quality standards of the international marketplace.

- **Morale problems** have led to alcoholism and absenteeism. The difficulty here seems to be lack of incentives, partly because a higher income can only be used to purchase inferior goods.

Problems in Moving any Marxist Economy toward Freer Markets

The Soviet Union or any other Marxist country will have to address a number of very difficult issues in moving from a government-controlled system to freer markets:

- Will firms face a **hard budget restraint?** That is, will the inefficient be allowed to go bankrupt? If they are not, waste and inefficiency will persist.

- **Will prices be set free?** They must be or allocative inefficiency and disguised unemployment will continue; shoes that won't fit will continue to be made.

- **Will the economy be opened to foreign competition?** This is needed to get the gains from trade and to pressure Soviet firms into improving quality.

- **How much private ownership will be allowed?** If there isn't a major shift towards private ownership, incentives to produce more and better goods will remain weak.

- **Will foreign ownership be allowed?** Foreign investment can bring large benefits because foreign firms:

  ° bring in new technology

  ° bid up wages

  ° pay taxes

But foreign ownership would severely compromise Marxism. The philosophical problems of allowing the **Soviets** to own Soviet industry would be magnified if Soviet industry can be owned by firms in **capitalist** countries.

- **Will agriculture or industry by reformed first?**

  ° The Chinese chose agriculture and this reform was, by and large, successful

  ° The Soviets started with industry, and found it much more difficult.

- Should reform be **phased-in** by sector or be **across-the-board?** There's a problem with phased-in reform: It may be like a phased-in change of traffic from the right lane to the left — cars this year, trucks the next. For example, if the most efficient firm in the economy still has its price frozen, but its input prices are allowed to rise, it will go bankrupt.

- Can the **institutions** required for a free market be developed, such as civil courts to settle disputes? (These have never been adequately developed because of the assumption that conflicts don't exist in a Marxist state.)

- Can government **regulations** be developed? For example:

  ° antitrust regulations to prevent monopoly abuse by private firms.

  ° controls to prevent pollution by private firms.

- **Can aggregate demand be constrained?** Recent financing of the large Soviet fiscal deficit by printing money has increased inflationary pressure. Because prices are controlled this has meant more severe scarcity and longer queues. If this "suppressed inflation" is not dealt with, prices will rise rapidly once they are set free. If inflationary pressure cannot be contained, this may destroy the whole reform process.

- **As democracy develops, will it be possible to set prices free?** In our democratic society, the public will often not allow a single price — rent — to be decontrolled because it would rise. How can **all** prices be allowed to rise in the Soviet Union if the public is allowed to vote? But isn't political reform even more important than economic reform?

IMPORTANT TERMS

Match the term in the first column with the corresponding explanation in the second column.

_____ 1. Capitalism
_____ 2. Socialism
_____ 3. Communism
_____ 4. Labor theory of value
_____ 5. Subsistence wage theory
_____ 6. Surplus value
_____ 7. Hard budget restraint
_____ 8. 5-year plan
_____ 9. Proletariat
_____ 10. Bourgeoisie
_____ 11. Dictatorship of the proletariat
_____ 12. Disguised unemployment
_____ 13. Soft budget restraint

a. The Marxist term for the working class
b. The situation that exists if people are employed, but in useless tasks.
c. In Marxist theory, this is the ideal system in which all means of production and other forms of property are owned by the community as a whole and the central government has "withered away".
d. An economic system in which most physical capital is privately owned.
e. A plan that sets up production and investment targets for each industry.
f. The theory that, in a capitalist economy, workers' wages can never rise, except temporarily, above a socially-defined subsistence level.
g. The transitory stage, according to Marx, that follows the worker's revolution, before the government withers away and the ideal state of communism is achieved.
h. An economic system in which physical capital and other means of production, such as land, are owned by the state.
i. The Marxist term for the capitalist class.
j. The difference, according to Marx, between the total value of output (all of which "belongs" to labor) and the wages actually received by labor.
k. The theory that the value of any good is determined solely by the amount of labor that goes into producing it, including the labor embodied in the capital used to produce the good.
l. The ability of a firm that has continuously suffered losses to stay in business.
m. The requirement that a firm that has continuously suffered losses should go bankrupt.

TRUE-FALSE

T   F   1. According to Marx, labor in a capitalist system receives a socially-defined subsistence income barely sufficient to meet the workers' basic needs.

T   F   2. The government of the Soviet Union does not regard itself as having achieved communism.

T   F   3. According to Marxist theory, a communist society is one in which the state has withered away.

T   F   4. A major reason why it has been difficult to control the abuse of personal power in the Soviet Union is that there have not been free elections in which the public can remove the party in power and replace it with another.

T   F   5.   Marx believed that the labor time spent on producing machinery and the income earned by capitalists on that machinery were both surplus value

T   F   6.   According to Marx, economic history was a story of the proletariat exploiting the bourgeoisie in a class struggle

T   F   7.   According to Marx, the amount of labor going into the production of a good includes the labor spent on (or congealed in) the machinery used to produce the good.

T   F   8.   Marx's analysis is positive, rather than normative.

T   F   9.   Marx spent a great deal of time discussing how, in his communist society, conflicts would be resolved by groups with conflicting interests.

T   F   10.   The Soviet planning system leads to more efficient production.

T   F   11.   Many workers in the Soviet Union (as well as in the United States) have become capitalists, in the sense that they have accumulated substantial quantities of human capital.

MULTIPLE CHOICE

1. Marx's analysis was based on:

   a. the labor theory of value
   b. the theory that wages tended towards a socially-defined subsistence level
   c. the marginal productivity theory of wages
   d. both a and b
   e. both b and c

2. Marx's recommended system for production and income distribution was:

   a. from each according to his need; to each according to his ability
   b. from each according to his ability; to each according to his need
   c. from each according to his ability; to each according to his wants
   d. from each, and to each, according to his ability
   e. from each, and to each, according to his need

3. Marx believed that once a communist society was established:

   a. power would corrupt, and absolute power would corrupt absolutely
   b. power would corrupt, but absolute power would provide freedom
   c. the power of the state would increase, but the power of any individual would decrease
   d. the power of the state and all individuals would increase
   e. the state would wither away

4. Marx charged that capitalism was unfair because of its:

   a. income payments to capitalists; he recommended having ownership of capital by the state
   b. income payments to capitalists; he recommended taxing capitalists' income more heavily
   c. inadequate income payments to capitalists; he recommended the transfer of some labor income to capitalists
   d. high income payments to highly skilled workers; he recommended paying unskilled workers more
   e. high income payments to highly skilled workers; he recommended paying highly skilled workers less

5. Marx argued that:

   a. surplus value goes to labor under a capitalist system
   b. surplus value goes to capitalists under a capitalist system
   c. surplus value goes to capitalists under a communist system
   d. deficit value goes to capitalists under a communist system
   e. deficit value goes to capitalists under a capitalist system

6. In Marxist countries, communism refers to:

   a. a period of violent class struggle
   b. a transitional period leading to socialism
   c. a period in which the means of production (capital equipment, etc) are owned by the state
   d. a period in which the means of production are owned by the community as a whole
   e. a period in which there is a dictatorship

7. Historically, the Soviet system has:

   a. provided enormous political power to its leaders, but inadequate means of controlling them
   b. provided its leaders with enormous political power, but inadequate economic power to do the job
   c. provided its leaders with enormous political power, but inadequate income
   d. provided its leaders with enormous political power, but inadequate financial power to do the job
   e. not provided employment opportunities

8. In the Soviet Union, profits:

   a. exist and play a more important role in allocating resources than in the U.S.
   b. exist and play as important a role in allocating resources as in the U.S.
   c. exist but they don't play as important a role in allocating resources as in the U.S.
   d. don't exist
   e. exist and are paid out to managers of Soviet plants

9. Human capital is owned by:

   a. the state in a capitalist system
   b. the state in a communist system
   c. the employing firm in a communist system
   d. the employing firm in a capitalist system
   e. neither state nor employing firm in either system

10. The Soviet Union has:

    a. more overt unemployment than the U.S., but less disguised unemployment
    b. less overt unemployment than the U.S., but more disguised unemployment
    c. more overt and disguised unemployment
    d. less overt and disguised unemployment
    e. the same overt and disguised unemployment

11. According to Marx:

    a. under socialism there is democracy; under communism there is dictatorship
    b. under socialism there is dictatorship; under communism there is no state
    c. under both there is dictatorship
    d. under both there is democracy
    e. under both there is no state

12. The savings necessary to finance the expansion of automobile factories:

    a. is provided voluntarily in our system. (Those whose incomes are low are not required to save at all.)
    b. is provided voluntarily in the Soviet Union
    c. is "forced saving" in the Soviet Union. (It is paid in taxes to the government by all the public, whether or not they wish to save.)
    d. a and b
    e. a and c

13. The Soviet system of political dictatorship:

    a. is not consistent with Marx's views
    b. is consistent with Marx's views that the overthrow of capitalism would be followed by a dictatorship
    c. makes it more difficult for central planners to impose their authority
    d. makes it more difficult to divert resources from consumer goods to heavy industry
    e. none of the above

14. In the Soviet system:

    a. the state owns most productive assets
    b. prices are determined largely by a central planning agency
    c. consumers choose from a relatively narrow selection of goods
    d. preference in production is given to heavy industry over consumer goods
    e. all of the above

15. Bottlenecks arise in the Soviet Union because:

    a. of the problems of setting up a completely consistent system of production quotas
    b. workers receive all the income
    c. there is no disguised unemployment
    d. investment is a smaller percentage of GNP than in the United States
    e. the overt unemployment rate is higher than in the U.S.

16. Between 1980 and 1985, the Chinese government moved:

   a. from the Cultural Revolution to the Great Leap Forward
   b. towards more orthodox Marxism
   c. away from more orthodox Marxism to the Great Leap Forward
   d. away from more orthodox Marxism toward Stalinism
   e. towards a greater degree of free enterprise

17. In the Soviet Union there is:

   a. private ownership but long queues to buy consumer goods
   b. private ownership but no queues to buy consumer goods
   c. state ownership and no queues to buy consumer goods
   d. state ownership but long queues to buy consumer goods
   e. state ownership and uncontrolled prices

18. In the Soviet Union, compared to the United States:

   a. production is more responsive to consumer preferences, and there is less overt unemployment
   b. production is more responsive to consumer preferences, and there is more overt unemployment
   c. production is less responsive to consumer preferences, and there is more overt unemployment
   d. production is less responsive to consumer preferences, and there is less overt unemployment
   e. production is less responsive to consumer preferences, and there is the same amount of overt unemployment

19. Soviet planners direct production away from consumption by:

   a. giving investment priority, and imposing no tax on consumer goods
   b. giving investment priority, and imposing a tax on consumer goods that accounts for about 10% of their price
   c. giving investment priority, and imposing a tax on consumer goods that accounts for about a third of their price
   d. giving investment priority, and imposing a tax on consumer goods that accounts for over half of their price
   e. imposing no priorities and an insignificant tax on consumer goods

20. A firm that doesn't face bankruptcy if it continues to make losses is subject to a:

   a. steel budget restraint
   b. soft budget restraint
   c. inflexible budget restraint
   d. hard budget restraint
   e. fixed budget restraint

21. The Chinese iron rice bowl system guaranteed:

   a. all families protection against an increase in the price of food
   b. all families protection against an increase in all prices
   c. all farmers protection against imports of rice
   d. all farmers protection against imports of all food
   e. all workers protection against unemployment

EXERCISES

1. Marx contended that in a free enterprise system (workers, capitalists) exploit (workers, capitalists) by acquiring the surplus value—that is, the difference between _____. Marx's solution was a (violent, non-violent) revolution in which the (proletariat, bourgeoisie) would seize the property of the (proletariat, bourgeoisie). A (communist, socialist) system would then follow in which there would be a (democratic government, dictatorship) of the (bourgeoisie, proletariat) and property would be owned by the (community as a whole, state). Eventually, this would pave the way for a (communist, socialist) system in which the state would (wither away, further consolidate its political power) and all property would be owned by the (community as a whole, state).

2. In the Soviet Union, investment is largely financed by (forced, voluntary) saving in the form of (taxation, subsidization) of (consumer, producer) goods. The big surprise is that the (high, low) investment in the Soviet Union has recently generated such a (high, low) rate of growth. The central planning agency often miscalculates in setting investment and output targets, and these errors lead to (excess supply, bottlenecks). In such circum-

stances, it is (producers, consumers) who do without. This group is also at a disadvantage because decisions on the models, styles, sizes, etc., of what should be produced are not determined by the (marketplace, hired managers) but instead by (the marketplace, hired managers).

In the Soviet Union, the problem of inequality (has, has not) been solved, in large part because workers have been investing in (physical, human) capital which (can, cannot) be owned by the state.

ESSAY QUESTIONS

1. "A communist society inevitably follows a dictatorship of the proletariat". Explain the degree to which you agree or disagree.

2. What are the problems facing Soviet planners that do not arise in our system?

3. It was often argued in the 1960s that Soviet growth exceeded that of the United States because the Soviets were playing "catch-up ball." Growth is easier in a less advanced economy because it's easier to copy technology than to develop it. Explain why you agree or disagree with this view.

4. "The growth of the labor union movement has severely damaged the credibility of Marxist theory in two respects: First, it has played a role in invalidating one of Marx's predictions. Second, events in Poland in the early 1980s made it clear that a Marxist government does not necessarily represent the interests of the working class." Explain why you agree or disagree? Explain.

5. Describe what is, in your view, the ideal organization of society. Try to ensure that the system you suggest would work in practice as well as in theory.

6. The Soviets do not appear to suffer as seriously from inflation as we do. In what sense do you think that the Soviets have replaced measured inflation with a less obvious kind? Hint: Is the value of your money really constant if prices remain the same but bottlenecks make goods harder to find?

7. Can the labor theory of value explain why land has value? Why oil deposits have value? (You may wish to review the discussion in chapter 37 of how land and resource values are determined.)

8. What do you think the practical problems are in defining a "subsistence wage"? (Hint: do you think the problems of defining a poverty line in Chapter 38 apply here as well?)

9. Suppose you are a non-communist politician in an African state. For the last 20 years the communist members of your parliament have been recommending a switch to a Soviet-type system because it offers a more rapid growth rate. What is your view?

ANSWERS

Important Terms: 1 d, 2 h, 3 c, 4 k, 5 f, 6 j, 7 m, 8 e, 9 a, 10 i, 11 g, 12 b, 13 l

True-False: 1 T (p. 745)
2 T (p. 746)
3 T (p. 746)
4 T (p. 753)
5 F (p. 746)
6 F (p. 746)
7 T (p. 745)
8 F (p. 746, FOOTNOTE)
9 F (p. 759)
10 F (p. 750)
11 T (pp. 752, 753)

Multiple Choice:	1 d (p. 745)
	2 b (p. 749)
	3 e (p. 746)
	4 a (pp. 745, 749)
	5 b (p. 746)
	6 d (p. 746)
	7 a (p. 753)
	8 c (p. 750)
	9 e (pp. 752, 753)
	10 b (p. 754)
	11 b (p. 746)
	12 e (p. 747)
	13 b (p. 753)
	14 e (pp. 749-751)
	15 a (p. 751)
	16 e (p. 757)
	17 d (p. 749)
	18 d (pp. 750, 754)
	19 c (p. 751)
	20 b (p. 755)
	21 e (p. 757)

Exercises

1.   capitalists, workers, what labor produces and what it is paid, violent, proletariat, bourgeoisie, socialist, dictatorship, proletariat, state, communist, wither away, community as a whole.

2.   forced, taxation, consumer, high, low, bottlenecks, consumers, marketplace, hired managers, has not, human, cannot.

Chapter 1

Chapter 3

Chapter 8

Chapter 10

Chapter 12

Chapter 15

Chapter 16

Chapter 18

Chapter 21

Chapter 24

Chapter 26

Chapter 28

Chapter 31

Chapter 33

Chapter 35

Chapter 37

Crossword Puzzle Solutions
476

NOTES

NOTES

NOTES

NOTES